Integrating Usability Engineering for Designing the Web Experience:
Methodologies and Principles

Tasos Spiliotopoulos
National and Kapodistrian University of Athens, Greece

Panagiota Papadopoulou
National and Kapodistrian University of Athens, Greece

Drakoulis Martakos
National and Kapodistrian University of Athens, Greece

Georgios Kouroupetroglou
National and Kapodistrian University of Athens, Greece

INFORMATION SCIENCE REFERENCE

Hershey · New York

Director of Editorial Content:	Kristin Klinger
Director of Book Publications:	Julia Mosemann
Development Editor:	Joel Gamon
Publishing Assistant:	Kurt Smith
Typesetter:	Callie Klinger, Jamie Snavely
Quality Control:	Jamie Snavely
Cover Design:	Lisa Tosheff
Printed at:	Yurchak Printing Inc.

Published in the United States of America by
Information Science Reference (an imprint of IGI Global)
701 E. Chocolate Avenue
Hershey PA 17033
Tel: 717-533-8845
Fax: 717-533-8661
E-mail: cust@igi-global.com
Web site: http://www.igi-global.com/reference

Library of Congress Cataloging-in-Publication Data

Integrating usability engineering for designing the web experience: methodologies and principles / Tasos Spiliotopoulos ... [et al.].
     p. cm.
  Includes bibliographical references and index.
  Summary: "The book provides a link between theoretical research and web engineering, presenting a more holistic approach to web usability"--Provided by publisher.

  ISBN 978-1-60566-896-3 (hardcover) -- ISBN 978-1-60566-897-0 (ebook) 1. Web sites--Design. 2. Web site development. I. Spiliotopoulos, Tasos.
  TK5105.888.I5714 2010
  658.8'7201--dc22
                                        2009045211

British Cataloguing in Publication Data
A Cataloguing in Publication record for this book is available from the British Library.

All work contributed to this book is new, previously-unpublished material. The views expressed in this book are those of the authors, but not necessarily of the publisher.

Editorial Advisory Board

Table of Contents

Section 1
Integrating Usability Methods in the Web Development Process

Mikael B. Skov, Aalborg University, Denmark
Jan Stage, Aalborg University, Denmark

Juan Manuel González-Calleros, Université catholique de Louvain, Belgium
Jean Vanderdonckt, Université catholique de Louvain, Belgium
Jaime Muñoz-Arteaga, Universidad Autónoma de Aguascalientes, México & CENIDET, México

Steve Hogg, SELEX Sensors and Airborne Systems Limited, Scotland
Patrik O'Brian Holt, Robert Gordon University, Scotland
Jim Aitchison, SELEX Sensors and Airborne Systems Limited, Scotland

Matija Pipan, Jozef Stefan Institute, Slovenia
Tanja Arh, Jozef Stefan Institute, Slovenia
Borka Jerman Blažič, Jozef Stefan Institute, Slovenia

Section 2
Universal Usability

Section 3
Theoretical Approaches

Section 4
Usability Methods and Techniques

Detailed Table of Contents

Section 1
Integrating Usability Methods in the Web Development Process

Chapter 1

    Mikael B. Skov, Aalborg University, Denmark
    Jan Stage, Aalborg University, Denmark

Support to website developers without formal training in human-computer interaction that enable them to conduct their own usability evaluations would radically advance integration of usability engineering in web development. This chapter presents experiences from usability evaluations conducted by developers and results from an empirical study of means to support non-experts in identifying usability problems. A group of software developers who were novices in usability engineering analyzed a usability test session with the task of identifying usability problems experienced by the user. In their analysis they employed a simple one-page tool that has been developed to support identification of usability problems. The non-experts were able to conduct a well-organized usability evaluation and identify a reasonable amount of usability problems with a performance that was comparable to usability experts.

Chapter 2

    Juan Manuel González-Calleros, Université catholique de Louvain, Belgium
    Jean Vanderdonckt, Université catholique de Louvain, Belgium
    Jaime Muñoz-Arteaga, Universidad Autónoma de Aguascalientes, México & CENIDET, México

Effective and satisfying Web usability is crucial for successfully built Web applications. Traditionally, Web development considered 2D User Interfaces (2D UI) based on Graphical User Interfaces (GUI).

Since the end of the 90's, the evolution of technology and computers capacity introduced a new paradigm, the Web 3D. Similarly to traditional web development, Web 3D development requires an interdisciplinary approach and a profound theoretical background. In this chapter the authors attempt to structure a methodology to support 3DUIs development. The development methodology is articulated on three axes: models and their specification language, method, and tools that support the methodology based on the underlying models. The method considers guidelines to support its correct use towards producing usable 3DUIs.

Chapter 3

Steve Hogg, SELEX Sensors and Airborne Systems Limited, Scotland
Patrik O'Brian Holt, Robert Gordon University, Scotland
Jim Aitchison, SELEX Sensors and Airborne Systems Limited, Scotland

The work discussed in this chapter is a case study of real application of usability engineering and Agile methods in the defence industry. The area of application is the monitoring of legal compliance to import and export of technology (ITAR). Manual compliance for an organization like BAE SYSTEMS presents serious challenges and is prone to errors, which can potentially lead to serious penalties. BAE decided to automate the compliance process using intranet technology with a time scale of three months. Several factors contributed to the successful development of the system and these include detailed but flexible planning, close and intense involvement of users and stakeholders and real time iteration of prototypes. The system is currently in use and while not without limitations, is seen as successful and provides a methodological framework for future similar work.

Chapter 4

Matija Pipan, Jozef Stefan Institute, Slovenia
Tanja Arh, Jozef Stefan Institute, Slovenia
Borka Jerman Blažič, Jozef Stefan Institute, Slovenia

The chapter deals with a complex decision-making problem, the selection and evaluation of Learning Management Systems (LMS) in which several objectives - referring to the definite group of users - like social, technical, environmental, and economic impacts, must be simultaneously taken into account. We introduce Evaluation Cycle Management (ECM), a support methodology aimed at the evaluation of options that occur in the decision-making processes. ECM is based on Multi-attribute decision making (Criteria Evaluation) and Usability Testing (Usability Evaluation). The Multi-attribute decision making in the first phase of ECM presents an approach to the development of a qualitative hierarchical decision model that is based on DEX, an expert system shell for multi-attribute decision support. The second phase of ECM is aimed at Usability Testing on end users. ECM illustrates its usefulness by showing its main features and its application to the above problem. It is based on the theoretical and practical expertise related to the quality and usability assurance of LMS.

Chapter 5

The purpose of this chapter is to provide an overview of usability and usability techniques. It discusses interaction design with a bias on web-based technologies, focusing on usability and usability definitions. Usability principles are discussed with a particular focus on web usability, and some of the techniques that can be used to incorporate usability design and testing. The chapter also considers aspects of electronic commerce usability. These techniques are divided into usability evaluation, (heuristic evaluation, checklists, usability tests, think aloud approaches) followed by designing with usability in mind (including user and task analysis, walkthroughs, user experience and scenario-based usability). Several E-commerce case studies, from a developing economy perspective, are then analysed, before finally discussing E-commerce usability.

Chapter 6

This chapter discusses a research project that focused on the development of a new methodology for creating more effective websites for marketing purposes. After reviewing existing methodologies, it was noted that some key aspects were under-utilized, including user participation and "real interaction" (i.e. monitoring of user interaction with a prototype site). This situation can lead to deficiencies in the resulting website and hence user frustration. A study was carried out to examine various methodologies, from different disciplines, and their integration, to select the strongest aspects of the various methodologies to be combined into a new methodology. This methodology was assessed by interviews and a questionnaire. Proposed further research will develop a website describing the new methodology; incorporate a software tool to assist in tailoring the methodology to a particular project.

Section 2
Universal Usability

Chapter 7

This chapter presents methodologies and techniques for performing accessibility evaluations on web applications. These methodologies are discussed in the context of performing them within a web engineering process, be it a traditional, unified or agile process. In this chapter the case is made that website commissioners and web engineers cannot afford to overlook accessible practices as they risk alienating an increasingly large user base who may require accessible web features.

Chapter 8

This chapter presents the state-of-the-art in usability issues and methodologies for spoken dialogue web interfaces along with the appropriate designer-needs analysis. It is planned to unfold a theoretical perspective to the usability methodology and provide a framework description for creating and testing usable content and applications for conversational interfaces. Main concerns include the problem identification of design issues for usability design and evaluation, the use of customer experience for the design of voice-web interfaces and dialogue, and the problems that arise from real-life deployment. Moreover, it discusses the hands-on approaches for applying usability methodologies in a spoken dialogue web application environment, including methodological and design issues, resource management, implementation using existing technologies for usability evaluation in several stages of the design and deployment.

Chapter 9

This chapter defines accessibility in the broader context of usability and explains the importance of making websites accessible as well as usable. It then focuses on one particular aspect of website accessibility – the accessibility statement, which is a declaration on a website about the accessibility of the site to disabled people and others with accessibility needs. This chapter argues that accessibility statements can play an important part in website accessibility if they are appropriately designed and targeted. Based on an extensive literature review and detailed examination of a large sample of accessibility statements, the chapter presents an overview of current practice and usage, raises and discusses the problematic issues that arise when developing accessibility statements, and provides recommendations for best practice.

Chapter 10

In this chapter the authors discuss the growing relevance of audio on the World Wide Web, and show how new issues of accessibility and usability are coming to the fore. Web designers are employing an increasingly rich palette of sounds to enhance the user "experience", but apart from guidelines for facilitating screen-readers, very little exists in the way of design strategies for non-speech sound content. Although their primary focus is on web accessibility for visually disabled users, the same issues are increasingly applicable to sighted users accessing the web via WIFI enabled mobile devices with small screen real estate. The authors present an auditory user interface model aimed at conceptualizing the perceptual issues involved when presenting a rich soundscape to the user, and show how this model can help web designers to consider issues of accessibility and usability without detracting from the "experience". Non-speech sound is not only a means of entertainment or background enhancement, but can also efficiently relay useful information to the user – a function that is still underutilized on the web.

Tania di Mascio, University of L'Aquila, Italy
Rosella Gennari, Free University of Bozen-Bolzano, Italy

The need of literacy tools for deaf people is well documented in the literature of deaf studies. This chapter aims at drawing the attention of the HCI and AI worlds on the need of intelligent web tools for the literacy of deaf people. It reviews several such e-tools. The review tries to cover complementary and diverse literacy aspects, ranging from word knowledge to global reasoning on texts. The authors assess whether the tools conform to the User Centred Design Methodology, and put forward a first set of usability guidelines based on such a methodology for the design of more intelligent web e-tools for the literacy of deaf people. The chapter concludes by eliciting a debate on the need of a deaf user centred design.

Section 3
Theoretical Approaches

Horia D. Pitariu, Babes-Bolyai University, Romania
Daniela M. Andrei, Babes-Bolyai University, Romania
Adriana M. Guran, Babes-Bolyai University, Romania

The present chapter focuses on the idea of rethinking the concept of usability moving from the traditional view of usability expressed in the internal characteristics of the product towards usability understood as deriving from the quality of interactions between humans, their work and the web design product. Usability is not only an add-on or a final result in the design process but it is embedded as a main concern within the design process itself. Related to this perspective on usability, the authors discussed the design models which can support it and argued on the importance of using social research tools for a better understanding of the people and their needs starting with the very first stage of design. Further on the authors have provided a brief description of the most frequently used research methods in user needs analysis (interviews, focus groups and surveys) together with short guidelines in preparing and using these methods. The last part is dedicated to the illustration of user needs analysis taken from two of their research projects.

Konstantina Vassilopoulou, Harokopio University, Greece
Kathy K. Keeling, University of Manchester, UK
Linda A. Macaulay, University of Manchester, UK

The motivation for this research effort is the failure of usability in Human Computer Interaction (HCI) to consider the needs of users as potential consumers. The hypothesis underlying this research is that it is possible to construct a framework based upon the needs of computer users who are at the same time consumers. The aim of this research is to build a theoretical framework that addresses the needs of a retail site user as a potential consumer. To achieve this we examined the literature relating to usability in HCI as well as Social Attitude Theories. Two empirical studies were conducted using existing sites. The first aimed at incorporating attributes from the fields of Social Attitude Theories and Retail Marketing the second at developing a theoretical framework measuring the usability of retail sites.

Chapter 14

This chapter aims to study the effects of the colors of e-commerce websites on consumer behavior, in order to better understand website usability. Since color components (Hue, Brightness and Saturation) affect behavioral responses of the consumer (memorization and buying intention), this research reveals the importance of the interaction between hue and brightness, in enhancing the contrast necessary to ensure an easy navigation. By comparing graphic chart effects according to their level of saturation and brightness depending on the hue, it aims at focusing on particularly important consideration of webdesign, linked to choices of color. The obtained results were conveyed through the changes in internal states of the organism, which are emotions and mood. The interaction of hue and brightness, using chromatic colors (as opposed to Black & White) for the dominant (background) and dynamic (foreground) ones, supports memorization and the intent to purchase, reinforcing the importance to attach to usable websites. This is even more evident when contrast rests on a weak situation of brightness. The data collection was carried out during a laboratory experiment so as to ensure the accuracy of measurements regarding the color aspects of e-commerce websites.

Section 4
Usability Methods and Techniques

Chapter 15

This chapter focuses on the adoption and adaptation of methodologies drawn from research in psychology for the evaluation of user response as a manifestation of the mental processes of perception, cognition and emotion. The authors present robust alternative conceptualizations of evaluative methodologies which allow the surfacing of views, feelings and opinions of individual users producing a richer, more informative texture for user centered evaluation of software. This differs from more usual user questionnaire systems such as the Questionnaire of User Interface Satisfaction (QUIS). The authors present two different example methodologies so that the reader can firstly, review the methods as a theoretical exercise and secondly, applying similar adaptation principles, derive methods appropriate to their own research or practical context.

Chapter 16
    Petros Georgiakakis, ITisART.Ltd, Greece
    Symeon Retalis, University of Piraeus, Greece

Scenario based inspection methods are currently widely used for evaluating the usability of web-based information systems (e-systems). However, it is neither easy nor cheap to find usability experts who possess the competencies for performing a usability inspection while at the same time have deep knowledge of the context for which each e-system has been developed. Moreover, the effectiveness of these methods depends on the quality of the inspection scenarios. These issues can be tackled by finding potential users of the e-systems under inspection who have basic knowledge about human-computer interaction and adequately support them to execute the appropriate scenarios. Towards this goal, a new usability evaluation method called DEPTH along with a web based tool that supports its application, have been created. This chapter describes DEPTH's underlining philosophy which is the re-use of inspection scenarios per feature of genres of e-systems as well as the re-use design expertise which can be encoded in terms of design patterns.

Chapter 17
    Tayana Conte, Federal University of Amazonas, Brazil
    Verônica T. Vaz, PESC – COPPE/UFRJ, Brazil
    Jobson Massolar, PESC – COPPE/UFRJ, Brazil
    Andrew Bott, Fundação COPPETEC, Brazil
    Emilia Mendes, University of Auckland, New Zealand
    Guilherme H. Travassos, PESC – COPPE/UFRJ, Brazil

This chapter presents the WDP (Web Design Perspectives-based Usability Evaluation), an inspection technique specifically designed to assess the usability of Web applications. This technique combines Web design perspectives and the heuristic evaluation method proposed by Nielsen (1994b). In addition to describing the components of the WDP technique this chapter also illustrates its use in practice by means of an industrial case study where the technique is applied to inspect a real Web application. In this case study, developers and requirement assessment staff applied the WDP technique to evaluate the usability of modules developed from scratch for a Web application. The results of this case study indicate the feasibility of performing usability inspections with the participation of a software project's stakeholders, even when stakeholders are not usability experts.

Chapter 18

Borchuluun Yadamsuren, University of Missouri, USA
Anindita Paul, University of Missouri, USA
Sanda Erdelez, University of Missouri, USA
Joi L. Moore, University of Missouri, USA

Web developers and usability specialists face the challenge of dealing with the cost and quality of usability testing that must be implemented in a short period of time. Multiple-User Simultaneous Testing (MUST) can reduce usability testing time by allowing data collection from many users at the same time. This chapter reviews the literature on MUST and related methodologies for group users. It describes on a conceptual level two methods for setting up the MUST testing environment: self-paced and moderated. The authors do not aim to present which method is better from the empirical standpoint. Instead, the chapter describes the authors' comparative experiences with these methods, with a focus on the laboratory set up, data collection protocols, and data analysis issues. The chapter concludes with suggestions for future research and recommendations for usability specialists on how to conduct well designed MUST studies.

Foreword

We are definitely living the web era where we are all increasingly becoming users of applications with web interfaces. With the continuing advancements of ICT, these applications increase in number as well as complexity. But what about usability? Although the concept is not new and its importance has been long recognized, a lack of usability can be noticed in the web environment. This undoubtedly calls for a thorough understanding of how usability, both in theoretical and practical aspects, can be integrated into web development.

I was really glad to read "Integrating Usability Engineering for Designing the Web Experience: Methodologies and Principles" and realize that it skillfully addresses this issue and in many ways fills the existing gap.

Having the responsibility for the past three years of the organization of the "Usability and Accessibility Days" in Athens, Greece (http://www.media.uoa.gr/usability), I have come to believe, as it is clearly put in a chapter of the book in hand that "usability is not only an add-on or a final result in the design process but it is embedded as a main concern within the design process itself".

The book provides a holistic perspective regarding usability and the web, covering a wide range of topics along four main axes. First, it explores how usability methods can be integrated in the web development process. Second, it presents the relationship between usability and accessibility. Third, it shows how usability principles and practice can be informed by various disciplines and applied in various domains. Finally, it examines selected examples of innovative usability methods and techniques.

I believe that the book will be valuable to researchers as well as practitioners in diverse fields, as the web constitutes a key means for any ICT-related activity. I hope you enjoy reading it as much as I did.

Professor Michael G. Meimaris
Director, Laboratory of New Technologies in Communication, Education and the Mass Media
National and Kapodistrian University of Athens

Athens, October 2009

Michael Meimaris is the founder and director of the New Technologies Laboratory in Communication, Education and the Mass Media of the Faculty of Communication and Media Studies of the University of Athens. He is currently the Director of the University Research Institute of Applied Communication. He has been awarded Chevalier de l'Ordre des Palmes Académiques of the French Democracy. He has studied Mathematics at the University of Athens and Data Analysis at the University of Paris VI - Pierre et Marie Curie. His scientific interests involve the application of New Technologies in Communication, Education and the Mass Media, the New Technological Communication Environment and its design, Open and Distance Education, Digital Game-Based Learning. He is a member of the International Committee and President of the National Committee of the Möbius Awards, member of the Scientific Board of the Maison des Sciences de l'Homme Nord of France, as well as of C.I.T.I. of the University of Lisbon.

Preface

INTRODUCTION

System usability is defined as the extent to which a product can be used by specified users to achieve specified goals with effectiveness, efficiency and satisfaction in a specified context of use. Usability is regarded as one of the aspects of software quality, and as such it can be described alternatively as "quality in use". Since usability is only defined within a certain context of use, we can deduce that it cannot be considered as an inherent attribute of a product, but it has to be studied by studying the users themselves.

Ease of use has long been a major concern within software development and the industry has realized that in order to achieve such a quality, a user-centered approach is needed. However, User-Centered Design (UCD) constitutes a considerable paradigm shift in the development process and this has hindered the adoption of UCD methods. Thus, it is fairly recently that more systematic approaches have been considered and efforts have been made to integrate such methods in the software development process. Moreover, the proliferation of the World Wide Web has increased the need for developing usable systems, since the designers have to cater for a much more diversified user base. In addition, the Internet has lead to an increase in the number of people that develop software and has shrunk the amount of time from the inception of an idea to its development as an application and its deployment to the market. Advances in ICT have complicated modern applications and their interfaces, making them harder to use. As a consequence of all the above, a considerable lack of usability can be observed in the Web today, despite the fact that the importance of the concept has been widely acknowledged.

Since usability, and Human-Computer Interaction (HCI) in general, has to study the users of computer systems, researchers and practitioners have traditionally drawn upon principles from a wide range of scientific fields in order to devise effective UCD methods. Apart from computer science, such fields include cognitive psychology, social psychology, ergonomics, linguistics, philosophy, anthropology, industrial design etc. In addition, several theoretical approaches are being adapted from these disciplines to computer science in order to give insights on the design of the interaction between computers and their users.

Usability methods for the web, that is methods that enable or facilitate the development of usable systems for the web, can be classified as inquiry, prototyping, inspection and testing methods.

Inquiry methods investigate the usability attributes of a system by noting down the user's opinions of it. It should be taken into account, however, that the users' opinions are always subjective and therefore not of as much value as one would expect. These methods include user questionnaires, interviews, focus groups, personas, card sorting, field observations etc.

Prototyping methods aim at modeling the final system, thus making it possible to study and test it, even if its development has not finished yet. It is possible to have high or low fidelity prototypes and horizontal or vertical prototypes. Moreover, prototypes can be classified as reusable or evolutionary and modular or incremental. Some usability methods in this category are paper prototyping, storyboards, video prototyping, rapid prototyping and parallel design.

Inspection methods refer to the inspection of a system or a prototype of the system by one or more usability experts. The inspection can be either a simple review by the expert or it can be based on certain scenarios that constitute a walkthrough of the system. Such methods include heuristic, expert, guideline and cognitive reviews and walkthroughs.

Testing methods involve the participation of actual users in testing the system. Their interaction with the system is recorded and analyzed later, in order to obtain useful conclusions. Some methods for usability testing are thinking aloud protocol, constructive interaction, retrospective testing, coaching method, wizard of Oz and logging actual use of the system.

Other characteristics of such usability methods include:

- The stages of the development process that the method can be used in, i.e. requirements analysis, design, implementation, formative or summative evaluation. Of course, a usability method can be applied in more than one stage in the web development process.
- The type of results obtained from the method, i.e. qualitative or quantitative
- Bias of the method, i.e. objective or subjective results
- The resources necessary, such as equipment, implementation of a prototype, number of users or usability experts needed and trips
- Level of the information obtained, i.e. high or low level
- Location, i.e. laboratory or real work environment
- Immediacy of response, i.e. how quickly the feedback is available
- Intrusiveness of the method

Since usability methods can provide complementary results, it is important to examine the ways that these methods can be combined and integrated in the development process, in order to achieve increased efficiency. This book aims at providing a holistic approach to web usability methods, allowing the readers to obtain a better understanding of usability in the context of the development process for the web.

ORGANIZATION OF THE BOOK

Section 1 of the book focuses on the integration of usability methods in the web development process. This part of the book examines the reasons that advances in usability research do not find their way easily into the web industry and attempts to provide valuable insights to all the stakeholders in the development of a web system. Section 2 examines universal usability for the web and explores ways of enabling all citizens to succeed using communication and information technology in the web. In doing so, this section studies designs that gracefully accommodate a diversity of user needs and circumstances. Section 3 focuses on the theoretical aspects of usability for the web. This part of the book acknowledges the inherent interdisciplinarity of usability in order to provide a deeper understanding of the scientific principles in the field and to investigate their application in web design. Finally, the last section of the book examines and appraises particular examples of usability methods and techniques in more detail.

Section 1: Integrating Usability Methods in the Web Development Process

Chapter 1, *Supporting Web Developers in Evaluating Usability and Identifying Usability Problems* is written by Mikael B. Skov and Jan Stage. In this chapter, the authors propose to facilitate the integration of usability in the web development process by enabling website developers without formal training in human-computer interaction to conduct their own usability evaluations. The authors' own experiences and results from such usability evaluations are presented, where they employed a simple tool that has been developed to support identification of usability problems.

Chapter 2, *A Structured Methodology for Developing 3D Web Applications* is written by Juan Manuel González-Calleros, Jean Vanderdonckt and Jaime Muñoz-Arteaga. This chapter tackles the issue of designing usable 3D web applications. In order to achieve this aim, the authors develop a user-centred methodology as an alternative to content-centric methodologies for developing 3D user interfaces, which considers a step-wise development life cycle where usability guidelines could be considered implicitly or explicitly at each development step.

Chapter 3, *A Case Study of Usability Engineering in the Defence Industry* is written by Steve Hogg, Patrik O'Brian Holt and Jim Aitchison. This chapter discusses a case study of how a company used modern system design and development approaches, agile software development and usability engineering to produce and deploy a solution to a problem that is critical to the organization. The authors describe in detail this endeavor, explaining the usability issues encountered, and conclude with a discussion providing useful guidance for future work, based on the lessons learned.

Chapter 4, *The Evaluation Cycle Management Method Applied to the Evaluation of Learning Management Systems* is written by Matija Pipan, Tanja Arh and Borka Jerman Blažič. This chapter introduces ECM, a support methodology based on multi-attribute decision making and usability testing, which is aimed at the evaluation of options that occur in the decision-making process. This method is subsequently employed for evaluating the suitability of Learning Management Systems for a defined target group.

Chapter 5, *Usability Techniques for Interactive Software and Their Application in E-Commerce* is written by Shawren Singh. This chapter attempts an overview of usability and usability techniques, focusing on the development of e-commerce systems. It examines usability evaluation techniques and techniques for designing with usability in mind before presenting and discussing several e-commerce studies from a developing economy perspective.

Chapter 6, *Development and Evaluation of a Methodology for Developing Marketing Websites* is written by Tomayess Issa, Martin West and Andrew Turk. In their work, they select the strongest aspects of various development methodologies from several disciplines and combine them into a new, participative methodology for the development of marketing websites, with a focus on usability.

Section 2: Universal Usability

Chapter 7, *Integrating Accessibility Evaluation into Web Engineering Processes* is written by Christopher Power, André Pimenta Freire and Helen Petrie. This chapter presents the relationship between usability and accessibility and argues for the importance of accessibility evaluation in web engineering. The authors present the major types of accessibility evaluation that are available to web engineers and explain how to integrate these evaluations into existing development processes.

Chapter 8, *Usability Methodologies for Spoken Dialogue Web Interfaces* is written by Dimitris Spiliotopoulos and Georgios Kouroupetroglou. This chapter investigates usability issues for spoken dialogue web interfaces. The authors describe the background of such systems, before discussing hands-on approaches for applying usability methodologies in a spoken dialogue web application environment.

Chapter 9, *Website Accessibility and the Role of Accessibility Statements*, written by C.M. Parkinson and Wendy Olphert, defines accessibility in the broader context of usability and describes the key drivers for website accessibility. It then goes on to focus on accessibility statements and explain their importance for website accessibility. The main goal of the chapter is to present an overview of the current practice and usage of accessibility statements and to provide guidance for their development.

Chapter 10, *Considering the Perceptual Implications of Auditory Rich Content on the Web* is written by Flaithrí Neff, Aidan Kehoe and Ian Pitt. This chapter explores design strategies for non-speech sound content for the web. In order to help web designers to consider issues of accessibility and usability without detracting from the overall user experience, the authors present an auditory user interface model aimed at conceptualizing the perceptual issues involved when presenting a rich soundscape to the web user.

Chapter 11, *A Usability Guide to Intelligent Web Tools for the Literacy of Deaf People* is written by Tania di Mascio and Rosella Gennari. This chapter reviews several literacy e-tools for deaf people and assesses whether the tools conform to the User Centred Design Methodology. Based on these assessments, the authors stress the need for the introduction of guidelines for developing tools that are usable by deaf people and propose a set of such guidelines.

Section 3: Theoretical Approaches

Chapter 12, *Social Research Methods Used in Moving the Traditional Usability Approach Towards a User-Centered Design Approach* is written by Horia D. Pitariu, Daniela M. Andrei and Adriana M. Guran. This chapter provides a social scientist's perspective on usability, portraying web usability as deriving from the quality of interactions between humans, their work and the web design product. The authors discuss the design models that can support usability and argue on the importance of using social research tools for a better understanding of the people and their needs starting with the very first stage of design. They describe user needs analysis methods and provide guidelines in preparing and using these methods. Finally they demonstrate the use of these methods in user needs analysis through two empirical studies.

Chapter 13, *A Theoretical Framework Measuring the Usability of Retail Sites* is written by Konstantina Vassilopoulou, Kathy K. Keeling and Linda A. Macaulay. This chapter attempts to determine the extent to which usability succeeds in addressing the needs of the user as a consumer, and subsequently develops a theoretical framework that suggests future use intention as a new type of measurement of usability of retail sites and identifies appropriate usability attributes for retail sites.

Chapter 14, *The Influence of E-commerce Website Colors on Usability* is written by Jean-Eric Pelet. This chapter explores the effect of the colors used on e-commerce websites on consumer retention of information and buying intention, in order to better understand website usability. After an extensive laboratory experiment, the author concludes that the graphic composition of a website can indeed affect the representation that the consumer retains when shopping, providing some useful insights for web designers.

Section 4: Usability Methods and Techniques

Chapter 15, *Whose Questionnaire Is It, Anyway?* is written by Andrew Saxon, Shane Walker and David Prytherch, who provide a much needed social scientist's view on evaluative methodologies for web software. The authors examine two different example methodologies for addressing the psychological needs of the users, the Motivation Systems Theory and the Repertory Grid Technique.

Chapter 16, *DEPTH: A Method and a Web-Based Tool for Designing and Executing Scenario-Based Usability Inspections of E-Systems* is written by Petros Georgiakakis and Symeon Retalis. In this chapter, the authors provide an overview of DEPTH, an innovative method and the corresponding tool for performing scenario-based expert heuristic usability evaluation for web based systems. The distinguishing characteristic of this method is the fact that it uses the added value of design patterns in a very systematic way within the usability evaluation process.

Chapter 17, *Applying the WDP Technique to Usability Inspections in Web Development Organizations* is written by Tayana Conte, Verônica T. Vaz, Jobson Massolar, Andrew Bott, Emilia Mendes and Guilherme H. Travassos. This chapter presents a usability inspection technique for Web applications, the process to execute an inspection using this technique and the results of the execution of a usability inspection in a software development project. This technique combines web design perspectives and heuristic evaluation, while the results of its application indicate the feasibility of performing usability inspections with the participation of a software project's stakeholders, even when stakeholders are not usability experts.

Chapter 18, *Multiple-User Simultaneous Testing: Experience with Two Methods* is written by Borchuluun Yadamsuren, Anindita Paul, Sanda Erdelez and Joi L. Moore. This chapter examines two different approaches for multi-user simultaneous usability testing; self-paced and moderated. The authors describe the two methods in detail and their comparative experiences, while concluding with recommendations for practitioners on how to design and conduct similar studies.

Acknowledgment

This book is the result of a long and exciting process, which involved the combined effort of a number of individuals who kindly agreed to participate in the project.

The editorial team would like to thank all the chapter authors for their excellent contributions, as well as their cooperation and enthusiasm throughout this process. We hope that this publication makes you proud!

A special word of thanks goes to everyone involved in the review process. Their comprehensive and insightful reviews were invaluable to the quality of the book.

Finally, special thanks go to the staff at IGI Global who supported this publication with their excellent administrative skills, kind words of encouragement and their enthusiasm.

Tasos Spiliotopoulos
Panagiota Papadopoulou
Drakoulis Martakos
Georgios Kouroupetroglou

Section 1
Integrating Usability Methods in the Web Development Process

Chapter 1
Supporting Web Developers in Evaluating Usability and Identifying Usability Problems

Mikael B. Skov
Aalborg University, Denmark

Jan Stage
Aalborg University, Denmark

ABSTRACT

Support to website developers without formal training in human-computer interaction that enable them to conduct their own usability evaluations would radically advance integration of usability engineering in web development. This chapter presents experiences from usability evaluations conducted by developers and results from an empirical study of means to support non-experts in identifying usability problems. A group of software developers who were novices in usability engineering analyzed a usability test session with the task of identifying usability problems experienced by the user. In their analysis they employed a simple one-page tool that has been developed to support identification of usability problems. The non-experts were able to conduct a well-organized usability evaluation and identify a reasonable amount of usability problems with a performance that was comparable to usability experts.

INTRODUCTION

Over the last decade, software usability as a discipline has made considerable progress. An important indicator of this is that more and more software organizations are beginning to take usability seriously as an important aspect of development. Yet there are still significant obstacles to a full integration of usability engineering into software development

DOI: 10.4018/978-1-60566-896-3.ch001

(Bak et al., 2008). The average developer has not adopted the concern for usability, and evaluators are not being involved until late in development, when most substantial changes are too costly to implement (Anderson et al., 2001).

There are several areas of software development where the limited integration of usability efforts is apparent. Development of sites for the World Wide Web is one such area. It is usually argued that the web is qualitatively different from conventional software systems. For the typical web application, the user group is more varied and fluent, and it has a considerably shorter lifetime compared to other kinds of software. For web development, the main difference is that it is done by a broad variety of companies, ranging from one or two person companies to large corporations, and many of the development companies, in particular the smaller ones; do not have any usability experts available. Budget constraints prohibit hiring specialists, and the development schedule does not leave time for usability testing and feedback to iterative design (Scholtz et al., 1998). Research indicates that work practices in web-site development seem to largely ignore the body of knowledge and experience that has been established in the disciplines of software engineering, human-computer interaction, and usability engineering (Sullivan and Matson, 2000). Conventional usability evaluation is expensive, time consuming and requires usability experts. This is incompatible with web development, where many web sites are designed and implemented in fast-paced projects by multidisciplinary teams that involve such diverse professions as information architects, Web developers, graphic designers, brand and content strategists, etc. Such teams are usually not familiar with established knowledge on human-computer interaction (Braiterman et al., 2000). The consequence of this is clear. A large number of websites have severe usability problems that prohibit effective and successful use (Spool et al., 1999). An investigation of usability through content accessibility found that 29 of 50 popular web sites were either inaccessible or only partly accessible (Spool et al., 1999; Sullivan and Matson, 2000).

At least two ways exist for organizing usability expertise in website development projects. First, developers can adapt and use tailored usability heuristics in the evaluation and let these heuristics guide the usability work in the development team (Agarwal and Venkatesh, 2002; Sutcliffe, 2001). The practical implications of usability heuristics in software design have been discussed for several years, but traditional heuristics is not of focus in

this paper. Secondly, a possible solution to the limited integration of usability in software development is to involve non-experts in the usability engineering activities. This could be accomplished by offering ordinary software developers means for creating usable web sites and for evaluating them in a systematic manner (Skov and Stage, 2001). This would bring usability into the earliest possible phases of software development where it could have most impact by improving initial design and eliminating rework. It would also solve a potential problem with availability of usability experts. The professional evaluator resource is very scarce. Evaluating the usability of just a fraction of all new web sites would be well beyond their capacity.

This chapter presents an empirical study of a specific means to support non-experts in web usability in conducting a web site usability evaluation. We have explored to what extent a simple one-page usability problem identification tool can support and stimulate the analytical skills of novice usability evaluators. By doing this, we wish to explore whether people with a basic foundation in software engineering and programming through methodological support can build a capability to identify, describe and classify usability problems. The following section gives an overview of existing literature on identification of problems. The next section describes the design of an empirical study we have conducted in order to examine the usefulness of the usability problem identification tool we have developed for problem identification. Then the results of the empirical study are presented and discussed. Finally, we conclude on our study.

BACKGROUND

With the prevalent role of contemporary websites in today's societies, website usability has received increased attention over the last years and several textbooks on website usability has been published

(Badre, 2002; Krug, 2000; Nielsen, 2000; Nielsen and Tahir, 2002). While such literature primarily focuses on specific elements of usability in websites, e.g. Nielsen and Tahir (2002) analyze 50 different websites on their usability; some references in the research literature provide methodological support of the usability evaluation process for web sites. Primarily, some research attempts have proposed heuristics for website evaluation (Agarwal and Venkatesh, 2002; Sutcliffe, 2001). On the other hand, the more general literature on usability evaluation practices and means to support it is varied and rich. On the overall level, there are methods to support the whole process of a usability evaluation, e.g. (Rubin, 1994). The literature that compares usability evaluation methods also includes detailed descriptions of procedure for conducting evaluations, e.g. how to identify, group and merge lists of usability problems (Hornbæk and Frøkjær, 2004; Jeffries et al., 1991; Karat et al., 1992). All of this deals with user-based usability evaluation.

Heuristic methods for usability evaluation have been suggested as means to reduce the resources required to conduct a usability evaluation. In many cases, strong limitations in terms of development time effectively prohibits conventional usability testing as it is described in classical methods (Dumas and Redish, 1993; Fath et al., 1994; Nielsen, 1993; Nielsen et al., 1992; Rubin, 1994). Such evaluations are very time-consuming, and considerable costs arise when a large group of users is involved in a series of tests. Heuristic inspection evolved as an attempt to reduce these costs (Lavery et al., 1997; Nielsen, 1993; Nielsen et al., 1992). The basic idea is that a group of usability experts evaluate an interface design by comparing it to a set of guidelines, called heuristics (Nielsen, 1992). The first heuristics consisted of nine principles (Lavery et al., 1997), which have been developed further over the last ten years. The literature on heuristic inspection also includes empirical studies of its capability for finding usability problems. The first studies indicated that

the method was very effective (Agarwal and Venkatesh, 2002; Lavery et al., 1997; Nielsen, 1992; Nielsen et al., 1992). Other studies have produced less promising results as they conclude that a conventional user-based usability test yields similar or better results compared to inspection (Karat et al. 1992), and heuristic inspection tends to find many low-priority problems (Jeffries et al., 1991). But usability heuristics designated for website design and evaluation have been proposed and successfully adapted in some research studies (Agarwal and Venkatesh, 2002, Sutcliffe, 2001). Finally, the basic idea in heuristic evaluation is also the key characteristic of the usability evaluation method called MOT, where five metaphors of human thinking are used as a basis for evaluation (Hornbæk and Frøkjær, 2004).

There is also research that describes how usability experts actually conduct evaluations. It has been established that expert evaluators find different usability problems. This has been denoted as the evaluator effect (Hertzum and Jacobsen, 2001; Jacobseb et al., 1998). There is a remarkable difference both in the number of problems and the specific problems they find. The strength is that if we introduce more evaluators, we find more problems. The weakness is that it seems random and difficult to trust.

Changes in software development with new development approaches such as open source development, global software development and outsourcing are challenging conventional usability evaluation practices. With outsourcing and global software development, developers, evaluators and users are distributed across multiple organizations and time zones. This also characterizes several website development projects and makes conventional user-based usability testing considerably more complex and challenging (Murphy et al., 2004). This makes remote usability testing increasingly important as an alternative to conventional usability testing (Andreasen et al., 2007). Remote usability testing denotes a situation where "the evaluators are separated in space and/or time from users" (Castillo et al., 1998). The first methods for remote usability testing emerged about ten years ago. At that time, some empirical studies were conducted that showed results comparable to conventional methods (Hartson et al., 1998). A very interesting method was based on the idea that users should report the critical incidents they experienced while using the system (Hartson et al., 1996; Hartson et al., 1998). A recent study of remote usability evaluation methods concluded that users report significantly fewer problems compared to a classical usability evaluation but the method imposes considerably less effort on the evaluators (Andreasen et al., 2007; Bak et al., 2009).

A related line of research has inquired into the ability of novice usability evaluators to identify usability problems. Based on a comparison with experts it is concluded that novice evaluators can quickly learn to plan and conduct user-based usability evaluations and to write up the related reports. However, when it comes to identification, description and categorization of usability problems, they perform at a significantly lower level than expert evaluators (Skov and Stage, 2001; Skov and Stage, 2004).

The amount of research on user-based usability evaluation conducted by novices is very limited. We have only been able to find one reference where novices conducted the evaluation, and this was heuristic evaluation and not user-based (Slavkovic and Cross, 1999). An effort with training focused on transfer of developers' skills in design of user interfaces from one technology to another (Nielsen et al., 1992).

These streams of research emphasize a need for methodological support to novice or non-expert usability evaluators in identifying usability problems. They also illustrate that the literature is limited in this area.

CONCEPTUAL TOOL FOR USABILITY PROBLEM IDENTIFICATION

During a series of courses on usability testing for under-graduate students, we discovered a clear fundamental need for support on usability problem identification for novice usability evaluators. Especially, we found that even though test participants experienced usability problems, novice evaluators were incapable of identifying and classifying such problems (Skov and Stage, 2001). As a solution, we came up with the idea of the usability problem identification tool (see Table 1).

The basic idea in the usability problem identification tool is that it provides a conceptual or overall interpretation of what constitutes a

Table 1. Usability problem identification tool

	Slowed down *relative to normal work speed*	**Understanding**	**Frustration**	**Test monitor intervention**
Critical	Hindered in solving the task	Does not understand how information in the system can be used for solving a task. Repeats the same information in different parts of the system.		Receives substantial assistance (could not have solved the task without it).
Serious	Delayed for several seconds	Does not understand how a specific functionality operates or is activated. Cannot explain the functioning of the system.	Is clearly annoyed by something that cannot be done or remembered or something illogical that you must do. Believes he has damaged something.	Receives a hint.
Cosmetic	Delayed for a few seconds	Does actions without being able to explain why (you just have to do it).		Is asked a question that makes him come up with the solution

problem. Inspired by previous research (Molich, 2000; Nielsen, 1993; Rubin, 1994) and our own practical experiences with usability test teaching, we identified four overall categories of usability problems as experienced by users:

1. slowed down
2. understanding
3. frustration
4. test monitor intervention.

These four episodes often reveal some sort of usability problem. 1) The first category includes problems where the test participant is being slowed down relatively to normal speed. Several usability problems denotes and describes some sort of users being slowed down while interacting with a website. Thus, they are not able to complete assigned tasks in an efficient manner. 2) The second category of problems deals with users' understanding of the website. Often users find it difficult to understand how website are constructed, what functionality the website offers, and how information is organized in the website. 3) The third category describes problems related to the user's level of frustration. This is a classical metric in usability evaluation studies where researchers focus on the user frustration as an indicator of website usability. Users may (or may not) show their frustration during a usability test session, however if they do so, it is often due to interaction problems with the interface. 4) The fourth category shows problems where the test monitor has intervened or helped the test participant in order to complete the assigned tasks. A good acting test monitor will intervene (and only intervene) if the participant experience severe problems in task completion.

On the other dimension, we distinguish between three severities of problem namely critical problem, serious problems, and cosmetic problems – inspired by previous research (Molich, 2000).

EMPIRICAL STUDY

We have conducted an empirical study with a usability problem identification tool that is intended to support novice or non-expert evaluators in identifying usability problems in a user-based evaluation. The purpose of the empirical study was to examine whether this tool was useful for such inexperienced evaluators.

Setting: The empirical study was conducted in relation to a course that one of the authors of this paper was teaching. The course was an introduction to design and implementation of user interfaces. It consisted of the following three modules:

A. Introduction to human computer interaction and a method for user interaction design
B. Implementation of user interfaces in Java
C. Usability evaluation of interactive systems

Each module consisted of five class meetings with a two-hour lecture and an equal amount of time for exercises. The experiment was part of the last module (module C). The content of that module was a presentation of the activities of a usability evaluation and techniques that are relevant in each activity. The main literature was (Preece et al., 2002) supplemented with selected articles. The five lectures of this module had the following contents:

1. The purpose of a usability evaluation, the concept of usability and overview of the activities involved in a usability evaluation
2. Basic decisions, field versus lab, the test monitor role and the test report
3. Creation of test context, tasks assignments, conducting the test and the think-aloud technique
4. Interpretation of data, the ISO definition, task load, identification of usability problems, exercises in identification and categorization of usability problems

5.   Presentation of experiences from our evaluation, heuristic evaluation, comparison with think-aloud and training of novices in usability evaluation

Subjects: The participants in the experiment were 24 undergraduate second-year students in computer science. They had a basic qualification in programming and software engineering. They were offered to participate in this experiment as a voluntary exercise, and they were promised feedback on their products.

Usability problem identification tool: The empirical study involved a one-page usability problem identification tool that the authors had developed during earlier usability evaluations, see Table 1. The authors also used this tool in their own data analysis

Experimental procedure: The empirical study was conducted between lecture 3 and 4. The students were only told in advance that there would be an exercise about usability problems, but no details were given. The empirical study lasted for three and a half hour. All students came into the class at 8:30. They were handed a CD-ROM with the same recording of a usability test session and a few practical guidelines for carrying out the exercise. The test session was app. 30 minutes. The students also received the usability problem identification tool they were asked to use, cf. Table 1. The recording was of a user that solved a series of tasks on a web site for a large furniture store. The think-aloud technique was used. The empirical study ended at noon when they delivered their problem lists and diaries by email.

The students were asked to work individually on the task. They would see the recording and note down usability problems as they occurred. In doing so, they were encouraged to use the usability problem identification tool. Thus the tool gave a practical definition of usability problems, and it was supposed to be used in the detailed analysis. For each usability problem they identified, they were also asked to record in the diary if they used the tool and which field in the table the problem was related to.

Data collection: The main result was the problem list from each student. In addition, they were asked to maintain a diary with reasons why they decided that something was a usability problem and why they categorized it at a certain level. In this paper, we only deal with the problem lists.

Data analysis: The two authors of this paper analyzed the recording independently of each other and produced an individual problem list where each problem was described as illustrated in Table 2. The first column contains the unique number of the problem. The second column specifies the window or screen where the problem occurred. The third column contains the description of the way the user experiences the problem. In the individual problem lists, each evaluator also made a severity assessment for each usability problem. This was expressed on a three-point scale, e.g. cosmetic, serious, or critical (Molich, 2000). The individual problem lists from the two authors were merged through negotiation into one overall list of usability problems. The resulting problem list was the basis for evaluating the problem lists produced by the participants in the experiment. Thus the problem list from each student was compared to the authors' joint problem list.

Validity: The specific conditions of this study limit its validity in a number of ways. First, the

Table 2. Example of a usability problem

No.	Window	Description	Severity
13	Product page	Does not know how to buy the article that is described in the page; is uncertain about the procedure to buy an article on-line	Serious

students participated in the empirical study on a voluntary basis receiving no immediate credit for their participation. Thus, motivation and stress factors could prove important. This implies that students did not have the same kinds of incentives for conducting the usability test sessions as people in a professional usability laboratory. Secondly, the demographics of the test subjects are not varied with respect to age and education. Most subjects were students of approximately 22 years of age with approximately the same school background and recently started on a computer science education.

RESULTS

This section presents the key results from our empirical study. First, we present the problem identification by the 24 participants and compare their reporting with the usability experts. Second, we analyze the identified problems according to their categorization as done by the participants.

Identifying and Reporting Usability Problems

The participants identified very different numbers of usability problems. This is illustrated by two participants reporting no usability problems while one participant identified and reported 18 different usability problems. On average, the participants identified 8.00 usability problems (SD=4.63). This is illustrated in Table 3. The high variety in numbers of reported problems suggests strong presence of the evaluator effect. Therefore, the

Table 3. Mean numbers of identified problems and non-problems

	Problems	Non-Problems	Sum
Tool Participants (N=24)	8.00 (4.63)	2.95 (2.87)	10.39 (5.83)

usability problem identification tool did not in itself remove this effect and indicates that some participants only marginally used the tool.

From our data it seemed from the reporting of usability problems that our participants could be divided into three different groups regarding numbers of reported problems. The first group reported no or very few problems (0-3), the second group reported up to ten problems (4-10), and the third group reported more than ten problems (>10). Six participants belonged to the first group, and 11 participants belonged to the second group, while seven participants belonged to the third group. Interestingly, we saw a gap between participants from the first group compared to the second group as the "best" participants in group one identified three problems whereas none in the second group reported less than seven problems

As stated earlier and further illustrated above, novice evaluators often find it difficult just to see and identify usability problems. Additionally, they are typically faced with challenges when trying to describe (or illustrate) identified problems. Several participants reported issues from the usability test as problems but it was impossible for us to figure out or extract the actual problem from the descriptions. We denote such issues as non-problems (see Table 3). In several cases, these issues were even described in a non-problematic way (e.g. as a positive or neutral feature of the tested system). The participants reported on average 2.95 non-problems (SD=2.87). Again, the numbers of reported non-problems were very diverse between participants having some participants reporting zero non-problems while one participant reported 10 non-problems.

Having discussed numbers of problems identified per participant, we will now outline the reporting of problems for all participants as one group. Two usability experts also conducted a video analysis of the test session and reported usability problems. We will in the following compare the participants in the experiment with these usability experts.

Table 4. Total numbers of identified problems for the two approaches

	Usability Experts (N=2)	Participants (N=24)	Sum (N=26)
Critical	2	2	2
Serious	19	16	19
Cosmetic	17	12	18
Total	38	28	39

The 24 participants together identified and reported a total of 28 different usability problems. Thus on one hand, they were not able to identify all known problems as reported by the usability experts, but they were able to report on a substantial amount of these problems (72%). When looking at problem severity, we found that the participants were able to identify many of the more severe problems. As a group, they identified 86% of the most severe problems (critical and serious problems) where they identified both critical problems and 16 out of the 19 serious problems. On the other hand, they reported on the identification of 12 cosmetic problems out of a total of 18 problems. One participant identified a usability problem not identified or reported by any of the two usability experts. In summary, the participants as a group were able to identify most severe problems as reported by the usability experts while they missed some cosmetic problems in their reporting.

Considering numbers of participants reporting the 28 problems, further analysis show that problem severity had an impact on identification and reporting. Thus, the more severe a problem was the higher the chance of identification and reporting. On average, the critical problems were reported by 67% of the participants. The two critical problems were reported by 18 participants respectively 14 participants. The same figures are considerably lower for the serious and cosmetic problems. In fact, our analysis show that a critical usability problem was significantly

more likely to be reported by a participant than a serious or a cosmetic usability problem according to two-tailed Chi-square tests ($\chi^2[1]=47.691$, $p=0.0001$; $\chi^2[1]=66.012$, $p=0.0001$). However, we only discovered a tendency towards a serious problem being more likely to be reported than a cosmetic problem, but this finding was not significant ($\chi^2[1]=3.725$, $p=0.0536$). Summarized, it appeared that severity had considerable impact on identification as severe problems were more likely to be reported.

Categorization of Usability Problems

As an integrated part of the usability problem identification tool, problems should be categorized according to severity. The usability problem identification tool integrates three levels of severity namely critical, serious, and cosmetic problems (see Table 1). The categorization was characterized by some diversity but also by agreement between the participants. All problems had been categorized according to severity by the two usability experts.

The two problems categorized as critical by the usability experts were identified by 18 respectively 14 participants out of the total number of 24 participants (as discussed previously). However, the two problems were categorized very differently by the participants. The first critical problem (reported by 18) was unanimously categorized as critical by all participants who identified it. This particular problem is that the test subject was unable to complete a purchase on the website. Interestingly, the second critical usability problem was categorized rather differently, where only one participant categorized it as critical, and nine participants categorized it as serious, while four categorized it as cosmetic. This problem is subtle as it reflects how the test subject understands interface elements which make her navigate wrongly. The problem was categorized as critical by both of the usability experts as it delayed her task completion for several minutes. Either the participants did not see this long delay or they disagreed that she was delayed this long. This is not clear from the descriptions, but their reporting typically lacked information on task delay in this situation. This was quite the opposite for the other problem where she failed to complete the task and the delay was obvious.

The remaining 26 serious and cosmetic problems were categorized quite differently by the participants compared the categorization made by the usability experts. Three problems received all three categorizations ranging from critical to cosmetic, but most problems were categorized as either serious or cosmetic. Also, five problems received unanimously categorizations by the participants. Summarized, our analysis of usability problem categorization confirms that this is a highly difficult and challenging task. Furthermore, it seems that individual differences between evaluators are very prominent.

DISCUSSION

Our aim with the usability problem identification tool is to provide software designers and programmers support in constructing more usable interfaces. Thus, we strive to contribute to the body of knowledge within discount usability evaluation by integrating the activities of usability testing into the knowledge of the software developer. In addition, we are interested in providing software projects that are distributed physically with tools or techniques that can support remote usability testing. Inspired by previous research on usability evaluation and particularly on the challenges related to usability problem identification, we developed a usability problem identification tool for use in user-based usability evaluations. The tool is supposed to support evaluators during video analysis of user interaction with a computerized system by emphasizing different levels of problems and modes of experiencing problems. We evaluated the usability problem identification

tool in an experiment with 24 participants. All participants had only introductory knowledge of human-computer interaction issues and no specific training in analysis of usability test sessions.

Our empirical study shows that the participants were able to identify and report many of the more severe problems from the test session. Two critical problems were identified by more than half of the participants; in fact, one critical problem was discovered by 75% of the participants. Several participants used and applied the tool in the identification of the problems and tried to express the problems in terms of the different suggested modes. Especially user delay was commonly used in the reporting. Not surprisingly, less severe problems were not identified to the same extent as the critical problems. More of these problems were only reported by one or two participants, while only four problems were reported by at least ten participants. No problem was reported by all participants partly as a consequence of the fact that two participants reported no usability problems at all.

Promoting remote or distance usability testing conducted by the users themselves require some sort of framework to guide the testing or the analysis. As a group, somewhat surprisingly the participants performed well by identifying a substantial amount of the usability problems. In fact, the most severe problems namely the critical and serious problems were identified almost completely by the group taken as a whole.

A major challenge in usability problem identification and categorization is the so-called evaluator effect. Previous studies have found that the evaluator effect is challenging in user-based usability evaluations such as think-aloud tests as evaluators identify substantial amounts of unique problems (Hertzum and Jacobsen, 2001; Jacobsen et al., 1998). Furthermore, evaluators also suffer from the fact that they identify very few common problems. Our results seem to confirm the evaluator effect as our participants identified several unique problems. This is not surprising.

At this stage, we cannot conclude whether the tool addressed or solved some of the inherent problems of the evaluator effect, but we can see that participants in several cases used the tool actively in their descriptions. But further studies are needed to confirm or reject the effects of different evaluators.

Categorization of usability problems is very difficult and challenging. This was confirmed in our experiment. It seemed that the tool only marginally supported the categorization. The tool was designed to integrate key aspects of severity by illustrating different modes of usability problems for different severity ratings. In certain situations, it seemed to help the participants in understanding the situation and therefore more easily being able to categorize the observed problem. As an example, most participants actively used the tool in the categorization of one of the critical problems. However, several problems were categorized rather differently by the participants sometimes reflecting differences in the assessed scope of the problem.

We have only involved novice evaluators as participants in our study, just like the studies in (Hornbæk and Frøkjær, 2004). Studies involving expert evaluators tend to identify more and different kinds of problems (Nielsen, 1992). However, to compensate against this potential problem, we measured the participants' performance against experienced usability evaluators. The participants taken together identified a significant proportion of the problems identified by the experts.

FURTHER DEVELOPMENT

The usability problem identification tool used in this experiment has been developed entirely through introspective observation of our own problem identification and categorization process in other usability evaluations. In addition, certain parts are still vaguely defined. In other domains, there is a considerable confidence in the use of checklists. Schamel (2008) present the history behind introduction of checklists in aviation.

Hales and Provonost (2006) describes a checklist as a list of action items or criteria that are arranged in a systematic manner, which allow the user to record the presence/absence of the individual items listed to ensure that all of them are considered or completed. They emphasize that the objectives of a checklist may be to support memory recall, standardization and regulation of processes or methodologies. They present an overview of the use of checklists in the areas of aviation, product manufacturing, healthcare and critical care.

Hales et al. (2008) have conducted a systematic study of literature on checklist. They provide a categorization of different checklists with examples from medicine. Some of these categories are clearly relevant for usability evaluation. The tool we have presented in this chapter resembles what they call a Diagnostic checklist or a Criteria of merit checklist. They also provide guidelines for development of checklists. This could be a useful basis for enhancing our problem identification tool.

Verdaasdonk et al. (2008) argue that the use of checklists is a promising strategy for improving patient safety in all types of surgical processes. They present requirements and guidelines for implementation of checklists for surgical processes. Helander (2006) describes checklists in relation to HCI. He emphasizes the checklist as a memory aid that can be used to support systematic assessment of ergonomics in a workplace.

All of these examples deals with checklists for professionals. Our tool can be considered as a simple checklist. It has been shown that a usability problem identification tool like the one presented in this chapter combined with education provides solid support to problem identification and categorization (Skov and Stage, 2005). The results presented in this chapter show that even without training, the tool provides some assistance. However, the results also indicate that the tool could be improved. Other researchers in the HCI area have worked with definition of usability problems from a usability problem identification platform (Cockton et al., 2004; Lavery et al., 1997). It may be possible to combine this with the guidelines for developing checklist in order to create an enhanced usability problem identification tool.

CONCLUSION

This paper has presented results from an empirical study of methodological support to identification of usability problems as part of a usability evaluation. The key element of the support was a usability problem identification tool for identification of usability problems.

The non-expert participants in the experiment found on average 8 usability problems, but with substantial differences between them. Two usability experts found 38 problems. Compared to this, the performance of the participants is limited. On the other hand, the 24 participants together identified 72% of the problems found by the experts. And they found nearly all critical and serious problems. This is very interesting given that the time spent on data analysis of the problem lists produced by the participants is very limited. This indicates that even with a very limited expert effort you are able to get a large proportion of the severe problems provided that you involve a group of participants that is larger than what we normally are used to. This gives a reason to be optimistic about the ideas of having developers report usability problems.

The idea of this approach is to reduce the efforts needed to conduct usability testing. This is consistent with the ideas behind heuristic inspection and other walkthrough techniques. On a more general level, it would be interesting to identify other potential areas for reducing effort.

These conclusions are based on a single experiment with 24 participants. Unfortunately, there are very few results in the literature to compare

with. Therefore, it would be interesting to repeat the empirical study. The usability problem identification tool could also be developed further, especially in order to support categorization of usability problems.

ACKNOWLEDGMENT

The work behind this paper received financial support from the Danish Research Agency (grant no. 2106-04-0022). We would especially like to thank all the participating test subjects. Finally, we want to thank the anonymous reviewers for comments on the draft of this paper

REFERENCES

Agarwal, R., & Venkatesh, V. (2002). Assessing a Firm's Web Presence: A Heuristic Evaluation Procedure for the Measurement of Usability. *Information Systems Research*, *13*(2), 168–186. doi:10.1287/isre.13.2.168.84

Anderson, J., Fleek, F., Garrity, K., & Drake, F. (2001). Integrating Usability Techniques into Software Development. *IEEE Software*, *18*(1), 46–53. doi:10.1109/52.903166

Andreasen, M. S., Nielsen, H. V., Schrøder, S. O., & Stage, J. (2006). Usability in open source software development: Opinions and practice. *Information Technology and Control*, *35A*(3), 303–312.

Andreasen, M. S., Nielsen, H. V., Schrøder, S. O., & Stage, J. (2007). What Happened to Remote Usability Testing? An Empirical Study of Three Methods. In *Proceedings of CHI 2007*. New York: ACM Press.

Badre, A. N. (2002). *Shaping Web Usability – Interaction Design in Context*. Boston: Addison-Wesley.

Bak, J. O., Nguyen, K., Risgaard, P., & Stage, J. (2008) Obstacles to Usability Evaluation in Practice: A Survey of Software Organizations. In *Proceedings of NordiCHI 2008*. New York: ACM Press.

Benson, C., Muller-Prove, M., & Mzourek, J. (2004). Professional usability in open source projects: Gnome, openoffice.org, netbeans. In *Proceedings of CHI 2004* (pp. 1083-1084). New York: ACM Press.

Braiterman, J., Verhage, S., & Choo, R. (2000). Designing with Users in Internet Time. *Interactions, 7*(5, September–October), 23-27.

Bruun, A., Gull, P., Hofmeister, L., & Stage, J. (2009). Let your users do the testing: a comparison of three remote asynchronous usability testing methods. *Proceedings of CHI 2009*. New York: ACM Press.

Castillo, J. C., Hartson, H. R., & Hix, D. (1998). Remote usability evaluation: Can users report their own critical incidents? In *Proceedings of CHI 1998*, (pp. 253-254). New York: ACM Press.

Cockton, G., Woolrych, A., & Hindmarch, M. (2004) Reconditioned Merchandise: Extended Structured Report Formats in Usability Inspection. In *CHI 2004 Extended Abstracts*, (pp. 1433-36). New York: ACM Press.

Dempsey, B. J., Weiss, D., Jones, P., & Greenberg, J. (2002). Who is an open source software developer? *Communications of the ACM, 45*(2), 67–72. doi:10.1145/503124.503125

Dumas, J. S., & Redish, J. C. (1993). *A practical guide to usability testing.* Norwood, NJ: Ablex Publishing.

Fath, J. L., Mann, T. L., & Holzman, T. G. (1994). A Practical Guide to Using Software Usability Labs: Lessons Learned at IBM. *Behaviour & Information Technology, 13*(1-2), 25–35.

Frishberg, N., Dirks, A. M., Benson, C., Nickell, S., & Smith, S. (2002). Getting to know you: Open source development meets usability. In *Proceedings of CHI 2002,* (pp. 932-933). New York: ACM Press.

Hales, B. M., & Provonost, P. J. (2006). The checklist. A tool for error management and performance improvement. *Journal of Critical Care, 21*, 231–235. doi:10.1016/j.jcrc.2006.06.002

Hales, B. M., Terblanche, M., Fowler, R., & Sibbald, W. (2008). Development of medical checklists for improved quality of patient care. *International Journal for Quality in Health Care, 20*(1), 22–30. doi:10.1093/intqhc/mzm062

Hartson, H. R., & Castillo, J. C. (1998). Remote evaluation for post-deployment usability improvement. In *Proceedings of AVI 1998*, (pp. 22-29). New York: ACM Press.

Hartson, H. R., Castillo, J. C., Kelso, J., & Neale, W. C. (1996). Remote evaluation: The network as an extension of the usability laboratory. In *Proceedings of CHI 1996*, (pp. 228-235). ACM Press

Helander, M. (2006). *A Guide to Human Factors and Ergonomics*, (2nd ed.). Boca Raton, FL: CRC Press.

Hertzum, M., & Jacobsen, N. E. (2001). The evaluator effect: A chilling fact about us-ability evaluation methods. *International Journal of Human-Computer Interaction, 13*(4), 421–443. doi:10.1207/S15327590IJHC1304_05

Hornbæk, K., & Frøkjær, E. (2004). Usability Inspection by Metaphors of Human Thinking Compared to Heuristic Evaluation. *International Journal of Human-Computer Interaction, 17*(3), 357–374. doi:10.1207/s15327590ijhc1703_4

ISO 9241-11. (1997). *Ergonomic Requirements for Office Work with Visual Display Terminals* (VDTs), (Part 11: Guidance on usability). ISO.

Jacobsen, N. E., Hertzum, M., & John, B. E. (1998) The Evaluator Effect in Usability Tests. In *Proc. CHI'98*. New York: ACM Press

Jeffries, R., Miller, J. R., Wharton, C., & Uyeda, K. M. (1991) User Interface Evaluation in the Real World: A Comparison of Four Techniques. In *Proceedings of CHI '91*, (pp. 119-124). New York: ACM Press.

Karat, C.-M., Campbell, R., & Fiegel, T. (1992) Comparison of Empirical Testing and Walk-through Methods in User Interface Evaluation. In *Proceedings of CHI '92*, (pp. 397-404). New York; ACM Press

Krug, S. (2000) *Don't Make Me Think – A Common Sense Approach to Web Usability*. Circle. com Library, USA

Lavery, D., Cockton, G., & Atkinson, M. P. (1997). Comparison of Evaluation Methods Using Structured Usability Problem Reports. *Behaviour & Information Technology*, *16*(4), 246–266. doi:10.1080/014492997119824

Molich, R. (2000). *User-Friendly Web Design* (in Danish). Copenhagen: Ingeniøren Books.

Murphy, J., Howard, S., Kjeldskov, K., & Goschnick, S. (2004). Location, location, location: Challenges of outsourced usability evaluation. In *Proceedings of the Workshop on Improving the Interplay between Usability Evaluation and User Interface Design, NordiCHI 2004*, Aalborg University, Department of Computer Science, HCI-Lab Report no. 2004/2, (pp. 12-15).

Nielsen, J. (1992). Finding Usability Problems Through Heuristic Evaluation. In *Proceedings of CHI '92*, (pp. 373-380). New York: ACM Press.

Nielsen, J. (1993). Usability Engineering. San Francisco: Morgan Kaufmann Publishers.

Nielsen, J. (2000). *Designing Web Usability*. New York: New Riders Publishing.

Nielsen, J., Bush, R. M., Dayton, T., Mond, N. E., Muller, M. J., & Root, R. W. (1992). Teaching experienced developers to design graphical user interfaces. In *Proceedings of CHI 1992*, (pp. 557-564). New York: ACM Press.

Nielsen, J., & Tahir, M. (2002). Homepage Usability – 50 Websites Deconstructed. New York: New Riders Publishing.

Preece, J., Rogers, Y., & Sharp, H. (2002). *Interaction Design: Beyond Human-Computer Interaction*. New York: John Wiley and Sons.

Rohn, J. A. (1994). The Usability Engineering Laboratories at Sun Microsystems. *Behaviour & Information Technology*, *13*(1-2), 25–35. doi:10.1080/01449299408914581

Rubin, J. (1994). *Handbook of Usability Testing: How to plan, design and conduct effective tests*. New York: John Wiley & Sons, Inc.

Schamel, J. (2008). *How the pilot's checklist came about*. Retrieved from http://www.atchistory.org/History/checklst.htm

Scholtz, J., Laskowski, S., & Downey, L. (1998). Developing Usability Tools and Techniques for Designing and Testing Web Sites. In *Proceedings of the 4th Conference on Human Factors & the Web*. AT&T.

Skov, M. B., & Stage, J. (2001). A Simple Approach to Web-Site Usability Testing. In *Proceedings of 1st International Conference on Universal Access in Human-Computer Interaction*, (pp. 737-741). Mahwah, NJ: Lawrence-Erlbaum.

Skov, M. B., & Stage, J. (2004) Integrating Usability Design and Evaluation: Training Novice Evaluators in Usability Testing. In K. Hornbæk & J. Stage (Eds.), *Proceedings of the Workshop on Improving the Interplay between Usability Evaluation and User Interface Design, NordiCHI 2004*, (pp. 31-35), Aalborg University, Department of Computer Science, HCI-Lab Report no. 2004/2.

Skov, M. B., & Stage, J. (2005) Supporting Problem Identification in Usability Evaluations. In *Proceedings of the Australian Computer-Human Interaction Conference 2005 (OzCHI'05)*. New York: ACM Press.

Slavkovic, A., & Cross, K. (1999). Novice heuristic evaluations of a complex interface. In *Proceedings of CHI 1999*, (pp. 304-305). New York: ACM Press.

Spool, J. M., Scanlon, T., Schroeder, W., Snyder, C., & DeAngelo, T. (1999). *Web Site Usability – A Designer's Guide*. San Francisco: Morgan Kaufmann Publishers, Inc.

Sullivan, T., & Matson, R. (2000). Barriers to Use: Usability and Content Accessibility on the Web's Most Popular Sites. In *Proceedings of Conference on Universal Usability*, November 16-17, Washington, (pp. 139-144). New York: ACM.

Sutcliffe, A. (2001). Heuristic Evaluation of Website Attractiveness and Usability. *Interactive Systems: Design, Specification, and Verification*, (. *LNCS, 2220*, 183–198.

Verdaasdonk, E. G. G., Stassen, L. P. S., Widhiasmara, P. P., & Dankelman, J. (2008) Requirements for the design and implementation of checklists for surgical processes. *Surgical Endoscopy*.

Chapter 2
A Structured Methodology for Developing 3D Web Applications

Juan Manuel González-Calleros
Université catholique de Louvain, Belgium

Jean Vanderdonckt
Université catholique de Louvain, Belgium

Jaime Muñoz-Arteaga
Universidad Autónoma de Aguascalientes, México CENIDET, México

ABSTRACT

Effective and satisfying Web usability is crucial for successfully built Web applications. Traditionally, Web development considered 2D User Interfaces (2D UI) based on Graphical User Interfaces (GUI). Since the end of the 90's, the evolution of technology and computers capacity introduced a new paradigm, the Web 3D. Similarly to traditional web development, Web 3D development requires an interdisciplinary approach and a profound theoretical background. In this chapter the authors attempt to structure a methodology to support 3DUIs development. The development methodology is articulated on three axes: models and their specification language, method, and tools that support the methodology based on the underlying models. The method considers guidelines to support its correct use towards producing usable 3DUIs.

INTRODUCTION

Three-dimensional (3D) interaction is an exciting field of research that promises to allow users to perform tasks freely in three dimensions rather than being limited by the two-dimensional (2D) desktop metaphor of conventional graphical interfaces. For

DOI: 10.4018/978-1-60566-896-3.ch002

some computer-based tasks, pure 3D representations are clearly helpful and have become major industries: medical imagery, architectural drawing, computer-assisted design and scientific simulations, (Shneiderman, 2003). Those systems traditionally are associated to complex and expensive technologies. Games industry is leading the market and showing the potential of rendering 3D graphics in a desktop computer and for the Web.

In *Human-Computer Interaction* (HCI) several structured methods (Wilson, Eastgate, & D'Cruz, 2002); Celentano & Pittarello, 2001; Gabbard, Hix, & Swan, 1999; Kaur, 1998; Witmer & Singer, 1998); Bowman, Kruijff, & Laviola, 2004) have been introduced to develop *Three Dimensional User Interfaces* (3DUIs), decomposing *User Interface* (UI) software development life cycle into steps and sub-steps. Despite this situation, these methods rarely provide any form of design knowledge that should be typically used for achieving each step. This is primarily caused by the fact that the development life cycle is more focusing on the programming issues (content-centric approach) rather than on the design and analysis phases. This is also reinforced by the fact that available tools for 3DUI development are content-centric, typically toolkits, interface builders, rendering engines.

We argue that developing 3DUIs is an activity that would benefit from the application of a methodology which is typically composed of:

1. a set of models gathered in an ontology;
2. a method manipulating the involved models based on guidelines;
3. a language that express models in the method.

Our goal is not to prove that Web 3DUI are better or worse than 2DUI or any other Information System, rather, we consider the benefits and shortcomings as granted and rely on them. Some studies (Cockburn and McKenzie, 2001; Shneiderman, 2002) concluded that 3D presentation is not just more attractive for the users but also provide a best option for developers to manage the information visualization issue. In their review of applications, Cockburn (2001) offer some examples of user performance in 3D applications. They found that user preferences are on the use of 3D systems, as users found them more natural to use. Also, that 3D user interfaces are better to use for cognitive reasons, as it exploits the spatial memory and cognition of humans.

Model-Driven Development of User Interfaces (MDDUI) is finding its way from academic research to practical applications in industrial projects. As opposed to a content-centric approach, MDDUI involves users in the requirements analysis and evaluation. Separating the conceptual part from the rest of the life cycle to identify and manage the *Computing-Independent Models* (CIM as defined in the Model-Driven Engineering–MDE) from the Computing-Dependent part. This part is in turn typically decomposed into issues that are relevant only to one particular development environment (*Platform-Specific Models* –PSM) as opposed to those issues which remain independent from any underlying software (*Platform-Independent Models*–PIM). In the MDE paradigm promoted by the Object Management Group (www.omg.org), it is expected that any development method is able to apply this principle of separation of concerns, is able to capture various aspects of the problem through models, and is capable of progressing moving from the abstract models (CIM and PIM) to the more concrete models (PSM and final code).

By expressing the steps of the method through transformations between models, the method adheres to MDE paradigm where models and transformations are explicitly defined and used. Models are uniformly expressed in the same *User Interface Description Language* (UIDL), which is selected to be UsiXML (User Interface eXtensible Markup Language – www.usixml.org (Vanderdonckt, 2005), any other UIDL could be used equally provided that the used concepts are also supported. The use of a formal specification technique is extremely valuable, because it provides non-ambiguous, complete and concise ways of describing the behaviour of the systems. Finally, different principles are used to guide designers while applying the methodology, including usability guidelines when appropriate. For instance, a set of transformation rules are applied to support the concretization of the development steps of the method where Usability guidelines are encoded as a subset of transformation rules that are applied at the different steps of the method.

The reminder of this chapter is structured as follows: background section presents a review on existing methods for 3DUI development. After reviewing exiting work, the proposed methodology is presented including: models, development steps, transformation rules, and principles (e.g., guidelines, patterns, canonical task types) supporting the use of the methodology. Afterwards, the software to support the automatic use of the methodology is described. Finally, we conclude this chapter by summarizing the benefits of this methodology.

BACKGROUND

There is a plethora of methodologies for developing 3DUIs using different models, methods, and evaluation tools. Due to the diversity of existing works comparing them without a common ground would be time consuming and probably without any significant result. The *Cameleon Reference Framework* (CRF) (Calvary et al., 2003) was chosen as a common ground in order to compare evaluation methods in existing methodologies, among other reasons, because: is the result of an European project; it has been used as theoretical background in subsequent related projects in different countries; is structured according to four basic levels of abstractions that are compliant with OMG recommendations: task & concepts (CIM), abstract UI (PIM), concrete UI (PSM) and final UI (source code); the scientific community has reached some consensus about using this CRF (even if they diverge in the respective implementations of this CRF); finally, w have experience using it.

Some authors, of 3DUI methodologies, introduced usability evaluation in intermediate development steps. Some others just evaluate the final result. There is a wide set of techniques used for evaluating 3DUI. Those techniques have

been proved to be good not just in immersive applications but also in other context of use, such as: desktop UIs, Web UIs. If fact none of exiting tools and methods used in 3DUI evaluation are new or unique (Bowman, Kruijff, & Laviola, 2004), they have been used for 2DUI evaluation. A set of methodologies for 3DUI development were selected, analyzed and gathered. Evidently, there is a plethora of methods and we might have skipped some significant work in this area. However, our goal is not to be exhaustive but to show exiting work in this area.

A Comparison of 3DUI Development Methodologies

Wilson, Eastgate & D'Cruz (2002) introduced different actions at early development steps to evaluate usability: Feedback definition (this characteristic is used to reinforce the comprehension on the 3DUI); then, a survey of *Interaction Techniques* (IT) is done. Based on the selected IT, task analysis is performed over task models to evaluate speed and applicability of the 3DUI. Once implemented, the 3DUI is evaluated to check: the fidelity, compared to the real life stuff it represents; and the validity, if the 3DUI corresponds to the real life phenomenon.

In Gabbard, Hix, & Swan (1999), Guideline-based expert evaluation, when task are described that is later evaluated using task analysis. In late development phases a heuristic evaluation is performed based on guidelines and expert evaluation on prototypes. This step is really important before going into implementation. Finally, expert guidelines are used to evaluate the resulting 3DUI.

In Bowman, Kruijff, & Laviola (2004), User task (task properties) scenarios are used to validate the usability of the task models. The possible use of IT is evaluated based on taxonomy, metaphor-based (Poupyrev et al., 1997) or IT-based, decomposition, an interesting approach that theoretically evaluate composition of exiting and proved IT. The context of use (environment, user, system) is analyzed. Early requirements end with a summative evaluation of IT (similarly to: Hix, & Hartson, 1993; Poupyrev et al., 1997). The concretization of the task modelling is evaluated on prototypes of low-fidelity (similarly to: Hix, & Hartson, 1993) and IT using Wizard of OZ. The Final result uses the widely used testbed evaluation, including summative evaluation (similarly as Poupyrev et al., 1997).

Finally, there are some other methodologies that just evaluate the final 3DUI and not intermediary steps, for instance, evaluation of the 3DUI with end-users and experts (Celentano, & Pittarello, 2001; Neale, 2001); presence questionnaires (Witmer, & Singer, 1998); simulator sickness questionnaire (Kennedy et al., 1993). Similarly, other methodologies just evaluate early stages of the development, for instance, Task analysis (Hackos, & Redish, 1998); multidimensional design spaces (Card, Mackinlay, & Robertson, 1990).

In this review of the literature (Table 1), evaluation method used in each development step was analyzed. Taking into account the development step where such evaluation is performed considering the CRF as common ground. A dotted line (----) means that the development step is not supported by the methodology. The letters at the beginning of each paragraph denotes whether the method is respectively: *automatic* (A), *manual* (M) or *both* (B).

From the aforementioned survey we notice that most of the methods apply evaluation just at the end of the development process. Some others introduce early evaluation based on task analysis, scenarios, prototyping. A survey on usability evaluation methods for virtual environments conducted by Bowman, Gabbart and Hix (2002) shows that the most well known and used methods classified according to three axes: *User involvement*, this characteristic illustrates methods that require users either beta or experts and those that do not; *type of results*, this characteristic identifies whether or not a given usability evaluation method produces qualitative or quantitative data; and *context of evaluation*, this characteristic represents the type of context in which the evaluation is conducted, it can be a generic context of use or simply an application-specific one, for which results remain specific. As observed by Bowman, Gabbard, & Hix (2002) the characteristics are not mutually exclusive: on the contrary as they all form a design space for evaluation design. The present work is situated on different axes, depending on the development step. The evaluation at each step can be performed manually or automatically. More details on the different techniques used to assure usability are found in the next section.

We conclude this section by referring to existing approaches for usability evaluation and their diversity. As Bowman, Kruijff, & Laviola (2004) identified, most of the times evaluation is linked with the budget of the project. In most of research projects it is always better to have some sort of evaluation, even informal, than nothing. Some methodologies rely on expert evaluation, at different steps of their methodologies, which is not an asset easy to find, not just for the cost but also for their availability. Another problem found in this review is the lack of modality independence: the development is often linked to a particular interaction modality since the early development stages are themselves bound to some interaction techniques, referring to the modality (mode=sense + device) of interaction. The most complete set of guidelines for 3DUI development that covers different development steps was probably presented by Kaur (1998). This set of guidelines was reused in this chapter. In order to provide yet another possibility to evaluate 3DUI our method, introduced below, could be an option to cope with the budget problem.

A METHODOLOGY FOR DEVELOPING 3D USER INTERFACES

Web Engineering for 3D Web application is an area in which model-driven software development can be successfully applied in a similar way as for GUIs (Moreno, Romero, & Vallecillo, 2007). Our methodology relies on our previous work (Gonzalez, Vanderdonckt, & Muñoz, 2006) (Figure 1), which is decomposed into four development steps:

1. *Task & Concepts (T&C):* describe the various users' tasks to be carried out and the domain-oriented concepts as they are required by these tasks to be performed.

Table 1. Review of existing evaluation methods

	Usability Evaluation Method			
	Task & Concepts	**AUI**	**CUI**	**FUI**
Wilson et al., 2002	(M) Feedback definition (B) Task analysis (M) Interaction techniques selection based on survey of available interactions.	----	----	(M) Fidelity and validity of the virtual environment.
Celentano & Pittarello, 2001	----	----	----	(M) User and Expert experience evaluation
Gabbard et al., 1999	(B) Task analysis (M) Guideline-based expert evaluation	----	(M) Heuristic evaluation based on guidelines expert evaluation on prototypes	(M) Experts guidelines evaluated on the VE
Nedel & Freitas, 2006	(M) Usability aspects to be evaluated are defined	----	(M) Design User experiments	(M) User experience evaluation based on questionnaires
Neale & Nichols, 2001	----	----	----	(M) Evaluation on user and expert experience
Kaur, 1998	(M) Guideline-based evaluation	----	(M) Guideline-based evaluation	(M) Guideline-based evaluation
Hackos, & Redish, 1998	(B) Task analysis	----	----	----
Witmer, & Singer, 1998	----	-----	----	(M) Presence Questionnaire
Kennedy et al., 1993	----	-----	----	(M) Simulator sickness questionnaire
Bowman et al., 2004	(M)User task (task properties) scenarios. (M) Interaction Technique evaluation based on taxonomy decomposition (M) Context (environment, user, system) analysis (B) Summative evaluations of IT	----	(M)Evaluation on low-fidelity prototyping. (M)Wizard of OZ.	Summative evaluation (M) Testbed evaluation
Hix, & Hartson, 1993	(B) Summative evaluations of IT	----	(M) Formative evaluation with Prototyping	----
Card et al., 1990	(B) Multidimensional design spaces	----	----	----
Poupyrev et al., 1997	Metaphor-based classifications	----	----	Summative evaluation
Steed, & Tromp, 1998	----	----	(M) Guideline-based expert evaluation on prototypes	Cognitive Walkthrough
Our Proposal	(B) Evaluation based n guideline rules	(B) Evaluation based on guideline rules	(B) Evaluation based on guideline rules	(B) Evaluation based on guideline rules

Figure 1. Outline of the method for developing 3D UIs

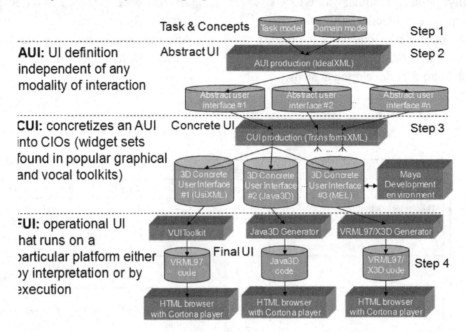

2. *Abstract UI (AUI):* defines abstract containers (AC) and individual components (AIC) (Limbourg, 2004), two forms of Abstract Interaction Objects (AIO), introduced by Vanderdonckt & Bodart (1993), that group subtasks according to various criteria (e.g., task model structural patterns, cognitive load analysis, semantic relationships identification), a navigation scheme between the container and selects abstract individual component for each concept so that they are independent of any modality.

3. *Concrete UI (CUI):* concretizes an abstract UI for a given context of use into Concrete Interaction Objects (CIOs) (Vanderdonckt & Bodart, 1993), so as to define widgets layout and interface navigation. It abstracts a FUI into a UI definition that is independent of any computing platform. For example, in Envir3D (Vanderdonckt et al., 2004), the CUI consists of a description of traditional 2D widgets with mappings to 3D by relying on different mechanisms when such a mapping is possible.

4. *Final UI (FUI):* is the operational 3DUI i.e. any 3DUI running on a particular computing platform either by interpretation (e.g., through a Web browser) or by execution (e.g., after compilation of code in an interactive development environment.

The method still has some open issues (De Boeck et al., 2006), including, but not limited to:

- From a technological point of view it involves an integration of technologies to support the *complete* process. A transformation engine to support the transformational approach, high-level editors to support the design of concepts at each development step, a change tracking system (reverse engineering process) to identify changes in dependent models are also beneficial in a mature model-based approach.
- From a methodological point of view, there are quite some open issues for which the solution is not straightforward.

Figure 2. Architecture for the usability evaluation system

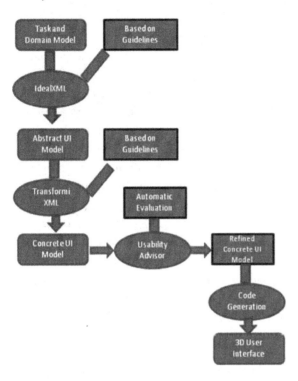

This chapter focuses on the methodological aspects addressing guidelines and heuristics that can be manually or automatically incorporated in the development steps in order to contribute on the creation of usable 3DUI. The next subsection discusses each sub-step and how guidelines can be incorporated.

Step1: Task and Concepts Modelling

The task model is today at the core of many design activities carried out during the UI development life cycle, such as: user task analysis (Hackos, & Redish, 1998), user task scenarios, design space based on taxonomies (Card, Mackinlay, & Robertson, 1990), metaphor-based classification (Poupyrev et al., 1997) and technique decomposition taxonomy (Bowman & Hodges, 1999). Modelling a task based on well-defined semantics and using a well-understood notation are key aspects, but the many degrees of freedom offered by task

modelling should not let us to forget the quality of the resulting task model. Over time, we observed the following potential shortcomings:

- *Incompleteness*: labels, definitions, goals, and properties used for a task suffer from many drawbacks such as short name, name without action verb or without object (and therefore non-compliant with the traditional interaction paradigm of action+object), name that is incompatible with its definition, no usage of standard classification.
- *Inconsistency*: labels, definitions, goals, and properties used for a task do not have unique names (e.g., a label or a goal is duplicated), there are some homonyms, and there are some synonyms (e.g., tasks having the same semantics but wearing different names).
- *Incorrectness*: labels, definitions, goals, and properties used for a task violate some of Meyer's seven sins (1985) of specification, i.e., noise, silence, overspecification, contradiction, ambiguity, forward reference, and wishful thinking.

The aforementioned shortcomings are not just observed while modelling task. They could be propagated, if not amplified, throughout the rest of the UI development life cycle since it is effectively based on the task model. The potential damages are even more important if they reach the stage of the FUI. Indeed, several approaches, Frank and Foley (1993), Paternò (1999), Puerta (1997) and Vanderdonckt (2005), use task models to specify and generate UIs. The way of selecting the widgets to be used or the interaction techniques is rather intuitive in Frank and Foley (1993), Paternò (1999), Puerta (1997), while Vanderdonckt (2005) takes this decision on specific attributes of the task model.

In Vanderdonckt (2005), the UI interaction (UII) is characterized by two elements: (1) the task type (sometimes called action or activity in the literature) and (2) the item manipulated/ required in the action. Both attributes are relevant to designing interactive systems using task models that later are transformed in UIs.

In 2003, Constantine introduced an abstract set of task types used in common UII. However, an extension to the set of proposed action types is needed, as they do not express a complete abstraction including existing UI action tasks. Due to the fact that most tasks are application dependent it is not feasible to include all tasks types for each existing interaction techniques. So, in order to reduce the design space UI action types from patterns and common UIs are proposed. The benefit of such taxonomy is applied when designing the concrete model.

User Interface Interaction Taxonomy

Existing UII taxonomies are modality-dependent, some examples are: the abstract interaction of 2DUI by Constantine (2003) and Limbourg et al. (2004); Web interaction taxonomy by Jansen (2006); haptic interaction taxonomy, Bodart and Vanderdonckt (1994), Bleser and Silbert (1990), Hutchinson et al. (1989) and Limbourg (2005); input devices by Greenstein and Arnaut (1988). Some other taxonomy is modality-independent such as: user/system-actions/activities taxonomy such as Johnsgard, Page et al. (1995) and Foley, Wallace and Chan (1984). After comparing these taxonomies, their related action types defined and looking at their definition, we propose a new taxonomy of action types (Gonzalez, Vanderdonckt, Muñoz, 2009) that encompasses all the task types found in these references. In this taxonomy, each action type is named, defined, exemplified, and comes with some related UI actions (Table 2).

Task Patterns for 3DUI Modelling

HCI patterns has been used to specify and to capitalize good practices to design graphical UIs in different domains, such as: interactive patterns (Welie et al., 2000), usability patterns (Mahemoff

et al., 2001), task patterns (Pribeanu et al., 2003), games design patterns (Davidsson et al., 2004) and design patterns (Gamma et al., 1995). The idea of using patterns for task models is not new. The goal is to simplify designer's workload and to have just one single representation of well known tasks (patterns). By using this approach, it can be ensured, in some way that further reifications of the task models to UIs found in the subsequent levels (i.e., AUI, CUI, and FUI) are valid.

There has been a lot of work regarding the modelling that captures the essence of successful solutions for 3DUI development, majorly for interaction techniques. Modelling interaction at the task model require a level of abstraction that is independent of the modality, thus interaction techniques should not be detailed in a task model. Rather, the user task to be performed in the 3DUI. Findings from Bowman et al. (2004) showed that interaction in 3DUI can be expressed in four main tasks. The so called Universal 3D interaction tasks are: Navigation, Selection, Manipulation and System control. In Bowman et al. (2004), they when through a detailed description of the different interaction techniques that exists for each Universal 3D interaction task. While removing the lower branches of the task models they propose, those including modality and device dependant characteristics, the pruned tree showed a solution pattern for each 3D Universal interaction task.

Even that the use of pattern-based development life-cycle is contradictory to model- driven, as patterns are poorly structured or in many different ways. Yet this is the case of the patterns collected in next subsections. However, there has been some works (Gaffar, Sinnig, Seffah, & Forbrig, 2004) showing the potential of modelling patterns for task models and to reuse successful solutions. In the remaining subsections, the 3D Universal interaction tasks patterns are expressed in terms of our task model. It is not the scope of this chapter to go beyond this description since most issues related to pattern-based design is extensively addressed in the literature. The description is limited to the *problem body* (accordingly to Alexander's pattern notation), including the empirical background, and the task model. This could be easily extended into more detailed pattern Markup languages such as PLML (Pattern Language Markup Language), as it was done in (Montero & Vanderdonckt, 2008).

Navigation Pattern

Bowman et al. (2004) define navigation as the composition of two concurrent tasks travel and way finding (Figure 3).

Travel pattern. Travel is the motor component of navigation and just refers to the physical

movement from place to place (Figure 4) with a common pattern *indicate position* and to *translate the view*. The set of specialisations expressed as IT are:

- *Gaze-directed steering using head tracking* (Mine, 1995). The involved tasks are: *Indicate direction*, the user move his head toward the desired direction, the system track the direction and *translate to the selected viewpoint*.
- Pointing using hand tracking (Mine, 1995; Bowman, Koller, & Hodges, 1997). The

Table 2. Canonical list of User Interface Action task types

Action Type	Refer to User Interface Actions	Definition	Examples
Convey	Communicate, Transmit, call, acknowledge, respond/answer, suggest, direct, instruct, request	The action to exchange information	Show details, Switch to summary
Create	Input/Encode/Enter Associate, name, group, introduce, insert, (new), assemble, aggregate, overlay (cover), add	Specifies the creation of an item instance	New customer, blank slide
Delete	Eliminate, Remove/cut, ungroup, disassociate, ungroup	The action of deleting an item	Break connection, Delete file/slide
Duplicate	Copy	Specifies the copy of an item	copy address, duplicate slide
Filter	Segregate, set aside	The action of filtering an item	Filter email, segregate any modification on a data base when backing up
Mediate	Analyze, synthesize, compare, evaluate, decide	The action of intercede task items	Compare products characteristics on a online store
Modify	Change Alter, transform, tuning, and rename, segregate, resize, and collapse/expand	An action of modifying an item	Change shipping address, Tuning volume
Move	Relocate, Hide, show, position, Orient, Path or travel	the action to change the location of an item	Put into address list, move up/down?
Navigation	Go/To	the action to find the way through containers	Navigation bar on a Web browser
Perceive	Acquire/detect/search for/scan/extract, identify / discriminate / recognize, Locate, Examine, monitor, scan, detect,	The action of identifying items and/or information from the items	Locate a destination in a map, observe the status bar while installing
Reinitialize	Wipe out, Clear, Erase	The action of cleaning an item	Clear form,
Select/choose	Pick	selection between items	group member picker, object selector
Trigger	Initiate/Start, Play, Search, active, execute, function, record, purchase	Specifies the beginning of an operation	Play audio/video file
Stop	End / finish/exit/suspend/complete /Terminate/ Cancel	Specifies the end of an action	Stop searching/playing, cancel register
Toggle	activate/ deactivate, /switch	The existence of two different states of an item	Bold on/off, encrypted mode,

involved tasks are: *Indicate direction*, the User move arm toward the desired direction, System track direction, and *Translate to the selected viewpoint*.

- *Map-based* (Bowman et al., 1998). The involved tasks are: *Indicate direction*, Select icon on the map, Drag icon, Release icon, the system translate to the selected viewpoint.
- Grabbing the air (Mapes & Moshell, 1995). The involved tasks are: Indicate direction, Select position (pinch or click on it), Translate to view point selected, Stop selection, and Release button or stop pitching.

Figure 3. Navigation pattern

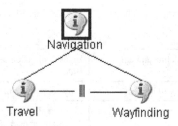

Figure 4. Travel pattern

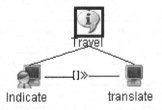

Figure 5. Wayfinding pattern

Wayfinding pattern. Wayfinding is part of the navigation task because it represents the cognitive task to decide where to go (Bowman et al. 2004). To help the user on this task the system must provide enough information to answer basic question: where am I? Where can I go? The involved tasks for Wayfinding are: The system *extract Information on User position*, the system *build up spatial* world structure and the user uses the spatial knowledge to *make a decision*.

Select Pattern

The select pattern (Figure 6) refers to objects selection in a 3DUI. Bowman et al. (2004) identified four interaction techniques for task selection:

- *Virtual Hand*. The most common technique is the virtual hand metaphor, which consists in representing the hand to touch objects as we do in the real world. There are two types: with or without any haptic feedback. The involved tasks are: the user *indicates position* by moving their hand, the system *identifies intersect/collision* depending on hand position with objects, and system provide feedback of the *selected object*.
- *Ray-Casting* (Mine, 1995). This is another common technique that uses the metaphor of a laser pointer, an infinite ray extending from the virtual hand. The involved tasks are: the user *indicates position*, user move hand, system determines ray direction, the system *identify intersect/collision*

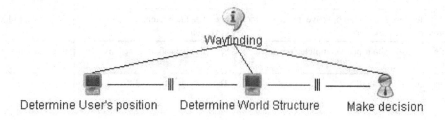

Figure 6. Select pattern

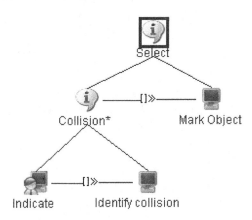

and system provide feedback of *selected object*.

- *Sticky finger* (Pierce, Forsberg, & Conway 1997). This is a technique that let users reach occluded objects. The involved tasks are: the user *indicates position*, user move head, user move hand, the system determine ray position by subtracting hand position, the system *identify intersect/collision*, and system shows provide feedback of selected object.
- *Go-go*. The go-go interaction technique (Poupyrev et al., 1996) is inspired by the character "Inspector Gadget" in the so-called cartoon, which had the ability to extend its arm to reach objects. This technique introduces a non-linear mapping between arm extension and virtual hand position. The involved tasks are: the user *indicates position*, user move hand, system determines hand position based on its extension, *identify intersect/collision*, and provide feedback of *selected object*.

Manipulation Pattern

There is a strong link between the manipulation task and the selection task. An object cannot be manipulated if in some way it has not been previously selected. The manipulation task is,

in some cases, bound to the selection technique. The virtual hand is used in all the family of hand techniques (e.g., go-go, ray-casting, any arm extension), involves: select object, transform object and release object, depending on the technique the position of the object will be calculated. Some ITs for manipulation are:

- *The Hand-Centred Object Manipulation.* Extending Ray-Casting (Homer) technique of Bowman and Hodges (1997). The tasks involved are: *select* using ray-casting, translate the hand to the selected object, *transform* object, *release* object and translate the hand back to its normal position
- *Scaled-world grabs*. This technique is related to the occlusion techniques for selecting. The tasks involved are: select using occlusion technique, translate the user or world to the selected object, transform object, release object and translate the user or world to their previous position.
- *World-in-miniature*. This technique, discussed in Stoakley, Conway, & Pausch (1995) and in Pausch, Burnette, Brockway, & Weiblen (1995), uses a small "doll house" version of the world that allows the user to perform indirect manipulation. The tasks involved are: select object using any virtual hand technique, attached mini-object to the hand, transform object, and release object. The position of the object will be calculated depending on the technique.

System Control Pattern

The system control pattern, Figure 8, is quite complex as there is a wide range of operations that cover system control. The pattern deals with menus, buttons, speech, tracking, existing, and new input devices. Bowman et al. (2004) identified that this pattern involves a sort of selection pattern but not just limited to that as it also needs a sort of system feedback.

Guidelines for Task Modelling

This section contains guidelines for conducting an appropriate task modelling according to the aforementioned terminology. The letters at the beginning of each paragraph denotes whether the guideline can be followed or evaluated: automatically (A), manually (M) or both (B).

(A) Ambiguity avoidance. The ambiguity problem (Paternò, 1999) indicates that a task model should be clear on what it is modelled. The idea is

to avoid situations task has task operators before and after that might lead to an ambiguity. When it is the case, a sub tree should be used in order to avoid any ambiguity. This problem is illustrated in Figure 9. Tasks T2 .. T6 are sibling tasks in the task tree. The task T2 enables T3 which becomes available right after T2 is finished. However, task T4 is related to T3 with a concurrency operator, which means that T4 can be performed before T3. If T4 is performed first, then it enables and passes information to T5, which might be a problem as T3 was not performed. The solution, depicted in the right hand side of Figure 9, consists in creating a new level when a new operator is introduced. Notice that T2 enables T3', which enables and passes information to T5'. Then, the whole first level is related to enabling operators and without any ambiguity. In this new scenario, even if T4 starts and is performed first, then T3 must be finished in order to complete T3' and enable the execution of the next task.

(A) Task Model Labelling. Our empirical experience reveals that authors modelling tasks normally end in similar structures of the task model with minimal variations. However, the way authors label tasks may vary considerably. While authors set task names without following any rule – which is a sign of flexibility-, automatic transformation of task models to UIs becomes almost impossible considering the infinite variety of names that authors can choose for tasks. In previous sections a canonical list of User Interface action types were

Figure 7. Manipulation pattern

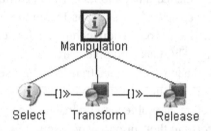

Figure 8. System control pattern

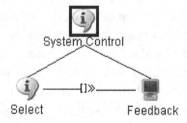

Figure 9. Ambiguity avoidance on task modelling

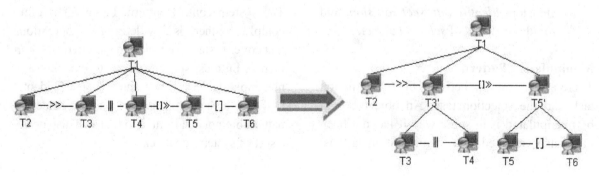

Figure 10. Guideline for task naming

Figure 11. Guideline for task naming

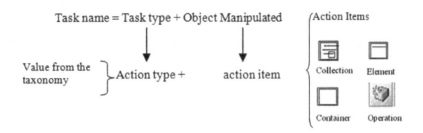

introduced from which the set of names (i.e., the task type, synonyms and sub-types) can be used for setting task names. Ideally, a task should be labelled with two elements: its name that reflect the task type and the object it manipulates (Figure 10). Task modellers could use for the task type any action from the taxonomy. Moreover, if the names are not considered correct or representative to the task, modellers are not forced to use this methodological guidance to name their tasks, they may add a new name at any time. Our goal is to strive for homogeneity for the set of action types. The action types' names were kept independent from any interaction modality or IT. Modellers may however label their task using any synonym. For instance, users could label a task "Show results", as the verb "show" refers to any sort of visual representation and the purpose of the taxonomy is to remain independent of any interaction modality, consequently, for the task labelled "Show results", its attribute action type should be "Convey". Notice that the relevance of keeping such naming for further concretization of

the task model: if the final UI is vocal or physical, the action *"Convey"* is still representative while *show* is not since it may induce that a visual modality will be exploited.

(B) Selection of action type. So far, action types have been discussed in the taxonomy. Once the modeller names the task using the previous guideline, the next step consists on assigning a value to two task attributes: the *action type* and the *action item*. The action type can be automatically derived from the task type if the modeller chooses any abstract value for the action types, such as those found in the first column of Table 2. When it is not the case, a synonym can be used instead. The corresponding action type for that synonym is then assigned. Regarding the task item, the decision of which value must be assigned is based on the object the task manipulates. In this case, we refer to the domain model of the problem and we have to look at the class(es) that the task manipulates, including the attributes and methods of interest. The assignation of this parameter is decided as follows:

- *Operation*: if the task manipulates a method, for instance "Insert a customer".
- *Element*: if the task manipulates a data item that is bound to an attribute of a class belonging to the domain model, for instance "the name of a person".
- *Container*: if the task manipulates an aggregation of elements, each element being an attribute of the same class or from several different classes. For instance, the attributes describing a book could be considered as a container of different elements (book title, book authors, book year).
- *Collection of elements*: if the task manipulates an item that is a list of elements or containers. For instance, customer registration container ("customer name", "customer address") and the shopping list ("item reference", "item description", "item quantity", "item price").

(B) Selection of task category. While authors concur on the need for separating the task types depending on the actor involved in the execution, it is not clear how to make this assignment. Lenorovitz et al. (1984) ended his review of the HCI discipline with a taxonomy of frequent interactive tasks. Johnsgard et al. (1995) separated the task categories into: user *interactive actions, user actions* and *system actions*. While *user actions* are more related to cognitive issues, *user interactive actions* correspond to the tangible manipulation of a system and *system actions* normally are transparent to the user. The user does not know what is happening at the system level. Therefore, a selection has a different impact depending on who is performing the task. At the *user action* level means choosing something after considering several options, for instance, decide which flight ticket you want to buy. If we consider the same selection task at the *user interactive action* level, it means the interaction with the system to be decided, could be selecting a desired flight from a combination box. Finally considering

the selection as a *system action* means that the system automatically will perform this action. For instance, the flight ticket could be bought using an agent that already know the end user's preferences and selects the best flight according to these preferences.

(B) Selection of task item. The combination of task categories and UI action types (which itself consists of an action type and an action item) provides precise information for UI derivation. In order to understand the mean of the combinations between task item and user categories, a survey was conducted for each task type. As an example of the way task types have been investigated, Figure 12 illustrates this for the task category "Mediate". For each task, there is a different meaning while being combined with different user's categories so as the task item they manipulate. The combination of these elements is useful for further concretization of the task. The "Reinitialize" task refers to an item that either erases or cleans certain fields (e.g., a text field in a graphical modality, a text input in a vocal modality, or a gesture area in a tactile modality). This impacts the visual part but this action might have also some impact at the data level. At the data level, it implies restoring the default value. Reinitialize an element, a collection, or a container on a UI represents almost the same. However, the agent performing the task whatever that is (i.e., the user interacting with the system, the system or the cognitive decision making of the user), may hold different interpretations. System and user categories might have, in principle, no representation in the UI. When the task becomes interactive, the user might need an explicit mechanism in order to reinitialize the task item, i.e. an *Abstract Interaction Object* (AIO) (Vanderdonckt and Bodart, 1993; Bodart, & Vanderdonckt, 1994) that will be concretized in further steps. In some cases the reinitialize task is implicit in the nature of some other task types: for instance, in a mailing website, creating a new user account normally involves the use of a form where users should fill a set of fields with personal data. Each element

Figure 12. Guideline for task naming

Task Type	Task Item	User category		
		Interactive	System	User
Mediate	Collection	Compare products by price	Google search evaluating the best ranked pages to present the results of a query.	Analyze the data details (author, name, publisher, ...) of a book
	Container	Compare side by side documents in word	Decide the layout of a slide when creating a new one	Compare a list of books
	Element	Evaluate a video watched on YouTube	Evaluate the security risk of a password	Determine the date of a trip
	Operation	Decide which operation to apply to a combination of CTRL keys.	Propose different arrangement of the results of a query.	Decide which operation will be used with a special key on a joystick

on the UI, unless something else is predefined, can be reinitialized by the user without the use of a reinitialize task for each element. It is always possible to erase any entry in a form and this does not mean that for each entry there will be a need for a supplementary task to specify that it can be reinitialized. This is what is usually assumed at the implementation level.

The set of guidelines and task patterns that have been introduced here do not guarantee the usability of the future system but at least some consistency between proved solutions and new design for task models is established. Moreover, if the developers would like to perform some transformation on the task model, the concepts introduced in this section would contribute in further reifications of the 3DUI following where more guidelines, considering usability aspects, are applied in the selection of the corresponding concretization of the task model and domain aspects.

Step 2: Abstract User Interface Modelling

An AUI model can be generated automatically or produced manually from a task model following a set of heuristics. Various set of heuristics may fit this purpose depending on the type of AUI to be obtained: an AUI that reflects the task structure, an AUI minimizing navigation, an AUI compacting input/output. Some of these heuristics have been discussed in Gonzalez et al. (2006) for 3DUIs. Even if this level is independent of the modality, some guidance is still required on how AUI might be structured considering further reifications into concrete objects. For this purpose, design guidelines are discussed.

Guidelines for Abstract User Interface Modelling

This section contains guidelines for producing an AUI model based on previous models, such as task model and, if any, domain model (e.g., a UML class diagram).

(B) *Navigation incorporation.* In 3DUIs, several metaphors have been introduced in order to display information or windows. If we imagine for instance a cube to render the different tasks as an Abstract Container (AC), then authors need to add inputs with navigation facets (Figure 13) in order to guarantee the transitions between the different faces of the cube.

(M) *Facets selection.* Similarly to the task model, the AUI model uses the same attributes in to specify the UI action: action type and task item. In addition, the abstract level incorporates the facet concept. The "action type" attribute of

Figure 13. Adapting an AUI that further will need navigation facets

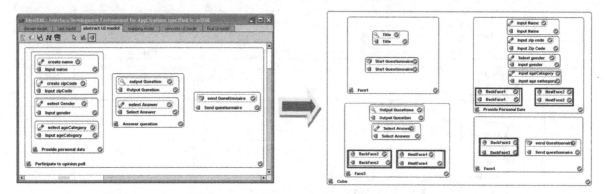

a facet enables specifying the type of action that an AIC is allowed to perform. The "action item" attribute characterizes the item that is manipulated by the AIC. The AUI Model as well as the Task Model is independent of any modality of interaction. The set of possible AUI facets are:

- An input facet describes the input action supported by an AIC.
- An output facet describes what data may be presented to the user by an AIC.
- A navigation facet describes the possible container transition that a particular AIC may enable.
- A control facet describes the links between an AIC and system functions i.e., methods from the domain model when existing.

The abstract layer has few guidelines listed but the set is more than these two. More rules, described as transformation rules in Gonzalez (2006), are applied in order to transform a task model into an AUI model. The set of rules was conceived considering guidelines as well trying to ensure the creation of a usable guideline-based 3DUI in the next steps of the development methodology.

Step 3: Concrete User Interface Modelling

As depicted in Figure 14, AIOs can be selected based on the *facet* of the *Abstract individual component* (AIC), the *action type* and *action item*. Unfortunately, it is not enough while the *action type* and *action item* combined with the *facet* to properly select the AIO. An example can be used to clarify this situation. Assuming that the UI action type corresponds to a select of a collection of elements, then, several are the potential AIOs that can be used such as: combo box, radio button group, text fields. The problem became then on deciding the appropriate AIO depending on the context of use, the type of value to be selected, and the domain. For that purpose, the rest of UsiXML meta-models can be used. While models already exist and have been extensively detailed in other papers, e.g., Limbourg et al. (2004), Vanderdonckt (2005), our aim consists of using them and providing guidelines on the relevant selection of AIOs. How to differentiate 2D and 3D tasks working on 2D or/and 3D objects? Another question is related to the final code. What is the appropriate representation of 3DUIs? Should the 2D desktop metaphor still be used or are there alternative visualizations or metaphors. Several attempts go towards defining a new toolkit of 3D objects (Andujar, Fairén, & Argelaguet 2006) which are natively appropriate to 3D applications. Again, this represents an advantage to have a predefined collection of such 3D-widgets, but then the interaction is reduced by what they offer natively.

Guidelines for Concrete User Interface Modelling

This section contains guidelines for producing a CUI model based on the AUI model obtained in

the previous step. The primary problem to solve at this level of abstraction consists in determining which mapping rules can be defined in order to transform an AUI into one or several CUIs. This is one of the most complex tasks in an MDE approach in general, but also more specifically in the domain of 3DUIs. This problem can be stated more specifically to 3DUIs as follows: 'how to define spatial positions to place 3DUI elements or objects in a 3D scene', which is not an easy task to automate due to the lack of semantic properties that define these spatial relations and the difficulty of finding empirically-validated usability guidelines: Bowman et al. (2005) have argued that generalizing usability guidelines from the world of 2D GUI to 3DUIs is not straightforward and may also not consider the specific characteristics of 3DUIs: «*3DUIs are still often a 'solution looking for a problem.' Because of this, the target user population or interaction technique to be evaluated may not be known or well understood… Presence is another example of a measure often required in VE evaluations that has no analogue in traditional UI evaluation.* »

Figure 14. Meta-model of the AUI model

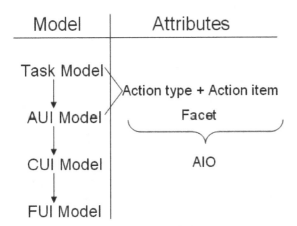

Figure 15. Graphical representation for a toggle button

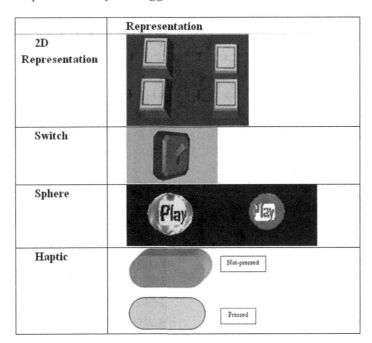

Table 3. Questions and answer criteria to select a toggle button

Question	Answer	Score	Options
What will be the representation of the 3D Toggle Button?	*Switch*	-	(1) 2D-3D Consistency
		--	(3) Easy to develop
		+	(4) Intuitional
		~	(5) Usability
	Sphere	~	(1) 2D-3D Consistency
		~	(3) Easy to develop
		~	(4) Intuitional
		~	(5) Usability
	2D representation	++	(1) 2D-3D Consistency
		+	(3) Easy to develop
		+	(4) Intuitional
		+	(5) Usability
	Haptic	+	(1) 2D-3D Consistency
		+	(3) Easyto develop
		+	(4) Intuitiona
		+	(5) Usability

Maybe the use of aforementioned taxonomy can be of some help to solve this problem as discussed in Bowman et al. (2004). Designers can be benefit from the taxonomy as the design space of UI actions is reduced to a set that is easier to handle. During a second phase of the process of developing 3DUIs, the task action can be mapped to a corresponding CUI. We have discussed the process of selecting 3D presentations based on the questions and answers method (MacLean et al., 1991) in Kaklanis et al. (2008). We illustrate below how the taxonomy can be used for proper selection of the representation of the widget. The meaning of the links are: the darkest solid line (++) means strongly supported, dark solid line (+) means supported, solid line (~) means neutral, dash lines (-) means denied and dot lines (..) means strongly denied.

Unfortunately, the problem is not just a matter of widget representation, but also the selection of the widget itself. The possible mappings and guidelines to support the correct transfer from task model to UI widgets, as shown in Bodart et al. (1994) and Johnsgard et al. (1995), is also relevant. Because it is not enough just to use any arbitrarily selected widget, say a combo box for selecting a value, it is important to precisely define the conditions under which a particular widget may be selected: Bodart et al. (1994) propose that the concretization of the select task must be based on the number of values to be selected (Figure 16). While these characteristics are relevant in further transformations, following model-driven methods to derive UIs, examples can be found in (Limbourg et al., 2004), (Paternò, 1999) and (Puerta, 1997), describing the task types using a good characterization of UI actions provides good basis for the concretization of the UI. As shown in Figure 12, the select of a simple value can be mapped to a radio button group or a list box, the difference relies on the number of possible values to select. This characteristic could be part of the design, as used in Limbourg et al. 2004, the domain model in combination with the task model provide semantic information that can be further used on the specification of an AUI.

Step 4: Final User Interface Modelling

At this stage of the development, any traditional usability method can be applied in principle. We are not aware of any system that performs usability evaluation directly on the code of a 3DUI (e.g., on VRML), although this could be a future avenue for automated evaluation. This is because at this stage, it is very complicated to analyze the code in a meaningful way. However, several methods can be used (Table 1). Some of the usability guidelines collected in Bach (2004) could be evaluated at this stage, such as:

(M) Realism of the objects. Virtual objects should be similar as much as the real objects (Kaur, 1998).

(M) Compatibility with the navigation. When the user is expected to navigate in a virtual word

Figure 16. Which widget to select for which element of the domain model

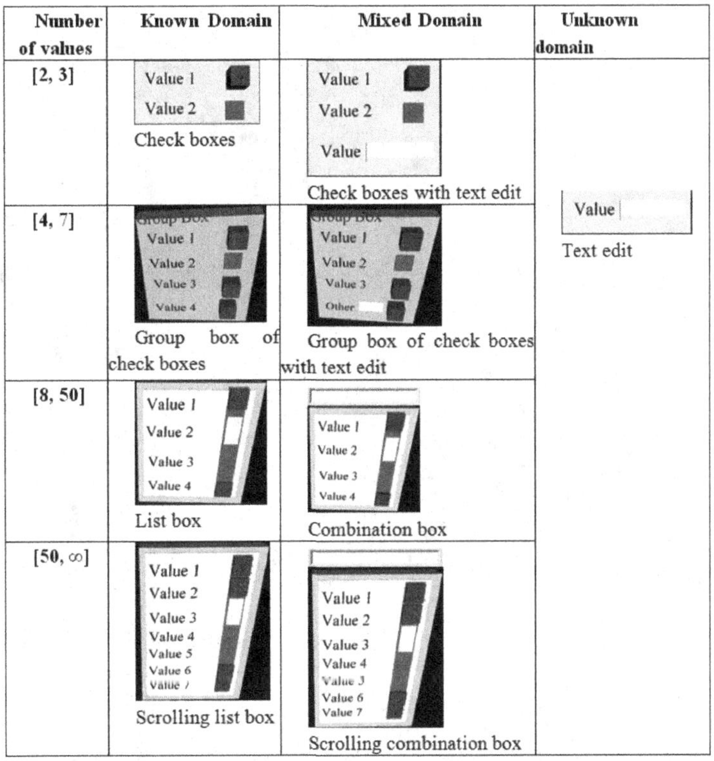

Number of values	Known Domain	Mixed Domain	Unknown domain
[2, 3]	Value 1 ▢ Value 2 ▪ **Check boxes**	Value 1 ▢ Value 2 ▪ Value ⬚ **Check boxes with text edit**	Value ⬚ Text edit
[4, 7]	Group Box Value 1 Value 2 Value 3 Value 4 **Group box of check boxes**	Group Box Value 1 Value 2 Value 3 Other ⬚ **Group box of check boxes with text edit**	
[8, 50]	Value 1 Value 2 Value 3 Value 4 **List box**	Value 1 Value 2 Value 3 Value 4 **Combination box**	
[50, ∞]	Value 1 Value 2 Value 3 Value 4 Value 5 Value 6 Value 7 **Scrolling list box**	Value 1 Value 2 Value 3 Value 4 Value 5 Value 6 Value 7 **Scrolling combination box**	

with a vast surface extension, it is important to let her navigate using different perspectives such as: egocentric and exocentric views (Gabbart et al., 1999).

(B) Movement metaphors compatible. The user might walk its avatar through the virtual world using the most appropriate metaphors, such walking, flying, virtual carpet (Gabbart et al., 1999). Today most of the renders of 3D Web applications allows fast movements. However, the flying property or virtual carpet should be added to the avatar.

(B) Speed of the movement compatible. Similarly the speed of the movement should be in harmony with the metaphor used, to fly faster speed than when walking (Gabbart et al., 1999). The speed attribute of the avatar or virtual carpet can be checked to be different and with a virtualCarpetSpeed > avatar Speed.

(M) The nature of the user movement compatible the human nature. It is important that the user

uses his body to interact in a virtual world in correspondence to the movements that they normally do (Kaur, 1998). This guideline is particularly important when gloves, head mounted displays or any other input device is used. However, it is applicable and relevant to Web application as the use of the keyboard and mouse should try to consider this issue as well. This is the case when using the augmented reality toolkit that can track the head movements so the viewpoint of the virtual world could be attached to the head movements.

(M) Compatibility with the task and the guidance offered. It is important that accordingly to the task some guidance should be provided (Kaur, 1998). This can be assured as the task model should be modelled considering the desired scenario. If it is a learning application then highlighting to guide the user must be explicitly determined in the task model then this information will be automatically considered when concretizing the 3DUI. Figure 17 depicts a navigation in a virtual

Figure 17. Guidance offered in virtual reality for requesting navigation help (Source: Alterface.com)

reality scene where the user is moving thanks to arm movements. The navigation direction (or pointer) is represented by a plot of dots that is moving according to the navigation. When the user requests some help, the pointer is transformed into a phone icon in the nearest environment in order to provide guidance.

(B) Pointer should reflect when an object can be manipulated. The pointer must provide a feedback when an object is different from the rest so that the user knows that there she can perform

some action (Kaur, 1998). In many existing Web sites, a 3DUI is rendered that associates an object to a sensor so that this object changes when the sensor is activating this object (e.g., when the mouse pointer is over an object, this object may change). Of course, more sophisticated rendering could be associated to the pointer, such as voice feedback.

(B) Objects and actions needed to perform a task must be available. The user must be capable to perform the desired action using the objects needed

Figure 18. Virtual office with an interactive table

to execute a task (Kaur, 1998). It is important to consider that a task model could incorporate aspects that might not be possible to perform on some applications, such as in a Web application. Then a task model incorporating those elements may trigger some warning of usability guideline violation, e.g. notifying that the task is not compatible with the available resources.

(M) Actions available must be compatible with what the user expects. In a virtual world, the user expects to have some sort of actions available to perform her tasks (Kaur, 1998). This is the case of a user searching on the Web using a 3DUI (Kaklanis et al., 2008) that combines capabilities for both sighted and sight-impaired users: when the user is sight-impaired, the actions available are represented by haptical widgets (so-called 'hapgets', concatenation of haptic and widget) that the user can feel, differentiate, and manipulate, while the sighted user is merely using the normal widgets of the browser.

(M) Spatial organization of the virtual environment. It is important to keep the spatial distribution of the objects in a virtual world devoted to training or to be the mock-up of a place as similar as the real space. On the right part of Figure 18, a virtual office is used to mock-up a virtual world with an interactive table that is combined with some

part of the reality (the corridor and the entrance depicted in the left part of Figure 18).

(M) Spatial organization of the virtual environment. Related to the previous guideline, this guideline refers to the need to represent a virtual world in a way that end users may easily discover some other areas related to the main one (Kaur, 1998). As in the previous example, authorities may want to know where the office is located and walk through the corridors before getting in the studio (left part of Figure 18).

(M) Decoration appropriate to the context. Decoration of the virtual world should be compatible with the context of use that is represented (Gabbart & Hix, 1999). In Figure 18, the decoration is exactly the same as the building, carpet and walls colour, posters.

(A) Provide avatar depending on the context. There are certain tasks where an avatar may be useful to use (Kaur, 1998). For instance, in an electronic commerce Web site, an avatar may represent the customer so as to try items to buy. In an aircraft, such an avatar may become irrelevant.

(B) Natural objects behaviour. Objects manipulated in the virtual world must keep their natural behaviour unless something different is defined. By natural behaviour, it is meant that they should obey to physical laws, gravity laws, etc. This

guideline can be linked to the behaviour model, where it can be checked that different behaviours are available. For instance, in the context of a space ship, objects may follow the gravity laws on earth but when outer space objects must float. By default, objects should follow the natural behaviour designed by the programmer. The realm of this behaviour cannot be tested automatically.

SOFTWARE SUPPORT FOR AUTOMATIC USABILITY EVALUATION

So far, usability guidelines have been introduced for each development step. In this section, we show how such usability guidelines can be evaluated in different ways: manually (M) when the guideline can be evaluated only by human evaluators, automatically (A) when the guidelines can be tested

by software (Usability Adviser in this case), or both (B). The Usability Adviser (Vanden Bossche, 2006) concretizes our previous experience in the usability evaluation (Vanderdonckt, 1999) and (Vanderdonckt and Beirekdar, 2005).

A 3DUI CUI specification is parsed by the tool and examined against a set of usability guidelines encoded in GDL (Guideline Definition Language). The Usability Advisor uses logical grammars to expresses usability guidelines. For instance, considering the guideline of proper colour combination that is illustrated in Figure 20 that states: when the colour of the slider is white then the colour of the slider's label must not be yellow, instead a different colour should be used for the slider, blue in our example (Figure 19). The guideline is written in logical grammar notation as follows:

i ∈ Slider: ¬ (SliderColor(i,white) ∧ LabelColor (i,yellow)).

Figure 19. Adaptation based on ergonomic rule

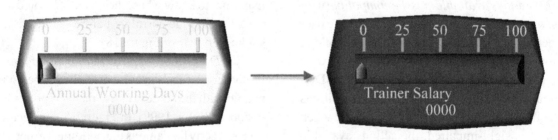

Figure 20. Bad colour combination

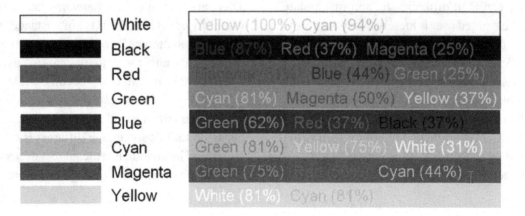

Usability guidelines can be added, removed, and edited from a configuration file that stores the set of logical expressions. This software is primarily used at the CUI level where AIOs (Figure 2) are mapped to CIO by relying on information hold at more abstract levels. The main window of the Usability Advisor is shown Figure 21.

Usability guidelines for 3D applications have been introduced in several research papers, for instance: for guidance during navigation in augmented virtual environments (Grammenos, Mourouzis, & Stephanidis, 2006; Smith, & Marsh, 2004); to design objects for reduced spaces (Kaur, 1997) and user interaction in virtual environment (Kaur, Maiden, & Sutcliffe, 1999). Even if many similar usability guidelines exist for the Web, many of them can also be used for 3DUIs after some adaptation. In (Bodart et al. 1994), the problem of selecting a widget from information contained at the abstract level is addressed. For instance, a selection task can be mapped onto different widgets depending on: the number of possible values, the number of values to be selected, the domain whether is known or not or a mixture of both.

From the compilation of guidelines from Bach (2004), a set of guidelines for automated evaluation was extracted. Notice that for Web 3D applications there are no immersion and sophisticated input devices available in general. Here are some significant examples:

Objects availability. Objects associated to a task must be available to perform the task (Kaur 1998). Objects in the virtual world are directly associated with the task model so that in theory they will not be missing.

Object's highlight for guidance. Relevant objects for the task must be highlighted to guide users on their task (Kaur 1998). The domain of the problem provides some sort of information of the purpose of the virtual world. If an object was chosen to be highlighted for a specific purpose, this can be checked by referring to the highlighted object's property at the concrete level (CUI).

Object transparency feedback. Objects in the virtual world which are solid should provide a feedback to the user in order to let the user know their limits (Kaur, 1998). This property can be checked automatically with the rule: if a solid property is defined, then the feedback property must be defined.

Different exploration facilities available. The application must provide facilities to explore the virtual world in different modalities (Gabbart et al., 1999). Most existing browsers provide means to jump into predefined viewpoints that might be relevant for the user or useful if they are lost.

Many more guidelines are applicable, not just for 3DUI for the Web in general. Again, this is beyond the scope of this chapter.

Figure 21. Usability advisor interface

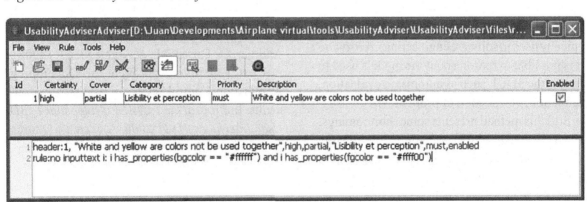

CONCLUSION

This chapter was aimed at presenting a MDE-compliant method that is user-centred as an alternative to content-centric methods for developing 3DUIs. The approach considers a step-wise development life cycle where usability guidelines could be considered implicitly or explicitly at each development step. Also, the method proposes the use of automatic usability evaluation where guidelines can be stored as rules and subsequently tested during the transformation process. In general, model transformation holds the promise that each step could be achieved by applying a limited set of transformations, which are declaratively stated. It is a fundamental research problem to assess that the declarative power of such transformations, at least equal the procedural capabilities of algorithms traditionally used to produce a final UI. With this method, it is expected that the development of usable systems, like for the 3D Web, will be facilitated.

The potential advantages of using this method are: *modifiability* (if there is a change in a model then the 3DUI changes accordingly), *reduced complexity* (as it provides ways to address complexity, huge quantity of code, as well as the reliability), *safety critical* (models are needed to ensure the behaviour of safety critical systems), *formality* (the use of a formal specification technique is extremely valuable, because it provides non-ambiguous, complete, and concise ways of describing the behaviour of the systems), *rigorousness* (the development life cycle of the 3DUI involves the same level of rigorousness that is typically used in software engineering), *reasoning* (it is possible to reason about the models used to specify the 3DUI, such as automated evaluation, simulation, verification of properties).

Still this method presents some shortcomings. It is likely that the model transformations of large systems will be more complex to discover and to apply, so it is not clear if the solution is computationally feasible and scalable considering the amount of operations needed to perform graph transformations. Finally, empirical data coming from an evaluation of the methodology is required. Such data would emphasize the value added by this methodology to develop 3DUIs. An evaluation is planned as part of the future work.

Resources

All resources related to UsiXML can be found at: http://www.usixml.org.

ACKNOWLEDGMENT

We gratefully acknowledge the support of the CONACYT program (www.conacyt.mx) supported by the Mexican government, the HUMAN European project (Model-based Analysis of Human Errors during Aircraft Cockpit System Design, project funded by FP7-AAT-2007-RTD-1/CP-FP-211988 from European Commission), and the ITEA2 Call 3 UsiXML project under reference 20080026, the PROMEP net Project under Contract UAA-CA-48. Finally, the authors are very grateful to the reviewers for their comments on earlier version of this chapter.

REFERENCES

Alexander, C. Ishikawa, S., Silverstein, M., Jacobson, M., Fiksdahl-King, I. & Angel, S. (1977). *A Pattern Language.* New York: Oxford University Press.

Andujar, C., Fairén, M., & Argelaguet, F. (2006). A Cost Effective Approach for Developing Application-Control GUIs for Virtual Environments. In *Proc. of the 1st IEEE Symposium of 3D User Interfaces 3DUI'2006,* Alexandria, March 25-26, pp. 45-52. Washington, DC: IEEE Comp. Society Press.

Bach, C. (2004). *Elaboration et validation de Critères Ergonomiques pour les Interactions Homme-Environnements Virtuels*. Ph.D. Thesis, Metz University, France.

Bleser, T. W., & Sibert, J. (1990). Toto: a tool for selecting interaction techniques. *In Proc. of user interface software and technology,* Snowbird, Utah, Oct.3-5, pp. 135-142. New York: ACM.

Bodart, F., & Vanderdonckt, J. (1994). On the Problem of Selecting Interaction Objects. In G. Cockton, S.W. Draper, G.R.S. Weir (eds.), *Proc. of BCS Conf. HCI'94 "People and Computers IX",* Glasgow, 23-26 August, (pp. 163-178). Cambridge, UK: Cambridge University Press.

Bowman, D. Koller, D., & Hodges L. (1997). Travel in Immersive Virtual Environments: an Evaluation of Viewpoint Motion Control Techniques. In *Proceedings of Virtual Reality Annual International Symposium.*

Bowman, D., Gabbard, J., & Hix, D. (2002). A Survey of Usability Evaluation in Virtual Environments: Classification and Comparison of Methods. *Presence (Cambridge, Mass.),* *11*(4), 404–424. doi:10.1162/105474602760204309

Bowman, D., & Hodges, L. (1997). An evaluation of techniques for grabbing and manipulating remote objects in immersive virtual environments. In *Proceedings of Symposium on Interactive 3D Graphics,* (pp. 35-38).

Bowman, D., & Hodges, L. (1999). Formalizing the design, evaluation, and application of interaction techniques for immersive virtual environments. *Journal of Visual Languages and Computing,* *10*(1), 37–53. doi:10.1006/jvlc.1998.0111

Bowman, D., Wineman, J., Hodges, L., & Allison, D. (1998). Designing Animal Habitats Within an Immersive VE. *IEEE Computer Graphics and Applications,* *18*(5), 9–13. doi:10.1109/38.708555

Bowman, D. A., Kruijff, E., & Laviola, J. J. (2004). *3D User Interfaces: Theory and Practice.* Reading, MA: Addison Wesley Publishing Company.

Calhoun, G. C., Arbak, C. L., & Boff, K. R. (1984). Eye-controlled switching for crew station design". In *Proceedings of the Human Factors Society 28th annual meeting,* (pp. 258-262). Santa Monica, CA: Human Factors Society.

Calvary, G., Coutaz, J., Thevenin, D., Limbourg, Q., Bouillon, L., & Vanderdonckt, J. (2003). A Unifying Reference Framework for Multi-Target User Interfaces. *Interacting with Computers,* *15*(3), 289–308. doi:10.1016/S0953-5438(03)00010-9

Card, S. K., Mackinlay, J. D., & Robertson, G. G. (1990). The design space of input devices. In *Proceedings of the SIGCHI conference on Human factors in computing systems: Empowering people,* (pp. 117-124). New York: ACM press.

Celentano, A., & Pittarello, F. (2001). A content centred methodology for authoring 3d interactive worlds for cultural heritage. *International Cultural Heritage Informatics Meeting, 2,* 315-324.

Cockburn, A. & McKenzie (2001). 3D or not 3D? Evaluating the Effect of the Third Dimension in a Document Management System. In *Proceedings of the SIGCHI conference on Human factors in computing systems,* Seattle, WA. (pp. 434 – 441). Retrieved from http://www.cosc.canterbury.ac.nz/andrew.cockburn/papers/chi01DM.pdf

Constantine, L. L. (2003). Canonical Abstract Prototypes for Abstract Visual and Interaction. In *Proceedings of the 10th International workshop on Design, Specification and Evaluation of Interactive Systems DSV-IS,* (LNCS Vol. 2844, pp. 1-15). Berlin: Springer Verlag.

Davidsson, O., et al. (2004). *Game Design Patterns for Mobile Game.* Project report to Nokia Research Center, Finland.

De Boeck, J., González-Calleros, J. M., Coninx, K., & Vanderdonckt, J. (2006). Open Issues for the development of 3D Multimodal Applications from an MDE perspective. In A. Pleuss, J. Van den Bergh, H. Hussmann, S. Sauer, A. Boedcher, (ed.), *Proc. of 2nd Int. Workshop on Model Driven Development of Advanced User Interfaces MD-DAUI'2006,* Geneva, October 2, (pp. 11-14).

Eastgate, R. (2001). *The Structured Development of Virtual Environments: Enhancing Functionality and Interactivity.* Ph.D. Thesis, York University.

Foley, V. W., & Chan, V. (1984). The human factors of computer graphics interaction techniques. *IEEE Computer Graphics and Applications,* (4): 13–48.

Frank, M., & Foley, J. (1993). Model-based user interface design by example and by answering questions. In *Proc. INTERCHI, ACM Conference on Human Factors in Computing Systems,* (pp. 161-162).

Gabbard, J. L., Hix, D., & Swan, J. E. (1999). User-Centered Design and Evaluation of Virtual Environments. *IEEE Computer Graphics and Applications, 19*(6), 51–59. doi:10.1109/38.799740

Gamma, E., Helm, R., Johnson, R., Vlissides, J., & Booch, G. (1995). Design Patterns: Elements of Reusable Object-Oriented Software. Reading, MA: Addison-Wesley Professional Computing.

Gonzalez-Calleros, J. M. (2006, June). *A Method for Developing 3D User Interfaces for Information Systems.* DEA thesis, UCL, Louvain-la-Neuve.

González-Calleros, J. M., Vanderdonckt, J., & Arteaga, J. M. (2006). A Method for Developing 3D User Interfaces of Information Systems. In *Proc. of 6th Int. Conf. on Computer-Aided Design of User Interfaces CADUI'2006* (Bucharest, 6-8 June 2006), (pp. 85-100). Berlin: Springer-Verlag.

González-Calleros, J. M., Vanderdonckt, J., & Arteaga, J. M. (2009). Towards Canonical Task Types for User Interface Design. In *Proc. of 4th Int. Conf. on Latin-American Conference on Human-Computer Interaction CLIHC'2009,* Merida, November 9-11. Los Alamitos, CA: IEEE Computer Society Press.

Grammenos, D., Mourouzis, A., & Stephanidis, C. (2006). Virtual prints: Augmenting virtual environments with interactive personal marks. *International Journal of Man-Machine Studies, 64*(3), 221–239.

Greenstein, J. S., & Arnaut, L. Y. (1988). Input devices. In M. Helander, (Ed.), *Handbook of Human-Computer Interaction* (pp. 495-519). Amsterdam: North-Holland.

Hackos, J. T., & Redish, J. C. (1998). *User and Task Analysis for Interface Design.* Dover, TN: Crystal Dreams Pub.

Hix, D., & Hartson, H. R. (1993). *Developing user interfaces: Ensuring usability through product and process.* New York: John Wiley & Sons.

Hutchinson, T. E., White, K. P. Jr, Martin, W. N., Reichert, K. N., & Frey, L. A. (1989). Human-Computer Interaction Using Eye-Gaze Input. *IEEE Transactions on Systems, Man, and Cybernetics, 19*(6), 1527–1533. doi:10.1109/21.44068

Jansen, B. J. (2006). Using Temporal Patterns of Interaction to Design Effective Automated Searching engines. *Communications of the ACM, 49*(4), 72–74. doi:10.1145/1121949.1121986

Johnsgard, T. J., & Page, S. R., Wilson, R.D. & Zeno, R., J. (1995). A Comparison of Graphical User Interface Widgets for Various Tasks. In *Proceedings of the Human Factors & Ergonomics Society - 39th Annual Meeting, Human Factors and Ergonomics Society,* (pp. 287-291).

Kaklanis, N., González Calleros, J. M., Vanderdonckt, J., & Tzovaras, D. (2008). Hapgets, Towards Haptically-enhanced widgets Based on a User Interface Description Language. In *Proc. of Workshop on Multimodal Interaction Through Haptic Feedback MITH'2008* Naples, May 31. New York: ACM Press.

Kaur, K. (1997). Designing Virtual Environments for Usability. *INTERACT, 1997*, 636–639.

Kaur, K. (1998). *Designing virtual environments for usability*. Ph. D. Thesis, City University, London.

Kaur, K., Maiden, N. A. M., & Sutcliffe, A. G. (1999). Interacting with virtual environments: an evaluation of a model of interaction. *Interacting with Computers, 11*(4), 403–426. doi:10.1016/S0953-5438(98)00059-9

Kennedy, R. S., Lane, N. E., Berbaum, K. S., & Lilienthal, M. G. (1993). Simulator sickness questionnaire (SSQ): A new method for quantifying simulator sickness. *The International Journal of Aviation Psychology, 3*, 203–220. doi:10.1207/s15327108ijap0303_3

Lenorovitz, D. R., Phillips, M. D., Ardrey, R. S., & Kloster, G. V. (1984). A taxonomic approach to characterizing human-computer interaction. In G. Salvendy (Ed.), *Human-Computer Interaction*, (pp. 111-116). Amsterdam: Elsevier Science Publishers.

Limbourg, Q. (2004). *Multi-path Development of User Interfaces*. Ph.D. thesis, Université catholique de Louvain Press, France.

Limbourg, Q., Vanderdonckt, J., Michotte, B., Bouillon, L., & Lopez, V. (2004): UsiXML: a Language Supporting Multi-Path Development of User Interfaces. In R. Bastide, P. Palanque, & J. Roth (Eds.), *Engineering Human Computer Interaction and Interactive Systems*. (LNCS Vol. 3425, pp. 200–220).

MacLean, A., Young, R. M., Bellotti, V., & Moran, T. P. (1991). Questions, Options, and Criteria: Elements of Design Space Analysis. *Human-Computer Interaction, 6*(3-4), 201–250. doi:10.1207/s15327051hci0603&4_2

Mahemoff, M. J., & Johnston, L. J. (2001). Usability Pattern Languages: the ``Language'' Aspect. In Hirose M. (ed.), *Human-Computer? Interaction: Interact '01, Tokyo, Japan*, (pp. 350-358). Amsterdam: IOS Press.

Mapes, D., & Moshell, J. (1995). A Two-Handed Interface for Object Manipulation in virtual Environments. *Presence (Cambridge, Mass.), 4*(4), 403–426.

Meyer, B. (1985). On Formalism in Specification. *IEEE Software*, 6–25. doi:10.1109/MS.1985.229776

Mine, M. (1995). *Virtual environment Interaction techniques*. UNC Chapel Hill CS Dept., Technical Report TR95-018, Chapel Hill, NC.

Molina Massó, J. P. (2008). *A Structured Approach to the Development of 3D User Interfaces*. Ph.D. thesis, University of Castilla-La Mancha, Albacete, Spain, February 29.

Montero, F., & Vanderdonckt, J. (2008). *Generative Pattern-Based Design of User Interfaces*. Working paper 08/13, Louvain School of Management, Université catholique de Louvain, Louvain-la-Neuve, April 2008. Accessible at http://www.uclouvain.be/cps/ucl/doc/iag/documents/WP_08-13.pdf

Moreno, N. Romero, J. R. & Vallecillo (2007), A. An overview Model Driven Web Engineering and the MDA. In L. Olsina, O. Pastor, & G. D. Schwabe, (Eds.), *Web Engineering and Web Applications Design Methods*, (vol. 12 of Human-Computer Interaction Series). Berlin: Springer.

Neale, H., & Nichols, S. (2001). *Designing and Developing Virtual Environments: Methods and Applications*. Visualization and Virtual Environments Community Club (VVECC) Workshop: Design of Virtual Environments, Oxfordshire, England.

Nedel, L. P., & Freitas, C. M. D. S. (2006). 3D User Interfaces: from Pragmatics to Formal Description. *Research in Interactive Design*, *1*, 1–13.

Paternò, F. (1999). Model-based design and evaluation of interactive applications. *Applied Computing*. Berlin: Springer.

Pausch, R., Burnette, T., Brockway, D., & Weiblen, M. E. (1995). Navigation and locomotion in virtual worlds via flight into hand-held miniatures. In *Proceedings of ACM SIGGRAPH 95*, (pp. 399-400).

Pierce, J. S., Forsberg, A. S., & Conway, M. J. (1997), Image Plane Interaction Techniques in 3D Immersive Environments. In *Proceedings symposium on Interactive 3D graphics*, 39-ff.

Poupyrev, I. Weghorst, S., Billinghurst, M., & Ichikawa, T. (1997). A framework and testbed for studying manipulation techniques for immersive VR. In *Proceedings of the ACM symposium on Virtual reality software and technology*, (pp. 21-28).

Poupyrev, I., Billinghurst, M., Weghorst, S., & Ichikawa, T. (1996), The Go-Go Interaction Technique: Nonlinear Mapping for Direct Manipulation in VR. In *Proc. UIST'96*, (pp. 79-80).

Pribeanu, C., & Vanderdonckt, J. M. (2003). A Pattern-based Approach to User Interface Development. In *Proceedings of the Tenth International Conference on Human-Computer Interaction 2003*, (pp. 1524-1528).

Puerta, A. R. (1997). A Model-Based Interface Development Environment. *IEEE Software*, *14*(4), 41–47. doi:10.1109/52.595902

Shneiderman, B. (2002). 3D or Not 3D: When and Why Does it Work? Human-Computer Interaction Laboratory & Department of Computer Science University of Maryland. *Talk in Web3D*. Phoenix, AZ, February 26, 2002.

Shneiderman B. (2003). Why Not Make Interfaces Better than 3D Reality. *Virtualization Viewpoints*, (November-December).

Smith, S. P., & Marsh, T. (2004). Evaluating design guidelines for reducing user disorientation in a desktop virtual environment. *Virtual Reality (Waltham Cross)*, *8*(1), 55–62. doi:10.1007/s10055-004-0137-x

Steed, A., & Tromp, J. (1998), Experiences with the evaluation of CVE applications. In *Proc. of the conf. Collaborative Virtual Environments (CVE'98)*, Manchester, UK, June 17-19th.

Stoakley, R., Conway, M. J., & Pausch, R. (1995), Virtual Reality on a WIM: Interactive Worlds in Miniature. In *Proceedings of ACM CHI 95*, (pp. 265-272).

Vanden Bossche, P. (2006). Développement d'un outil de critique d'interface intelligent: UsabilityAdviser. M.Sc. thesis, *Université catholique de Louvain*, Louvain-la-Neuve, Septembre 1, 2006.

Vanderdonckt, J. (1999). Development Milestones towards a Tool for Working with Guidelines. *Interacting with Computers*, *12*(2), 81–118. doi:10.1016/S0953-5438(99)00019-3

Vanderdonckt, J. (2005), A MDA-Compliant Environment for Developing User Interfaces of Information Systems. In *Proc. of 17th Conf. on Advanced Information Systems Engineering CAiSE'05*, Porto, June 13-17, 2005, (LNCS Vol. 3520, pp.16-31). Berlin: Springer-Verlag.

Vanderdonckt, J., & Beirekdar, A. (2005). Automated Web Evaluation by Guideline Review. *Journal of Web Engineering*, *4*(2), 102–117.

Vanderdonckt, J., & Bodart, F. (1993), Encapsulating Knowledge for Intelligent Automatic Interaction Objects Selection. In: *Proc. of the ACM Conf. on Human Factors in Computing Systems* I*N*TERCHI'93, Amsterdam, 24-29 April 1993, (pp. 424–429). New York: ACM Press.

Vanderdonckt, J., Bouillon, L., Chieu, K. C., & Trevisan, D. (2004): Model-based Design, Generation, and Evaluation of Virtual User Interfaces. In *Proc. of 9th ACM Int. Conf. on 3D Web Tech. Web3D'2004,* Monterey, April 5-8, 2004. New York: ACM Press.

Welie, M., & Trćtteberg, H. (2000). Interaction Patterns in User Interfaces. In *Proc. Seventh Pattern Languages of Programs Conference: PLoP 2000*, Allerton Park Monticello, IL.

Wesson, J., & Cowley, N. L. O. (2003). Designing with patterns: Possibilities and pitfalls. In *2nd Workshop on Software and Usability Cross-Pollination: The Role of Usability Patterns 2003*.

Wilson, J. R., Eastgate, R., & D'Cruz, M. (2002). Structured Development of Virtual Environments. In J. Jacko (ed.), *Handbook of Virtual Environments: Design, Implementation, and Applications*. Mahwah, NJ: Lawrence Erlbaum Associates.

Witmer, B. G., & Singer, M. J. (1998). Measuring Presence in Virtual Environments: A Presence Questionnaire. *Presence (Cambridge, Mass.),* 7(3), 225–240. doi:10.1162/105474698565686

Chapter 3
A Case Study of Usability Engineering in the Defence Industry

Steve Hogg
SELEX Sensors and Airborne Systems Limited, Scotland

Patrik O'Brian Holt
Robert Gordon University, Scotland

Jim Aitchison
SELEX Sensors and Airborne Systems Limited, Scotland

ABSTRACT

The work discussed in this chapter is a case study of real application of usability engineering and Agile methods in the defence industry. The area of application is the monitoring of legal compliance to import and export of technology (ITAR). Manual compliance for an organization like BAE SYSTEMS presents serious challenges and is prone to errors, which can potentially lead to serious penalties. BAE decided to automate the compliance process using intranet technology with a time scale of three months. Several factors contributed to the successful development of the system and these include detailed but flexible planning, close and intense involvement of users and stakeholders and real time iteration of prototypes. The system is currently in use and while not without limitations, is seen as successful and provides a methodological framework for future similar work.

Good ideas are not adopted automatically they must be driven into practice with courageous patience -Admiral Hyman Rickover (1900-1986)

DOI: 10.4018/978-1-60566-896-3.ch003

INTRODUCTION

The work described and discussed in this case study relates to how BAE SYSTEMS, a multinational defence company, applied usability engineering and web technology to address mission critical control and monitoring arising from the International Trade in Arms Regulations (ITAR) imposed by the USA. The regulations require strict monitoring of the export of technology from the USA. The project does not involve new technology or methodologies but rather demonstrates how industrial organisations can take an eclectic approach to solving problems through the application of user centred design methods and web technology, resulting in novel and innovative solutions, demonstrating high degrees of usability and user satisfaction.

The work is often characterized by the pressures that frequently apply in industrial settings, where more principled and academic approaches are acknowledged but cannot be utilised fully due to impending deadlines and tight delivery schedules. It is not the intention of the authors to advocate an applied approach that "cuts corners" and rejects other approaches. Rather, we hope to show that it is possible to design and deliver effective and usable systems in an industrial context and which are guided in their design by more principled approaches and design methods. In the sections that follow we will outline the problems that faced the design team, the solutions adopted, the building of the system and finally the evaluation of the prototype. We finish with a discussion that places the project in a wider context. The focus of the discussion is on the design, task analysis and usability, but not on detailed implementation issues relating to the BAE SYSTEMS intranet.

BACKGROUND

What Is ITAR?

The International Trade in Arms Regulations (ITAR) relate to export controls, which are designed to protect items and information important to the interests of the United States. The regulations refer specifically to government controls that govern the transfer of the following to non-US entities or individuals, regardless of where or how the transfer takes place:

1. Goods (systems, components, equipment, or materials).
2. Technologies (technical data, information, or assistance).
3. Software/codes (commercial or custom).

In 1999 the International Arms Sales Code of Conduct Act enacted in the USA obliged the administration to establish an international regime to ensure global transparency with regards to arms transfers. In December 2000 the EU and the United States issued a "Declaration by the European Union and the United States on the Responsibilities of States and on Transparency Regarding Arms Exports (www.basicint.org/WT/armsexp/USEUCoop.htm 23.05.09). Since 9/11 the nature of the international security environment has changed markedly, with implications for the relative weight applied to export control criteria and perceived foreign-policy imperatives in arms export licensing decisions. At the same time, governments and their export licensing authorities are having to confront rapid consolidation of the defence industry, both within and across borders. Traditional anti-proliferation concerns have been challenged by arguments for streamlining export licensing processes for transfers to economic, as well as strategic allies.

Within these relatively wide categories it is often not obvious what is export sensitive, and therefore, impacted by export controls. Export controls serve multiple purposes - from guarding US national security, to protecting the US economy, to supporting US foreign policy. As a result, different government agencies have different rules and lists, specifying what may be considered export sensitive, or where export controls apply. Furthermore, these rules and lists are updated frequently, and in a given situation any, or none, may apply. This obviously invites potential confusion and complexity for organisations involved in the defence trade. Most

US exports however, take place under expressly defined exceptions or waivers and therefore do not require a specific export license or other special authorization. However, recording and monitoring is always required and these arrangements inevitably add further complexity to an already complex system.

Companies like BAE SYSTEMS that trade globally have international partners, and collaborators are heavily impacted by regulations like ITAR. Non-compliance could result in suspension of current or future licensing privileges, creating a challenge for companies to meet some of its contractual obligations. Non-compliance could also result in administrative or criminal penalties for companies like BAE SYSTEMS and/or individual employees.

Therefore, import and export is an area with very high stakes. Companies that ignore ITAR do so at their peril as penalties for export violations can be severe. Criminal penalties for wilful violations may include fines of up to $1 million per violation for companies, and up to ten years imprisonment for individuals. Civil penalties may also be assessed up to $500,000 per violation, and multiple violations can arise from the same program or project.

ITAR Administration and Compliance at BAE SYSTEMS

The ITAR control and compliance process that was in place prior to this project was mainly paper based notification of technology and hardware transfers from the US to the UK, relying heavily on UK users reading the end-user restrictions endorsed on the documentation accompanying the technology. There were no formal means of confirming that the transfer of the technology had been received in the UK, or that the UK end-user had seen and read the restrictions endorsed on the documentation accompanying the transfer.

BAE SYSTEMS Head Office in Washington DC collected the transfer information from mul-

tiple sites spread throughout the United States. Each site had their own method of providing this information, usually as electronic spreadsheets and text files. This information was then re-keyed into a master database in Washington, printed and sent to the BAE SYSTEMS corporate compliance officer in the UK. When received, the printed copies were sent out to the data managers at each UK site who then had to trace each transfer and ensure that the end-user had complied with end-user restrictions. This was a system that was slow, cumbersome and open to errors, no matter how careful and diligent the staff. These were the core issues addressed in the project reported here.

ADDRESSING THE CORE PROBLEM

As mentioned above the perceived problem lay in the procedure, i.e. how to administer ITAR without errors and in a way that allowed progress to be monitored and audited. In addition to the core problem, BAE SYSTEMS wanted a new and more effective procedure to be available in a matter of months. The core issues were defined to belong to five categories:

1. Identification, receipt and tracking of ITAR controlled items or technical data.
2. Re-exports and re-transfers.
3. Record keeping.
4. Internal monitoring.
5. Sharing and monitoring of activity at any or all of BAE's worldwide locations (also including collaborators and partners).

It had been stipulated from the onset that any new procedure must be in place within three calendar months. The project began with brainstorming about new ways of working with the ITAR procedures and a number of options were discussed and these broadly included:

1. Continuing with a manual system but with enhancements.
2. Obtain a COTS (Commercial **Off** **T**he **S**helf) system.
3. Design and implement a new software solution.

Each of these options was analysed in detail and compared on the basis of viability, cost and future impact on the company. The option of continuing with the current manual system was rejected early in the analysis process. Even with enhancements and improved organisation and procedure, the manual approach was still regarded as unacceptably time consuming and therefore costly. It was also accepted that the large amount of re-keying and paper communication (even if electronically transferred, e.g. using secure email) would be likely to contribute to human errors and the loss of data. Additionally, the distributed nature of the activity made it hard to monitor and audit the process. The idea of obtaining a COTS system seemed quite attractive but despite an extensive search, no suitable system was found for evaluation. This left the option of designing and implementing an in-house system.

An organisation like BAE SYSTEMS is clearly very experienced at designing and delivering new software solutions both for clients and for internal use, including solutions using web technology. The particular division of the company that led this work specialises in improving production and has extensive experience in experimenting with various kinds of technology and design methods. Some of these projects are done in collaboration with universities and the team responsible for the ITAR project had collaborated previously. In those projects, modern user centred design approaches and web technology had been used, as had very advanced technology such as virtual reality (see e.g. Day, Ferguson, Holt, Hogg, & Gibson 2005). Faced with developing an in-house system, it was therefore very natural to consider the use of web technology, in this case intranet, and usability engineering.

It was therefore decided to design and implement a prototype ITAR support system based on web technology (BAE SYSTEMS intranet). The basic ideas were that web technology would greatly aid communications and sharing of information and data relevant to ITAR compliance, and would allow enhanced monitoring of compliance processes. The formal adoption of user centred design was based on the wish to produce a highly usable system that would be perceived as the "property" of the users or stakeholders who carry out the work relevant to ITAR compliance. The system must also be easy to learn and simple to maintain.

DESIGNING THE ITAR SYSTEM

Choice of Specific Methodology and Refining the Approach

Having decided to adopt user centred design which would be characterised by an early and intense involvement of users, prototyping and iterative evaluation, it was necessary to refine the approach to suit the task at hand and in particular the tight time scale of 12 weeks from inception to delivery of a working prototype.

A serious consideration was given to using scenario-based design (see e.g. Rosson and Carroll, 2002), as it would allow the wider context of stakeholders to be taken into account and incorporated into the design. The scenario-based approach was thought more likely to capture the various organisational issues associated with modes of working and traditions while at the same time facilitating the design of a robust system that could monitor the ITAR transactions. However, the team concluded that, while a powerful and attractive option, it was unlikely that the various necessary stages could be completed in 12 weeks. However, some aspects of scenario-based design were adopted. This included a focus on stakeholders and an emphasis on devising methods for more or less continuous communications between the design team and the stakeholders, using examples (scenarios). An important decision was to adopt overall the star model of design and development proposed by Hartson and Hix (1989) and shown in Figure 1 below. While this model is one of the most frequently cited life cycle models in HCI and therefore not new, the formal adoption was important as it acknowledged the need to carry out many essential tasks in parallel. In particular, detailed requirements capture, design and prototyping would all need to be done at the same time. Equally important was the acknowledgement that continuous formative evaluation with users would guide, drive and control the progress of the various components.

When comparing traditional software development methods (e.g. Waterfall) with more modern approaches (e.g. Agile), Szalvay (2004) likens software development to the development of new products. With the Waterfall approach, plans are typically laid out in advance of the development

so that in essence a complex software system can be built in a sequential, step-by-step manner. All the necessary information is gathered at the beginning, the system is then designed, and lastly there is the production phase. Figure 2 shows a typical diagram of this methodology.

Szalvay concludes, as have many others, that with the Waterfall method, it is practically impossible to accurately gather all project requirements at the beginning. In fact Szalvay states that only between 9% and 16% of projects are on time and within budget. In the US the RAND corporation has claimed that the reason for many defence projects going over budget is changes to the requirements introduced during the life cycle of the project (Younossi, Arena, Leonard, Roll, Jain, Sollinger 2007).

Szalvay promotes the Agile approach in which software development is done in small steps and each phase or stage can be revisited. These are characteristics shared with user centred ap-

Figure 1. The Star Model (adapted from Hartson and Hix 1989)

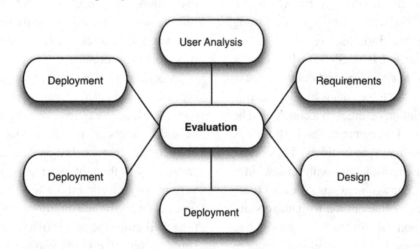

Figure 2. Traditional methods: sequential phased approach

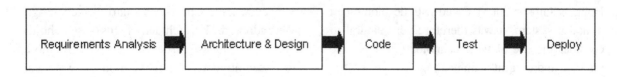

proaches as can e.g. be seen in the Hartson and Hix (1989) star model and in scenario based design (Rosson and Carroll 2002). This concept of iterative development can be traced back to the "lean development" era of the 1980s, where Japanese auto manufacturers using this innovative approach, made substantial efficiency gains. Figure 3 shows how prototypes were developed for short-term milestones.

Agile methods promote an iterative methodology for producing software, with short design-code-test loops. Another important feature is that they allow developers to set aside the notion of having a complete design in favour of designing iteratively based on user needs that emerge through the process of working with prototypes or mock-ups. The frequent demonstration and release of software encourages formative evaluation and feedback from stakeholders to guide the design and enhance the requirements.

In the work described here, the Agile approach described by Highsmith (2004) was adopted along with the iterative stakeholder involvement and concurrent development. This allowed the ITAR monitoring system to be designed and implemented incrementally and in close consultation with users and other stakeholders. With continuous and rich feedback from users, all components of the system are continuously revised throughout the development process.

Refining the Requirements

At the start of the project high-level requirements were put forward in the form of five questions:

1. How was the company going to ensure that BAE SYSTEMS North America informed the 101 UK sites in a timely fashion of ITAR controlled data and hardware?
2. How could these sites in turn instruct BAE SYSTEMS North America that they had received and understood the notice?
3. How was this data or hardware stored and controlled or disposed of, and if forwarded on to someone else, how could you ensure that these customers met the strict compliance with the ITAR regulations?
4. How could we ensure that this system was accessible, and open to an audit either internally or by US State Department?
5. Could the system be developed, tested and implemented in a very short time scale, in this case 12 weeks?

A key characteristic of the requirements was the focus on the process of compliance. This allowed the team to decompose the tasks required to initiate, generate, monitor and complete any compliance process. This covered issues relevant to hardware, software, designs and communications between staff, in fact all aspects of technology related work that needed to be included in ITAR compliance. The detailed decomposed tasks served as a task model, which guided the identification and design of the web-based software modules required for the system.

The initial requirements were refined through interviews and group problem solving sessions that were largely conducted through teleconferencing. While this was time consuming and often

Figure 3. Iterative approach - overlapping phases of development

Phase 1 2 3 4 5 6

Table 1.

Role	No of Persons
Technical Design	1
US / UK Users and Admin processes	6
US / UK Legal requirements	4

took place at odd times of day or night due to time differences between the UK and the USA, the requirements were clarified and fleshed out effectively. In total 11 people participated and formed the "Process Requirements Team". The key to the team was the expertise of the members. Table 1 shows the constitution of the team:

During the 12-week design and development period formal international teleconference calls were held once a week for about one hour each time. These calls were primarily for progress updates, but were also used for clarification and interpretation of process and legal requirements. Informal phone calls between specific members of the team accounted for about two hours per week, but the main communication mechanism was email. From the start of the project to the formal launch of the system, there were in excess of 300 email communications just between Technical Designer and other members of the Process Requirements Team.

The original outline specification of the system is shown below:

1. Provide an on-line interactive database/ toolset to record the transfer of military controlled technology and hardware from any BAE SYSTEMS facility in the USA to any BAE SYSTEMS facility worldwide.
2. Export Control Management in the US and UK will provide a list of the input fields required.
3. Access to the toolset needs to be made available to every BAE SYSTEMS location worldwide.
4. Dual type access will be required. Password control for admin rights and the general staff view only.
5. Input of data must be by means of forms not tables, (i.e. data should be entered through specifically designed forms, dealing with one export transaction at a time).
6. Data and information added to or amended in the toolset by the BAE SYSTEMS US

initiator must be automatically notified by some form of electronic means to a designated official at the BAE SYSTEMS site receiving the transfer.

7. Send and receive confirmations of electronic notifications must be included in the process.
8. The toolset must record the details of the persons approved at each US site who are approved to input and/or amend data in the database and restrict the use of that facility only to those persons.
9. Administrative rights to add, amend, or update, the list of US sites, and the approved persons at these sites, must be made available to the designated export control officers located in the BAE SYSTEMS, Head Office, Washington DC.
10. Dropdown selection boxes to be made available to pick-up site and person.
11. Site selection must return only the approved persons at that site.
12. Provide metrics showing frequency of transfers by site, by month, and by country.
13. Usability must be high – the system should be easy to use, efficient and error free.

From the system requirements specification, the overall process had to be broken down into smaller, more manageable stages that would be easier to implement, and be testable as separate prototypes, in fact a modular design approach where the concept of step-by-step modular design is synchronised with the progress of the design process (Aoyama and Uno 2003). This resulted in a three-stage design shown in Figure 4 below. This approach allowed for stage 1 of the process to be prototyped, tested and evaluated by US users, whilst work on stages 2 and 3 could be conducted in parallel. This would in the longer term enable a more rapid implementation and deployment of the finished system.

Stage 1: Create a user interface for US initiators, with some "smart" functionality e.g.

Figure 4. Simplified process model of control and compliance

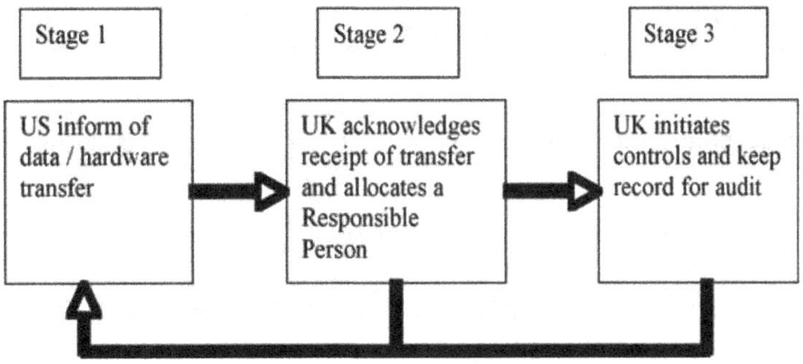

Stage 1	Stage 2	Stage 3
US inform of data / hardware transfer	UK acknowledges receipt of transfer and allocates a Responsible Person	UK initiates controls and keep record for audit

choosing a US business group in one dropdown menu would automatically populate only the appropriate US sites in another dropdown menu. Care had to be taken to ensure that the user input form flowed in a logical manner to suit the user, with enough help facilities built-in, to provide error free guidance.

Stage 2: Enable UK recipient of transfer information to allocate a Responsible Person (RP) from a form embedded within the automated email, i.e. by submission of the form. The system would automatically send an email to the appropriate UK recipient, with another automatic email notification being sent back to the USA initiator for their own record keeping.

As there would be no easy way that the USA person creating an entry into the system would know who the UK RPs are, the most sensible option was to use the contact name that initiated the original purchase order for the hardware. Contact names would be known for technical data and design services.

Stage 3: Create a user interface for UK RP to track and update received transfer information, with the system automatically mailing back to the US that the process was complete. Again, care had to be taken to ensure that the user input form flowed in a logical manner to suit the user, and again with enough help.

Detailed Planning

As previously stated, the implementation of this system had to be done in 12 weeks, a considerable challenge for a project of this size and potential impact. After an initial meeting, seven development stages were planned (Figure 5 below shows the modular structure of the system):

1. **Understanding the Process:** Procedural meetings between all concerned stakeholders to ensure that everyone understood the requirements.

Figure 5. Basic modular architecture

2. **Stage Designs:** Site design and coding created within a development environment

3. **Stage Testing:** Design/development testing of code modules.

4. **Stage UAT:** User acceptance testing, formative evaluation.

5. **Full System Functionality Test**: Design/development testing to ensure technical working, and no conflicts between the different modules. Page loading tests, connectivity checks, mailing systems, and correct data transfers.

6. **Full System UAT:** Full user acceptance testing, following the process from start to finish, and analysing data captured, reviewing built in metrics, usability testing and evaluation.

7. **System Readiness Review**: Complete review of the system process, working and data capture. Confirm system delivers what was expected, and then obtain Management approval for formal launch of system.

Before writing any code, the following questions were posed to generate a "to do" list. The list was adapted from *It's a Different World from Web Site Design* (www.digital-web.com 03.04.07), and is a list most projects may find useful:

1. Have I recognised the aim of the project and the problem it addresses?

2. Have appropriate analysis tools been used?

3. Is the background to the project understood?

4. Has the scope of the solution been determined?

5. Have the boundaries to and the constraints on the solution been recognised?

6. Have the hardware and software requirements of the solution been identified and their availability determined?

7. Is there an appropriate contingency plan?

8. Are there media constraints?

9. Has the user view of the system been considered?

10. Has a design for the solution been prepared?

11. Has there been a discussion of the rejected options?

12. Have the various elements of the system been justified?

13. Have the potential benefits of the proposed computerised solution been presented?

14. Is there a clear understanding of the limitations of the proposed solution?

15. Is there evidence of the recording (e.g. sketches, notes and other visual data) of ideas and observations from a range of appropriate sources?

16. Have I made perceptive connections between my personal work and that of others?

17. Have alternative ideas and solutions been considered and developed visually with originality and personal style?

18. Is there a detailed testing strategy and plan?

The list was used to ensure that the development team were addressing all aspects of the project that were thought to merit attention.

User Interface Design

As part of the requirements capture and early formative feedback from users, it seemed almost common sense to adopt form-based interfaces underpinned by a desktop metaphor, i.e. a GUI. All users are very familiar with forms and form structures of various kinds and this can perhaps be characterised by the interface widely used in Microsoft Excel. General HCI principles were applied to the look and feel and information layout (see e.g. Shneiderman, Byrd & Croft, 1997; Rosson & Carroll 2002). The design process was divided into three stages, which were carried out in parallel:

Figure 6. Example form user interface

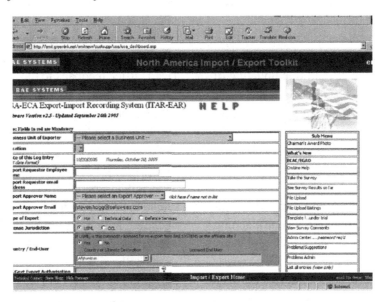

1. Stage 1 – The User Input Form
2. Stage 2 – Receipt Acknowledgement
3. Stage 3 - End User Controls

An example screenshot is shown in Figure 6 below.

It is not possible for reasons of confidentiality and perhaps not relevant to show all the form based interfaces here. It is however worth noting that the key issues that determine the usability of the system lie in the task functionality and support for that functionality.

Implementation

A detailed description of the implementation of the ITAR system is outside the scope of this chapter and some aspects are subject to confidentiality restrictions. However, a key characteristic of the approach was to use standard, "off-the–shelf", tools. The system uses a Microsoft Access Database to store data. Implementation was done with the VBScript language within Active Servers Pages (ASP) and Javascript was used to implement client side interactions. The system is hosted on a BAE

SYSTEMS secure intranet, which uses a Microsoft Internet Information Server (IIS v6.0).

TESTING AND EVALUATION

The system was tested and formatively evaluated throughout the development process and this approach was an important component of the overall approach. It is clear that the testing and evaluation contributed significantly to the system being delivered on time and fit-for-purpose. Although testing and evaluation continue, the focus in this section is on the work done during the 12-week period of prototyping.

Understandably, a great deal of testing was carried out to ensure that the system was running without bugs, errors or indeed crashes. Much of this is not directly relevant to usability and will not be discussed here. However, some of the software testing does have implications for usability, in particular, the user experience and is of relevance.

Overall, the testing and evaluation fall into five main relevant categories:

1. Analysis of user feedback on various aspects of usability and the user experience.
2. Monitoring the connectivity between USA users and the UK Web Server.
3. Testing of continuous and true updating of the database.
4. Measurements of page loading times for the USA users.
5. Testing of responsiveness of automatically generated emails.

The overall methodology and approach to testing was conventional and based e.g. upon planning advocated by Satisfice (Virginia, USA), a company at the forefront of testing methodologies (www.satisfice.com 25.09.06). This typically consists of a test plan, a test plan document, strategy and implementation.

Usability Issues

User feedback was collected continuously during the development period through informal and semi-structured interviews with users and other stakeholders. These took place face-to-face, through teleconferences and through email. Most commonly, users did structured walkthroughs of particular interfaces or functions, guided by a developer. Additionally, users and stakeholders were encouraged to provide feedback on any and all aspects of the system and this was again done through direct contact, teleconferencing and email.

Formative feedback from users was extensive and indicated no problems with usability after various initial observations had been taken on board. Only two major and five minor systems problems relating to usability were identified while three minor process problems were highlighted. The major problems noted here resulted in several days work to satisfy users suggestions on improving the system by providing a facility to auto-populate certain fields with email addresses and to provide an on-line edit facility where the user can store partially filled in forms, then retrieve these at a later date for full submission.

The minor system problems required very little work, and the minor process data only required Head Office feedback to the user on etiquette and formality. In fact, 80% of all user comments can be categorised as minor, with 30% of all comments being related to procedural issues. What users often reported as issues of usability were in fact related to how to work the ITAR rules. Typically, users on different sites had a different understanding of what information needed to be declared, how it should be declared and varying interpretations of ITAR related points of law. Perhaps these issues are not surprising in a company the size of BAE SYSTEMS where there are changes in staff roles as well as staff turnover. This is also a reflection of the immense complexity of the ITAR and related rules. These issues relate to ITAR rules one way or another and are addressed through staff training. In fact there is an annual conference for export control officers where such issues are addressed.

Connectivity, Data Integrity and the User Experience

Connectivity may not seem like an issue that relates to usability but it did impinge upon user experiences. We define user experience as an aspect of usability that goes beyond or is wider than interacting with user interfaces.

Users expressed concern that they were initially not sure if submissions to the database had been successful. This was regardless of any feedback provided through the user interfaces. Special tests were conducted where submissions were made in the USA and monitored real time in the UK. During the testing the staff in the USA and UK communicated via telephone and the tests were conducted more than 100 times in the first month of prototype development. The results of these tests were communicated to the users and stakeholders and this gave them increased confidence in the system and concerns over connectivity were then not expressed in the feedback.

Data integrity was similarly reported as an issue of negative user experience. The approach here was similar in that testing and feedback was obtained while developers and testers communicated via telephone. Typically the issues of concern were ensuring constraints on formats such as dates and numeric fields. The main user experience issues were trust in the system and allowing users to reassure themselves that the system was behaving in the manner expected. Once users had been directly involved in these live tests, the feedback changed from expressed concerns to positive support.

Other Issues Affecting User Experiences

Users in the USA expressed concern that the pages might not load fast enough and saw this as a potential issue that might adversely affect usability. The system uses dynamic pages with e.g. dropdown menus that are populated from a remote database, so this concern was seen as potentially real. Typically, acceptable loading times for commercial internet sites is anything less than 10 seconds on a standard 56k modem (www.1-hit.com 18.10.06). Page loading times were therefore tested extensively with USA users as participants. When the results showed that the concerns were unfounded, this issue disappeared off the usage and usability agenda.

A similar concern was expressed over email responsiveness. This issue is subject to various influences that are hard to monitor and control, e.g. because of the use of company email servers that are not under the control of the ITAR team, network congestion, etc. Monitoring email responsiveness is not a problem as it is done through comparing the date and time of submission with the date and time the user receives an email. The development team and users engaged in a detailed discussion about this issue and it was agreed that given the

problems of external factors, the delivery would simply be monitored. In summary, the users accepted that this was something that could not be resolved by the development team. Users were further assured by the observation that throughout the UK and USA BAE SYSTEMS sites mail was being delivered around 90% of the time, with around 10% of mail not being delivered due to users entering wrong email addresses.

CONCLUSION

The work discussed here is a case study of how one company used modern system design and development approaches, Agile software development and usability engineering to produce and deploy a solution to a problem that is critical to the organisation. At the onset the sheer scale of the project especially given the time constraints seemed to present a challenge that would be hard to meet. However, by adopting the right approaches and careful planning, the project has demonstrated a way of working that not only allowed the team to meet the challenges but has also influenced the way other projects are conducted within the company. The intense focus on users and involvement of stakeholders throughout the project is clearly a major factor in the successful completion of the work.

As with all projects the team look back and reflect on how the work could have been improved and what lessons are learned for the future. In addition to the obvious point of having had to develop the system in 12 weeks the main lessons can be summarised as follows:

1. More time and effort should have been devoted to collecting and incorporating user preferences regarding the design of the user interfaces. This would have improved human computer interaction in the first version of the system.

55

2. While it seemed a natural choice at the time to use Microsoft Access as a database platform, it is likely that there will be performance issues with increased usage, in particular concurrent usage. It would have been more appropriate to use a platform such as MySQL or Oracle.

3. There was a missed opportunity to reuse code modules to a greater extent, in particular style sheets.

4. Code annotations and commenting could have been more detailed, an important issue for future maintenance.

The lessons learned would not be complete without taking into account time scales and issues such as key stakeholders not being available at important times due to other duties being given higher priority, various flexible working arrangements that again made access to users a problem and working across different time zones.

It is clear that the project does provide a design and development framework for future work undertaken by the authors and this will also involve further developments of the ITAR system. The lessons can be summarised as eight points of advice:

1. Adopt aspects of Agile methodologies and merge these with user centred design approaches and usability engineering (e.g. scenario based design, star model, etc.).

2. Use a task model (e.g. as described by Welie 2001).

3. Adopt a prediction model (e.g. as described by Fewster and Mendes 2001).

4. Produce a very detailed but flexible plan that covers all aspects of the work.

5. Establish a way to review and change the plan frequently and easily.

6. Involve stakeholders and users from the start and continue that involvement.

7. Establish continuous and detailed communications between the stakeholders and the developers.

8. Prototype as early as possible, allow formative feedback and iterative development of prototypes.

The team regard the project as being successful but the influences of that success were not fully anticipated. It has become increasingly apparent that successful ITAR compliance depends on effective record keeping. The system, which has now been in place essentially unchanged for five years, has provided that essential underpinning and has contributed significantly to BAE SYSTEMS' compliance programme, including a satisfactory outcome to periodic audit, both internal and external.

From the user's point of view, the project has offered three principal benefits:

1. Unlike off-the-shelf applications (COTS), it has been possible to tailor it closely to the specific requirements of the business, which has contributed to high usability.

2. It was developed into a practical working system, which is both usable and fast.

3. It proved to be readily and quickly modifiable in response to user requests.

While the use of databases is now almost routine for ITAR compliance, this system retains, even after five years, one key and unique feature. No other, as far as we are aware, links both the exporter and the recipient in the same comprehensive way, providing a "one-stop-shop" for record keeping and an audit trail linking items from their departure from the US to their final disposal. This feature, initially seen as necessary as well as feasible because the same company, BAE SYSTEMS, was both exporter and recipient, could nevertheless offer clear attractions to other major transatlantic defence companies.

ACKNOWLEDGMENT

This project won a Silver Award in 2004 for the annual BAE SYSTEMS Chairman's Award for Innovation and Implementation. There were approx 4,000 entries world wide submitted into that year's event, with the eventual winners being presented by BAE SYSTEMS Chairman, Dick Olver.

REFERENCES

Aoyama, K., & Uno, Y. (2003). Modular design supporting system with a step-by-step design approach. In *Third International Symposium on Environmentally Conscious Design and Inverse Manufacturing, 2003 - EcoDesign '03.*

Day, P. N., Ferguson, R. K., & Holt, P. O'B., Hogg, S., & Gibson, D. (2005). Wearable Augmented VR for Enhancing Information Delivery in High Precision Defence Assembly: An Engineering Case Study. *Virtual Reality (Waltham Cross)*, *8*(3), 177–185. doi:10.1007/s10055-004-0147-8

Fewster, R., & Mendes, E. (2001) Measurement, Prediction and Risk Analysis for Web Applications. In *Proceedings of IEEE Metrics'2001-7th International Software metrics Symposium.* Washington, DC: IEEE CS Press.

Hartson, H. R., & Hix, D. (1989). Human-computer interface development: concepts and systems for its management. [CSUR]. *ACM Computing Surveys*, *21*(1), 5–92. doi:10.1145/62029.62031

Highsmith, J. (2004). *Agile Project Management: Creating Innovative Products*. New York: Addison Wesley.

Rosson, M. B., & Carroll, J. M. (2002). *Usability Engineering: Scenario-Based Development of Human-Computer Interaction*. San Francisco: Morgan Kaufmann.

Shneiderman, B., Byrd, D. & Croft, W.B. (1997). Clarifying Search: A User-Interface Framework for Text Searches. *D-Lib Magazine, January*.

Szalvay, V. (2004). *An Introduction to Agile Software Development*. Bellevue, WA: Danube Technologies, Inc.

van Welie, M. (2001). *Task-Based User Interface Design*. PhD Thesis, Vrije Universiteit, Amsterdam.

Younossi, O., Arena, M. V., Leonard, R. S., Roll, C. R., Jain, A., & Sollinger, J. M. (2007). Is Weapon System Cost Growth Increasing? *(A Quantitative Assessment of Completed and Ongoing Programs), (Monograph MG-588-AF)*. Santa Monica, CA: RAND Corporation.

NOTE: BAE SYSTEMS AND SELEX

BAE SYSTEMS Avionics Division in Edinburgh, Scotland carried out the work reported and discussed in this chapter. Subsequently, BAE SYSTEMS sold the majority holding of the Avionics Division to Finmeccanica to form SELEX S&AS (SELEX Sensors and Airborne Systems). Key staff involved in this project transferred to SELEX and continue involvement in the work. The system is of importance to both BAE SYSTEMS and SELEX, and both share the current system and future developments.

Chapter 4
The Evaluation Cycle Management–Method Applied to the Evaluation of Learning Management Systems

Matija Pipan
Jozef Stefan Institute, Slovenia

Tanja Arh
Jozef Stefan Institute, Slovenia

Borka Jerman Blažič
Jozef Stefan Institute, Slovenia

ABSTRACT

The chapter deals with a complex decision-making problem, the selection and evaluation of Learning Management Systems (LMS) in which several objectives - referring to the definite group of users - like social, technical, environmental, and economic impacts, must be simultaneously taken into account. We introduce Evaluation Cycle Management (ECM), a support methodology aimed at the evaluation of options that occur in the decision-making processes. ECM is based on Multi-attribute decision making (Criteria Evaluation) and Usability Testing (Usability Evaluation). The Multi-attribute decision making in the first phase of ECM presents an approach to the development of a qualitative hierarchical decision model that is based on DEX, an expert system shell for multi-attribute decision support. The second phase of ECM is aimed at Usability Testing on end users. ECM illustrates its usefulness by showing its main features and its application to the above problem. It is based on the theoretical and practical expertise related to the quality and usability assurance of LMS.

DOI: 10.4018/978-1-60566-896-3.ch004

INTRODUCTION AND RELATED WORK

Considering the abundance of e-learning systems that have offered education over the Internet during the past decade, it is not surprising that there has been growing interest in identifying design principles and features that can enhance user satisfaction. User satisfaction with technologies related to distance and collaborative learning applications has been found to be significantly associated with usability, that is, the effectiveness, efficiency and satisfaction that it gives to its user in a given context of use and task. The usability of an educational environment is related to its pedagogical value (Kirkpatrick, 1994) and evaluation of its usability is part of the processes of establishing its quality. In the literature, there are numerous recommendations for the design of pages, text, graphics, and navigation in Learning Management Systems (LMSs), but in spite of that, it is still recognized that "*severe usability problems are present and common*" (Brinck, Gergle & Wood, 2002). However, despite the increased awareness of these problems when adopting internet-based education (Johnson & Hegarty, 2003) the usability of e-learning systems has still not been sufficiently explored and solutions not yet provided.

These are some of the realizations that led us to perform the case study described in this chapter and to analyze the results. The case study was undertaken as part of an EU project centered on the issues of introducing internet-based education in a region that suffers from a low level of business-oriented usage of the Internet and related e-services together with a relatively high level of unemployment. We found the environment and the context of this study extremely suitable for an evaluation and assessment of the usability of the Learning Management Systems, and to try to identify the "*threshold of acceptability beyond which users can begin to interact productively and voluntarily instead of simply acting and reacting*" (Hémard, 2003).

The usability of a Learning Management System is often perceived to be the province of the technical expert rather than the content expert; however, technical knowledge is insufficient when it comes to designing and testing systems intended for e-learning. A recent survey (Pulichino, 2004) shows that e-learning practitioners perceive usability a key factor in e-learning systems planning and use. The results of that survey indicate three aspects (Inversin, Botturi & Triacca, 2006): (a) usability is an essential consideration when designing e-learning systems; (b) e-learning systems and applications should always be tested for usability; and (c) e-learning systems and applications effectiveness can be greatly enhanced through user-centred design methodologies.

From the perspective of LMS selection, adoption and maintenance, the investigating the usability of LMS can be very interesting also for at least three reasons. (1) it may reveal usability breakdowns and provide indications for enhancing the application itself, by creating workarounds or by fixing the code – a possible alternative with Open Source; (2) it allows LMS manager to create guidelines for course authors and instructors that are actually supportive for their practice and focus on their problems instead of being (only) general introductions to the tool; (3) it allows user-oriented instead of system-oriented comparison and assessment of LMSs.

There are different methodologies for evaluating the usability of e-learning systems and applications. Basically they fall within two main categories: (a) usability inspection methods, and (b) empirical testing. Usability Inspections methods, also called expert review methods, include a set of methods based on having expert evaluators instead of final users inspect or examine usability-related aspects of a user interface (Cato, 2001, Holzinger, 2005). The main systematic inspection techniques are: Heuristic Evaluation (Cato, 2001), Cognitive Walkthrough (Brinck, Gergle & Wood, 2002) and Formal Usability Inspections (Holzinger, 2005). Empirical testing methods, also called user-based methods, investigate usability through direct observation of a sample of users interacting with the application (Whiteside, Bennet & Holtzblatt, 1988). This method we used in our empirical study. The most used techniques are Thinking Aloud Protocol (Lewis & Rieman, 2007; NIARNIAR: Think Aloud Protocol, 2007) and Contextual Inquiry (Nielsen & Mack, 1994).

There has to be some comparative analysis and assessment of LMSs, which clearly probes their features in the context of pedagogy, open learning and instructional design. Consequently instructional designers that are called upon to solve a specific instructional problem with explicit needs and requirements will be assisted in choosing a specific LMS that fits closer to their problem. A number of comparative reviews are available on the World Wide Web. To our knowledge, the most important are:

- a review and comparison of the current Campus LMS with alternative management learning systems and recommendation of a standard strategy with a general implementation timeline and description of needed resources (LMS Evaluation Committee, 2009),
- a comprehensive presentation of technical characteristics of LMSs and an on-line tool for the automatic comparison of systems, based on certain criteria (EduTools, 2009),
- a review that provides a full framework for the evaluation of LMSs based on pedagogy and system organization, applied on 12 systems (JISC, 2009),
- an LMS check list for Schools produced by the European Schoolnet (European Schoolnet, 2009),
- a multi-stage evaluation of next-generation Learning Management Systems (The Learning Technologies Resource Centre, 2009).

These reviews mainly present tables of features supported by selected LMSs. They usually focus on the mere presentation of the features supported by the LMSs being examined, as well as on the comparison between them according to specific criteria.

A variety of different evaluation models are presented in the evaluation literature, but they do not involve a selection of the most relevant LMS and later on usability evaluation into one single methodology. For this reason we have developed a new methodology named ECM (Evaluation Cycle Management) which presents one attempt to select and evaluate different Learning Management Systems in the framework of single methodology and also to discuss the findings in an assessment of the *learnability, effectiveness, efficiency* and level of *satisfaction* of an LMS (Lai-Chong Law, Jerman Blažič & Pipan, 2007). Results of the case study can provide a better understanding of the ECM methodology, development of *multi-attribute decision making* and *usability testing*.

To achieve the proposed objectives, this chapter is organized as follows: to begin, we will describe the theoretical framework which we have applied in this research. We will present and describe *Evaluation Cycle Management (ECM)*, a novel methodology aimed at the evaluation of options that occur in decision-making processes. This section presents a brief introduction to the Multi-attribute decision making (*Criteria evaluation*) as a first phase of ECM and *Usability evaluation* as the second phase of ECM. Each of the applied methods is followed by a description of the scenario and a study of the results. Finally, the chapter ends with a discussion of the overall results, conclusions and implications.

EVALUATION CYCLE MANAGEMENT (ECM)

What is ECM?

To assure that a product is good enough to satisfy all the needs and requirements of the users and other potential stakeholders, such as the users' clients or managers, we need to verify the products' characteristics and assess its acceptability within various categories. Several unique methods and techniques for evaluating products/systems are known, as well as many possible ways of combining various evaluation methods.

Evaluation Cycle Management (ECM), which was developed by the authors, can be classified as a combined evaluation system, because it is composed of two independent evaluation methods: *Multi-attribute decision making (Criteria evaluation)* and *Usability testing (Usability evaluation)*. A detailed description of these two evaluation methods and validation of ECM on the case study follows.

Architecture of ECM

The principal feature that characterizes the Evaluation Cycle Management (ECM) is a two-phase evaluation method with a feedback loop. The first phase of ECM includes Multi-attribute decision making and the second, Usability evaluation. The results gained from the Multi-attribute decision making model (first phase), developed by experts, is being verified on users as well. In case user usability testing (second phase) shows overly significant changes between the presupposed and the gained results, we return to the first phase and correct the multi-attribute model on the basis of the analysis results. When an observed product/system gains good results with the user testing, or only minor corrections are needed, such a system is recommended. The key advantage of the ECM methodology as seen by the authors is that in the first phase of evaluation (evaluation using a multi-attribute decision making model) only one – the most suitable solution – is chosen which leads to lowered costs and decreased use of time regarding continued evaluation in the second phase (usability testing), for only one solution is subjected to testing and not all (Pipan, Arh & Jerman Blažič, 2006).

The First Phase of ECM: Criteria Evaluation

Decision making is a process of selecting a particular option from a set of possibilities, so as to best satisfy the aims or goals of the decision maker (Efstathiou & Mamdani, 1986; Rajkovič, Bohanec & Batagelj, 1988). In practice, the *options* (also called *alternatives*) are objects or actions of (approximately) the same type, such as different computer systems, different people applying for a particular job, different investment strategies, and different e-learning technologies. Supporting humans in making complex decisions has long been a goal of many researchers and practitioners. A number of methods and computer-based systems have been developed (Humphreys & Wisudha, 1987). They are mainly studied in the framework of decision support systems (Alter, 1980; Keen & Scott Morton, 1978; Turban, 1988), operations research and management sciences, decision theory (French, 1986) or decision analysis (Phillips, 1986).

One of the approaches to decision support, which is widely used in practice, is multi-attribute decision making (Chankong & Haimes, 2008; Keeney & Raiffa, 1976). The basic principle is a decomposition of the decision problem into smaller, less complex sub-problems (Figure 1). Options are decomposed onto different dimensions X, usually called *attributes, parameters* or *criteria*. According to this decomposition, each option O is first described by a vector of values v of the corresponding attributes. The vectors are then evaluated by a *utility function F*. This function should be previously defined by the decision maker(s),

Figure 1. Architecture of ECM

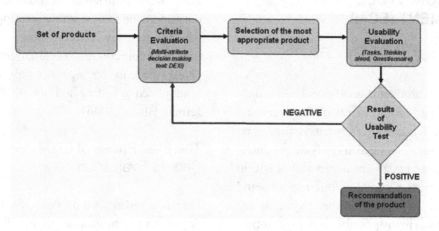

representing his, her or their *goals*. When applied upon a particular option *O*, the function F yields a *utility F(O)*. According to this value, the options can be ranked and/or the best one chosen. In the multi-attribute paradigm, the decision makers' knowledge about a particular decision problem is therefore *described* by *attributes X* and a *utility function F*. In addition, there is a data base of options, consisting of vectors *v*.

The methodology of hierarchical decision models has been developed and extensively applied in relation to decision support (Nagel, 1993). There, the decision-makers are often faced with the problem of choice (Simon, 1977): to choose an option from a set of available options so as to best satisfy the decision-makers' goals. In complex real-life decision processes, the problem of choice can be extremely difficult, mainly because of complex, interrelated or even conflicting objectives. To support the decision-maker, a decision model is designed to evaluate the options. Also, it can be used for the analysis, simulation, and explanation of decisions. In practice, this approach has been most often used for technical or economical decision problems, such as project or investment evaluation, portfolio management, strategic planning, and personnel management.

The contribution to these fields has been the development of an expert system shell for multi-attribute decision support DEX (Bohanec & Rajkovič,

1990). DEX itself is designed as an interactive *expert system shell* that provides tools for building and verifying a knowledge base, evaluating options and explaining the results. The structure of the knowledge base and evaluation procedures closely correspond to the multi-attribute decision making paradigm. This makes the system specialized for decision support (Bohanec & Rajkovič, 1995).

Some recent developments have made the hierarchical decision model approach very attractive also for problems in web based education and e-learning. In particular, some newly developed methods, including DEX, facilitate the design of qualitative (or symbolic) decision models. In contrast to traditional quantitative (numeric) models, the qualitative ones use symbolic variables. These seem to be better suited for dealing with 'soft' decision problems, which are typical for education and e-learning: less structured and less formalized problems that involve a great deal of expert judgments as opposed to exact formal modeling and computation. In next section we present the approach to the development and application of qualitative hierarchical decision models that is based on the DEX shell.

Knowledge Representation in DEX

A particular knowledge base of DEX consists of (1) a tree of attributes and (2) utility functions (Figure 3).

Figure 2. General concept of multi-attribute decision making

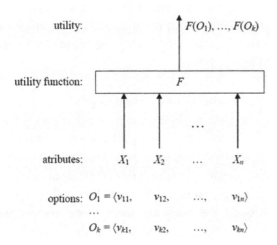

Figure 3. Tree of attributes with utility functions and options

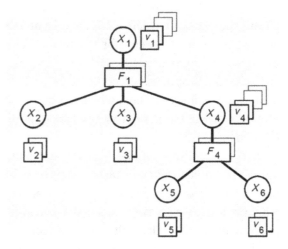

A tree of attributes represents the structure of a given decision problem. The attributes are structured according to their interdependence: a higher-level attribute depends on its descendants (sons) in the tree. Leaves of the tree, referred to as *basic attributes*, depend solely on the characteristics of options. Internal nodes of the tree are called *aggregate attributes*. Their values are determined on the basis of utility functions. The most important aggregate attribute is the root of the tree. Its purpose is to represent the overall *utility* of options. *Utility functions* define the process of aggregation of lower-level attributes into the corresponding higher-level fathers. For each aggregate attribute X, a utility function F that maps values of sons of X into values of X, should be defined by the decision maker.

Utility functions are represented by *elementary decision rules*. Let X_1, X_2, ..., X_k be the sons of an aggregate attribute Y. Then, the function $Y = F(X_1, X_2, ..., X_k)$ is defined by a set of rules of the form

$$\textbf{if} X_1 = x_1 \textbf{and} ... \textbf{and} X_k = x_k \textbf{then} Y = y_m : y_M$$

where x_i, y_m and y_M represent the values of the corresponding attributes. "$y_m : y_M$" stands for an interval of values between y_m and y_M, inclusive. Most commonly, $y_m : y_M$ is a single-value interval. In this case, the rule is simplified to

$$\textbf{if} X_1 = x_1 \textbf{and} ... \textbf{and} X_k = x_k \textbf{then} Y = y.$$

Sets of elementary decision rules are grouped into tables. In case when more decision making *groups* with different objectives are involved in the decision process, each group can define their own set of utility functions. In Figure 2, two such groups are assumed. *Options* are represented by the values of basic attributes, i.e. by values v_1, v_2, ..., that are assigned to the leaves of the tree. In Figure 2, two options are assumed. Regardless of the number of groups, there can be only one value v_i assigned to a basic attribute for each option.

In the final stage of the decision making process, the above described components of the knowledge base are utilized in order to *evaluate options*, i.e. to determine the values of the root and the remaining aggregate attributes in the tree. Since there can be more than one group of utility functions, the evaluation process can result in several sets of aggregate evaluation results, as shown by separate sets of squares in Figure 3.

The Second Phase of ECM: Usability Evaluation

Usability is most often defined as the ease of use and acceptability of a system for a particular class of users carrying out specific tasks in a specific environment. Ease of use affects the users' performance and their satisfaction, while acceptability affects whether the system or product is used (Holzinger, 2005).

In the case of Evaluation Cycle Management, only the usability evaluation on end users reveals the real value of the observed system/product, which has been chosen on the first evaluation phase with the aid of the multi-attribute decision making technique. Testing with end users is one of the most fundamental usability methods and one which is irreplaceable in the second phase of the ECM methodology, because it provides direct information about how people use the system/product, what their exact problems are with the concrete interface and it verifies its expected usefulness for the system user.

In usability testing it is very important to pay attention to the issues of reliability and validity (Holleran, 1991). Reliability is the question of whether one would get the same results if the test were to be repeated, and validity is the question of whether the result actually reflects the usability issues one wants to test. To ensure reliability and validity of the usability evaluation outcome, several points need to be considered: representativeness of test participants for real users of the system, realness of testing tasks as compared to actual tasks performed by real users, accuracy of observations of test participants behaviors, and sensitivity of measuring tools.

There are several unique methods and techniques for testing usability as well as many possible ways of combining various usability methods. A combination of methods and techniques used in the second phase of ECM usually contains: task scenarios, think aloud, field observations, questionnaires and participant debriefing (Law, Hvannberg & Cockton, 2008; Pipan, 2007).

The most important thing that we need to do before any testing is conducted is writing down a test plan and addressing the following issues (Nielsen, 1993):

• **Usability Evaluation Goals**

The usability testing of the system/product evaluates the potentials for errors and difficulties involved in using the system for human resource activities. Some of the areas that will be tested through the usability evaluation process are derived from the criteria evaluation in the first phase of ECM; other concerns are identified from the observed system functionalities (i.e. Can users successfully navigate through the system? Can they easily locate the information they are looking for? Can the application be used with only the on-line help? etc.). Specific usability goals are determined from the above concerns. These goals allow the creation of evaluation scenarios and tasks that let us know if the observed system is: *effective, efficient* and *satisfactory*. During the task creation and selection we need to be very attentive because one of the essential requirements of every usability test is that the test participants attempt tasks that real users of the system will want to perform with it and also probe potential usability problems (Dumash & Redish, 1999).

• **Target Audience**

The selection of participants whose background and abilities are representative of the products' intended end user is a crucial element of the evaluation process. Valid results will be obtained only if the selected participants are typical end users of the product, or are matched as close to a selected set of characteristics as possible.

- **Preparing the Testing Environment**

Before you are ready to conduct the pilot test, which is the last step before conducting the usability evaluation, you have to prepare the physical test environment. The evaluation team needs to prepare the test room and observation room, procure required equipment (hardware, software), network connections and establish communications between the participant and the helpdesk (Philips & Dumas, 1990).

- **Experimental Design**

Each participant receives a short, scripted verbal introduction and orientation to the evaluation. This material explains the purpose and objective of the evaluation, and additional information about what is expected of them. They are assured that the product is the center of the evaluation and not themselves, and that they should perform the test in whatever manner is typical and comfortable for them. The participants will be informed that they are being observed and videotaped and asked to fill out a short background pre-test questionnaire. The scenario is as follows:

  - After the orientation, the participants are asked to sit down at the computer. The evaluation administrator gives the participants the task scenario booklet and instructs them on the use of the help desk.

  - After the participants begin working through the evaluation scenario, they are encouraged to work without guidance except for the provided material and the product itself. The evaluation administrator may ask the participant to verbalize his or her thoughts if the participant becomes stuck or hopelessly confused. These occurrences will be noted by the evaluation administrator, and will help to pinpoint the cause of the problem.

  - All test participants are required to think aloud when performing the task scenarios. It enables administrators to identify where participants are in a series of tasks, follow their thought processes, and identify points in the task flow where users deviate from the ideal path. As participants are providing feedback while completing a task, this method vividly reveals users' conceptions and misconceptions regarding a system (Wickens & Hollands, 2000).

  - To gather additional insights from the participants about performed scenarios, participants are asked to fill out a post-scenario questionnaire: the After-Scenario Questionnaire (ASQ). The ASQ is a 3-item questionnaire which assesses participant satisfaction after the completion of each scenario (Lewis, 1991). The items address three important aspects of user satisfaction with system usability: *ease of task completion, time to complete a task,* and *adequacy of support information (on-line help, messages, and documentation).*

- **Data Collection Methodology**

Usability evaluation data is usually a combination of two types of measurements: *performance measures* and *subjective measures.* Performance measures are obtained primarily through observations. These measures concern counts of actions and behaviors observed and consist of several aspects (Lai-Chong Law & Pipan, 2003), e.g.: *timing* (time to finish a scenario), *errors* (number of wrong menu choices, selections and other errors), *seeking help* (number of screens of on-line help and number of times help is solicited from the evaluation administrator) and *emotional expression* (observations of frustration). Subjective measures are obtained mainly through participants' self-reporting. These measures concern people's perceptions, options and judgments and consist of two aspects: *quantitative aspect* (Computer System Usability Questionnaire - CSUQ - and After-Scenario Questionnaire - ASQ) and *qualitative aspect* (participants think aloud all the time when carrying out the task scenarios and participants debriefing).

• **Participant Debriefing**

After all tasks are completed or the time expires, each participant is debriefed by the evaluation administrator. The debriefing is recorded and usually includes the following:

  ○ Participant's overall comments about his or her experience,
  ○ Participant's responses to probes from the evaluation monitor about specific errors or problems encountered during the evaluation.

The debriefing session serves several functions. It allows the participants to say whatever they like, which is important if tasks are frustrating. It provides important information about each participant's rationale for performing specific actions, and it allows the collection of subjective preference data about the application and its supporting documentation. After the debriefing session, the participants will be thanked for their efforts, and released.

VALIDATION OF ECM–CASE STUDY: SELECTION OF THE MOST APPROPRIATE LEARNING MANAGAMENT SYSTEM

Identification of the Problem

In accordance with the fact that human resource development has been recognized as one of the most important elements for the further development of modern societies, the current demands for new knowledge and skills has constantly increased. Parallel to the wide range of possibilities offered by new generations of educational technologies, a number of Learning Management Systems (LMSs) which support e-learning have been developed and are available on the market. Consequently, customers are often faced with the dilemma of how to choose the optimum LMS for the implementation of the education process for a definite target group. Precisely defined strategy in the sense of "who and what", sets the basis for further decision making and usability evaluation: *Does the LMS gives proper and sufficient support for the execution of the exercises which lead to the planned objective realization.* The usability evaluation then presents the real value of the system, its effect on communication, the anticipated benefits for the owner and user, and justification for the investment.

Recent studies of student perceptions of online education point to a number of benefits, such as convenience and flexibility, greater motivation to work, better understanding of the course material, more student communication, and immediate and extensive feedback. Some studies also note some of the disadvantages of a Web-based education, such as technical, logistical and usability problems, some frustration, lack of instructor interaction, etc.

The general aim of our case study was focusing on the usability and applicability aspects of LMSs in relation to definite target group and users: employees in the Drava-Mura Region SMEs with a basic knowledge of ICT. In the next sections, Evaluation Cycle Management will be tested through the case study. In the first phase of ECM, the multi-attribute decision making model for evaluation of LMSs will be developed, in the second phase of ECM, we will examine the satisfaction associated with the selected LMS.

Development of the Multi-Attribute Decision Making Model

In this section we present the approach to the development and application of qualitative hierarchical decision models that is based on the DEX shell. It helps in the creation of decision models that consist of non-numerical (qualitative) criteria. The criteria are hierarchically ordered into a tree structure. The aggregation of partial evaluations into the final evaluation is then carried out by decision rules of the *if-then type*. The weights are replaced by rules that define the interdependence of the criteria and their influence on the final evaluation. Thus the influence of a criterion can depend on its value, which corresponds in utility theory (Bohanec & Rajkovič, 1995; Chankong & Haimes, 2008; French, 1986) to the variability of the weights (Mandić & Mamdani, 1984). The decision-making model is based on a chosen list of criteria, parameters, variables or factors, which we are going to monitor in the decision-making process (Bohanec & Rajkovič, 1999).

The decision-making process was divided into four phases: *(1) criteria identification and criteria structuring, (2) utility function definition (decision rules), (3) description of variants, (4) LMS evaluation and analysis.* Individual decision-making phases are presented in detail below.

Identification, Description and Criteria Structuring

This section provides descriptions of criteria which are the components of the decision-making model. When creating this model we tried to meet the requirements set by Bohanec & Rajkovič (1999). We have taken into account the principle of *criteria integrity* (inclusion of all relevant criteria), *appropriate structure, non-redundancy, comprehensiveness* and *measurability* (Baker, Bridges, Hunter, Johnson, Krupa, Murphy & Sorenson, 2002). Comprehensiveness means that all the data about the subject are actually present

in the database. Non-redundancy means that each individual piece of data exists only once in the database. Appropriate structure means that the data are stored in such a way as to minimize the cost of expected processing and storage (Awad & Gotterer, 1992).

The criteria are divided into three main scopes: *Student's learning environment, System, technology & standards and Tutoring & didactics.* These three scopes represent the skeleton of the multi-attribute model. The criteria can include the following values: 'low', 'average' or 'high'; the only exception being the criteria where it is impossible to determine an intermediate value. All values have an increasing range (low value is worst than high value).

The first group of criteria is merged into the *Student's learning environment* category composed of four basic attributes: *Ease of use, Communication, Functional environment* and *Help*. Web-supported communication tools and new technologies ensure and promote continuous communication and interaction processes between tutors and education participants. Information infrastructure enables *synchronous* and *asynchronous communication*, which is why the best LMSs combine both.

The second group of attributes is merged into the *System, technology & standards category.* These groups of criteria are assessed through the basic attributes of *Technological independence, Security and privacy, Licensing & hosting* and *Standards support.* The attribute of technological independence is used for the evaluation of an LMS from the prospective of its technological accessibility, which is a pre-condition that has to be met if we wish to talk about system applicability and efficiency.

The Security and privacy criterion focuses on two issues: *User security and privacy* and *security and privacy of an LMS*. User security and privacy should be at the forefront of attention; therefore an LMS must keep communication and personal data safe and avoid dangers and attacks on user computers. Application security and privacy

Figure 4. Tree of attributes for assessment of applicability of LMS

assessment is made using authentication, authorization, logging, monitoring and validation of input. It is also important to consider *e-learning standards* – standards for description of learners' profiles and standards for the description of learning resources (Jerman Blažič & Klobučar, 2005). In the context of e-learning technology standards are generally developed to be used in system design and implementation for the purposes of ensuring interoperability, portability and reusability, especially for learning resources as they require for their preparation qualified professionals and are very time demanding (IEEE Computer Society, 2002).

Third group of criteria is merged into *Tutoring & didactics*. The tutor's quality of environment is assessed using the *Course development, Activity tracking* and *Assessment criteria*. Activity tracking undoubtedly provides important support to the tutor in the learning process. Here we have focused on monitoring students in the process of learning and the possibility of displaying students' progress, analysis of presence data, sing-in data and time analysis.

Utility Function

The tree of criteria defines the structure of the evaluation model by defining the criteria and their interdependence. In the final outcome, this means that the overall evaluation of the LMS depends on 57 criteria. On the other hand, the criteria tree does not define the aggregation, i.e., the procedure that combines the values for the final evaluation.

Figure 5. Utility function for criterion, Student's learning environment

	Ease of use	Communication	Functional environment	Help	Student's learning environment
	39%	29%	21%	11%	
1	low	low	<=average	*	low
2	low	low	*	low	low
3	low	<=average	low	*	low
4	low	<=average	<=average	low	low
5	<=average	low	low	low	low
6	>=average	*high*	*high*	*high*	*high*
7	*high*	>=average	>=average	*high*	*high*
8	*high*	>=average	*high*	*	*high*
9	*high*	*high*	*	*high*	*high*
10	*high*	*high*	>=average	*	*high*

In DEX, the aggregation procedure is defined by decision rules, an example of which is shown in Figure 5.

The rules determine the evaluation of the criterion, *Student's learning environment*, based on four criteria: *Ease of use, Communication, Functional environment,* and *Help*. The first five rules determine the conditions by which the Student's learning environment is evaluated as unsuitable (low grade). This is for example whenever: the LMS does not conform to ease of use, communication and help (regardless of the evaluation of the remaining criteria, denoted by an asterisk) (rule 2). On the other hand for example the Student's learning environment is suitable (high grade) whenever the LMS respects the case of use criterion at least on the average level (average grade) and the quality of the attributes communication, functional environment and help assessment are high (rule 6). The remaining rules can be interpreted similarly, with the symbols <= and >= representing "worse or equal" and "better or equal", respectively.

Obviously, there are many more such rules in the model. For each aggregate criterion (such as *Student's learning environment*), a similar table is defined. In the entire model there are 108 rules defined in this way.

The tables were defined by a group of experts at the Jozef Stefan Institute using the DEX computer system. Experts contributed the contents of the rules, and the system made sure that the tables were complete (covering all possible combinations of the evaluation criteria) and consistent (an improvement of a single lower-level criterion could never decrease the overall value of the LMS). Decision rules therefore define the conditions under which an LMS is ranked.

Description of Variants

The multi-attribute decision making model was tested on three Learning management systems: *Blackboard 6* (www.blackboard.com), *CLIX 5.0* (www.im-c.de) and *Moodle 1.5.2* (www.moodle. org). Blackboard is among the most perfected and complex LMSs on the market. The system offers various communication options (both synchronous and asynchronous) within the learning environment. The Blackboard LMS is designed for institutions dedicated to teaching and learning. Blackboard technology and resources power the online, web-enhanced, and hybrid education programs at more than 2000 academic institutions (research university, community college, high school, virtual MBA programs etc. CLIX is targeted most of all at big corporations, because it provides efficient, manageable, connected and expandable internet-based learning solutions. This scalable, multilingual and customizable software aims at providing process excellence for educational institutions. For educational administrators, CLIX offers powerful features for course management and distribution. Addition-

Figure 6. Examples of evaluation and analysis of Blackboard, CLIX and Moodle

Criterion	Blackboard 6	CLIX 5	Moodle 1.5.2
Applicability of LMS	average	*high*	low
Student's learning environment	average	*high*	average
Ease of use	average	*high*	average
Keyword search	*high*	*high*	low
Metadata search Engine	*high*	*high*	low
Navigation	average	*high*	*high*
Print current page	low	low	*high*
Communication	*high*	*high*	*high*
Asynchronous communications	*high*	*high*	*high*
Internal mailing system	*high*	*high*	*high*
Instant messaging	*high*	*high*	*high*
Discussion forums	*high*	*high*	*high*
Synchronous communications	average	average	average
Chatrooms	*high*	*high*	*high*
Chatroom logfile	*high*	*high*	*high*
Audio/videoconferences	low	low	low
Functional environment	*high*	average	average
Configurable environment	*high*	average	average
Network search	average	*high*	low
Collection of tools	*high*	*high*	*high*
Browser bookmarks	low	low	*high*
Help	average	*high*	average
System, technology & standards	*high*	*high*	average
Technological independence	*high*	*high*	*high*
Compliant with common web technology	*high*	*high*	*high*
Transfer speed	*high*	average	*high*
Graphical independence	average	*high*	*high*
Advanced technologies	average	average	average
Security & privacy	*high*	*high*	average
User security and privacy	*high*	*high*	average
Security and privacy of LMS	*high*	*high*	average
Authentication	*high*	*high*	average
Authorization	*high*	*high*	average
Logging and monitoring	average	*high*	average
Validation of input	average	*high*	average
Licensing & Hosting	*high*	*high*	*
Standards support	*high*	*high*	average
ADL SCORM	*high*	*high*	*high*
IMS QTI	*high*	*high*	low
IMS LIP	*high*	low	low
AICC CMI	*high*	*high*	low
Tutoring & didactics	*high*	*high*	*high*
Course development	*high*	average	*high*
Online editor for course organization	average	*high*	*high*
Up/download of resource packages	*high*	low	*high*
Linking	*high*	*high*	*high*
Activity tracking	average	*high*	*high*
Monitoring student in the learning process	*high*	*high*	*high*
Activity tracking during the learning process	*high*	*high*	*high*
Statistical reports of student progress	*high*	*high*	*high*
Course analysis	low	*high*	*high*
Participant administration	*high*	*high*	*high*
Login analysis	low	*high*	*high*
Time analysis	low	*high*	*high*
Assessment	*high*	*high*	*high*
On-line quiz editor	*high*	*high*	*high*
Extensible quiz engine	*high*	*high*	*high*
Quizzes import	*high*	low	*high*

ally, it provides personalized learning paths for students, a tutoring centre for lectures and a whole bunch of innovative collaboration tools for both user groups, e.g. a virtual classroom. Altogether, CLIX makes planning, organizing, distributing, tracking and analyzing of learning and teaching a smooth and efficient process. Moodle is a free, open source PHP application for producing internet-based educational courses and web sites on any major platform (Linux, UNIX, Windows and Mac OS X). The fact that it is free of charge is especially attractive for schools and companies which always lack resources for the introduction of new learning technologies. Furthermore, the Moodle system is not only price-efficient – it can easily be compared to costly commercial solutions on all aspects. Courses are easily built up using modules such as forums, chats, journals, quizzes, surveys, assignments, workshops, resources, choices and more. Moodle supports localization,

Figure 7. Evaluation results for Blackboard 6, CLIX 5.0 and Moodle 1.5.2

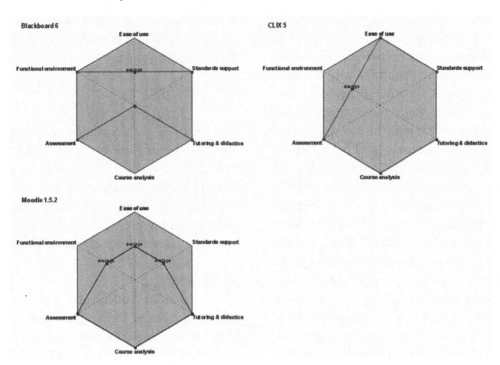

and has so far been translated into 34 languages. Moodle has been designed to support modern pedagogies based on social constructionism, and focuses on providing an environment to support collaboration, connected knowing and a meaningful exchange of ideas. The greatest disadvantage of the system is certainly support to e-learning standards, which is reflected on Figure 7, showing evaluation results according to different assessment criteria for Blackboard, CLIX and Moodle Learning management systems.

LMS Evaluation and Analysis

The evaluation is carried out according to the tree of criteria from the basic criteria up. The method of aggregation is determined by the decision rules. The variant which is awarded the highest grade should be the best one. To illustrate the use of the decision model, we consider Blackboard, CLIX and Moodle Learning Management Systems. The results of assessment are given in Figure 6. The

systems obtained high, average and low grades in the evaluation assessment process.

Due to the complexity of LMSs and a large number of criteria it is essential that the decision-making model allows us to obtain not only the final assessment, but also a detailed partial analysis of individual elements (Figure 7). In this way we can detect weak points and disadvantages of the system, which can be used as the basis for system improvements. We can anticipate how specific criteria improvements would influence quality and we can achieve a more optimal distribution of resources at our disposal. The immense importance of individual criteria and their autonomy prevents the average of one or more criteria to automatically become the average of the entire system. For example, an LMS that was awarded an average grade in all three criteria (e.g. *average Student's learning environment, System, technology & standards, Tutoring & didactics*), cannot be called average, because it could be even worse, under average. On the other hand, a system with excellent technological and standardization solutions cannot be considered of high quality also from the methodology and didactics point of view, if the system does not provide an adequate Student's learning environment, which is essential for e-learning users, since it does not fulfill their objectives. Besides these, there are also some excluding factors that must be met in order for an LMS to achieve a certain level from the point of view of security and privacy for example. We can renounce the safe SSL transfer in order to enhance the operational speed (this is especially important for users still using modems to connect to the Internet) and consequently positively influence applicability of the system. However, such a system does not meet security requirements, which are important in e-learning (they are considered important also by the decision-making model). The advantages and disadvantage of the systems are reflected in Figure 7, showing evaluation results according to attributes: Functional environment, Ease of use, Course analysis, Tutoring & didactics, Assessment and Standards support for Blackboard, CLIX and Moodle LMS.

Usability Evaluation of LMS CLIX 5.0.

According to the results of the first phase of ECM (criteria evaluation), where the LMS CLIX 5.0 got the highest assessment among three different Learning Management Systems and methodology of Evaluation Cycle Management, we performed the second phase of evaluation: Usability testing (usability evaluation) of the LMS CLIX 5.0.

Usability Testing

Standard user test procedures were adopted (Dumas and Redish, 1999) and were conducted by the respective evaluation administrators, who were responsible for recording the data, transcribing think-aloud protocols of the participants, asking them to fill out pre-test, post-task and post-test questionnaires and participant debriefing.

Participants

We selected 10 participants, who were typical representatives of the target audience or were matched as closely to the criterion as possible. They possessed a certain level of experience and knowledge of information and communication technologies (ICT), experience in using software applications and had some basic knowledge about e-learning.

Testing Environment

For the purpose of the usability test we prepared a usability room and set up the required hardware and software equipment (Table 1).

Table 1. Testing environment

Device	Attribute	Equipment
Computer Configuration	Model	PC Pentium 4, 2.80GHz, 1 GB RAM
	OS Version	MS Windows XP Professional
	Browser	Internet Explorer 6.0
	Networking	LAN
Display Device	Screen Size	21 inches
	Resolution	1280 x 1024
Recording Device	Hardware	CD audio recorder
	Software	HyperCam v.2.13
Communication	Phone	Cordless telephone

Test Objectives

Usability goals for the LMS CLIX 5.0 were referred to on the hypothesis that users can utilize the services of the observed learning management system quickly, easily and accurately to accomplish their tasks in the way to attain the optimum level of effectiveness and efficiency, and find the navigation design comprehensive and user-friendly to attain an optimum level of satisfaction.

Task Scenarios

A set of seven tasks covering the core functionalities of the LMS CLIX 5.0 and also presenting the potential usability problems. Here below is the list of the tasks:

(T1) Updating a personal profile
(T2) Booking a course
(T3) Accessing the learning resources of a booked course
(T4) Taking an e-test
(T5) Joining and contributing to the discussion forum
(T6) Making a post in the Chat-room
(T7) Creating a personal Bookshelf

Each of the above seven tasks was translated into task scenarios, which render the test more realistic and problem oriented. (e.g. *T1 Scenario: A personal profile is a record of user-specific data that define the user's working environment. The basic data of your personal profile has been entered by the portal administrator. Your task here is to verify and, as necessary, update the existing data, upload your picture and enter your personal interests. These data are indispensable for collaborative working in CLIX communities*).

In addition, for each of the task scenarios, an experienced user of the LMS CLIX 5.0 assessed the range of acceptable time for completing a single task and determined maximum number of errors. These data can serve as references or baselines for data analysis.

Measurements and Usability Metrics

Quantitative Data
a. Effectiveness: *completion rate* (percentage of participants who completed each task correctly with/without assistance from a usability administrator), *errors* (number of errors: in menu choice, selecting an item from a list and other) and *assists* (number of times looking up on-line help and from a usability administrator).
b. Efficiency: *task time* (mean time of completion of each task, range and standard deviation of times) and *completion rate efficiency* (mean task time only for unassisted tasks).

Qualitative Data
c. Satisfaction: ratings and comments obtained through ASQ, CSUQ and participant debriefing.

Table 2. Time-on-task of the participants

	Task 1	Task 2	Task 3	Task 4	Task 5	Task 6	Task 7	TOTAL
Mean	5.20	4.94	3.95	11.27	9.06	5.38	7.85	47.65
Std. Dev.	0.994	0.781	1.189	2.094	1,455	1.354	1.253	4,453
Min	3.78	3.67	2.38	7.88	7.33	3.97	6.14	40.74
Max	7.12	6.02	7.12	15.63	12.56	8.82	10.06	55.02

The Results of the Usability Test

Quantitative Data

    a.   Effectiveness and Efficiency

Each participant was required to perform 7 tasks and fill out enclosed questionnaires. Based on the data (Table 2), the mean time over 7 tasks is 47.65 minutes, with the range from 40.74 to 55.02 and a standard deviation of 4.453. Altogether, participants performed 70 tasks, 59 (84,3%) were correctly completed without assistance and 11 (15,7%) with assistance (on-line help, advice) from the usability administrator (Table 3). Task 4 (Taking an e-exam) was found to be the most problematic. The mean time for Task 4 is 11.27 minutes and exceeds the time for completing the task (9 minutes), assessed by the experienced user, by 25,2%.

Furthermore, effectiveness and efficiency per task were computed. Effectiveness presents the rate that a task is correctly completed without intervention from the usability administrator or any other help. Efficiency is presented as the percentage of task completion per minute and it is calculated through dividing an unassisted completion rate by the corresponding unassisted average time-on-task. The average effectiveness (Table 4) over 7 tasks is 84,28%, ranging from 70% (Task 4, 5, 7) to 100% (Task 2, 3). The average efficiency over 7 tasks is 14.94%/minute, ranging from 6.78%/min (Task 4) to 25.32%/min (Task 3). From these data it is evident once again that Task 4 potentially should be problematic.

    b.   Errors

There are three types of errors that the participants may commit: *Menu choice error (M), Select from list error (L)* and *Other error (O)*. As shown in Table 5, the total number of errors committed by 10 participants is 90, with the Menu choice Error being the highest (53), followed by Select from list error (30) and Other error (7). The average number of errors over 10 participants is 9, ranging from 7 to 16. One of the measured attributes was also a frustration per task and Task 4 has caused much higher frequency of frustration (4) than the other tasks. These results are consistent with other findings that Task 4 evoked the highest number of errors and amount of frustration and had the longest time-on-task.

Qualitative Data

    a.   After Scenario Questionnaire (ASQ)

For measuring satisfaction Lewis (1991) has developed a three-item questionnaire called the

Table 3. Assistance from the usability administrator

Tasks completed without assistance	59
Tasks completed with assistance	11
Failed tasks	0
TOTAL	**70**

Table 4. Effectiveness and efficiencies per task

Task	Effectiveness (%)		Total Completion		Efficiency (%/min)	Total number of assists
	Rate	Mean Time	Rate	Mean Time		
T1	90%	4.99	100%	5.20	18.04	1
T2	100%	4.94	100%	4.94	20.24	0
T3	100%	3.95	100%	3.95	25.32	0
T4	70%	10.32	100%	11.27	6.78	5
T5	70%	8.32	100%	9.06	8.41	5
T6	90%	4.99	100%	5.38	18.04	1
T7	70%	7.15	100%	7.85	9.79	3

Table 5. Types of errors and frustration

Number of:	T1	T2	T3	T4	T5	T6	T7	TOTAL
Error (M)	5	4	2	19	11	4	8	53
Error (L)	3	5	3	7	6	2	4	30
Error (O)	1	0	1	2	1	2	0	7
TOTAL	9	9	6	28	18	8	12	90
Frustration	0	0	0	4	2	1	1	8

After Scenario Questionnaire (ASQ). The ASQ was developed to be used immediately following scenario completion in scenario-based usability studies. The three questions of ASQ unequivocally measure one single underlying aspect of participants' perceptions of how easily and quickly the scenarios were completed and the contribution of support information to carrying out the tasks. Each item is rated with a 7-point Likert scale, with 1 being "Strongly agree" and 7 "Strongly disagree". The items are phrased in a positive manner. Hence, the lower the score gained out of the 7-point Likert scale, the higher the satisfaction with the observed system. The psychometric evaluation of ASQ has excellent internal consistency, with coefficient alphas across a set of scenarios ranging from 0.90 to 0.96. The overall satisfaction rate over 10 participants is above the average with the mean value of 2.14 out of the 7-point Likert scale. The lowest rating of satisfaction, with the mean value 4.67, was for Task 4, which indicates that this functionality is difficult and complex for general users to manage.

b. Computer System Usability Questionnaire (CSUQ)

We adopted the Computer System Usability Questionnaire (CSUQ) from IBM to measure participants' satisfaction with system usability at a global system level (Lewis, 1996). The publicly available questionnaire contains 19 questions with a 7-point Likert scale for each answer. The CSUQ has excellent internal consistency with an overall coefficient alpha of 0.97. CSUQ can gauge three factors of satisfaction: *System Usefulness*

(SYSUSE), Information Quality (INFOQUAL), and *Interface Quality (INTERQUAL),* with corresponding coefficient alphas of 0.96, 0.91, and 0.91, respectively. A higher score gained out of a 7-point Likert scale means higher satisfaction with the system. In addition to the 19 questions from CSUQ, we also had after test debriefing with each participant. The average overall satisfaction over 10 participants is 5.68, with a standard deviation 0.48. The implication of the value is that the users' general satisfaction with the LMS CLIX 5.0 is good. Both the system usefulness (mean=6.03, SD=0.37) and interface quality (mean=5.94, SD=0.74) were above the system average, whereas the information quality (mean=5.07, SD=0.82) was a little bit below the average. A little lower assessment for the INFOQUAL should be attributed to the fact that most of the 10 participants were not satisfied with the supporting on-line help and feedback massages.

c. Participant debriefing

The debriefing session is an extremely important portion of the usability evaluation as it allows participants to convey their exact feelings about the product being tested. In addition, it allows the usability administrators to ask direct questions about murky points of each participant's evaluation, i.e. any sticking points they encountered during the testing, any specific problems with wording, etc. From these interviews usability administrators were identified some usability problems and acquired very useful information and recommendation from the real users (e.g. not enough clear taxonomy, lack of on-line help, the graphical user interface is confusing due to many colors and fonts etc.).

Analysis of Results and Findings

The main goal of the case study was the selection of the most suitable and appropriate LMS among the three available (BlackBoard 6, Moodle 1.5.2 and CLIX 5.0), which would to the greatest degree possible, satisfy the requirements and needs of the target group: employees in small and medium-sized enterprises with a basic previous knowledge of information-communication technologies.

As was already expected at the commencement of evaluation, a system which would entirely satisfy the target group of users was extremely difficult to find. Each system observed had its strengths and weaknesses, thus the choice of the most suitable system was that much harder. The ECM methodology in the first phase – development of a multi-attribute decision-making model – foresees the choice of only one of a number of solutions, namely that which best satisfies the criteria defined especially for the aforementioned target group. Furthermore this solution, selected as most suitable in the second ECM phase was then also validated by testing its usability on end users whereby the actual usefulness of the system was ascertained confirming that the LMS chosen offers sufficient and proper support for execution of the exercises which will lead to the realization of the planned objective. The advantage of ECM lies in the fact that only one – the most suitable – solution (LMS) is chosen during the first phase of evaluation allowing a decrease in costs and time used, for continued evaluation of its usability is subject to only one solution and not all.

Based on the results acquired with the aid of the first phase ECM methodology (criteria evaluation) it is evident (Figure 6) that the LMS CLIX 5.0 obtained the best marks of all three main criteria, at the same time coming closest to the criteria of an optimal solution. Due to the extreme complexity of Learning Management Systems and

the large number of criteria used it was essential that in addition to the final assessment, a detailed analysis of individual elements (Figure 7) impacting quality and the suitability of the LMS was also obtained from the decision-making model. Thus we were able to precisely define the weak points and deficiencies of the system or respectively, where the system could be improved. Since it was, however, the second ECM phase (usability evaluation) which supplied the answer of whether the selected LMS CLIX 5.0 was really the most suitable solution for the selected target group, it was additionally subjected to the testing of its usability. Ten participants participated in the test, which, on the basis of 7 tasks, verified the key functionalities of the system. The LMS CLIX 5.0 also proved to be an extremely suitable system for the target group of users in the second phase of evaluation according to ECM methodology. While performing usability testing several deficiencies were ascertained which, according to experts, represent merely minor corrections (e.g. *facilitation of navigation to e-testing, improvement of on-line help features, facilitation of terminological support texts in on-line documents, better colour reconciliation and fonts for the user server, etc.*). The main strengths and weaknesses of the LMS CLIX 5.0 are presented in Table 6 below.

Based on the results of the study implemented according to ECM methodology we concluded that the selected LMS, CLIX 5.0 (with several minor corrections) was suitable for the chosen target group of users – employees in small and middle-sized companies and was also recommended for use by us. Since CLIX 5.0 received good marks both in the first and second phases of ECM and in terms of feedback, consequently modification of the multi-criteria decision-making model was not required.

Table 6. The strengths and weaknesses of the evaluated system CLIX 5.0

Strong points	Weaknesses
Large palette of tools	Insufficiency and unintelligibility of help-texts
Good support for external content	Navigation to the e-tests
Syllabus/learning plan with branching options	Terminology of supporting information given in the on-line documents, limited support for e-learning specifications
Powerful rights management system	No search function in contents (only in descriptions of elements)
"Mandanten" concept (one installation for several units with their own courses)	Too many different colours and fonts in the graphical user interface

CONCLUSION AND RECOMMENDATIONS

Evaluation Cycle Management which represents a two-phase method for evaluating the suitability and usability of a certain system/product proved extremely suitable in the case of the choice of the most suitable Learning Management System for a defined target group. The success of the method used was evident both in the choice of LMS as well as its economic justification. On the basis of the findings acquired with the aid of the ECM methodology the selected LMS, CLIX 5.0 with smaller corrections later proved as extremely adequate for the training of employees in small and medium-sized enterprises. The economic justification for using the ECM methodology is especially supported in that already in the first phase regarding the development of a multi-attribute decision making model with relatively low costs, we choose from among all available solutions (systems) only the solution which will most satisfy the requirements of the target group of users while in the second phase of evaluation (usability testing) the testing of all possible solutions is avoided which certainly means a considerable savings in terms of finances and time. Taking into account the number of observed systems/products in the first phase, the advantage of the ECM methodology is even more evident.

We should also emphasize the versatility of the ECM methodology meaning that this method is not intended merely for evaluating and selecting the most appropriate Learning Management System as presented in the case study but is also suitable for evaluating and choosing numerous other solutions whether software, products, personnel, etc. The multi-attribute decision making model must be suitably adapted in the first phase of evaluation according to ECM methodology depending on the specifics of the observed products, and in the second phase of evaluation, those usability testing methods and techniques must be selected which in the given situation are most suitable.

REFERENCES

Alter, S. L. (1980). *Decision Support Systems - Current Practice and Continuing Challenges.* London: Addison-Wesley.

Awad, E. M., & Gotterer, M. H. (1992). *Database management.* Danvers, MA: Boyd & Fraser.

Baker, D., Bridges, D., Hunter, R., Johnson, G., Krupa, J., Murphy, J., & Sorenson, K. (2002). *Guidebook to Decision-Making Methods.* USA, WSRC-IM-2002-00002, Department of Energy.

Bohanec, M., & Rajkovič, V. (1990). DEX: an expert system shell for decision support. *Sistemica, 1,* 145–157.

Bohanec, M., & Rajkovič, V. (1995). Večparametrski odločitveni modeli. *Organizacija, 28,* 427–438.

Bohanec, M., & Rajkovič, V. (1999). Multi-Attribute Decision Modeling: Industrial Applications of DEX. *Informatica, 23*, 487–491.

Brinck, T., Gergle, D., & Wood, S. D. (2002). *Usability for the Web: Designing Web Sites that Work.* San Francisco, CA: Morgan Kaufmann.

Cato, J. (2001). *User-Centered Web Design.* Reading, MA: Addison Wesley.

Chankong, V., & Haimes, Y. Y. (2008). *Multi-objective Decision Making: Theory and Methodology.* New York: Dover Publications.

Dumash, J., & Redish, J. C. (1999). *A Practical Guide to Usability Testing.* Exeter, UK: Intellect Books.

EduTools. (2008). *EduTools Course Management System Comparisons – Reborn.* Retrieved March 17, 2008, from http://www.edutools.info/course/index.jsp

Efstathiou, J., & Mamdani, E. H. (1986). *Expert Systems and How They are Applied to Industrial Decision Making.* North Holland: Computer Assisted Decision Making, Elsevier Science Publishers.

European Schoolnet. (2008). Virtual Learning Environments for European Schools. *A Survey and Commentary*, (pp. 1-36). Retrieved April 10, 2008, from http://www.eun.org/etb/vle/vle_eun_feb_2003.pdf

French, S. (1986). *Decision theory: An Introduction to the mathematics of rationality.* New York: Wiley.

Hémard, D. (2003). Language Learning Online: Designing Towards User Acceptability, In Felix, U. (Ed.) *Language Learning Online: Towards Best Practice* (pp. 21–42). Hawaii, USA: University of Hawaii, National Foreign Language Resource Center.

Holleran, P. A. (1991). A methodological note on pitfalls in usability testing. *Behaviour & Information Technology, 10*, 345–357. doi:10.1080/01449299108924295

Holzinger, A. (2005). Usability Engineering Methods for Software Developers. *Communications of the ACM, 48*, 71–74. doi:10.1145/1039539.1039541

Humphreys, C. P., & Wisudha, D. A. (1987). *Methods and Tools for Structuring and Analysing Decision Problems, Decision Analysis Unit* (Tech. Rep. No. 87-1). London: The London School of Economics and Political Sciences.

IEEE. Computer Society. (2002). *Learning Technology Standards Committee LTSC, IEEE, Draft Standard for Learning Objects Metadata (LOM)* (Tech. Rep. 1484.12/D4.0). Washington, DC: IEEE Computer Society.

Inversini, A., Botturi, L., & Triacca, L. (2006). Evaluating LMS Usability for Enhanced eLearning Experience. In *the proceedings of EDMEDIA 2006,* (pp. 595-601), Orlando, GA.

Jerman Blažič, B., & Klobučar, T. (2005). Privacy provision in e-learning standardized systems: status and improvements. *Computer Standards & Interfaces, 27*, 561–578. doi:10.1016/j.csi.2004.09.006

JISC. (2008). *JISC Technology Applications Programme.* Retrieved February 8, 2008, from http://www.leeds.ac.uk/educol/documents/00001237.htm

Johnson, R., & Hegarty, J. R. (2003). Websites as Educational Motivators for Adults with Learning Disability. *British Journal of Educational Technology, 34*(4), 479–486. doi:10.1111/1467-8535.00344

Keen, P. G. W., & Scott Morton, M. S. (1978). *Decision Support Systems – An Organizational Perspective.* Reading, MA: Addison-Wesley.

Keeney, R. L., & Raiffa, H. (1976). *Decisions with Multiple Objectives*. New York: John Wiley & Sons.

Kirkpatrick, D. (1994). *Evaluating Training Programs*. San Francisco, CA: Berrett Koehler Publishers Inc.

Lai-Chong Law, E., Jerman Blažič, B., & Pipan, M. (2007). Analysis of user rationality and system learnability: Performing task variants in user tests. *Behavior & Information Technology, 7, 26*(5), 421-436.

Lai-Chong Law, E., & Pipan, M. (2003). *International Usability Tests on the Multilingual EducaNext Portal - Universal Exchange for Pan-European Higher Education* (Usability Tech. Rep. v.2.0). Zurich, Switzerland: Swiss Federal Institute of Technology Zurich.

Law, E., Hvannberg, E., & Cockton, G. (Eds.). (2008). *Maturing Usability: Quality in Software, Interaction and Value*, (Human Computer Interaction Series). Berlin: Springer Verlag.

Lewis, C., & Rieman, J. (2007). *Task-Centered User Interface Design: A Practical Introduction*. Retrieved May 17, 2007, from http://hcibib.org/tcuid/tcuid.pdf

Lewis, J. R. (1991). Psychometric evaluation of an after-scenario questionnaire for computer usability studies: the ASQ. *SIGCHI Bulletin, 23*(1), 78–81. doi:10.1145/122672.122692

Lewis, J. R. (1996). IBM Computer Usability Satisfaction Questionnaires: Psychometric evaluation and instructions for use. *International Journal of Human-Computer Interaction, 7*(1), 57–78. doi:10.1080/10447319509526110

LMS Evaluation Committee. (2009). LMS Evaluation Committee Report. *University of North Carolina at Charlotte*. Retrieved January 15, 2009, from http://www.lmseval.uncc.edu

Mandić, J. N., & Mamdani, H. E. (1984). A multi-attribute decision-making model with fuzzy rule-based modification of priorities. In Zimmerman, Zadeh, & Gaines (Ed.), *Fuzzy Sets and Decision Analysis* (pp. 285-306). North-Holland: Elsevier Publishers.

Nagel, S. (1993). *Computer-Aided Decision Analysis: Theory and Application*. Westport, CT: Quorum Books.

NIAR - National Institute for Aviation Research. (2007). *Think-Aloud Protocol*. Retrieved July 6, 2007, from http://www.niar.wichita.edu/humanfactors/toolbox/T_A%20Protocol.htm

Nielsen, J. (1993). *Usability Engineering*. San Diego, CA: Morgan Kaufman, Academic Press.

Nielsen, J., & Mack, R. (1994). *Usability Inspection Methods*. New York: John Wiley & Sons.

Philips, B., & Dumas, J. (1990). Usability testing Functional requirements for data logging software. In Human Factors Society (Ed.), *Proceedings of the Human Factors Society 34th Annual Meeting: Countdown to the 21st Century,* (pp. 295–299). Santa Monica, CA: Human Factors & Ergonomics Society.

Phillips, L. D. (1986). Decision Analysis and its Applications in Industry. In G. Mitra (Ed.), *Computer Assisted Decision Making*. North-Holland: Elsevier Science Publishers.

Pipan, M. (2007). *Methods and techniques for usability evaluation of software solutions*. Unpublished dissertation, University of Ljubljana, Ljubljana, Slovenia.

Pipan, M., Arh, T., & Jerman Blažič, B. (2006). Development of the model for a usability and applicability assessment of learning management systems. In Lillemaa, T (Ed.), *Is information technology shaping the future of higher education?: Proceedings of the 12th International Conference of European University Information Systems EUNIS 2006* (pp. 325-332). Tartu, Estonia: University of Tartu press.

Pulichino, J. (2004). *Usability and e-learning.* The E-learning Guide Survey series: Vol. January 2004.

Rajkovič, V., Bohanec, M., & Batagelj, V. (1988). Knowledge Engineering Techniques for Utility Identification. *Acta Psychologica*, *68*, 37–46. doi:10.1016/0001-6918(88)90060-1

Simon, A. H. (1977). *The New Science of Management Decision*. New York: Prentice-Hall.

The Learning Technologies Resource Centre. (2008). *LMS Evaluation Information*. Retrieved March 30, 2008, from http://www.ltrc.mcmaster.ca/lmseval/index.html

Turban, E. (1988). *Decision Support and Expert Systems*. New York: Macmillian.

Wickens, C., & Hollands, J. (2000). *Engineering Psychology and Human Performance*. Upper Saddle River, NJ: Prentice-Hall.

Chapter 5
Usability Techniques for Interactive Software and Their Application in E-Commerce

Shawren Singh
University of South Africa, South Africa

ABSTRACT

The purpose of this chapter is to provide an overview of usability and usability techniques. It discusses interaction design with a bias on web-based technologies, focusing on usability and usability definitions. Usability principles are discussed with a particular focus on web usability, and some of the techniques that can be used to incorporate usability design and testing. The chapter also considers aspects of electronic commerce usability. These techniques are divided into usability evaluation, (heuristic evaluation, checklists, usability tests, think aloud approaches) followed by designing with usability in mind (including user and task analysis, walkthroughs, user experience and scenario-based usability). Several E-commerce case studies, from a developing economy perspective, are then analysed, before finally discussing E-commerce usability.

The dependability of computing is a problem with which our societies will continue to have to wrestle. Donald MacKenzie

INTRODUCTION

For a system to be usable an interface must let users of the system, working in their own physical, social and cultural environments, accomplish their goals and tasks effectively and efficiently (Hackos & Redish, 1998).

Meeting the needs of users who demand power without complication has made the computer industry increasingly sensitive to the design of the user interface. The user interface could be the most important determinant of success for *electronic commerce* (Singh & Erwin, 2002). In fact, to many users, the interface *is* the system (Turban & Aronson, 1998). The success of any interactive product or system is ultimately dependent on it providing the right facilities for the task at hand in such a way that they can be effectively used, at an appropriate price (Dillon, 1994). To achieve success, good design is essential. In relation to *E-commerce,* Cockton

DOI: 10.4018/978-1-60566-896-3.ch005

(2005) advocates Value-Centred Design–the intent to create value must be incorporated as early as possible at the initial design stage.

To enable development methodologies to be Value-Centred, Cockton advocates a design philosophy that is intended to create value–for the enterprise (and the consumer in relation to *E-commerce*). To become Value-Centred, Cockton stresses the necessity for opportunity identification, where the intended value of a digital product is identified, agreed, and specified–the virtual 'gap in the market.'

There are several reasons why we should consider interaction design in any system. MacKenzie (2000), for example, provides a list that documents the cases of possible computer-related accidental death (to end of 1992). Prominent on the list is what MacKenzie (2000) labels the 'human-computer interaction problem'. Examples include problems with medical equipment, mission controls, airplanes, robotics and general work equipment that have 'malfunctioned' due to problems in the interface, and caused the loss of human life. Although electronic commerce users will not die from using poorly designed electronic commerce web sites, designers should consider the impact of poorly designed user interfaces. This idea reinforces the arguments of Pressman (2000), discussed later.

Another reason for considering interaction design is that of dependability. Computer systems' dependability is intrinsically multifaceted. Dependable hardware is patently of limited value unless accompanied by dependable software - which may not be very helpful if the human interaction with the hardware and software system is fault-prone. The resulting effect is that the dependable socio-technical performance of an inappropriate task may cause wider damage (MacKenzie, 2000). The usability factor is a critical aspect of the dependability puzzle (Scholtz, 1995). Yet another reason why one should adopt a human-centred design approach is the increasing legal regulations for designing safe systems, which do not harm the health or the well-being of their intended users (ETSI ETR-095, 1993).

HUMAN-COMPUTER INTERACTION AND INTERACTION DESIGN

Human-computer interaction aims at designing, constructing and evaluating computer-based interactive systems, including hardware, software, input/output devices, displays, training and documentation, so that people can use these computer-based interactive systems efficiently, effectively, safely and with satisfaction (Baecker & Buxton, 1987; Carroll, 2003; Cox & Walker, 1993; Dix, Finlay, Abowd, & Beale, 2004; Downton, 1993; Hartson & Hix, 1989; Hartson, 1998; Kotze & Johnson, 2001; Newman & Lamming, 1995; Preece, Rogers, & Sharp, 2002; Preece *et al.*, 1994; Shneiderman, 1998; Sutcliffe, 1988). Human-computer interaction is cross-disciplinary in its conduct and multidisciplinary in its roots. Human-computer interaction draws on, synthesises and adapts from several fields, including:

- Human factors (e.g. the roots for task analysis and designing for human error in HCI)
- Ergonomics (e.g. the roots for design of devices, workstations and work environments)
- Cognitive psychology (e.g. the roots for user modelling)
- Behavioural psychology and psychometrics (e.g. the roots of user performance metrics)
- Systems engineering (e.g. the roots for much pre-design analysis)
- Information systems (the development of user-centric computer artifacts)
- Computer science (the roots for graphical interfaces, software tools and issues of software architecture) (Hartson, 1998)

USABILITY

Usability means different things to different stakeholders. Usability is generally regarded as ensuring that interactive products, such as electronic commerce applications are easy to learn, effective to use, and enjoyable from the user's perspective, and involves the optimisation of user interaction with these interactive products (Preece et al., 2002). Over time, several researchers have produced sets of generic usability principles which can be used in improving electronic commerce web sites, as well as showing how to test usability and how to design software products, bearing usability in mind (for example, (Dix et al., 2004; Badre, 2002; Bevan, 2006; Cato, 2001; Falk & Sockel, 2005; Mayhew, 1999; Nielsen, 1993, 2000; Preece *et al.*, 2002; Preece *et al.*, 1994; Shneiderman, 1998; Thimbley, 1990)). These principles include aspects such as effectiveness, efficiency, safety, utility, learnability, flexibility, robustness, memorability, etc.

Usability Definitions

There are a number of definitions of usability, (e.g. those set out by ISO, RACE, ETSI and Preece *et al.* (2000)). The ISO 9241 standard describes ergonomic requirements for office work with visual display terminals (Abran, Khelifi, Suryn, & Seffah, 2003; ISO 9241, 1998; Travis, 2003), defining aspects such as how to specify and measure the usability of products, and defines the factors which have an effect on usability, including effectiveness, efficiency and satisfaction, (the former echoing Cockton's value-centred approach)

The standard sets out the following criteria for specifying/measuring usability:

- A description of the intended goals
- A description of the components of the context of use, including users, tasks, equipment and environments. This may be a description of an existing context, or a

specification of intended contexts. The relevant aspects of the context and the level of detail required will depend on the scope of the issues being addressed. The description of the context needs to be sufficiently detailed so that those aspects of the context which may have a significant influence on usability could be reproduced.

- Target or actual values of effectiveness, efficiency, and satisfaction for the intended contexts

The context of use defined by the standard includes the following factors: description of users, description of tasks, detailed description of the activities and processes may be required, description of equipment, description of environment and usability measures

A designer's perspective of usability – what designers need to do to ensure that usable systems and services are developed – is adopted by RACE (RACE 1065-ISSUE, 1992). Design guidance is offered to ensure that the appropriate enabling state exists for each of the user's goal tasks, and to reduce or minimise user costs.

Conversely, a purely ergonomic perspective is adopted by the European Telecommunications Standards Institute (ETSI ETR-095, 1993) rather than a cost orientation. Usability, together with the balance between the benefit for the user and the financial costs, form the concept of utility. Thus the downside of an ergonomic-driven orientation, is that a highly usable ergonomic system may have a low utility for a user who considers the cost to be excessive in relation to his/her needs.

Measures of usability are assumed to be of two kinds:

- **Performance measures:** Objective measures or observations of user behaviour and are focused on task performance, i.e. how well the user can achieve a specific task
- **Attitude measures:** Subjective measures or observations of the users' opinion of

working with the system, i.e. how much they like to use the system

These two measures of usability are subjective and dependent on the scenario. This means that a system or a service can get a high score on performance measures and a low score on the attitude measures. The two measures can, however, be dependent through sharing a common set of physical characteristics. The scores on these two usability measures may vary independently for a given system if either the task or the user category is changed. In conclusion, these two measures are highly dependent on the context, task and type of users concerned.

Performance and attitude measures are also complementary in the sense that both contribute to the complete evaluation of the usability of a human/machine system. An assessment in both dimensions is therefore necessary, unless it can be shown that one attribute remains constant over different implementations of a concept.

It is important to remember that the usability definition given here refers to a specific kind of task, user and environment. Usability in this sense cannot be generalised over different kinds of tasks, users and environmental conditions. Variations in these aspects are expected to give different values of usability for the same system, and require separate evaluations.

A more user-centred perspective is offered by Preece et al. (2002) who define interactive usability in terms of the following criteria: easy to learn, effective to use, and enjoyable from the user's perspective. Thus (in part following Cockton's value centred approach), Preece *et al* categorises usability into effectiveness, efficiency, safety and efficacy.

There are various overlaps with the different definitions of usability. Usability is a specific function of the particular task; usability can be broadly defined or can be narrowly defined to suit a particular task, event or set of circumstances. From these different definitions we can conclude

that usability is subjective. However, usability does not automatically translate into efficacy.

Usability Principles

In order to untangle these definitions, several researchers have over the years produced sets of principles or guidelines aimed at improving the usability of interactive systems. Usability guidelines are lists of rules about when and where to do things, or not to do things, in an interface. These guidelines can take a variety of forms and may be obtained from several sources such as journal articles, general textbooks, company in-house style guides, etc.

Dix *et al*. (2004), for example, puts forward principles to support usability in three categories:

- **Learnability:** Referring to the ease with which new users can begin effective interaction and then to attain a maximal level of performance. Usability principles related to learnability include predictability, synthesisability, familiarity, generalisability, and consistency.

- **Flexibility:** Referring to the multiplicity of ways in which the user and the system exchange information. A user is engaged with a computer in order to achieve some set of goals in the work or task domain. Usability principles related to flexibility include dialogue initiative, multi-threading, task migratability, substitutivity, and customisability.

- **Robustness:** Referring to the level of support provided to the user in determining successful achievement and assessment of goals. Usability principles related to robustness include observability, recoverability, responsiveness, and task conformance.

Shneiderman (1998) also focuses on this aspect. He advocates three groups of principles some of which overlap with those of Dix *et al.*(2004). He focuses on the recognition of diversity, the prevention of errors, and the use of the eight golden-rules of interface design (see below) applicable to most interactive systems. These underlying principles must be interpreted, refined and extended for each environment. The rules include: consistency, use of shortcuts, informative feedback, design dialogues, error prevention and handling, easy reversal of actions, and reduction of short-term memory load.

Usability of E-Commerce

Usability has assumed a much greater importance in the Internet economy than it has in the past (Seilheimer, 2004). In traditional physical product development, customers did not get to experience the usability of the product until *after* they had already bought and paid for the software product. Usability is an essential consideration for *E-commerce*.

In relation to *E-commerce*, Nielsen (2000) identifies the following common errors:

- **Business models:** Companies see the web as an electronic brochure instead of considering that there is a fundamental shift in the way business is conducted in the networked economy
- **Project management:** Web-based software projects are managed as if it they were traditional corporate projects. The consequences are that it may lead to an internally focused design with an inconsistent user interface. An *E-commerce* web site should be managed as a single customer-interface project.
- **Information architecture:** The web sites' structure reflects that of the company's. Ideally an *E-commerce* website should be structured in such a way that it reflects the users' tasks and their views of the information space

- **Page design:** Pages are not designed to optimise the *E-commerce* consumer's experience under realistic circumstances
- **Content authoring:** Written content should be optimised for online consumers who scan text quickly and need product information and/or payment details, (with secondary information relegated to supporting pages)
- **Linking strategy:** Develop a linking strategy that clearly identifies the company's content and links to *E-commerce* web sites (e.g. E-Bay and Amazon) or during a Google Search Function when a search term is entered seeking information about a product or service, a related 'sponsored link' appears on the same search return – a subliminal linking strategy

To bridge the common problems identified by Nielsen (2000), there are various techniques that can be used to incorporate usability into the design of interactive software. There are two groups of techniques that can be used to incorporate usability design and testing in the *E-commerce* development process.

The first group is usability evaluation. Under the auspices of usability evaluation we will discuss heuristic evaluation, checklists, usability tests and think aloud approaches. The second group is designing with usability in mind. Each approach has its own set of advantages and disadvantages (Maria et al., 2003).

Usability Evaluation

Usability evaluation is a process of evaluating a web site against a group of well defined criteria, such as easy to learn, effective, efficient, safe and satisfying [Preece *et al.*, 2002]. In this section we will discuss heuristic evaluation, checklist, and usability testing. These techniques can be used to improve the usability of an interactive software product.

Heuristic Evaluation

Heuristic evaluation is sometimes referred to as 'discount usability engineering.' Heuristic evaluation is a form of usability inspection where usability specialists evaluate whether an interface follows established usability guidelines, or heuristics. Heuristic evaluation is best conducted in the early, prototype stages of an electronic commerce project, and repeated as significant design changes are implemented.

Usability heuristics are general user interface design principles. The most widely used heuristics are the ones defined by Jakob Nielsen. He originally developed the heuristics evaluation in collaboration with Rolf Molich in 1990 (Molich & Nielsen, 1990; Nielsen & Molich, 1990). The set of heuristics can be used in expert evaluation as they provide a guideline and checklist for user interface designers. Nielsen (1994) presents a list of ten usability heuristics based on an analysis of 249 usability problems. These are: visibility of system status, match between system and the real world, user control and freedom, consistency and standards, error prevention, recognition rather than recall, flexibility and efficiency of use, aesthetic and minimalist, help users recognise, diagnose and recover from errors, and help and documentation.

The above set of heuristics is however very general – it can be seen as a set of guidelines rather than being regarded as synoptic for all circumstances. Heuristic evaluators are not like typical users – there is gap between the test and user needs that can affect the user experience substantially, either positively or negatively (Park, 2008). Thus Nielsen's usability heuristics may not be sufficient in *all* circumstances and may need to be enhanced to take cognizance of the *E-Commerce* era.

Checklist

A usability evaluation can also be conducted by going through a checklist of guidelines. Using checklists is a subjective evaluation method, and is closely related to the heuristic evaluation methods as examined previously. It is based on training, field experience and an examination of human factors data (Van Dyk, 1999). Holmes (2002) provides an extensive checklist that covers the following aspects of web page design: content, information architecture, navigation design, and screen design.

Checklists can be short or long, general or special purpose. For example, consistency of page layouts throughout the site; page titles with link names; consistent syntax, capitalisation and punctuation; images should have identical stylistic treatment; and logos that should conform to strict corporate standards throughout the site.

A short checklist takes less time and, with practice, can substitute single, broad principles for a long list of specific guidelines that all follow the same general principle. For example, there are many ways in which a web site can be consistent, and if one has learned to check for all the different types of consistency, the checklist only needs to mention 'consistency,' rather than a whole list of specific principles, (Brinck, Gergle, & Wood, 2002).

In relation *E-commerce,* specific checklists have also been developed. Perry and Schneider (2001), for example, suggest the following checklist for an *electronic commerce* web site:

- Design the site around how the users will navigate the site, not around the company's organisational structure
- Use small graphics and keep file sizes small so that pages load quickly
- Place frequently used links at the top of the page
- Clearly show the company's name and contact details on the home page; ensure that all pages include a link back to the home page for visitors who do not enter the site through the home page
- Avoid using business jargon and terms that visitors might not understand
- Design for legacy systems, i.e. older browsers, older computers, etc; be consistent

with the use of design features and colour on all web pages within the site

- Ensure that the navigation links are clearly indicated to the user and check that text and background colour combinations are visible to colour-blind users

However, it must be noted that checklists are only broad guidelines and may not solve all usability issues.

Usability Tests

Another approach often used for usability evaluation is usability testing. Usability testing is one of the cornerstones of user-interface design (Cox & Walker, 1993; Nielsen, 1993). Various researchers suggest different variations to usability testing (Cato, 2001; Hackos & Redish, 1998; Mandel, 1997; Nielsen, 1993; Preece *et al.*, 2002, Redmond-Pyle & Moore, 1995; Shneiderman, 1998; Spool, Scanlon, Schroeder, Snyder, & DeAngelo, 1999). Usability tests are conducted with actual end users, ideally

in their own environment, while performing real tasks. Only three to five users are needed to obtain a significant amount of valuable data. Research conducted by Nielsen (1993) has shown that as much as 85% of usability problems can be identified in the first usability test with a small group. Nielsen (1993) suggest that when the site is redesigned based on the initial usability test results, it must be tested again to ensure that prior problems were eliminated and new problems have not been created. Usability evaluators also gather data on problems that arise, such as, errors, confusion, frustrations and complaints. These can be noted and discussed with the user. It is useful to have the user talk aloud about what they are doing. Usability tests identify serious or recurring problems (Galitz, 1997).

Table 1 is an overview of some usability testing approaches that can be used and the particular circumstances in which each test can be used.

In Table 2 a summary is provided of some usability considerations (Cox & Walker, 1993), these considerations provide a basis for usability testing.

Table 1. An overview of usability testing (Cox & Walker, 1993)

Testing	Things to test (see Table 2) Users to test (naïve, novice, skilled or expert) Approaches to take (see test methods)	Testing methods	Task analysis Questionnaires Interviews Against standard Against guidelines Aesthetic judgement Observation of free use
When to test	Pre-design testing Testing concepts Testing task design Testing task definition Implementation	Benchmarks	Existing system Competitive systems Manual system Absolute scale

Table 2. Summary of some usability considerations (Cox & Walker, 1993)

Functionality	Can the user do the required task?
Understanding	Does the user understand the system?
Timing	Are the user tasks done within a reasonable time?
Environment	Do the tasks fit in with other parts of the user environment?
Safety	Will the system harm the user, either psychologically or physically?
Errors	Does the user make too many errors?
Comparisons	Is the system comparable with other ways the user might have of doing the same task?
Standards	Is the system similar to others the user might use?

To summarise, Cox and Walker (1993) state that:

- Usability testing requires a user
- Usability testing is done by observing people doing tasks with the products being tested
- Very importantly, Cox and Walker stress that usability measures are imprecise and there is no prescription that tells us how usable an artefact can be. Interpreting observations always requires judgment and will vary depending on the circumstances

Nielsen (1993) and Shneiderman (1998) point out that there are several methodological pitfalls in usability testing. One needs to pay attention to the issues of reliability and validity. Reliability is the question of whether one would get the same results if the test were to be repeated, and validity is the question of whether the results actually reflect the usability issues that are tested.

Think Aloud Approaches

The think aloud approach requires the user of an interactive application to verbally express themselves while performing a computer-related task or solving a computer-related problem (Jaspers, 2006).

Holmes (2002) suggests the following quick and easy usability tests. There are a few important rules and steps to follow when doing the testing:

- Get a person who fits the user profile for the site. Do not get someone who has extensively worked on the site; sit them down in front of a computer, give them the URL, and give them a small scenario, e.g. "I am testing this CV (curriculum vitae) site. Imagine you are a person looking for a job, and try to enter your CV." Also, tell them to think aloud, especially when

they are wondering about something; then silently observe; watch them use the site. If they ask you something, tell them you are not there. Then silently observe; start noting all the things you are going to have to change and afterwards ask them what they thought.

The National Cancer Institute, on the other hand, presents a variation on the above approach, which they refer to as an informal test. The informal test can be conducted in any space with or without specialised recording equipment. The approach can be summarised as follows (National Cancer Institute, 2002):

- Sit with the user. The tester may have another person sitting nearby to take notes; let the user do the work, encouraging the user to think aloud. The tester may also ask clarifying questions while the user is working; the tester may probe the user on how they interpret a screen or what they would expect to happen if they clicked a particular item and collect primarily qualitative data.

These techniques can be adapted to suite the particular circumstances of a particular project.

DESIGNING WITH USABILITY IN MIND

In this section we will discuss user and task analysis, walkthroughs, user experience and scenario based usability, as techniques used for designing with usability principles in mind.

User and Task Analysis

User and task analysis is the process of learning about ordinary users by observing them in action (Diaper, 2006). User task analysis is conducted before design begins. The results of the analysis will be used to create the information architecture, navigation structure and labelling schemes that make sense to users.

A detailed task analysis can be conducted to understand the current system and the information flows within it. These flows are important to the maintenance of the existing system and should be incorporated in any new or replacement system (Maguire, 1997). Kirwan and Ainsworth (1992) present a similar definition as the previous but they substitute 'to achieve a task' with 'to achieve a system goal'. Newman and Lamming (1995) also emphasise the goal-directed nature of tasks when they state succinctly that 'a task is a unit of human goal-directed activity'. There is no real consensus amongst practitioners concerning what is task analysis (Shepherd, 1989).

Formal task analysis yields the following benefits (Maguire, 1997):

- It provides knowledge of the tasks that the user wishes to perform; it is a reference against which the value of the system functions and features can be tested; it is a cost-saving exercise because failure to allocate sufficient resources to the task analysis activity increases the potential for costly problems arising in later phases of development; task analysis makes it possible to design and allocate tasks appropriately and efficiently within the new system; the functions to be included within the system and the user interface can be more accurately specified.

Formal task analysis has one major limitation in that it can be time-consuming and produce a large volume of data which may require considerable effort (and skill) to analyse (Van Dyk, 1999).

Task decomposition, knowledge-based techniques, and entity-relationship-based analysis are three different but overlapping approaches to task analysis (Dix et al., 2004):

- **Task decomposition:** This consists of defining the overall task in terms of sub-tasks and their sequence. Hierarchical task analysis (HTA) is such an approach and produces a hierarchy of tasks, subtasks and plans, or a description of task conditions (when a subtask is performed), and a task sequence or order of execution.

- **Knowledge-based techniques:** This builds a conceptual model of the way the user views the system and the task, and what a user needs to know about task objects and actions. One technique (TAKD or task analysis for knowledge description) uses an either/or (AND, OR and XOR) branch based taxonomy (TDH or task descriptive hierarchy) of all objects and actions in the task, which differs from the HTA methods (based on 'how to') in that it is based on task and object similarities (i.e. genericity).

- **Entity-relationship-based analysis:** The emphasis is on identifying objects and actors, and their relationships and operations, rather than on object similarities. Objects are classified as being either actors (usually human entities), concrete objects (all the other 'things'), and composite objects (sets or combinations of the previous two groups). Attributes of objects and actors are listed only when it is relevant to a human or computer task.

- **Task analysis echniques:** There are a number of techniques used to conducting task analysis. Under the GOMS (Goals, Operators, Methods and Selection rules) approach there are a family of techniques such as (John, 2003): hierarchical task analysis; link analysis; operational sequence diagrams; timeline analysis and cognitive work analysis.

Structured Walkthroughs

The goal of a structured walkthrough in HCI design is to detect problems very early on, so they can be eliminated (Preece et al., 1994).

Structured walkthroughs involve constructing carefully defined tasks from a system specification or screen mock-ups. A typical example would be to walk through the activities (cognitive and operational) that are required to get from one operational screen to another to complete a specified task. Before doing a walkthrough, experts determine the exact task that will be done, the context in which it will be done and their assumptions about the user population. They then walk through the task, review the actions that are necessary to achieve the task, and attempt to predict how the user population would most likely respond to the problems that they may encounter (Preece *et al.*, 2002; Preece *et al.*, 1994).

There are various techniques for conducting a walkthrough, for example:

- **Cognitive walkthroughs:** A cognitive walkthrough involves simulating a user's problem-solving process at each step in the human-computer dialogue, checking to see if the user's goals and memory for actions can be assumed to lead to the next correct action. The defining feature is that they focus on evaluating design for ease of learning – a focus that is motivated by observation that users learn by exploration (Brinck *et al.*, 2002; Nielsen, 1993; Preece *et al.*, 2002).

- **Pluralistic walkthroughs:** A process in which users, developers and usability experts work together to step through a (task) scenario, discussing usability issues associated with dialog elements involved in the scenario steps. Each group of experts is asked to assume the role of typical users (Brinck *et al.*, 2002; Nielsen, 1993; Preece *et al.*, 2002).

- **Group walkthroughs:** a group walkthrough brings together several people to review the web site jointly. The group walks through the web site for each major task a user would perform, trying to touch on every page that will be commonly used. For each task the group steps through every page on a web site to experience everything that a user would encounter (Preece et al., 1994).

From the various abovementioned walkthrough, HCI researchers tend to adapt methods that best fit their particular circumstances (Casaday, 2001).

User Experience

Advances in technology have encouraged usability engineers to design and develop systems that have the potential to enhance the user experience (Preece et al., 2002) so that they can be: satisfying; enjoyable; fun; entertaining; helpful; motivating; aesthetically pleasing; supportive of creativity; rewarding; and emotionally fulfilling.

'User experience is not about how a product works on the inside (although that sometimes has a lot of influence). User experience is about how it works on the outside, where a person comes into contact with it and has to work with it' (Garrett, 2003). User experience goes beyond web site functionality and works emotionally on the basis of the interactivity.

Usability can also be personal and emotional. 'Although most people think that design is about what we see – the form, shape, proportion, colour, and finish – the aesthetic value comes from the whole experience, including gesture and ritual, what we feel and hear, perhaps even what we taste and smell' (Moggridge, 1999). Since many usability tests have been focused on the examination of functionality of a website, the user's aesthetic and emotional experience has been excluded in the design process or dealt with as the graphic designer's task. Unfortunately, many designers have a tendency to be constrained within the information provided by the developer or the mood and feeling of the whole website separated from the user experience of design elements. There may be mutually conflicting objectives while they develop a web site so that they can anticipate the client and user's expectation from their designer's expertise and experience (Chevalier & Ivory, 2003).

Scenario-Based Usability

Mandel (1997) states that it is difficult to define exactly what a scenario is, but a scenario is typically a high-level description of what the user does. Mandel (1997) further describes a scenario as a sequence of user tasks or events that make up a common transaction. Rosson and Carroll (2002) simply define scenario-based usability as 'a scenario is simply a story about people carrying out an activity; problem scenario is a story about the problem domain as it exits prior to technology introduction'. Rosson and Carroll (2002) further unpack the meaning of scenario-based methods as 'that description of people using technology are essential in discussing and analysing how the technology is (or could be) reshaping their activities.' Scenario based usability is case specific and scenario dependent. For scenarios to be effective, developers must have a rich picture of the context. This requires many iterations with users to enable a 'rich-picture' to be drawn – not an exact science in the same way as Schniederman or Dix envisage.

Examples Illustrating the Need for Web Usability

The following are cases from a multi-lingual and developing economy that help illustrate the importance of usability in the design of web-based systems:

Case 1: South African Revenue Services (SARS)

In an effort to streamline the tax collection process, SARS has introduced e-filing. Page 1 is the index/welcome page to the SARS website. Page 2 is the login page for registered users. From a consistency perspective this page looks different. Pages 3 and 4 are consistent with page 2. Page 4, which is an actual tax return is an Adobe fill-in-form. With the SARS website, there are several usability problems. The essential aspect to note, however, is that the website is aimed at facilitating taxpayers to pay their tax. SARS and taxpayers in South Africa must either overcome usability issues, or face extremely long lines at the tax office – a major disincentive in efficient tax collection in a developing economy.

A radically transformed revenue collection system was envisaged by the commissioner of SARS. SARS believes that E-Filing will enable employers to use SARS's own payroll software, in a simplified process, and in a form that will allow employers to do their own reconciliations of deductions and tax return forms (W1, 2009).

The reason for shifting to a more electronic based system is to shift the burden onto the tax payer, and away from SARS itself, reducing a costly and slow administrative process on the part of the state. This is only possible if South African tax payers – typically the higher income groups in a developing economy – are themselves online, familiar with the internet, and can understand the SARS tax forms. Thus usability is critical if SARS is to achieve the target of increasing its future tax take. 'Reconciliations will need to increase in frequency over the next few years,' according to the Tax Commissioner. Currently, only an annual account is all that is necessary, but in future reconciliations will have to be done every six months, and from 2010 it will be every quarter.

Eventually says SARS, 'we shall move to real-time reconciliation', and thus interfaces, ease of use and user needs will all be essential. By 2012, it is thought that the tax filing system

Figure 1. The SARS Web Page

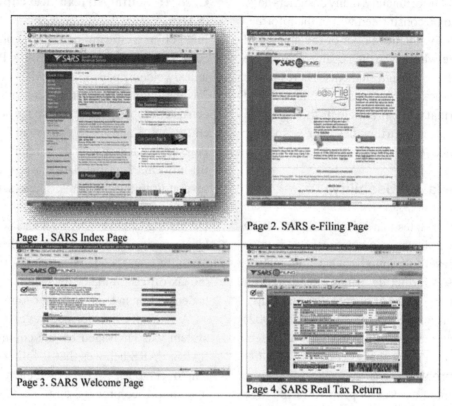

Page 1. SARS Index Page

Page 2. SARS e-Filing Page

Page 3. SARS Welcome Page

Page 4. SARS Real Tax Return

would have become so automated, that the tax could be assessed and paid and refunds automatically transferred into taxpayers' bank accounts, without filling in a form at all. Thus usability is all the more critical.

The E-Filing system is necessary, because of the huge waste of money sending out forms to the millions of tax payers who could file their returns electronically. SARS agrees that the shift to *E-filing* will require a culture shift, so it will need to be as sensitive as possible to public reaction.

Eventually, the returns received by taxpayers will already have their tax data filled in – 'pre-populated'. This overcomes a key problem. Taxpayers frequently make mistakes when copying figures from their tax form, as well as the staff at SARS. Broadly speaking, using these 'simplified' techniques adds a level of acceptable usability to the tax application for the user. This conforms

to the *golden rules* of usability (as advocated by Shneiderman and others above).

Case 2: The Olympic Games

In Australia, in June 1999, Bruce Maguire lodged a complaint with the Human Rights and Equal Opportunity Commission under a law called the Disability Discrimination Act (Travis, 2003). His complaint concerned the poor web site design of the Sydney Organising Committee for the Olympic Games, which Maguire alleged was inaccessible to visually impaired persons.

Maguire used a refreshable Braille display, as opposed to a screen reader, to view web pages. Braille displays and screen readers lack the sophistication to convert images into a text equivalent. The Sydney Organising Committee for the Olympic Games was fined in a court of law for not having made provision for blind us-

Figure 2. The Unisa Web Page

Page 1: Unisa's index page

Page 2: Index page with Quick Reference Drop-down Menu

Page 3: Search Page

Page 4: Results from Search

Page 5: First result option from Search

Page 6: Second result option from Search

ers and ordered to add alt text to all images on its website.

The above case points out that the design team and other stakeholders did not consider the diversity of their intended users.

Case 3: A University Website

While an academic institution is not an overtly commercial activity, it also needs to follow the value-centred design ethos advocated by Cockton

(referred to earlier). Intended value need not be purely monetary - it may relate to relevant stakeholders. In the case of a University, this includes management, students, parents and academics, the primary value being "the provision of appropriate, adequate and effective help with the choice of course and its delivery," Cockton (2005). This is even more critical in a Distance Learning University. The University of South Africa (Unisa) both delivers its courses electronically, and allows its

Figure 3. The CS/IS Web Page

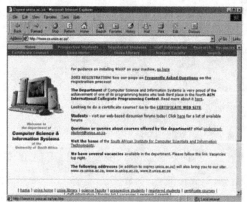
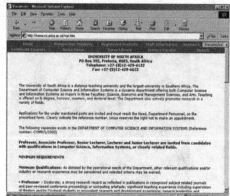

Page 1: CS/IS Web Page   Page 2: Vacancies

students to upload their assignments via its Web Portal. Clearly the usability of its interface is of vital importance.

The following is a brief case study of user experience for putative staff and academics – the UNISA vacancy pages. Unisa advertises various academic and administrative posts. In the advertisement, the University's URL was supplied. The assumption was that prospective candidates could go to the web site, obtain further information and download the relevant application forms. Figure 2 is a storyboard that relates to the authors attempts to find the relevant information for the advertised posts.

Upon arriving at the Unisa web page (see Page 1), the user tried in vain to find the advertised posts and application forms. The user tried the drop-down quick (see Page 2) reference menu with no success. The simplest thing to do was to try the search option provided on the Unisa web page (see Page 3). The user keyed in as the search string the word 'vacancies' (also tried the words 'job', 'jobs' and 'vacancy'. The results for vacancies were not shown in the storyboard, but the same results appeared as shown in Page 4). Page 4 had some promising results to explore. With a ranking of 224, there was the option 'Vacancies/bursaries' and with a ranking of 40 was the option 'Employment' (The current researcher is still not sure how and why the ranking was placed next to the found options or how it worked). Both

options took me to unrelated pages (see Pages 5 and 6). At this stage it was safe to conclude that the advertised post and related information was not on the Unisa web page.

Purely by chance the user saw the drop-down menu (see Page 2) and clicked on the option 'About Unisa' (with the intent to read about Unisa's 130-year history) and saw the option 'employment' (see Page 7). Clicking the option took the user to the 'Vacancies' page (see Page 8).

It can be concluded that this site was not subjected to a usability test, there was no clearly defined development methodology and there is no logical information structure. The search strategy seems to be a brute force strategy. Thus it appears that the UNISA website designers may not have followed the value-based authoring, value statements and value delivery scenarios advocated by Cockton – the above case-study reveals that the University has largely failed to deliver 'appropriate, adequate and effective' help with staff recruitment. This would be even more problematic if it related to student recruitment, a university's key revenue generating source.

Case 4: University of South Africa – School of Computing

In contrast, on the same site, the School of Computing had the following 'well-designed' web page, as illustrated in Figure 3.

There is no information hiding on this page. The 'blue line' menu runs consistently throughout all the CS/IS related web pages. This is a one-stop shop - prospective students, registered students, certificate students and prospective employees can visit this page and find the information that they are looking for (see Page 1, Figure 3). The original quest to find the information regarding the advertised post can be found on these pages under the option 'vacancies' (See Page 2, Figure 3).

Case 4: I paid you

Electronic Internet payments have made life that bit easier, or so they say. In this case study the current researcher relates the experience of a user (whom we will call John) with the local town council in a multi-lingual society where both English and Afrikaans are commonplace, and his ordeal in paying them. To pay his outstanding account, John chose to do an Internet payment. He made the payment, everything went well and he even printed out a receipt for proof of payment. One month later John received a statement claiming that he did not settle his outstanding account, and that interest and delivery charges had been added to the account. John verified that he did make the payment, and sent an e-mail confirming it. This e-mail resulted in the following string of communications:

- John's e-mail in English stating his claims and providing evidence
- The reply he received in English
- John re-sent e-mail, in English
- The reply he received in Afrikaans. It is presumed that the reply was in Afrikaans because John signed his previous e-mail with his full name and surname, and his surname happened to be that of Afrikaans descent.
- John response in Afrikaans

To no avail, John resorted to calling the call centre. After several calls, and speaking to second-language English speakers, John's problem was solved by speaking to an Afrikaans-speaking person who claimed that they were aware that the system did not work as effectively as they originally expected.

Many of the above problems can be attributed to poor design, testing and usability. Often these 'shopping' sites cater for the mythical ideal customer who enjoys the navigational adventure of securing a product.

Focused Electronic Commerce Usability

The usability techniques discussed previously clearly relate to *electronic commerce* applications. Various researchers have, however, also suggested specific methods to improve electronic commerce usability (Atterer & Schmidt, 2005; Nielsen, 1996, 2000; Schaffer & Sorflaten, 1999; W2, 2004). Travis (2003) makes the following recommendations for electronic commerce websites:

- Understand the needs of the customer for your project; understand the current web site that is in use; get different people on your project team to profile the website that is being developed. Compare these profiles; use representative customers to test the web site; contact customers who recently e-mailed the webmaster and ask them questions so that you can understand the customer profile; understand the environment that your system will be operating in; identify the key objectives of the web site and try to benchmark these activities; conduct task analysis on one important activity on the web site; conduct heuristic evaluation on one screen of the website, and consider the implication on the next cycle of the development process; conduct a walkthrough test on a frequently expected task on the web site.

Kuan *et al.* (2003) argue that there are four main *E-commerce* usability dimensions:

- **Perceived website usability:** Designers should implement features that enhance the customer's shopping experience. For example, a travel website can allow customers to book flights, accommodation, car rental and purchase travel insurance all within one website.
- **Perceived interface quality:** Designers should work upon increasing the ease of navigation and consistency of interface interaction
- **Perceived information quality:** Developers should work on accuracy of content, format and timeliness. For content, developers should provide sufficient relevant information for customers to make a good decision for purchase.
- **Perceived service quality:** Designers can work on responsiveness, interactivity, security and privacy policies, and search and comparison facilities

Rohn (1998) suggests the following design guidelines (including usability issues) for the design of E-commerce applications:

- **General navigation:** Website navigation should answer three key questions: Where am I in the website? Where have I been on the website? and, Where can I go in the website?
- **Browsing and searching:** There are several issues that should be considered for browsing and searching, such as: use category pages for products; do not over-classify; enable sorting (e.g. Amazon.com allows users to sort products by price value from cheapest to most expensive); and, comparison of similar products.
- **Product pages:** These pages should show extensive product images, display prices, provide details about the product, show product availability and provide information on guarantees and conditions.

- **Search engines:** Designers should consider: including keywords into the page titles, filling pages with meaningful content, using meta tags, and submitting the website into directories and related websites.
- **Checkout and shopping cart guidelines:** An effective cart would show items, all costs and subtotal; allow users to modify quantities and remove items; explain/show the steps of the checkout process; show shipping charges earlier; provide field for shipping instructions; enable separate shipping and billing fields; preserve entered information; provide order summary before committing the purchase; and, send a confirmation e-mail.

Recalling Cockton's Value-Centred design methodology, Rohn (1998) argues that to produce a highly usable and successful electronic commerce site, usability is a key factor. Rohn relies heavily on electronic commerce usability heuristics relating for: site introduction, content, navigation, product selection, shopping cart, international issues, ordering, downloads, feedback and errors, help, and rewarding customer loyalty. Rohn suggests that the following factors should also be considered:

- Utilise usability engineering methods, prepared by experienced usability engineers, throughout the design and development of the site; understand what the goals of the site are; decide on the target population; research and profile the target customer population and update the profiles of the target customer population, including attributes, context of use, goals, tasks, and priorities; create a specification based on functionality and design requirements derived from customer research and perform interactive design and usability evaluation to drive functionality and design decisions.

Tilson *et al.* (1998) point out that researchers and practitioners know little about the habits of virtual shoppers or how to create effective electronic commerce sites. Tilson *et al.* concentrate on the following aspects that will improve usability: structure and navigation, and obviousness and feedback. For the structure and navigation to be effective the following factors have to be accounted for:

- The number of clicks required to view an item; helpful product organisation; scanning and selecting an item from a list of products and returning to different levels after adding an item to the shopping cart.

For the obviousness and feedback to be effective the following factors have to be accounted for:

- Feedback on saved items; obviousness of 'Order' links; presentation of additional features (such as wish list) and security messages.

Kubilus (2000) reports that slow response time, lack of user-friendliness, poor navigation and poor web site design affect the success of electronic commerce web sites. The factors that would improve electronic commerce success are: customer's previous experience should have been positive, fast response time, and relevant frequently updated content. Kubilus suggest the following strategy to improve electronic commerce web site usability:

- Understand the conceptual model of the user and the system: How does the user perceive the system?
- Develop an information presentation strategy.
- Provide feedback.

Huang (2002) also argues that usability is an important aspect in electronic commerce systems.

He brings to our attention the following issues that need to be considered in the electronic commerce usability saga:

- Users of electronic commerce web sites are located at remote locations, making it difficult to access hands-on help from technical support personnel.
- If an electronic commerce site is riddled with poor usability, the user will switch to a more usable site.
- Users are heterogeneous - an electronic commerce website should accommodate these users.
- Poor usability presents a bad image for a company.
- Poor usability could increase running costs, e.g. toll free numbers.
- Users are not trained to use electronic commerce websites.
- Users of electronic commerce websites may not know what they are looking for, or not know if the electronic commerce system can solve their particular problem.

Huang (Huang, 2002) further reinforces the notion that developing a usable electronic commerce web site is not an easy task. There are various factors that need to be considered. He points out that there is no well-defined set of usability principles available. Most usability principles are vague. He further points out the concept of usability as subjective as well as scientific. Usability is dependent on the computing environment.

Tzanidou *et al.* (2005) argue that the majority of the existing electronic commerce website design guidelines have been derived from expert heuristic evaluation, apparently without involving the users themselves. Their research contradicts Nielsen's (1996) heuristics that 'place important information at the top of the page'. Their eye tracking research indicated that users looked at the center of the screen when information was downloading and not the top of the screen. Tzanidou *et al.* (2005) point out several defects relating to heuristics. They, in particular, focus on banner advertisements, product images and design layout. Their research also reveals that users adapt quickly to unexpected design layouts. This does question the concept of consistency. Bark *et al.* (2005) indicate that different human-computer interaction practitioners are using different techniques in their projects. The uses of these different usability techniques affect the usability of the final product.

There is thus no formula for the effective application of usability to an electronic commerce web page. Overall electronic commerce researchers, agree that electronic commerce websites should be consistent in the interface design, follow an understandable navigation strategy and the information should be presented in a structured format. It seems to us that usability is part craft, part art and part science. Usability is only one aspect of the success formula for the development and maintenance of a viable electronic commerce website. Nielsen (2001) poses the question 'Did poor usability kill electronic commerce?' His answer is 'no', but he points out various factors such as uncontrollable costs as a possible answer to the problems associated with poor electronic commerce. Nielsen argues that electronic commerce sites lose almost half their potential sales because the user cannot use the site. He clearly states that "even a site that scores well on usability guideline compliance and enjoys the resulting good sales can go under." This is probably because other uncontrollable factors affect the economic environment.

SUMMARY

In this chapter we considered usability in the context of interaction design and the various ways in which usability can be employed in the design of interactive products such as electronic commerce. We have noticed the following:

- The traditional approach of soliciting sales in a brick-and-mortar commerce environment, such as atmosphere, placement of goods, lighting, etc., do not automatically transfer to online commerce. It is interaction and participation that are the emotional hooks for electronic commerce, and the developers of electronic commerce sites should bear this in mind in their development strategies.

- *Electronic commerce* users have evolved to become more sophisticated and now demand powerful uncomplicated applications. Developing a usable user interface is one main facet of developing these successful powerful applications.

However, usability means different things to different role players. While some see usability as an additional expense, some see it as an essential expense. With regard to usability guidelines, we have found that:

- There are general usability guidelines that can be applied to *electronic commerce* websites. However, usability guidelines and principles tend to be very vague and generalistic. There are certain specific usability guidelines and principles for *electronic commerce*.

- There are a few methods to apply and evaluate usability in an *electronic commerce* application, each with its own unique pros and cons. There are no universally accepted standards for *electronic commerce* evaluation.

Usability is only one piece of the puzzle in the development of a successful electronic commerce website. As has been seen, designing with usability in mind is not the 'silver bullet' for the design of successful *E-commerce* websites. There are other factors that need to be considered and incorporated into design of the website. A holistic socio-technical approach should be adopted in the design of interactive products that interact with the wider society. The practical reality is that applying usability and designing *E-commerce* applications is part science (which can be measured), and part art and craft (which cannot be measured).

ACKNOWLEDGMENT

The author is grateful to Mr Niall Levine, School of Computing, for the discussions and comments on how to improve this chapter. The author thanks the two anonymous reviews for their comments as well.

REFERENCES

W1. (2009). The South African Revenue Services Retrieved 10 June, 2009, from http://www.sars.gov.za/

W2. (2004). *e-Commerce Usability Guide*. Retrieved 7 October, 2005, from http://www.bonasource.com/print/page/e-commerce-usability-guide.htm

Abran, A., Khelifi, A., Suryn, W., & Seffah, A. (2003). Usability Meanings and Interpretations in ISO Standards. *Software Quality Journal, 11*, 325–338. doi:10.1023/A:1025869312943

Atterer, R., & Schmidt, A. (2005). *Adding Usability to Web Engineering Models and Tools*. Paper presented at the Fifth International Conference on Web Engineering (ICWE 2005), Sydney, Australia.

Badre, N. A. (2002). *Shaping Web Usability: Interaction Design in Context*. Boston: Addsion-Wesley.

Baecker, M. R., & Buxton, A. S. W. (Eds.). (1987). *Readings in Human-Computer Interaction: A Multidisciplinary Approach*. Los Altos, CA: Morgan Kaufmann.

Bark, I., Folstad, A., & Gulliksen, J. (2005, 5-9 September). *Use and Usefulness of HCI Methods: Results from an Exploratory Study among Nordic HCI Practitioners*. Paper presented at the Human-Computer Interaction 2005: People and Computers XIX - The Bigger Picture, Edinburg.

Bevan, N. (2006). International Standards for HCI. In C. Ghaoui (Ed.), *Encyclopedia of Human-Computer Interaction*. Hershey, PA: Idea Group Reference.

Brinck, T., Gergle, D., & Wood, D. S. (2002). *Designing web sites that work: Usability for the web*. San Francisco: Morgan Kaufmann.

Carroll, J. M. (Ed.). (2003). *HCI Models, Theories, and Frameworks: Towards a Multidisciplinary Science*. Amsterdam: Morgan Kaufmann Publishers.

Casaday, G. (2001). Whiteboard: online shopping: or, how I saved a trip to the store and receive my item in just 47 fun-filled days. *Interaction, 8*, 15–19.

Cato, J. (2001). *User-Centered Web Design*. Harlow, UK: Addison-Wesley.

Chevalier, A., & Ivory, M. (2003). Web site design: Influences of designer's expertise and design constraints. *International Journal of Human-Computer Interaction Studies, 58*, 57–87. doi:10.1016/S1071-5819(02)00126-X

Cockton, G. (2005). A development framework for value-centred design, Paper presented at the Conference on Human Factors in Computer Systems: CHI'05. Portland, USA.

Cox, K., & Walker, D. (1993). *User Interface Design* (2 ed.). New York: Prentice Hall.

Diaper, D. (2006). Task Analysis is at the Heart of Human-Computer Interaction. In C. Ghaoui (Ed.), *Encyclopedia of Human-Computer Interaction* (pp. 579-587). Hershey, PA: Idea Group Reference.

Dillon, A. (1994). *Designing Usable Electronic Text: Ergonomic aspects of human information usage*. London: Taylor & Francis Ltd.

Dix, A., Finlay, J., Abowd, G., & Beale, R. (2004). *Human-Computer Interaction* (3 ed.). Harlow, UK: Prentice Hall.

Downton, A. (Ed.). (1993). *Engineering the Human-Computer Interface* (Student Ed.). London: McGraw-Hill.

ETSI ETR-095. (1993). *Human Factors: Guide for Usability Evaluations of Telecommunications Systems and Services*. Sophia Antipolis, France: European Telecommunications Standards Institute.

Falk, L. K., & Sockel, H. (2005). Web Site Usability. In M. Pagani (Ed.), *Encyclopedia of Multimedia Technology and Networking* (Vol. 2, pp. 1078-1083). Hershey, PA: Idea Group reference.

Galitz, O. W. (1997). *The Essential Guide to User Interface Design: A Introduction to GUI Design Principles and Techniques*. New York: John Wiley & Sons.

Garrett, J. (2003). *The Elements of User Experience: User-Centered Design for the Web*. New York: New Riders.

Hackos, T. J., & Redish, C. J. (1998). *User and Task Analysis for Interface Design*. New York: Wiley.

Hartson, H. R., & Hix, D. (1989). Human-Computer Interface Development: Concepts and Systems for Its Management. *ACM Computing Surveys*, *21*(1), 5–92. doi:10.1145/62029.62031

Hartson, R. H. (1998). Human-Computer Interaction: Interdisciplinary Roots and Trends. *Journal of Systems and Software*, *43*(2), 103–118. doi:10.1016/S0164-1212(98)10026-2

Holmes, M. (2002). *Web Usability & Navigation: A Beginner's Guide*. New York: McGraw-Hill.

Huang, H. A. (2002). *A Research Taxonomy for e-Commerce System Usability*. Paper presented at the Eight Americans Conference on Information Systems.

ISO 9241. (1998). Ergonomic requirements for office work with visual display terminals: The International Organization for Standardization.

Jaspers, M. W. M. (2006). The Think Aloud Method and User Interface Design. In C. Ghaoui (Ed.), *Encyclopedia of Human-Computer Interaction* (pp. 597-602). Hershey, PA: Idea Group Reference.

John, E. B. (2003). Information Processing and Skilled Behavior. In J. M. Carroll (Ed.), *HCI Models, Theories and Frameworks: Towards a Multidisciplinary Science* (pp. 55-101). Amsterdam: Morgan Kaufmann.

Kirwan, B., & Ainsworth, L. K. (Eds.). (1992). *A Guide to Task Analysis*. London: Taylor and Francis.

Kotze, P., & Johnson, C. W. (2001). *Human-Computer Interaction 1*. Study Guide for INF120-8, INF120-8/502/2001, University of South Africa.

Kuan, H. H., Vathanophas, V., & Bock, G. (2003). *The Impact of Usability on the Intention of Planned Purchases in e-Commerce Service Websites*. Paper presented at the 7th Pacific Asia Conferece on Information Systems, Adelaide, South Australia.

Kubilus, N. J. (2000). Designing an e-commerce site for users. *Crossroads*, *7*, 23–26. doi:10.1145/351092.351099

MacKenzie, D. (2000). *A View from the Sonnenbichl: On the Historical Sociology of Software and System Dependability*. Paper presented at the International Conference on the History of Computing: Software Issues, Paderborn, Germany.

Maguire, M. (1997). *RESPECT User Requirements Framework Handbook*. Leicester, UK: HUSAT Research Institute.

Mandel, T. (1997). *The Elements of User Interface Design*. New York: John Wiley & Sons.

Maria, E., Alva, O., Ana, B., Martínez, P., Juan, M., Cueva, L., et al. (2003). Comparison of Methods and Existing Tools for the Measurement of Usability in the Web. In J. M. Cueva Lovelle (Ed.), *Lecture Notes in Computer Science* (Vol. 2722/2003, pp. 386–389). Berlin: Springer-Verlag.

Mayhew, D. J. (1999). *The Usability Engineering Lifecycle: a practitioner's handbook for user interface design*. San Francisco: Morgan Kaufmann.

Moggridge, B. (1999). Design, expressing experience in design. *Interaction, 6*(July), 17–25. doi:10.1145/306412.306430

Molich, R., & Nielsen, J. (1990). Improving a human-computer dialogue. *Communications of the ACM, 33*(3), 338–348. doi:10.1145/77481.77486

National Cancer Institute. (2002, 5 August 2002). *Is Usability Testing Always Conducted the Same Way?* Retrieved 12 August, 2003, from http://usability.gov/methods/same_way.html

Newman, W. M., & Lamming, M. G. (1995). *Interactive System Design*. Wokingham: Addison Wesley.

Nielsen, J. (1993). *Usability Engineering*. San Diego: Morgan Kaufmann.

Nielsen, J. (1994). *Enhancing the explanatory power of usability heuristics*. Paper presented at the SIGCHI conference on Human factors in computing systems, Boston, MA.

Nielsen, J. (1996). *Top Ten Mistakes in Web design*. Retrieved 25 June, 1999, from http://www.useit.com/alerbox/9605.html

Nielsen, J. (2000). *Designing Web Usability: The Practice of Simplicity*. Indianapolis, IN: New Riders.

Nielsen, J. (2001). *Did Poor Usability Kill e-Commerce*. Retrieved 3 June, 2003, from http://www.useit.com/alertbox/200110819.html

Nielsen, J., & Molich, R. (1990, 1-5 April). *Heuristic evaluation of user interfaces*. Paper presented at the ACM CHI'90 Conf, Seattle, WA.

Park, J. Y. (2008). A model of experience test for web designers: Design Principles and Practices. *International Journal (Toronto, Ont.), 2*(1), 175–182.

Perry, T. J., & Schneider, P. G. (2001). *New Perspectives on E-Commerce*. Australia: Thomson Learning.

Preece, J., Rogers, Y., & Sharp, H. (2002). *Interaction Design: Beyond human-computer interaction*. New York: John Wiley & Sons.

Preece, J., Rogers, Y., Sharp, H., Benyon, D., Holland, S., & Carey, T. (1994). *Human-Computer Interaction*. Harlow, UK: Addison-Wesley.

Pressman, R. S. (2000). What a Tangled Web We Weave. *IEEE Software, 17*(1), 18–21. doi:10.1109/52.819962

RACE. 1065-ISSUE. (1992). *ISSUE Usability Evaluation Guidelines*. Brussels: Commission of the European Communities.

Redmond-Pyle, D., & Moore, A. (1995). *Graphical User Interface Design and Evaluation: A Practical Process*. London: Prentice Hall.

Rohn, J. A. (1998, September). Creating Usable e-Commerce Sites. *StandardView, 6*, 110–115. doi:10.1145/324042.324046

Rosson, M. B., & Carroll, J. M. (2002). *Usability Engineering: Scenario-Based Development of Human-Computer Interaction*. San Francisco: Morgan Kaufmann Publishers.

Schaffer, E., & Sorflaten, J. (1999). Web Usability Illustrated: Breathing Easier with Your Usable E-Commerce Site. *Journal of Economic Commerce, 11*(4), 1–10.

Scholtz, J. (1995). Usability: What's it all about? *Software Quality Journal, 4*(2), 95–100. doi:10.1007/BF00402713

Seilheimer, S. (2004). Productive development of World Wide Web sites intended for international use. *International Journal of Information Management, 24*(5), 363. doi:10.1016/j.ijinfomgt.2004.06.001

Shepherd, A. (1989). Analysis and Training in Information Technology Tasks. In D. Diaper (Ed.), *Task Analysis for Human-Computer Interaction* (pp. 15-55). Chichester, UK: Ellis Horwood Limited.

Shneiderman, B. (1998). *Design the User Interface: Strategies for effective Human-Computer Interaction* (3 ed.). Reading, MA: Addison-Wesley.

Singh, S., & Erwin, J. G. (2002, 4-5 April). *Electronic Business Accepted Practices (e-BAP): Standardized HCI for E-Commerce.* Paper presented at the ISOneWorld, Las Vegas, NV.

Spool, M. J., Scanlon, T., Schroeder, W., Snyder, C., & DeAngelo, T. (1999). *Web Site Usability: A Designer's Guide.* San Francisco: Morgan Kaufmann.

Sutcliffe, A. (1988). *Human-Computer Interface Design.* London: Macmillan Education LTD.

Thimbley, H. (1990). *User Interface Design.* Wokingham, UK: Addison-Wesley.

Tilson, R., Dong, J., Martin, S., & Kieke, E. (1998). *A Comparison of Two Current e-Commerce Sites.* Paper presented at the 16th Annual International Conference on Computer Documentation, Quebec, Canada.

Travis, D. (2003). *Bluffers' Guide to ISO 9241.* Retrieved 19 August, 2003, from www.userfocus.co.uk

Travis, D. (2003). *e-Commerce Usability: Tools and Techniques to Perfect the On-line Experience.* London: Taylor & Francis.

Turban, E., & Aronson, J. E. (1998). *Decision Support Systems and Intelligent Systems.* Englewood Cliffs, NJ: Prentice Hall.

Tzanidou, E., Minocha, S., Petre, M., & Grayson, A. (2005, 5-9 September). *Revisiting Web Design Guidelines by Exploring Users' Expectations, Preferences and Visual Search Behaviour.* Paper presented at the The 19th British HCI Group Annual Conference: the Bigger Picture, Edinburgh.

Van Dyk, T. (1999). *Usability and Internet-Based Banking.* Unpublished Masters, University of South Africa, Pretoria.

Chapter 6
Development and Evaluation of a Methodology for Developing Marketing Websites

Tomayess Issa
Curtin University of Technology, Australia

Martin West
Curtin University of Technology, Australia

Andrew Turk
Murdoch University, Australia.

ABSTRACT

This chapter discusses a research project that focused on the development of a new methodology for creating more effective websites for marketing purposes. After reviewing existing methodologies, it was noted that some key aspects were under-utilized, including user participation and "real interaction" (i.e. monitoring of user interaction with a prototype site). This situation can lead to deficiencies in the resulting website and hence user frustration. A study was carried out to examine various methodologies, from different disciplines, and their integration, to select the strongest aspects of the various methodologies to be combined into a new methodology. This methodology was assessed by interviews and a questionnaire. Proposed further research will develop a website describing the new methodology; incorporate a software tool to assist in tailoring the methodology to a particular project.

INTRODUCTION

This chapter describes the development of a new methodology for developing websites for marketing purposes that meet the requirements of the users and designer simultaneously. These days, businesses are using the Internet as a tool to develop new and enhanced aspects of business, including vendor contact, provision of information, recruitment, customer service, research, entertainment and of course marketing and promotion. Ellsworth & Ellsworth(1997, pp. 51-52) declared that marketing on the WWW must *"take place in reaction to interest from customers and other site visitors"*. Therefore, the marketing website must *"first attract customers to the page by providing services and information*

DOI: 10.4018/978-1-60566-896-3.ch006

Figure 1. Current methodologies

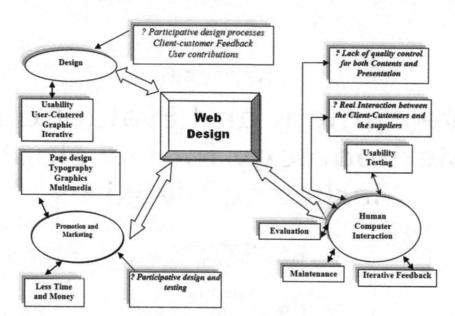

that will be useful to the users". Successful marketing on the World Wide Web relies on careful use of appropriate methodologies to create an effective website, with expenditure of minimum time and money (Lazar, 2006).

The key principles behind designing a website are "*to help people find the content they need quickly and to present content in the most readable format*" (Mankelow, 2006, p.53). However, some people try to mimic successful sites by copying attractive images off the internet and they create their own website without the basic knowledge of design principles. Hence, the website will never have a kind of unity, since the graphics and the texts were written and created by different writers and designers, and it will "*stay a jumble of loose parts, lacking coherence*". However, "*If you make your own site, it is your work. It will radiate something of your personality, your preferences and your taste*" (Hoekstra, 2000). To create an effective website, designers need to work with a specific methodology, which meets the requirements of the users and encourages them to revisit the website. The users need to feel comfortable, confident and satisfied while working with the website.

The informal and formal website development methodologies currently utilized include the following stages: establish the need, gather information, develop site, implement, maintain and usability test (Abels, White, & Hahn, 1998; Cunliffe, 2000; IBM, n.d; Vora, 1998). However, it is noted that formal methodologies are either not used in industry practice or are inadequate, since many users are still frequently frustrated and confused when using websites. The problems experienced relate especially to navigation, interactivity and downloading. "*Users are frustrated because of an inability to find the information sought, disorganized pages and confusing information, pages under construction and disconnected links, the lack of navigation support and other problems*" (Borges, Morales, & Rodriguez, 1998 p.137). Such problems negatively influence users' confidence in the site and their desire to explore it: "*the barriers imposed in the poorly designed interface and the user's lack of trust or faith on the site will discourage further exploration of the site*"(Borges, Morales, & Rodriguez, 2008).

The current methodologies (see Figure one) do not adequately support participative design processes for content and presentation. User contributions may therefore be limited and ad-hoc. In Figure 1, items in *italics* are the under-utilized stages in current methodologies. Designers need to involve the users from the beginning and to keep focused on the requirements of the target audience (Boyer, 1999, p.113). According to Kambil & Eselius (2000, p.36) *"When companies get their customers involved in the creation of their products, it can play out in two ways: as a collective contribution from many customers, or as a self-directed effort from a focused individual"*. Mumford stresses the importance of user participation to enable a *"shared learning process to take place in which each of the interest groups can contribute to the problem-solving process. The various interest groups are likely to have different values, needs and objectives, and these can be brought into the open, discussed and attempts made to reconcile them as part of the participative process"* (Mumford, 1995, pp.15-16). Participation in general can play an important role in the development process since the users will contribute significantly to the decision-making about the new system and will be able to test and evaluate the new system before it is implemented.

To generate an efficient website, designers need to work with a precise methodology, which identifies the requirements of the users and designs the website appropriately. Van Duyne, Landay and Hong (2003 p.32) state that *"to understand your customers, consider the completing elements of every design: your customers, their tasks, their technology and their social context. Each of these elements has certain capabilities and limitations that exert forces on your design. To create a successful site, you must understand and balance these forces so that none dominates and each is considered in your final decision"*. Furthermore, Holzinger (2005 p.74) stated that *"many aspects of usability can best be studied by querying the users. This is especially true for issues related to the subjective satisfaction of the users and their possible anxieties, which are difficult to*

measure objectively". This research sought to identify and evaluate a more effective, participative methodology for developing websites used for marketing.

The practicality of the proposed approach was assessed through interviews and questionnaires with representatives of website development companies in Western Australia. The proposed new methodology has been developed in the context of "for profit" organizations, however, it may well be useful also for development of websites for "not-for-profit" organizations.

BACKGROUND

Problems with Websites

The Internet offers huge opportunities for enhanced marketing; however, there are also many potential problems. Websites, which meet users' expectations, in terms of content and ease of use, will enjoy many advantages as a result of their effective design. According to Donahue (cited in (McCracken & Wolfe, 2004)) the four most important advantages are: *Gaining a competitive edge; Reducing development and maintenance costs; Improving productivity; and Lowering support cost.* Other advantages of good website design are that they facilitate the users to enjoy working with websites without any frustrations and aggravation. Studies have indicated that usable websites consistently have the highest conversion rates (completion of sales and repeat visits) *"if customers have an enjoyable experience, they are likely to spend more time on a site, [to] make purchases, and return to the site for further shopping"* (McCracken & Wolfe, 2004, p.2).

Frustration can result from failure to complete a task when working with a website, hence goals are not achieved. For example, reading a web site to find information which will *"allow you to take some type of action and get stuck wading through long sentences and paragraphs"* (Spyridakis,

2000, p.360). Failure can also take place if the users: "*Spend a lot of time hitting the wrong buttons; Get error messages; Feel confused; Curse at the screen; and Need to ask customer support for help*" (McCracken & Wolfe, 2004, p.xii). Designers should provide clear instructions to the users concerning the purpose and limitations of the site. For example, 'this web site will serve only local and not global users'. By providing this information, users "*may not be happy about your inability to serve them*", however, "*they will certainly appreciate saving time and frustration by learning your site's interests and limitations up front*" (Clare, 2002, p.25). These days, users are "*becoming more sophisticated and as they do so, their expectations and behaviors are changing; don't get caught designing for yesterday's audience - stay on the cutting edge with this kind of research so that you can design for tomorrow's audience!*" (Sheridan, 1999). Moreover, "*users are in control of their own destiny. Get over it, you don't own them*" (Nielsen, 2000, p.66).

For these reasons, designers need to work with a specific methodology to create an effective website that meets the requirements of the users and to encourage them to revisit the website (Gardner, 2003).

HCI and Usability

Human-Computer Interaction (HCI) "*is a discipline concerned with the design, evaluation and implementation of interactive computing systems for human use and with the study of major phenomena surrounding them*" (Preece et al. 1994). Therefore, the reasons for studying HCI in the development process are to create interactive computer systems that are usable and practical (Head, 1999). HCI is specifically relevant to several stages in the development process, including the design, implementation and evaluation of interactive systems, in the "*context of the user's task and work*" (Dix, Finlay, Abowd, & Beale, 2004, p. 4). The implementation of HCI can be

perceived as an art as well as a science because it requires a comprehensive range of skills, including an understanding of the user, an appreciation of software engineering capabilities and application of appropriate graphical interfaces. "*If we are to be recognized as developers with professional capabilities, as competent practitioners, then it is critical to understand what makes an application interactive, instructional and effective*" (Sims, 1997). HCI "*is concerned with the design of computer systems that are safe, efficient, easy and enjoyable to use as well as functional*"(Preece et al. 1993, p.11). Vora (1998) describes a framework, which provides for effective HCI for websites, with the main task being to have a clear understanding of user needs: who the users are, and what their tasks and environments are.

Usability refers to the "*quality of the interaction in terms of parameters such as time taken to perform tasks, number of errors made and the time to become a competent user*"(Benyon, Turner, & Turner, 2005, p. 52). Usability "*is a quality attribute that assesses how easy user interfaces are to use. The word "usability" also refers to methods for improving ease-of-use during the design process*" (Nielsen, 2003). The usability evaluation stage of a methodology is an effective method by which a software development team can establish the positive and negative aspects of a prototype system, and make the required changes before the system is delivered to the target users (McGovern, 2003). It is "*based on human psychology and user research*" (Rhodes, 2000). HCI specialists "*observe and talk with participants as they try to accomplish true-to-life tasks on a site (or system), and this allows them to form a detailed picture of the site as experienced by the user*" (Carroll, 2004).

From the user's perspective, usability is considered a very important aspect in the development process as it can mean the difference between "*performing a task accurately and completely or not*" and the user "*enjoying the process or being frustrated*" (Bullet, 2002). Alternatively, if usability is not highlighted in website design, then users will become very frustrated working with the website. For example, according to Nielsen (2003), people will leave the website: (a) if is difficult to use; (b) if the users get lost on a website; (c) the information is hard to read; (d) it does not answer users' key questions; (e) and lastly, if the homepage fails to define the purpose and the goals of the website. *"Usability rules the web. Simply stated, if the customer cannot find a product, then s/he will not buy it. In addition, the web is the ultimate customer-empowering environment. S/he who clicks the mouse gets to decide everything. It is so easy to go elsewhere; all the competitors in the world are but a mouse-click away"* (Nielsen, 2000, p.9).

Usability is a critical issue for websites as it improves competitive position and customer loyalty and drives down costs (Rhodes, 2000). Therefore, if usability is highlighted in website design, it will keep the organization in a powerful position compared with their competitors, as *"Usability = simplicity = user satisfaction = increased profits"* (Rhodes, 2000). However, it is critical that the most effective form(s) of usability design and evaluation be determined for any particular website and the evaluation processes should incorporate a high level of user participation (Turk, 2001).

User Participation

Participation refers to the role that users can play in assisting with the design and development of an effective website or system. According to Hartwick & Barki (1994, p.441), participation in information systems development (ISD) is defined as the *"behaviors, assignments, and activities that users or their representatives perform during the ISD process"*. This helps the designer to understand *"what specific behaviors are performed, how many of these behaviors are performed and how often they are performed"* (Hartwick & Barki, 2001, p.21). If the designers work very closely with the

users to produce a successful system (or website), then less time will be required for the implementation and testing stages, and this will lead to the user working with this system (or website) with less frustration and dissatisfaction. However, *"few empirical studies have clearly demonstrated a relationship between user participation and two key indicators of system success: system usage and user information satisfaction"* (Olson & Ives, 1981, p.183). Hence, a clear methodology incorporating user participation needs to be developed and evaluated.

The research discussed in this chapter distinguishes between two types of users: end-users (internal to the client organization) and client-customer users (external). End-users (Internal) are the real users in the client organization, who test and evaluate the website and use it to respond to the client-customer's queries. The client-customer users (external) are those who interact with the website to accomplish their goals such as purchasing goods or services from the client organization. It is important to understand the needs, desires and characteristics of both types of users. To date, most designers of websites have *"assumed that their users had the same background and expectations that they did"*; therefore, *"the more you know about your users and their work, the more likely it is that you will develop a usable and successful website"* (McCracken & Wolfe, 2004, p.37).

Both of these two types of users should participate in the development process under the methodology developed during this research, to make sure that the website meets the requirements of end-users, client-customers and designers simultaneously. This participation has various benefits: (1) to reduce the time in the implementation and testing stages; (2) to familiarize the end-users and client customers with the new system before the implementation; (3) to provide job satisfaction and meet the task effectiveness needs of the end-users and client-customers.

Real Interaction

Another aspect that needs to be addressed in website design is 'real interaction'; that is, the actual way that real users interact with the site. Real interaction can be tracked to trace the performance of website visitors, either at the prototype stage or after initial implementation. For example, according to Ramey (2000), real interaction can be tracked by using the server log file data (the record of user activity on a website) to enhance the design of the website. The following types of data can be analyzed: dates and times of transactions; number of hits and number of page views; amount of time spend on each page; search terms used to hit the website pages; search terms used to search within the website; most frequent paths through the site; the most and least frequently visited pages and the IP addresses, translated into domain names and/or counties of origin. This type of analysis *"focuses on marketing or technical issues rather than rhetorical issues like audience analysis"* (Ramey, 2000, p.397). However, website designers cannot easily utilize these processes unless they are incorporated into an appropriate website development methodology.

RESEARCH METHODOLOGY

The first step in this study was to explore the main objective of the research i.e. *Can an integrated design methodology help designers and users to create effective websites, which meet the requirements of end-users, client-customers, and designers?* This was achieved by examining various methodologies for website design to identify the reasons why many users are frustrated and confused when working with websites. The researcher also reviewed the basic concepts behind a wide range of methodologies used in information systems development and marketing. From this information, the draft version of a New Participative Methodology for Developing Websites from the Marketing Perspective was developed - see Section 4 below.

This study predominantly used an Interpretive (Qualitative) research approach. The qualitative method is centered mainly on an ethnographic approach (Myers & Avison, 2002) through which data is collected mainly from interviews and observation. Interviews were utilized in this research to explore the type of methodology, tools and techniques that are adopted by website development industry personnel in Western Australia and to learn more about their technical expertise and knowledge of how to develop a website. The interviews identified existing problems and provided an indication of the likely usefulness of the principles behind the proposed new methodology. The data from the interviews was also used to generate the questionnaire for the second phase of this research. The interview phase is described in Section 5.

The second approach used in this research was an on-line questionnaire, which was generated and developed from the qualitative research after *"analyzing the interviews and observations to derive categories for questions that focused on the primary expectations expressed by interviewees"* (Kaplan & Duchon, 1988, p.578). The purpose of using the questionnaire approach in this research was: (1) to evaluate the "practicality" and "benefits" of adopting the proposed new methodology in the website industry in Western Australia; (2) to consider the various requirements for promotion and adoption of the methodology; and; (3) to evaluate whether it is possible to achieve effective user participation in website design, via the new methodology. The questionnaire phase is described in Section 6.

CREATING THE NEW WEBSITE DEVELOPMENT METHODOLOGY

In order for systems (or websites) to be widely accepted and used effectively, they need to be well designed. To achieve this, designers need to use a specific methodology to produce the system (or website). A methodology *"should tell us what steps to take, in what order and how to perform those steps but, most importantly, the reasons, 'why' those steps should be taken, in that particular order"* (Jayaratna, 1994, p.242). This indicates that each methodology should have a set of stages and steps, which need to be followed if the work is to be done successfully. 'Stage' is a *"convenient breakdown of the totality of the information systems life cycle activity"*, while 'step' is *"the smallest part of a design process"* (Olle et al., 1988, p.21). Each stage consists of a set of steps. The sequence of the stages may not always be fixed. In some projects, iteration between stages will occur and this may have a different impact on the methodology (Olle et al., 1988). According to Avison & Fitzgerald (1993, p.261), the main requirement is for methodologies that can lead to improvements in the following three aspects: *"A better end product; A better development process; and A standardized process"*. For these reasons, a designer needs to understand users' requirements for the project before choosing the most appropriate methodology; this is a 'contingency-based' approach.

In this research study, various existing models of system development and methodologies were analyzed, including:

Lifecycle Models:

- **The Waterfall Lifecycle Model:** This is basically a linear model of system development stages, where each stage must be completed before the next stage can be started (Darlington, 2005);(Preece, Rogers, & Sharp 2002)
- **The Spiral Lifecycle Model:** This model combines the waterfall model with an element called "risk analysis". It is divided into three major stages: (1) planning - to define the objectives, alternatives and constraints; (2) Risk Analysis - for each of the

alternatives solutions risks are identified and analyzed; and if this information is not enough, then the prototyping approach will be adopted, before finally, (3) Engineering the solution (Preece et al., 2002).

- **Rapid Application Development (RAD):** This approach takes a user-centered view. It minimizes the risk caused by requirements changing during the course of the project by completing each of the five stages as rapidly as possible (Dix et al., 2004); (Preece et al., 2002)
- **Systems Development Life Cycle:** This lifecycle is a *"project management technique that divides complex projects into smaller, more easily managed segments or phases"* (FFIEC IT Examination Handbook, 2005).
- **The Star Lifecycle Model:** The Star Lifecycle Model was proposed by (Hix & Hartson, 1993) to address Human Computer Interaction issues in system development in a more flexible way. The evaluation activity is at the centre of this model, since, before moving to another activity, one need to pass through the evaluation activity to evaluate the result from the previous stage.
- **The Usability Engineering Lifecycle:** Deborah Mayhew proposed the Usability Engineering Lifecycle in 1999, and the purpose of this model is to focus more on how usability design and evaluation tasks may be performed alongside more traditional software engineering activities (Preece et al., 2002).

Information Systems Development Methodologies:

- **Structured Systems Analysis and Design Methodology:** This methodology is classified into two major parts: three stages of systems analysis and three stages of systems design. The purpose behind this classification is to *"make it easier to judge the proportion of time to spend on analysis"* (Avison & Fitzgerald, 1993, p.192).

- **Soft Systems Methodology:** Checkland proposed the Soft Systems Methodology (SSM) in 1981. SSM provides a *"way of tackling messy situations in the real world"* (Checkland & Scholes, 2003, p.1).

- **User-Centered Development Methodology:** This methodology involves numerous stages, which focus on *"gathering information, designing, building and testing of a prototype of the interface"* (McCracken & Wolfe, 2004, p.5).

- **ETHICS Methodology:** Mumford defines a specific methodology with high levels of stakeholder participation called "ETHICS", standing for *"Effective Technical and Human Implementation of Computer-based Systems"* (Mumford, 1995, p.3). Designers need to involve the users from the beginning, to keep focused on the target audience, to evaluate their activities, and to see if they address their needs. Users, through involvement in the development process, may be able to help to *"shape design decisions in ways that deal with their concerns or make their work easier"* (Doll & Torkzadeh, 1989, p.1156).

Methodologies for Developing Web Sites:

- **Human Factors Methodology for Designing Web Sites:** Vora (1998) describes a methodology which provides for the development of effective HCI for websites, with the main task being to have a clear understanding of user needs, with particular attention given to: the types of users and their characteristics; and their specific tasks and environments.

- **Relationship Management Methodology:** Isakowitz, Stohr and Balasubramanian (1995) describe a methodology, which provides for the development of effective websites for highly structured applications such as online conference proceedings, directories, academic journals, courseware and electronic-commerce.

- **The W3DT Design Methodology:** Bichler, Nusser and Wien (1996) describe the W3DT (World Wide Web Design Technique), a methodology especially for designing a large-scale Web-based hypermedia application. This methodology focuses on two main parts: modeling techniques and computer-based design.

- **Information Development Methodology for the Web:** John December (1996) describes a methodology which provides for the development of effective websites for technical communicators, writers, designers and software developers. The main task of this methodology is to decrease difficulty and make the website easy to navigate, maintain, and more attractive to the users.

- **The Web Site Design Method:** Olga De Troyer (1998)describes a methodology for web site design. The main goal for this new methodology is to develop a site which provides information *'in such a way that both the provider and the inquirer benefit from it"* (Troyer & Leune, 1998, p.88).

Marketing Methodologies:

- **E-Marketing Plan:** The E-Marketing plan is a *"guiding, dynamic document that links the firm's e-business strategy with technology-driven marketing strategies and lays out details for plan implementation through marketing management"*(Strauss, El-Ansary, & Frost, 2006, p.46). The main ideas behind an e-Marketing plan are: (1)

to achieve an effective and efficient e-business objective; (2) to increase revenues and reduce costs; (3) to serve *" as a roadmap to guide the direction of the firm, allocate resources, and make tough decisions at critical junctures"* (Strauss, El-Ansary, & Frost, 2003).

- **The Advertures Company Methodology:** The Advertures Company (2004) released a process methodology to enhance the development of websites from a marketing perspective in 2004. This methodology has five stages, each of which should be completed before moving to the next stage.
- **The Market-Vantage (Internet Performance Marketing) Methodology:** The Market-Vantage Company introduced a new methodology for developing websites in order to *"reduce cost, increase customer loyalty and market analysis"*(Market Vantage, 2003).
- **EnSky's Unique Methodology:** EnSky Company initiated a methodology for developing websites from the marketing perspective (EnSky, 1997).

Additional Detailed Techniques:

- **Task Analysis:** Task analysis is the *"process of building a complete description of the [users'] and (their) duties"*(McCracken & Wolfe, 2004, p.44).
- **The Object-Oriented Hypermedia Design Model:**Schwabe and Rossi (1995) describe an (Object-Oriented Hypermedia Design Model) OOHDM, a new model especially for designing a complex Web-based hypermedia application.
- **Implementation Methodology:**Sampson et al., (2001) describe a methodology which provides for the development of effective websites for counseling and career services. This methodology is very useful as it

"can be used to consider opportunities for enhancing the design and use of the site" (Sampson et al., 2001) and it incorporates organizational aspects of implementation.

There are numerous similarities with respect to the stages between methodologies for developing information systems, websites, or marketing strategies; however, integrating stages from information systems methodologies into website and marketing methodologies is very beneficial in order to develop websites that are more effective and efficient. Human factors experts should be involved in these methodologies to make sure that transaction processes, tracking, maintenance and updating of the website meet the users' requirements.

The researcher reviewed each of the above methodologies to identify two aspects: (1) the stages needed for the system development process; and (2) the utilization of four key principles (user participation, usability, iteration, real interaction (i.e. monitoring of user interaction with a prototype site). These principles were chosen to address the main deficits identified in existing website development methodologies; to produce a new methodology, which will assist in development of websites with high usability.

After reviewing the Information Systems Development Methodologies and Methodologies for Developing Web Sites, the researcher identified the strongest stages. The five major stages, identified are Planning, Analysis, Design, Testing, and Implementation. The extra minor steps are: Promotion, Prototyping, Budget, ROI (return on investment) and Measurement. The main purposes of these extra steps are to:

1. Identify the 4Ps (product, pricing, place and promotion) for the E-Marketing;
2. Identify the time frame to accomplish the job;

3. Define the expected returns from investment;
4. Produce the first trial of the system; and
5. Learn about the audience by tracking their visits and the purpose behind each visit.

In order to develop the new methodology the researcher studied additional detailed techniques to understand the website, structure – that is, the connection between the front and back ends of the website (i.e. the interface and the database and analysis structures). The additional stages are: Task Analysis, Navigation Design, Staff Training, Prototyping, Promotion, and Measurement of outcomes. These extra stages were added to the methodology.

The specific parts from the different methodologies are listed in Table one, grouped into the major stages (first column). Participation (second column) is rated from 0 to 3 – indicating zero participation to maximum user participation. The researcher adopted the (Mumford, 1995) classification of user participation approaches in the system development process. In this research, the researcher used only the Consultative Approach and the Representative Approach. Both of these approaches are very appropriate in all the stages in order to secure agreement between users and designers at the beginning and to identify the key aspects, such as system objectives, problems, and the creating of various solutions to the system requirements. The Consensus Approach was not adopted in this research as it "*does not always emerge easily and conflicts which result from different interests within a department may have to be resolved first*" (Mumford, 1995, pp. 18-19)

The four right hand most columns in the table rate each of the reviewed methodology stages in terms of the four key research principles: "user participation", "usability", "iteration" and "real interaction". These key principles were either not fully considered in some methodologies, or were totally ignored. These principles are identified as being fundamental to the proposed system development process of a website for marketing purposes. The ratings used for these four key principles are from 0 to 3. The former presents zero availability while the latter is the maximum.

The first of these four columns is "user participation". High levels of user participation can have a positive impact on the development process. The second column is "usability". Usability is very important in the system development process in terms of "*support for needs such as ease of use, ease of learning, error protection, graceful error recovery, and efficiency of performance*"(Carroll 2002, p.193). The third column is "iteration". This aspect is also important in the system development process, as it can occur in each stage to ensure that the web site is meeting the user requirements and company objectives. This will enable the designers to build up the new website and make sure that the project will be tested repeatedly until it meets user requirements. The fourth column is "real interaction". This aspect occurs in the evaluation and maintenance stages to ensure that user requirements are being met, by tracking use of the website by real users to achieve their specific objectives.

The draft version of the new participative framework for developing websites was constructed from the stages and steps listed in Table one. Two techniques were used for combining stages from different methodologies: grafting and embedding (Miles, 1992). The stages in the new methodology were constructed from the strongest stages of the various methodologies with a view to combining approaches with minimal epistemological damage to their philosophical foundations. Figure two illustrates the stages and steps for the draft new participative methodology for developing websites. Figure two was adapted from the Star Lifecycle model (Hix & Hartson, 1993), as the evaluation stage is at the centre of the methodology. The final version of the new methodology is summarized in Section seven

Table 1. Stages from methodologies reviewed

Stage	Partici-pation rating	Methodologies	Principles			
			User Par-ticipation	Usability	Iteration	Real Inter-action
Planning	3	Soft System Methodology	1	0	2	0
		Human Factor Methodology for Designing Websites (HFMDW)	1	2	1	0
		Relationship Management (RMM)	0	0	1	0
		The Website Design Method (WSDM)	1	2	0	0
		E-Marketing Plan	1	0	0	0
		The Market-Vantage (Internet Performance Marketing) Methodology	0	0	0	0
Analysis	2	Software Methodology (SSM)	3	0	2	0
		User Centered Development Methodology (UCDM)	1	0	0	0
		Ethics Methodology	3	0	0	0
		Human Factor Methodology for Designing Websites (HFMDW)	0	3	1	2
		The Web Site Design Method (WSDM)	1	2	0	2
		Task Analysis				
Design	3	Structured Systems Analysis and Design Methodology (SSADM)	1	0	1	0
		Software Systems Methodology (SSM)	2	0	2	0
		User Centered Development Methodology (UCDM)	1	3	1	0
		Relationship Management Methodology (RMM)	0	0	2	0
		The W3DT Design Methodology	0	0	0	0
		The Web Site Design Method (WSDM)	1	2	0	2
		Navigation				
		Prototyping				
Testing	3	User Centered Development (UCDM)	1	3	1	0
		Human Factor Methodology for Designing Websites (HFMDW)	1	3	2	0
		The Adventures Company Methodology	0	0	2	0
Imple-menta-tion	2	Information Development Methodology for the Web	1	0	0	0
		E-Marketing Plan	1	0	0	0
		The Market-Vantage (Internet Performance Marketing) Methodology	0	0	2	0
		Construction				
		Promotion				
		Staff Training				
Evalua-tion	3	User Centered Development Methodology (UCDM)	2	3	1	0
		Human Factor Methodology for Designing Websites (HFMDW)	0	3	2	0
		E-Marketing Plan	0	0	0	3
		Measurement				
Mainte-nance	2	Human Factor Methodology for Designing Websites (HFMDW)	0	0	1	3
		The Market-Vantage Methodology	2	0	0	2
		EnSky's Unique Methodology	1	0	0	1

Figure 2. Draft new participative methodology for developing websites

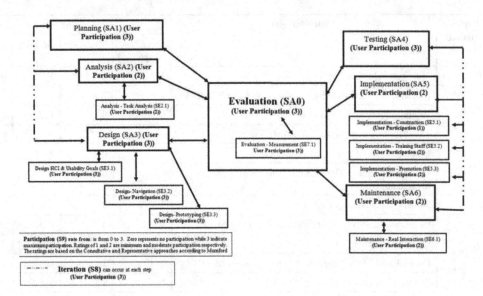

(7) below. The most important aspect of this new methodology is that, before moving to the next stage, each completed stage must be evaluated and tested to ensure that the users' requirements are being met. If they are met, the designers can move to the next stage, if not, they need to return to the previous stage. This process continues until the last stage in the new methodology.

Interview Phase

To implement the qualitative approaches for this research, the researcher collected information about the website development industry in Western Australia so as to address the main research objectives. This research was divided into two phases; interviews and questionnaire.

The researcher interviewed representatives of nine companies (about 1/4 of all website development companies in Western Australia) asking the interviewees questions concerning their methodology, tools and techniques for developing a website. The researcher also discussed the four key principles behind this research, which are user participation, real interaction, usability and iteration. The researcher was interested to know whether

or not, and to what extent, these key principles are reflected in the companies' methodologies. It was noted that most of the industry methodologies are based on experience and knowledge derived from past projects, rather than on academic theory perspectives. The researcher provided details of her prototype new methodology and discussed it in detail with the interviewees. The interviewees raised questions concerning the prototyping, testing, evaluation, implementation and maintenance stages, and about tools to provide user feedback. The researcher noted that most industry representatives indicated that the new methodology has all the stages and steps which are needed to develop a website, and that the new methodology is very much a user-centered methodology. Table two summarizes some of key results of the interviews with industry representatives.

After examining the data gained from all the interviews, the researcher identified the new information about methodologies provided by industry, for input to the New Participative Methodology for Developing Websites. This will allow it to become more practical. New techniques were added to the real interaction step (under the maintenance stage), to allow the users to give positive or negative

Figure 3. Summary of questionnaire phase

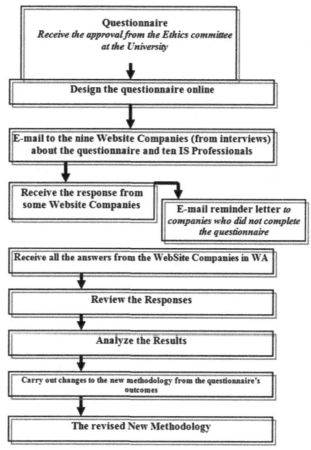

feedback about the website. Under the prototyping step, in the design stage, it was suggested that two initial sketch prototypes of the website (instead of three) be created to reduce expenditure of time and money. A new step (Project Review) was added under the maintenance stage to ensure that the website is running without any problems. This means that one week after implementing the website online, the website will be checked by the designer to ensure if it is operating properly. The potential use of Content Management Systems (CMS) was added to the new methodology to allow the client to manage the content of a website. This approach will allow clients to be able to more easily create, modify, or remove information from the website. According to Guenther (2006, p.54),

the CMS can provide the following functionality: *"....streamline the front-end process of managing content through well-defined work-flows and templates and allow more effective management of back-end processes to include defining, standardizing, controlling, staging, routing, storing and delivering content"*.

Questionnaire Phase

Designing the questionnaire involved interpretation of the interview data and analysis in the context of the research questions. The method for phase two of this research consisted of the steps summarized in figure three. The questionnaire was divided into seven parts: User Participation;

Table 2. Summary of interviews

Aspects	Industry responds
User Participation	*Most companies in Western Australian are encouraging their clients to be involved in the development process not only the top management, but also the users who are dealing and interacting with the website.*
Real interaction	*Is becoming more popular and an increasing number of clients are prepared to deal with it. However, other clients neglect this technique, since it is very expensive; and they need more knowledge and experience in their team to be able to understand the outcomes of the log reports.*
Usability and Human Computer Interaction	*Most companies in Western Australia agreed that Usability is critical in the development process to produce websites where users can find information quickly and easily. Human Computer Interaction is the interaction between the user and computer to achieve easily your tasks and goals.*
Iteration	*Iteration should be available in the any methodology to ensure that the website meets the user requirements.*
Prototyping	*Most developers use one or two sketches in the low fidelity prototyping stage for the website; however, some companies indicated that the nature of the low fidelity prototype would depend on the client, project and the budget.*
Testing and Evaluation	*Both evaluation and testing are available in the design process, after implementation, to ensure the website meets the goals.*
Implementation and Maintenance	*Most of the clients have Content Management Systems (CMS) which will allow them to maintain their website by themselves. Therefore, the development company will encourage their client to maintain not only their information but also the functionality and navigation of their websites.*
Tools to Encourage Feedback	*Most of the companies agreed that these tools should be available in the website structure i.e. forms, content forms, survey, discussion forums, E-mail and Telephone. However, the only feedback tool which is not popular in the industry is "Chat" since this tool requires a person to be available 24/7 and most of the clients are not prepared to pay extra money to provide this service.*

Real Interaction; Usability and HCI; Iteration; New Participative Methodology for Developing Websites; General Questions; and Background Information.

A Likert five-point scale was used in each part of the on-line questionnaire (Sekaran, 2003, p. 197). The researcher also provided a section for participants to write down other comments regarding each part of the questionnaire. The 16 participants who completed the questionnaire were drawn (in equal numbers) from the website companies who participated in the interview phase and IS professionals (to obtain the IS perspective regarding the New Participative Methodology for Developing Websites, since most of the industry participants had degrees in multimedia and communication technology, but few had an academic background in Information Systems). Each participant received (via e-mail) a PDF file containing information about the New Participative Methodology for Developing Websites so that the participant could assess the new methodology. To analyze the outcomes from the questionnaire the researcher used the mean percentages of responses, and the mean rating and standard deviation were also calculated for each question (in each part) of the questionnaire. In addition, the participant's comments were analyzed. Table 3 summarizes some key results from the questionnaire.

From the second phase for this research it was indicated that the industry participants and IS Professionals agreed that all aspects of the new participative methodology for developing websites (structure, stages, steps, tools and techniques) are needed to develop a website successfully. The only key additional insight gained from the questionnaire was moving Human Computer Interaction (HCI) to a separate step under the design stage, since most of the industry participants and IS Professional agreed that adopting HCI principles and practices in the website development process will significantly enhance the website development process.

Table 3. Results from questionnaire

Aspects	Industry responds
User Participation	*The outcomes indicated that both types of users (end-users and client-customers) should take part in the website development process. Most of industry's participants and IS Professionals agreed that the website development process will benefit from user participation.*
Real interaction	*The results indicate that the real interaction aspect is important in the website development process, since this tool provides useful information to the designers to assist them to understand the performance of the website with real users.*
Usability and Human Computer Interaction	*The most important aspect in section three was that 94% of responses from the industry and IS Professionals agreed that Human Computer Interaction(HCI) techniques should be part of the website development process since it is concerned with design, evaluation and implementation of interactive computer-based systems. This outcome is considered very important to the research since current industry's methodologies were missing key HCI aspects.*
Iteration	*Of sixteen responses form the industry's participants and IS Professional 88% agreed that iteration is a very important aspect in the website development process. The new participative methodology will allow iteration to be available in each stage and step to ensure that users' requirements are met. This approach was agreed to by 87.5% of participants.*
New Participative Methodology for Developing Websites	*The outcomes from part five indicated that most of the industry participants agree that this new methodology satisfies the needs of the website industry in Western Australia with the methodology having all the necessary stages and steps, which are mandatory when building up a website effectively. Furthermore, 50% of participants agree that this new methodology is contingent which means the designers and clients can choose the specific tools and techniques which suit the problem situation since every project has different requirements and needs. The researcher calculated the mean for the IS Professionals and Industry Participants separately to distinguish the difference in response regarding contingency. It was noticed that 62.5% of IS professionals agreed that this new methodology is contingent compared to 37.5% of the industry participants. This outcomes indicated that IS professionals were more experienced with, and informed about, the term" contingent "(with respect to the website development processes) because most of the other industry participants have degrees in non-IS disciplines.*
General Questions	*62.5% agree that evaluation (of Usability) and Testing (of Functionality) should be carried out at each stage of the website development process.* *87.5% agree that feedback tools should be available on the website to track user behaviors.* *69% agree that the cost issue is the main concern for clients when choosing a methodology to develop a website.* *75% agree that low fidelity prototyping should be used in the website development methodology.* *100% agree that project review steps should be available in the website development process.* *68.75% agree it is very important to review the website one week after going "live" to ensure it meets the project requirements.* *81% agree that Content Management Systems (CMS) is a very important aspect in website development.* *94% agree that using Content Management Systems (CMS) in the website development process will reduce the time to update the website by the clients (following implementation).*

Figure 4. New participative methodology for developing website

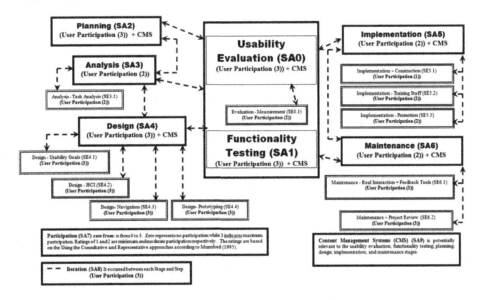

FINAL VERSION OF NEW METHODOLOGY

The draft methodology, which was reviewed in the Interview and Questionnaire phases, was revised to produce the final version of the new website development methodology. It is summarized in the following figure and tables. Figure four shows the final structure of the new participative methodology for developing websites and table four summarizes the major stages and steps. Further details are available in the first author's PhD thesis (Issa, 2008)

Table 4. Summary of major stages and steps of the new participative methodology for developing websites

Stage/Step	Description
Usability Evaluation (SA0)	*This stage is located at the center of the New Participative Methodology for Developing Websites, as before moving to another stage, it is necessary to evaluate the results from the previous stage, where appropriate materials have been produced (i.e. "formative evaluation"). This may involve use of usability guidelines, heuristic evaluation and/or user testing. Measurement (SE0.1): this step is an ongoing evaluation of the website to ensure it meets the website goals.*
Functionality Testing (SA1)	*This stage is located at the center of the New Participative Methodology for Developing Websites to test the results from the previous stage before moving to another stage. Expert-based and user-based evaluation will test the website to ensure that the web site functions effectively from the technical perspective.*
Planning (SA2)	*This stage allows the designer and users to address various project-scoping issues such as requirements for developing a website; the nature of the product; the buyers; the firm's competitors; the location of the site; and how to promote the website.*
Analysis (SA3)	*Users, analysts and designers expand their findings into adequate detail to illustrate exactly what will and will not be built into the website design and to add, improve, and correct the initial website requirements if they are not meeting the user's desires. Task Analysis (SE3.1): this step will define the purpose of developing the website, the user type, the type of work users will do with the website, users' goals and their activities.*
Design (SA4)	*This stage will utilize the requirement specification from the previous stage to define the website requirements: how the website will work; future users and usability requirements; and also user involvement in decision-making. Under this stage there are three steps: Usability Goals (SE4.1) will allow users (end-user and client-customer), analysts and designers (internal and external) to confirm that the website design is efficient, effective, safe, has utility, is easy to learn, easy to remember and easy to evaluate. HCI (SE4.2), HCI goals are usable,, practical, visible, job satisfaction and provide extra techniques such as text style, fonts, layout, graphics and color. Navigation (SE4.3) is to define the specific navigation paths through the website between the entities and to establish the communication between the interface and navigation in the hypermedia application. Prototyping (SE4.4) (low and high fidelity) is essential..*
Implementation (SA5)	*This stage involves the implementation of the website design. Construction (SE5.1) involves implementation of the website design via a Technical Application (i.e. HTML, Dreamweaver; Cold Fusion and ASP) n. Training Staff (SE5.2) will give necessary training to the staff about the new website. Promotion (SE5.3) will use various tools (such as press releases, link building and banner-ad campaigns, paid search engine, directory listing campaigns and traditional marketing) to promote the website.*
Maintenance (SA6)	*Ongoing maintenance to the website includes update changes and the correction of errors in the website. Real Interaction and Feedback Tools (SE6.1) involves tracking by using a server log file. In addition, feedback tools should be available on the website to allow the users to be able to contact the website owner for information or personal communication and to provide feedback about the website i.e. forms, survey, discussion forum, contact form, and telephone number. Project review (SE6.2) should be available to ensure that the website is working within the project goals.*
User Participation (SA7)	*This aspect is a very important concept in the New Participative Methodology for Developing Websites, as the main purpose is to allow user participation in the website development process to gain more information about the problems and alternative solutions from the users and to familiarize them with the system before it is released.*
Iteration (SA8)	*Occurs potentially between each Stage and Step in the new participative methodology for developing websites to ensure that the website does indeed meet users' (end-user and client-customer) requirements and company objectives before moving to another stage. This will result from evaluation of results of the previous stage, if appropriate (i.e. if an evaluation can be carried out and if it reveals problems).*
Content Management Systems (CMS) (SA9)	*CMS will allow the users to manage the web contents by allowing them to add, edit, remove, and submit information by using various templates and workflows without needing any previous knowledge of website editing tools. The CMS operates within parameters determined during the website development process. Inevitably, after sufficient rounds of updating via the CMS, a review of the website usability will be required.*

PROPOSED FUTURE RESEARCH AND DEVELOPMENT

Further research will be carried out with the website development industry and the education sectors. From the interviews and the questionnaire, the researcher noted that most of the participants have limited knowledge with respect to the Usability and HCI aspects, and most of the industry organizations paid little attention to these aspects in their methodologies. Currently the researcher is running a postgraduate course to introduce the benefits of the adoption of the usability and HCI in the website development process. In addition, the new methodology will be introduced as a part of these courses, by providing detailed information about how this methodology was created and discussing the stages, steps, tools and techniques, which are part of this methodology. The course will also discuss how the new integrated methodology needs to be "contingent" (Turk, 2001) and how to implement this approach.

A website describing this methodology (in a similar style to the UsabilityNet (www.usability-net.org) website) will be developed. This website will incorporate a software tool to facilitate selection of particular stages, steps and techniques from the contingent methodology to produce a tailored methodology to suit the situation for any specific project. The situation will vary with respect to website type, type(s) of users, budget, time, etc. The effectiveness of this approach will be evaluated.

CONCLUSION

This research focused on investigating, developing and evaluating a new methodology for designing more user-friendly websites. The framework for the new participative methodology for developing websites was developed by identifying the strongest stage of each of various: lifecycles models; Information Systems methodologies; methodolo-gies with explicit human factors aspects; websites methodologies; marketing methodologies and additional detailed techniques to allow both designers and users (end users and client-customers users) to work collaboratively for developing websites. The most important aspect of this new participative methodology for developing websites is to assist users to participate from the beginning. This should result in avoiding frustrations for the users; making the website more user-friendly and interesting; and winning the trust of the site visitors by meeting users' requirements. To assess the new methodology the researcher used two phases, interviews and a questionnaire. The responses from the two phases supported the new methodology structure and style. This study identified the need for further research, including the development of a website describing the new participative methodology.

REFERENCES

Abels, E. G., White, M. D., & Hahn, K. (1998). A user-based design process for Web sites. *Internet Research: Electronic Networking Applications and Policy, 8*(1), 39–48. doi:10.1108/10662249810368879

Advertures. (2004). *Process Methodology.* Retrieved 16 Sept 2004, from http://www.advertures.cz/alt/index_en.php?cat=company&sub=methodology

Avison, D. E., & Fitzgerald, G. (1993). *Information Systems Development: Methodologies, Techniques and Tools.* Oxfordshire, UK: Alfred Waller Ltd, Publishers.

Benyon, D., Turner, P., & Turner, S. (2005). *Designing Interactive Systems.* Upper Saddle rver, NJ: Pearson Education Limited.

Bichler, M., Nusser, S., & Wien, W. (1996). *Modular Design of Complex Web-Applications with W3DT.* Paper presented at the 5th International Workshops on Enabling Technologies: Infrastructure for Collaborative Enterprises (WET ICE'96), Standord, CA.

Borges, J. A., Morales, I., & Rodriguez, N. J. (1998). Page Design Guidelines Developed Through Usability Testing. In E. G. J. R. Chris Forsythe (Ed.), *Human Factors and Web Development* (pp. 137-152). Mahwah, NJ: Lawrence Erlbaum Associates.

Borges, J. A., Morales, I., & Rodriguez, N. J. (2008). *Page Design Guidelines Developed through Usability Testing.* Retrieved 15 April, 2009, from http://ece.uprm.edu/hci/papers/Chapter.pdf

Boyer, M. A. (1999). Step 1: Satisfy the consumer. *Supermarket Business, 54*(4), 112.

Bullet, D. (2002). *Introduction to Usability.* Retrieved 14 April 2004, from http://www.usabilityfirst.com/intro/index.txl

Carroll, J. M. (2002). *Human-Computer Interaction in the New Millennium.* New York: Addison-Wesley.

Carroll, M. (2004). *Usability testing leads to better ROI.* Retrieved 14 April 2004, from http://www.theusabilitycompany.com/news/media_coverage/pdfs/2003/NewMediaAge_270303.pdf

Checkland, P., & Scholes, J. (2003). *Soft Systems Methodology in Action.* London: John Wiley & Sons, LTD.

Clare, S. (2002). Worldwide-friendly sites draw returns. *Marketing News, 36*(18), 24.

Cunliffe, D. (2000). Developing usable Web sites - a review and model. *Internet Research, 10*(4), 295. doi:10.1108/10662240010342577

Darlington, K. (2005). *Effective Website Development.* Upper Saddle River, NJ: Pearson Education Limited.

December, J. (1996). An information development methodology for the World Wide Web. *Technical Communication, 43*(4), 369.

Dix, A., Finlay, J., Abowd, G., & Beale, R. (2004). *Human-Computer Interaction* (3rd ed.), Upper Saddle River, NJ: Pearson Education Limited.

Doll, W. J., & Torkzadeh, G. (1989). A Discrepancy Model Of End-User Computing Involvement. *Management Science, 35*(10), 1151. doi:10.1287/mnsc.35.10.1151

Ellsworth, J. H., & Ellsworth, M. V. (1997). *Marketing on the Internet.* Mahwah, NJ: John Wiley & Sons, Inc.

EnSky. (1997). *EnSky's Unique Methodology.* Retrieved 16 Sept 2004, from http://www.ensky.com/company/process/methodology.php

FFIEC IT Examination Handbook. (2005). *Systems Development Life Cycle.*

Gardner, D. (2003). Cool customer response? Hit their hot buttons! *Agri Marketing, 41*(4), 74.

Guenther, K. (2006). Content Management Systems as "Silver Bullets". *Online, 30*(4), 54–55.

Hartwick, J., & Barki, H. (1994). Explaining the role of user participation in information Systems. *Management Science, 40*(4), 440. doi:10.1287/mnsc.40.4.440

Hartwick, J., & Barki, H. (2001). Communications as a Dimension of User Participation. *IEEE Transactions on Professional Communication, 44*(1), 21–36. doi:10.1109/47.911130

Head, A. J. (1999). *Design Wise.* Medford, NJ: Thomas H Hogan Sr.

Hix, D., & Hartson, H. R. (1993). *Developing user Interfaces: Ensuring Usability through product & Process.* New York: John Wiley & Sons.

Hoekstra, G. (2000). *History of Web Design*. Retrieved 27 May 2003, from http://www.weballey.net/webdesign/history.html

Holzinger, A. (2005). Usability Engineering Methods for Software Developers. *Communications of the ACM*, *48*(1), 71–74. doi:10.1145/1039539.1039541

IBM. (n.d). *Web Design Guidelines*. Retrieved 1 Aug 2006, from http://www-3.ibm.com/ibm/easy/eou_ext.nsf/Publish/572PV

Isakowitz, T., Stohr, E. A., & Balasubramanian, P. (1995). RMM: A Methodology for Structured Hypermedia Design. *Communications of the ACM*, *38*(8), 34–44. doi:10.1145/208344.208346

Issa, T. (2008). *Development and Evaluation of a Methodology for Developing Websites - PhD Thesis, Curtin University, Western Australia*. Retrieved from http://espace.library.curtin.edu.au.1802/view/action/nmets.do?DOCCHOICE=17908.xml&dvs=1235702350272~864&locale=en_US&search_terms=17908&usePid1=true&usePid2=true

Jayaratna, N. (1994). *Understanding and Evaluating Methodologies - NIMSAD - A Systemic Framework*. London: McGraw-Hill International.

Kambil, A., & Eselius, E. (2000). Where the interaction is. *Across the Board*, *37*(10), 36.

Kaplan, B., & Duchon, D. (1988). Combining Qualitative and Quantitative Methods in Information Systems Research: A Case Study. *MIS Quarterly/December 1988*, 571 - 586.

Lazar, J. (2006). *Web Usability*. Upper Saddle River, NJ: Pearson Education, Inc.

Mankelow, T. (2006). Optimal Usability. *NZ Business*, *20*(1), 53.

Market-Vantage. (2003). *Internet Marketing Methodology*. Retrieved 16 Sept 2004, from http://www.market-vantage.com/about/methodology.htm

McCracken, D. D., & Wolfe, R. J. (2004). *User-Centered Website Development A Human-Computer Interaction Approach*. Upper Saddle River, NJ: Pearson Education, Inc.

McGovern, G. (2003). *Usability is good management*. Retrieved 14 April 2004, from http://www.gerrymcgovern.com/nt/2003/nt_2003_04_07_usability.htm

Miles, R. (1992). Combining 'Hard' and 'Soft' systems practice: Grafting and Embedding Revisited. *Systemist*, *14*(2), 62–66.

Mumford, E. (1995). *Effective Systems Design and Requirements Analysis*. London: Macmillan Press Ltd.

Myers, M. D., & Avison, D. (2002). *Qualitative Research in Information Systems* (1st, Ed.). London: SAGE Publications Ltd.

Nielsen, J. (2000). *Designing Web Usability*. New York: New Riders Publishing.

Nielsen, J. (2003). *Usability 101*. Retrieved 14 April 2004, from http://www.useit.com/alertbox/20030825.html

Olle, T. W., Hagelstein, J., Macdonald, I. G., Rolland, C., Sol, H. G., Assche, F. J. M. V., et al. (1988) *Information Systems Methodologies "A framework for understanding."*: Reading, MA: Addison-Wesley Publishing Company.

Olson, M. H., & Ives, B. (1981). User Involvement in System Design: An Empirical Test of Alternative Approaches. *Information & Management*, *4*(4), 183. doi:10.1016/0378-7206(81)90059-8

Preece, J., Rogers, Y., Benyon, D., Holland, S., & Carey, T. (1994). *Human Computer Interaction*. Reading, MA: Addison-Wesley.

Preece, J., Rogers, Y., Keller, L., Davies, G., & Benyon, D. (1993). A Guide to Usability. In J. Preece (Ed.), *Human Factors in Computing*. London: Addison Wesley.

Preece, J., Rogers, Y., & Sharp, H. (2002). *Interaction design: beyond human-computer interaction*. New York: John Wiley & Sons.

Ramey, J. (2000). Guidelines for Web Data Collection: Understanding and Interacting with Your Users. *Technical Communication, 47*(3), 397–410.

Rhodes, J. S. (2000). *Usability can save your company*. Retrieved 5 Dec 2003, from http://webword.com/moving/savecompany.html

Sampson, J. P., Carr, D. L., Panke, J., Arkin, S., Minvielle, M., & Vernick, S. H. (2001). *An Implementation Model for Web Site Design and Use in Counseling and Career Services*. Retrieved 14 June 2004, from http://www.career.fsu.edu/documents/implementation/Implementing%20Web%20Sites.ppt.

Schwabe, D., & Rossi, G. (1995). The Object-Oriented Hypermedia Design Model. *Communications of the ACM, 38*(8), 45–46. doi:10.1145/208344.208354

Sekaran, U. (2003). *Research Methods for Business "A Skill Building Approach"* (4th ed.). Mahwah, NJ: John Wiley & Sons.

Sheridan, W. (1999). *Web Design is Changing*. Retrieved 27 May 2003, from http://www3.sympatico.ca/cypher/web-design.htm

Sims, R. (1997). *Interactivity: A Forgotten Art?* Retrieved 4 Dec 2003, from http://www.gsu.edu/~wwwitr/docs/interact/

Spyridakis, J. H. (2000). Guidelines for authoring comprehensible Web pages and evaluating their success. *Technical Communication, 47*(3), 359.

Strauss, J., El-Ansary, A., & Frost, R. (2003). *E-Marketing*. Retrieved 28 May 2005, from www.nd.edu/~mkt384/mark461/powerpoints3/chapter3F.ppt

Strauss, J., El-Ansary, A., & Frost, R. (2006). *E-Marketing* (4th ed.). Upper Saddle River, NJ: Pearson Prentice Hall.

Troyer, O. D. (1998). *Designing Well-Structured Websites: Lessons to Be Learned from Database Schema Methodology*. Paper presented at the Conceptual Modeling – ER '98: 17th International Conference on Conceptual Modeling, Singapore.

Troyer, O. M. F. D., & Leune, C. J. (1998). *WSDM: a user centered design method for Web sites*. Paper presented at the Computer Networks and ISDN systems, Proceedings of the 7th International World Wide Web Conference, Elsevier, Vrijdag.

Turk, A. (2001). *Towards Contingent Usability Evaluation of WWW Sites*. Paper presented at the Proceedings of OZCHI, Perth, Australia.

Van-Duyne, D. K., Landay, J. A., & Hong, J. I. (2003). *The Design of Sites: Patterns, Principles and processes for Crafting a Costumer-Centered Web Experience*. Boston: Addison-Wesley.

Vora, P. (1998). Human Factors Methodology for Designing Web Sites. In E. G. J. R. Chris Forsythe (Ed.), *Human Factors and Web Development* (pp. 153 - 172). Mahwah, NJ: Lawrence Erlbaum Associates.

Section 2
Universal Usability

Chapter 7
Integrating Accessibility Evaluation into Web Engineering Processes

Christopher Power
University of York, UK

André Pimenta Freire
University of York, UK

Helen Petrie
University of York, UK

ABSTRACT

This chapter presents methodologies and techniques for performing accessibility evaluations on web applications. These methodologies are discussed in the context of performing them within a web engineering process, be it a traditional, unified or agile process. In this chapter the case is made that website commissioners and web engineers cannot afford to overlook accessible practices as they risk alienating an increasingly large user base who may require accessible web features.

INTRODUCTION

Accessibility is becoming a required feature of web applications for commerce, health care and government. For website commissioners and engineers who are unfamiliar with it, accessibility can be a word that conjures up spectres of legal obligations, litigation and increased costs in development. For those who are familiar with the technical side of accessibility,

images of long documents of guidelines, regulations and criticisms of both are come to mind. Finally, for people with disabilities, accessibility can inspire either dread, due to the current state-of-the-art in accessibility in web technology, or hope, for the future of web applications, or both.

Faced with all of these views, what are web engineers to do? Many want to make their applications available to as many people as possible; however, just as many have thrown up their hands in dismay at the current perceived state of acces-

DOI: 10.4018/978-1-60566-896-3.ch007

sibility, and the seeming impenetrability of the process. These web engineers often take the road of conformance with guidelines and checklists, a route that does not necessarily guarantee accessibility (DRC, 2004). While this is often the route that leads to the largest acceptance within an organization, there are larger implications to the website engineer of which they should be aware. An inaccessible website has the potential to alienate a large audience that the organization could reach to offer their products and services. As a result, managers, designers and developers all must be concerned about accessibility itself, not just guideline conformance.

The goal of this chapter is to present the concept of accessibility and what it means to the web engineer. In particular, it will focus on the development and evaluation of web applications for accessibility, ensuring that the largest number of people of the web audience can use them.

This chapter will present the relationship between usability, a concept well understood by the web engineering community, and accessibility. It will discuss how these two concepts interact, and how they are achieving the same end goal: allowing users to use web applications.

In the sections following, the authors have chosen to ignore conventional wisdom regarding discussing web problems via guidelines, checkpoints and specific technologies. Instead, the focus is placed on the users and their interactions with web applications. After all, technology continues to change, but humans change very slowly, and the challenges and issues associated with accessibility will remain long after the current crop of web technologies is gone.

The chapter will present different types of evaluation available to the web engineer: expert inspection, automatic tools and user evaluation. An analysis of where these evaluation processes can be applied in web engineering processes is discussed as well as structured unified processes and flexible agile processes.

BACKGROUND

In order to understand the techniques discussed later in this chapter, it is important to understand what accessibility is and why it is important. This chapter presents several different views of accessibility. This is followed by a discussion regarding why accessibility is a factor that must be considered by the web engineer and website commissioners. Hereafter, a *web site* consists of many interconnected *web pages* all belonging to the same domain address. Further, a *web application* is a website that has interactive components for completing complex tasks.

The Accessible Web versus the Usable Web versus Using the Web

With web engineering being focused on the design and development of both content and structure in websites, it is perhaps unsurprising that usability is well represented in the web engineering literature and in experience reports (Mariage & Vanderdonckt, 2005; Martens, 2003; Agarwal, 2002; Becker, 2002; Palmer, 2002; Ivory & Hearst, 2001).

In general, it is reasonable to say that the web engineering community has taken on board the concept of usability, addressing different aspects of effectiveness, efficiency and satisfaction[1] (Shneiderman, 1998). In comparison, the uptake of accessible design and evaluation slow to come into common practice. In some cases, this is a result of the definition of accessibility being unclear and at times contradictory, making it difficult for web engineering teams to adopt a culture of accessibility. Petrie and Kheir (2007) provide an extensive discussion of these definitions a portion of which is included here for completeness.

In this chapter, *technical accessibility* refers to the checking of features of a website for conformance against a set of guidelines specifying what is and what is not accessible to people with disabilities (Petrie and Kheir, 2007). The guidelines typically used for such evaluations are the

Web Content Accessibility Guidelines (WCAG) (Chisholm, 1999; Caldwell *et al.*, 2008) from the Web Accessibility Initiative (WAI) of the World Wide Web Consortium (W3C). Indeed, it is often the case that legislation or company policies are based on this view of accessibility.

Unfortunately, it has been demonstrated that accessibility is not so simple. Indeed, the extensive study performed for the Disability Rights Commission in the UK (2004) concluded that there was no relationship between technical accessibility and the success of users with disabilities in achieving their goals on a particular website. Clearly a more user-based definition is required to truly capture the essence of what it means for a website to be accessible.

There have been several attempts to define what accessibility means to the user, from Shneiderman's (2000, 2003) *universal usability* which presents accessibility as a precursor to usability; to Thatcher *et al.* (2003) who defines accessibility as being a disjoint subset of problems of people with disabilities from mainstream users. Unfortunately, neither of these definitions appears to be sufficient to describe the issues encountered by people with disabilities on the web. Petrie and Kheir (2007) demonstrated that there is a common subset of problems that are shared between web users with disabilities and mainstream users, as well as those that are disjoint between the two groups. It is also the case that there is evidence that certain types of usability problems are amplified for people with disabilities (Harrison and Petrie, 2006; Petrie, King and Hamilton, 2005; DRC, 2004), with this research showing a "usability bonus", where websites become more usable for all users due to good accessibility practices. Clearly, the issue about what is or is not accessible is not as clear as the technical accessibility enthusiasts would have us believe.

For purposes of this chapter, the authors adopt the term *accessibility* to mean that people with disabilities and other user groups such as older adults are able to successfully perceive, understand and interact with websites and web applications[2].

Modern Web Audiences Impact on Website Use

There is a segment of the design and development community that contends that there are not enough users that would benefit from accessible practices to warrant their inclusion in development cycles. In this section, the case will be made that there are too many web users in the broader audience who can be reached through accessible practices to ignore.

A report prepared for the Royal National Institute of Blind People (RNIB) by the University of York (Kennaugh and Petrie, 2006) discusses the demographics of the UK population of potential users of interactive online services. In that report, calculations of potential market sizes were derived from estimates of the number of people in the overall population of the UK who fall into one of two broad categories of people who can benefit from accessible applications. The first, core group of users consists of those who are: over 75; people with severe visual disabilities; people with profound hearing loss; people with severe dyslexia; people aged 16-74 with dementia and people aged 16-74 with the tremor related illness of Parkinson's. This core group is estimated to be approximately 7,797,000 people.

A further secondary group of approximately 13,382,000 users was also identified as people whose lives would benefit from the provision of accessible digital applications. This user group consists of those people who have: mild to moderate hearing loss; learning difficulties; mild dyslexia; arthritis aged 16-74 of 75; and people with low literacy.

Certainly, it would not be expected that all individuals in these user groups would adopt accessible digital services through either television or the web; however, if only 10% of the potential users gain access to digital services on the web, this could mean millions of additional users.

In an online marketplace that is largely usage-based for generating revenue, driven by funding through online advertising, these numbers cannot be overlooked for much longer. With the overall average population age increasing, we are moving into a crucial phase where the majority of people using the internet will experience some mild to moderate accessibility problems, these numbers are expected to increase over time.

Companies, web commissioners and web engineers have a unique opportunity to integrate accessibility and evaluation practices into their businesses now, before the massive shift in population demographics occurs.

Accessible Practices for Modern Web Applications

In the last decade the web has changed from a source of information for a small audience, to a necessity for a business, education and leisure. In the same way that the audiences of the web have evolved, so has the content with which they interact. Text and static pictures have been augmented with multimedia, animation and interactive components. This section explores some of the features that make up the modern web and discusses some of the accessibility issues that can arise due to them. As there are several good resources on implementation of accessible designs (Thatcher *et al.*, 2003), and as accessibility needs often do not change as the underlying web technology evolves, the web features are discussed from the user centric point of view, with examples of current technology provided, where appropriate, that both satisfies users and WCAG 2.0.

Text

Text is still perhaps the most common form of information available on the web. Text is still the main medium of presentation, with a marked increase recently in participatory web communities such as blogs and wikis. This is fortunate, as text is relatively easy to transform from symbols into synthetic speech, thus solving many of the

perceptual problems associated with graphics and other types of media that occur for people with visual disabilities or people with specific learning difficulties; however, this does not mean that text is always accessible to users.

For example, the use of text decoration, such as bold, italics or font colour, needs to be implemented in such a way that screen readers[3] and other assistive technologies can determine that it is in fact intended for emphasis. In current technology this means using (X)HTML elements such as *strong* and *em(phasis)* in combination with cascading style sheets to provide access to the semantic information to both mainstream users and people with visual disabilities.

Text size remains a problem for many users, and thus in browser options are often used to view text. However, if implemented incorrectly, this resizing can be a disaster! For example, Figure 1 demonstrates that text can be rendered unreadable in large font if a fixed spacing layout is used.

A further example, which often affects mainstream users as well as older adults or people with specific learning difficulties, is the use of large blocks of complicated text that are difficult to parse (Kurniawan, 2003). Smaller, more organized, sections of text, or simpler text can be easier to perceive and understand for many users.

Images

On the web, the use of images varies between *informative* and *decorative. Informative images* are those that contain information critical to undertaking tasks on a given website. These could be graphics that provide instruction, or those that require direct interaction from the user (such a graphic links).

One group that is severely affected by images on websites are people with visual disabilities, who require alternative text on informative images to describe the contents of images for interpretation and understanding of their contents. Indeed, this is perhaps the most studied issue in regards to

Figure 1. An example of a website created with fixed spacing of (X)HTML div elements resulting in poor rendering of enlarged text.

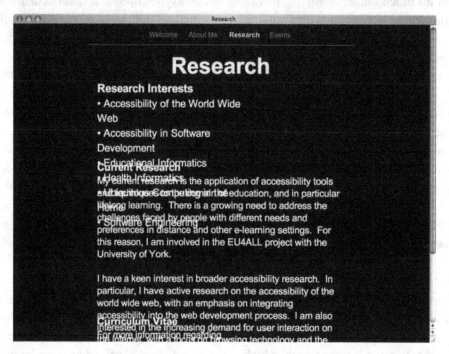

accessibility, with several studies citing serious problems with the lack of alternative text for informative images on websites (DRC, 2004; Harrison and Petrie, 2006).

In comparison, *decorative images* are those that provide no direct information to the user about the contents or use of the web page and as a result do not need to be voiced. In current practice, this means that alternative text attributes in (X)HTML should be included with empty character strings. This will result in most screen readers skipping over the image.

Beyond this, forced direct manipulation of very large images or very small images can cause accessibility issues for anyone with tremor or dexterity disabilities including older adult users and users with physical disabilities.

Multimedia

Multimedia, which can include audio content or video content, provides interesting challenges in accessibility. There are not only the challenges in making sure that the content is accessible, but also the media players and other technology (e.g. Flash, SCORM players) that are used to deliver the content must themselves be accessible. While this chapter is primarily concerned with the aspects of the web engineering process (i.e. content, structure etc.), it is worth noting that in the procurement process for a multimedia player, a web engineer should place accessibility in its requirements.

For audio content, it is essential that text equivalents in the form of either captioning or a transcript be provided. This is similar for audio tracks in a video. When using the transcript, people with certain specific learning difficulties can be further supported by using time dependent highlighting, with text being highlighted during relevant points in the video. On the other hand, some sign-language using people who are deaf would prefer captioning be done with sign-language (Fels *et al.*, 2004; Petrie, Weber and Fisher, 2005).

Video does add a further potential barrier for people with visual disabilities as the visual content must also be augmented with audio description. These descriptions provide information regarding the activities happening in the video for a person with visual disabilities (Petrie, Weber and Fisher, 2005).

Tables

When presented visually, tables can provide an efficient means of organizing and viewing data. In audio formats, this form of data presentation can be arduous when it is linearized without audio cues about table headings and table columns. In current practice this can be accomplished through the *TH* element in (X)HTML. Further, use of the caption and summary attributes of tables can help orient all users to the purpose of the table(s) and information about the contents, respectively.

In other cases, where tables are more complex, sophisticated reading strategies may be required to make sense of the data through audio. Many of these types of strategies, and a more in-depth discussion of the impact of linearization of tables for people with visual disabilities can be found in the work by Yesilada *et al.* (2004). In general, it is recommended that tables are kept as simple as possible for aid all users in understanding their contents.

In regards to the use of tables for layout on websites: a developer should never use tables for layout on websites[4].

Links

Links would seem like an easy thing to get right on web pages. By adding a web address, some text, or a graphic, a designer provides a user with a way to navigate to a new web page. Unfortunately, in addition to the problems already associated with text and graphics mentioned above, there is a need to be careful regarding the labeling of links in a web application. First there is the problem of the sheer number of links on a web page. If the complete list of links is overly long, it is difficult to navigate for all users[5]. Further, if these links are not labeled appropriately, with meaningful identifiers, they will be impossible to interpret in a list of links such as those used by screen reader users. Consider the following screenshot of such a links list from the phone sales page on a major UK phone company's website.

As can be seen, there were (at least) four phones on the page being viewed, with links to select a specific phone, or links to the details regarding a phone. However, it is impossible to tell from this listing *what* phone would be viewed when a link is followed.

Figure 2. Screen shot of a screen reader style links list for the website of a UK based mobile phone company.

This type of problem of overloading of link text is not unique to the audio browsing user. Mainstream users can run into similar problems if links are not sufficiently distinguished from one another either explicitly through their labels, or implicitly by the context in which they are used.

Headings

Even the earliest markup languages included heading elements for indicating divisions in a web document. However, as technology evolved, it became easier to add visual emphasis to words to indicate sections of the website. Unfortunately, this visual information is often not implemented in such a way that it can be detected by assistive technologies such as screen readers. In order to make a website easy to navigate for someone using such technology, the developer should use appropriate markup, such as the heading elements (e.g. *H1*, *H2*) available in (X)HTML. Proper indication of headings, in both visual and screen reader detectable markup has been shown to increase performance for both mainstream users and users who are blind (Watanabe, 2007).

Forms

The possibility of including forms to provide features in websites was provided in early versions of the HTML, and has played a key role for the implementation of interaction in the web. Although forms have been widely used since early applications were available, many web systems still have many inaccessible forms.

When designing a form, a web designer or developer must ensure that the form is accessible through keyboard and mouse input, with *onfocus* events replacing *onclick*. Further, proper association between fields and their *label* elements such that the two are linked is also important. This will allow screen readers users to detect the labels associated with one or more fields; however, it will also benefit mouse users as they can click on the

associated label to select the field. In this way, web engineers can use graphical positioning as they wish without concern that the labels will become disassociated with their appropriate fields.

ACCESSIBILITY EVALUTION TECHNIQUES

The techniques presented above provide web engineers with practical advice regarding how to build accessible websites. However, without proper evaluation techniques it is impossible for web engineers to know whether or not they have been successful in providing accessible designs and implementations. In this section, techniques for evaluating web accessibility are presented.

Throughout this section examples are provided from accessibility evaluations performed on a number of UK museum websites by the authoring team during a recent contract[6].

Conformance Evaluations and Accessibility Evaluations

As was mentioned previously, the evaluation of a web page, website or web application for its conformance to the Web Content Accessibility Guidelines (WCAG) is one measure of the accessibility of a website. *Conformance evaluation* consists of checking the features of a website as to whether they satisfy aspects of accessibility that are specified in WCAG. For web engineers who are familiar with accessibility, this is the most common type of evaluation done due to the influence that WCAG has had on the legal and political landscape.

The first version of WCAG (Chisholm, 1999) was produced by the Web Accessibility Initiative (WAI) of the World Wide Web Consortium (W3C) as a recommendation for practice on the web. The primary goal of these guidelines was to increase awareness of accessibility as well as to provide best practices for developers to help them make the web available to all users. The first version of the guidelines had 14 guidelines with 65 checkpoints. Each checkpoint had a *Priority* from 1 to 3 that indicated its importance to making the website accessible to user groups. If a website met all Priority 1 checkpoints it was said to meet *Level A* conformance. Further, if a website met all Priority 1 and 2 checkpoints, it was conformant to *Level AA*. Finally meeting all of the checkpoints meant that a website was conformant to *Level AAA*.

In December, 2008 the second version of WCAG was released. This substantial update included a reorganization of the guidelines. In WCAG 2.0 there are four guiding principles, specifically that a website should be: perceivable to the senses of the user, operable by the user, understandable to the user, and robust in that it can function when used with a variety of technologies. Within these four principles are 12 guidelines, within which there are success criteria (SC). Each SC has a priority attached to it, where priorities are now A, AA, AAA. As a result, conformance levels of A, AA, and AAA are met by meeting all guidelines of the same priority and lower.

A *conformance evaluation* can be undertaken through *conformance tests* conducted via *automated evaluation tools* and *inspection methods*. When such an evaluation is undertaken, the evaluator goes through each guideline checking the features of a website against the criteria of that guideline[7]. Some of these criteria, such as the presence or absence of alternative text, can be checked with an automatic evaluation tool. In other cases, such as criteria relating to the clarity of the contents of the alternative text, the evaluation can only be conducted using human judgment.

Further information regarding conformance tests is contained in the following sections. However, while conformance evaluations are perhaps the most common evaluations conducted in industry, it is unclear that conformance to WCAG leads to an accessible website. Indeed, there is evidence from the DRC report that there is no relation between WCAG 1.0 and user reported

problems on websites. As a result, the following sections also provide information regarding evaluation methodologies that are not based on guideline conformance checking.

Automated Evaluation

Automated evaluation for the verification of accessibility issues provides an efficient way of checking a subset of WCAG and are heavily used by practitioners (Ivory, 2003). This broad use of automated evaluation tools has resulted in a wide range of tools, including the previously widely used *Bobby*, *Wave*[8], *Hera* (Benavidez et. al, 2006), *Imergo* (Mohamad et. al 2004) and many others. All of these tools provide similar functionality through the processing of the markup of web pages.

First, these tools can check the validity of (X) HTML mark up and the use of style sheets. This can include checking features such as the correct nesting of elements in tables and headers, and proper use of other W3C recommended technologies. This first step helps ensure that a web page can be read by assistive technologies.

Beyond the technical tests regarding the technology, automated testing can check things that are, in general, deterministic. They can check the presence or absence of features, such as alternative text attributes and headings, or can check values against known standards, such as values for colour contrast. The results of all these tests are usually presented to the user in the form of a report that details problem areas of the web page(s) for the developer.

However, in context of an evaluation, it is important to highlight that automated evaluation tools are very limited in their capabilities. Although they may help a lot to identify problems that otherwise would very tedious to test, there is only a small number of WCAG guidelines that can be tested automatically. For WCAG 1.0 checkpoints, the Unified Web Evaluation Methodology (UWEM) (WAB Cluster, 2007) defines a set of methods and

Figure 3. A summary document provided by the automated evaluation tool HERA.

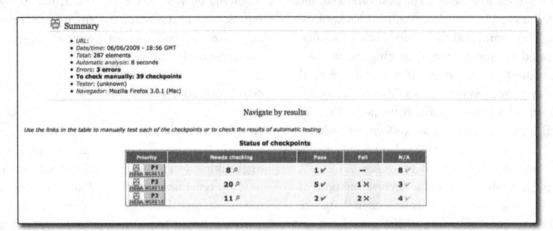

accessibility test cases. From the 108 test cases listed at UWEM for the WCAG 1.0 checkpoints only 26 of the tests (less than 20%) can be checked with an automatic tool. Although many of these automatable tests may help considerably to reduce time and effort spent in evaluation, it is clear that, even for evaluation based on checkpoints review, relying exclusively on automated tools covers only a very limited number of problems users may encounter. As an example, consider the use of text alternatives for images. Although it is possible for an automatic tool to identify whether an image element has an *alt* attribute, the tool cannot identify if the text contained within that attribute describes the image appropriately.

Figure 3 presents summary outputs from one such automatic evaluation tool HERA[9], which displays the errors and warnings on a particular web page. Further to this, Figure 4 displays an expanded view of the Priority 3 errors, with a description of the checkpoint violated and the location in the code of the violation.

Understanding the outcomes of an automated evaluation tool is also frequently a challenge to evaluators and developers (Choi et. al, 2006). Even experienced evaluators very often face problems in comprehending what the messages provided from them mean. Although the so called "warning messages" may help find potential errors in a manual checking, these messages are often vague and obscure, and end up not clearly showing where the problem may be, or more importantly, how to repair it.

Finally, there is a question of validity of automatic evaluation tools. The implementation of the checking algorithms varies substantially between different tools, and validation tests for the tools are often not available. This can lead to inaccuracies in checks, such as those found by Brajnik (2004) where he identifies reporting errors in various tools.

The proper use of automated evaluation tools can be an asset to the web engineering team. However, evaluators should bear in mind not only the advantages of such tools, but their severe limitations to broadly cover all possible accessibility problems. Performing expert evaluations and user tests are essential for creating accessible websites.

Inspection Methods

Along with tests with automated evaluation tools, *inspection methods* by expert evaluators play an important role in the evaluation process of web applications. The use of inspection methods is important to help finding barriers in web resources that cannot be checked automatically. Inspection

Figure 4. An expanded view of the accessibility errors for Priority 3 checkpoints.

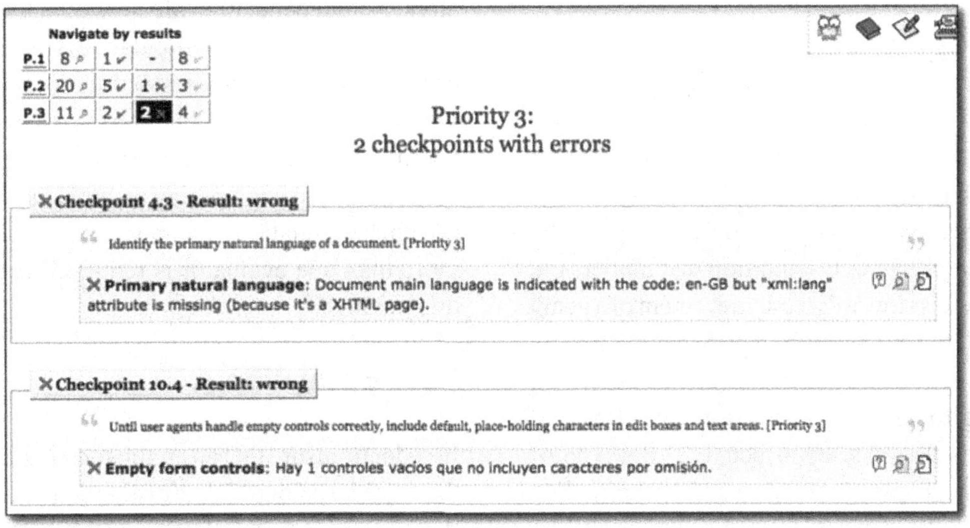

methods may be integrated within the development cycles of web projects, as they do not demand the recruiting of a large range of users with a wide range of different disabilities and restrictions. Although they cannot uncover all the problems that users may encounter, these tests are good at finding problems early in development.

Expert Checklist Review

In this chapter, an *expert checklist review* refers to the inspection method where a human checks the conformance of a website against a set of guidelines such as WCAG. Expert checklist reviews can be difficult for non-experienced evaluators, as the checkpoints are usually related to issues that cannot be automatically checked require

in-depth knowledge of accessibility. Additionally, the guidelines and checkpoints may not always be clear and easy to understand and may cause confusion even to experienced evaluators (Colwell and Petrie, 1998). As a result, training and experience are needed to be able to do these checklists well.

With this in mind, if a web engineering team wishes to achieve conformance of their website to WCAG, or another set of guidelines, it is essential that they perform a checklist review as some problems can only be detected through human inspection.

As an example, Table 1 presents two violations that were discovered through an expert conformance review of one of the mentioned UK museum websites.

Table 1. Example violations of errors on a web page along with comments from the evaluator

Violation: Checkpoint 6.3 (P1) – Ensure that pages are usable when scripts, applets, or other programmatic objects are turned off or not supported. If this is not possible, provide equivalent information on an alternative accessible page.	Example: It is not possible to navigate through the objects in the left column when JavaScript is disabled.
Violation: Checkpoint 3.4 (P2) – Ensure that text size values are relative than absolute.	Example: Absolute sizing is used in many elements in the CSS. The size of the items in the upper menu do not resize when changing the size preferences in the browser. This may be a problem for people with low vision.

Barriers Walkthrough

The Barriers Walkthrough method (Brajnik, 2006) was inspired in the use of usability heuristics to perform walkthrough evaluations. The method is based on the concept of detection of *barriers* for users with different types of disabilities.

The method adopts the concept of an *accessibility barrier* as "any condition that hinders the user's progress towards the achievement of a goal" (Brajnik, 2006). The method provides evaluators with a list of possible barriers, which are described according to 1) the types of users and types of disabilities that may be affected, 2) the type of assistive technology being used, 3) the *failure mode* (activity or task that may be impacted by the barrier) and 4) the consequences of the occurrence of the barrier. The list of barriers to be used with the method is classified according to groups of users separated by types of disabilities.

With a pre-defined list of barriers defined by the method, the evaluation process involves four steps:

1. Define the relevant user categories
2. Define the user goals to be analysed with the correspondent pages to be tested and scenarios to be considered
3. Check the relevant barriers (according to the user categories defined) in the selected web pages
4. Assign a severity level for each of the occurrence of a barrier

In two experiments (Brajnik, 2006, 2008), a comparison between the checklist review and barriers walkthrough method showed the latter to be better in several aspects. The barriers walkthrough showed to be more precise (problems found are more prone to be true problems), to produce to a smaller number of reports of false problems and to be better to identify more severe problems.

However, according to the second experiment comparing the methods (Brajnik, 2008), barriers

walkthrough had low reliability between evaluators, as independent evaluators tend to produce different results. In particular, the barriers list provides a level of understanding to the evaluator as to what each of the barrier means, which could be advantageous for raising knowledge of accessibility in engineering teams. This is similar to other evaluation methods, and implies that more than one evaluator is required when using this method.

User Evaluation

In order to ensure that an application is accessible, the "gold standard" for evaluation is the *user evaluation*. In this section, the steps to preparing a typical user evaluation are discussed (Monk *et al.*, 1993, Stanton *et al.*, 2005) along with advice from the authors regarding minimum numbers of users to engage based on experience in evaluating websites for accessibility.

User Recruitment

One key aspect to user evaluation is recruiting people who are representative of those who are likely to use the web application. For purposes of evaluation, many web engineers will select people who surround them; in particular, people within the office or within the business. However, one of the key problems with this type of recruitment is that the participants such as these will bring biases to the table. These internal users share a common vocabulary and set of knowledge with the engineer that users do not have available. This type of bias can cause simple errors that would otherwise be revealed to go undetected as the internal participants rely on their own experiences and knowledge to compensate for errors.

Instead of this type of internal recruitment, it is critical that a target population of users be identified. This target audience should be people who will use the web application, but are separate from the development team. Similarly, if there are particular types of errors that are attempting to be detected, such as accessibility errors, then it is important that users who are likely to encounter these errors be engaged in evaluation. Indeed, it is only through users experiencing the web application through their own user agents and assistive technologies that the engineering team can truly understand accessibility errors.

Again, due to the daunting nature of having to recruit from such a large and varied population, evaluation may be bypassed entirely by a team. However, recent results, such as in the study conducted by the Disability Rights Commission (2004), showed that there was a large overlap between disability groups in terms of accessibility problems. While it is advisable to have as many people as possible evaluate a web application, *a minimal set* of 5 people from each of the following groups will reveal *some* of the critical accessibility errors:

- People who are blind and use a screen reader
- People who have low-vision and use a screen magnifier
- People who have severe dyslexia
- People who have upper body physical disabilities
- Mainstream users with no identified disability as a control group

While this set is not complete, notably missing people with hearing disabilities, it does account for individuals who will encounter many of the most common accessibility errors on web applications. Of course, it would be preferable to have people with hearing disabilities in the user group, and to have as many people as can be recruited participate in the evaluation.

Task Preparation

It is insufficient to seat a participant in front of a website or web application and ask them to "play around" on it. For proper data collection, and for proper identification of errors in the web application, it is necessary for the evaluator to prepare tasks in advance for people to complete. These tasks should be representative of the types of things that users are likely to do on the website, and should provide coverage of critical tasks.

When preparing tasks, it is essential that all members of the design team be involved so that the aspects of the web application (e.g. the web store, the contact information) that are most important to the stakeholders be evaluated. Once the critical tasks have been identified, broader tasks that are complex (such as a multi-page shopping page) may need to be broken down into sub-tasks and detailed instructions prepared for the participants. These tasks should be written in the users' language, not business terms, and they should be piloted with a few users to ensure that they are understandable. Finally, task length needs to be estimated to ensure that users are not conducting overly long evaluations[10]. An example of tasks that were created for the UK museum websites is presented in Table 2.

From these initial pilot tests, the evaluators can check to ensure that the data they are receiving makes sense as per what they are trying to find out about the web application. A simple example

Table 2. Tasks used to evaluate a set of museum websites

1. What time is the museum open on Sundays?
2. Are all floors of the museum accessible via a lift?
3. What will you find in the Wilkinson Collection?
4. Find the page to join the mailing list for the museum. Fill in the form, but only submit it if you actually do want to join the mailing list!
5. How much is a copy of "Getting Better: Stories from the History of Medicine" from the Museum shop?

is: if the evaluator is concerned about the time to completion of a task, a time record should be kept[11].

Running the Evaluation

When running an evaluation, the participant should be brought in at a time convenient for both the evaluator and the participant. They should be made comfortable[12] and given the opportunity to read a briefing form regarding the evaluation. This form should inform the participants what they will be doing, how they will be compensated, how their information will be used and what the risks to them, if any, are expected. This form should not provide detailed information about what the evaluation is attempting to uncover, as that may influence the participant. Finally, the participant should be informed that they may leave the evaluation at any point.

When the participant begins the tasks, the evaluator should record any issues they may encounter. The participant should be encouraged to voice their thoughts about what they are doing and why they are doing it, and in particular what problems they are encountering, in what is termed a "think-aloud protocol". This protocol will allow the evaluator to determine when problems occur, and provide an opportunity for questions to be asked. One possible way to record errors encountered is with a description of the magnitude of the problem encountered as per Nielsen's ratings (Nielsen & Mack, 1994):

- **Cosmetic:** A small problem that does not hinder the task
- **Minor:** A small problem that hinders the task, but the participant can continue
- **Major:** A large problem that hinders the task and the participant has difficulty recovering, but could complete the task if needed
- **Catastrophic:** A large problem that hinders the task to the point that the participant

would give up if it was encountered in the real world

When the tasks are completed, the participant should be provided with a debriefing form. This form should provide more detail about what the participant has completed and provide them with contact information if they have any further questions.

Summarize Results

It is beyond the scope of this chapter to discuss detailed techniques for qualitative and quantitative data analysis. However, the collection of comments and the magnitude rankings from the participants can be summarized to provide feedback to the web engineering team. This summarization should provide:

- An overall description of what types of participants were recruited
- a description of the tasks undertaken by the evaluation team
- a general statement about the web application in terms of what was evaluated (e.g. accessibility, usability etc.)
- a detailed list of problems encountered by participants, with magnitude ratings averaged

With this information the web engineering team can move into revision of their web application.

FUTURE TRENDS: INTEGRATING EVALUATION

The rapid growth of the number of web applications produced has motivated the specification of a number of approaches to make the development of such systems more disciplined. In the context of the Software Engineering discipline, the different aspects attributed to the development of web applications and websites have motivated the establishment of a special set of techniques and methods, which are the body of the Web Engineering discipline (Ginige & Murugesan, 2001). However, despite this rapid growth, evaluation of a website or web application is seldom mentioned as a concern.

In this section, the open question regarding where accessibility evaluation fits in existing Web Engineering and Software Engineering approaches is explored. Existing approaches are analysed in regards to their features, their proposed phases and the methodologies that are typically applied. Currently, there are no major case studies available discussing the success of integrating accessibility practices into any of the processes mentioned in this section. As such, the authors do not prescribe adopting any particular approach discussed in this section and instead opt to present possible places where accessibility could be integrated into each approach.

Web Engineering Processes

According to Deshpande *et al.* (2002), Web Engineering is regarded as "the systematic, structured and quantifiable application of methodological proposals to the development, evaluation and maintenance of web applications". Accordingly, a Web Engineering approach or method should provide basis for a solid process from requirements to evaluation for websites and web applications.

As a basis for this discussion, consider that Pressman (2005) defines that Web Engineering processes should involve activities covering Formulation, Planning, Analysis, Design (Architecture, Navigation and Interface), Generation, Testing and Evaluation. Although many of the existing methods provide good resources for some of these tasks, they do not provide enough guidance for all activities involved in the development cycle (Escalona *et al.*, 2007) (Domingues *et al.*, 2008), and the activities related to testing and evaluation are particularly pointed out as being

poorly addressed by current methods (Domingues *et al.*, 2008).

Early Web Engineering methods were mainly concerned with modelling issues. For example, the HDM (Hypermedia Design Model) (Garzotto *et al.*, 1993) presented an approach for modelling hypermedia applications by extending the entity-relationship model from database design. According to an analysis performed by Escalona *et al.* (2007), subsequent methods later extended methodological coverage to include implementation and page generation issues. These methods include: RMM (Relationship Management Method) (Isakowitz et. al, 1995), OOHDM (Object Oriented Hypermedia Design Method) (Schwabe & Rossi, 1998) and the WSDM (Website Design Method) (Troyer & Leune, 1998).

Besides the strong emphasis on modelling, the evolution of new methods has brought the inclusion of new tools and methods of the Web Engineering development life cycle. Languages such as WebML (Web Modelling Language) (Ceri *et al.*, 2000) and methods like OO-H (Object-Oriented Hypermedia Method) (Gómez *et al.*, 2001), have also included activities related to analysis and refinement of web application architectures. The methods W2000 (Baresi et. al, 2001) and UWE (UML-Based Web Engineering) (Koch, 2001) each include activities for analysis, design and implementation and also provide resources to help the activities for requirements elicitation.

However, while many of the above methods cover the development aspects of Pressman's description, they still fail to provide a solid foundation on which to perform testing and evaluation. Even the methods that do provide some sort of high-level guidance for testing are restricted to code testing issues (Domingues et. al, 2008). Evaluation with users and evaluation of accessibility issues seems to be absent from most of the methods. As a result, the current Web Engineering methodologies will need substantial extension to encompass and address accessible development.

Evaluation in Unified Processes for Web Engineering

For comparison to Web Engineering processes, the Unified Processes (UP) are examined here regarding their potential to have accessibility evaluations integrated into them.

Unified Processes provide a structure for managing both the risks incurred by a web engineering project and for addressing key issues such as requirements and testing. UPs can be adopted either formally through the use of particular techniques such as Use Cases and UML, as recommended by the Rational Unified Process (RUP) (Kruchten, 2003), or through a set of development principles as is seen in the Open Unified Process (OpenUP)

initiatives of the open source development community (Borg *et al.*, 2007).

Unified Processes focus on disciplines that consist of three key components: roles, work products and tasks. The roles that can be adopted within a project are key to understanding responsibility and accountability for particular tasks. Work products are the outputs of any particular task. There are several standard disciplines that are adopted in UP: business modeling, requirements, analysis and design, implementation, testing (code verification) all as core tasks, and deployment, management and maintenance practices as additional tasks (Kroll & Kruchten, 2003).

Figure 5 depicts an idealized version of UP (adapted from Kruchten, 2003). Each track in the

Figure 5. An idealized version of the UP lifecycle including the 6 disciplines of business modeling, requirements, analysis and design, implementation, test and deployment.

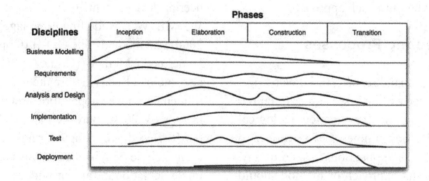

Figure 6. An idealized version of UP where evaluation has been added as a discipline to be managed in the project.

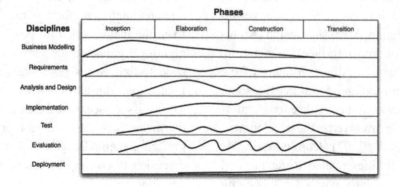

Figure 7. An idealized version of evaluation being included across disciplines in a project.

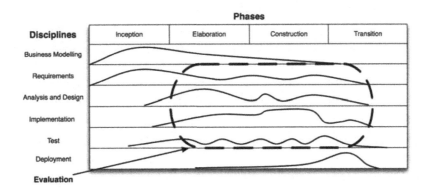

diagram represents the amount of team activity along the vertical axis, with one track per discipline. The horizontal axis represents the timeline of a project, with a website or web application moving four different phases. Inception focuses on the gathering and analysis of basic business case and capability that will be provided by the web application. Elaboration allows designers and developers to move initial designs and use cases into more detailed designs and prototypes. Construction focuses on the building of complex, hi-fidelity prototypes and then Transition moves the web application into a production ready state for deployment.

One approach to including accessibility evaluations would be to include accessibility professionals on the team who provide detailed evaluation reports as their only work products. These team members would review the outputs of other disciplines for accessibility concerns. This approach is depicted in Figure 6, where evaluation could be considered its own discipline, which has a flow similar to testing, where after initial elaboration there is a crucial evaluation of prototypes before entering into major implementation details. An iteration of construction would be followed by a period of code verification and then accessibility evaluation. Finally, it would be necessary to have a large integrated user evaluation just before deploying the software to end users, in the first transition period. This project configuration matches well

with the existing work in the literature on the Usability Engineering Lifecycle where emphasis is placed on design and evaluation of prototypes in iterative stages (Nielsen & Mack, 1994; Lif & Goransson, 2007).

In contrast, if each team member is familiar with accessibility evaluation practices, evaluations could be integrated into each of the design and implementation iterations. An idealization of this situation is presented in Figure 7. As can be seen, concerns about accessibility could also be integrated into the requirements phase, with careful review of the users and their needs and preferences being considered early in the project.

While this chapter focuses on primarily accessibility evaluation in the unified processes, it is perfectly reasonable that evaluation of other aspects such as usability or user experience could be integrated in a similar way to the two described project configurations.

Evaluation in Agile Processes for Web Engineering

In comparison to the heavy-weight processes associated with UP, the proponents of Agile Processes (AP) to software emphasize the need for flexibility when working in environments with volatile requirements. With the emphasis largely being on the process for producing software artifacts, agility has come to be embraced by people in various sectors, including business processes, management and production lines. All of these areas have taken on board aspects of the Agile Manifesto (Beck *et al.*, 2001), usually focusing on the fast turn around of prototypes and End-User engagement. One critical point is that the focus of AP is on the products being produced, not the process and roles that produce them.

Web engineering has long discussed the importance of such flexibility due to the very nature of web applications. With the need to flexibly build the software, infrastructure, information structure and the actual content, often centered on the needs of a particular business or domain model, makes web engineering projects perfect candidates for an AP (McDonald & Welland, 2004). Indeed, McDonald and Welland (2004) provide an overview of different Agile approaches in commercial web engineering systems, in which they identified 7 key characteristics that must be met by Agile Web Engineering (AWE) processes. Among these key characteristics, are:

- Evaluation with End-Users
- Rigorous validation testing against requirements

While the former encompasses the broader functional aspects of consulting End-Users on domain specific issues, such as business rules, there are examples where this includes evaluation of the usability aspect (Haire *et al.*, 2001). As such, the case certainly can be made that accessibility evaluation can be integrated seamlessly into AP. Further, the second characteristic emphasizes the importance of validation of user requirements for web applications. For accessibility to properly integrated into development approaches, it is essential that it become a fundamental aspect of requirements work, focusing on the needs of the users, and then on the systems to address them.

User-Centred Design (UCD) methodologies in AP have been introduced in several different places by usability researchers and practitioners with no

overarching vision of where these methodologies fit into AP emerging. Beyer *et al.* describe several different challenges with UCD in AP (Beyer *et al.*, 2004) and indirectly suggest that an ethnographic observation of users in context can provide much needed insights into user needs. Memmel *et al.* (2007) demonstrate in their work how AP can incorporate into Universal Access Design for older adults with rapid prototyping. Similarly, Meszaros and Aston (2006) provide an experience report on incorporating UCD and in particular evaluations through paper prototyping into an AP. Further work is presented regarding requirements acquisition for UCD in the paper by Duchting *et al.* (2007) where they observe neither Extreme Programming or Scrum based processes have sufficient focus on evaluation of usability principles. However, they also point to these AP as having the opportunity of exploiting the close ties between the development and design activities for purposes of delivering a high-quality, evaluated product. In the following, a selection of APs are presented with an examination of their key concepts and a discussion of how these concepts can be leveraged for evaluation of web applications.

Feature Driven Development (FDD) (Palmer & Felsing, 2002) presents a process that organizes development of web (and other) applications by feature. It concentrates on the identification of key features, and then the team focuses on designing and building a particular feature (or small set of features). FDD is unique in agile approaches in that it has a comprehensive management focus at the beginning of the process that allows designers and developers to focus on particular aspects of the software that is of particular concern. One challenge for accessibility proponents, much like the challenges faced by usability proponents, is to move accessibility requirements to be one of these chief concerns (Ambler, 2008).

The focus of FDD on fast turnaround teams for individual features provides a unique synergy with the above evaluation methodology in that accessibility can be addressed in each step in the FDD model for each individual feature. This provides for the opportunity to isolate particular pieces of an application and perform accessibility evaluations on it before integration. This results in a much smaller set of accessibility issues at integration time with, in theory, only transitions between features needing to be checked for accessibility requirements. All of the types of accessibility evaluations can rigorously applied to each feature in the FDD process, with the advantage that user evaluations for individual features will lessen the time commitment for each individual participant at any given time. However, due to the need to conduct user evaluations on the smaller components and then, most importantly, at integration, there are challenges that must be addressed in recruitment and retention of users for testing.

The Dynamic Systems Development Method (DSDM) being one of the oldest of the APs has some of the highest uptake in industry, and thus has some of the best understood processes (Stapleton, 2003). With DSDM, the project begins with an understanding of the domain in which the application is to be built, with a focus on understanding the feasibility and business cases for the application being developed. DSDM provides three broad states that a prototype moves through. The Functional Model Iteration focuses on the rapid development of prototypes for review, after which the prototype can evolve in the Design and Build state in which the prototype is evaluated iteratively by users. Finally, in the Implementation state the prototype is transferred from development to production, with users being trained in its operation.

Certainly DSDM contains many of the broad aspects of evaluation model above, and the basic principles of understanding the needs of the users, conducting prototype design development and then evaluation. Indeed, it perhaps embodies best the ideals behind user involvement and evaluation, introducing users and their input in the process from the beginning. Indeed, this is supported

by the large number of developers who concern themselves with usability aspects of their software (Bygstad *et al.*, 2007).

For purposes of accessibility testing, there are more difficult challenges that need to be managed in comparison to FDD. In DSDM, the entire system is being developed in a sequence of small, fast iterations. This results in relying more heavily on automated and expert testing as having users test an entire large application at each iteration is likely infeasible.

Extreme Programming (XP) (Beck, 2000) is inherently centered on the development of software (and thus web) artifacts. A combination of practices, such as pair programming, refactoring and the use of metaphors for development are used in short cycles of iterative development. With XP being one of the most well-known APs it is natural to ask: where in this development centric process the evaluation model presented fit?

There are several practices within XP that could be exploited for purposes of including all aspects of the evaluation methodology above. Certainly, there is a case to be made that users are represented and understood through the use of user written *User Stories* detailing how the application should behave in real-world environments. Much like FDD, these User Stories drive the development, allowing users and develops to select functionality that will be developed in the next iteration of development. Further, user stories mesh nicely with many well-known scenario based design techniques used in UCD (Wolkerstorfer *et al.*, 2008). The engineering systems with minimal design, foregoing the inclusion of future extension, and a practice of refactoring to keep functionality sets relatively small and fit-to-purpose certainly indicate that evaluation of prototypes with a critical eye is already being done in this AP. Finally, the necessity of keeping short releases of small chunks of functionality seems to blend the advantages of FDD with some of the process advantages of DSDM for purposes of evaluation.

When looking at accessibility, it is clear that automated testing is an option for XP teams. With the heavy emphasis in XP that is placed on the output of working code, it is natural, and indeed within the philosophy of many APs, for developers to use automated tools to produce reports on accessibility. However, the responsibility of interpretation of these reports and the impact of such analysis is unclear as the role responsible for such analysis is not clear in XP. Certainly there are places where expert evaluation and user evaluation of accessibility could be integrated into an XP environment, but whether this is in scope of XP, where the focus is code artifacts, also remains unclear. Finally, the key XP practice of adopting coding standards for a given application is very attractive in web application development; however, for accessibility professionals this raises the concern of developers slavishly following coding guidelines for conformance, which is insufficient for access, as opposed to being focused on the outcomes for the user.

When looking at Agile Processes, there is a lot of potential for integrating accessibility and other types of UCD criteria into the processes. Indeed, there is a great deal of interest from the UCD community in the increased presence of users and their needs into APs. However, there are several reports of challenges that have yet to be addressed in agile environments. There have been experience reports of developer dominance, where developers override the judgment and expertise of other types of analysts (Gerber *et al.*, 2007). Given the challenges already faced in getting accessibility concerns into development environments, this is very concerning. Further, there are reports of coding standards being poorly adopted, which is of concern when considering the technical accessibility of a website (Tingling & Saeed, 2007). Finally, the role of interface design and evaluation in APs is relatively poorly understood, with only a moderate amount of work investigating these crucial aspects of software design (Ferreira *et al.*, 2007; Lee, 2007; Obendorf & Finck, 2008; Wolkerstorfer *et al.*, 2008).

CONCLUSION

In this chapter, the authors have presented an overview of accessibility evaluation and its role in the web engineering process.

It has presented a view of accessibility from the point of view of the users and their goals, and what challenges they are presented with when interacting with web applications. These challenges were related to the technologies through which the user interacts with as well as the types of content present in web applications. A case has been made that users that encounter accessibility issues on websites, be they people with disabilities or older adults, represent a large market that is going to become more important in the knowledge economy.

This chapter has presented the major types of accessibility evaluation that are available to web designers/developers. The evaluation techniques, whether they involve expert inspections, automated evaluation tools or users evaluations all provide the opportunity to identify accessibility issues that may arise after a website or web application is deployed.

Finally, the chapter presented an analysis of the current state of web engineering and software engineering processes regarding evaluation. This analysis has produced a list of opportunities for web engineers as to how to integrate accessibility evaluations into existing processes in order to ensure that web pages, websites and web applications are created that everyone can use, independent of user preferences for access.

REFERENCES

Agarwal, R., & Venkatesh, V. (2002). Assessing a Firm's Web Presence: A Heuristic Evaluation Procedure for the Measurement of Usability. *Information Systems Research, 13*(2), 168–186. doi:10.1287/isre.13.2.168.84

Ambler, S. W. (2008). Tailoring Usability into Agile Software Development Projects. In *Maturing Usability* (pp. 75-95). Berlin: Springer.

Baresi, L., Garzotto, F., & Paolini, P. (2001). Extending UML for modeling Web applications. In *Proceedings of the 34th Annual Hawaii International Conference on System Sciences* (pp. 1285-1294).

Beck, K. (2000). *Extreme Programming Explained--Embrace Change*. Reading, MA: Addison-Wesley.

Beck, K., Beedle, M., van Bennekum, A., Cockburn, A., & Cunningham, W. (2001). *Manifesto for agile software development: Agile Manifesto Website*. Retrieved 01/2009 from http://agile-manifesto.org/

Becker, S. A. (2002). An Exploratory Study on Web Usability and the Internationalizational of US E-Businesses. *Journal of Electronic Commerce Research*, *3*(4), 265–278.

Benavídez, C., Fuertes, J. L., Gutiérrez, E., & Martínez, L. (2006). Semi-Automatic Evaluation of Web Accessibility with HERA 2.0. In *Proceedings of the 10th International Conference on Computers Helping People with Special Needs (ICCHP 2006)* (pp. 199-106). Berlin: Springer.

Beyer, H., Holtzblatt, K., & Baker, L. (2004). An Agile Customer-Centered Method: Rapid Contextual Design. In *Extreme Programming and Agile Methods - XP/Agile Universe 2004. Proceedings,* (pp. 50-59). Berlin: Springer.

Borg, A., Sandahl, K., & Patel, M. (2007). Extending the OpenUP/Basic Requirements Discipline to Specify Capacity Requirements. In *15th IEEE Internationalm, Requirements Engineering Conference, 2007 (RE '07), Proceedings*. Washington, DC: IEEE.

Brajnik, G. (2004). Comparing accessibility evaluation tools: a method for tool effectiveness. *Univers. Access Inf. Soc.*, *3*(3), 252–263. doi:10.1007/s10209-004-0105-y

Brajnik, G. (2006). Web Accessibility Testing: When the Method Is the Culprit. In *Proceedings of 10th International Conference on Computers Helping People with Special Needs* (pp. 156-163). Berlin: Springer.

Brajnik, G. (2008). A comparative test of web accessibility evaluation methods. In *Assets '08: Proceedings of the 10th international ACM SIGACCESS conference on Computers and accessibility* (pp. 113-120). Berlin: ACM.

Bygstad, B., Ghinea, G., & Brevik, E. (2007). Systems Development Methods and Usability in Norway: An Industrial Perspective. In *Usability and Internationalization. HCI and Culture. Proceedings,* (pp. 258-266). Berlin: Springer.

Caldwell, B., Cooper, M., Reid, L. G., & Vanderheiden, G. (2008). *Web content accessibility guidelines 2.0*: World Wide Web Consortium. Retrieved June, 2009 from http://www.w3.org/TR/WCAG20/

Ceri, S., Fraternali, P., & Bongio, A. (2000). Web Modeling Language (WebML): a modeling language for designing Web sites. *Computer Networks, 33*(1-6), 137 - 157.

Chisholm, W., Vanderheiden, G., & Jacobs, I. (1999). *Web content accessibility guidelines 1.0: World Wide Web Consortium*. Retrieved June, 2009 from http://www.w3.org/TR/WCAG10/

Choi, Y. S., Yi, J. S., Law, C. M., & Jacko, J. A. (2006). Are universal design resources designed for designers? In *Assets '06: Proceedings of the 8th international ACM SIGACCESS conference on Computers and accessibility* (pp. 87-94). New York: ACM.

Cluster, W. A. B. (2007). *Unified Web Evaluation Methodology (UWEM 1.2)*. Retrieved 01/2009 from www.w3c.org

Deshpande, Y., Murugesan, S., Ginige, A., Hansen, S., Schwabe, D., & Gaedke, M. (2002). Web Engineering. *Journal of Web Engineering, 1*(1), 3–17.

Disability Rights Commission. (2004). *The Web: access and inclusion for disabled people*. London: The Stationery Office.

Dix, A., Finlay, J. E., Abowd, G. D., & Beale, R. (2003). *Human-Computer Interaction* (3rd ed.). Upper Saddle River, NJ: Prentice Hall.

Domingues, A. L. S., Bianchini, S. L., Re, R., & Ferrari, R. G. (2008). A Comparison Study of Web Development Methods. In *Proceedings of the 34th Latin-American Conference on Informatics* (pp. 10).

Düchting, M., Zimmermann, D., & Nebe, K. (2007). Incorporating User Centered Requirement Engineering into Agile Software Development. In *Human-Computer Interaction. Interaction Design and Usability. Proceedings.* (pp. 58-67). Springer.

Escalona, M. J., & Torres, J., MejÌas, M., GutiÈrrez, J. J., & Villadiego, D. (2007). The treatment of navigation in web engineering. *Advances in Engineering Software, 38*(4), 267–282. doi:10.1016/j. advengsoft.2006.07.006

Fels, D. I., Richards, J., Hardman, J., Soudian, S., & Silverman, C. (2004). American sign language of the web. In *CHI '04 Extended Abstracts on Human Factors in Computing Systems* CHI '04 (pp. 1111-1114). New York: ACM.

Ferreira, J., Noble, J., & Biddle, R. (2007). Agile Development Iterations and UI Design. In *Proceedings AGILE Conference,* (pp. 50-58). Washington, DC: IEEE.

Freire, A. P., Goularte, R., & de Mattos Fortes, R. P. (2007). Techniques for developing more accessible web applications: a survey towards a process classification. In *SIGDOC '07: Proceedings of the 25th annual ACM international conference on Design of communication* (pp. 162-169). New York: ACM.

Freire, A. P., Russo, C. M., & Fortes, R. P. M. (2008). A survey on the accessibility awareness of people involved in web development projects in Brazil. In *W4A '08: Proceedings of the 2008 international cross-disciplinary conference on Web accessibility (W4A)* (pp. 87-96). New York: ACM.

Garzotto, F., Paolini, P., & Schwabe, D. (1993). HDM--a model-based approach to hypertext application design. *ACM Transactions on Information Systems, 11*(1), 1–26. doi:10.1145/151480.151483

Gerber, A., Van Der Merwe, A., & Alberts, R. (2007). Practical implications of rapid development methodologies. In *Proceedings Computer Science and Information Technology Education Conference.*

Ginige, A., & Murugesan, S. (2001). Web engineering: an introduction. *Multimedia, IEEE, 8*(1), 14–18. doi:10.1109/93.923949

Ginige, A., & Murugesan, S. (2001). Guest Editors' Introduction: Web Engineering - An Introduction. *IEEE MultiMedia, 8*(1), 14–18. doi:10.1109/93.923949

Gómez, J., Cachero, C., & Pastor, O. (2001). Conceptual Modeling of Device-Independent Web Applications. *IEEE MultiMedia, 8*(2), 26–39. doi:10.1109/93.917969

Haire, B., Henderson-Sellers, B., & D., a. L. (2001). Supporting web development in the OPEN process: additional tasks. In *Proceedings COMPSAC'2001: International Computer Software and Applications Conference.* New York: ACM.

Harrison, C., & H., P. (2006). Impact of usability and accessibility problems in e-commerce and e-government websites. In *Proceedings HCI 2006.* (Vol. 1). London: British Computer Society.

Hesse, W. (2003). Dinosaur meets Archaeopteryx? or: Is there an alternative for Rational's Unified Process? *Software and Systems Modeling, Springer, 2*(4), 240–247. doi:10.1007/s10270-003-0033-y

Isakowitz, T. a., Stohr, E. A., & Balasubramanian, P. (1995). RMM: a methodology for structured hypermedia design. *Communications of the ACM, 38*(8), 34–44. doi:10.1145/208344.208346

Ivory, M. Y. (2003). *Automated Web Site Evaluation: Researchers and Practitioners Perspectives.* Amsterdam: Kluwer Academic Publishers.

Ivory, M. Y., & Hearst, M. A. (2001). The state of the art in automating usability evaluation of user interfaces. *ACM Computing Surveys, 33*(4), 470–516. doi:10.1145/503112.503114

Kennaugh, P., & Petrie, H. (2006). *Enhanced Access to Television (EAT): humanITy.*

Koch, N. (2001). *Software engineering for adaptive hypermedia applications.* Munich, Germany: Uni-Druck Publishing Company.

Koch, N., & Kraus, A. (2003). Towards a Common Metamodel for the Development of Web Applications. In *Web Engineering* (pp. 419-422). Berlin: Springer.

Kroll, P., & Kruchten, P. (2003). *The Rational Unified Process Made Easy: A Practitioner's Guide to the RUP.* Reading, MA: Addison-Wesley.

Kruchten, P. (2003). *The Rational Unified Process: An Introduction.* Reading, MA: Addison-Wesley.

Kurniawan, S. H. (2003). Aging. In *Web Accessibility: A foundation for research* (pp.47-58). Berlin: Springer

Lazar, J., Dudley-Sponaugle, A., & Greenidge, K. (2004). Improving Web Accessibility: A Study of Webmaster Perceptions. *Computers in Human Behavior, 20*(2), 269–288. doi:10.1016/j.chb.2003.10.018

Lee, J. C., & McCrickard, D. S. (2007). Towards Extreme(ly) Usable Software: Exploring Tensions Between Usability and Agile Software Development. In *Proceedings AGILE Conference,* (pp. 59-71). Berlin: IEEE.

Lif, M., & Goransson, B. (2007). Usability Design: A New Rational Unified Process Discipline. In *Proceedings Human-Computer Interaction; INTERACT 2007,* (pp. 714-715). New York: ACM.

Mariage, C., & Vanderdonckt, J. (2005). Creating Contextualised Usability Guides for Web Sites Design and Evaluation. *Computer-Aided Design of User Interfaces, IV,* 147–158. doi:10.1007/1-4020-3304-4_12

Martens, A. (2003). Usability of Web Services. *International Conference on Web Information Systems Engineering Workshops,* (pp. 182-190). Washington, DC: IEEE.

McDonald, A., & Welland, R. (2004). Evaluation of Commercial Web Engineering Processes. In *Web Engineering* (pp. 166-170). Berlin: Springer.

Memmel, T., Reiterer, H., & Holzinger, A. (2007). Agile Methods and Visual Specification in Software Development: A Chance to Ensure Universal Access. In *Proceedings of Universal Access in Human Computer Interaction Coping with Diversity.* (pp. 453-462). Berlin: Springer.

Meszaros, G., & Aston, J. (2006). Adding usability testing to an agile project. In *Proceedings of Agile Conference, 2006.* Washington, DC: IEEE.

Mohamad, Y., Stegemann, D., Koch, J., & Velasco, C. A. (2004). imergo: Supporting Accessibility and Web Standards to Meet the Needs of the Industry via Process-Oriented Software Tools. In *Proceedings of the 9th International Conference on Computers Helping People With Special Needs (ICCHP 2004)*, (pp. 310-316). Berlin: Springer.

Monk, A., Wright, P., Haber, J., & Davenport, L. (1993). *Improving your human-computer interface: a practical technique*. Bath, UK: Redwood Books.

Motschnig-Pitrik, R. (2002). Employing the Unified Process for Developing a Web-Based Application - A Case-Study. In *Practical Aspects of Knowledge Management: 4th International Conference, PAKM 2002 Vienna, Austria, December 2-3, 2002, Proceedings*, (pp. 97-113). Berlin: Springer.

Ncube, C., Lockerbie, J., & Maiden, N. A. M. (2007). Automatically Generating Requirements from \it * Models: Experiences with a Complex Airport Operations System. In *Proceedings REFSQ*, (pp. 33-47).

Nielsen, J., & Mack, R. (1994). Usability Inspection Methods (pp. 448p). New York, NY.

Obendorf, H., & Finck, M. (2008). Scenario-based usability engineering techniques in agile development processes. In *CHI '08: CHI '08 extended abstracts on Human factors in computing systems* (pp. 2159-2166). New York: ACM.

Paddison, C., & Englefield, P. (2004). Applying heuristics to accessibility inspections. *Interacting with Computers*, *16*(3), 507–521. doi:10.1016/j.intcom.2004.04.007

Palmer, J. W. (2002). Web site usability, design, and performance metrics. *Information Systems Research*, *13*(2), 151–167. doi:10.1287/isre.13.2.151.88

Palmer, S. R., & Felsing, J. M. (2002). *A Practical Guide to Feature-Driven Development*. Upper Saddle River, NJ: Prentice Hall PTR.

Petrie, H., Hamilton, F., King, N., & Pavan, P. (2006). Remote usability evaluations with disabled people. In *CHI '06: Proceedings of the SIGCHI conference on Human Factors in computing systems* (pp. 1133-1141). New York: ACM.

Petrie, H., & Kheir, O. (2007). The relationship between accessibility and usability of websites. In *CHI '07: Proceedings of the SIGCHI conference on Human factors in computing systems* (pp. 397-406). New York: ACM.

Petrie, H., King, N., & Hamilton, F. (2005). *Accessibility of museum, library and archive websites: the MLA audit*. Retrieved 01/2009 from http://www.mla.gov.uk/webdav/harmonise?Page/@id=73&Document/@id=23090&Section%5B@stateId_eq_left_hand_root%5D/@id=4302

Petrie, H., Weber, G., & Fisher, W. (2005). Personalization, interaction and navigation in rich multimedia documents for print disabled users. In *IBM Systems Journal*. Armonk NY: IBM.

Pressman, R. (2006). *Software Engineering: A Practitioner's Approach* (6th ed.). New York: McGraw-Hill.

San Murugesan, Y. D., Hansen, S., & Ginige, A. (2001). Web Engineering: A New Discipline for Development of Web-Based Systems. In *Web Engineering Managing Diversity and Complexity of Web Application Development*, (LNCS Vol. 2016, pp. 3-13). Berlin: Springer.

Schwabe, D., & Rossi, G. (1998). An object oriented approach to web-based applications design. *Theory and Practice of Object Systems*, *4*(4), 207–225. doi:10.1002/(SICI)1096-9942(1998)4:4<207::AID-TAPO2>3.0.CO;2-2

Shneiderman, B. (1998). *Designing the User Interface*. Reading, MA: Addison-Wesley.

Shneiderman, B. (2000). Universal usability. *Communications of the ACM, 43*(5), 85–91. doi:10.1145/332833.332843

Shneiderman, B. (2003). Promoting universal usability with multi-layer interface design. In *Proceedings of the 2003 Conference on Universal Usability (CUU 2003)*. New York: ACM.

Soares, K., & Furtado, E. (2003). RUPi - A Unified Process that Integrates Human-Computer Interaction and Software Engineering. In *Workshop Bridging the Gap Between Software-Engineering and Human-Computer Interaction at ICSE 2003, Proceedings,* (pp. 41-48).

Sousa, K., & Furtado, E. (2005). A Unified Process Supported by a Framework for the Semi-Automatic Generation of Multi-Context UIs. In *12th International Workshop on Design, Proceedings*.

Sousa, K., Mendonça, H., & Vanderdonckt, J. (2007). Towards Method Engineering of Model-Driven User Interface Development. In *Task Models and Diagrams for User Interface Design* (pp. 112-125). Berlin: Springer.

Stanton, N. A., Salmon, P. M., Walker, G. H., Baber, C., & Jenkins, D. P. (2005). *Human Factors Methods: A Practical Guide for Engineering and Design*. London: Ashgate.

Stapleton, J. (2003). *DSDM: Business Focused Development* (2nd ed.). Harlow, UK.: Addison-Wesley.

Thatcher, J., Waddell, C. D., Henry, S. L., Swierenga, S., Urban, M. D., Burks, M., et al. (2003). *Constructing accessible web sites*. San Francisco: glasshaus.

Tingling, P., & Saeed, A. (2007). Extreme Programming in Action: A Longitudinal Case Study. In *Human-Computer Interaction. Interaction Design and Usability, Proceedings,* (pp. 242-251).

Troyer, O. M. F. D., & Leune, C. J. (1998). WSDM: a user centered design method for Web sites. *Computer Networks and ISDN Systems, 30*(1-7), 85 - 94.

Watanabe, T. (2007). Experimental evaluation of usability and accessibility of heading elements. In *Proceedings of International Cross-Disciplinary Conference on Web Accessibility (W4A)* (pp. 157-164). New York: ACM Press.

Wolkerstorfer, P., Tscheligi, M., Sefelin, R., Milchrahm, H., Hussain, Z., Lechner, M., et al. (2008). Probing an agile usability process. In *CHI '08: Extended abstracts on Human factors in computing systems Proceedings,* (pp. 2151-2158). New York: ACM.

Yesilada, Y., Stevens, R., Goble, C. A., & Hussein, S. (2004). Rendering tables in audio: the interaction of structure and reading styles. In *Proceedings of the ACM SIGACCESS Conference on Computers and Accessibility (ASSETS),* (pp. 16-23). Berlin: Springer.

ENDNOTES

[1] The authors acknowledge that even though the community may have taken on board the concept of usability it is often the case that usability is not achieved in websites.

[2] This is the original definition of accessibility used by the Web Accessibility Initiative.

[3] Screen readers are assistive technology software that transform text, controls and other aspects of the screen into audio.

[4] The authors recommend the website http://shouldiusetablesforlayout.com/ which has a discussion on this topic.

[5] During preparation of this chapter the authors checked one UK mobile phone company website and found over 100 links on the home page.

6   These evaluations were completed using WCAG 1.0 guidelines.

7   Checkpoints in WCAG 1.0, Success Criteria in WCAG 2.0.

8   Available at http://wave.webaim.org, last access on June 1, 2009

9   http://www.sidar.org/hera/index.php.en, last access on June 1, 2009

10   The authors strive for keeping evaluations for each participant under 1 hour for the completion of all tasks. Experience has shown that beyond this will affect the concentration level of the participant.

11   Sadly, the authors have seen this particular error in several evaluation protocols that have already been completed testing with their users with no time data being recorded.

12   Comfortable within reason; some older books comment that participants should be offered a cigarette. The authors find a cup of tea is often sufficient.

Chapter 8
Usability Methodologies for Spoken Dialogue Web Interfaces

Dimitris Spiliotopoulos
University of Athens, Greece

Georgios Kouroupetroglou
University of Athens, Greece

ABSTRACT

This chapter presents the state-of-the-art in usability issues and methodologies for spoken dialogue web interfaces along with the appropriate designer-needs analysis. It is planned to unfold a theoretical perspective to the usability methodology and provide a framework description for creating and testing usable content and applications for conversational interfaces. Main concerns include the problem identification of design issues for usability design and evaluation, the use of customer experience for the design of voice-web interfaces and dialogue, and the problems that arise from real-life deployment. Moreover, it discusses the hands-on approaches for applying usability methodologies in a spoken dialogue web application environment, including methodological and design issues, resource management, implementation using existing technologies for usability evaluation in several stages of the design and deployment.

INTRODUCTION

Web technology is rapidly reaching maturity making its use practically possible for most applications by the majority of potential users in the recent years. With high speed internet availability providing access to demanding multimodal services to all homes, most people can reap the benefits of real-time services ranging from voice banking to online socialising and beyond. Most high-level services are provided solely through web pages in the traditional point-and-click manner. In an effort to boost *customer experience* most providers deploy spoken dialogue interfaces as a means to increased naturalness of information access.

Due to the complexity of natural language interaction, it is becoming very important to build spoken language interfaces as easily as possible using the enabling technologies. However, not all technologies involved in the process are of the same

DOI: 10.4018/978-1-60566-896-3.ch008

maturity, let alone standardisation. Furthermore, there are only a handful of platforms available for building such systems. Given the range, variability and complexity of the actual business cases it is obvious that the enabling technologies may produce working systems of variable usefulness due to design and/or implementation limitations.

As with all human-computer interfaces, speech-based interfaces are built with the target user in mind, based on the requirements analysis. However, they differ from the traditional graphical user interfaces and web interfaces. The use of speech as the main input and output mode necessitates the use of *dialogue* for the human-machine communication and information flow. Information is received by the speech interface and presented to the user in chunks, much alike a dialogue between two humans. The input is recognised, interpreted, managed, and the response is constructed and uttered using speech. The naturalness is indeed far more enhanced than using forms and buttons on a traditional web interface. But, is the user satisfaction similarly improved? Does the performance of the resulting application meet the user requirements? How is usability ensured by design and verified by evaluation in a spoken dialogue web interface?

This chapter discusses the background of speech-based human-computer interaction and elaborates on the spoken dialogue interfaces. It explores what usability is and how it is ensured for natural language interaction interface design and implementation, both from the designer and the application deployment (business use) points of view. Finally, it presents methodologies for usability testing of spoken dialogue web interfaces.

BACKGROUND

People use the web and engage in several different activities, information retrieval, problem solving, entertainment, social interaction, personal, work, etc. Human-computer interaction is the study of interactive communication between humans and computers. People acquire communicative skills over time through the experience of using and operating the user interfaces. As the level of user adeptness rises, the speed and accuracy of the operation increases. The user adapts to the system and interacts more efficiently. The level of absolute efficiency corresponds to the actual system design, and can be assessed either as a full system or as a breakdown of its fundamental design modules or processes. In order to evaluate usability of such interfaces it is important to understand their design requirements and their architecture. The architecture of most applications falls into specific interaction frameworks, described below.

Multimodal Interaction

A general framework (Larson et al., 2003) for the description and discussion of multimodal interaction on the web is developed by the World Wide Web Consortium (W3C). It describes the input and output modes that can be used in a relational abstractive architecture that includes all component types required for the interaction.

In such framework, an application may handle several requests through one or more input modes and respond accordingly. The user may use their input options to make a request for an archive retrieval, the system may respond by either requesting an explicit verification or present all options from the retrieval function, the user may specify or select their preference, allowing the application to present the information. Consider the following examples:

Example 1:

User: "I would like to see highlights from the 2008 Olympic Games, please." [spoken input]

System: "Please specify the sport category." [spoken output]

User: "Tennis." [spoken input]

System: (*starts showing highlights*) [screen output]

Figure 1. The multimodal interactive framework

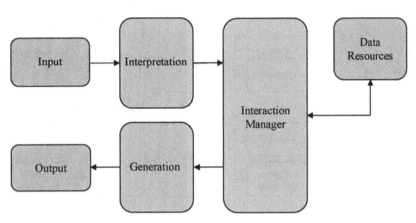

Example 2:

User: (*selects event: olympic_games, sport: tennis, action: highlights*) [keyboard input]

System: (*shows available video thumbnails for selection sorted by date*) [screen output]

User: (*clicks a thumbnail*) [pointing device input]

System: (*starts showing highlights*) [screen output]

The above short examples illustrate how a web interface handles an interaction. In the former example the interaction is achieved through speech, while in the latter using other input methods. Both examples can be serviced by an application within the multimodal interaction framework. Figure 1 illustrates the basic components:

- **Input and output:** The entry and exit points of the information. In multimodal environments the input may be through various modes such as haptics, keyboard, pointing devices, speech, audio, handwriting, special accessibility devices, Dual-Tone Multi-Frequency (DTMF) signal, etc.

- **Interpretation:** Processes the input using specialized modules for each type of input. In effect, the input is analyzed and its semantic and pragmatic meaning is channeled to the system manager.

- **Generation:** Creates the appropriate output for the system response. It translates from the internal system representation to a usable response for the user. It decides how that information would best be rendered by the most suitable output mode or combination of output modes.

- **Interaction manager:** It is the most complicated component comprising of several modules that handle the interaction state, the system information, the data resources, the validation and verification of input and response data, the process management, the business model, the user experience, the application functions, the environment variables, and many more.

- **Data resources:** The data pools, databases, web services and any external information needed or requested by the system in order to fulfill the information requests and data flow.

More information on multimodal dialogue can be found in the latest literature (Kuppevelt et al., 2005; Walster, 2006).

Speech-Based Interaction

The use of speech as input/output for interaction requires a spoken language oriented framework

Figure 2. Spoken dialogue interface framework

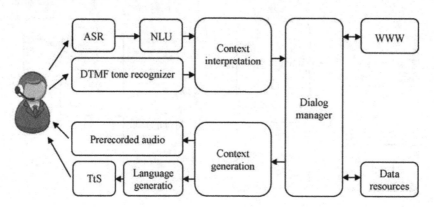

that adequately describes the system processes. W3C has defined the Speech Interface Framework to represent the typical components of a speech-enabled web application (Larson, 2000).

Speech-based interaction is context-dependent. The context of the user input is analysed by the system in an attempt to understand the *meaning* and *semantics* within the application domain. The interaction itself is called a *dialogue*. Spoken dialogue interfaces handle human-machine dialogue using natural language as the main input and output. A general depiction of a Spoken Dialogue Interface is shown in Figure 2.

Broadly speaking, a generic dialogue system comprises of three modules:

- **Input:** Commonly includes automatic speech recognition (ASR) and natural language understanding (NLU). The ASR converts the acoustic user input into text while the NLU parses the text in order to semantically interpret it. Additionally, a DTMF tone recognizer may be included in order to allow for such input.
- **Dialogue management:** Is the core of the dialogue system. It handles a unique and complete conversation with the user, evaluating the input and creating the output. In order to do that, it activates and coordinates a series of processes that evaluate

the user prompt. The dialogue manager (DM) identifies the communicative act, interprets and disambiguates the NLU output and creates a specific dialogue strategy in order to respond. It maintains the state of the dialogue (or belief state), formulates a dialogue plan and employs the necessary dialogue actions in order to fulfil the plan. The DM is also connected to all external resources, back-end database and world knowledge.

- **Output:** Usually includes a natural language generator (NLG) coupled with a text-to-speech synthesizer (TtS). The NLG renders the dialogue manager output from communicative acts to proper written language while the TtS engine converts the text to speech and/or audio. A lot of applications, for the sake of customer satisfaction, use prerecorded audio queues instead of synthetic speech for output. In that case, the dialogue manager forms the output by registering all text prompts and correlating them with prerecorded audio files.

More on the speech-based interaction enabling technologies can be found in respective textbooks (Dybkjær et al., 2007; Dybkjær & Minker, 2008; Tatham & Morton, 2005)

Spoken Dialogue Web Interfaces and Voice Browsers

Before entering the usability realm, there are several principles and notions governing the spoken dialogue web interfaces and voice browsers. Humans have the ability to communicate with certain complexity. The most natural way of doing so is with the use of natural language. Speech is the direct product of the communication and dialogue denotes the interaction between two or more participants. Non-speech web interfaces use modalities other than speech to communicate. The underlying philosophy of the web interface designer is directly dependent on the mode of communication. In effect, the same service would be designed and implemented in much different way if the hosting platform was a traditional point-and-click web interface than a speech-based one.

For a spoken language dialogue system, the communicative skills of the system are explicitly encoded by a dialogue designer. A good designer defines the core methods that are collectively known as dialogue management according to the given requirements. The design requirements are set by the application functional requirements. All applications have intrinsic *business logic* associated with their basic functions. This means that any application interface should accommodate and handle all functions in a specific way.

Let us consider a request for a typical customer service speech-based application. Such request includes specific directives about handling the various user types, the type of dialogue and attitude for the interaction, the actual tasks that the system should perform (perhaps even comparing to existing services), performance requirements and, most importantly, *acceptance criteria*. The acceptance criteria typically include the performance and reliability factors as well as the user experience evaluation. The latter would most probably count twice as much towards the final product acceptance. It is only fair, after all, for the user experience to be the most valuable factor in a human-machine interface evaluation.

When building a speech-based human-computer interaction system, certain basic modules must be present. The Dialogue Manager is responsible for the system behavior, control and strategy. In general, a dialogue with a machine is a sequential process and contains multiple turns that can be initiated by the machine (system initiative), the user (user initiative), or both (mixed initiative). The ASR and NLU recognize the spoken input and identify semantic values. The language generator and TtS or the prerecorded audio generator provides the system response. The dialogue is usually restricted within the thematic domain of the particular application. The performance of the particular modules is an indication of usability issues. The ASR accuracy and the lack of language understanding due to out-of-grammar utterances or ambiguity hinder the spoken dialogue. Moreover, the lack of pragmatic competence of the dialogue manager (compared to the human brain) and the response generation modules sometimes overcomplicate the dialogue and frustrate the user.

In our analysis, voice browsers can be considered as a subset of the spoken dialogue web interface description. Voice browsers are, by design, system-directed (or even user-directed) dialogue applications with a very limited domain and limited dialogue strategy. They are meant to provide the means to browse information and navigate web documents. In this case, dialogue management complexity is not a demand. In this respect, the usability requirements and evaluation methods for spoken dialogue web interfaces discussed later in this chapter also apply to voice browsers.

Interested readers may are refer to spoken dialogue textbooks for further reading (Bernsen et al., 1998; Jurafsky & Martin, 2000; Huang et al., 2001; McTear, 2004).

USABILITY FOR SPEECH-BASED SYSTEMS

The term usability has been used for many years to denote that an application or interface is *user friendly, easy-to-use*. These general terms apply to most interfaces, including web interfaces and more importantly speech-based web interfaces. Usability is measured according to the attributes that describe it, as explained below (Rubin & Chisnell, 2008):

- **Usefulness:** Measures the level of *task enablement* of the application. As a side result, it determines the *will* of the user to actually use it for the purpose it was designed for.
- **Efficiency:** Assesses the *speed, accuracy* and *completeness* of the tasks or the user goals. This is particularly useful for evaluating an interface sub-system since the tasks may be broken down in order to evaluate each module separately.
- **Effectiveness:** Quantifies the system *behaviour*. It is a user-centric measure that calculates whether the system behaves the way the users expect it to. It also rates the system according to the level of *effort* required by the user to achieve certain goals and respective *difficulty*.
- **Learnability:** It extends the effectiveness of the system or application by evaluating the user effort required to do specific tasks over several repetitions or time for training and expertise. It is a key measure of user experience since most users expect to be able to use an interface effortlessly after a period of use.
- **Satisfaction:** It is a subjective set of parameters that the users are asked to estimate and rank. It encompasses the user overall *opinion* about an application based on whether the product meets their *needs* and performs *adequately*.
- **Accessibility:** In the strict sense, it is not part of the usability description. As a starting point, it is a totally different approach on system design. Accessibility is about access to content, information, and products

by everyone, including people with disability. *Design-for-all* is a term that denotes that an application is designed in such way so that everyone can use it to full extent (Stephanidis, 2001). An accessible web site should be implemented according to specification in order to enable voice browsers to navigate through all available information. An accessible web interface should allow for everyone to use. A blind user, for instance, could use certain modalities for input but the system should never respond by non-accessibly visual content (Freitas & Kouroupetroglou, 2008). Accessibility is a very important and broad discipline with many design and implementation parameters. It can be thought as an extension of the aforementioned usability attributes to the universal user. Universal Accessibility (Stephanidis, 2009) strives to use most modalities in order to make the web content available to everyone. Speech and audio interfaces are used for improved accessibility (Fellbaum & Kouroupetroglou, 2008; Duarte & Carriço, 2008). For example, spoken dialogue systems are considered as key technological factors for the universal accessibility strategies of public terminals, information kiosks and Automated Teller Machines (ATMs) (Kouroupetroglou, 2009). It is mentioned here for completeness; however, it is out of the scope of this chapter.

Interaction Design Lifecycle (Interfaces) and Usability

The basic interaction design process is epitomized by the main activities that are followed for almost every product. There are five activities in the lifecycle of a speech interface (Sharp et al., 2007):

- Requirements specification and initial planning

Figure 3. Typical interface lifecycle of a speech-based dialogue system.

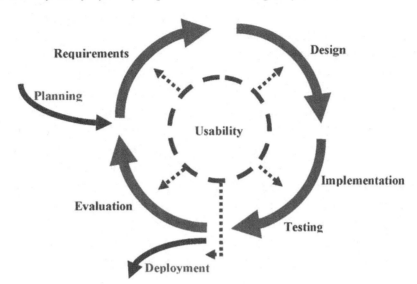

- Design
- Implementation and testing
- Deployment
- Evaluation

In terms of usability there are three key characteristics pertaining to user involvement in the interaction design process (Sharp et al., 2007):

- User involvement should take place throughout all five stages
- The usability requirements, goals and evaluation parameters should be set at the start of the development
- Iteration through the five stages is inevitable and, therefore, should be included in the initial planning

Figure 3 shows how usability generally integrates with the development of a speech-based dialogue interface.

Spoken dialogue interfaces may be of three types depending on their design:

a. DTMF replacement

b. Simple system or user-directed question-answering
c. Open-ended natural language mixed-initiative conversational system.

Type (a) systems are the very basic menu-driven interfaces where a static tree-based layout is presented to the user. The user may respond with yes/no and navigate through the menu via options. Such systems are not user-friendly, typically used for very limited domain services, and require patience and time from the user in order to complete a task. The main advantage is that they are very robust, since the user is presented with only a few options at any time, and can only go forward or backwards in the tree-structured menu.

Type (b) systems use more advanced techniques in order to accommodate a more natural interaction with the user. The menus may be dynamic, have confirmation and disambiguation prompts as well as more elaborate vocabulary. Still, the system or the users have to use voice responses within the grammar. Such systems have reusable dialogue scripts for dialogue repair. The small grammars keep the system relatively robust. Such systems are used for most applications at the moment, providing a trade-off between efficiency and robustness.

Type (c) systems are used for large scale applications. These systems are targeted for user satisfaction and naturalness. The users may respond to natural "how may I help you" system prompts with equally natural replies. The utterances may be long, complex and exhibit great variety. The dialogue is dynamic and the demand for successful ASR is high, as is the use of statistical or machine learning methods for interpretation. The dialogue management is task-based, the system creating tasks and plans of actions to fulfil. The users expect high-level natural interaction, a very important element to factorise in usability parameterisation.

It is obvious, now, that each type of design entails particular usability expectations. Each type is expected to excel in certain aspects.

Based on the analysis of our-own involvement through the development and testing of a number of nationwide-size spoken dialogue business applications, we present in Table 1 how usability is taken into account in each stage of the product lifecycle. The development of such applications is an iterative process, as mentioned before. Reliant on own experience as described above, we can declare that practitioners in industrial settings agree that usability parameters, as well as testing, are also part of the iterative process. Type (c) systems possess the highest potential for usability integration. In that respect, the remainder of this chapter refers mostly to type (c) systems and less to the other two. These days, such systems are the centre of the attention by researchers, developers and customers alike, focusing on advanced voice interaction and high user satisfaction. The use of natural voice response (both acoustic and syntactic) and the natural dialogue flow constitute the state-of-the-art in spoken dialogue interfaces. The web provides the means for the application deployment and the system-world communication, aiming to provide stability and vast amount of available information.

Typical Requirements for Real-Life Spoken Dialogue Interfaces

In systems engineering the term *non-functional requirements* is used to denote the requirements that specify the criteria for assessing the operation of a system, while *functional requirements* define the behaviour. In this context, usability is one of the major functional requirements. Non-functional requirements do not encompass usability per se, however they are effective constraints on the design of the system and may indirectly affect the user experience.

Before the start of the design phase, there are certain accustomed typical requirements pertaining to the areas that the design should focus, i.e. the actual issues that the spoken dialogue system is asked to realize or abide with. Some of them are specifically usability-oriented while others are domain-dependent or generic system-oriented. These typical requirements for Voiceweb interfaces are:

- **User satisfaction:** Users should be satisfied or very satisfied either as standalone users or comparing their input from using an earlier interface.
- **Quality of service offering:** Improvement on the quality of the way the requested services/tasks are presented. For example, a large DTMF tree-based dialogue may require the users to navigate through several menu layers to achieve their goal, while a natural language dialogue may identify the initial user request and retrieve the requested service right at the start.
- **State-of-the art solution:** The system should deploy cutting edge technology.
- **Ability to provide customised behavioural or personalised interaction for specific user groups:** A common example is the use of a preferred type of interaction (formal, casual, friendly, entertaining, etc.) set specifically for the application domain.

Table 1. Usability impact on spoken dialogue interface development lifecycle

Type	Requirements	Design	Implementation	Deployment	Evaluation
a	low	medium	low	Low	low
b	medium	medium	low	Low	medium
c	high	high	medium	high	high

- **Complete access to all services or business units that are supported:** By design, the system should be able to provide the users the same high quality interaction for all services that the interface is used for.
- **Reliability:** Extends to the system providing the intended functions continuously without failing.
- **Continuity of processing:** Also includes problem recovery. In this case a natural language interface should cater for the interaction when a system problem occurs.
- **Auditability:** Ensures the transparency of the system providing supporting evidence to trace processing of data.
- **Performance requirements:** Describes the capacity of the system to perform certain functions or process certain volume of transactions within a prescribed time.
- **Usability-related factors:** The operator of a spoken dialogue interface may find these prudent to stress upon to the designer.

These requirements are usually followed by a list of mandatory *acceptance tests* that the final system should pass before it is deployed to the web. The format imposed for the acceptance tests is generally comprised of *key performance indicators* (KPIs) for ASR and TtS success. These should be developed by the designer and be available on production to use also for tuning purposes. Furthermore, acceptance tests include task completion evaluation for all requested tasks that are to be tested.

For average size/complexity spoken dialogue interfaces, a magnitude of 10-15 trialists should be

sufficient for the acceptance tests. There are two main areas that the tests are carried out in:

1. *Functional assessment* of the system respective modules and functions such as accuracy of information relayed to the user, start/end of dialogue or sub-dialogue flow, service/information provision accuracy, and so on.
2. *User Experience assessment* in terms of:
   a. Quality issues
      i. Speech or dialogue pause length between activities such as voice request, system search, information retrieval, information relay/output, and prompt delays between responses
      ii. Output voice (natural or synthetic) consistency and naturalness for all stages of dialogue as well as in special cases where critical information or explicit help is required
      iii. Choice of presenting output voice, clear and non-breaking, during loudspeaker mode or in noisy environments
      iv. Correct pronunciation and focus placement in sentences
   b. User interaction
      i. Ease of use, navigation through the interface
      ii. Instructions and help prompt quality
      iii. Smart recovery from misinterpretations or misrecognitions

iv. Disambiguation and confirmation function performance

v.   Dialogue flow cohesion

vi. Overall satisfaction.

Since all this information is available to the designer beforehand, it can be put to good use especially during the design. Most of these requirements are the constraints set by the operator so that the design should be built around them. A good design should take those into account in order for the final system to pass the acceptance test assessments.

USABILITY EVALUATION FOR SPEECH-BASED SYSTEMS

Usability evaluation can be formative or summative and thus it can be performed either during or at the end (or near the end) of the development cycle. The methodologies that can be used for that differ in their scope, their main difference being that, when a product is finished (or nearly finished), *usability testing* serves for fine-tuning certain parameters and adjusting others to fit the target user better. During the design phase, usability evaluation methods can be used to probe the basic design choices, the general scope and respective task analysis of a web interface. Some of the most common factors to think about when designing a usability study are:

- Simulate environment conditions closely similar to the real world application use
- Make sure the usability evaluation participants belong to the target user group
- Make sure the user testers test all parameters you want to measure
- Consider onsite or remote evaluation

These factors are referenced later in this section.

Methodologies

Usability evaluation for speech-based web interfaces is carried upon certain evaluation methods and approaches on the specific modules and processes that comprise each application. Each approach measures different parameters and goals. They all have the same goal, to evaluate usability for a system, sub-system or module. However, each approach targets specific parameters for evaluation. The main two usability evaluation classes for spoken dialogue systems include the Wizard-of-Oz (WOZ) formative testing (Harris, 2005) and the summative usability testing.

The Wizard-of-Oz Formative Evaluation

It is a common formative approach that can be used not only for speech-based dialogue systems but for most web applications. It enables usability testing during the early stages by using a human to simulate a fully working system. In the case of speech-based dialogue systems, the human "wizard" performs the speech recognition, natural language understanding, dialogue management and context generation. Cohen et al. (2004) list the main advantages of the WOZ approach:

- **Early testing:** It can be performed in the early stages in order to test and formulate the design parameters as early in the product lifecycle as possible.
- **Use of prototype or early design:** Eliminates problems arising later in the development such as integration.
- **Language resources:** Grammar coverage for the speech recognition (ASR) and respective machine learning approaches for interpretation (NLU) are always low when testing a non-finalised product. Low scoring for ASR-NLU may hinder the usability evaluation, however, the use of the human usability expert eliminates such handicap.

- **System updates:** The system, being a mock-up, can be updated effortlessly to accommodate for changes imposed from the input from the test subjects, making it easier to re-test the updated system in the next usability evaluation session.

The WOZ approach is primarily used during the initial design phase to test the proposed dialogue flow design and the user response to information presentation parameterisation. Since errors from speech recognition and language interpretation are not taken into account, the resulting evaluation lacks the realistic aspect. Expert developers usually know what to expect from the speech recognition and interpretation accuracy because these are domain dependent.

There are two requirements for successful usability testing, the design of the tasks and the selection and training of participants. The participants must be representative of the end-user population, taking into account age, demographics, education. Other criteria may be set depending on the actual application domain, for example users of a specific web site. Moreover, novice and expert users can be recruited in order to provide the means of applying the system design to the worst-case (low experience level) and best-case (high experience level) population.

The participants are required to complete a number of tasks that are carefully selected to test the system performance. In a dialogue system the primary concern to evaluate is the dialogue flow. Two sets of scenarios should be designed, one asking the participants to perform specific actions or pursue predetermined goals and another asking for uncontrolled access of the system pursuing goals of their own choice. The controlled predetermined scenarios are used to evaluate the behaviour of the participants against the behaviour expected by the designer, exposing possible flaws of the design. The uncontrolled interaction is used to evaluate the generic performance of the participants revealing

basic design faults, such as non-obvious availability of *help* function or *ambiguous* interaction responses from the system.

The results of the WOZ tests are both from the user subjective feedback and the examination of the objective performance measures. The performance measures include:

- **Task completion:** Whether the participants completed the specified tasks that were set within the scenarios successfully
- **Efficiency:** Whether the participants chose the most direct route to the goal, using the predetermined scenario feedback to compare against the optimal path for the same scenario that was expected by the designer
- **Dialogue flow:** How the participants chose to interact with the system, the number of times the help was requested and how informative it was, as well as the number of times disambiguation, confirmation and error recovery sub-dialogues were enabled

The subjective input of the participants is recorded through questionnaires that the participants fill in after each task completion as well as at the end of the evaluation. The questions are used to assess the user experience asking about complexity, effort required, efficiency, linguistic clarity, simplicity, predictability, accuracy, suitable tempo, consistency, precision, forgiveness, responsiveness (see Ward & Tsukahara, 2003), appropriateness, overall impression and acceptance of the system, either regarding particular tasks or the full system (Weinschenk & Barker, 2000). The participants are usually asked to mark the level of their agreement to the questions through a 1-to-5 or 1-to-7 scales (for example, 1 being "totally disagree" and 7 "totally agree" and the rest in between), commonly known as Likert scales.

The data are analysed and problems are prioritized in terms of type, severity, and frequency. The subjective feedback also indicates behavioural flaws in the design. Both results enable the designer to take certain action to fix or eliminate those flaws from the design and proceed to implementation.

The Summative Usability Testing of Voiceweb Systems

At the end of the implementation, pre-final versions of the system should be tested by potential users in order to evaluate the usability. Usability testing at this stage is not much different to WOZ in terms of planning. But now there is no human actor (wizard) but the full system interaction with the user. This means that the ASR, Context interpretation and generation, and TtS are now part of the usability metrics.

At this stage, the usability tests play a much more pivotal role since the development of the system is near completion. There are three distinct purposes for usability testing of a working system: the *development*, *testing* and *tuning*. During the development the users test a nearly finished product, during testing a finished product, and during tuning a finished and already deployed product. Regardless of purpose, the tests focus on all aspects that the WOZ handled as well as several aspects that the WOZ ignored:

- Grammar testing
- Interpretation testing
- Dialogue management/flow
- System response adequacy
- Output speech quality.

For spoken dialogue interfaces, the following 15 objective (both quantitative and qualitative) and subjective usability evaluation criteria have been proposed (Dybkjær & Bernsen 2000):

1. Modality appropriateness
2. Input recognition adequacy
3. Naturalness of user speech relative to the task(s) including coverage of user vocabulary and grammar
4. Output voice quality
5. Output phrasing adequacy
6. Feedback adequacy
7. Adequacy of dialogue initiative relative to the task(s)
8. Naturalness of the dialogue structure relative to the task(s)
9. Sufficiency of task and domain coverage
10. Sufficiency of the system's reasoning capabilities
11. Sufficiency of interaction guidance (information about system capabilities, limitations and operations)
12. Error handling adequacy
13. Sufficiency of adaptation to user differences
14. Number of interaction problems (Bernsen et al. 1998)
15. User satisfaction

Bernsen & Dybkjær (2000) have proposed the use of the *evaluation templates*, i.e. "models of what the developer needs to know in order to apply an evaluation criterion to a particular property of a Spoken Language Dialogue System or component", in their methodology as best practice guides. Later, they formed a set of guidelines for up-to-date spoken dialogue design, implementation and testing, covering seven major aspects: informativeness, truth and evidence, relevance, manner, partner asymmetry, background knowledge, repair and clarification (Bernsen & Dybkjær, 2004). These aspects can be used as the basis for usability testing strategies and for evaluation frameworks (Dybkjær & Bernsen, 2001; Dybkjær et al., 2004). One of them is the PARADISE evaluation framework (Walker et al., 1998; Hajdinjak & Mihelic, 2006) with general models developed for it (Walker et al., 2000).

As with WOZ, usability testing needs participants. The recruitment procedure is pretty much the same as described earlier in WOZ, with a few additional parameters. The participants use the real system, which means that, at this stage, functional parameters in speech recognition and speech synthesis should be tested, measured and decided upon. There is extensive work on the comparison of usability evaluation feedback between in-house recruited participants versus real users. The differences are mainly on the use of barge-in, explicit requests, the use of help and dialogue acts preference/selection (Ai et al., 2007). Moreover, parameter measurements in speech recognition rejection, choice of interaction ending, help and repeat requests, user interruptions and silence timeouts, show that there users behave differently in the first month of their interaction. After that, the users become accustomed to the system, experienced and their behaviour becomes more or less stabilised (Turunen et al., 2006).

Kamm et al. (1998) stress the importance of a successful quick tutorial on the users before using a speech-based application. They show that the initial user experience can be ensured when the first-time users are trained on the use of the system. The user satisfaction and the system performance were significantly improved in this case. Also, there is significant differentiation between onsite and remote evaluation. Participants recruited for onsite evaluation know that they are required to evaluate the system and may behave unexpectedly or even use extreme caution when using the system, a behavior much dissimilar to that of real users.

Apart from task completion and dialogue flow, depending on the domain, as a general rule, functional measurements should be recorded for at least the following indicative parameters:

- Average call duration
- Peaks and valleys of usage per hour per day
- Successful speech recognitions
- Misrecognitions
- No-inputs
- Timeouts
- Rejections
- Early hang-ups
- Successful interpretations

- Failed interpretations (no-matches)
- Successful repairs
- Failed repairs.

Performance metrics may be derived by calculating parameters such as the number of user and system turns, elapsed time, number of help requests, number of timeout prompts, mean ASR accuracy and number of speech recognition rejections (Kamm & Walker, 1997; Kamm et al. 1999). Generally, the above parameters can indicate functional problems with the application and the degree that each of those affects the user experience (Walker et al., 1999). Furthermore, the data can be automatically processed using appropriate methods (Hartikainen et al., 2004), used to train models for evaluation-based problem prediction that leads to an adaptive spoken dialogue interface (Litman et al. 1998; Litman & Pan, 2002).

The user subjective feedback is also very important at this stage. It illustrates the user experience as perceived by the user (to be compared with automatically-derived user experience level from the performance metrics analysis) and stresses the points where the users were not satisfied. By analysing the questionnaires down to the usability factors (Larsen, 2003) the designer can even, to an extent, predict the quality and usability of spoken dialogue services (Moller et al. 2006; 2008).

Functional Assessment and Usability Testing for Deployed Systems

In the recent years, there has been a need for designers to examine how a deployed system behaves and be able to alter the system output in real time, for testing, updating (observing user behavioural transformation after major updates) and fine-tuning. Expensive, large-scale systems enter the market by incremental deployment to groups of real users. Between the increments, the designing team evaluates the functional aspects of the system as well as the user experience of first-time or advanced users. That is also the case for

Figure 4. Wizard-based usability testing for a deployed Spoken Dialogue Interface.

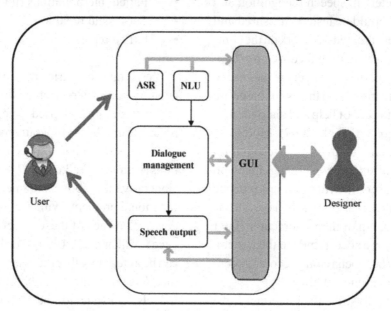

when major updates or supplemental features are implemented and released to target users for the first time. To do that, the application framework should be able to support a WOZ-like mode that allows the designer to intervene on the dialogue process during an interaction. This is especially suitable for spoken dialogue web interfaces where the implementation of such feature would enable the web interface designer to try out alternative routes to the interaction tasks and goals. Figure 4 shows the layout of a real-time wizard-based testing environment for already deployed systems.

Using this framework any member of the design and implementation team can perform real time inspection of the interaction, watching for speech recognition, interpretation and dialogue management parameters, observing the dialogue flow, history, user input and system responses. They can intervene at any time by involving themselves in the decision process of the dialogue manager, overriding the system response to change an interpreted request or redirect the dialogue flow. Even more, the wizard may validate the user input or trigger a disambiguation sub-dialogue to test the user and system responses.

CONCLUSION

Natural language dialogue web interfaces interact with the users in a natural and convenient way. Usability integration and evaluation is a fundamental requirement for such delicate interaction. This chapter presented the guidelines and methodologies for designing, developing, testing and deploying usable spoken dialogue interfaces. As technology advances, the use of natural language interfaces requires more sophisticated approaches to enhance the user experience with high-level linguistic input-output and advanced dialogue management. Such endeavour necessitates the use of equally advanced usability methodologies during all stages of the system development.

This chapter discussed the theory behind usability evaluation methods and approaches as well as the frameworks that incorporate usability evaluation and testing for speech-based web interfaces. Moreover the major methods used for formative and summative evaluation have been examined and analyzed in the context of voiceweb systems.

Usability evaluation is used during the requirements analysis, design, implementation, testing deployment and evaluation of speech-based dialogue interfaces. The requirements/design stages of development are benefited by the input of potential user groups. The designer can use the feedback to formulate an interface that provides all the requested services in a suitable user-approved interaction design. The finished or nearly finished systems are put to test in order to assure the quality of interaction, as well as performance, completeness and naturalness. At this stage the functional tests are also performed and included in the usability evaluation.

Finally, the already deployed systems need to be re-evaluated at any time during their life on the market for either testing or updating purposes. At this point the existing functional and non-functional parameters are taken for granted. The new or updated technologies or dialogue flow can be evaluated by the designer or tester using a graphical user interface, a front-end for dialogue overview and control that enables the designer to monitor all dialogue processes and override, manipulate, confirm or dismiss any input or output of the system. The importance of such application framework as part of the integrated design and implementation approach facilitates a professional after-release support and development for the ever growing requirements of spoken dialogue web interfaces.

ACKNOWLEDGMENT

The work described in this chapter has been funded by the Special Account for Research Grants of the National and Kapodistrian University of Athens under the KAPODISTRIAS program.

REFERENCES

Ai, H., Raux, A., Bohus, D., Eskenazi, M., & Litman, D. (2007). Comparing spoken dialog corpora collected with recruited subjects versus real users. In *Proc. of the 8th SIGdial workshop on Discourse and Dialogue* (pp. 124–131).

Bernsen, N. O., Dybkjaer, H., & Dybkjaer, L. (1998). *Designing Interactive Speech Systems: From First Ideas to User Testing*. New York: Springer-Verlag.

Bernsen, N. O., & Dybkjær, L. (2000). A Methodology for Evaluating Spoken Language Dialogue Systems and Their Components. In *Proc. 2nd International Conference on Language Resources & Evaluation - LREC 2000* (pp.183-188).

Bernsen, N. O., & Dybkjær, L. (2004). Building Usable Spoken Dialogue Systems: Some Approaches. *Sprache und Datenverarbeitung, 28*(2), 111–131.

Cohen, M., Giancola, J. P., & Balogh, J. (2004). *Voice User Interface Design*. Boston: Addison-Wesley Professional.

Duarte, C., & Carriço, L. (2008). Audio Interfaces for Improved Accessibility. In S.Pinder (Ed.), *Advances in Human Computer Interaction* (pp. 121-142). Vienna, Austria: I-Tech Education and Publishing.

Dybkjær, L., & Bernsen, N. O. (2000). Usability Issues in Spoken Language Dialogue Systems. *Natural Language Engineering, 6*(3-4), 243–272. doi:10.1017/S1351324900002461

Dybkjær, L., & Bernsen, N. O. (2001). Usability Evaluation in Spoken Language Dialogue Systems. In. Proc. *ACL Workshop on Evaluation Methodologies for Language and Dialogue Systems*, (pp. 9-18).

Dybkjær, L., Bernsen, N. O., & Minker, W. (2004). Evaluation and Usability of Multimodal Spoken Language Dialogue Systems. *Speech Communication, 43*(1-2), 33–54. doi:10.1016/j.specom.2004.02.001

Dybkjær, L., Hemsen, H., & Minker, W. (Eds.). (2007). *Evaluation of Text and Speech Systems*. Berlin: Springer-Verlag.

Dybkjær, L., & Minker, W. (Eds.). (2008). *Recent Trends in Discourse and Dialogue*. Berlin: Springer-Verlag.

Fellbaum, K., & Kouroupetroglou, G. (2008). Principles of Electronic Speech Processing with Applications for People with Disabilities. *Technology and Disability*, *20*(2), 55–85.

Freitas, D., & Kouroupetroglou, G. (2008). Speech Technologies for Blind and Low Vision Persons. *Technology and Disability*, *20*(2), 135–156.

Hajdinjak, M., & Mihelic, F. (2006). The PARADISE evaluation framework: Issues and findings. *Computational Linguistics*, *32*(2), 263–272. doi:10.1162/coli.2006.32.2.263

Harris, R. A. (2005). *Voice Interaction Design: Crafting the New Conversational Speech Systems*. San Francisco: Morgan Kaufmann.

Hartikainen, M., Salonen, E.-P., & Turunen, M. (2004). Subjective Evaluation of Spoken Dialogue Systems Using SERVQUAL Method. In *Proc. 8th International Conference on Spoken Language Processing - ICSLP*, (pp. 2273-2276).

Huang, X., Acero, A., & Hon, H.-W. (2001). *Spoken Language Processing: A Guide to Theory, Algorithm and System Development*. Upper Saddle River, NJ: Prentice Hall PTR.

Jurafsky, D., & Martin, J. H. (2008). *Speech and Language Processing. An Introduction to Natrural Language Processing, Computational Linguistics, and Speech Recognition*. Upper Saddle River, NJ: Prentice-Hall.

Kamm, C. A., Litman, D. J., & Walker, M. A. (1998). From novice to expert: The effect of tutorials on user expertise with spoken dialogue systems. In *Proc. 5th International Conference on Spoken Language Processing - ICSLP*.

Kamm, C. A., & Walker, M. A. (1997). Design and Evaluation of Spoken Dialogue Systems. In Proc. *IEEE Workshop on Automatic Speech Recognition and Understanding*, (pp. 14–17).

Kamm, C. A., Walker, M. A., & Litman, D. J. (1999). Evaluating spoken language systems. In *Proc. Applied Voice Input/Output Society Conference - AVIOS*, (pp. 187–197).

Kouroupetroglou, G. (2009). Universal Access in Public Terminals: Information Kiosks and Automated Teller Machines (ATMs). In C. Stephanidis (Ed.), *The Universal Access Handbook*, (pp. 761-780). Boca Raton, FL: CRC Press.

Larsen, L. B. (2003). Issues in the Evaluation of Spoken Dialogue Systems using Objective and Subjective Measures. In *Proc. 8th IEEE Workshop on Automatic Speech Recognition and Understanding -ASRU*, (pp. 209-214).

Larson, J. A. (2000). *Introduction and Overview of W3C Speech Interface Framework*. Retrieved August 2, 2009, from http://www.w3.org/TR/voice-intro/

Larson, J. A., Raman, T. V., & Raggett, D. (2003). *W3C Multimodal Interaction Framework*. Retrieved August 2, 2009, from http://www.w3.org/TR/mmi-framework/

Litman, D. J., & Pan, S. (2002). Designing and evaluating an adaptive spoken dialogue system. *User Modeling and User-Adapted Interaction*, *12*(2-3), 111–137. doi:10.1023/A:1015036910358

Litman, D. J., Pan, S., & Walker, M. A. (1998). Evaluating Response Strategies in a Web-Based Spoken Dialogue Agent. In *Proc. 36th Annual Meeting of the Association for Computational Linguistics and 17th International Conf. on Computational Linguistics (ACL/COLING)*, (pp. 780–786).

McTear, M. F. (2004). *Spoken Dialogue Technology: Towards the Conversational User Interface.* London: Springer-Verlag.

Moller, S., Engelbrecht, K., & Schleicher, R. (2008). Predicting the quality and usability of spoken dialogue services. *Speech Communication, 50*(8-9), 730–744. doi:10.1016/j.specom.2008.03.001

Moller, S., Englert, R., Engelbrecht, K., Hafner, V., Jameson, A., Oulasvirta, A., et al. (2006). MeMo: Towards Automatic Usability Evaluation of Spoken Dialogue Services by User Error Simulations. In *Proc. 9th International Conference on Spoken Language Processing - ICSLP,* (pp. 1786-1789).

Rubin, J., & Chisnell, D. (2008). *Handbook of Usability Testing: Howto Plan, Design, and Conduct Effective Tests.* Indianapolis, IN: Wiley Publishing, Inc.

Sharp, H., Rogers, Y., & Preece, J. (2007). *Interaction Design: Beyond Human-Computer Interaction.* West Sussex, UK: John Wiley & Sons, Inc.

Stephanidis, C. (Ed.). (2001). *User Interfaces for All: Concepts, Methods and Tools.* Mahwah, NJ: Lawrence Erlbaum Associates.

Stephanidis, C. (Ed.). (2009). *The Universal Access Handbook.* Boca Raton, FL: CRC Press.

Tatham, M., & Morton, K. (2005). *Developments in Speech Synthesis.* West Sussex, UK: John Wiley & Sons, Inc.

Turunen, M., Hakulinen, J., & Kainulainen, A. (2006). Evaluation of a Spoken Dialogue System with Usability Tests and Long-term Pilot Studies: Similarities and Differences. In *Proc. 9th International Conference on Spoken Language Processing - INTERSPEECH* (pp. 1057—1060).

van Kuppevelt, J., Dybkjær, L., & Bernsen, N. O. (Eds.). (2005). *Advances in natural multimodal dialogue.* Dordrecht, The Netherlands: Springer.

Wahlster, W. (Ed.). (2006). *SmartKom: Foundations of Multimodal Dialogue Systems.* Berlin: Springer-Verlag.

Walker, M. A., Borland, J., & Kamm, C. A. (1999). The utility of elapsed time as a usability metric for spoken dialogue systems. In *Proc. IEEE Automatic Speech Recognition and Understanding Workshop - ASRU,* (pp. 317–320).

Walker, M. A., Kamm, C. A., & Litman, D. J. (2000). Towards developing general models of usability with PARADISE. *Natural Language Engineering, 6*(3-4), 363–377. doi:10.1017/S1351324900002503

Walker, M. A., Litman, D. J., Kamm, C. A., & Abella, A. (1998). Evaluating spoken dialogue agents with PARADISE: Two case studies. *Computer Speech & Language, 12*(3), 317–347. doi:10.1006/csla.1998.0110

Ward, N., & Tsukahara, W. (2003). A Study in Responsiveness in Spoken Dialog. *International Journal of Human-Computer Studies, 59,* 603–630. doi:10.1016/S1071-5819(03)00085-5

Weinschenk, S., & Barker, D. T. (2000). *Designing effective speech interfaces.* New York: John Wiley & Sons, Inc.

Chapter 9
Website Accessibility and the Role of Accessibility Statements

C. M. Parkinson
Loughborough University, UK

C. W. Olphert
Loughborough University, UK

ABSTRACT

This chapter defines accessibility in the broader context of usability and explains the importance of making websites accessible as well as usable. It then focuses on one particular aspect of website accessibility – the accessibility statement, which is a declaration on a website about the accessibility of the site to disabled people and others with accessibility needs. This chapter argues that accessibility statements can play an important part in website accessibility if they are appropriately designed and targeted. Based on an extensive literature review and detailed examination of a large sample of accessibility statements, the chapter presents an overview of current practice and usage, raises and discusses the problematic issues that arise when developing accessibility statements, and provides recommendations for best practice.

INTRODUCTION

The overall aim of this book is to explore the crucial role that usability plays in the design of successful and effective websites. In this chapter we argue that websites must not only be usable but they must also be accessible. The definition of usability provided by ISO 9241 is: "the extent to which a product [or website] can be used by specified users to achieve specified goals with effectiveness, efficiency and satisfaction in a specified context of use" (International Standards Organisation, 1992/2000). While there is no single standard definition of accessibility as there is for usability, there is consensus that the goal of accessibility is to ensure that a product, system or service can be used by people with a wide range of abilities and disabilities. Therefore, as suggested by Petrie and Kheir (2007 p.397), accessibility can be considered as "usability for people with disabilities". An accessible website will be one that has been designed so that people with functional limitations (e.g. visual, motor, cognitive

DOI: 10.4018/978-1-60566-896-3.ch009

and auditory impairments) and situational limitations (e.g. those using alternative web-access equipment) can freely access the content of the site. An accessible website is "perceivable, operable and understandable", without barriers, for all people (Thatcher et al, 2002, pp. 8-13).

The chapter begins by making the case for website accessibility. It will go on to review the guidance that is available for designers seeking to create accessible websites, and will then focus on the role that an accessibility statement can play in this process.

Why is Website Accessibility Important?

There are now a number of key drivers for website accessibility. The first of these is legislation: in many countries, a website which is not accessible, in other words which cannot be accessed freely and fully by people with functional limitations, is likely to be breaking anti-discrimination laws.

The right of all persons to equality before the law and protection against discrimination is acknowledged by the United Nations' Universal Declaration of Human Rights (1948) and many countries have incorporated these rights within their laws. For example, the European Commission Directive 2000/78/EC of 27 November 2000 (European Commission, 2000) prohibits any direct or indirect discrimination based on religion or belief, disability, age or sexual orientation against individuals in the workplace throughout the member states of the European Community. Furthermore, numerous countries around the world have introduced specific legislation relating to disabled people. In the United States, the Americans with Disabilities Act (ADA) has been law since 1990 and was amended in 2008. In the United Kingdom, the Disability Discrimination Act has been in place since 1995 and was amended in 2001 to cover provision of post-16 education, and again in 2005 primarily to cover transport and public services. In India the Persons with

Disabilities (Equal Opportunities, Protection of Rights and Full Participation) Act was passed in 1995. Many other countries have similar laws.

While much of the legislation initially aimed to prevent discrimination against disabled people in terms of access to work and the workplace, the thrust of recent laws and amendments has been to prevent such discrimination in other aspects of life. For example, the European Commission Directive mentioned above was extended in July 2008 to provide protection beyond the workplace. This new directive aims to ensure equal treatment in the areas of social protection, including social security and health care, education and access to and supply of goods and services which are commercially available to the public. Websites, which are increasingly being used to deliver such services, are included under disability discrimination legislation. A Code of Practice produced by the Disability Rights Commission in the UK specifically mentions websites in relation to the Disability Discrimination Act: "An airline company provides a flight reservation and booking service to the public on its website. This is a provision of a service and is subject to the Act". (Disability Rights Commission, 2002, cited by Massie, 2005). There are already examples of prosecutions being brought under disability discrimination legislation against organisations who fail to make their websites accessible. For instance, an influential case in Australia (Maguire v Sydney Organising Committee of the Olympic Games - SOCOG) found SOCOG to have failed in its obligations to make its website accessible (Sloan, 2001).

A second driver for website accessibility is to prevent social exclusion. Although internet use is increasing across the globe, accessibility problems contribute to 'digital divides' (Ellison, 2004) in society between those who can and those who cannot make full and effective use of this technology and the benefits that it can provide. The internet and web-based services have tremendous potential for disabled people. A survey carried out for the

US National Organisation on Disability in 2000 (Taylor, 2000) found that 48% of disabled people said that going online significantly increased their quality of life, compared to 27% of non-disabled people. In the UK, a study for the Leonard Cheshire Foundation (Knight, Heaven & Christie, 2002) found that 54% of disabled people sampled considered Internet access essential, compared with only 6% in the general population. Yet by contrast, a survey in the US found that 28% of disabled non-users said that their disability made it difficult or impossible for them to go online (Lenhart et al., 2003). As more and more services and applications become web-based, web accessibility will be crucial to ensuring that such 'digital divides' do not worsen. As noted above, not only commercial services but, increasingly, public services are being delivered through the web. Barriers to full access to these services affect the civil rights of people both with and without disabilities (Yu, 2002) and, as many governments across the world are putting their activities online, accessibility is now also an issue of equal access to democracy (Wallis, 2005).

Besides these imperatives, however, there are other advantages to be gained from creating accessible websites. Attention to accessibility issues can benefit both the organisation providing the website (in terms, for example, of customer satisfaction, repeat sales and brand image), and consumers, who are able to make use of the wide variety of products, services and activities that are now available online (Davies, 2006; Hackett, Parmanto & Zeng, 2004; Robb, 2005). For example, the financial company Legal & General found that the redesigning their website to make it accessible led to a surge in online traffic (the number of visitors doubled within three months), conversion rates increased by 300%, site maintenance costs were reduced by 66% and the entire project delivered 100% return on investment within 12 months (Socitm Insight, 2007). Disabled people may have considerable spending power (AbilityNet 2004a; Loiacono & McCoy 2004),

and represent an often neglected potential market for companies. It has also been argued that there are many circumstances and contexts in which people who do not consider themselves as disabled are situationally impaired – for example because of lighting conditions, noise, task overload etc. (Iwarsson & Stahl 2003; Newell & Gregor, 2000). Consequently considering accessibility problems and designing websites appropriately is likely to bring benefits not only to disabled people but to other users as well.

Thus there are compelling reasons for making websites accessible. In the following section, we provide some information about the prevalence of disabilities, to indicate how many disabled people could be affected by website inaccessibility.

Incidence of Disability

Firstly it is important to state that there is no single and widely accepted definition of disability. Many definitions have been proposed, stemming from different purposes and from different perceptions, or models, of the features and causes of disability. Models that are medically-based define disability at an individual level, emphasise physical or mental deficits in their definitions of disability and seek medical interventions to relieve disability. Socially-based models, in contrast, make a distinction between the impairments of the individual and the disabling effects of an inaccessible environment. Social models define disability at the societal level, emphasise the environmental barriers to access in their definitions of disability and seek social interventions, such as increased accessibility and removal of barriers, to prevent disability. However the World Health Organisation (WHO) has made a concerted effort to arrive at a 'universal' definition and developed the International Classification of Functioning, Disability and Health (ICF). In May 2001 this was endorsed by all 191 members of the WHO as the international standard to describe and measure disability. The ICF definition (World Health Organisation, 2009) is as follows:

Disability is a decrement in functioning at the body, individual or societal level that arises when an individual with a health condition encounters barriers in the environment.

By this definition, disability is not something that happens to only a minority of people, as it acknowledges that any individual can be disabled for many different reasons. The definition highlights the importance of context and environment for understanding the causes of disability, and opens the way for an increased focus on accessibility and the removal of barriers in the environment.

At a global level, the World Bank (2009) estimates that about 10-12% of the population of the world is disabled. However rates vary widely between countries, being higher in developed countries such as the US and Canada (19.4% and 18.5% respectively) and lower in developing countries. In Kenya and Bangladesh for example the reported rates are below 1%. Statistics from the EU (European Commission, 2003) suggest that around one in six persons between the ages of 16 and 64 has a long standing health problem or impairment. Such variation between the reported rates in different countries is most probably due to variations in definitions and measures. The table below is an example derived from the United States Census Bureau figures from 1997 (IGDA, 2004) relating to people aged 15 and above.

Of course it must be remembered that impairments vary in their impact on a person's function, from severe to moderate or mild; and not all impairments will have an impact on a person's ability to access and effectively use a website. With reference to the above table, it is likely that not all of the of the 18 million people who have hand problems, 7.7 million people who have difficulty reading, or 3.5 million people with a specific learning disability, would experience difficulties operating a keyboard or mouse, or reading or comprehending website content. Nevertheless it is clear that the number of people who are likely to be affected by poor website accessibility is potentially very large.

Carey (2005) clusters disabilities into four main groups, in descending order of incidence, as follows:

* learning/cognitive/developmental
* physical/motor
* deafness/hearing impairment
* blindness/visual impairment

Carey argues that a 'functionality gap' arises due to a combination of the "lack of skills or incentive on the part of the human user" and the "deficiency in the design of the system and its user interface". He describes the functional gap as "the inadequate transactional outcome between digital

Table 1. Examples of the incidence of different types of impairment in the US population in 1997

Impairment	Number
People who have difficulty lifting 10 pounds or grasping small objects	18 million
People with hearing impairments	8 million
People who have difficulty reading even with glasses	7.7 million
People who use a cane, crutches or walker	6.4 million
People with a specific learning disability	3.5 million
People who have a mental/emotional condition	3.5 million
People with speech impairments	2.2 million
People who use a wheelchair	2.2 million

information systems and people". He points out that, for PC-based systems largely presenting text and static graphics, the functionality gap between disabled people and information systems widens by cluster as follows:

- deafness/hearing impairment
- physical/motor
- learning/cognitive/developmental
- blind/visually impaired

However he also notes that with the growth of multi-media products without sub-titling or captioning, it would be expected that this ranking would change, with problems for deaf and hearing impaired people increasing. (Carey, 2005).

A further important factor which is likely to have an impact on rates of disability is the growing proportion of older people in the population. Across the world, the population's average age is increasing. While the global working-age population is expected to remain fairly constant at around 223 million in 2025, the over-65 population is anticipated to rise. In the EU it is expected to increase from 15.4% of the population in 1995 to 22.4% by 2025 (BBC News, 2002a) but it is estimated that by the year 2050, Asia will be home to almost two-thirds of the world's population of people over 60 (BBC News, 2002b). As people age, they are more likely to experience functional impairments, for example, due to failing eyesight, poor hearing and mobility, as well as to have greater difficulties with learning and memorising new materials. Compared to an incidence of about 16% in the general population, the European Commission (2001) has found that between 20% - 52% of the population in the age group 55-64 report an impairment (depending on the country). Thus the percentage of the population who are disabled is likely to rise as the population ages, increasing the requirement for accessible websites and services.

In the following sections we shall review the support and guidance which is available to designers aiming to create accessible websites.

Designing an Accessible Website

There are numerous sources of advice for those seeking to design an accessible website. It is not the intention of this chapter to provide detailed guidance about how to do this, but to refer the reader to sources of information. Key texts include: Chisholm and May (2008), Clark (2003), Slatin (2002), Paciello (2000) and Thatcher et al. (2006). In 2009, a new British Standard (BS 8878, Web Accessibility – Building Accessible Experiences for Disabled People) will be published which will provide guidance for organisations in considering the needs of web users with physical impairments or learning disabilities.

However the principle source of information for those seeking to design an accessible website is likely to be the guidance produced by the World Wide Web Consortium's (W3C) Web Accessibility Initiative (WAI) which has, over the course of several years, been working to establish standards and guidance for web accessibility. Version 2.0 of the Web Content Accessibility Guidelines (WCAG 2.0) was published in December 2008. Although other guidelines exist[1], the WCAG guidelines are so influential that web accessibility is often defined as conformance to them (Kelly, Sloan, Phipps, Petrie & Hamilton, 2005). WCAG 2.0 has only four principles at the top level under which more specific guidelines, called success criteria, are organized (WebAIM, 2009a). These four principles require that, in order to be accessible, websites must be:

1) perceivable
2) operable
3) understandable
4) robust

Figure 1. Summary of Guidelines for Web Accessibility (Source: http://www.w3.org/TR/WCAG20/, accessed 25.06.09). Copyright © World Wide Web Consortium, (Massachusetts Institute of Technology, European Research Consortium for Informatics and Mathematics, Keio University). All Rights Reserved. http://www.w3.org/Consortium/Legal/2002/copyright-documents-20021231.

Principle 1: Perceivable: Information and user interface components must be presentable to users in ways they can perceive.

Guideline 1.1 Text Alternatives: Provide text alternatives for any non-text content so that it can be changed into other forms people need, such as large print, braille, speech, symbols or simpler language.

Guideline 1.2 Time-based Media: Provide alternatives for time-based media.

Guideline 1.3 Adaptable: Create content that can be presented in different ways (for example simpler layout) without losing information or structure.

Guideline 1.4 Distinguishable: Make it easier for users to see and hear content including separating foreground from background.

Principle 2: Operable - User interface components and navigation must be operable.

Guideline 2.1 Keyboard Accessible: Make all functionality available from a keyboard.

Guideline 2.2 Enough Time: Provide users enough time to read and use content.

Guideline 2.3 Seizures: Do not design content in a way that is known to cause seizures.

Guideline 2.4 Navigable: Provide ways to help users navigate, find content, and determine where they are.

Principle 3: Understandable - Information and the operation of user interface must be understandable.

Guideline 3.1 Readable: Make text content readable and understandable.

Guideline 3.2 Predictable: Make Web pages appear and operate in predictable ways.

Guideline 3.3 Input Assistance: Help users avoid and correct mistakes.

Principle 4: Robust - Content must be robust enough that it can be interpreted reliably by a wide variety of user agents, including assistive technologies.

Guideline 4.1 Compatible: Maximize compatibility with current and future user agents, including assistive technologies.

Detailed guidance about how to achieve these principles is provided by the W3C (Web Accessibility Initiative, 2008a). The guidelines are summarised in Figure 1.

Guidance about assessing accessibility is provided by the WAI (Web Accessibility Initiative, 2008b). Designers have a wide choice of automated testing tools to check the accessibility of a website. Examples of tools include RAMP (Deque, 2008), InFocus (SSB BART Group, 2006), A-Prompt (Adaptive Technology Resource Centre, n.d.) the WAVE (WebAIM, 2009b), the Web Developer Toolbar (Pederick, 2009) and more

specific tools like the Colour Contrast Analyser (Web Accessibility Tools Consortium, 2005). However, while automated testing goes some way towards assessing the accessibility of a website, it is universally recommended that sites should be tested by users with accessibility needs, since ultimately accessibility - as is usability - is based on the experience of the user (Kelly et al., 2005; Nielsen 2009). The WAI suggest that the user of the site also plays a part in the accessibility process, as they must be aware of the assistive technology that can enable them to access the web (screenreaders, alternative keyboards, switches, scanning software etc.) and must also bring their "knowledge, experiences and ... adaptive strategies" to the website (Web Accessibility Initiative, 2005).

Accessibility of Websites in Practice

The strong drivers for website accessibility described above, together with the availability of expert guidance for designers, would be expected to lead to a corresponding proliferation of accessible websites. Unfortunately however this does not seem to the case. Numerous research studies investigating the levels of accessibility of websites in different sectors and countries have consistently shown that organisations are failing to make their sites accessible.

A large-scale investigation into website accessibility in the UK commissioned by the Disability Rights Commission (DRC) in 2004 involved testing the homepages of 1,000 websites for compliance with the WAI checkpoints. The investigation was an important milestone in UK web accessibility since, as the DRC noted, with a few exceptions "the evidence of Web inaccessibility had in the past been largely anecdotal or derived from comparatively small-scale studies." (Disability Rights Commission 2004, p.5). The investigation's findings indicated an "unacceptable" state of Web accessibility, with 81% of websites tested failing to meet the most basic Web Accessibility Initiative category.

Such problems appear to be widespread. AbilityNet has conducted surveys of websites across many sectors, using automated and manual testing, (for example UK newspapers (2003a), UK airlines (2003b), UK premiership football clubs (2004a), UK banks (2004b), UK supermarkets (2004c), UK retail companies (2004d), online dating websites (2007a), UK utility and switching companies (2007b), and social networking websites (2008a)), consistently finding that a high proportion failed to meet a basic level of accessibility. AbilityNet also looked at the Beijing Olympics website (2008b)

which, despite all the problems with the website of the Sydney Olympic Games, had poor levels of accessibility.

Possible Reasons for Poor Accessibility in Practice

There are multiple reasons given in the literature for poor website accessibility. Some suggest that it is due to a lack of awareness amongst web designers of the importance of accessible design and recommend training in accessible design techniques to solve the fundamental problem (Rosmaita 2006), or say that web designers tend to design for people like themselves (often young, male, computer literate and not disabled) and are unable to empathise with disability, age or impairment (Thatcher et al., 2000). Designers may also have an unconscious fear of disability, and this "discomfort and ignorance" could lead to the exclusion of disabled people from the perceived audience of the site (Clark, 2002, p.16). Others argue that false presumptions can lead to poor accessibility, that accessible websites are too expensive to produce (Clark, 2002), or that accessible websites have to be bland, "vanilla" sites with no room for design and creativity (Harper, Yesilada & Goble 2004, p.2, Petrie, Hamilton & King 2003, p.13). This view is held by Olson, who says that the obligation to make accessible websites "...was a nearly perfect way to stifle creative freedom and slam the brakes on the Internet's expansion" (2000, p.49, quoted by Oravec 2002, p.455), and by the Boston Herald, which suggested that "not only will handicapped access on the Web be expensive to achieve, but it will stifle creativity and innovation ... and may force some Web masters to keep displays static and dull" (1999, p.26, quoted by Oravec 2002, p.455).

The Disability Rights Commission suggests that awareness of accessibility issues is no longer the core issue, rather "what [developers] lack is training in, and the resulting confidence in the use of, accessibility features." (Disability Rights Commission, 2004, p.41.) Others, such as Sloan, Heath and Hamilton (2006) and Kelly et al (2005), believe that although guidelines such as WCAG can be difficult to understand and need to be interpreted in the context of specific development settings, further problems arise from the way the WCAG is worked into organisational policy. Clark (2003) argued that the first version of the W3C's Web Content Accessibility Guidelines (WCAG 1.0), which were in effect until the latest version (WCAG 2.0) was released in December 2008, were "unrealistic guidelines divorced from real-world web development that are at once too vague and too specific." (The new version of the guidelines, WCAG 2.0 aims to have addressed some of the criticisms about the ease of use of previous versions, but at the point of writing little evidence is available on which to judge the extent to which this aim has been achieved). Alongside this argument is a view that the problems are exacerbated by the misuse of automated testing tools. These are easy to use on a site, but can produce false reassurance of accessibility, as organisations may fail to apply manual checks or user tests (Kelly et al., 2005).

What Can Be Done to Improve Website Accessibility?

In view of the significant numbers of people likely to be affected by inaccessible websites, it is clearly of vital importance to address these shortcomings in website accessibility. Problems with the usability of the accessible design guidance, coupled with a lack of training and the fact that there are many misconceptions about the costs and design restrictions of implementing an accessible site, may all have contributed to the slow uptake in accessible design practice. The emphasis in designing for website accessibility has tended to be on the features and functions of the website. Yet the addition of an accessibility statement, as long as it is user-centered and offers practical help, is an

important additional way of making a website more accessible. In the following sections we shall focus on the role of the accessibility statement as an aid to website accessibility and provide guidance for the design of effective accessibility statements. In addition to the published literature about accessibility statements, we draw on a comparative study of 110 websites carried out by Parkinson (2007) which investigated the use, nature and content of website accessibility statements in two different sectors in the UK – local government and high street retailers.

ACCESSIBILITY STATEMENTS AND THEIR ROLE IN WEBSITE ACCESSIBILITY

What Is an Accessibility Statement?

An accessibility statement is most often a single page or group of pages on a website that is dedicated to declaring the accessibility of the website for disabled people and others with accessibility needs. Accessibility statements are not a compulsory feature of websites and indeed are not present on every site. In the sample of 110 websites surveyed by Parkinson (2007), 55 (50%) did have an accessibility statement, with public sector organisations providing them more often than private sector/commercial organisations. As will be evident from inspection of accessibility statements where they are provided on a website, there is wide variation in terms of their content, style and tone, their location and visibility on the website, their level of detail and in the audience that is addressed.

With regard to content, our research found some or all of the following features in the accessibility statements surveyed:

- a statement of the organisation's commitment to accessibility
- an outline of the accessibility features of the site

- a statement about how the website complies with accessibility standards and legislation
- information about how the user can make accessibility adjustments, by altering their browser settings or using access keys as keyboard shortcuts
- details of the process undertaken to make the website accessible
- an explanation of accessibility problems within the website and a promise of resolution
- details of how to contact the webmaster if accessibility problems are encountered
- links to external tools or information that may be of assistance

It is possible to see how some of these features are utilised in an accessibility statement by looking at the example accessibility statement provided as an appendix at the end of this chapter. This accessibility statement comes from the website of the Royal National Institute of Blind People (RNIB), an organisation that supports blind and partially sighted people in the UK. This statement includes a declaration of the organisation's commitment to accessibility:

We are committed to ensuring everyone can access our website. This includes people with sight problems, hearing, mobility and cognitive impairments as well as users with dial-up, older browsers or newer technologies such as mobiles and PDAs. It outlines the accessibility features of the site under the heading "How the site is built for accessibility" by explaining how the layout and content of the site has been designed to be accessible and what the implications of these design decisions are for the user. The statement also outlines the process of testing the accessibility of the website "by users with a range of disabilities including mobility, hearing and cognitive impairments as well as users with sight problems", to further explain the process undertaken to make the website accessible. The statement includes a

section which explains how the website complies with accessibility standards and legislation and external links are also provided to the organisation's 'See it Right' checkpoints and the WAI's guidelines.

A particular feature of this accessibility statement is the user help that it provides, with information about how the user can make accessibility adjustments, together with information about how to navigate and search within the site. A means of contacting the web team with feedback about the use of the site is also provided.

Although there is considerable diversity, our survey of accessibility statements found could broadly be classified into the following different 'types':

- *Minimal* statements are brief, and only contain one or two elements within them, such as a short statement of commitment to accessibility or a few conformance logos
- *Declarative* statements make announcements about the website's accessibility; the statement is used to inform others (who may be the website user with accessibility needs or may be an alternative audience) of the ways in which the website conforms with accessibility standards or with the accessibility policy of the organisation. Such statements do not contain instructions for the user (or contain little or no instructions for the user).
- *User centered* statements direct their commentary towards the website user and tend to provide more practical instructions and assistance to help the user to make the website more accessible; providing instructions on how to alter the text size, for example, or to set other personal preferences
- *Specialist* statements are defined by their vocabulary, which is often highly technical. Due to this terminology, the statements are difficult to understand for those who are not web designers.

- Finally, *mixed* statements take on multiple combined roles of user support, policy declaration, technical detail and others

The accessibility statement from the RNIB is a good example of a user-centered statement, that provides practical assistance to aid the user of the website. Any material that is related to policy, legislation or design technicalities is written in a clear and simple way, to avoid alienation of the user.

It would appear from the evident differences between accessibility statements in practice, as well as from the literature (discussed below) that there is little consensus about what a statement is for, and which audience it is intended for. Nevertheless research suggests that accessibility statements that enable communication between the designer/organisation and the user, and that are written in a user-centred way, have an important role to play in website accessibility.

Role of the Accessibility Statement in Website Accessibility

There are a number of ways in which a good accessibility statement can play a part in making a website accessible. The statement can act as a contract between the organisation and the user and offer an opportunity for the organisation to express their commitment to meeting the accessibility needs of their users. As Hochheiser and Shneiderman (2001, p.16) say, this is "a powerful means of building user confidence". However an accessibility statement that solely provides assurances of commitment to accessibility and offers no other material is of little value in improving accessibility. It must provide or at least link to further useful information for the website user – and must also be part of a website that is accessible. In our research we have come across several accessibility statements on inaccessible websites that declare their commitment to accessibility and effectively ask the website user to

'watch this space' for accessibility developments. Such statements have a hollow ring to them and can, justifiably, make the disabled web user feel dismissed. A good accessibility statement, on the other hand, can establish an open commitment of good practice that can be the basis for the relationship between the disabled web user and the organisation's website.

As shown in Figure 2 below, an important but under-recognised aspect of an accessibility statement is providing information to the user about the accessibility of the website – for example, telling the user what steps have been taken to make the website accessible, what accessibility standards and evaluation have been used, and what the user can do themselves in order to adapt the website to make it more accessible for their particular needs. This diagram also highlights the fact that accessibility is not just the responsibility of the *designer* (who needs awareness, appropriate skills and resources to create an accessible site, in addition to motivation – which may be provided by the legislation described above) but involves also the *provider* of the website (who may commission the website design, maintain the website, and is primarily responsible for content and delivery of services through the website) and the *user* who brings their own awareness, skills, resources and motivation to their use of the website. Many disabled users will be informed and skilled and have access to resources (for example screen readers) which will enable them to access websites in a particular way, but that bring with them their own accessibility requirements. Other users may be less aware of the impact of their impairments, less aware about and skilled in how to access websites and not have any assistive technology to help them. Both kinds of users (and many other variations in between these two somewhat extreme examples) will have different requirements for accessibility which need to be taken into account.

If the accessibility statement is available in some form at the beginning of the process of website development, it can also be useful in

Figure 2. The role of the accessibility statement in website accessibility

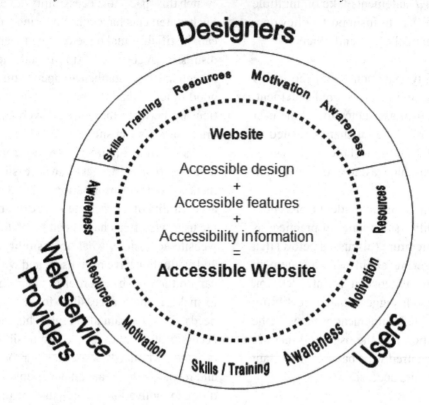

holding the organisation to account in upholding accessible web design principles. The statement is the 'public face' of the accessibility policy, and, as such, its very presence can be a driver for the development and maintenance of an accessible website. The UK's PAS 78 document 'Guide to Good Practice in Commissioning Accessible Websites', acknowledges that an accessibility statement can have an important role at the beginning of the design process as it can be "referenced in tender and contract documents" (British Standards Institution, 2006, p.17).

An accessibility statement can provide an opportunity for the organisation to communicate with the website user about the accessibility features of the website. It can inform the user of the levels of accessibility of the website, so that the user can find out whether the website will meet their accessibility needs. It can also be a place where existing accessibility barriers are

acknowledged and explained, which is useful for disabled website users if alternative methods of accessing inaccessible material on the site are also provided. Most importantly of all, the accessibility statement can inform and educate the user of the website, explaining the accessibility features of the site and instructing the user on how to make changes to the site through their own browser settings to enhance accessibility. When used in this way, the accessibility statement becomes a tool for enhanced accessibility of the website.

Accessibility statements also provide a means of communication from website user to web developer, so that the user can provide feedback on their experience of using the website. Website users may encounter barriers when using the site, and should be provided with a means of reporting these barriers and asking for solutions to be provided to inaccessible content. A good accessibility statement will have a link that allows the user to contact someone who is responsible for website maintenance, rather than a generic 'contact us' link, to enable communication about the technical and practical aspects of the website experience to occur with the appropriate person.

It is clear that accessibility statements have the potential to fulfil a range of useful roles in website accessibility. The challenge for website developers and providers is to produce a quality statement that matches up to this potential.

We review below the guidance that is available to provide direction on producing a good accessibility statement.

Guidance for the Development of Accessibility Statements

In the guidance available for web designers on creating an accessible website there is generally little mention of accessibility statements. Statements are discussed in places on the WAI website, for example as a means of informing the user of the policy on retrofitting the website (Web Accessibility Initiative, 2006a), but this is buried deep within the site and there are no documents specifically devoted to accessibility statements.

Many accessibility statements include claims of conformance to some kind of accessibility standard or level. The WCAG 2.0 (Web Accessibility Initiative, 2008a) includes a section that provides guidance for how to make a claim of conformance to the WCAG guidelines on a website. They make it clear that making a conformance claim is strictly optional. However, they stipulate that if a claim of conformance to the WCAG 2.0 is made, it must contain certain 'required' elements, and they provide examples of conformance claims to illustrate the form that conformance claims should take (Web Accessibility Initiative 2008c). The elements that they list as required for a conformance claim are the date of the claim, the conformance level reached – A, AA or AAA, the full name of the guidelines with a link to them, a list/description of the web pages referred to and a list of

the web content technologies relied upon (e.g. HTML, CSS, JavaScript, etc.). They also provide suggested optional components as follows (Web Accessibility Initiative, 2008a):

- "A list of success criteria beyond the level of conformance claimed that have been met. This information should be provided in a form that users can use, preferably machine-readable metadata.
- A list of the specific technologies that are '*used but not relied upon*'.
- A list of user agents, including assistive technologies that were used to test the content.
- Information about any additional steps taken that go beyond the success criteria to enhance accessibility [2]
- A machine-readable metadata version of the list of specific technologies that are re-lied upon.[3]
- A machine-readable metadata version of the conformance claim."

They also encourage the reporting of any efforts that have been made to attain a higher conformance level, when that level is not yet been attained.

Figure 3 below shows the examples that are provided in the WCAG 2.0 guidance of conformance claims containing only required components, and Figure 4 below provides an example for claims including optional components:

These examples contain a considerable amount of technical information, in a set format, that may be of benefit for the web developer or the organisation in making a claim of conformance. However, such material may potentially 'frighten off' the average user with accessibility needs who they may wish to help with the practical instructions in the rest of their accessibility statement.

Statements of conformance can be one component of an accessibility statement, but as is evident from the observations above, an accessibility statement which in itself makes a contribution to the

Figure 3. Example of Required Components of Conformance Claims – W3C Understanding Conformance (Source: http://www.w3.org/TR/UNDERSTANDING-WCAG20/conformance.html#uc-conformance-requirements-head. Accessed 25.06.09) Copyright © World Wide Web Consortium, (Massachusetts Institute of Technology, European Research Consortium for Informatics and Mathematics, Keio University). All Rights Reserved. http://www.w3.org/Consortium/Legal/2002/copyright-documents-20021231.

Examples of Required Components of Conformance Claims

Example 1: On 20 September 2009, all Web pages at http://www.example.com conform to Web Content Accessibility Guidelines 2.0 at http://www.w3.org/TR/2006/REC-WCAG20-20081211/. Level A conformance.

- The documented set of accessibility-supported content technologies **relied upon** for this claim is a subset of ISA- AsCTset#1-2008 at http://ISA.example.gov/AsCTsets/AS2-2008.

Example 2: (using a regular expression) On 12 August 2009, pages matching the pattern http://www.example.com/(marketing|sales|contact)/.* conform to Web Content Accessibility Guidelines 2.0 at http://www.w3.org/TR/2006/REC-WCAG20-20081211/. Level AA conformance.

- The technologies that this content **"relies upon"** is: XHTML 1.0 Transitional, CSS 2.0 and JavaScript 1.2.

Example 3: (using boolean logic) On 6 January 2009, http://example.com/ AND NOT (http://example.com/archive/ OR http://example.com/publications/archive/) conforms to Web Content Accessibility Guidelines 2.0 at http://www.w3.org/TR/2006/REC-WCAG20-20081211/. Level AA conformance.

- The documented set of accessibility-supported content technologies **relied upon** for this claim includes XHTML 1.0 and SMIL from ISA- AsCTset#1-2008 at http://ISA.example.gov/AsCTsets/AS2-2008.

accessibility of the website must have additional elements. The document PAS 78 'Guide to Good Practice in Commissioning Accessible Websites' (British Standards Institution, 2006), written for website commissioners, is the only piece of formal guidance at present that comes close to recommending and describing an accessibility statement which meets these criteria. It encourages the development of a formal accessibility policy, provides recommendations for the content of the policy and states that a summary should be placed on the website. However the new full British Standard (BS 8878, Web Accessibility – Building Accessible Experiences for Disabled People) which is currently being developed and is due to be published in late 2009, is expected to contain text that organisations can extract and use in their accessibility or procurement statement (British Standards Institution, 2009). Other articles in the academic and professional literature do offer advice on how to write a state-

ment based upon research about web accessibility and usability (Gibson, 2004; Hochheiser & Shneiderman, 2001; Phipps, Harrison, Sloan, & Willder, 2004; Phipps, Witt & McDermott, n.d.; Providenti, 2005; Sloan, Dickinson, McIlroy, & Gibson, 2006). Similar articles offering advice have also been written by web design practitioners based on their expertise in accessible design (e.g. Lemon, 2005; Pilgrim, 2002).

The most comprehensive mention of accessibility statements in books about web accessibility comes from Joe Clark, who offers some detailed instructions on the content and purpose of statements (2002, pp.335-343). Other website accessibility textbooks (e.g. Ruse, 2005; Thatcher et al., 2002) mention validation and recommend logos, but do not deal with accessibility statements. Most of the academic articles on 'how to make your website accessible' do not mention accessibility statements. Of those that do, Burgstahler (2006)

Figure 4. Example of Conformance Claims Including Optional Components – W3C Understanding Conformance (Source: http://www.w3.org/TR/UNDERSTANDING-WCAG20/conformance.html#uc-conformance-requirements-head Accessed 25.06.09) Copyright © World Wide Web Consortium, (Massachusetts Institute of Technology, European Research Consortium for Informatics and Mathematics, Keio University). All Rights Reserved. http://www.w3.org/Consortium/Legal/2002/copyright-documents-20021231.

Examples of Conformance Claims Including Optional Components

Example 1: On 5 May 2009, the page "G7: An Introduction"
http://telcor.example.com/nav/G7/intro.html conforms to Web Content Accessibility Guidelines 2.0 at
http://www.w3.org/TR/2006/REC-WCAG20-20081211/. Level AA conformance.

- The following additional Success Criteria have also been met: 1.1.2, 1.2.5, and 1.4.3.
- The documented set of accessibility-supported content technologies used for this claim is AsCTset#1-2006 at http://UDLabs.org/AsCTset#1-2006.html.
- The technologies that this content **"relies upon"** is: XHTML 1.0 (Strict), and Real Video.
- The technologies that this content **"uses but does not rely upon"** are: JavaScript 1.2, CSS2.

Example 2: On 21 June 2009, all content beginning with the URI http://example.com/nav and
http://example.com/docs conform to Web Content Accessibility Guidelines 2.0 at
http://www.w3.org/TR/2006/REC-WCAG20-20081211/. Level AAA conformance.

- The documented set of accessibility-supported content technologies used for this claim is SMITH- AsCTset#2-2008 at http://smithreports.example.com/AsCTsets/AS2-2008.
- The technologies that this content **"relies upon"** are: XHTML 1.0 (Strict), CSS2, JavaScript 1.2, JPEG, PNG.
- The user agents, including assistive technologies, that this content has been tested with can be found at http://example.com/docs/WCAG20/test/technologies.html.

Example 3: On 23 March 2009, all content available on the server at
http://www.wondercall.example.com conforms to Web Content Accessibility Guidelines 2.0 at
http://www.w3.org/TR/2006/REC-WCAG20-20081211/. Single-A conformance.

- The technology that this content **"relies upon"** is: HTML 4.01.
- The technologies that this content **"uses but does not rely upon"** are: CSS2, and gif.
- This content was tested using the following user agents and assistive technologies: Firefox 1.5 on Windows Vista with Screenreader X 4.0, Firefox 1.5 on Windows XP SP 2 with Screenreader X 3.5, IE 6.0 on Windows 2000 SP4 with Screenreader Y 5.0, IE 6.0 on Windows 2000 SP4 with Screenreader Z 2.0, and Firefox 1.5 on Windows XP SP2 with Screenreader X 4.0, Safari 2.0 with OS X 10.4.

and Chavan and Steins (2003) are good examples. They offer little advice on content, but recommend their use as part of an overall strategy.

The patchy mention of accessibility statements in official advice results in a lack of clarity for those looking for official endorsement of accessibility statements and advice on their content and use. It may be one explanation for the lack of uniformity in the content and execution of statements in practice. The lack of guidance is evident in forum discussions, where web designers are turning to each other and offering their own advice and support to help with writing accessibility statements (Accessify, 2005; WebAim, 2005).

The range of advice provided by authors on how to produce a good accessibility statement is mixed in quality and contains significantly different emphases. The authors recommend different content and approaches. Clark's (2002) recommendations, for example, are web-designer centered, and have no elements of customer help, education or assurance. In contrast, both Sloan et al (2006) and Lemon's advice (2005) are wholly user-focused. Hochheiser and Shneiderman's recommendations (2001) are broad, addressing accessibility and usability elements. Gibson (2004) and Phipps et al's (2004) advice focuses on accuracy of conformance claims and clarity of information, whilst Providenti (2005) concentrates on organisational and technical elements.

Many writers agree that the statement should be easy to locate and many advocate simple, clear writing that is easy to read and understand. Despite their agreement about clarity, several writers include complex technical information in their examples of good accessibility statements:

This site validates as XHTML 1.1... This site uses structured semantic markup. <h3> tags have been used to identify subsections within each page... Relative links have been defined... Alternate style sheets have been used... (Providenti, 2005, p.59)

All pages on this site use structured semantic markup... All content images... include descriptive ALT attributes... Complex images include LONGDESC attributes or inline descriptions... (Pilgrim, 2002).

It would be unfortunate if, as a result of the WCAG 2.0 guidance, web developers confined their accessibility statements to claims of conformance, or made this the first part of an accessibility statement, since this kind of technical language is potentially alienating for website users and could deter users from reading any other help material on the statement page.

Our research uncovered not only conflicting possible roles and purposes for the statements, and a lack of clear and consistent guidance about how to write a statement, but, apart from Sloan et al (2006), also an absence of research into how they are used by people who may benefit from the information in a statement. The result is that someone trying to write a statement has many difficult issues to contend with. They may not be clear about the best reasons for writing a statement, or who the statement should be written for. They also may not know how best to write the statement or how to present it. These dilemmas are evident from the discussion in online discussion forums and from the

statements that were observed in our research; the results showed a lack of consistency in statement content, use of statements for multiple purposes, statements that were not always directed at the user and poor, inaccessible delivery of statements.

Specific additional failings of accessibility statements in practice that were observed in our research (Parkinson, 2007), included statements which were buried deep within a website without effective and obvious links to help the website user locate them. When there were links to the statement, they were often located at the bottom of the home page in a small font and a pale colour with similar links to legal pages and other 'small print' on the site. Of the statements themselves, we found many with highly complex and technical language, that included considerable computer and web design jargon, with few explanations of the terms or acronyms (such as W3C, WAI, DDA and DRC) that were included. Some of the statements presented their information in an 'unintelligible jumble', mixing up many different elements for different audiences (such as conformance declarations, technical information and practical instructions) into a single complex paragraph. Many were in danger of 'turning off' the average website user by beginning the statement with the technical information. Many others seemed to avoid providing practical help and instructions at any cost. A few statements included completely irrelevant material, such as service opening hours and statistics, demonstrating considerable confusion about the purpose of the accessibility statement. If accessibility statements in practice are so badly produced, it is little wonder that some web-designers consider them to be irrelevant.

Despite Chavan and Steins' (2003, p.13) assertion that adding an accessibility statement is "the easiest step to take" in making a website more accessible, it is clear from our findings above that producing a good accessibility statement is anything but easy. It appears that there is little consensus about content and emphasis from those offering advice about how to write a good accessibility statement, and those seeking direction from the advice that is available will develop very different accessibility statements depending on the source of advice that they consult. Furthermore, we would argue that, even if the guidance were clear and coherent, an accessibility statement is only a positive contribution towards accessibility if it is directed towards the user and makes a practical contribution to their ability to use the website.

Below we present a set of recommendations which attempt to overcome these problems. The recommendations are distilled and synthesised from previous advice provided in the literature and our analysis of features of the statements reviewed as part of our own research.

RECOMMENDATIONS

These recommendations are divided into four categories. Recommendations about access relate to where the accessibility statement is positioned and how the user navigates to it. The next set of recommendations relate specifically to the content, and wording of statements. The third category relates to ensuring that the style and tone of the statement are appropriate to the target audience. The final category relates to the way that the content is organised and structured.

Access

- Ensure that the statement is clearly signposted, with links from every page, especially the homepage
- Make the links to this statement clear and apparent. Put them at the top of the page, with clear colour contrast and good size.
- Use a practical, solution-orientated phrase for the link. Avoid 'disability' and 'accessibility'. Consider a 'how to' phrase instead, perhaps including the word 'help'.

- Make your statement page accessible. Remember to make the rest of your site accessible too – people will be using the whole site, not just the accessibility statement.

Content

- Include, if you want to, a statement about how important accessibility is to your company. But don't just leave it at that. Include as a minimum:
- Practical instructions about how to use the accessibility features on the site, including access keys, browser changes and instructions on how to navigate around the site.
- Information and links to tools that can help the user to get the most from the site, for example the BBC website 'My Web, My Way' (BBC, 2009).
- An acknowledgement of current accessibility problems with the site and an explanation of how users can access the content in an alternative way.
- Contact details that connect directly with the webmaster rather than a general customer service point. Encourage users to report accessibility difficulties with the site and include a commitment to resolving these difficulties.
- Details of compliance with guidelines (but consider including a plain English explanation of the meanings of this material and do not make this the first thing you mention).
- Avoid writing too much about what you have done to make the site accessible. This material often becomes overly technical. Instead focus on the solutions for the user.
- Do not include extra, irrelevant material in the statement, like opening hours.

Audience, Language and Style

- Write the statement for the user of the website, not for other web designers or policy makers.
- Write the statement for a broad audience base, including older people. Avoid writing just for disabled people.
- Remember that access issues cover a broad spectrum of areas – do not only write for visually impaired people or people who cannot use a mouse.
- Keep it really simple – use simple language and plain English.
- Avoid specialist terminology at all costs – something that you consider easy to understand may not mean anything to the reader.
- Write it directly to the user who is facing accessibility difficulties with your website Use phrases like "if you want to make the text bigger …" "if you need to listen to the text…" rather than "changing browser settings."
- If you need to write about people with impairments, use 'disabled people' rather than 'people with disabilities' or 'the disabled' - this is in line with the Social Model of Disability, which is the model which many disabled people prefer.

Presentation

- Avoid one really long paragraph for your statement. Divide the text into clearly headed paragraphs. Make sure that each paragraph contains only one idea.
- Use visual clues or pictograms for each paragraph for easy identification of the contents by users with reading or concentration difficulties.
- Put practical instructions first and make them the main focus on the page. Sideline other information that is not aimed at the average website user (for example, highly technical conformance information) by putting it in a separate section on the page, or by creating a link for further information.
- Put links to every section of the statement at the top of the page, to enable users to quickly jump to the section they need. Make the links meaningful and simple.
- Use diagrams and/or screenshots to explain how to change browser settings.
- Consider providing 'instant buttons' that generate an immediate change in text size or text/background colour.

CONCLUSION

Accessibility statements have not been without their critics, and a small but vocal number of web developers have asserted that they are unhelpful, and would be better left out of websites (see, for example, Rosie Sherry's (2006) article 'Showing web accessibility statements the door' in Usability News). One of the main arguments of critics is that the user-related help information in accessibility statements designed to enable web users to make adjustments to their browser settings are unnecessary and that providing this information is simply 'stating the obvious'. The danger with this argument, however, is that it presumes a level of knowledge about making accessibility-related adjustments that is not always held by those who use websites. Research has shown that people testing accessibility statements do not always have the knowledge that critics believe to be obvious. They do not know how to adjust their browser settings, are afraid of breaking the computer by making alterations, and will devise alternative ways of improving their online experience such as copying and pasting text into other applications or adjusting ambient lighting, because they are unaware of the accessibility options available to them (Sloan et al, 2006).

We have argued in this chapter that accessibility statements are not superfluous, but, if written in a certain way, can be a useful vehicle for making websites more accessible and usable for disabled people. Accessibility is important because it can help to avoid the 'digital divide' whereby some individuals are excluded from access to digital technologies, and in many cases the providers of websites and web-based services could be breaking anti-discrimination legislation by failing to make their sites accessible. Furthermore making websites accessible can offer a number of other benefits for providers as well as customers.

So what should be done to ensure that the potential benefits offered by a well-written and well-designed accessibility statement are realised? Firstly, accessibility statements should be more than dry, policy documents and instead offer real, practical help. The recommendations contained in this paper provide a starting point for this. Better communication of this message to web designers and organisations, and persuasion of the possible benefits to the user of accessibility statements is clearly needed. Further regulation may not be the best way forward, as requiring a statement may lead to 'tokenistic' or 'copy-cat' statements that are not related to the actual website or the intended users. A preferable approach would be to raise awareness both of their potential for contributing to improved accessibility and of the principles for producing helpful and effective statements. A clear message of support from the W3C and WAI and other influential bodies may be useful, positioning statements as user-centred help and explaining how to accomplish this. Website providers can exercise influence by requiring the production of high-quality accessibility statements that act as an additional tool for their website accessibility. In this way they would be moving closer to providing quality services for their website users, meeting their legal obligations and widening their customer base. The resulting benefits for all would be clear.

ACKNOWLEDGMENT

We would like to thank our anonymous reviewers for their helpful suggestions for revision of this chapter, and also Dr David Sloan of the School of Computing at the University of Dundee for his expert advice and guidance.

REFERENCES

AbilityNet. (2003a). *State of the e-nation report: UK on-line newspapers.* Retrieved June 1, 2009, from http://www.abilitynet.org.uk/content/one-offs/Newspaper%20eNation%20report.pdf

AbilityNet. (2003b). *State of the e-nation report: UK airlines.* Retrieved June 1, 2009, from http://www.abilitynet.org.uk/content/oneoffs/Airlines%20eNation%20report.pdf

AbilityNet. (2004a). *State of the e-nation report: Premiership clubs.* Retrieved June 1, 2009, from http://www.abilitynet.org.uk/content/oneoffs/eNation%20report%20-%20Football%20Clubs.pdf

AbilityNet. (2004b). *State of the e-nation report: Online banks.* Retrieved June 1, 2009, from http://www.abilitynet.org.uk/content/oneoffs/eNation%20report%20-%20Online%20banks.pdf

AbilityNet. (2004c). *State of the e-nation report: Online supermarkets.* Retrieved June 1, 2009, from http://www.abilitynet.org.uk/content/oneoffs/eNation%20report%20-%20supermarkets.pdf

AbilityNet. (2004d). *State of the e-nation report: Retail websites.* Retrieved June 1, 2009, from http://www.abilitynet.org.uk/content/oneoffs/eNation%20report%20-%20Retail%20Sites.pdf

AbilityNet. (2007a). *State of the e-nation report: Online dating sites.* Retrieved June 1, 2009, from http://www.abilitynet.co.uk/docs/enation/2007datingSites.pdf

AbilityNet. (2007b). *State of the e-nation report: Utility and switching sites.* Retrieved June 1, 2009, from http://www.abilitynet.co.uk/docs/enation/2006utilitySites.pdf

AbilityNet. (2008a). *State of the e-nation report: Social networking sites.* Retrieved June 1, 2009, from http://www.abilitynet.co.uk/docs/enation/2008SocialNetworkingSites.pdf

AbilityNet. (2008b). *State of the e-nation report: The Beijing Olympics.* Retrieved June 1, 2009, from http://www.abilitynet.co.uk/docs/enation/2008BeijingSpecialReport.pdf

Accessify. (2005). *Accessibility statement.* Retrieved May 10, 2009, from http://www.accessifyforum.com/viewtopic.php?t=2307

Adaptive Technology Resource Centre. (n.d). *Web accessibility verifier: Ensuring that your web pages are accessible to all people.* Retrieved November 21, 2008, from http://aprompt.snow.utoronto.ca/

Americans with Disabilities Act. (1990). Retrieved May 20, 2009, from http://www.ada.gov/pubs/adastatute08.htm

BBC. (2009). *My web, my way.* Retrieved June 26, 2009, from http://www.bbc.co.uk/accessibility/

British Standards Institution. (2006). *PAS 78: 2006. Guide to good practice in commissioning accessible websites.* Retrieved June 1, 2009, from http://www.bsonline.bsi-global.com/server/PdfControlServlet/bsol?pdfId=GBM02%2F30129227&format=pdf

British Standards Institution. (2009). *BS 8788 Web accessibility: Building accessible experiences for disabled people* (in preparation). Retrieved June 26, 2009, from http://www.bsigroup.com/en/Standards-and-Publications/Industry-Sectors/ICT/ICT-standards/BS-8878/

Burgstahler, S. (2006). Web accessibility: Guidelines for busy administrators. *Handbook of Business Strategy, 7*(1), 313-318. Retrieved June 1, 2009, from http://www.emeraldinsight.com/Insight/viewContentItem.do?contentType=Article&hdAction=lnkpdf&contentId=1523742

Carey, K. (2005). Accessibility: The current situation and new directions. *Ariadne, 44.* Retrieved June 5, 2009, from http://www.ariadne.ac.uk/issue44/carey/

Chavan, A., & Steins, C. (2003). Doing the right thing. *Planning, 69*(7), 10-13. Retrieved June 1, 2009, from http://proquest.umi.com/pqdweb?did=379258791&Fmt=3&clientId=5238&RQT=309&VName=PQD

Chisholm, W., & May, M. (2008). *Universal design for web applications.* Sebastopol, CA: O'Reilly.

Clark, J. (2002). *Building accessible websites.* Indianapolis: New Riders Publishing.

Clark, J. (2003). *How to save web accessibility from itself.* Retrieved June 10, 2009, from http://www.alistapart.com/articles/saveaccessibility/

Davies, M. (2006). *Isolani, PAS 78 launch, 2006.* Retrieved June 10, 2009, from http://www.isolani.co.uk/blog/access/Pas78Launch

Deque, (2008). *Deque RAMP™ product family.* Retrieved November 21, 2008, from http://deque.com/products/ramp/index.php

Disability Discrimination Act. (1995). (c.50) London: HMSO. Retrieved May 20, 2009, from http://www.opsi.gov.uk/acts/acts1995/ukpga_19950050_en_1

Disability Rights Commission. (2004). *The web, access and inclusion for disabled people: A formal investigation conducted by the Disability Rights Commission.* London: TSO. Retrieved May 25, 2009, from http://83.137.212.42/sitearchive/drc/PDF/2.pdf

Ellison, J. (2004). Assessing the accessibility of fifty United States government web pages. *First Monday, 9*(7). Retrieved April 23, 2009, from http://firstmonday.org/issues/issue9_7/ellison/index.html

European Commission. (2000). *Directive 2000/78/EC*. Retrieved May 20, 2009, from http://ec.europa.eu/employment_social/news/2001/jul/dir200078_en.html

European Commission. (2001). *Eurostat: Disability and social participation in Europe*. Retrieved June 11, 2009, from http://epp.eurostat.ec.europa.eu/cache/ITY_OFFPUB/KS-AW-01-001/EN/KS-AW-01-001-EN.PDF

European Commission. (2003). *Eurostat: One in six of the EU working-age population report disability*. Retrieved June 11, 2009, from http://epp.eurostat.ec.europa.eu/cache/ITY_PUBLIC/3-05122003-AP/EN/3-05122003-AP-EN.HTML

Gibson, L. (2004). *Writing an accessibility statement*. Retrieved June 1, 2009, from http://www.dmag.org.uk/resources/design_articles/accessibilitystatement.asp

Hackett, S., Parmanto, B., & Zeng, X. (2004). *Accessibility of internet websites through time*. Paper presented at the 6th International ACM SIGACCESS Conference on Computers and Accessibility, 18-20 October 2004, Atlanta. Retrieved June 1, 2009, from http://delivery.acm.org/10.1145/1030000/1028638/p32-hackett.pdf?key1=1028638&key2=0515277511&coll=ACM&dl=ACM&CFID=486951&CFTOKEN=79021637

Harper, S., Yesilada, Y., & Goble, C. (2004). Workshop report: W4A - International Cross Disciplinary Workshop on Web Accessibility 2004. *ACM SIGCAPH Computers and the Physically Handicapped, 76*, 2-3. Retrieved June 1, 2009, from http://portal.acm.org/ft_gateway.cfm?id=1037130&type=pdf&coll=ACM&dl=ACM&CFID=486951&CFTOKEN=79021637

Hochheiser, H., & Shneiderman, B. (2001). Universal usability statements: marking the trail for all users. *Interactions, 8*(2), 16-18. Retrieved June 1, 2009, from http://portal.acm.org/citation.cfm?id=361897.361913

IGDA. (2004). *Accessibility in games: motivations and approaches*. Retrieved May 29, 2009, from http://www.igda.org/accessibility/IGDA_Accessibility_WhitePaper.pdf

Insight, S. (Producer), & Tibbetts, J. (Director). (2007). *A world denied* [DVD]. Extract retrieved June 26, 2009, from http://www.socitm.gov.uk/NR/rdonlyres/8B648F2B-B602-4224-8DA9-FD70BD822CAE/0/Aworlddeniedvideo.wmv

International Standards Organization. (1992 - 2000). *Standard 9241: Ergonomic requirements for office work with visual display terminals*. Retrieved November 21, 2008, from http://www.iso.org

Iwarsson, S., & Stahl, A. (2003). Accessibility, usability and universal design: Positioning and definition of concepts describing person-environment relationships. *Disability and Rehabilitation, 25*(2), 57–66.

Kelly, B., Sloan, D., Phipps, L., Petrie, H., & Hamilton, F. (2005). *Forcing standardization or accommodating diversity? A framework for applying the WCAG in the real world*. Paper presented at the International Cross-Disciplinary Workshop on Web Accessibility (W4A), 10-14 May 2005, Chiba, Japan. Retrieved June 1, 2009, from http://portal.acm.org/citation.cfm?id=1061811.1061820

Knight, J., Heaven, C., & Christie, I. (2002). *Inclusive citizenship*. London: Leonard Cheshire.

Lemon, G. (2005). *Writing a good accessibility statement*. Retrieved June 1, 2009, from http://juicystudio.com/article/writing-a-good-accessibility-statement.php

Lenhart, A., Horrigan, J., Rainie, L., Allen, K., Boyce, A., & Madden, M. (2003). *The ever shifting internet population: A new look at internet access and the digital divide.* Retrieved May 28, 2009, from http://www.pewinternet.org/~/media//Files/Reports/2003/PIP_Shifting_Net_Pop_Report.pdf.pdf

Loiacono, E., & McCoy, S. (2004). Web site accessibility: An online sector analysis. *Information Technology & People, 17*(1), 87-101. Retrieved June 1, 2009, from http://www.emeraldinsight.com/Insight/ViewContentServlet?Filename=/published/emeraldfulltextarticle/pdf/1610170105.pdf

Massie, B. (2005). *Bert Massie BSI Conference, London July 2005.* Retrieved August 30, 2006, from http://www.drc-gb.org/library/drc_speeches/bert_massie_-_bsi_conference_.aspx

Newell, A. F., & Gregor, P. (2000). Designing for extra-ordinary people and situations. *CSERIAC Gateway, 11*(1), 12–13.

News, B. B. C. (2002a). *Europe's ageing workforce.* Retrieved November 21, 2008, from http://news.bbc.co.uk/1/hi/world/europe/2053581.stm

News, B. B. C. (2002b). *Asia strained by ageing population.* Retrieved November 21, 2009, from http://news.bbc.co.uk/1/hi/world/south_asia/3025289.stm

Nielsen, J. (2009). *useit.com: Jakob Nielsen's website.* Retrieved June 11, 2009, from http://www.useit.com/

Oravec, J. A. (2002). Virtually accessible: Empowering students to advocate for accessibility and support universal design. *Library Hi Tech, 20*(4), 452-461. Retrieved June 1, 2009, from http://www.emeraldinsight.com/Insight/ViewContentServlet?Filename=/published/emeraldfulltextarticle/pdf/2380200407.pdf

Paciello, M. G. (2000). *Web accessibility for people with disabilities.* Lawrence, KS: CMP Books.

Parkinson, C. M. (2007). Website accessibility statements: a comparative investigation of local government and high street sectors. *Library and Information Research, 31*(98), 29-44. Retrieved November 19, 2008, from http://www.lirg.org.uk/lir/ojs/index.php/lir/article/viewFile/40/50

Pederick, C. (2009). *The web developer toolbar.* Retrieved June 26, 2009, from http://chrispederick.com/work/web-developer/

Persons with Disabilities (Equal Opportunities, Protection of Rights and Full Participation) Act. (1995). Retrieved May 28, 2009, from http://www.disabilityindia.org/pwdacts.cfm

Petrie, H., Hamilton, F., & King, N. (2003). *Tension? What tension?: Website accessibility and visual design.* Paper presented at the 2004 International Cross-Disciplinary Workshop on Web Accessibility (W4A) 17-22 May, 2004, New York. Retrieved June 1, 2009, from http://portal.acm.org/citation.cfm?id=990660&coll=ACM&dl=ACM&CFID=486951&CFTOKEN=79021637&ret=1#Fulltext

Petrie, H., & Kheir, O. (2007). *The relationship between accessibility and usability of websites.* Paper presented at the SIGCHI Conference on Human Factors in Computing Systems 28 April-03 May 2007, San Jose, CA. Retrieved June 1, 2009, from http://portal.acm.org/citation.cfm?id=1240624.1240688

Phipps, L., Harrison, S., Sloan, D., & Willder, B. (2004). Developing and publicising a workable accessibility strategy. *Ariadne, 38.* Retrieved June 1, 2009, from http://www.ariadne.ac.uk/issue38/phipps/intro.html

Phipps, L., Witt, N., & McDermott, A. (n.d.). *To logo or not to logo?* Retrieved June 1, 2009, from http://www.techdis.ac.uk/index.php?p=3_8_8

Pilgrim, M. (2002). *Dive into accessibility: 30 days to a more accessible website. Day 30: creating an accessibility statement.* Retrieved June 1, 2009, from http://diveintoaccessibility.org/day_30_creating_an_accessibility_statement.html

Providenti, M. (2005). The art of the accessibility statement. *Internet Reference Services Quarterly, 10*(1), 47–62. doi:10.1300/J136v10n01_04

Robb, D. (2005). One site fits all: Companies find web sites that comply with accessibility guidelines mean more customers. *Computerworld, 39*(13), 29-30. Retrieved June 1, 2009, from http://www.computerworld.com/action/article.do?command=viewArticleBasic&articleId=100607

Rosmaita, B. (2006). *Accessibility first! A new approach to web design.* Paper presented at the 37th SIGCSE Technical Symposium on Computer Science Education, 1-5 March 2006, Houston, Texas. Retrieved June 1, 2009, from http://portal.acm.org/citation.cfm?id=1124706.1121426

Ruse, K. (2005). *Web standards design guide.* Boston: Charles River Media.

Sherry, R. (2006). *Showing web accessibility statements the door.* Retrieved October 19, 2008, from http://www.usabilitynews.com/news/article3516.asp

Slatin, J. (2002). The imagination gap: Making web-based instructional resources accessible to students and colleagues with disabilities. *Currents in Electronic Literacy, 6.* Retrieved June 26, 2009, from http://www.cwrl.utexas.edu/currents/spring02/slatin.html

Sloan, D., Dickinson, A., McIlroy, N., & Gibson, L. (2006). *Evaluating the usability of online accessibility information.* Retrieved June 1, 2009, from http://www.techdis.ac.uk/index.php?p=3_10_10_1

Sloan, D., Heath, A., & Hamilton, F. (2006). *Contextual web accessibility: maximizing the benefit of accessibility guidelines.* Paper presented at the International Cross-Disciplinary Workshop on Web Accessibility (W4A), 10-14 May 2005, Chiba, Japan. Retrieved June 1, 2009, from http://portal.acm.org/citation.cfm?id=1133242&coll=ACM&dl=ACM&CFID=553412&CFTOKEN=75424160&ret=1#Fulltext

Sloan, M. (2001). *Institutional websites and legislation.* Retrieved June 1, 2009, from http://www.techdis.ac.uk/index.php?p=3_8_14

SSB BART Group. (2006). *InFocus suite overview.* Retrieved November 21, 2008, from http://ssbtechnologies.com

Taylor, H. (2000). *How the internet is improving the lives of Americans with disabilities.* Retrieved June 1, 2009, from http://www.harrisinteractive.com/harris_poll/index.asp?PID=93

Thatcher, J., Waddell, C., Henry, S., Swierenga, S., Urban, M., Burks, M., et al. (2002). *Constructing accessible websites.* Birmingham: Glasshaus.

The World Bank. (2009). *Disability and development.* Retrieved May 29, 2009, from http://go.worldbank.org/19SCI890L0

United Nations General Assembly. (1948). *Universal declaration of human rights.* Retrieved November 21, 2008, from http://www.un.org/Overview/rights.html

Wallis, J. (2005). The web, accessibility and inclusion: Networked democracy in the United Kingdom. *Library Review, 54*(8), 479-85. Retrieved June 6, 2009, from http://www.emeraldinsight.com/Insight/viewPDF.jsp?Filename=html/Output/Published/EmeraldFullTextArticle/Pdf/0350540806.pdf

Web Accessibility Initiative. (2005). *Involving users in web accessibility evaluation*. Retrieved June 11, 2009, from http://www.w3.org/WAI/eval/users.html

Web Accessibility Initiative. (2006a). *Improving the accessibility of your web site*. Retrieved June 11, 2009, from http://www.w3.org/WAI/impl/improving.html

Web Accessibility Initiative. (2008a). *Web content accessibility guidelines (WCAG) 2.0*. Retrieved June 10, 2009, from http://www.w3.org/TR/WCAG20/

Web Accessibility Initiative. (2008b). *Evaluating web sites for accessibility: Overview*. Retrieved June 10, 2009, from http://www.w3.org/WAI/eval/Overview.html

Web Accessibility Initiative. (2008c). *Understanding conformance*. Retrieved June 24, 2009, from http://www.w3.org/TR/UNDERSTANDING-WCAG20/conformance.html#uc-conformance-claims-head

Web Accessibility Tools Consortium. (2005). *Colour contrast analyser*. Retrieved June 26, 2009, from http://www.wat-c.org/tools/CCA/1.1/

WebAIM. (2005). *Check of an accessibility statement*. Retrieved May 10, 2009, from http://www.webaim.org/discussion/mail_thread.php?thread=2341&id=6773

WebAIM. (2009a). *The web content accessibility guidelines*. Retrieved June 11, 2009, from http://www.webaim.org/standards/wcag/

WebAIM. (2009b). *The WAVE web accessibility evaluation tool*. Retrieved June 26, 2009, from http://wave.webaim.org/

Witt, N., & McDermott, A. (2004). Web site accessibility: what logo will we use today? *British Journal of Educational Technology, 35*(1), 45-56. Retrieved June 1, 2009, from http://www.blackwell-synergy.com/doi/pdf/10.1111/j.1467-8535.2004.00367.x

World Health Organisation. (2009). *International classification of functioning, disability and health (ICF)*. Retrieved May 22, 2009, from http://www.who.int/classifications/icf/en/

Yu, H. (2002). Web accessibility and the law: recommendations for implementation. [from http://www.emeraldinsight.com/Insight/viewPDF.jsp?Filename=html/Output/Published/Emerald-FullTextArticle/Pdf/2380200403.pdf]. *Library Hi Tech, 20*(4), 406–419. Retrieved May 10, 2009. doi:10.1108/07378830210452613

ENDNOTES

[1] Other guidelines for specific sectors include Section 508 guidelines for US federal websites, and 'Guidelines for UK Government Websites' for UK government websites, although both of these are heavily influenced by the Web Content Accessibility Guidelines.

[2] "This can include additional Success Criteria that have been met, advisory techniques that were implemented, information about any additional protocols used to aid access for people with particular disabilities or needs, etc. Any information that would be useful to people in understanding the accessibility of the pages may be included." (Web Accessibility Initiative 2008c).

[3] "The most useful way of attaching conformance claims to content would be to do so in standard machine readable form. When this practice is widespread, search tools or special user agents will be able to make use of this information to find and provide content that is more accessible or so the user agents can adjust to the content" (Web Accessibility Initiative 2008c).

APPENDIX 1

Accessibility Statement from the RNIB (Royal National Institute of Blind People, UK)

This page is reached by clicking 'Help' from a menu at the top left hand side of the RNIB home page (www.rnib.org)

Site tools: Help

Summary: Information about our site, how to change how it looks and tips for people using screen readers.

- Using the site
- Audio help
- Where to start
- Search tips
- How the site is built for accessibility
- Conformance statement

We are committed to ensuring everyone can access our website. This includes people with sight problems, hearing, mobility and cognitive impairments as well as users with dial-up, older browsers or newer technologies such as mobiles and PDAs. If you have any comments and or suggestions please don't hesitate to contact us about the site (email webteam@rnib.org.uk).

Using the Site

- Change your browser settings - find out how to change the font type, colour and size to suit your needs.
- You may prefer the convenience of our font size changer which appears as three A's in the top right hand of every page.
- Tips for screenreader users about how the site is structured.
- Our 'jump to site navigation' and 'jump to site tools navigation' links (at the top left of each page) help people using screen readers to skip around the page.

Audio Help

We have a number of audio clips on the site, including an audio logo. Read our audio files help page if you are experiencing problems.

Where to Start

Use the sitemap to get an overview of what is on the site or try one of the audience pages:

- Friends or family
- General public
- Members
- Older people
- People with sight problems
- Professionals
- Supporters
- Teenagers

Each of the main navigation areas – Good Design, About us, Eye info, Support us, Daily life and Shop have sub-sections. All of these sections can be accessed quickly from the homepage, using the drop-down menu in the left-hand column called "Browse by section".

© RNIB, 2009 *(Source:*http://www.rnib.org/xpedio/groups/public/documents/publicwebsite/public_pubsitemap.hcsp) *(Accessed 01.06.09)*

Chapter 10
Considering the Perceptual Implications of Auditory Rich Content on the Web

Flaithrí Neff
University College Cork, Ireland

Aidan Kehoe
University College Cork, Ireland

Ian Pitt
University College Cork, Ireland

ABSTRACT

In this chapter the authors discuss the growing relevance of audio on the World Wide Web, and show how new issues of accessibility and usability are coming to the fore. Web designers are employing an increasingly rich palette of sounds to enhance the user "experience", but apart from guidelines for facilitating screen-readers, very little exists in the way of design strategies for non-speech sound content. Although their primary focus is on web accessibility for visually disabled users, the same issues are increasingly applicable to sighted users accessing the web via WIFI enabled mobile devices with small screen real estate. The authors present an auditory user interface model aimed at conceptualizing the perceptual issues involved when presenting a rich soundscape to the user, and show how this model can help web designers to consider issues of accessibility and usability without detracting from the "experience". Non-speech sound is not only a means of entertainment or background enhancement, but can also efficiently relay useful information to the user – a function that is still underutilized on the web.

INTRODUCTION

Many services and sources of information now reside solely on the web, from the acquisition of software serial keys and updates to social event registration and webinars. Given the plasticity of digitized content, people with disabilities should have the same access to facilities as able-bodied web users. Although officially and unofficially there is improved appreciation of the need for equal ac-

DOI: 10.4018/978-1-60566-896-3.ch010

cess for all, it is seldom put into practice. It seems that the more web content advances in terms of entertainment value and service provision, the wider the gap between able-bodied and disabled web users becomes.

This problem can be demonstrated in relation to visually disabled users with the web evolution from a primarily text-based environment to a rich-media environment. Text-to-Speech (TTS) software allowed a visually disabled web user to interpret text-based content, as well as graphics featuring descriptive *alt* attributes. However, as screen-readers started to become technologically and aesthetically advanced, the web moved on to include videos, animation, CAPTCHAs[1] and other forms of information presentation that is unfriendly to TTS. These new visual-oriented features, together with widespread lack of compliance with accessibility guidelines, make using screen-readers on the web increasingly difficult and unusable.

We are not advocating the simplification of web content and technologies but we do believe that a more concise encapsulation of how we all interpret and interact with sonic information will allow for the development of new ways of complying with accessibility issues without reducing the visual effects and appeal of creative web design. In fact, we believe that appropriate use of sound can dramatically enhance the web experience for all hearing-abled users. Not only is good sound design relevant to visually disabled web users, it is progressively relevant for hearing-abled sighted users visiting rich-media sites on standard laptop, desktop and mobile devices. Many websites now enhance their visual content with background sonic effects, soundtracks and environmental sounds with little consideration as to how sound impacts on general usability. With a better understanding of how the auditory perceptual system processes and deals with sonic information (including the perceptual interaction between concurrent visual and aural content), tools and guidelines may be developed to solve issues relating to accessibility

and usability while positively enhancing access to information and quality of entertainment for all web users.

Properly understanding how the human auditory system works is, of course, a significant challenge. Therefore, in order to aid in the development of guidelines for developers and designers, we introduce a user-model in this chapter that specifically examines the perceptual implications of audio-rich content on the web. The end-goal of the user-model is to allow guidelines to emerge that will help designers build audio-rich web content that will maintain the "experience" but reduce auditory *clutter* through detailed understanding of how users process sounds presented to them.

BACKGROUND: AUDIO ON THE WEB

The Web Accessibility Initiative (WAI) makes a strong case for tackling issues of accessibility and usability at the early stages of web-design. However, the areas of accessibility, usability and associated web-standard guidelines, means that documentation is vast and sometimes difficult to comprehend and fully implement. Coupled with staying up-to-date with the rapid evolution of web-technologies (standard and non-standard), the task of thoroughly studying the Web Content Accessibility Guidelines (WCAG) can be daunting, especially when designers are under commercial time constraints and client demands. However, this should not be an excuse for the sometimes obvious disregard for large sections of the web-using population, and web-designers should at least be aware of the primary recommendations outlined by the WAI and some third party tool developers. The guidelines outlined in the WCAG (Vanderheiden et al, 2008) offer designers a lot of commonsense instruction on how to make their websites more accessible, and provide simple pointers that can make a big difference for visually disabled web-users.

Much of the reference to audio within the WCAG alludes to facilitating screen-readers and other forms of assistive technologies. Speech output (either as pre-recorded speech or synthetic TTS) plays an extremely important role in relation to visually disabled web-users. Many of the issues surrounding audio on the web relate to non-speech sound that may overpower screen-reader output or distract the user from the important speech content. Another primary issue concerning video-only information online is allowing screen-readers access to descriptive text equivalent information. Without a text equivalent, the visually disabled user is essentially barred from interpreting the video content. This is becoming an even more vital issue given the large number of websites that are solely designed and implemented using Flash animation (Adobe®). However, when used with screen-readers in mind, Flash can actually be rendered very accessible and it is essentially down to the intentions of the designer regarding issues of accessibility.

Silverlight (Microsoft®) is another potential minefield for web accessibility, but once again, assistive technology can be very readily integrated with Silverlight-based sites. Since the release of version 2.0, many improvements have been made to allow screen-readers access to text-based information and it satisfies many of the criteria laid down in the WCAG (WAI Working Group, 2008). Silverlight provides accessibility support using the Usability Interface Automation API as well as bridges to the older Microsoft Active Accessibility API utilized by Flash for screen-reader access. It is clear in relation to visually disabled web-users that speech is the primary mode of communication and navigation online, and needs to be more tightly integrated and further enhanced in the various development environments. Many more issues remain un-chartered, however, around the perceptual implications of audio-rich web presentation (speech plus non-speech sound), which we will discuss later in the chapter.

The Role of Speech Technology on the Web

Speech output has frequently been incorporated as a static element in multimedia content on the web, e.g., speech included in audio and video recordings that are played in the context of a visual web browser. Such applications of speech have typically used human speech recordings, in preference to speech generated by a speech synthesizer. In the past, studies have shown that people find synthesized speech more difficult to understand (CCIR-5, 1999) and that it imposes a significantly higher cognitive load on the listener (Luce, 1983). The current generation of high-quality speech synthesizers (e.g., AT&T Natural Voices, Nuance RealSpeak, Microsoft Vista Anna, etc.) use a concatenative synthesis approach. Concatenative synthesis works by joining together segments of pre-recorded human speech in an attempt to create output that is intelligible and natural. Intelligibility refers to the ease with which the speech output is understood by humans. Naturalness describes how closely the speech output seems like human speech. So even while speech synthesis quality has improved significantly over the last decade, it has yet to achieve the quality level of natural human speech, especially with respect to prosodic content.

Beyond including human speech recordings as an element in multimedia content, there are two additional approaches to enabling broader speech-based access to information and services hosted on the web. The first approach, which is currently only used in narrow application domains, is to design web pages and services that have integral support for speech using technologies such as VoiceXML (Voice Extensible Markup Language) and XHTML+Voice. The second approach, and this is the method used by people with visual disabilities, is for a person to use a screen-reader software application (JAWS, 2008) or an audio browser (HearSay, 2008).

The past decade has seen the emergence of a number of competing standards and technologies that enable voice access to the web. Prior to the emergence of these standards, the development of speech-enabled web applications required the use of proprietary API-level programming techniques. These new standards allowed developers to leverage existing web infrastructure and many existing protocols. VoiceXML is a W3C XML-based standard for specifying interactive voice dialogues between a human and a computer. While HTML documents are generally interpreted and presented by a visual web browser, VoiceXML documents are interpreted by a voice browser. VoiceXML allows telephone users to interact with voice applications hosted on the web. Commercially deployed applications include banking services, package tracking, driving directions, voice access to email, and national directory assistance. Even though VoiceXML has been primarily focused on form-based telephony applications, researchers have recently begun to explore its application in other fields including E-commerce and E-learning (Reusch, 2005).

Several popular books covering the topic of commercial speech-enabled service development recommend the use of human speech recordings, in preference to speech synthesis engines, when possible (Abbott, 2001; Cohen, 2004, Kotelly, 2003; Weinschenk, 2000). These books emphasise the possibilities for creation of high quality, easy-to-understand material in a voice that is appropriate for the application, and in sync with a company's brand. When people hear a voice they infer numerous attributes including items such as the speaker's gender, age, geographic origin, etc. (Cohen, 2004). As a result, commercial speech-enabled applications often deliberately create a persona for their Voice User Interface (VUI) that is suitable for the product or service being offered.

XHTML+Voice, also promoted by the VoiceXML forum, enables multimodal access to web pages. Input is primarily by voice and keyboard; output is primarily via visual display and speech. VoiceXML is widely deployed in successful commercial applications, but at the moment this is not the case for XHTML+Voice.

Recorded speech is used in many of the most widely deployed commercial IVR (Interactive Voice Response) and VoiceXML applications. However, the use of human speech recordings is possible only if the system has a limited amount of possible outputs. As a result, screen-readers and audio web browsers, which must be capable of rendering dynamic web pages, create their output using speech synthesis. While screen-readers and audio web browsers have continued to evolve and improve, these applications have typically lagged behind the latest technologies used to enable richer graphical content on the web. This results in a widening accessibility gap between visually impaired and sighted users.

Selection of an appropriate voice introduces a number of challenges. The voice must be appropriate for the application and the audience (Larson, 2002), and different users may have different preferences (Nass, 2005). For example, children prefer voices with more prosodic variation (Bell, 1999) and older people prefer slower speaking rates (Morrissey, 2001). The selection of the voice may even impact the users' perception of the reliability and the value of the material presented (Dahlbäck, 2007).

Speech synthesizers, implemented as part of products such as JAWS (Freedom Scientific®) and Microsoft® Narrator, have already been very successful in enabling users with visual disabilities to access information available on the web and in documents created by word processors. The speech synthesizers most widely used with screen-reader products have some special requirements. Regular users of these products accept less natural sounding speech as a trade-off for being able to listen to intelligible speech at higher spoken word rates (Asakawa, 2003). Users of these products tend to be very motivated, and tolerant of poorer speech synthesis quality and errors (Holmes, 2002).

Audio & Speech in the Web Content Accessibility Guidelines 1.0 and 2.0

The Web Content Accessibility Guidelines 1.0 was published in 1999, when both Flash Player and QuickTime (Apple®) were already on version 4, and so the markers for rich-media web-content were already laid. With a pressing need for some form of procedure in relation to accessible design using rich-media content, the WCAG formulated some valid fundamental guidelines. Many of these guidelines focus on the use of audio (speech and non-speech) in web-design. The most fundamental guideline associated with audio content in WCAG 1.0 is providing a text equivalent that clearly explains or summarizes pre-recorded audio, video etc (Checkpoint 1.1 & 1.3, see Figure 1 for description). This is necessary for visually disabled users utilizing screen-readers and for hearing disabled users to read about the content being aurally presented. Although a very achievable task in the design process, and something already well established in relation to still-images, designers often continue to forego adding this facility to time-based content (audio samples and video), even though the guideline is specified as having Priority 1 in the WCAG 1.0. This criterion is again described in greater detail in the WCAG 2.0 (Guideline 1.2), published in 2008 with the addition of animation within this context.

Guideline 1.2 breaks accessibility for time-based media into nine subsections. Each subsection includes detailed guidance for designers with links to 'Understanding 1.2.x' and 'How to Meet 1.2.x' – a feature found uniformly throughout the WCAG 2.0, allowing for a much clearer layout compared with the WCAG 1.0. Fulfilling Guideline 1.2.1 entails making any pre-recorded audio-only and video-only media (except if these are functioning as alternatives for some other content already) accessible to all web-users. In order to achieve this, the WCAG clearly recommends a text equivalent so that screen-readers and Braille devices can relay the content to visually disabled users. It defines using filenames, placeholder names and irrelevant text in place of a proper text equivalent as being the most common reasons for failing to satisfy this criterion. The importance of a correct text equivalent cannot be overstated. A text equivalent allows hearing disabled users to interpret an audio-only file while it allows visually disabled users to use assistive technologies (i.e. most commonly a screen-reader) to relay information on video-only content.

The WCAG in Guideline 1.2.3 also tackles the possibility that user agents (screen-readers, for example) may be unable to relay a text equivalent for visually presented material, and in such cases the designer is required to supply an auditory description in the form of a pre-recorded or synthesized speech output. This audio output should be synchronized to the visuals of the presentation, explaining key points on actions, body language, graphics, scene changes etc. If the visuals already include an audio track containing speech, then the designer must carefully choose moments where there are sufficient pauses to insert the supporting audio. Where this is not possible, Guideline 1.2.7 advices the designer to set key points in the video/audio presentation to pause the entire material and render the supporting audio at those key points.

Checkpoint 1.3 (WCAG 1.0) also specifies the use of non-audio synchronization with time-based multimedia using text captions for when a hearing impaired user requires information about the audio content of a presentation. Guideline 1.2.2 (WCAG 2.0) explains in greater detail how to achieve captioning using a variety of different video formats. With the general expansion of bandwidth infrastructure, the web is now commonly used for live conferencing and live presentation. Given this trend, the WCAG 2.0 go into much greater detail in terms of captioning in live scenarios with Guideline 1.2.4 and Guideline 1.2.9. Not only is captioning an important feature for hearing disabled web users, but it is often vital for visually disabled users when relying on their

Figure 1. This table describes Checkpoints 1.1. & 1.3 in the Web Content Accessibility Guidelines 1.0 published in 1999.

WCAG 1.0.		
CHECKPOINT 1.1	**OPTIONS IN USE:**	**PRIORITY**
Provide a text equivalent for every non-text element. This includes: images, graphical representations of text (including symbols), image map regions, animations (e.g., animated GIFs), applets and programmatic objects, ascii art, frames, scripts, images used as list bullets, spacers, graphical buttons, sounds (played with or without user interaction), stand-alone audio files, audio tracks of video, and video.	*Use "alt" for IMG, INPUT and APPLET elements.* *Provide text equivalent in content of OBJECT and APPLET elements.* *For complex content (e.g. chart), use "longdesc" with IMG or FRAME.* *Provide a link inside OBJECT element or a description link. (see Checkpoint 1.3).*	*1*
CHECKPOINT 1.3	**OPTIONS IN USE:**	**PRIORITY**
Until user agents* can automatically read aloud the text equivalent of a visual track, provide an auditory description of the important information of the visual track of a multimedia presentation. **User Agent = assistive technology such as screen readers.*	*Description link may be an auditory description of the key visual elements of a presentation. This can be a prerecorded human or synthesized voice. Auditory description should be synchronized with the audio track of the presentation, during natural pauses in the audio track. Auditory descriptions = information about actions, body language, graphics, and scene changes.*	*1*

screen-readers to inform them of non-speech events during a live web-cast. Promoting this form of online information presentation seems to be of genuine interest to the WAI and may feature in more detail in future guidelines or even as part of emerging technologies during the development of Web 3.0. Figure 2 outlines Guideline 1.2.

Issues of Accessibility: Audio in Flash

Adobe® Flash (formerly Macromedia® Flash) has come under much criticism over the years for its visual bias and dependence on mouse interaction. However, since Flash Player 6, the format has steadily introduced many key features for assisting designers in making Flash accessible. As with most other web development environments, this option is not automatically enforced. That said, by default, Flash 10 exposes all text elements to

Figure 2. This table describes Guideline 1.2 (which is broken into none distinct subsections), in the Web Content Accessibility Guidelines 2.0 published in 2008.

Guideline 1.2 Time-based Media: Provide alternatives for time-based media		
	DESCRIPTION	IMPLEMENTATION
1.2.1 Audio-only. Video-only. *(Prerecorded).*	Provide an alternative for time-based media (audio-only) that presents equivalent information. Provide an alternative for time-based media (video-only) such as an audio track that presents equivalent information.	Create a document that tells the same story and presents the same information as the prerecorded audio-only content. The document serves as a long description for the content and includes all of the important dialogue and as well as descriptions of background sounds etc. For video-only, provide either an audio-track or a document that describes scenery, actions, expressions, etc. Preferably, give multi-lingual option.
1.2.2 Captions. *(Prerecorded).*	Provide captions for all prerecorded audio content in synchronized media, except when the media is a media alternative for text (and clearly labeled as such).	Provide embedded text in the video track describing all dialogue and important sounds. Closed-captions also an option – users do not see captions unless requested. Synchronized Multimedia Integration Language 3.0 (SMIL 3.0) – XML-based standard allowing authors to write interactive/accessibility elements into media content.
1.2.3 Audio Description. Media Alternative. *(Prerecorded).*	Provide an alternative for time-based media. Provide an audio description for prerecorded video content, except when the media is a media alternative for text (and clearly labeled as such).	Adjacent to the non-text content, place a link to a collated document of captions. Insert "End of document" at the end and a "Back" button facility. Provide an audio description of visual content, also with a "Back" button facility.
1.2.4 Captions. *(Live).*	Provide captions for all live audio content in synchronized media.	Provide open (always viewable) or closed (requested by user) captions. Various third-party software options available as well as the SMIL standard.
1.2.5 Audio Description. *(Prerecorded)*	Provide an audio description for all prerecorded video content in synchronized media.	Provide a second, user-selectable audio track that includes audio descriptions. Provide a version of a movie with audio descriptions via SMIL 1.0, SMIL 2.0 or SMIL 3.0. Preferably, multi-lingual options should be provided.
1.2.6 Sign Language. *(Prerecorded).*	Provide sign language interpretation for all prerecorded audio content in synchronized media.	Include a sign language interpreter in the video stream, or provide a sign language interpreter in a different viewport or overlaid on the image of the player. Can be implemented via SMIL. Future link to be implemented so that metadata can provide a service to different languages.
1.2.7 Extended Audio Description. *(Prerecorded).*	Where pauses in foreground audio are insufficient to allow audio descriptions to convey the sense of the video.	Achieved by freezing the synchronized media in order to allow an audio description to update the listener. Future link to provide multi-lingual options via SMIL.
1.2.8 Media Alternative. *(Prerecorded).*	Provide alternative for time-based, prerecorded synchronized media and for all prerecorded video-only media.	Similar to 1.2.3.
1.2.9 Audio-only. *(Live).*	Provide an alternative for time-based media that presents equivalent information for live audio-only content.	Similar to 1.2.3.

screen-readers, but relies on designer choice to implement text equivalents for a hierarchy of non-text elements in a Flash movie. Text equivalent for movie, parent and child objects are available in the Flash Accessibility Panel, and although this feature remains limited to browsers and screen-reader applications using Microsoft Active Accessibility, it is at least a move in the right direction. Of course, other complicated issues also need to be addressed by the designer when opening Flash movie content to screen-readers, such as reading order, which requires some extra planning prior to design implementation.

Audio is an intricate part of the Flash development environment, and is being increasingly utilized in Flash movies to enhance the visual impact of websites. Many popular sites include environmental sounds, background music scores and other functional sonic assets associated with mouse-over events. For sighted individuals, this certainly adds to the entertainment value, but for the visually impaired user the complex soundscape can be very confusing. A lot of the sounds incorporated into a Flash movie are associated with specific visual elements, such as when hovering over buttons or when an animated character runs across the screen. Although purely for entertainment purposes, this can have a negative impact on users who rely on sound for information purposes - something that is acknowledged in the Adobe® Flash documentation (Adobe®). This is especially true when considering the potential interference with screen-reader output.

However, the designer can take some extra steps within the Flash development environment to reduce the negative impact on users of screen-readers while retaining the entertainment aspect. These range from incorporating play, pause, mute and volume buttons with associated keyboard shortcuts to writing ActionScripts that recognize screen-reader presence and subsequently mute or reduce background sound automatically.

AUDIO-RICH WEB CONTENT: PERCEPTUAL IMPLICATIONS

Although very comprehensive and accurate, the Web Content Accessibility Guidelines are not a perfect solution and cannot keep entirely up-to-date with constantly re-changing trends online. The entertainment value of the web has dramatically increased from the days of text and static images, and the end-user's expectations put more pressure on designers and tool developers to push the limits of technology in order to present information on the web as richly as possible. This means that we are now faced with a huge number of popular sites outputting concurrent streams of audio, video and animation. Two important issues arise –

a. The effectiveness of screen-readers and other assistive technologies is dramatically reduced, as entertainment sound can over-power text-to-speech output. Furthermore, as already mentioned, time-based media often lacks any form of proper text equivalent as a result of decisions made by designers.

b. All web-users run a risk of cognitive over-load as they are bombarded with too much information that needs to be perceptually segregated and processed. Even concurrent information in different perceptual domains (visual and auditory) can interfere and interact with each other.

There is clearly a need for comprehensive user-models to cater for new approaches to web-design and that examine the perceptual implications of rich-media content. From such models, guidelines could be developed and integrated into design tools. As rich-media content is here to stay – evident from the expected developments from Web 2.0 to Web 3.0 – it is likely that rich-audio content will become more common and elaborate. If left unguided, there is a significant risk that designers could render functional auditory information inaccessible and cognitively tasking by cluttering the soundscape with inappropriately designed entertainment-based sound. However, we do believe that sound for entertainment value can co-exist with screen-readers and concurrent visual content, if presented in the right manner.

Non-speech sound is often used only as a background/ambient element, but it can also relay important information to the user, giving it an added function other than solely for entertainment purposes. Armed with knowledge of how all users interpret a rich soundscape and with tools that coach designers to arrange sound in a perceptually-friendly format, designers can start from the outset with the confidence that their rich-media website will fulfill official accessibility and usability guidelines and maximize functionality and entertainment values.

Interestingly, in relation to our proposed user-model, the WCAG itself does not consider in much detail the perceptual implications of outputting concurrent speech and non-speech information. Guideline 1.2.5 in the WCAG 2.0 does state that audio descriptions (speech-based) should be placed between pauses in the original soundtrack dialogue. Guideline 1.2.7 extends on 1.2.5 in relation to situations where there are insufficient pauses in the foreground audio to facilitate continued audio description. In such cases, the user should have the option to freeze-frame the media to allow audio descriptions to explain the scene. On further investigation of this recommendation by the WCAG, the foreground audio is specified as dialog and therefore restricted to speech-on-speech interference. Both of these guidelines do not specify any concern with regard to concurrent speech and non-speech sound. There is sufficient evidence that non-speech sound and speech do often interact unless presented in a compatible way to the end-user (Jones, 1992, 1993).

Guideline 1.4.2 goes some way toward acknowledging potential interference between non-speech and speech content. This relates to background sound that plays automatically and which may interfere with clear screen-reader output. The guideline specifies that some form of user control over volume (that is independent from system volume), or indeed an option for turning audio off completely, should be attached. It seems that web designers intuitively implement this guideline to some degree, especially in relation to Flash players, but this may be more of an aesthetic decision rather than insight into accessibility issues. In relation to guideline 1.4.2, it goes on to recommend the avoidance of using background sound that starts automatically and instead states that sound should be voluntarily activated by the user. This recommendation may indeed be the most sensible in terms of functionality, but web-design is often more about aesthetics than functionality. Having to voluntarily initiate background audio may very well take away from the user's web "experience" in those vital first few seconds. Just as it may be difficult to turn audio off, depending on where and how clearly this function is positioned on the page, it may be equally difficult or awkward to turn audio on. As we have already stated, we believe that the web "experience" need not be compromised when trying to evoke proper functionality and equal access for all. Our approach, in relation to guideline 1.4.2, is that background sound (if designed appropriately) can reside and function alongside text-to-speech output. Guideline 1.4.7 has an option that allows for some concurrency of background sound and speech, but only in relation to volume ratio between background and foreground sound. However, there are many other sonic dimensions to consider in relation to auditory perception in this regard. By allowing properly designed background sound to play automatically, the designer can maintain the web "experience" for the sighted user and the visually disabled user also. The visually disabled web-user appreciates web "experience" just as much as the sighted web-user.

Another issue relating to the perceptual implications of an audio-rich web environment concerns Guideline 1.2.2. This guideline considers the differences between closed caption and open caption options, but does not explain the perceptual implications of concurrent audio (speech or non-speech) with visual content in the form of textual captions. While reading text, the user perceptually *vocalizes* the text string, meaning the potential for interference between concurrent lexical information and sonic information is possible. This is a concern for users who can both hear and see the content being presented, especially when open captioning is employed by the designer. Accessibility also extends to web-users who can both see and hear material, and therefore any content that has the potential to inhibit proper functionality for this portion of the online community needs equal investigation.

Designers can implement many of the guidelines outlined in the WCAG using applications like Flash with clever ActionScript development. For example, scripts can be used to determine if the user is utilizing a screen-reader, in which case background sound can be automatically adjusted. However, two issues spring to mind with regard to this approach. Even with volume adjustment, some sounds may still impact on screen-reader clarity due to their inherent attention-grabbing nature. Therefore, the actual design of sonic elements still needs to be addressed. The second issue relates to the wasteful use of sonic elements. Although sound used on the web is, for the most part, purely for entertainment, it is still a valid and effective mode of communication. Many sounds can have very important functional roles for all users. This feature is extremely underutilized in website development, because the vast majority of designers are trained in the visual medium and most of the development tools do not highlight functional sound design. To fully exploit sound in terms of both entertainment and functionality, we need to understand the perceptual issues involved in order to reduce interference and enhance sonic usability. We believe that this can be achieved by employing an auditory user-model.

Auditory User-Model for Rich-Media Audio Content

Auditory environments in the digital domain are becoming increasingly complex and ubiquitous in our daily lives, and the web is no different in this regard. For most sighted users of technology, audio has a strong entertainment value but it can, at the same time, serve a deeper meaning. Sound, in the context of music, is entertaining but can also convey functional information such as the mood of a scene. In fact, sound in all its guises is used to relay information to the user on devices that are becoming more powerful but that have reduced visual feedback (i.e. mobile devices with small screen real estate). For visually disabled users, sound is of course also a form of entertainment, but in addition it serves as one of the primary mechanisms for interacting with any digital device (Stevens, 1996). However, the more complex our sonic environment becomes, the less regulated and organized it seems to be.

Background music, environmental sounds, mouse-over sound events, music players etc., are just some of the features commonly found on websites today. Couple that with screen-reader output, and the soundscape quickly becomes very complex and potentially unusable. Entertaining sonic enhancements on websites are not going to be easily disregarded by web designers, since sound is a very effective means of ornamenting the web "experience". However, with proper understanding on how our perceptual system traditionally evaluates and organizes the sonic environment, we can guide designers in the effective use of sound online. To achieve this we need to model the auditory perceptual system and adapt our online sound environment accordingly.

Once an understanding of how we perceive sound is accomplished, it becomes possible to even further expand the use of sound on the web.

Sound is often used to serve a single, straightforward function or simply used to enhance the web "experience". Many elements, such as buttons, now have sounds associated with them, but for the most part, little thought is given to how that sound can relay extra information to the user besides just augmenting the button's presence. For example, on Flash sites a sound typically indicates to the user that they have moved their mouse over the area where the button is located, but the functional information usually stops there. With correct use of sound, more information could be relayed, telling the user if the button is an internal or external link, or whether the button has subcategories etc. The use of sound in this manner is an active area of research in auditory display technology (ICAD), where earcons and auditory icons (non-speech sound with some form of meaning) convey multilayered information to the user. This type of research relies on psychoacoustic understanding and is an effective means of using the human auditory system to a higher potential. A similar approach could be employed online, but again, a model is required to direct designers on what type of sound within the overall soundscape could be used, and when to employ these techniques.

Model Structure: Overview

The auditory user-model that we have developed relies on a combination of various contemporary cognition-based theories. The most important of these construct the four main blocks of the model – Auditory Scene Analysis (Bregman, 2002), Schema theory (Baddeley, 1996), the Attention Mechanism (Wrigley & Brown, 2000) and the Changing-State Hypothesis (Jones et al., 1992; Jones & Macken, 1993) (see Figure 3). Each block is of extreme importance and relies sequentially and cyclically on the other. From a sound-design point of view, perhaps the most vital stage in the model is the perceptual entry-point. If sound is inappropriately designed from

Figure 3. Overview of our Auditory User Model for audio-rich content on the Web. The user navigates to a website containing a rich soundscape. This may include background music, sounds associated with buttons, and perhaps a screen-reader. The sound is output via speakers/headphones to the user. The user's perceptual system interprets the soundscape. According to our model, the perceptual system organizes and filters the soundscape along several stages. Based on the processing done in the perceptual system, the user reacts by interacting with an input device (keyboard). This has an affect on the soundscape of the website, and the process begins again.

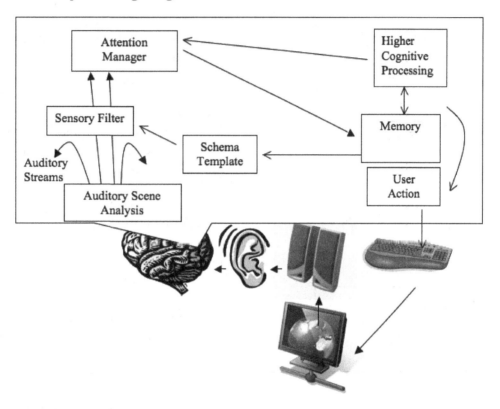

the outset, then this entry-point will not correctly organize the soundscape (perceptually speaking) and this will have a negative knock-on affect on the effectiveness of the other stages in the model. This entry-point is not only the most peripheral of auditory perceptual processes, but is also the most primitive. It is an instinctive, automatic process and so has some level of predictability involved based on the rules of Auditory Scene Analysis (Bregman, 2002).

Peripheral Organization of Sound: Auditory Scene Analysis

This stage of the model reflects the theory of auditory scene analysis. The organization of sound at this stage is critical in the design of the sonic environment created online, since it is at this moment that the human perceptual system begins to interact with all the sounds presented. Because this stage is instinctive and less vulnerable to individual differences, the sonic scene can be manipulated to suit particular intentions of the designer. Any of the stages beyond this point are

Figure 4. Auditory scene analysis is performed on a complex stream, resulting in the scene being broken into smaller, more manageable components called streams. However, not all streams can be allowed into the auditory perceptual pathway, as this would result in cognitive overload. Therefore, a mechanism is required to filter unimportant streams – in our model, this is referred to as the Sensory Filter.

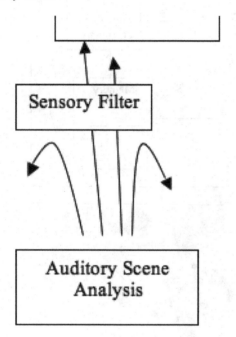

heavily influenced by individual differences (for example, experience). Therefore, with knowledge as to how this peripheral perceptual mechanism works, the designer can form a sonic scene that will be perceptually organized in an intended manner.

Understanding how sounds are organized at this stage of the model is key. A complex sonic scene contains too many elements for the perceptual system to cope with. Therefore, the scene needs to be organized and broken into several, smaller components called streams. Robust rules govern how the smaller components come into being – essentially, this means the perceptual system has a specific mechanism for grouping and seg-

regating sounds within a complex scene based on the acoustic structure of the scene. The types of rules that allow the perceptual system to organize a complex sonic scene into several smaller streams have some basis in Gestalt principles of perception. For example, sounds that emanate from the same location have a better chance of being grouped than those emanating from very different locations. Sounds within a similar pitch range or timbre may be grouped together. These are very simple examples and many other complex acoustic traits are influential in governing stream segregation and amalgamation. Once a complex scene has been organized into several streams, the perceptual system needs to consult with higher mechanisms in order to determine which streams are deemed important and which streams can be blocked from continuing along the auditory perceptual pathway.

Individual differences now begin to become an important factor. Not all streams can be allowed to enter the auditory perceptual pathway, as doing so would result in cognitive overload. Therefore, some form of filter is required to allow designated important streams to pass while blocking others (Figure 4).

THE SENSORY FILTER AND THE SCHEMA TEMPLATE

The Sensory Filter in our model is tasked with the decision of blocking what it deems as unimportant streams, and allowing streams it deems important to pass to the next stage in the auditory perceptual pathway. How the Sensory Filter determines this is based on a Schema Template (see Figure 5). Essentially a Schema Template is based on the user's experience over time with a particular problem or task. One particular Schema Template out of many is called from Memory and imposed on the Sensory Filter. Over time, a user may have gained experience with a certain task, environment or problem of which certain information pertaining

Figure 5. The Sensory Filter determines what stream to block and what stream to pass. How it determines this is based on a Schema Template pulled from Memory. A user's experience of a particular task will determine how accurate their allocated Schema Template will be, and subsequently determine how well the Sensory Filter performs.

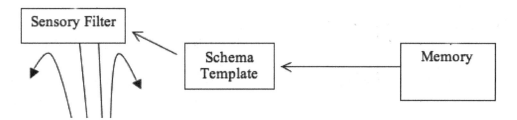

to the situation was encoded into Memory at every exposure. The more exposure, the more defined and refined the Schema Template becomes and subsequently, the more accurate the Schema Template is when called upon for the same task, environment or problem. Therefore, an inexperienced user of a particular website will have a less refined Schema Template or even none at all for navigating that particular site. Therefore, their Sensory Filter will make errors in choosing which streams to block and which to allow to pass. An experienced user, on the other hand, will have a much more suitable Schema Template pulled from Memory, and therefore his/her Sensory Filter will accurately deal with the situation at hand. This can be clearly demonstrated when comparing screen-reader speeds between visually impaired users and sighted users who have little exposure to high speech rates.

THE ATTENTION MECHANISM

Once a selection of streams has been allowed to pass the Sensory Filter, they are sent to the Attention Mechanism (see Figure 6). Some degree of stream prioritization is required as only one stream can be encoded into Memory at a time. The Attention Mechanism is controlled by higher

cognitive processes and the most important stream is allocated to Focused Attention, while all other streams are queued in Peripheral Attention (see Figure 7). Only the stream in Focused Attention gains privileged access to Memory for encoding (implemented using a higher cognitive process called Rehearsal). Streams in Peripheral Attention, on the other hand, do not have access to Memory, but can loiter waiting for the switch from Peripheral Attention to Focused Attention.

Again, the acoustic makeup of a stream can pull on Focused Attention, which may draw Focused Attention away from an important stream. For example, a speech stream (being emitted from a screen-reader) is typically denoted as the important stream since it transmits factual information. However, high-pitched sounds (such as a siren-type sound) can very quickly draw attention away from the speech stream. Therefore, in our model, the speech stream had been allocated to Focused Attention and was being encoded into Memory. However, some time during that process, a high-pitched sound was emitted from the webpage that grabbed attention. For a moment, the speech stream was de-allocated from Focused Attention to Peripheral Attention, while the high-pitched sound forced its way into Focused Attention. This means that for that moment, a portion of the speech string was not encoded into Memory, and so the high-pitched sound interfered with the user's attention to the screen-reader.

MEMORY ENCODING: THE CHANGING STATE HYPOTHESIS

The more consistently and often a stream is in Focused Attention, the more vivid an imprint that stream will leave in Memory. In our model, the Rehearsal process 'engraves' (metaphorically speaking) the stream into Memory. Although streams in Peripheral Attention do not have access to memory itself, they can interfere with the higher cognitive process, such as Rehearsal. This is commonly experienced when background speech is present in the soundscape while at the same time the listener is trying to focus on another speech stream concurrently. This is referred to as the *Irrelevant Speech Effect*, but investigations

Figure 6. Some streams are allowed to pass the Sensory Filter and onto the Attention Mechanism. The Attention Mechanism is controlled by higher cognitive processes. There are two categories of attention – Peripheral Attention and Focused Attention (which has access to Memory facilities).

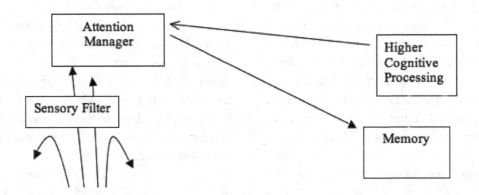

Figure 7. There are two components in the Attention Mechanism – Peripheral Attention and Focused Attention. Streams deemed less important are queued in Peripheral Attention, while the most important stream is sent to Focused Attention. Focused Attention is subsequently connected to Memory where the stream can be encoded using the Rehearsal Process.

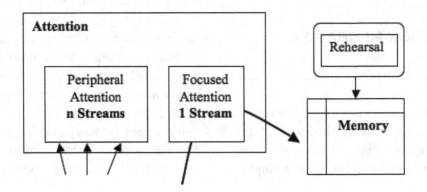

(Jones & Macken, 1993) have also shown this to be the case when non-speech sound is present the background. Therefore, the phenomenon is now referred to as the *Irrelevant Sound Effect*. Jones et al. (1992) further revealed that the reason behind this type of interference, between irrelevant and relevant streams, was due to the acoustic structure of the interfering streams. They revealed that an acoustically changing sound stream interferes with speech in focused attention, while unchanging streams does not.

USING THE AUDITORY USER MODEL IN PRACTICAL DESIGN

The Auditory User Model we have presented is an overview, based on contemporary perceptual investigation, of the auditory perceptual pathway. We believe that in order to maintain entertaining audio for the web, whilst vastly reducing the possibility for interference with screen-reader technology, requires an understanding of the perceptual implications when combining many different sound sources in one space. Of course, the model needs to be integrated into some form of interactive application for the designer, so that its rules can be implemented in real-time during the design process. The model identifies a number of key design strategies when using concurrent audio sources.

The first relates to auditory scene analysis where a designer can force sonic segregation/amalgamation depending on the acoustic traits of the sounds used. This type of approach could be useful in relation to audio CAPTCHAs for example, where some level of sonic scene complexity is required to ensure security. Like many visual CAPTCHAs, audio CAPTCHAs are either too simplistic or too complicated. Audio CAPTCHAs that are very easy to interpret consist of two voices outputting content sequentially - one voice relays instructional information while the other relays the security code. The

problem with this method is that speech recognition software has no trouble interpreting the output. In order to ensure some level of security, more complicated audio CAPTCHAs employ several background voices performing nonsense utterances while the primary voice sits on top relaying the security code. Google® employs this type of security measure (Google), but it can also be very difficult for a human user to interpret the complex auditory scene. Using our Auditory User Model, this type of CAPTCHA could be formatted to more closely conform to natural scene analysis processes. Using the rules of auditory scene analysis, a designer could create a complex auditory scene that conforms to human auditory perception but which may be too complicated for a web-bot to crack. Given the complexity of the rule sets associated with human perception, this could be a promising auditory security measure.

Other practical applications using the model's rules relate to attention and memory (rehearsal). Concurrent sounds can co-exist given the correct acoustic structures of each sound. Being aware of what sound types might simply remain in the background (in peripheral attention) and what sounds will grab attention (force their way into focused attention) is of immense importance to the web designer. In order to keep attention on screen-reader output for example, the designer can concurrently retain some level of non-intrusive, unchanging environmental sounds in order to maintain a sense of atmosphere or "experience" for all users.

Another advantage to utilizing our model in the web environment concerns perceptual streaming. Given that several streams can co-exist, designers who conform to the rules of the auditory perceptual system can relay several streams of information to the user at once. This type approach would not only be beneficial to visually disabled users, but is also increasingly relevant to users with small mobile devices. Mobile users accessing full web services often find interacting with the web difficult due to the visual limitations of the device. Several streams of information could be presented to the user, including a mixture of auditory and visual streams to relay data instead of relying on visual-only methods.

Non-speech sound can be used in several other useful ways. It can be used to relay structural information, such as bullet points or lists, as well as conveying a quick overview of certain types of information, such as the hierarchy of a menu item. Instead of waiting for speech to linearly progress down a list, non-speech sound can very quickly summarize this type of information to the user. Again, careful consideration to the perceptual implications when using a rich palette of sound for functional tasks is required. We believe that using our Auditory User Model to exploit these under-utilized resources can be incorporated into web design, and that this could help visually disabled users navigate a webpage more effectively. It could also aid sighted users who operate web-enabled devices with restricted visual feedback.

CONCLUSION

The WCAG are a useful source for designers looking to comply with accessibility and usability protocols. Most of the methods required for designing accessible websites are very well explained and documented. However, they require extensive study and time to fully appreciate and absorb. One of the primary problems perhaps, is the static nature of the WCAG when designers are more used to interactive design procedures. That said, the WCAG are not a web design tool and so the onus lies with the many commercial, third party tools to implement services within their frameworks that comply with the WCAG.

Many of the commonly used web design tools have some accessibility options. However, these are typically only the most basic suggestions, such as signifying to the designer to include *alt* tags when displaying images. Furthermore, many other relevant guidelines are simply ignored and intel-

ligent assessment of the actual text included in the *alt* element does not feature at all. For example, some tools will be happy that accessibility issues are entirely fulfilled when an *alt* tag contains any sort of text, even if that text makes absolutely no sense. Many of the accessibility options within the design tools have to be initiated by the designer, and are not setup automatically by default. Therefore, the complacency regarding accessibility guidelines in many major design tool packages means that all the blame cannot fall on designers alone. Some online validation tools incorporating a standards compliance test and accessibility test (WCAG & US Section 508) are available, but once again, these tools are mostly implemented after a web page has been designed and built. The need for a more interactive, intelligent, 'on-by-default' web design tool that directs designers from the ground up is required if accessibility is become the de facto on the web.

Although making a website more accessible initially entails much more consideration to the finer details during design, the process does not just fulfill moral or legal obligations, but it can actually enhance the web experience for all users and help dramatically with search engine optimization. Because of the lack of comprehensive, robust and intuitive accessibility options in web design tools, ensuring compliance with accessibility guidelines is often viewed similarly as compliance with strict web standards. It is often viewed as being an extra cost, time-consuming and reducing the web experience for the end-user. However, if design tools allowed designers to implement these features from the start, the opposite is actually true. Search engine robots and spiders would be able to index more data from elements on the website (resulting in higher hit results), the target audience is no longer restricted to just able-bodied users, and rich-media content could be included since it would provide either an equivalent or alternative source for relaying the information. Usually, the trouble with making a webpage accessible is that the designer has to patch up a design that originally only catered for one particular audience.

Although the WCAG are indeed comprehensive, some new issues come to the fore given the fast evolution of web technologies. Web pages are becoming increasingly complex in terms of visual and auditory presentation. Therefore, we need to consider the perceptual implications of presenting concurrent information to all users, but in particular disabled users who rely on extra assistive technology to navigate and interact with the web. Having audio-rich content on a website can have a very negative impact on users utilizing screen-readers, but there is also a need to advance the entertainment value of online content. Using an auditory perceptual model may help to identify areas where entertainment related sound and screen-readers can co-exist without interference.

Indeed, accessibility is also becoming an issue for sighted users accessing the web using small screen mobile devices. Using all sound types (earcons, auditory icons, music, speech etc.) as a means of relaying functional information is becoming a valid issue for all hearing-abled users of this type of technology. Severe workarounds such as cutting background audio out completely if a screen-reader or mobile device is detected may not be the fruitful way forward. Accessibility concerns everyone, and everyone should enjoy the web "experience". Therefore, investigations into the nature of our perceptual system may allow designers to attain full accessibility whilst maintaining the experience.

REFERENCES

Abbott, K. R. (2001). *Voice Enabling Web Applications: VoiceXML and Beyond*. Berkeley, CA: Apress. Adobe Systems Incorporated. (n.d.). Retrieved from http://www.adobe.com/accessibility/products/flash/

Apple Inc. (n.d.). Retrieved from http://www.apple.com

Asakawa, C., Takagi, H., Ino, S., & Ifukube, T. (2003). Maximum listening speeds for the blind. In Brazil, E. & Shinn-Cunningham, B. (Eds), *Proceedings of the 9th International Conference on Auditory Display 2003* (pp. 276-279). Boston: Boston University Publications Production Department.

Baddeley, A. D. (1996). *Your Memory – A User's Guide*. London: Prion.

Bell, L., House, D., Gustafson, K., & Johansson, L. (1999). Child-directed speech synthesis: evaluation of prosodic variation for an educational computer program. In G. Olaszy, (Ed), *Proceedings / Eurospeech '99, 6th European Conference on Speech Communication and Technology* (pp. 1843-1846). Budapest: Dep. of Telecomm. and Telematics, Techn. Univ. of Budapest.

Bregman, A. S. (2002). *Auditory Scene Analysis: Perceptual Organization of Sound*. Cambridge, MA: MIT Press.

CCIR-5. (1999). *User attitudes towards real and synthetic speech*. Edinburgh, UK: University of Edinburgh, Centre for Communication Interface Research.

Cohen, M., Giangola, J., & Balogh, J. (2004). *Voice User Interface Design*. Reading, MA: Addison-Wesley Professional.

Dahlbäck, N., Wang, O., Nass, C. I., & Alwin, J. (2007). Similarity is More Important than Expertise: Accent Effects in Speech Interfaces. In *Proceedings of the SIGCHI conference on Human Factors in Computing Systems* (1553–1556). New York: ACM.

Google, (n.d.). Retrieved from https://www.google.com/accounts/DisplayUnlockCaptcha

HearSay Browser, (n.d.). Stony Brook University, NY, NSF Award-IIS-0534419. Retrieved from http://www.cs.sunysb.edu/~hearsay/.

Holmes, J. N., & Holmes, W. (2002). *Speech Synthesis and Recognition*. New York: Taylor and Francis.

International Community for Auditory Display. (n.d.). Retrieved from http://www.icad.org

JAWS Screen Reader. (n.d.). Retrieved from http://www.freedomscientific.com

Jones, D. M., & Macken, W. J. (1993). Irrelevant Tones Produce an Irrelevant Speech Effect: Implications for Phonological Coding in Working Memory. *Journal of Experimental Psychology. Learning, Memory, and Cognition, 19*(2), 369–381. doi:10.1037/0278-7393.19.2.369

Jones, D. M., Madden, C., & Miles, C. (1992). Privileged access by irrelevant speech to short-term memory: The role of changing state. *Quarterly Journal of Experimental Psychology, 44*(4), 645–669.

Kotelly, B. (2003). *The Art and Business of Speech Recognition: Creating the Noble Voice*. Reading, MA: Addison-Wesley Professional.

Larson, J. A. (2002). *Voicexml: Introduction to Developing Speech Applications*. Upper Saddle River, NJ: Prentice Hall.

Luce, P. A., Feustel, T. C., & Pisoni, D. B. (1983). Capacity demands in short-term memory for synthetic and natural word lists. *Human Factors, 25*, 17–32.

Microsoft Corporation. (n.d.). Retrieved from http://msdn.microsoft.com/en-us/library/bb980024(VS.95).sapx

Morrissey, W., & Zajicek, M. (2001). Remembering how to use the Internet: An investigation into the effectiveness of VoiceHelp for older adults, In Stephanidis, C (Ed.) *Proceedings of the 9th International Conference on Human-Computer Interaction, New Orleans* (pp. 700-704). Mahwah, NJ: Lawrence Erlbaum

Nass, C., & Brave, S. (2005). *Wired for Speech: How Voice Activates and Advances the Human-Computer Relationship*. Cambridge, MA: MIT Press.

Reusch, P. J. A., Stoll, B., & Studnik, D. (2005). VoiceXML-Applications for E-Commerce and E-Learning. *Intelligent Data Acquisition and Advanced Computing Systems: Technology and Applications, 2005. IDAACS 2005,* (pp. 709-712). Washington, DC: IEEE.

Stephens, R. (1996). *Principles for design of auditory interfaces to present complex information to blind people*. Unpublished doctorial dissertation, University of York, UK.

Vanderheiden, G., Reid, L. G., Caldwell, B., & Henry, S. L. (Eds.). (2008), *The Web Content Accessibility Guidelines*, W3C. Retrieved from http://www.w3.org/WAI/

WAI Working Group (2008). Retrieved from http://www.w3.org/WAI/GL/WCAG20/implementation-report/Silverlight_accessibility_support_statement

Weinschenk, S., & Barker, D. T. (2000). *Designing effective speech interfaces*. New York: John Wiley & Sons, Inc.

Wrigley, S. N., & Brown, G. J. (2000). *A model of auditory attention*. Technical Report CS-00-07, Speech and Hearing Research Group, University of Sheffield, UK.

ENDNOTE

[1]   In its most common form, a CAPTCHA is a visual image generated by a server. The user is required to enter the characters embedded in the image, submit it to the server where it is validated. This is designed so that only human users can decipher the content and not an automated computer script. Variations exist such as "common-sense question" CAPTCHAs and audio CAPTCHAs.

Chapter 11
A Usability Guide to Intelligent Web Tools for the Literacy of Deaf People

Tania di Mascio
University of L'Aquila, Italy

Rosella Gennari
Free University of Bozen-Bolzano, Italy

ABSTRACT

The need of literacy tools for deaf people is well documented in the literature of deaf studies. This chapter aims at drawing the attention of the HCI and AI worlds on the need of intelligent web tools for the literacy of deaf people. It reviews several such e-tools. The review tries to cover complementary and diverse literacy aspects, ranging from word knowledge to global reasoning on texts. The authors assess whether the tools conform to the User Centred Design Methodology, and put forward a first set of usability guidelines based on such a methodology for the design of more intelligent web e-tools for the literacy of deaf people. The chapter concludes by eliciting a debate on the need of a deaf user centred design.

INTRODUCTION

Good literacy is essential for everyone. It ensures a continuous process of personal maturation and a positive social integration. Educators, linguists and psychologists working on deaf studies report that deaf and hard-of-hearing people encounter difficulties in learning to read and write with proficiency, e.g., see (Marschark & Spencer, 2003). However,

the level of literacy of deaf people is varied and can depend on several factors.

For instance, the degree of deafness as well as the age they become deaf can affect the communication abilities of deaf people (RIT, 2008). There are, basically, four degrees of deafness: mild, moderate, severe and profound. In this chapter, the term "deafness" refers to any of the aforementioned degrees. Even a mild hearing loss can be serious for children still learning to speak. People who are born deaf or who loose their hearing prior to the age at which

DOI: 10.4018/978-1-60566-896-3.ch011

speech is acquired learn a verbal language mainly through artificial means, i.e., reading.

Moreover, which education method is adopted can play a key role in the literacy of a deaf person in a *verbal language* (VL). Nowadays, there are education programs for teaching various the national *sign languages* (SL). Note that an SL is a full-fledged gestural-visual language with signs as lexical units, whereas a VL is an oral-auditive language with words as lexical units. Among the main literacy education methods for deaf people include, we have: oral education only to the national VL; oral education with manual aids such as lip-reading or finger-spelling; bimodal education to the national VL and SL. Other combinations are possible resulting in a richly varied spectrum of education methods (Reynolds & Fletcher-Janzen, 2001). Issues of language, literacy and integration often include debate and even controversy, with different viewpoints from within deaf and hearing circles (Marschark and Wauters, 2008).

Comprehensive research on SLs in modern linguistics dates back to the 1960s, mainly influenced by the communication mode of SLs, that is, the body instead of the voice, and by the fact that SLs are face-to-face unwritten languages. Recent research in information technology has concentrated on the creation of e-tools for SLs, mostly, on e-dictionaries (Branson & Miller, 1997).

There is a large amount of work that is being undertaken by organisations for deaf people to develop literacy in deaf people in VLs, e.g. (Brueggemann, 2004). In particular, "the research literature has shown that interactive storybook reading, sign print, extensive reading and writing experiences, and social interaction around literacy activities support the deaf child's emergent and early literacy development" (Schirmer & Williams, 2003, p. 119). However, information technologists seem to be paying less attention to e-tools for improving the literacy of deaf people. Literacy is also a critical issue, as substantiated by linguists and psychologists working in deaf studies, crucial for the integration of deaf people into the hearing society.

This chapter aims at eliciting the interests of Human Computer Interaction (HCI) and Artificial Intelligence (AI) researchers and practitioners on the creation of intelligent web tools that can contribute to the literacy of deaf people. Web-based architectures, being cross-platform, should make the tools as widely available as possible, overcoming geographical or technological constraints. The tools should be intelligent in that they adopt techniques or technologies from AI, with the aim of improving the interaction and feedback specific to deaf users.

More precisely, this chapter describes the state of the art in the literature of e-tools for the literacy of deaf people. This review tries covering complementary and diverse literacy aspects in a VL, ranging from word knowledge to global reasoning on texts. This chapter aims at highlighting the role that the user centred design methodology (UCDM) can play in their design and development.

Why Do We Propose the UCDM, Which Focuses on Usability?

To the best of our knowledge, there are no standard usability guidelines *specific* for designing and developing web tools that are *usable* by deaf people. When it comes to designing for people with disabilities (deaf people in particular), the popular terms are *adaptive* or *assistive*. For instance, (Berry, 2004) recommends to provide all auditory information visually, captions with all multimedia presentations, and ensure that all visual cues are noticeable even if the user is not looking straight at the screen; important information should catch the user's attention, even through peripheral vision in order to maintain user interfaces accessible by deaf people. (Fajardo, 2005) and others suggest that web resources should provide a translation of their contents into the SL of the intended deaf users, whenever possible.

Still, "just because a design is theoretically accessible, doesn't mean that it's easy to use"

(Nielsen, 2001). According to (Woodson, 1981), usability means the practice of designing products so that users can perform required use, operation, service, and supportive tasks with a minimum of stress and maximum efficiency. In particular, (Laurel, 1990) states that the goal of human interface design is to empower users by providing them with ease of use.

Given this, why is the UCDM an appropriate methodology for creating web tools that are usable by deaf users? Much of the accessibility efforts in Information and Communication Technologies (ICT) development is taken from a pan-disability perspective, whereas the issues that deaf e-learners face are often ignored. Deaf users have unique and highly variable characteristics, which depend on several factors, such as the degree of deafness, different language education methods as well as the level of socio-cultural integration. Defining them as well-known user types is difficult.

The UCDM can be helpful in this respect in that it places the users at the centre of the design process. It demands an analysis of the context of use and the user requirements, a necessary step if the user types are not well determined. A web tool becomes truly accessible by deaf users if it is designed and evaluated through iterations of design solutions and evaluations *with* and *for* deaf users.

Moreover, the UCDM foresees multidisciplinary competences. E-tools for the literacy of deaf people do require them. For instance, such tools are likely to demand linguists that are expert of deaf studies, or educators that work with deaf people, and primarily deaf people.

Our review of current of e-tools for the literacy of deaf people is also meant to substantiate such claims.

The above part serves as a light introduction to deaf studies, concentrating on the literacy of deaf people. It mainly draws on the work of psychologists, linguists and educators as well as deaf researchers. Albeit very concise for space limits and thereby not making justice to the richness and variety of their work, it can give a first glimpse of the challenges open for HCI researchers and practitioners alike, interested in designing web tools for deaf people.

The following section presents the strictly necessary information on the UCDM. It is primarily meant for experts of deaf studies not acquainted with the UCDM, or ICT experts working in a different area.

The chapter continues with a review of different e-tools for the literacy of deaf people. We outline them in brief, and then concentrate on the usability of the tools, assessing whether they conform to the UCDM.

Supported by the findings of deaf studies outlined in the opening of this chapter, by our own experience and by the review of e-tools for deaf people, we conclude with a challenging task: the final section proposes a first set of guidelines for designing usable web tools for deaf people, by following the UCDM.

The User Centred Design Methodology

Several different definitions of usability exist, but all focus on the users, and all stress that the users' perspectives should be incorporated in each critical point of the design process. In particular, Donald Norman describes the UCDM as a philosophy based on the needs and interests of the user, with an emphasis on making products usable and understandable (Norman, 1998). The user-centred design process was also formalised in the ISO standards. In (ISO, 1998), usability is characterised as the extent to which a product can be used with efficiency, effectiveness and satisfaction by specific users to achieve specific goals in a specific environment.

According to this, the UCDM is an iterative process, which is repeated until attaining the usability of the tool under development. The iterative design revolves around the following main activities: (a) understanding and specifying the context of use; (b) specifying the user requirements; (c) producing design solutions; (d) evaluating designs against requirements.

The characteristics of the users, tasks, the organisational environment and physical environment define the *context* in which the system is to be used. Relevant characteristics of the users include knowledge, skills, experience, education, training, physical attributes, habits and capabilities. Task description includes the overall goals of the use of the system, as well as the allocation of activities and operational steps between humans and technological resources. The description of the environment includes both physical and socio-cultural characteristics that may influence the usage and acceptance of the system. In most design processes, there is a major activity specifying the functional requirements as well as others for the product or system.

The UCDM requires that designers should explicitly specify the intended end-users and their *requirements*, in relation to the analysed context of use. This is done in terms of: the HCI and workstation design; the user tasks; task performance; work design and organisation; co-operation and communication between the users and other relevant parties; management of change, including training; required performance of the tool against operational and financial objectives. The user requirements are thus derived and objectives are set with appropriate trade-offs identified between the different requirements.

Once clearly specified the context of use, as well as the user requirements, the process of iterative *design* can start (Figure 1). The process is based on a continuous interaction with the users, involved in the design since the very beginning, by: a) showing them concrete realisations of design solutions in form of models, mock-ups, etc.; b) allowing them to simulate real tasks, and using their feedbacks for improving the design; c) realising new models and iterating the process until the usability goals are met.

In the interaction with users, it is essential to exploit the system prototypes, even paper and pencil drawings in the preliminary phase of the development. The prototypes are not demonstrators for showing users a preview of the design, on the contrary, they are meant for collecting the users' feedback.

With web tools, it is often best to carry out several iterations with a few users, rather than a few iterations with a number of users. However, in order to determine whether the overall objectives are met, one also needs to perform a formal evaluation in a realistic context, for example, without the assistance and interruptions of evaluators.

The evaluation is an essential step in the UCDM and should take place at all stages in the system's life cycle (Figure 1). Early in the design, the evaluation aims at obtaining feedback that can guide the design itself. Later, when a realistic prototype is available, the evaluation should aim at measuring whether user and organisational objectives have been achieved.

Since changes are less expensive in the early stages of design and development than in later stages, the evaluation has to be started as soon as the first design proposals are available. Depending on the development stage of the project, the evaluation could be used to select and validate the design options that best fit the user requirements, or to elicit feedback and further requirements from the users, or to diagnose potential usability problems and identify needs for improvement in the system.

In (Hartson *et al.,* 2001), the authors present a practical discussion of factors, comparison criteria, and performance measures for comparing different usability evaluation methods (UEMs). In particular, we can distinguish *expert-based* and *user-based* UEMs. In the expert-based UEMs, usability experts evaluate a prototype, comparing it against existing usability rules or guidelines; in the user-based UEMs, real users use or comment on a tool prototype.

Figure 1. UCDM cycle, based on the specifics of (ISO, 1999).

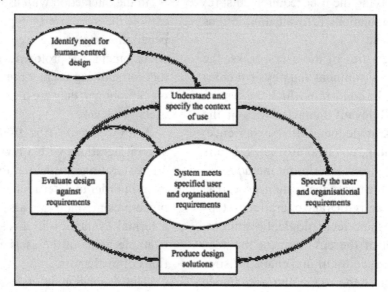

The expert-based UEMs include heuristic evaluation (Nielsen & Molich, 1990), cognitive walk-through (Yagita *et al.*, 2001).

A *heuristic* evaluation foresees a small set of usability evaluators that assess the system and judge its compliance with well known usability principles, namely, the heuristics. *Cognitive walkthrough* is typically performed by the system designer and a group of his or her peers (Wharton *et al.*, 1994).

The user-based UEMs include: observational evaluations, controlled evaluations (Yagita *et al.*, 2001), inquiries (Presser, 2004).

In the *observational* evaluations, users are observed while performing tasks with a prototype of the tool. Such evaluations offer a broad assessment of usability. Depending on the specific situation, one may either apply the observational evaluation by direct observation of the user, or record the interaction between the users and the system, e.g., via usability labs.

Inquiries include interviews, questionnaires and surveys. With *interviews*, designers directly queries users about their opinion on the tool, and act as discussion chairs. A *survey* evaluation re-

quires structured ad-hoc interviews, which do not demand the presence of the designer of the tool; a list of questions is asked and the users' responses recorded. Surveys differ from *questionnaires* in that surveys are interactive interviews. These and other inquiry methods offer a broad evaluation that allows for the identification of critical aspects at any stage of the design.

Controlled evaluations serve to test how a change in the design project could affect the overall usability. It may be applied in any phase during the development of a system. This method mainly aims at checking some specific cause-effect relations, and this is achieved checking as many variables as possible.

A Review of E-Tools for the Literacy of Deaf PEOPLE

This section reviews some literacy e-tools for the literacy of deaf people, which are web based or intelligent. Our review does not pretend to be an exhaustive list of all the available literacy e-tools; rather, it aims at covering diverse and

Table 1. Reviewed literacy e-tools for deaf people

Tool	Web	Use of Artificial Intelligence	Adults	Children	UCDM
CornerStones	No	No	No	Yes	No
LODE	Yes	Yes (constrain programming)	No	Yes	Yes
SMILE	No	No	No	Yes	Yes
ICICLE	No	Yes (natural language processing)	Yes	No	No
MAS	Yes	No	Yes	No	No
MM-DASL	No	Yes (database technologies)	Yes	Yes (old children)	No
Woordenboek	Yes	No	Yes	Yes (old children)	No
e-LIS	Yes	Yes (OWL ontology + query tool)	Yes	Yes (old children)	Yes

complementary literacy aspects that are considered in the development of such e-tools for deaf people, ranging from word knowledge to global reasoning on texts.

There is quite a literature on e-dictionaries for SL, which impels us to include them in our review although they are not, strictly speaking, e-tools for the literacy in a VL (Branson & Miller, 1997). In this chapter, we confine our analysis to three case studies, chosen because they are bimodal dictionaries, that is, dictionary from a SL to the VL of the same country and vice-versa, and because they are for the web, or are intelligent.

In the remainder of this section, we outline the tools, and afterwards we review them according to the UCDM.

Description

This subsection groups and describes the tools according to the intended end users. CornerStones, LODE and SMILE are e-tools specifically for children, ICICLE and MAS are for adults, e-LIS, MM-DASL, and Woordenboek are e-dictionaries for adults, but children could use them as well. Table 1 offers a bird-eye view of the tools, by assessing whether they are meant for children or adults.

Tools for Children

CornerStones is a tool for teachers of early primary-school children who are deaf, or have visual learning capabilities and literacy problems (Loeterman *et al.*, 2002) (CornerStones, 1998). Academic experts in literacy and deafness, along with teachers of deaf students participated in its development. An essential element of CornerStones is a story taken from the PBS's literacy series "Between the Lions", complemented by versions of the story in American SL and other visual-spatial systems for communicating with deaf children; word games are part of the tool. Cornerstones adopts storytelling to enrich the vocabulary and world knowledge of children, and improve their reading comprehension; however there is no artificial intelligence in CornerStones, which is essentially made up of a collection of web pages and games. Its interface is highly entertaining and visual, with catching images; text is always accompanied by a reference image. Overall the tool is well suited to children.

LODE is a web tool for children, primarily deaf children. It aims at stimulating children to globally reason on texts written in a VL, more specifically, Italian; (Gennari & Mich, 2008) (LODE, 2008). As in CorneStornes, LODE adopts storytelling. Deaf children often tend to reason on isolated concepts and not relate distant concepts in written texts; this attitude may also depend on the kind of "literacy interventions addressed to deaf children" which tend to "focus on single sentences and the grammatical aspects of text production" (Arfé & Boscolo, 2006). In its current version, LODE focuses on a specific type of reasoning, namely, on global temporal reasoning. LODE narrates temporally rich stories for children and then stimulates children to create a coherent network of temporal relations out of each story through apt exercises. Moreover, LODE invites children to create their own stories and then reason on their temporal dimension. To this end, the tool employs an automated reasoner, namely, a constraint programming system. A demonstrator of the tool is publicly available online (LODE, 2008). The last evaluated prototype of the tool embeds the constraint-based reasoner, and is available on demand.

SMILE has different educational goals than the tools mentioned so far: it is not an application for improving the literacy of deaf children; instead, it helps them learn mathematics and science concepts (Adamo-Villani & Jones, 2007) (SMILE, 2006). SMILE is an immersive game in which deaf and hearing children (aged 5–11) interact with fantasy 3D characters and objects. SMILE includes an imaginary town populated by fantasy 3D avatars that communicate with the child in written and spoken English, and American SL. The user can explore the town, enter buildings, select and manipulate objects, construct new objects, and interact with the characters. In each building the participant learns specific math or science concepts by performing hands-on activities developed in collaboration with elementary school educators and in alignment with standard science curriculum. SMILE is mentioned here because it adopts the UCDM.

Tools for Adults

The primary goal of **ICICLE** is to employ natural language processing and generation to tutor deaf students on the written English (Michaud & Mc-Coy, 2006) (ICICLE, 2008). ICICLE's interaction with the user takes the form of a cycle of user input and system response. The cycle begins when a user submits a piece of writing to be reviewed by the system. The system then performs a syntactic analysis on this writing, determines its errors, and constructs a response in the form of tutorial feedback. This feedback is aimed towards making the student aware of the nature of the errors found in the writing and giving him or her the information needed to correct them. At the moment of writing, ICICLE is not envisioned as a web tool, however it is an intelligent e-tool that exploits findings and technologies of artificial intelligence, more precisely, natural language processing. The current ICICLE prototype is not publicly available, thus we could not test it directly.

MAS (Making Access Succeed for deaf and disabled students) was a project for improving the reading comprehension of deaf signers (Ferrer *et al.*, 2002). SIMICODE 2002 (SIMICODE, 2002) is a web tool developed within MAS. The tool is made up of thirty hypertexts related to ten themes, e.g., leisure and free time, divided along three difficulty levels. Spanish SL is used as well. Each text is accompanied by a series of exercises that aim at improving morphological and syntactic aspects of texts that are difficult for deaf people, in order to increase their lexical repertoire and help them in locating essential information. As in CornerStones, there is no artificial intelligence in the exercises of SIMICOLE 2002, and the assistance of a human tutor is necessary for the feedback.

Tools for Adults and Old Children

MM-DASL (Multimedia Dictionary of American SL) was conceived in 1980 by Sherman Wilcox and William Stokoe (Wilcox, 2003). Albeit it was not a web dictionary (at the time of the creation of MM-DASL, the web was not an option), we report on it because it is a pioneering work in the world of e-dictionaries and because its interface is intelligent. MM-DASL has a user interface with film-strips or pull-down menus. The interface allows users to look up for a sign only reasoning in terms of its visual formational components, that is, the Stokoe ones—handshape, location and movement. In MM-DASL, linguistic information on the formational components constraints the query for the signs that one can create; users are not required to specify all the sign's formational components, nevertheless their query must be created along a specific order. Textual information is enriched with digital videos showing signing people in MM-DASL. Time is an important feature of SLs: sign components may vary in time, for instance, the signer's hands can assume different shapes while performing a single sign. MM-DASL allows its users to specify the changing hand shapes (up to five). The MM-DASL project was never merchandised for several reasons, explained in (Wilcox, 2003). For instance, platform independence of the system was a problem for MM-DASL. The profile of the expected user was not analysed in details before starting the development of the dictionary.

Woordenboek is a web bilingual dictionary for Flemish SL (VGT) (Woordenboek, 2004). Users search for a sign by selecting its sign components. However, in the current version of Woordenboek: (1) users are not expertly guided through the definition of the sign (i.e., there is no artificial intelligence in the tool), thus users can specify a gesture which corresponds to no VGT sign or a sign that does not occur in the dictionary database; (2) the sign components are not represented via iconic images; they are represented with symbols of the adopted transcription system. Thereby the dictionary from VGT to Flemish is hardly usable by those who are not expert of VGT or the adopted transcription system.

The creation of a web dictionary for Italian SL (Lingua Italiana dei Segni, LIS) is part of the **e-LIS** project, which commenced at the end of 2004 (Di Mascio & Gennari, 2008) (e-LIS, 2006). The e-LIS dictionary from LIS to verbal Italian

was conceived for expert signers searching for the translation of a LIS sign. At the start of 2006, when the development of e-LIS was already in progress, it was realised that the potential users of a web dictionary would also include non-experts of LIS, more specifically, of the formational rules of signs adopted in the dictionary. Then the idea of an ontology and the associated technology for the dictionary took shape: they aim to allow even non-expert signers who are learning LIS to use the dictionary. The e-LIS ontology formalises the decomposition rules of signs of the e-LIS dictionary. The ontology becomes the input of a DIG-enabled query tool; the tool allows the dictionary users to compose a conjunctive query for retrieving a sign by assembling components of the sign in an expert manner, e.g., the tool forbids the composition of sign components that are inconsistent according to the ontology. However, the interfaces of most of the query tools for ontologies are textual, flat, not colourful, and hence unlikely to suit deaf users. According to (Fajardo, 2005), deaf signers privilege spatial demanding hypertexts, in which texts is evenly and sparsely distributed along layers of nodes. The novel visual interface of the e-LIS dictionary allows users to query by browsing the e-LIS ontology, and is designed according to the analysed user requirements; for instance, the novel interface renders the ontology with colourful, 2.5D, dynamic, interactive tree-maps. Visually showing the effects of the users' choices can minimise the need of undo tools: the dictionary users will start a search path only if the prospected next choices are suitable to them.

The Tools and the UCDM

Table 1 summarises the main features of the reviewed e-tools, but it does not comment on the design methodology. SMILE, LODE and e-LIS explicitly refer to the UCDM. According to the available documentation and to the best of our knowledge, the remaining e-tools do not mention the UCDM or other methodologies with the user at the centre of the design process.

Table 2. Reviewed literacy e-tools and the UCDM.

Tool	Context of use	User Requirements	Design—last product	Evaluation
CornerStones	Primary school	Literacy in VL	Web demo	Yes
LODE	Home or primary school	Global reasoning in VL	Web demo, prototype with the constraint reasoner on demand	On-going
SMILE	Virtual world	Science	Downloadable	Yes
ICICLE	Home	English grammar	Not available	Unclear
MAS	Home	Literacy in VL	Not available	Yes
MM-DASL	Home	Literacy in SL	Discontinued	No
Woordenboek	Home	Literacy in SL	Web site prototype	Unclear
e-LIS	Home	Literacy in SL	Web site prototype	On-going

However, by analysing the literature, we can highlight other features of the tools related to the UCDM, namely, (a) the context of use, (b) the user requirements, if there is (c) a prototype and (d) its evaluation. The results of our analysis are summarised in Table 2.

The context of use is the primary context for which the tool is developed; home indicates any environment in which the user feels at ease. For instance, the context of use of SMILE is the virtual world, because SMILE includes an imaginary town in which the user is immersed. The user requirements are not necessarily those of the end user; they are usually the requirements that pertain to the user in the view of designers, that is, they coincide with the usability goals of the tool. As the table shows, not all the tools have a prototype yet. In some cases, the existing prototypes are still in the initial stages of development, and it is unclear whether they underwent any evaluation.

This may well depend on the intrinsic difficulties of developing tools for not well known users, and calls for a set of guidelines that can help designers in developing literacy e-tools *usable* by deaf people.

FUTURE WORK: TOWARDS A DEAF USER CENTRED DESIGN

Know Your Users

Deaf studies are mainly authored by psychologists, linguists and educators, and not by usability experts. The UCDM, as stated in the introduction of this chapter, is intrinsically an interdisciplinary methodology. Therefore, user centred designers should include such studies in their design and development of tools for deaf people, in particular for establishing the context of use and the user

Table 3. Types of users

User type	Description
End-user	Deaf people for which the tool is developed
Usability expert	HCI expert
Deaf study expert	An author of deaf studies, e.g., an SL linguist
Intermediary	A person that the deaf participant in a test trusts, and with whom the deaf participant can easily communicate, e.g., a teacher of deaf children
Control user	A hearing person with a profile similar to that of the intended deaf end-users

requirements. Interviewing experts of deaf studies and analysing the literature are necessary steps in the early stages of the UCDM. Of the e-tools reviewed in this chapter, only LODE and e-LIS clearly refer to the UCDM as their design methodology. Albeit several e-tools do not explicitly mention the UCDM, they implicitly follow it whenever experts of deaf studies are consulted and involved in the design. For instance, this is the case of Cornerstones or MAS.

As stressed in the opening of this chapter and witnessed by our own experience, it may be difficult to recruit and directly interview deaf users. Designers may have problems in communicating directly with deaf users, as these may prefer their SL to the verbal language or simply tend to distrust unfamiliar people. Therefore the design and evaluation of tools for deaf people may also require the intervention of SL interpreters or, more in general, intermediaries that deaf users trust, for instance, the parents or a teacher of a deaf child.

In designing and evaluating a web tool for deaf people, control groups of hearing people can also be of assistance or even necessary; in this setting, control groups are formed by hearing people with the same profile of the intended deaf users.

This is all in accordance with the UCDM, which foresees the presence of different users, besides the end-users, in the development process. Table 3 classifies the users that we believe are necessary in the UCD of a web tool for deaf people, in line with the literature of deaf studies and our review of e-tools for deaf people.

However, this is a coarse-grained classification. The assistance of experts of deaf studies and intermediaries is highly recommended for fine-tuning the classification for the specific tool under development, and its specific users. Therefore, in the remainder of this chapter, we propose some guidelines for developing a deaf user centred design methodology.

Guidelines

Given the types of users summarised in Table 3, the iterative process for designing the tool can start (Figure 2). First, the context of use is analysed, then the user requirements are established; a first prototype is designed and evaluated; the results of the evaluations are checked against the user requirements, which can be refined, and the iteration may restart. In the remainder, we provide a concrete guide to each step of the iteration and highlight some guidelines that designers could employ.

Context of Use

The design team should analyse the state of the art, mainly through the literature of deaf studies and ad-hoc inquiries with experts of deaf studies.

These and intermediaries are also essential for refining the classification of the tool's end users. For instance, let us consider a tool for the literacy in a VL, like LODE; the experts of deaf studies may help in focusing the range of application of the tool, as well as in understanding whether it makes sense to classify deaf children according to their language education, e.g., oral or bimodal, or whether the children's age is a more relevant factor.

Such experts and intermediaries can also assist in choosing the best context for evaluating or using the tool. Again, let us reconsider the case of LODE as example; experts and intermediaries may suggest whether the child's home is more apt than a school lab for testing or using the tool.

Suggested UEM's: inquiries with experts of deaf studies.

Definition and Analysis of the User Equirements

In order to establish the user requirements, designers should consult with experts of deaf studies and HCI. Experts in deaf studies help in setting on

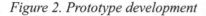

Figure 2. Prototype development

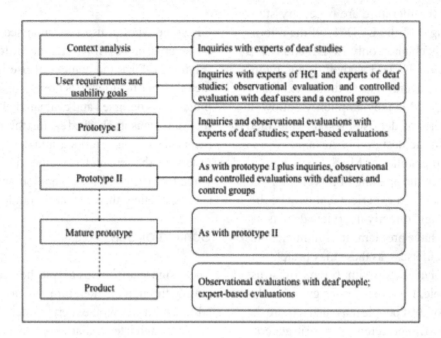

firmer grounds the requirements, e.g., if the tool is meant for correcting a specific type of grammatical errors, like ICICLE, then the experts could confirm whether the tool's end users commit such type of errors, or that the type of feedback of the tool is indeed useful.

Then the designers should assess the requirements with the end users, with the assistance of intermediaries. The assessment can be done via structured inquiries, or observational evaluations. These evaluations should be organised right at this stage of the project, even with small groups of end users given the difficulty in recruiting deaf users for tests, and possibly with control groups of hearing people; the results of the two groups should be compared through controlled evaluations. For instance, let us reconsider a web tool for improving the grammatical production of deaf signers. The observation and comparison of a group of deaf users and a group of hearing users working with the tool can serve to ascertain a significant difference between the grammatical productions of the two groups, and which gram-

matical interventions may be more suited to the former group of users.

One should also consider that deaf people, and deaf signers in particular are often organised in networks; a positive experience within the network can spread rapidly and elicit more deaf uses to participate in future evaluations of the tool. Moreover, such tests will also serve to assess the most comfortable environment for the users, the best test timing, hardware equipment etc.

With deaf signers, the assistance of a SL interpreter is highly desirable during the tests; similarly, deaf children may need the assistance of a person they trust and that can work as interpreter with them. To this end, the evaluators should gather information on the participants with questionnaires, prior to the observational evaluations; in this manner, the evaluators can assess if the their deaf participants need interpreters, their first language (VL or SL), their level of acquaintance with computers, …

Suggested UEM's: inquiries with experts of HCI and experts of deaf studies; inquiries, observational evaluations and controlled evaluations with even a small group of deaf users and a control group.

Design and Evaluation

The designers should produce several prototypes, even paper and pencil drawings. The schema in Figure 2 summarises the main steps in the development of the tool prototypes. We detail such steps in the remainder of this chapter.

Specific features of the first prototype should be evaluated with experts of deaf studies and HCI. As soon as possible, the subsequent prototypes should be evaluated with even a small number of the intended end users and a control group of hearing people, observed while interacting with the tool; the results should be then compared with controlled evaluations. For instance, let us reconsider the case of LODE. At around the age of 8, children start reading globally and summarising stories; such are critical steps for maturing a complete literacy in a VL. LODE aims at stimulating children to globally reason on the temporal dimension of stories, written in a VL; its usability is thus tested with control groups of hearing children, aged 7–8, and deaf children older than 8 years.

As the design cycle progresses, the evaluators should recruit a significant number of deaf users and observe them while they interact with the tool. It may be easier to have a number of these evaluations of the same tool prototype with few users.

In general, designers should consult with experts along the whole design process: experts of deaf studies help to ensure that the prototypes meet the end-user requirements; experts of HCI serve to ensure that the prototypes fulfil the usability goals. Intermediaries should assist designers along the observational evaluations; they can also help in structuring the inquiries for gathering information prior as well as post evaluations. For instance, let us reconsider the case of LODE: after the proper software evaluation, the evaluator administered a post-task interview using the sticky note critiquing method; children worked initially in pairs or small groups. The teams had approximately ten minutes for discussing and writing their notes concerning whether they liked or not the tool, and which games of the tool they enjoyed best. Then the evaluator opened a discussion on the notes themselves.

Suggested UEM's: expert-based evaluations with usability experts; observational evaluations and inquiries with experts of deaf studies; observational evaluations and inquiries with deaf users; observational evaluations and inquiries with control groups of hearing users; controlled evaluations.

CONCLUSION

Our review of literacy e-tools for deaf people showed that there are several projects covering diverse aspects of literacy, e.g., in-depth context-based knowledge of words, global reasoning on stories, grammatical aspects of text production. The review also puts forward that the majority of such tools do not have clearly designed or documented evaluations with deaf users. This may be possibly due to the absence of assessed guidelines for developing tools that are *usable by deaf people*, with deaf users at the centre of the design process as well.

Thereby this chapter concludes by proposing a first set of such guidelines, based on the UCDM and emerged from our own experience in developing web tools for deaf people, the multi-disciplinary findings of deaf studies, the analysis of the literature and of other literacy e-tools for deaf people.

The guidelines aim to ease the design of new tools for the literacy of deaf people, to improve the development of existing tools and, more ambitiously, to open a debate within HCI on the creation of a deaf user centred design. We hope that more HCI researchers and practitioners will take over the challenge, assess the guidelines, and contribute to the debate.

REFERENCES

Adamo-Villani, N., & Jones, D. (2007). A Study of Two Immotion Control Techniques. *Proc. of o Compuer Graphics and Visualization Conf, IADIS.*

Arfé, B., & Boscolo, P. (2006). Causal Coherence in Deaf and Hearing Students' Written Narratives. *Discourse Processes, 42*(3), 271–300. doi:10.1207/s15326950dp4203_2

Berry, D. (2004). Requirements for Maintaining Web Access for Hearing-Impaired Individuals. *Software Quality Control, 12*(1), 9–28.

Branson, J., & Miller, D. (1997). Research Methods for Studying the Language of the Signing Deaf. In N. Hornberger, & P. Corson (Eds), *Encyclopedia of Language and Education* (Vol. 8, pp. 175–184).

Brueggemann, B. J. (Ed.). (2004). *Literacy and Deaf People: Cultural and Contextual Perspectives.* Washington, DC: Gallaudet University Press.

Cole, R. (1999). New Tools for Interactive Speech and Language Training: Using Animated Conversational Agents in the Classrooms of Profoundly Deaf Children. In *Prof. of ESCA/SOCRA for Speech Science Education.*

CornerStones. (1998). Retrieved 2008, from http://ncam.wgbh.org/cornerstones/cornerstones.html

Crasborn, O., et al. (2008). Construction and Exploration of Sign Language Corpora. *E-proc. of the 3rd Workshop on the Representation and Processing of Sign Languages, LREC 2008l.*

Di Mascio, T., & Gennari, R. (2008). An Intelligent Visual Dictionary for Italian Sign Language. *Journal of Web Engineering, 7*(4), 318–338.

e-LIS (2006). Retrieved 2008, from http://elis.eurac.edu/index_it

Fajardo, I. (2005). *Cognitive Accesibility to Hypertext Systems.* PhD thesis. U. of Granada, Spain.

Ferrer, A., Romero, R., Martínez, M., Asensi, M., & Andreu, A. (2002). *Improving Reading Skills in Adult Deaf People: The Spanish MÀS Module.* Berlin.

Gennari, R., & Mich, O. (2008). Designing and Assessing an Intelligent E-Tool for Deaf Children. *Proc. of the IUI 2008 Conf.* ACM, pp. 325–328.

Hartson, H., Andre, T., & Williges, R. (2001). Criteria for Evaluating Usability Evaluation Methods. *International Journal of Human-Computer Interaction, 13*(4), 373–410. doi:10.1207/S15327590IJHC1304_03

ICICLE. (2008). Retrieved 2008, from http://www.eecis.udel.edu/research/icicle/.

ISO (1998). *Guidance on Usability,* (Vol. ISO 9141-11).

ISO (1999). *Human Centred Design Processes for Interactive Systems* (Vol. ISO 13407).

Laurel, B. (1990). *The Art of Human-Computer Interface Design.* Mountford S. Joy.

LODE. (2008). Retrieved 2008, from http://www.inf.unibz.it/lode

Loeterman, M., Paul, P., & Donahue, S. (2002). Reading and Deaf Children. *Reading Online, 6* (5). Retrieved 2008, from http://www.readingonline.org/articles/art_index.asp?HREF=loeterman/index.html.

Marschark, M., & Spencer, P. (Eds.). (2003). *Oxford Handbook of Deaf Studies, Language and Education.* New York: Oxford University Press.

Marschrak, M., & Wauters, L. (2008). *Language Comprehension and Learning by Deaf Students.* In M. Marschark & P.C. Hauser (Eds) *Deaf Cognition* (pp. 309–350). Oxford, UK: Oxford University Press.

Michaud, L., & McCoy, K. (2006). Capturing the Evolution of Grammatical Knowledge in a CALL System for Deaf Learners of English. [IJAIED]. *International Journal of Artificial Intelligence in Education, 16*(1), 65–97.

NCAM. (n.d.). *Accessible Digital Media: Design Guidelines for Electronic Publications, Multimedia and the Web.* Retrieved 2008, from http://ncam.wgbh.org/publications/adm/

Nielsen, J. (2001). *Beyond Accessibility: Treating Users with Disabilities as People.* Retrieved 2008, from Alertbox: Current Issues in Web Usability http://www.useit.com/alertbox/20011111.html

Nielsen, J., & Molich, R. (1990). Heuristic Evaluation of User Interfaces. In *Proc. of ACM CHI'90 Conf.*

Norman, D. (1998). *The Design of Everyday Things.* Cambridge, MA: MIT.

Presser, S. (2004). *Methods for Testing and Evaluating Survey Questionnaires.* New York: Wiley-IEEE.

Reynolds, C., & Fletcher-Janzen, E. (2001). Concise Encyclopedia of Special Education: A Reference for the Education of the Handicapped and Other Exceptional Children and Adults. Hoboken, NJ: Wiley.

RIT. (2008). *Hearing Loss.* Retrieved 2008, from RIT, Hearing Loss, http://www.ntid.rit.edu/media/hearing_loss.php

Schirmer, B. R., & Williams, C. (2003). Approaches to Teaching Reading. In M. Marschark, & P. Spencer (Eds), *Handbook of Deaf Studies, Language and Education* (pp. 110–122). Oxford, UK: Oxford University Press.

Shackel, B., & Richardson, D. (1991). *Human Factors for Informatics Usability.* Cambridge, UK: Cambridge University Press.

SIMICODE. (2002). Retrieved 2008, from http://acceso.uv.es/preacceso/typo/index.php/simicole.html

SMILE. (2006). Retrieved 2008, from http://www2.tech.purdue.edu/cg/i3/SMILE/

Wharton, C., Rieman, J., Lewis, C., & Polson, P. (1994). The Cognitive Walkthrough Method: a Practitioner's Guide. In J. Nielsen, & R. Mack (Eds), *Usability Inspection Methods* (pp. 105–140). Hoboken, NJ: John Wiley and Sons, Inc.

Wilcox, S. (2003). The Multimedia Dictionary of American Sign Language: Learning Lessons about Language, Technology, and Business. *Sign Language Studies, 3*(4), 379–392. doi:10.1353/sls.2003.0019

Woodson, W. (1981). *Human Factors Design Handbook.* New York: McGraw-Hill Education.

Woordenboek (2004). Retrieved 2008, from http://gebaren.ugent.be/information.php

Yagita, Y., Aikawa, Y., & Inaba, A. (2001). *A Proposal of the Quantitative Evaluation Method for Social Acceptability of Products and Services.* Tokyo: Ochanomizu University.

Section 3
Theoretical Approaches

Chapter 12

Social Research Methods Used in Moving the Traditional Usability Approach Towards a User–Centered Design Approach

Horia D. Pitariu
Babes-Bolyai University, Romania

Daniela M. Andrei
Babes-Bolyai University, Romania

Adriana M. Guran
Babes-Bolyai University, Romania

ABSTRACT

The present chapter focuses on the idea of rethinking the concept of usability moving from the traditional view of usability expressed in the internal characteristics of the product towards usability understood as deriving from the quality of interactions between humans, their work and the web design product. Usability is not only an add-on or a final result in the design process but it is embedded as a main concern within the design process itself. Related to this perspective on usability, the authors discussed the design models which can support it and argued on the importance of using social research tools for a better understanding of the people and their needs starting with the very first stage of design. Further on the authors have provided a brief description of the most frequently used research methods in user needs analysis (interviews, focus groups and surveys) together with short guidelines in preparing and using these methods. The last part is dedicated to the illustration of user needs analysis taken from two of their research projects.

DOI: 10.4018/978-1-60566-896-3.ch012

INTRODUCTION

Usability has become a topic of great interest to researchers in the field of human computer interaction and interaction design due to an increasingly strong connection between usability and the overall success of a given product, be it an object, software or a website (Kuniavsky, 2003; Nielsen, 1993; Norman, 2002). Although researchers agree that usability does not, in itself guarantee the success of such a product (Kuniavsky, 2003; Norman, 2002), they also underline the fact that the lack of usability and a low quality user experience may contribute substantially to the failure of a product or design (Kuniavsky, 2003; Norman, 2002). Together with a substantially grown interest in usability, even though the subject did not represent the focus of design process in its starting years (Norman, 2002, Jordan, 2002) a certain trend in the conceptualization of usability can be observed as the traditionally accepted view of usability is moving towards an integrated perspective in which usability is not just an end goal or attribute of the final product but is also represented by the quality of user experience it enables. Moreover, the maturation of this concept is seen in terms of quality in software, quality in interaction and quality in value (Law, Hvannberg, & Cockton, 2008) a perspective which clearly passes over the traditional view of usability as a validating measure for the design product (Dumas & Redish, 1999).

Taking into account this shift in conceptualization, this chapter is organized around the idea of rethinking the concept of usability,. This means moving from the traditional view of usability expressed in the internal characteristics of the product towards usability understood as deriving from the quality of interactions between humans, their work and the web design product (van Welie, 2001) or, in other words, from the better understanding of the user experience (Kuniavsky, 2003). More and more researchers argue that a user-centered approach or interactive design is the

kind of approach that can support this conceptualization of usability (Benyon, Turner & Turner, 2005; Kuniavsky, 2003; van Welie, 2001; Brink, Gergle & Wood, 2002). As a result, usability becomes a permanent concern for researchers and designers. Moreover, designing for usability starts precisely from the first stage of web design: user needs analysis.

In the first part of the chapter we will provide a short background on the trends and movements in research and design practices that have an impact on the way usability is defined and measured. We will also indicate that these trends influence the design stage when usability is taken into consideration. Aligned to these research trends, this chapter argues that instead of usability testing, which has been the focus of the majority of the publications in this field, researchers and designers should be primarily interested in usability building even from the beginning of the process by assuring the fact that their design will address the real and important needs and problems of future users. This goal cannot be achieved without a deep and accurate understanding of people, their world and their activities, their needs, problems or aspirations. This may appear very daunting to a web developer who has no training in research on and with people but can be very natural to a social scientist who has been trained in using all social research methods. We will argue that both in the traditional perspective on usability but even more now social research techniques are becoming indispensable for insuring a good design (and therefore usable products) and all known techniques become tools that can help us in attaining this goal (Dumas & Redish, 1999). As a result, in this chapter we are going to talk about the social research tools (or methods) that can be used during the first step of user-centered design in order to provide a deep and thorough understanding of the users, their needs, desires or problems, an understanding that will constitute the basis for usability building throughout the design process (Brink, Gergle & Wood, 2002). Some of the most popular methods are presented together with their relevance and applicability into this field. The final part of this chapter will be dedicated to the illustration of the way in which these methods have been used in our research and the benefits they generated for the further stages of the design process.

BACKGROUND

The history of usability research in the field of interactive systems design is rich and very interesting ranging from a point when it was barely acknowledged as relevant (Kuniavsky, 2003; Norman,2002) to a stage when usability became a business in itself (Rubin, 1994) and finally to the present day when even the term usability seems unable to encompass the developments regarding this concept and new concepts like user experience are taking over (Law et al., 2008). The transformations in the concerns for usability followed an ascending pattern but there are still authors arguing that we are not in the right place with the implementation of usability principles (Kuniavsky, 2003) or that there are very deep differences in usability practices between different organizations, some still at the beginnings of usability evaluation while other are influencing the development in this field (Rosenbaum, 2008).

The development of usability research in the field of web design started, just as in any other design fields, from a complete unawareness of its importance (Kuniavsky, 2003;, 2002). Kuniavsky (2003) underlines the fact that in the beginnings, web designers were more concerned with being the first ones on a certain market and with marketing and branding issues. The user was not important as there was no budget for such research. Things changed dramatically as technology developed and interactive systems (websites included) started being available to more people. The same reason for ignoring the user up to that point, the financial profit, became the reason for an increased attention

being given to usability aspects as usability started being seen as a competitive advantage (Baven, 2008; Kuniavsky, 2003). This increased attention led to the structuring of the research in this field. A structured body of research on the topic of usability was becoming visible. The characteristic of this development is the fact that usability research was still somehow technology-oriented. As a result, the traditional view of usability that became most popular among developers refers to the attributes of the interface that ease the use of product for its users (Bevan, 2008). This traditional view on usability can be seen by analyzing some of the most well-known definitions of usability which all refer to internal characteristics of technology. For example, Nielsen (1993) defines usability in terms of system attributes: learnability, efficiency, memorability, errors and satisfaction. Dix et al. (2004) describe usability in terms of learnability, flexibility and robustness which are primarily identified in the product and the features that enhance these properties. A short critical overview of these definitions can indicate that even during this prolific period in usability research most of the focus was on technology and not on people, or on users. Also, most of these conceptualizations reflect the efforts to develop standardized tools for measuring usability, and indeed, they are most suited for this purpose (Nielsen, 1993). The problem with this perspective on usability is neither the internal consistency of its elements nor the fact that it is not correctly defined, but the fact that the success of any product does not rely solely on usability and usability is not just an end product of the design process. Constraints coming from users are representing only one source of constraints for the success of a product and especially a web design product usability is seen more as the balancing of different and often conflicting constraints (Kuniavsky, 2003; Norman, 2002).

The view on usability started to change when another popular usability definition was proposed. usability was thought to represent the measure in which specified users can use a product to achieve certain goals with effectiveness, efficiency and satisfaction. (ISO, 1998). The change of focus is clear as the new definition doesn't rely anymore on the characteristics of the product but on the results of using the product. The characteristics the definition underlines (efficiency, effectiveness and satisfaction) refer as much to the product as to all the other elements of the system: users, their task and the environment in which they are performing their task (Bevan, 2008). This view on usability is more suitable to the present research and practice as it can more easily address business goals: efficiency, effectiveness and satisfaction are directly related to profitability (Bevan, 2005). With this definition, usability started to be seen from the inside-out and focus changed from technology characteristics to the ability of meeting the users' goals and needs (Bevan 2008). On the other hand, we must point out that a similar argument can be found in other classical work in the field. For example, Norman (2002) argues that usability is the result of balancing the needs of all stakeholders in the product development so the new focus is not entirely new but a returning to the essence of the concept. This returning is supported by the main challenges that the human computer interaction community is continually acknowledging. This community is focusing more and more not only on the way users are best supported by technology to meet their needs and goals, but also on the way users play a role in shaping the development of future designs. Other concerns are represented by the way user requirements are embodied in design products and also the support and measurement of the quality in use when nonfunctional attributes are also taken into account (Law, Hvannberg & Cockton, 2008) The present understanding of usability has reinforced the interest in the quality of interactions between humans, their work and the web design product (van Welie, 2001) or, in other words, in a better understanding of the user experience (Kuniavsky, 2003).

This trend is even more visible when we take into consideration web-design because in web-design customers have a greater power. If the traditional view set the usability experience after buying the product, on the web this situation is reversed: users can experience usability right from the beginning, before committing to any website and certainly before buying something (Nielsen, 2000). That is why a better understanding of user experience and usability has become central to the field of web design.

The Evolution of Usability Reflected in the Evolution of Design Models

These movements in the way researchers and designers think about usability have a correspondence in the way the design process has been remodeled over the years. The traditional way of thinking about usability is compatible to the traditional waterfall-type or corporation edict type of design process in which usability is taken into consideration only at the end of the design process when the product is already finished and launched on the market. The problem with this kind of design process is the fact that it does not afford for the early identification of possible design problems and, as a result, the balancing of different needs and constraints that creates a good user experience is very difficult. The alternative that developed to overcome the shortcomings of this design process was the iterative design. The underlying assumption of iterative development was the fact that it is practically impossible to create perfect solutions from the beginning, so we need several design cycle in which to alternate activities such as problem description, creating solutions and evaluating those solutions against problems described previously. This design method was more suitable for addressing the new perspective on usability as it is flexible and adaptable enough to incorporate different types of constraints that determine usability. The only weak point of it was the fact that, in its initial form, the iterative design process did not make the involvement of users necessary in the design process (Kuniavsky, 2003). Indeed, we can develop an iterative design process without talking to any end user at any stage if we assume that we already know everything there is to know about the user and the product.

As seductive as this assumption appears to be, the present orientation in design is based exactly on the observation that designers are not users, do not resemble the final user and cannot fully understand the user's needs and problems (Benyon et al., 2005; Kuniavsky, 2003; Norman, 2002). This is the argument that makes it necessary that end users be involved in the design process even from the very early stages and most of the literature argues the importance of user-centered design (Jokela, 2008, Brink et al., 2002; Rubin, 1994; van Welie, 2001). The main characteristic of this design process is the fact that users become partners in the design and are involved at every design stage. Most of all, the user-centered design contributes to the shift in user interest from the end of the design process to the beginnings. If the traditional design processes started with the specification of requirements for the new product, user-centered design places the needs analysis as the first phase in the design process and further retains the adaptability and flexibility of iterative design (Jokela, 2008; Benyon et al, 2005; Brink et al, 2002; Rubin, 1994). Moreover, researchers now agree that usability engineering has become more and more iterative, involving users throughout the design process (Dumas & Redish, 1999) and that usability should be followed throughout the entire design process (Brink et al., 2002).

Most researchers stress the need for a user-centered approach to design but very few of them offer operational design models that could inform practice. Even the ISO 13407 standards regarding user-centered design seem to offer only general principles that are not bound to specific phases in the development cycle (Jokela, 2008). Regarding the development cycle, a review of existing models

shows us that, with some differences in terminology and organization, all existing models of user centered design include a requirement analysis stage (or user analysis), conceptual design, prototype design and evaluation (mockups, prototypes, simulations), implementation and evaluation at every of these stages (Jokela, 2008; Brink et al, 2002; van der Veer, 1999; van Welie, 2001, Rubin, 1994). In a more simplified form, the core of these models is represented by a reiterative cycle of understanding the context of use, uncovering the user needs, developing design solutions and evaluating them against context and user requirements (Jokela, 2008, Benyon et al, 2005).

Although most of these authors agree that the main characteristics of user centered design are the importance given to an early involvement of users into the design process and the importance given to the first stages of the design model, they rarely include specifications for how to conduct the first stage of user need analysis within the model itself. We conducted a review of existing models of user centered design focusing mostly on the first stage of user needs analysis. The synthesis of these models (Jokela, 2008; Benyon et al, 2005; Pitariu, 2003; Brink et al, 2002) allowed us to articulate our own approach towards user need analysis which we have used in our research projects. The approach is presented in Figure 1 and it represents a systematization of existing models and guidelines on user-needs analysis in user centered design.

Qualitative vs. Quantitative Methods

These changes in the design process also generated modifications in the way usability was measured and the aspects that were measured. If the traditional usability concept generated well standardized measurement tools focused on the internal dimensions of the construct itself, user-centered design in its early focus on user needs and tasks created a need to develop and use less standardized methods that enable us to have a better understanding of people,

Figure 1. Our approach to user-needs analysis based on existing models

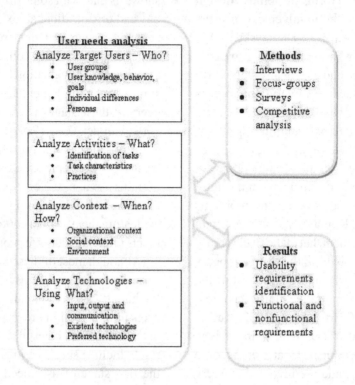

their activities, the context in which these activities take place, and their needs and values that could affect the design at every stage. A move from validating products toward understanding user experience and behavior can be identified in the research literature.

We can observe that the paradigm change in design is accompanied by a pressure of paradigm change in evaluation methodology. Signs of this paradigm change are highlighted in present literature, many researchers indicating a growing importance given to qualitative methods and to contextual, field research (Rosenbaum, 2008). A closer analysis of the scientific paradigms which fundament quantitative and qualitative methodology will support a better understanding of this growing emphasis on the qualitative.

Usually, quantitative methodology is associated with a positivist paradigm, which is the dominant paradigm in science. This paradigm is based on the ontological position that there is a single,

absolute, true, objective and independent reality which can be known using objective analysis and the tools of logical reasoning (Hatch & Yanow, 2008). The focus is on exact measures that could offer the researcher true and unbiased description of the reality. As a result, the preferred methodology is the quantitative one.

Qualitative methodology is associated to an interpretive or constructivist paradigm which assumes that reality does not exist independently outside of the human being. Reality is permanently constructed out of internal and external resources and the focus changes from true description of reality to different interpretations and meanings that constitute reality (Hatch & Cunliffe, 2006). As a result, researchers should not focus on discovering true facts of reality, but on understanding people, the way they interpret experience and the processes of meaning-making that contribute to reality building. The knowledge resulted in this paradigm will never constitute universal, abstract theories, but will allow for a deeper understanding of a given phenomenon in a given context and for explanations of specific situations. As a result, this knowledge should be judged in terms of its trustworthiness, credibility, transferability and confirmability (Denzin & Lincoln, 2005). As we can see, these evaluation criteria for qualitative research are concerned more with the applicability and credibility of results and less with internal and external validity.

A short analysis of the arguments given in the previous part of this paper shows us that such a paradigm shift from positivism to constructivism can be mirrored in the historical evolution of the usability research literature and practice. The beginnings of this field were marked by positivist and quantitative approaches in an effort to justify the concept (usability) and to contribute to a mature science. But the later growing emphasis on user involvement in the design process and formative usability evaluation changed the focus toward a deeper understanding of users and their needs. More and more researchers and practitioners consider that the value of usability evaluation is in diagnosing problems and not in validating products (Dumas & Redish, 1999). This emphasis marks the shift towards an interpretive/constructivist paradigm in human computer interaction which is also illustrated by a greater importance given to qualitative methods (Rosenbaum, 2008).

Although there seems to be a growing consensus in the research literature concerning the appropriateness of qualitative research methods in the present and future developments of the usability field (Rosenbaum, 2008), a short analysis of some well-known databases will show us that quantitative studies are still predominant in this field. This situation can be explained if we take into consideration the criteria by which research is judged and evaluated. Often, those who argue on the importance of using qualitative methodologies are also those who stress on the importance of solving the methodological uncertainties that accompany qualitative approaches (Dumas &

Redish, 1999). We would like to underline the fact that these methodological uncertainties or flaws are identified only when we are judging qualitative approaches by the same criteria we use to evaluate quantitative research. Given the different paradigm, qualitative research is based on different ontological and epistemic assumptions and therefore it has specific criteria against which it should be evaluated (Denzin & Lincoln, 2005). If we take these criteria into consideration, there should be no uncertainties related to the use of qualitative data in usability research and especially in user need analysis.

The characteristics of qualitative research make it very useful at this stage of user needs analysis and the literature shows indeed that qualitative methods are most indicated here as we are trying to better understand people and their experiences. The main characteristics are the descriptive nature of these methods, their interdisciplinary character and lack of formalizations which make it very accessible to researchers in different domains (Van Maanen, 1998). All these characteristics make qualitative research very suitable in this first stage of user-centered design when the focus is on a deep understanding of people.

In the following section we will briefly describe some of the qualitative methods used in the user needs analysis stage of user-centered design.

Review of Techniques and Methods

The literature on user-centered research shows that among the most frequently used methods in the first phase of the user-centered design process are interviews, focus groups, user diaries, surveys, case studies and competitive analysis (Kuniavsky, 2003; Brink et al, 2002; Dumas & Redish, 1999; Rubin, 1994,). In this section we will focus on some of these techniques that, by allowing for a better understanding of people, their goals and activities and the way they relate to them, can support a design for usability even from the start of the design process. The selection we have made does not illustrate all the social qualitative research techniques that could possibly inform the user needs analysis but are among the most popular techniques in user research and qualitative psychological research. Also, we will be able to draw some insights into the way we used them in two of our projects.

The user needs analysis is focused on acquiring a deep and accurate understanding of the people who will be involved in using the final web design product, the activities that the design will support, the context in which these activities will be performed as well as all the complex interactions between these elements. This deep understanding is crucial for the next stage of requirements development for the product which will be designed (Benyon et al., 2005). Moreover, we cannot consider this phase to be over when the design process begins and the first steps in design work are done. The user need analysis, requirements development, design process and evaluation are very tightly interrelated and constitute a permanent iterative process (Jokela, 2008; Benyon et al., 2005, Brink et al, 2002; Kuniavsky, 2003).

In conclusion, user needs analysis aims at getting to know the people, what they want, what they do, what problems they frequently encounter in their area of activity and how they might want to do things in order to help designers create a more usable and enjoyable product. The translation of these findings into requirements for a new design is not so straightforward and will often have to go back into the user research process to be validated.

As we have described earlier, the user research in the early stages of the design process can seem a very complex and difficult job (even more so for a designer not trained in this kind of research). The most common techniques imply observing people, interviewing them, organizing focus groups, in short, a qualitative, in depth approach to people involved and their needs, aspirations, experiences and problems. At the beginning, before any idea of the product is put forward, the user research has

to stay less structured and qualitative in essence. At more advanced stages other more structured techniques such as the structured interview or surveys can be used.

Interviews

Interviews are one of the most used research methods in social sciences and one of the best suited to gain a thorough understanding of peoples' wants and needs. Interviews can also provide a very flexible structure that can allow us to address multiple categories of stakeholders involved in the design process.

There are several types of interviews ranging from very structured interviews to unstructured ones. The structured interview closely resembles a survey as the researcher develops a fixed number of questions prior to the research. Those questions will be addressed in exactly the same way to every participant. Moreover, most of the time there are preset answers from which people have to choose. This type of interview can be very useful when the researcher needs to verify things but will become inappropriate when the focus is the in-depth understanding of people's needs and wishes as the high level of structure will not allow for unexpected responses and insights to arise.

Another type of interview is the unstructured interview which is, as its name suggests, completely dependent on what happens and develops during the interview itself. The researcher will not structure anything before the interview and will have no preset topic agenda besides the general topic of the project which is the focus of research. This type of interview can be very useful in projects which are less specified, for which there is very little information or when there is a great concern for putting aside the designer's preset solutions or preconceptions about the project.

Most of the time in user needs analysis and user research we will use semi-structured interviews. This type of interview is somewhere in-between the other two types being a degree more structured than the unstructured interview but still allowing for a great deal of unexpected, new information or insights to arise. The researcher will prepare in advance some questions or topics he/she will want to discuss during the interview, but the way in which these are brought into discussion is very flexible. Also, if new, unaccounted aspects arise during the interview, these can be further analyzed and included among the topics of interest. This form of open interview can be demanding for the researcher but it can produce a lot of valuable data to inform the design. More on how to prepare and conduct interviews can be found in King (2004).

When to Use Interviews

Most of qualitative research methods are in a way or another based on some form of interview, that is why interviews are so present in mostly all the stages of web design process. They are suited to address the first stage of user needs analysis and at this stage we will most probably use less structured or even unstructured interviews in order to uncover underlying experiences, beliefs and values. Interviewing is also present in later stages of development when it is more probable to use more structured interviews as we are trying to find out specific information and reactions to the design we have proposed. Besides the enormous advantages provided by this methods, we must also be careful to the problems that can arise during interviews and that can affect the results. We will have to remember that people do not always tell what they really believe but maybe the interpretation of this phenomenon could become relevant for our research project. Moreover, they can sometimes answer a completely different question than the one addressed. The researcher must very careful observe and assess these things in order to overcome this type of situation. As a result the data obtained using an interview is strongly dependent on the interviewer skills and mastery of the technique which is gained through exercising.

Focus Groups

Focus groups are related to interviews in the sense that they are more or less structured group interviews. Focus groups are a form of qualitative research based on creating a group interactive setting where people can be asked about their attitudes and feelings towards an idea, a product or a service. Also people are allowed to talk with each other, to question or develop each others' statements. The reason why focus groups can represent a valuable tool in this design phase is the fact that they are appropriate methods to gain access to people's needs, experiences, wishes and priorities. Although focus groups are most often associated with marketing research, they have been adapted to include social science research (Marshall & Rossman, 2006). As a social science research tool they are often very suitable for the study of people in their natural setting even more if they are used together with participant observation in order to elicit unexpected thoughts and issues for further exploration (Morgan, Krueger & King, 1998). As a result, the relevance of focus groups for the field of user research comes from both lines of research: focus on the product or service (marketing) or focus on understanding people, their attitudes and needs (social research). Due to its wide applicability in several stages of design, focus groups are one of the oldest methods of user research (Kuniavsky, 2003).

Literature on qualitative methods shows that focus groups have a high apparent validity (the result are trusted, believable, as it is very easy to see how people came to those results) and that they are also a very easy to learn and inexpensive method (Marshall & Rossman, 2006). There are also some shortcomings associated with this method and the first one relates to the power dynamics in group interaction that can affect the results obtained. The researcher will have to pay a great deal of attention to these aspects and be prepared to facilitate the interaction very well. Also, the researcher usually has less control over the interviewees during this kind of approach and unwanted discussions can take a part of the interviewing time. The groups can vary a great deal or can be more difficult to be assembled. At last, the method requires us to set up special rooms with highly trained observers or recording solutions in order to make the most of the data (Marshall & Rossman, 2006).

A focus group consists in a series of group discussions which are moderated by the researcher or collaborator according to a preset agenda. The focus of the entire interaction between the moderator and the group is to facilitate a group climate that will support opinion and feeling sharing among the participants. This method is appropriate both for a stage in which there is yet no idea regarding the final product and the main concern is the understanding of people's needs, problems, priorities and way of thinking and also for the stage in which some requirements are already translated into features and we need people to assess this translation or to prioritize these features.

When to Use Focus Groups

As we have already underlined, focus groups can be used at various stages in usability building and usability assessment. Their use can be seen at the very beginning of the design process where, together with contextual inquiry and task analysis can build a very detailed picture of how people are behaving right now and of their perceptions regarding important issues. At this stage, focus groups can be used as a method for analyzing the competition also. This use of the method can bring information related to the problems that our product is designed to solve, the reasons why it can be a more valuable resource than other similar products and the features that consumers perceive to be critical in the competition. All this information will enable us to set up requirements and features for our product that will be closer to what people want and value, and save a lot of resources from the beginning.

Focus groups can be also used at a later moment in the development cycle in order to identify and prioritize features or even in order to create or develop new features (Kuniavsky, 2003). They can also be used in the redesign process in order to improve present designs.

We also have to point out some instances in which this method is not suitable. We will not use focus groups as a usability assessment technique to generalize all the findings to a larger population or to justify a position or to prove a point (Kuniavsky, 2003).

Surveys

Even though very often surveys are considered to be mostly quantitative research, opposite to the qualitative research methods presented so far, we have to keep in mind that surveys are nothing more than very structured interviews: a very structured way of asking questions that enables us to address a large group of people and record their answers. The fact that the questions are always the same for everybody and that even responses can be given in a very structured format (multiple choice questions, checklists, Likert scales) allows the researcher to use statistical tools to examine the characteristics of the targeted population. On the other hand, the survey being rooted in qualitative research can still contain open ended questions where people are allowed to tell you what they want to communicate in the form they choose and these questions represent often valuable and rich information. The problem with open questions is that most often people have a very low response rate to them (Nielsen, 1993)

The types of information that can be obtained using surveys cover the characteristics of users groups and eventually, the identification of several user subgroups. We can also use surveys to find out which of the features of the product are more appealing or more important for the targeted users, the information and features that people look for in our product, problems that people have encountered while using our site or similar websites, the level of user satisfaction, suggestions for improvement and so on.

As we can see, most of this information relates to a stage where we have already designed a product and we want to test it or when we want to redesign our products. But surveys can be also used in the first stages of user needs analysis when the focus is on ensuring and building usability not on assessing it. At this stage surveys can be very useful to test and prioritize findings from earlier qualitative, in depth research. For example, insights and ideas obtained using a focus group can be tested to check if the value, needs and characteristics of the users identified using the focus-group results can also be met within a larger population. The survey results will enable us to see which of the developed requirements are the most important for the general population and should become priorities in the development process and which of the requirements developed so far are less relevant for further stages in design. The survey at this stage will also be very useful in helping us identify different groups of users for which the needs and preferences hierarchy is different and need to be addressed differently in the design process.

As we can seen surveys can be used at any design stage, ranging from the very first stage of user needs analysis, through the stage of the current design evaluation in order to begin a new design cycle and up to the last stage when, after releasing the product, we can use surveys to check if our design meets the user's needs and to identify possible improvements for the future.

When to Use Surveys

As we have already underlined, surveys are used when we want to test the preferences and needs of a broader population about a product or a potential product. As it involves a greater effort in planning and design and as it requires a higher level of standardization (Kuniavsky, 2003) it is

recommended to be used in design stages when in-depth information is not needed so much. As a result, we will use surveys when passing from the user needs analysis towards requirement specification in order to structure and prioritize the findings from interviews, observations and other less structured methods. Also, surveys can be very effectively used in testing preliminary ideas and designs as well as assessing the characteristics of the final product.

Two Example of User Needs Analysis from Our Own Research Projects

The Development of a Website Pattern

The results of this project have been presented in Onaca, Tarta, & Pitariu (2006), so here we will not emphasize them or the pattern proposed but the methodology we used to formulate this pattern. The illustration of this methodology is rather outside the main line of argument used here as we have focused mainly on user need identification for building a usable website within a user-centered design approach. The investigation we will present here was focused on proposing a design pattern for theatre and opera websites but the approach was still user-centered and the final focus was on advancing a design solution that would enhance the usability and acceptability of such websites. Therefore, we consider that this project constitutes an illustrative example of user needs analysis in the service of usability.

Van Welie & Traetteberg (2000) argue that the main concern in developing patterns should be on improving usability as many of the problems designers have during the design process and that are addressed in user interface design have no connection and produce no benefit for the end user. Researchers in UID underline the fact that developing a pattern in this field is not an easy task and the structure of such a pattern is different from an architectural pattern. One of the most important features of an UID pattern is that it is best suited to describe usability related problems (van Welie, Van der Veer & Eliens, 2000) so the development of a pattern should benefit from an increased attention paid to users and their needs.

User Needs Analysis

The research undertaken at this stage represented an exploratory study that aimed at identifying the categories of users, what are their usual actions related to a theatre/opera house, in what context do they perform those actions, what type of information they are using to perform those actions and what are the technologies they currently use or would like to use in the future.

The initial method we have used consisted in a semi-structured interview in which we have tried to cover all the above related aspects. We have started the interview without any references to theatre/opera houses websites and asked people to refer to their experiences going to the theatre/opera, their interests and needs in different aspects of the cultural life, the way they decide on what play/show to attend, difficulties that they have encountered in attending a play/show, details regarding the context of these activities. When the use of a website was mentioned, we used more in-depth questions related to their experience using different websites. The results of the interviews showed us that there were some aspects worth being taken into consideration as the social-nature of the attendance planning and also of the social-nature of experiencing the artistic act.

The analysis of the interviews focused on identifying specific user categories with specific goals and interests and here we have been able to take into consideration some categories which have been purely included in previous designs (artists, critics, people who collaborate with the theatre/opera). We have also discovered a wide range of activities related to the theatre, starting from the usual activity of play/show attendance to other activities such as discussing and debating

different performances, planning events (including photo shoots, galas, weddings) into the theatre building and also looking for job opportunities. The existent technologies used for accomplishing these activities have constituted a good indicator regarding possible opportunities and constraints to every theatre/opera house website.

In a second phase, we have directed our interview analysis towards prioritizing the needs of users in terms of actions and information which should be provided. A better way to do achieve this was considered to be the development of an exploratory survey based on the qualitative data obtained in interviews.

The dimensions we identified analyzing the interviews were mapped into the main features of some well-known theatre/opera websites and the main dimensions of the questionnaire were established:

1. Access/information about theatre's services
2. Communication, interaction, opinions exchange
3. Tourist information
4. Information about theatre's staff
5. Information about historical evolution of the theatre
6. Information about theatre's management
7. Information about present and future projects

For each of these dimensions a group of five experts generated items based on the initial qualitative data. Those items entered then in a procedure of redistribution on each dimension and only those items that met at least 70 percent in rating agreement were kept. In the end, a number of 43 items have been included in the questionnaire. Each item was rated on a 5 steps Likert scale ranging from completely useless to very useful information.

The questionnaire, designed in English, was administered to a non-random sample using an interactive web application. The sample included 112 volunteer participants. Their average age was 27.54 and 49.1% were men and 50.9% were women. Participants came from various countries: 67% Romania, 12% Netherlands, 8% Spain, 1.8% Switzerland, 1.8% Poland, 3.6% USA, 0.9% France, 0.9% Leetonia, 0.9% Indonesia, 0.9% Germany, 0.9% Austria, 0.9% Republic of Moldavia). Also, regarding their occupations, the distribution of the sample was: 0.9% pilot, 0.9% account manager, 2.7% actor/actress, 0.9% sales representatives, 30.4% students, 4.5% high school teachers, 13.4% university teachers, 31.3% IT, 0.9% retired, 10.7% psychologists, 1.8% MD doctors, 1.8% administration personnel.

Participants filled in the questionnaire voluntarily. The instructions that preceded the questionnaire were the following:

This questionnaire is designed to assess the most relevant types of information and actions that a theatre/opera website should provide. Please read carefully the statements and choose the answer that fits you best. There is no right or wrong answer and data collected through this survey are confidential and will be used only for academic purposes.

All fields are required and for every question you should choose only one answer.

A Short Description of Our Results

An important step in our analysis was represented by the descriptive results for each of the 7 dimensions in order to determine which categories of information and actions are perceived to be the most useful (most compatible to the user's needs) and should be included in a theatre/opera website.

Our data indicated that this information and these actions refer to a functional dimension –

granting access to performances, theatre's program, the price of tickets and having the option of booking them online, of checking the available seats, of accessing specialized information about shows, information about theatre's location, watching fragments of present and past performances and getting information about the author, cast, plot of the plays, about present and future projects, prizes and providing them with contact data and the possibility of searching the website. As a result we are suggesting that these information categories should be the main elements of the homepage when designing a website for a theatre/opera house and users should be able to access them rapidly, performing very few actions.

As we have already mentioned, this state of facts might be related to the fact that most of our sample used in the survey belonged to the audience category. If we question a different category of people connected to the theatre/opera world, like actors/actresses, critics, theatre specialists, people from show business, event's organizers, the information considered to be most relevant might be different, as previous suggested by interviews. In order to verify this assumption we need to further investigate the differences between user categories regarding their needs. If such differences are found we will be able to propose the design of websites which can adapt to the needs of different types of users.

Although at the beginning of the investigation we started with the assumption that there are different categories of people who might be interested in having information about theatre/opera houses and accessing this information on a website, we defined their interests and actions, our sample didn't comprise people from all these categories. As a result, the fact that our investigation indicated the information and actions related to the audience category to be the most relevant was not a surprise. A future direction of our investigation consists in analyzing the informational needs of people belonging to other categories of users.

As a result, we can observe that the richness

of our initial qualitative data has been partly lost in our effort of standardization. On the other hand, it is exactly this initial qualitative data that can indicate to us the *way* the informational need should be embedded in the design (for example it is not enough to provide the possibility of buying tickets, this process of buying must be accompanied by expert advices and commentaries on the performance to match the experience of buying tickets directly from the theatre's representative which can always inform you on the recent events related to the play and the cast). Also, these initial qualitative data made us aware that we must take into consideration different categories of people with different goals, different context in which people come into contact with theatres/opera houses. Although our effort of prioritizing needs excluded most of these categories, we are now aware of the fact that our solution serves only a specific goal and that future efforts should be directed towards the inclusion of other identified categories.

As a result, the pattern we proposed at the end of our project, based on these results is mainly suited for those situations when the main goal of the theatre/opera is to inform and attract the audience using their websites and also to facilitate the access of the audience to performances by allowing specific actions to be carried on their websites. For more complex objectives like facilitating the contact with suppliers, contractors, people from show business or organizers etc., a further investigation is necessary in order to identify these needs.

User Needs Analysis for Developing an Intelligent Web Assistant

The second project we analyze here which is to illustrate the usefulness of the techniques presented for user needs research refers to creating an intelligent web assistant for career-related decision making. The detailed results are presented in Onaca & Guran (2008) and here we will insist on

the way we have used the methodology described above for analyzing our possible users' needs. The project began when the university decided to award a research grant for creating an intelligent web assistant to help future students make their decision regarding which faculty to enroll to. The grant was awarded to a designer's team assisted by a psychologist and a human computer interaction expert. The idea the management had in mind was to deliver a webpage were high school graduates could test their abilities and compare their own profile to the profiles most suitable for different professions. Then, they should have the opportunity to find out which faculty can educate them for that profession and gather relevant information about that faculty. Moreover, the assistant had to be able to learn from past interactions and associate profiles with most requested information categories in order to personalize interaction.

The way the project was formulated followed a very traditional corporate edict (Kuniavsky, 2003) design process. Regardless of the very articulated request, we have managed to convince the research and design team to take into account a user-centered approach arguing that a great deal of effort and money could be spent with little results if we do not find first who are the people this product will address and which are their real needs. So, the first step taken was an extensive user-need analysis using several techniques from contextual inquiry to extensive interviews, focus-groups and survey. The results were partially contradictory to the initial request but very informing for the future steps of the project. For orienting this step we used the framework depicted in Figure 1 and analyzed the people who could become interested users, the activities that characterize the decision making process, the context in which these activities take place and what technology is now used or is considered to be best suited to support these activities.

The methodology we used was somehow unusual as we have decided to teach master students user-centered design by involving them as research teams in the project. We have formed 7 research teams all having no idea related to the way the project was initially formulated to prevent biases towards confirming the initial management idea. All the groups had the same research questions: *How do people choose the faculty they attend in our university* and *How do they perceive the idea of an assistant to help them make that decision.* More operational objectives included identifying the possible users, identifying specific actions, identifying the action sequence in this kind of decision making, identifying their difficulties and needs, their opinion and values related to this decision and all the contextual factors that come in at certain moments, and last but not least, how the process could be improved and by what type of technology.

The methods each group used were mostly qualitative but every group was gradually oriented to focus on a different aspect than the others in order to gain access to very diverse information (some focused on certain user category, some focused on gaining a deep understanding related to the process, some focused on structuring the initial qualitative data using surveys). The methods used were semi structured interviews, focus-groups, content analysis of educational forums and surveys.

All the methods used have been shaped by the initial operational objectives described earlier. We have instructed students to develop their methods focusing on people and the way they perceive this process of deciding the future of their education. That is why interviews and focus-groups have been designed to elicit personal concerns and difficulties related to the decision-making process and did not directly focus on the sequences of this process which is are not very easy to overtly explain without a process of post-decision justification. As a result participants in interviews were asked to reflect upon the process of choosing their faculty specialization (be it situated in the present for some or in the past for others). Main directions followed concerning the process itself, how they

have come to the decision, what emotions accompanied this process, who were the people they discussed these issues with, who did they trust for advice in this process and why, difficulties they had encountered on the way, how would they do things differently. Follow-up questions directed the discussion towards the main categories of information described in Figure 1.

We will not insist here on the methodology or exact results but we want to emphasize the importance of knowledge gathered during this phase of user needs analysis and the way it affected the project. The total number of participants involved in this research was 189 ranging from high school students, to undergraduate students, graduates, master students and other people involved in this process of decision making (high school head teachers and counselors, parents, teachers).

A Short Description of Our Results

The results: during the process we have identified several user categories which seemed very interested in tools to improve the process of decision making besides the initial one which was considered to be high school students. Moreover, we have identified that the most interested categories were not these students, but working people interested in continuing their education (and having less time to find information and compare it) and counselors and teachers who are often asked to assist their students in the decision making. Also, we have discovered that many of the undergraduate students or graduates were also possible users as they were very interested in following a Masters Program (or a second specialization) and needed support in identifying the best alternative.

Based on data gathered from interviews, we have been able to group characteristics and needs in 4 typologies: independent (they take decisions independently and only need information in order to make their mind), decided (the decision is already taken, the main needs involve support for implementing it), undecided (they can not decide between alternatives and the assistance needed consists in comparing and integrating information about alternatives and about self) and influenced (can change decisions depending on the others and the main needs refer to integrating information about self and finding social support for certain alternatives).

The results also lead us towards the design of a decision making process in this field of university program enrollment. The designed followed a model of rational decision supported by literature in the field of career management (Lemeni & Miclea, 2004). While building on this model we have realized that the information about their own abilities profile and the degree of fit with the profiles of the profession was only one information element needed in order to form and evaluate alternatives. Information regarding workforce, economical development in the area and economical perspectives were also highly invoked. Moreover, users did not want to have only the possibility of finding out this information but also the possibility to compare information using given or their own criteria.

Another surprising result was related to the implementation stage of the decision making process. Most of the users wanted to be assisted not only during the first phases of the decision making (as the project was formulated at the beginning) but also (and mostly) at the final stage of decision implementation. As a result, needs uncovered in this area were related to administrative details regarding admission procedures, automating some of these procedures, providing informational and social support for an easier and quicker adaptation to the new status and roles. The most surprising thing was that the needs of people related to this final stage were higher than the ones related to the earlier stages.

The last result that affected a lot the next stage was the fact that the decisions of Romanian people regarding their own educational career have a highly social character and are emotionally loaded. Very often people who participated

in the research would envision the assistant as a human expert providing personalized interaction and social and emotional support and they would very seldom think of technology supported assistance. That is why in the further development of requirements we had to take into account the fact that future features of the web assistant will have to support this kind of personalized interaction, expert advice and social support networks. Most probably if we hadn't taken into account this issue the final acceptance of our product would have been seriously endangered.

CONCLUSION

By these two final examples we have tried to illustrate both the "how" and the "why" aspects of using methodologies from social sciences in analyzing user needs for the development of successful and more usable designs.

With our first example we have tried to underline the process of creating and using a survey and the way we can correlate two different methods in the same research (interview and survey). In the second example we chose not to focus on the way we used the qualitative methodology but on the benefits we can obtain by focusing the entire initial research on discovering important user categories, their characteristics and needs.

The procedures and results which we have underlined come to complete the extensive literature body which is currently supporting the very early involvement of users into the design process in order to improve the outcome both in usability and acceptance as well as in their financial success. After all, the success of a product is determined by the degree in which it is needed and desired by the users, and the degree in which it can satisfy their needs and can be easily used by them (Kuniavsky, 2003). These are the characteristics of a web design product that can create its competitive advantage over other similar products. If by usability we understand a good design, then usability becomes critical for the success of a product. Designing for usability starts from the very first steps of understanding the users, their problems and needs in order to address them at further stages of development.

A last observation that can be made is the fact that the methods and tools discussed here represent only a small part of all social-research methods that can be used in user research. We chose to present only this three methods because they are the most popular and used methods in this field. Moreover, it is important to underline the fact that all methods of social research can become relevant and useful for user research but not everybody is prepared to properly and usefully design and conduct this kind of research. The results obtained from qualitative research depend a great deal on the researcher's training and expertise in using specific techniques and results analysis. As we have shown, many researchers still have difficulties in using qualitative methods mostly due to the fact that they are used to evaluate research depending on positivist criteria of internal and external validity. We wish to reemphasize here the fact that our results taken from the two projects do not represent universal truths and should not be judged in terms of their generalizability. They represent the level of understanding we have reached in relation to our targeted users and the specific problems we have addressed. They are useful and relevant to this given situation and we do not make (nor wish to make) any statement related to their value for other situations or design problems. On the other hand, the part that can be useful in other similar situations is the approach to user needs analysis which may end in different results every time but every time this results will be able to inform and direct future stages in design and ensure a more usable product. That is why we have to support more actively the importance of interdisciplinary design teams that could help us overcome the complexities involved in user-centered design and ensure the quality and success of the final design products.

REFERENCES

Benyon, D., Turner, P., & Turner, S. (2005). *Designing Interactive Systems, People, Activities, Context and Technology*. Edinburgh: Addison-Wesley.

Bevan, N. (2005). Cost benefits framework and case studies. In R.G. Bias, & D.G. Mayhew (Eds.) *Cost-Justifying Usability: An update for the internet age*. San Francisco: Morgan Kaufmann.

Bevan, N. (2008). A framework for selecting the most appropriate usability measures. In *COST 294-MAUSE Workshop: Critiquing Automated Usability Evaluation Methods*. March.

Brinck, T., Gergle, D., & Wood, S. D. (2002). *Usability for the Web: Designing Web Sites that Work*. San Francisco: Morgan Kaufmann.

Denzin, N. K., & Lincoln, Y. S. (2005). The discipline and practice of qualitative research. In N.K. Denzin & Y. S. Lincoln, (Eds.) *The SAGE handbook of qualitative research*, (3rd Ed.). London: Sage.

Dix, A., Finlay, J. E., Abowd, G. D., & Beale, R. (2004). *Human-Computer Interaction*. Upper Saddle River, NJ: Pearson Education.

Dumas, J. S., & Redish, J. C. (1999). *A Practical Guide to Usability Testing*. Bristol, UK: Intellect Books.

Hatch, M. J., & Cunliffe, A. L. (2006). *Organization Theory. Modern, Symbolic, and Postmodern Perspectives (2nd ed.)*. Oxford, UK: Oxford University Press.

Hatch, M. J., & Yanow, D. (2008). Methodology by Metaphor: Ways of Seeing in Painting and Research. *Organization Science, 29*(1), 23–44. doi:10.1177/0170840607086635

ISO 9241-11 (1998). *Ergonomic requirements for office work with visual display terminals* (VDTs), (Part 11: Guidance on usability). New York: ISO.

Jokela, T. (2008). Characterizations, Requirements, and Activities of User-Centered Design—the KESSU 2.2Model. In E. L-C. Law, E.T. Hvannberg & G. Cockton, (Eds.), *Maturing Usability. Quality in interaction, software and value*. London: Springer-Verlag Limited.

Jordan, P. W. (2002). *An Introduction To Usability*. London: Taylor and Francis.

King, N. (2004). Using interviews in Qualitative Research. In C. Cassell, & G. Symon, (Ed.), *Essential Guide to Qualitative Methods in Organizational Research*. Thousand Oaks, CA: Sage Publications.

Kuniavsky, M. (2003). *Observing the user experience. A practitioner's guide to user research*. San Francisco: Elsevier.

Law, E. L.-C., Hvannberg, E. T., & Cockton, G. (2008). A Green Paper on Usability Maturation. In Law, E. L-C., Hvannberg, E.T., & Cockton, G. (Eds). *Maturing Usability. Quality in interaction, software and value*. London: Springer-Verlag Limited.

Lemeni, G., & Miclea, M. (2004). *Consiliere şi orientare. Ghid de educaţie pentru carieră*. Editura ASCR, Cluj-Napoca.

Marshall, C., & Rossman, G. B. (2006). *Designing Qualitative Research*, 93rd Ed.). London: Sage

Morgan, D. L., Krueger, R. A., & King, J. A. (1998). *Focus Group Kit*. London: SAGE.

Nielsen, J. (1993). *Usability Engineering*. San Francisco: Morgan Kaufmann, Elsevier. Norman, D.A. (2002). *The design of every day things*. New York: Basic Books.

Onacă (Andrei), D.M., Tarţa, A.M., & Pitariu, H.D. (2006). The development of a theatre/opera website pattern based on a user need assessment approach. *Psihologia Resurselor Umane, 4*(1).

Onaca (Andrei). D.M., & Guran, A.M. (2008). A User-centred approach in developing an intelligent web assistant for supporting career related decision making. In *Proceedings of the Romanian Computer Human Interaction Conference,* Matrix Rom.

Pitariu, H.D. (2003). The influence of personality traits upon human computer interaction. *Cognition, Brain, Behavior, 8*(3).

Rosenbaum, S. (2008). The Future of Usability Evaluation: Increasing Impact on Value. In Law, E. L-C., Hvannberg, E.T., & Cockton, G. (Eds). *Maturing Usability. Quality in interaction, software and value*. London: Springer-Verlag Limited.

Rubin, J. (1994). *Handbook of usability testing. How to plan, design and conduct effective tests*. Montreal, Canada: John Wiley and Sons.

Van Maanen, J. (1998). *Qualitative studies of organizations*. The Administrative Science Quarterly, Series in Organization Theory and Behaviour. London: Sage Publications.

Van Welie, M. (2001). *Task-Based user interface design*. Amsterdam: SIKS.

van Welie, M., & Traetteberg, H. (2000). Interaction Patterns in User Interfaces. In *7th. Pattern Languages of Programs Conference*, 13-16 August, Allerton Park Monticello, Illinois. Retrieved June 20, 2005, from http://www.welie.com/about.html

van Welie, M., van der Veer, G. C., & Eliëns, A. (2000). Patterns as Tools for User Interface Design. In *International Workshop on Tools for Working with Guidelines*, (pp. 313-324), October 7-8, Biarritz, France. Retrieved June 17, 2005, from http://www.welie.com/about.html

Chapter 13
A Theoretical Framework Measuring the Usability of Retail Sites

Konstantina Vassilopoulou
Harokopio University, Greece

Kathy K. Keeling
University of Manchester, UK

Linda A. Macaulay
University of Manchester, UK

ABSTRACT

The motivation for this research effort is the failure of usability in Human Computer Interaction (HCI) to consider the needs of users as potential consumers. The hypothesis underlying this research is that it is possible to construct a framework based upon the needs of computer users who are at the same time consumers. The aim of this research is to build a theoretical framework that addresses the needs of a retail site user as a potential consumer. To achieve this we examined the literature relating to usability in HCI as well as Social Attitude Theories. Two empirical studies were conducted using existing sites. The first aimed at incorporating attributes from the fields of Social Attitude Theories and Retail Marketing the second at developing a theoretical framework measuring the usability of retail sites.

INTRODUCTION - POSITIONING THE RESEARCH

Forecasts for future growth in e-commerce sales are very promising and the benefits for both the retailer and the potential consumer are evident. At the same time there is evidence that users are

becoming more discriminating in their use of the Internet. Ward & Lee (2000) argue that more experienced users tend to be more proficient shoppers. At the same time, other studies indicate that the usability experience of using retail sites may often be less than satisfactory with studies carried out by Forrester and Jupiter revealing that sales growth is decreasing in a number of product categories (Richtell & Tedeschi, 2007).

DOI: 10.4018/978-1-60566-896-3.ch013

Many researchers have raised concerns about the lack of specific usability attributes and the lack of measurement validity for specific attributes in web site usability. To this end, it is argued that current usability evaluation frameworks for retail sites do not specifically address the needs of users as potential consumers, thus not evaluating critical consumer criteria and requirements unique to retailing or unique to the user as a consumer. This problem arises because researchers and practitioners in Human Computer Interaction (HCI) while carrying out numerous studies over the last decade (e.g. Ethier et al., 2008; Ho & Wu, 1999; Lavie & Tractinsky, 2004; Lee et al., 2000; Liang & Huang, 1998; Lin & Lu, 2000; Liu & Arnett, 2000; Zviran et al, 2006) have paid little, if any, attention to Social Attitude Theories. For example, Morris & Dillon (1997) argue that the otherwise well-known Technology Acceptance Model has received little attention by HCI researchers and practitioners. These authors conclude that "…*this is unfortunate because TAM appears to offer HCI professional a theoretically grounded approach to the study of software acceptability that can be directly coupled to usability evaluations*" (Morris & Dillon, 1997, p.59) This research examines the potential of these theories to add to the theoretical underpinnings and thus to better understanding of retail web site usability from the consumer's viewpoint.

Establishing the Role of Social Attitude Theories in Human Computer Interaction

In this section first a definition and dimensions of usability as viewed for Business –to-Consumer web sites will be given. The difficulties in defining these dimensions in the web environment will be discussed. From the consideration of these difficulties researchers and practitioners have made attempts to integrate material from the Social Attitude Theories, seeking to understand the web user as a potential consumer. These studies indicate that usability, as traditionally considered by HCI, is poorly defined and new attributes need to be considered.

Web Site Usability

Within HCI the need for evaluating the usability of traditional software has long been recognised. Shackel (1991) pointed out that as "*computers become cheaper and more powerful, usability factors will become more and more dominant in the acceptability decisions made by users and purchasers.*" A decade later Nielsen (2000), went a step further and reasoned that the importance of web usability can be simply viewed as an equation: "*In product design and software design, customers pay first and experience usability later. On the web, users experience usability first and pay later*" (p. 12). Thus, usability has become an imperative quality criterion when designing web user interfaces.

ISO (1995) defines usability as the effectiveness, efficiency and satisfaction with which specified users achieve specified goals in particular environments. To adapt this to the web user interface, Bevan (1997) adapts effectiveness, efficiency, and satisfaction and defines these three attributes for web user interfaces.

Aside from the attributes suggested by ISO (1995) and adapted by Bevan (1997) researchers have recognised that there are other attributes that also affect the usability of a web user interface: ease of navigation and content (Nielsen, 1999); attractiveness, control and learnability (Kirakowski et al., 1998); efficiency or accessibility (Helander & Khalid, 2000; Nielsen, 1999); helpfulness (Fleming, 1998; Kirakowski et al., 1998).

Further, usability has been recognised as a multi-dimensional property, the dimensions being: (i) the relevant attributes of the user; (ii) the tasks the user carries out; and (iii) the equipment and environment whereby the user uses a specific product (ISO, 1995; Shackel, 1991; Preece et al., 1994). Understanding these dimensions in the web environment raises several issues.

First are concerns regarding the relevant attributes of the user. User attributes are traditionally considered in terms of attitudes, occupation, computer experience and demographic variables such as gender and age (Hayes, et al., 1986). Unfortunately, this classification assumes that the designer knows the user prior to design. This is difficult in web site design. The user of a web site is portrayed by Hartson (1998) as "...*often remote and distributed*" (p. 110). These characteristics certainly do not make the job of the designer any easier in identifying the user.

Second, existing classifications and taxonomies of user tasks on websites are broad in context and do not alleviate the problems faced by the designer in identifying the tasks the user carries out when traversing a web site. Furthermore, in addition to the purpose and tasks that web sites are designed to support, users may access web sites to accomplish tasks that designers have not even contemplated. This can be an additional obstacle to the designer.

Finally, regarding the third dimension, Nielsen (1999) reasons that the web is a cross-platform design environment and "...*the ability to project a single design onto a wide variety of platforms presents User Interface challenges*" (p. 68). Thus, in an environment where a variety of hardware platforms and multiple servers are the norm, it is almost impossible to specify what equipment will be used by the user, or his or her working environment (Levi & Conrad, 1996).

Moreover, regarding the learning environment, the user is isolated and distributed, as characterised by Hartson (1998) and cannot discuss the problems he or she faces while using a web user interface with a co-worker. This may result in difficulties in learning how to use the web site.

To conclude, the dimensions identified in traditional user interfaces cannot be easily defined in a web user interface. Further, on the basis of the issues associated with usability and their role in evaluating a web site there is a danger in assuming that efficiency in terms of the time and resources required in finding information, and effectiveness in terms of achieving the desired tasks are the only goals of usability. A number of other issues contribute to the evaluation of the user interface of a web site for usability. The next section discusses how social attitude theories have been integrated into HCI to better understand the consumer and will describe how current studies can identify specific design issues for retail sites and their limitations.

Social Attitude Theories

Researchers and practitioners recognize that usability dimensions, i.e., users, tasks and web environment, are important factors. One research stream studies which factors affect users' satisfaction and intentions. Towards this direction, efforts have been made to integrate HCI and consumer behaviour models to better understand the potential consumer of retail sites.

In regard to on-line shopping, Limayem et al. (2000) showed that social attitude theories could throw light on the factors that affect online shopping. Social attitude theories include the Theory of Reasoned Action (TRA)(Fishbein and Azjen, 1975), the Theory of Planned Behaviour (TPB) (Ajzen 1991), and the Technology Acceptance Model (TAM) (Davis 1989). Limayem et al. (2000) augmented the TPB with two new constructs representing the effects of personal innovativeness and perceived consequences. The results of a longitudinal study revealed that in addition to attitude and subjective norms from the original TPB model, the two new constructs have significant effects on intentions to use a web site (Limayem et al 2000).

Other studies assess the factors affecting consumers' task fulfillment on retail sites from different theoretical perspectives. These include (a) a mix of user characteristics, perceived risk and the consumer experience (Liang and Huang, 1998; Kumar et al., 2004), (b) a mix of web site design characteristics, such as, information quality, response time and system acceptability (Lin & Lu, 2000), (c) logistical support, technological, product and information characteristics, and homepage presentation (Ho & Wu, 1999), (d) quality of information and service, system use, playfulness and system design quality (Liu & Arnett, 2000) and (e) comprehensive information about the products in the store and the opportunity for consumers to share more values with other consumers in the store (Lee et al., 2000). Ethier et al (2008) go a step further attempting to explain emotions experienced from the use of a B2C site. Evidence revealed that liking and joy were the two dominant emotions experienced by a substantial number of shoppers in their study.

These studies provide evidence that the measurement of usability for web user interfaces involves more than traditional usability attributes, in that it aims to provide the user with an experience that will potentially turn him or her into a customer. However, the results are largely general in content and, thus, cannot easily be used by a designer to evaluate and re-design a site.

In addition, consumers visiting the web more often they become more proficient shoppers and expect a level of design sophistication from web user interfaces. Finally, there is considerable ease with which consumers may switch sites, since they are only a click away from a competitor. Based on this evidence there is a clear need for usable web user interfaces that satisfy consumers, and promote repeat visits and repeat purchases.

Relevance of TAM and Diffusion of Innovations Theory in Developing a Theoretical Framework Measuring Usability

"Shopping on the Internet is a voluntary individual behaviour" (Limayem et al., 2000, p. 423). As discussed above, social attitude theories such as the TRA, TPB and TAM can be applied (and are) to explain the behaviour of the customer on retail sites. The TPB is the extension of the Theory of Reasoned Action (Fishbein & Ajzen, 1975). The TRA posits that a specific behaviour is a function of the individuals' intention (in this case, to purchase a product) and that intention is a product of the individual's attitude toward the particular behaviour occasion and perceptions of social influence (subjective norm). The TPB adds perceived behavioural control, i.e., the individual's perception of his or her ability to perform the behaviour as an additional influence on intentions and behaviour

The TAM adapts the TRA specifically for technological systems providing a parsimonious model positing that perceptions of usefulness and ease of use are instrumental in the development of attitudes, which lead to intentions, and eventually result in system utilisation behaviour.

The attributes of the TAM, i.e. perceived usefulness, perceived ease of use, attitude toward use and behavioral intention, are appropriate for use in developing a theoretical framework measuring usability for the following reasons. First, TAM is the specialisation in the domain of information systems of the TRA and TPB. Secondly, it relates constructs that are important for usability such as the ease of use of an information system and attitude towards the information system (user satisfaction), to future use intentions. Finally, TAM has been tested in different information technology environments (Adams et al., 1992; Mathieson, 1991; Thompson et al., 1991; Venkatesh & Davis, 2000) as well as the web (Morris & Dillon, 1997; Teo et al., 1999; Lederer et al. 2000; Lin & Lu, 2000) and consistently yields high explained variance in the adoption of systems.

Nevertheless, there is a caveat, the TAM was developed to predict future use intentions within an organisational context, outside of this context, consumer use of a web site is highly discretionary and may well be influenced by other factors. Thus, a major issue of concern with the straightforward adoption of the TAM is the consumer's acceptance of an innovation, in this case embodied by shopping on the web. To this end, *"...the process by which a new product, service, or idea spreads among the consumers in a market*" (Wells & Prensky, 1996, p. 489) is best described by a research area known as Diffusion of Innovations (Rogers, 1995; Wells & Prensky, 1996).

The Diffusion of Innovations Theory (DoI) is concerned with how innovations are spread and adopted by the consumer. Thus, two processes are involved: the diffusion process that is "... *concerned with the spread of a new product from its source to the consuming public*"; and the adoption process that "... *focuses on the stages through which an individual consumer passes when deciding to accept or reject a new product*" (Schiffman & Kanuk, 2000, p. 410). However, this chapter is concerned only with the attributes that affect a consumer's decision to adopt or reject the innovation.

The perceived attributes of an innovation are: relative advantage, compatibility, complexity, trialability and observability. These attributes have been shown to explain 49% to 87% of the variance in the rate of adoption of an innovation (Rogers, 1995).

The two attributes of usefulness and ease of use that were identified from TAM have strong similarities to the attributes of relative advantage and complexity from innovation. The use of a retail site must compete with 'bricks and mortar' purchasing and with other web sites. This competition takes place within a social context. To this end, when the uptake of innovations within their social context is considered, Rogers (1995) characterises the usefulness of an innovation as its relative advantage and ease of use as its complexity. Thus, the usefulness of a commercial web site can also be linked to the consumer's perceptions of the relative advantage of using that web site compared to other methods of achieving the same task.

The attribute of trialability as articulated by Rogers (1995) refers to a user's perception that he or she will be able to experiment with an in-

novation prior to making the decision to adopt it. However, Agarwal and Prasad (1997) point out that this attribute does not capture the notion of on-going trialability, which is referred to as continued accessibility. Culnan (1984) suggests that there are three dimensions of accessibility. The physical dimension refers to the physical access of the web. The interface dimension refers to ease-of-use of the interface. The information dimension refers to the ability to locate information within the web site.

Finally, the innovation attribute observability will not be measured in the present research since the degree of the customer observation of other people's behaviour on the web is outside the designer's control.

Attributes Predicting Consumer Acceptance of Retail Sites

On the basis of both TAM and the Diffusion of Innovations Theory the following attributes become capable of being tested as candidates for usability assessment of retail websites. Furthermore, these attributes can serve as predictors of consumer acceptance of retail sites, these are Relative Advantage, Compatibility and Learnability. Additionally, derived on the basis of established relationships found in a review of the HCI literature, a number of other usability attributes are considered. Those usability attributes that showed some correlation between web site characteristics, and consumers' satisfaction and future use intentions, were considered as candidate usability attributes for commercial web sites. These are Accessibility, Clarity of Communication, Navigation, Consistency, Visual Presentation, Content, Credibility, Affect, plus Security and Privacy Policies. Hence, the review identifies nine related usability attributes, together with the four attributes derived from TAM and DoI that had not been considered earlier in HCI literature also included as possible candidates (see Table 1).

Table 1. Candidate usability attributes and relevant literature

Usability attribute influencing future use intention	Literature
Accessibility	Eighmey & McCord (1998); Hamilton (1997); Lightner et al. (1996); Ramsay et al. (1998);
Clarity of Communication	Fleming (1998)
Navigation	Abels et al. (1997); Huizingh (2000); Rajani & Rosenberg (1999); Smith et al. (1997)
Consistency	Becker & Mottay (2001); Lin et al., (1997)
Visual Presentation	Lightner et al (1996)
Content	Dholakia & Rego (1998); Huizingh, (2000); Jarvenpaa & Todd (1997); Lee et al. (2000)
Credibility	Fogg et al., (2001); Lin & Lu (2000)
Security and Privacy Policies	Elliot & Fowell (2000); Furnell & Karweni (1999); Labuschagne & Eloff (2000); Novack et al., (2000); Liang & Lai (2000); Morganosky & Cude (2000).
Affect	Rice (1997); Teo et al. (1999)
Learnability	Lederer et al. (2000); Morris & Dillon (1997)
Habit	Keeling (1999); Raskin (2000)
Relative Advantage	Agarwal & Prasad (1997); Keeney (1999)
Compatibility with Lifestyle	Agarwal & Prasad (1997); Keeling (1999)

Relative Advantage

There is evidence of the importance of Relative Advantage to consumer purchase activity on the Internet. Keeney (1999) conducted a study suggesting that consumers must feel that they can get a better deal in order for them to transfer their shopping purchases to Internet acquisition. Keeney (1999: #535) further argues that "...*to a customer, the decision about whether to purchase over the Internet can be made with only a knowledge of how well the alternatives perform in terms of the fundamental objectives*".

Compatibility with Lifestyle

Another construct identified by Rogers (1995) as important in the uptake of innovations within the social context of use is Compatibility with Lifestyle. Agarwal & Prasad (1997) conducted a study where, among other issues, the results revealed that the compatibility of an innovation, in this case the web, as perceived by the members of a social system, is positively related to their future use intentions.

Learnability and the Establishment of Habit

Learnability measures the "*degree to which users feel they can get used to the site if they come into it for the first time, and the degree to which they feel they can learn to use other facilities or access other information once they have started using it*" (Kirakowski et al., 1998). Similarly, for web user interfaces, studies using the TAM show that learnability indirectly affects behavioural intention (Morris & Dillon, 1997; Lederer et al., 2000).

The traditional measurement of learnability may need to be extended to measure the extent to which users can interact with the web site using as little of their direct attention resources as possible. In 1993, Nielsen pointed out that users traditionally were required to "*pay close attention to the use of their computer and thus the focus of the user was not directed to the task at hand*" (Nielsen, 1993, p. 85). In order to allow users to focus on the task rather than the computer, user interfaces should be largely based on some form of non-command interaction principles (Nielsen, 1993). If consumers do not have to think about the details of every action to enable them to use a web user interface, this would free their attention and allow them to concentrate on the information and consequence aspects of the task, rather than the management of carrying out the task. The establishment of habitual operations during the use of an interface can smooth the flow of the work of a user (Raskin, 1997). Keeling (1999) measured the effects of the establishment of habit on consumer acceptance of electronic service delivery systems and the results revealed that the establishment of habitual operations has a direct effect on future use intentions.

Accessibility

Accessibility is a construct encompassing perception of speed, such as time it takes for a web page to download (Hamilton, 1997; Lightner, et al. 1996; Nielsen, 1999; Ramsay, et al., 1998), and time required to perform a specific task (Bevan, 1997). The time it takes for a document to download is recognised as an important determinant of user satisfaction (Conn, 1995; Jacko et al., 2000). Subsequent studies also show the importance of response time for a user's future intentions in the web environment (Eighmey & McCord, 1998; Lin & Lu, 2000).

Clarity of Communication

Fleming (1998) argues that the e-commerce world uses a lot of jargon. Therefore, sometimes it can be laborious for the consumer to understand its meaning. The purpose of the site needs also to be clearly communicated to the user to inform him or her about the kinds of tasks he or she can accomplish.

Navigation

Researchers consider ease of navigation as a very important quality factor of web site usability (Fleming, 1998; Nielsen, 2000; Shubin & Meehan 1997). Careful arrangement of information, not tempting the users to interrupt their work or to leave the site are all aspects that relate to efficient navigation. Clear structure of the site also allows for faster

accomplishment of tasks (Abels et al., 1997; Huizingh, 2000; Rajani & Rosenberg, 1999; Smith et al., 1997; Tilson et al. 1998). Clear indication where the user is at all times is imperative (Bevan, 1998; Lederer et al. 2000; Levi & Conrad, 1996).

Consistency

"Consistency is one of the most basic usability principles" (Nielsen, 1993, p. 132) and is probably one of the most-documented attributes in HCI (Lin et al., 1997; Bevan 1998). Consistency refers to the design layout, maintaining consistency of colours, and backgrounds (Lederer et al. 2000; Liang & Lai 2000; Becker & Mottay, 2001) of the site as well as the procedures used to perform a specific action (Gehrke & Turban, 1999).

Visual Presentation

Helander & Khalid (2000) argue that an important attribute of e-commerce web sites is that objects are clear and intuitive to control. Furthermore, the degree to which information is easy to read and see was measured by Lederer et al. (2000) and was found to have an indirect effect on behavioural intention. Information clutter has been reported as a significant issue affecting user satisfaction (Lightner et al., 1996).

Content

Gehrke & Turban (1999) note that content is the most commonly prescribed recommendation in the literature. Some researchers go a step further and distinguish content from the design of a web site (Huizingh, 2000). Content relates to depth and breadth of information as well as to updating of the information (Gehrke & Turban, 1999). Providing useful information regarding a company's services or products is an essential feature that can affect a user's perception (Abels et al., 1997; Jarvenpaa & Todd, 1997; Lee et al., 2000). Information provided about the products or services a company is offering through the web site must also be regularly updated. Studies reveal that regularly updating the content of the site has an effect on continued use (Dholakia & Rego, 1998; Maguire, 2000).

Credibility

Content is an important attribute that may affect intention to revisit and intention to purchase. However, even if the information is readily available to the consumer still there may be some uncertainty about the quality of the information (Burgoon et al., 2000). Information regarding the owner of the site and detailed information regarding the company itself could alleviate credibility issues (Eighmey, & McCord, 1998; Lin & Lu, 2000; Fogg et al., 2001).

Affect

Kirakowski et al. (1987) note that affect measures the degree to which a person likes to use the computer system. During a study conducted by Rice (1997) the results showed that repeat visits to a web site can be increased if consumers find the site enjoyable. Similarly Teo et al. (1999) and Henderson et al. (1998) found that perceived enjoyment directly affects future use intention.

Security and Privacy policies

Web sites, because of their communicative and interactive nature, also bring other credibility issues to the fore. There is a body of evidence that the lack of trust with respect to online payment, and consumer service constitutes a real psychological barrier to e-commerce (Elliot & Fowell, 2000; Furnell & Karweni, 1999; Novack, et al., 2000; Labuschagne & Eloff, 2000; Liang & Lai, 2000; Morganosky & Cude, 2000).

METHOD AND RESULTS

Instrument

The aim of this research is to develop a theoretical framework for measuring the usability of retail sites. In order to build this framework a questionnaire was designed. To construct the questionnaire two important questions must be answered: (1) what attributes representing usability are we going to measure (already discussed in previous section) and (2) which specific items will be included to represent the attributes.

The literature relating to social attitude theory argues that questionnaire items used in the prediction of behavior must be very specifically aimed at the behaviour in question. To identify the specific items for inclusion in each attribute discussed above we gathered criteria regarding web site design: (i) web site design guidelines based on Borges et al. (1996), IBM (1998), Keeker (1997), Lynch & Horton (1997), SUN (1996), Sullivan (1998); and (ii) a number of evaluation usability checklists, heuristics, and questionnaires based on Bevan (1998), December (1996), Kirakowski et al. (1998), Nielsen (1999) and Ravden & Johnson (1989).

Case Study 1

A first questionnaire was designed in order to assess the validity of using the attributes derived from the Social Attitude Theories.

After some demographic questions, respondent current use of the technology (computer, e-mail and the web) was ascertained so that some assessment of the respondents' level of familiarity with the medium could be made.

The second section concerned the measurement of the usability attributes identified in the previous section as well as the measurement of future use intentions. Respondents gave their opinions on a 5-point scale, where the anchors were 1, strongly disagree and 5 strongly agree. There was also space for free-form comments.

The web site under review was the student section of a local newspaper website, therefore the reviewers were the students of the HCI course in the Department of Computation in University of Manchester. The students were frequent users of the web site and had performed queries in the web site previously.

Results

The total number of respondents was 78. Sixty-six were male and 12 were female. The aim of the first case study was to test the relationship between the proposed usability attributes and the independent *variable future use intention* factor. A reliability analysis resulted in a high alpha (>.5) for all factors. Compatibility with Lifestyle was represented by one construct only, therefore no alpha was obtained. Additionally multiple regression was conducted in three stages. First, to test the validity of the use of the eleven proposed usability attributes distinguished from the literature, a multiple regression analysis was performed with 'Intention to use' as the dependent variable and the composite attributes taken from HCI literature: Accessibility, Clarity of purpose, Clarity of language, Navigation, Consistency, Content, Visual presentation, the two aspects of Credibility (Author and web site administrator information and Provision of Feedback), Learnability and Affect as independent variables. Entered together, these eleven attributes account for 23% of the variance. This was preliminary evidence of the validity of using these eleven attributes.

However, adding the additional constructs of Relative Advantage, Compatibility with Lifestyle and Privacy Security and Establishment of Habit to the regression achieves an Adjusted R^2 of .57, or 57% of the variance in future use intentions to use the web site. Thus, the new attributes add significantly to the explanation of intentions and are important when describing future use intentions to use commercial sites.

Case Study 2

A list of general usability guidelines, even including the four additional constructs only goes so far in providing understanding of the attributes considered important by the user *as a potential customer* rather than a navigator or browser of an internet *retail site*.

Thus, to identify the specific Internet retail site attributes related to usability of a retail website we first listed the attributes considered by shoppers in retail store selection in a physical environment. We used the widely accepted attributes identified by Arnold (1983) and Lindquist (1974). Lindquist (1974) compiled an attribute list of customer evaluation of a retail store from an aggregation of the work of 26 researchers in this field. Spiller & Lohse (1998) define objective online variables that map to the key retail store variables identified by Lindquist (1974) and Arnold et al. (1977) these are: (i) Merchandise; including product variety, quality, guarantees and price; (ii) Service: including general and sales clerk service, merchandise return, and credit and payment policies; (iii) Promotion: including 'sales', advertisement and promotion displays; (iv) Convenience: including store organisation and store hours; (v) Fast checkout and Ease of navigation: including, *navigation effort* features that influenced the amount of effort (time, number of steps, etc.) required to browse and navigate the online retail store and *interface variables* concerning consistency of navigation cues and layout and clarity of screens and pictures; and (vi) Store atmosphere. Seven main attributes were defined by associated criteria based on the HCI literature on web site guidelines (Table 2).

The resulting criteria corresponding to each attribute were assessed on a 5 point scale, where the anchors were 1, strongly disagree and 5, strongly agree. The questionnaire was administered online. The results were collected in MS Access and then imported into SPSS (Statistical Package for the Social Sciences) for analysis. The questionnaire was divided into three main sections similar to case 1.

Results

In order to test the questionnaire, students from the Information Systems course from the University of Canberra (UC) in Australia along with the

Table 2. Operationalisation of Usability definition and TAM for Internet retail stores

Usability Attributes	Usability criteria in internet retail sites
1. Merchandise *In HCI: Content; Relative Advantage*	I could find things on this site that I could not find easily elsewhere. The site gave enough depth of information about products. There was a good choice of products on this web site. The products on this site appeared to be of high quality. There were enough pictures of the products. This web-site had up-to-date information. Product information was presented in an easy to understand way. Using this site would save me time finding information.
2. Service *In HCI: Credibility, Security and Privacy*	There was a good search facility on this site. This site gave help on product selection. It was obvious to the user how to contact the administrator of the site. Precise information about delivery charges was clearly displayed. The site allowed the user to provide feedback about the site/product. Guarantees and contact information for returns/complaints were clear. Security and privacy policies were conspicuously displayed. There was sufficient information given about the company about who owns this web site. A currency conversion rate mechanism was provided.
3. Navigation Effort *In HCI: Learnability; Navigation; Accessibility* **Interface variables** *In HCI: Consistency; Screen Clarity*	From the beginning, it was clear how the site was organised. It was easy to learn how to use this web site. I could go where I wanted within a few steps on this site. When I followed a link (e.g., menu item, clickable picture or link in the text) I got what I expected. It was simple to manoeuvre among related pages and between different sections. I would be able to use this site again almost without thinking about it. The initial load time for the site to appear was too long. When moving around the site the individual pages take too long to appear. The site used the same procedure when you did similar or related things e.g. clicking the same shaped/coloured button on each page The page layout was consistent throughout the site (e.g., back "buttons" are in the same place on each page. The information was clearly organised on the pages. The text was easy to read. The pictures were clear and easy to see. I had difficulty with some pages that did not fit the screen.
4. Convenience and Fast checkout	It would take little time to order or purchase a product or service. The process of ordering products would be difficult. During the purchase process it is easy to keep track of what you are buying and spending.
5. Promotion	The site provided a place for users to exchange information and ideas with other users. This site has good promotions and incentives. Apart from the products, the site had links or other content of interest to me.
6. Store atmosphere *In HCI: Clarity of Language, Clarity of Purpose, Affect, Compatibility with Lifestyle and Establishment of Habit*	This web site was fun to use. I found this web site interesting. Using this web site fits well with my lifestyle. I felt in control of the shopping process on this site. The features of this web site fit well with how I like to shop. I felt comfortable on this web site. I would feel secure purchasing a product on this Web site. It was clear from the start just what the site offered. The language used was clear and easy to understand. The site gave a clear on-screen response to any actions I made. The "tone" of the language was friendly and welcoming. This web site aims at people like me. Using this site could become something of a habit.
7. Overall Evaluation on Intention	How likely is it that you would use this site to make a purchase? How likely is it that you recommend this site to a friend? How likely is it that you would use this site to get information about a possible purchase? How likely is it that you would visit this site again for any other reason?

students from the Electronic Commerce course from the University of Manchester in UK, were requested to participate. Both classes were divided into 7 groups and each student within a group was asked to evaluate two Web sites. Therefore, students that belonged in Group 1 from UC and Group 1 from University of Manchester would evaluate the same two Web sites.

The retail websites were selected based on Spiller & Lohse (1998) retail site classification: superstore, promotional, plain sales catalogue, one page catalogue, and product listing. Fourteen sites in total were selected. The aim of the study was to provide data for testing the validity of using the attributes in the questionnaire across a representative range of retail websites.

Two hundred responses were obtained; 72% between the ages of 18 and 24 and 28% between the ages of 25 and 54. Almost 66% were from UC and 34% were from UMIST. Around 75% were male and 25% were female. Considering that each student had to review two sites the total number of website reviews was 400.

A Principal Components Analysis with Varimax rotation revealed a ten-factor solution; Cronbach Alpha analyses provided evidence of the internal consistency of the factors (see Table 3).

Initially, the correlations between the dependent variable of Intention (likelihood of purchase, revisit, recommendation, etc., see Table 2) and the usability attributes identified from the data were examined to ensure that all attributes were related to Intentions (see Table 4). This was indeed the case, although the correlations for Consistency and Accessibility are relatively weak.

The table of correlations also helps to illustrate the effects of individual usability attributes on more comprehensive evaluations such as Store Atmosphere. It is clear that the content of the website (e.g., Merchandise and content) and help with Product Selection contributes to Store Atmosphere, which is expected. However, nearly as strong an influence is Clarity of Purpose and an even stronger influence is Navigation. Hence,

we argue that a careful examination of all the usability attributes identified in this chapter is a useful and information exercise for owners of retail websites.

It is also evident that, for all attributes, the correlation with the variable Store Atmosphere is higher than the correlation with Intentions (see columns Intent and '1' in Table 4). Combined with the presence of other higher correlations between Independent variables than with the Dependent variable (e.g., see Clarity of Purpose with Navigation), this is evidence for mediation/ moderation of the effects of some variables on the Dependent variable. For example, the strong relationship between Store Atmosphere and Intent means we can expect that most of the effects of the other usability attributes will be mediated (or at least moderated) by the evaluation of Store Atmosphere.

Consequently, a hierarchical regression for all store types was performed to evaluate the influence of the Usability Attributes on Intentions. The order of entry was decided on the basis of the most likely timing of evaluations of the attributes, e.g., logically, unless a respondent could access a website they could not evaluate the other Usability Attributes, hence, Accessibility is entered first in the regression (Model 1 in Table 5). Similarly, it is intuitive that an early evaluation of Navigation and Consistency (Model 2 in Table 5) is made whilst locating policies, evaluating clarity of purchase, locating merchandise, promotions, and making a product selection. Store Atmosphere is added last (Model 5 in Table 5) due to its high correlation with the dependent variable.

The results of the hierarchical regression in Table 5 show that Store Atmosphere evaluations do indeed fully account for the effects of eight of the nine other Usability Attributes on Intentions. 'Promotions' maintains a direct effect on Intentions but this is much weaker in the presence of Store Atmosphere. Hence, Store Atmosphere and Intentions are complex evaluations requiring high attention to detail in website design. It can be

Table 3. New questionnaire with associated alpha

Usability Attribute	Usability Items
Navigation: The extent to which this site is organised in terms of product information and obvious representation of links *a= 0.879*	From the beginning, it was clear how the site was organised It was easy to learn how to use this website I could go where I wanted within a few steps on this site When I followed a link (e.g., menu item, clickable picture or link in the text) I got what I expected It was simple to maneuver among related pages and between different sections I would be able to use this site again almost without thinking about it The site gave a clear on-screen response to any actions I made Product information was presented in an easy to understand way The information was clearly organised on the pages
Store Atmosphere: The extent to which the consumer feels "at home" while using this site. *a = 0.904*	This web site was fun to use I found this website interesting Using this web site fits well with my lifestyle The features of this website fit well with how I like to shop I felt comfortable on this website I would feel secure purchasing a product on this web site. Using this site could become something of a habit. Using this site would save me time finding information. This website aims at people like me
Merchandise and Content: The extend to which the site presents enough and up-to-date information of the products. *a = 0.762*	The site gave enough depth of information about products. There was a good choice of products on this website The products on this site appeared to be of high quality There were enough pictures of the products This web-site had up-to-date information The pictures were clear and easy to see
Clarity on policies: The extent of clarity on sales policies and after-sales contact. *a = 0.718*	It was obvious to the user how to contact the administrator of the site. Precise information about delivery charges was clearly displayed. The site allowed the user to provide feedback about the site/product. Guarantees and contact information for returns/complaints were clear. Security and privacy policies were conspicuously displayed. There was sufficient information given about the company that owns this website.
Product Purchasing: The extent to which the site helps with product purchasing. *a = 0.725*	It would take little time to order or purchase a product or service. The process of ordering products would be difficult. During the purchase process it is easy to keep track of what you are buying and spending. I felt in control of the shopping process on this site.
Promotions: The extent to which the extra services offered are perceived of interest to the consumer. *a = 0.603*	The site provided a place for users to exchange information and ideas with other users. A currency conversion rate mechanism was provided. I could find things on this site that I could not find easily elsewhere. Apart from the products, the site had links or other content of interest to me. This site has good promotions and incentives.
Clarity of Purpose: The extent to which the consumers perceive the purpose of the site. *a = 0.678*	It was clear from the start just what the site offered. The language used was clear and easy to understand. The text was easy to read. The "tone" of the language was friendly and welcoming.
Consistency: The perceived consistency of the interface interaction. *a = 0.703*	The site used the same procedure when you did similar or related things e.g. clicking the same shaped/coloured button on each page. The page layout was consistent throughout the site (e.g., back "buttons" are in the same place on each page.
Accessibility: The extend to which the consumer perceives accessibility *a = 0.723*	The initial time for the site to appear on screen was too long. When moving around the site the individual pages take too long to appear.
Product Selection: The extent to which the site helps with product selection. *a = 0.630*	There was a good search facility on this site. This site gave help on product selection

argued that it is not merely the type of merchandise provided for purchase, but *how* it is provided that is important in customer decisions to make a purchase. Good navigation, Clarity of Purpose and Policies and Help in Product Selection and Purchasing appear to be all equally necessary.

Finally, in order to test the validity of the use of the ten attributes distinguished from the literature

for each of the 5 store types, further regression analyses were performed with 'Intention to use' as the dependent variable and the ten attributes as independent variables. Table 6 presents the results from these regression analyses; these are consistent with the likely content of each store type.

Table 4. Intercorrelations between the constructs

	Intent	1	2	3	4	5	6	7	8	9
1. Store atmosphere	.784**									
2. Navigation	.465**	.601**								
3. Merchandise and content	.494**	.556**	.504**							
4. Clarity of policies	.357**	.447**	.384**	.384**						
5. Product purchasing	.375**	.453**	.425**	.408**	.339**					
6. Clarity of purpose	.383**	.515**	.655**	.471**	.326**	.368**				
7. Promotions	.442**	.457**	.233**	.419**	.362**	.266**	.177**			
8. Consistency	.225**	.327**	.493**	.248**	.270**	.247**	.405**	.050		
9. Accessibility (reversed)	.180**	.188**	.284**	.141**	-.091	.158**	.129*	.014	.084	
10. Product selection	.479**	.516**	.376**	.615**	.321**	.333**	.249**	.444**	.182**	.161**

**. Correlation is significant at the 0.01 level (2-tailed).

*. Correlation is significant at the 0.05 level (2-tailed).

Table 5. Hierarchical regression analysis results

	Model 1	Model 2	Model 3	Model 4	Model 5
Accessibility	.181***	.052	.061	.056	.035
Navigation		.454***	.313***	.169***	-.005
Consistency		.001	.035	.000	-.021
Clarity of policies			.203***	.054	-.019
Clarity of purpose			.117**	.081	-.032
Merchandise and content				.104*	.047
Product purchasing				.089*	.014
Promotions				.219***	.076**
Product selection				.182***	.058
Store atmosphere					.721***
R Square	.033	.221	.267	.409	.639
Adjusted R Square	.030	.215	.257	.395	.629

***. Coefficient significant at the 0.01 level (2-tailed).

**. Coefficient significant at the 0.05 level (2-tailed).

*. Coefficient significant at the 0.10 level (2-tailed).

Table 6. Regression statistics for all types of stores

Type of store	R square	Adjusted R square*
Superstore	60%	54%
Plain sales catalogue	62%	52%
One page catalogue	60%	54%
Product listing	69%	65%
Promotional	51%	45%

*lower adjusted R square are a function of the lower sample sizes for individual types of store

CONCLUSION

The objectives of this chapter were: (i) to examine the concept of usability, as currently applied to web sites, and thereby to identify its limitations in terms of addressing the needs of the user as a consumer; and (ii) to develop a theoretical framework that suggests future use intention as a new type of measurement of usability of retail sites and identified appropriate usability attributes for retail sites.

In order to achieve the first objective a thorough review of web usability was carried out. The review suggests that usability is not a single property. Usability is a multidimensional property where users, scenarios, environment and equipment need to be known to the designer. However, defining these dimensions in the web environment is not an easy task. Further, defining measurable usability attributes taking under consideration all kinds of web sites and users is difficult. The risk, of course, is that too many and too broad attributes can be confusing and frustrating to web site designers. Thus, it can be concluded that merely looking at traditional HCI analysis and design methods is not sufficient.

In order to achieve the second objective, finding usability factors associated with internet *retail* sites, we followed multidisciplinary approach. Our review on current practices in HCI reveals that researchers and practitioners are moving away from an emphasis on generalised usability principles and support frameworks and methods to specialized criteria and usability techniques in order to provide designers with specific attributes and reliable evaluation results respectively. While it is widely accepted that in order to assess users expectations we need to tailor specific usability factors to the web environment few attempts have been made to identify usability corresponding to web retail environment. Thus, a theoretical framework was built identifying important usability attributes for retail sites and at the same time focusing on the needs of the user as a potential consumer. We examined the fields of Social Attitude Theories and Retail Marketing to discover whether any of the research findings in these areas might be applied in HCI and thereby assist in better understanding the needs of the user as a *customer* making a purchase rather than browsing a website.

Two case studies were carried out in to test the proposed framework. The first aimed at collecting attributes from web site guidelines and studies carried out in the field of HCI and attributes derived from the field of Social Attitude Theories. The results revealed the importance of habit, affect, relative advantage and compatibility with lifestyle in explaining future use intention of a web site.

The second case study tailored this framework to the attributes defined from Retail Marketing for a bricks and mortar store. The results suggest a ten factor usability framework that combines Social Attitude, Retail Marketing and HCI principles for use by a web site designer to design or evaluate a functioning retail web site.

This chapter has contributed to the field of usability in HCI, through bringing a Social Attitude Theory and Retail Marketing perspective. The emphasis on the consumer within HCI is increasingly seen as important when evaluating the usability of retail sites. Contributions in this area have been made (i) by suggesting a new overall measurement of usability for retail websites, future use intentions, from Social Attitude Theories, thereby improving the accuracy of the prediction of customers' actual behaviour and (ii) by borrowing concepts from Social Attitude Theories and Retail Marketing, thereby expanding the scope of usability issues leading to a greater specific understanding of the user as a customer.

The empirical findings presented in this chapter provide helpful design guidelines that web designers within organizations can use to strengthen consumer enthusiasm and motivation to shop online. Further, the usability items within the framework can be used as a checklist (Table 3) in the web site design process.

FUTURE TRENDS

Web site designers are no longer simply designing usable interfaces but are seeking to engage the user. In the case of potential customers of internet retail sites, designers wish to provide a unique experience that will make customers return to that site. Thus, to measure future usage we need to look into other factors that might affect user's future intentions. The main aim of our framework is to identify distinct usability attributes that are possible to express in a quantifiable, objective and measurable manner. Within the framework it is possible to identify those attributes of usability that are important to users' future intentions for a particular website or particular retail sector and then associate each of them to specific design guidelines that are interpretable by a designer.

The proposed framework can be expanded through examining other issues that could have a bearing on the usability evaluation of retail sites. Possible suggestions in this direction are: Brand, Flow, Interactivity and Social Presence. The question here would be how building brand confidence affects the usability of a retail site, or indeed, vice versa, how website usability can affect perceptions of the brand. Thus, in addition to usable web user interfaces, companies may also wish to consider the retention and extension of any brand image

they possess or wish to achieve. There is some preliminary evidence that the user's perception of usability attributes does have an effect on brand confidence (Keeling et al., 2000). Impacting on brand confidence, in that study, were the quality of service perceived, navigation interface features, promotions and store atmosphere. In the future it would be useful to know exactly which design issues may affect brand confidence and protect brand image.

For e-commerce websites, increasing perceptions of 'social presence' is correlated to increased feelings of human contact and sociability (Hassanein and Head, 2006). Some research suggests that buying a complex product on the website requires a higher social presence (Jahng et al., 2006) as this reduces the perceived distance between buyers and sellers and the online exchange relationship feels closer to a traditional interpersonal relationship (Kumar and Benbasat, 2002). Many online stores are implementing strategies to increase social presence, for example, by including virtual reality as part of their web design.

One strategy for increasing perceptions of social presence is to introduce interactivity. Interactivity refers to the interaction between the website and a user who visits that site and "*goes to the core of a computer-mediated communication environment*" (Novack, et al., 2000). However, within this virtual hypermedia environment incorporating interactivity between people and computers, both experiential and goal directed behaviours compete for customer attention. The customer's capability in the virtual environment, as well as challenges posed by that environment introduces a competency issue that does not exist in the physical world (Novack, et al., 2000).

This competency issue involves flow, that is, the holistic sensation that people feel when they act with total involvement (Csikszentmihalyi, 1996). Novack, et al., (2000) suggest that flow state has been overlooked by most interactive marketers as a subset of interactivity. However, the work of Sicilia et al. (2005) shows that although there is an interactivity - flow state relationship, the two should be measured separately as this gives more precise information for website design and marketing.

Results from studies suggest that there is preliminary evidence that flow can be linked to web site design issues (Chen et al., 1999). The proposed theoretical framework also points towards design issues that might result in flow. For example, provision of feedback encourages the occurrence of flow (Chikszentmihalyi, 1996). Thus, research could seek a deeper understanding of the design issues that surround interactivity, flow and social presence while using a retail site.

REFERENCES

Abels, E., Domas, M., & Hahn, K. (1997). Identifying user-based criteria for Web pages. *Internet Research: Electronic Networking Applications and Policy*, 7(4), 252–262. doi:10.1108/10662249710187141

Adams, D., Nelson, R., & Todd, P. (1992). Perceived Usefulness, Ease of Use, and Usage of Information Technology: a Replication. *MIS Quarterly*, 16(2), 227–247. doi:10.2307/249577

Agarwal, R., & Prasad, J. (1997). The Role of Innovation Characteristics and Perceived Voluntariness in the Acceptance of Information Technologies. *Decision Sciences*, 28(3), 557–582. doi:10.1111/j.1540-5915.1997.tb01322.x

Ajzen, I. (1991). The Theory of Planned Behaviour: Some Unresolved Issues. *Organizational Behavior and Human Decision Processes*, 50, 179–211. doi:10.1016/0749-5978(91)90020-T

Arnold, S. J., Ma, S., & Tigert, D. J. (1978). A Comparative Analysis of Determinant Attributes in Retail Store Selection. *Advances in Consumer Research. Association for Consumer Research (U. S.)*, 5(1), 663–667.

Becker, S. A., & Mottay, F. E. (2001). A Global Perspective on Web Site Usability. *IEEE Software*, 18(1), 54–61. doi:10.1109/52.903167

Bevan, N. (1997). Usability Testing of World Wide Web Sites. *In Proceedings of Workshop at CHI'97: Usability Testing of World Wide Web Sites*, March 23-24, Atlanta, GA. Retrieved from http://www.acm.org/sigchi/webhci/chi97testing/bevan.htm

Bevan, N. (1998). Usability Issues in Web Site Design *In Proceedings of UPA'98: Usability Professional Association*. Online archive available at http://www.usability.serco.com

Borges, J. A., Morales, I., & Rodriguez, N. J. (1996). Guidelines for Designing Usabile World Wide Web Pages. In *Proceedings of CHI'96: Conference on Human Factors in Computing Systems*, Panel, (pp.277-278). New York: ACM Press/Addison Wesley.

Burgoon, J. K., Bonito, J. A., Bengtsson, B., Cederberg, C., Lundeberg, M., & Allspach, L. (2000). Interactivity in Human-Computer Interaction: A Study Of Credibility, Understanding and Influence. *Computers in Human Behavior*, 16(6), 553–574. doi:10.1016/S0747-5632(00)00029-7

Chen, H., Wigand, R. T., & Nilan, M. S. (1999). Optimal Experience of Web Activities. *Computers in Human Behavior*, 15(5), 585–608. doi:10.1016/S0747-5632(99)00038-2

Chikszentmihalyi, M. (1996). Go with the Flow. *Wired*. Online archive available at http://www.wired.com/wired/archive/4.09/czik_pr.html

Conn, A. (1995). Time Affordances: The Time Factor in Diagnostic Usability Heuristics. *In Proceedings of CHI '95: Human Factors in Computing Systems*, (pp. 1836-913). New York: ACM Press/Addison Wesley.

Culnan, M. (1984). The Dimensions of Accessibility to On-line Information: Implications for Implementing Office Information Systems. *ACM Transactions on Information Systems, 2*(2), 141–150. doi:10.1145/521.523

Davis, F. D. (1989). Perceived Usefulness, Perceived Ease of Use, and User Acceptance of Information Technology. *MIS Quarterly, 13*(3), 319–340. doi:10.2307/249008

December, J. (1996). An information development methodology for the World Wide Web. *Technical Communication in Cyberspace, 43*(4), 369–374.

Dholakia, U. M., & Rego, L. L. (1998). What Makes Commercial Web Pages Popular? An empirical investigation of web page effectiveness. *European Journal of Marketing, 32*(7/8), 724–736. doi:10.1108/03090569810224119

Eighmey, J., & McCord, L. (1998). Adding Value in the Information Age: Uses and Gratifications of Sites on the World Wide Web. *Journal of Business Research, 41*(3), 187–194. doi:10.1016/S0148-2963(97)00061-1

Elliot, S., & Fowell, S. (2000). Expectations versus Reality: A Snapshot of Consumer Experiences with Internet Retailing. *International Journal of Information Management, 20*(5), 323–336. doi:10.1016/S0268-4012(00)00026-8

Éthier, J., Hadaya, P., Talbot, J., & Cadieux, J. (2008). Interface design and emotions experienced on B2C Web Sites: empirical testing of a research model. *Computers in Human Behavior, 24*(6), 2771–2791. doi:10.1016/j.chb.2008.04.004

Fishbein, M., & Ajzen, I. (1975). *Belief, Attitude, Intention and Behaviour: An Introduction to Theory and Research.* Reading, MA: Addison-Wesley.

Fleming, J. (1998). *Web Navigation: Designing the User Experience.* Sebastol, CA: O'Reilly& Associates.

Fogg, B. J., Marshall, J., Laraki, O., Osipovich, A., Varma, C., Fang, N., et al. (2001). What Makes Web Sites Credible?: A Report on a Large Quantitative Study. In *Proceedings the SIG-CHI '01 Conference on Human Factors in Computing Systems,* (pp.61-680. Reading, MA: ACM Press/ Addison Wesley. Furnell, S. M., & Karweni, T. (1999). Security Implications of Electronic Commerce: A Survey of Consumers and Businesses. *Internet Research: Electronic Networking Applications and Policy, 9*(5), 372-382.

Gehrke, D., & Turban, E. (1999). Determinants of successful web-site design: Relative importance and recommendations for effectiveness. In *HICSS '99: Proceedings of 32nd Hawaii International Conference on System Sciences.* Washington, DC: IEEE Computer Society.

Hamilton, A. (1997). *Avoid The #1 Web Site Sin: Slow Loading Pages.* Online archive available at http://www4.zdnet.com/anchordesk/story/story/ story_1244.html

Hartson, H. R. (1998). Human-Computer Interaction: Interdisciplinary Roots and Trends. *Journal of Systems and Software, 43*, 103–118. doi:10.1016/S0164-1212(98)10026-2

Hassanein, K., & Head, M. (2006). The Impact of Infusing Social Presence in the Web Interface: An Investigation Across Product Types. *International Journal of Electronic Commerce, 10*(2), 31–55. doi:10.2753/JEC1086-4415100202

Hayes, P. H., & Rosson, M. B. Schneider, M. L., & Whiteside, J. A. (1986). Classifying Users: A Hard Look at some Controversial Issues. In *Panel Proceedings of CHI '86: Conference on Human Factors in Computing Systems,* (pp.84-88). Reading, MA: ACM Press/Addison Wesley.

Helander, M. G., & Khalid, H. M. (2000). Modeling the Customer in Electronic Commerce. *Applied Ergonomics*, *31*(6), 609–619. doi:10.1016/S0003-6870(00)00035-1

Henderson, R., Rickwood, D., & Roberts, P. (1998). The Beta Test of An Electronic Supermarket. *Interacting with Computers*, *10*, 385–399. doi:10.1016/S0953-5438(98)00037-X

Ho, C. F., & Wu, W. H. (1999) Antecedents of customer satisfaction on the Internet: An empirical study of online shopping. In HICSS '99 - *Proceedings of 32nd Hawaii International Conference on System Sciences*. Washington, DC: IEEE Computer Society.

Huizingh, E. K. R. E. (2000). The Content and Design of Web Sites: An Empirical Study. *Information & Management*, *37*(3), 123–134. doi:10.1016/S0378-7206(99)00044-0

IBM. (1998). *Ease of Use Web Design Guidelines*. Online archive available at http://www-3.ibm.com/ibm/easy/eou_ext.nsf/Publish/572

ISO. (1995). ISO/DIS 9241-11 *Draft International Standard, Ergonomic Requirements for Office Work with Visual Display Terminals (VDTs). Part 10: Dialogue Principles*. Genève, Switzerland: International Organisation for Standardisation.

Jacko, J. A., Sears, A., & Borella, M. (2000). The Effect of Network Delay and Media on User Perceptions of Web Resources. *Behaviour & Information Technology*, *19*(6), 427–439. doi:10.1080/014492900750052688

Jahng, J., Jain, H. K., & Ramamurthy, K. (2006). An Empirical Study of the Impact of Product Characteristics and Electronic Commerce Interface Richness on Consumer Attitude and Purchase Intentions. *Systems, Man and Cybernetics, Part A: Systems and Humans . IEEE Transactions*, *36*(6), 1185–1201.

Jarvenpaa, S. L., & Todd, P. A. (1997). Consumer reactions to electronic shopping on the World Wide Web. *International Journal of Electronic Commerce*, *1*(2), 59–88.

Keeker, K. (1997) *Improving Web site Usability and Appeal*. Online archive available at http://msdn.microsoft.com/workshop/management/planning/improvingsiteusa.asp

Keeling, K. A. (1999). *Customer Acceptance of Electronic Service Delivery: Extending the Technology Acceptance Model*. Unpublished PhD Thesis, School of Management, University of Manchester Institute of Science and Technology, Manchester, UK.

Keeney, R. L. (1999). The Value of Internet Commerce to the Customer. *Management Science*, *45*(4), 533–542. doi:10.1287/mnsc.45.4.533

Kirakowski, J., Claridge, N., & Whitehand, R. (1998) Human Centred Measures of Success in Web site Design, In *Proceedings 4th Conference on Human Factors and the Web*. Online archive available at http://www.research.att.com/conf/hfweb/proceedings/kirakowski/index.html

Kirakowski, J., Gould, J., Dillon, A., & Sweeny, M. (1987). *Parameters of Change in User Development. HUFIT Document Code:HUFIT/HFRG-2-2*.

Kumar, N. and Benbasat, I. (2002). Para-Social Presence and Communication Capabilities of a Web Site: A Theoretical Perspective. *e-Service Journal*, *1*(3), 5-24

Kumar, R. L., Smith, M. A., & Bannerjee, S. (2004). User interface features influencing overall ease of use and personalization. *Information & Management*, *41*(3), 157–178. doi:10.1016/S0378-7206(03)00075-2

Labuschagne, L., & Eloff, J. H. P. (2000). Electronic Commerce: The Information-Security Challenge. *Information Management & Computer Security*, *8*(3), 154–157. doi:10.1108/09685220010372582

Lavie, T., & Tactinsky, N. (2004). Assessing dimensions of perceived visual aesthetics of web sites. *International Journal of Human-Computer Studies*, *60*(3), 269–298. doi:10.1016/j.ijhcs.2003.09.002

Lederer, A. L., Maupin, D. J., Sena, M. P., & Zhuang, Y. (2000). The Technology Acceptance Model and the World Wide Web. *Decision Support Systems*, *29*(3), 269–282. doi:10.1016/S0167-9236(00)00076-2

Lee, J., Kim, J., & Moon, J. Y. (2000). What Makes Users Visit Cyber Stores Again? Key Design Factors for Customer Loyalty. In *Proceedings of CHI'2000: Computers and Human Interface*, (pp. 305-312). New York: ACM Press/Addison Wesley.

Levi, M. D., & Conrad, F. G. (1996). A Heuristic Evaluation of a World Wide Web Prototype. *Interaction*, *3*(4), 50–61. doi:10.1145/234813.234819

Liang, T. P., & Huang, J. S. (1998). An Empirical Study on Consumer Acceptance of Products in Electronic Markets: A transaction cost model. *Decision Support Systems*, *24*(1), 29–43. doi:10.1016/S0167-9236(98)00061-X

Liang, T. P., & Lai, H. (2000). Electronic Store Design and Consumer Choice: An Empirical Study. In *Proceedings of HICSS'00: 33rd Hawaii International Conference on System Sciences*. Washington, DC: IEEE Computer Society.

Lightner, N. J., Bose, I., & Salvendy, G. (1996). What is Wrong with the World-Wide Web? A Diagnosis of Some Problems and Prescription of Some Remedies. *Ergonomics*, *39*(8), 995–1004. doi:10.1080/00140139608964523

Limayem, M., Khalifa, M., & Frini, A. (2000). What makes Consumers Buy from Internet? A longitudinal Study of Online Shopping. *IEEE Transactions on Systems, Man, and Cybernetics. Part A, Systems and Humans*, *30*(4), 421–432. doi:10.1109/3468.852436

Lin, H. X., Choong, Y., & Salvendy, G. (1997). A Proposed Index of Usability: A Method for Comparing the Relative Usability of Different Software Systems. *Behaviour & Information Technology*, *16*(4/5), 267–278.

Lin, J. C., & Lu, H. (2000). Towards an Understanding of the Behavioural Intention to Use a Web Site. *International Journal of Information Management*, *20*(3), 197–208. doi:10.1016/S0268-4012(00)00005-0

Lindquist, J. D. (1974). Meaning of image: a survey of empirical and hypothetical evidence . *Journal of Retailing*, *50*(4), 29–38.

Liu, C., & Arnett, K. P. (2000). Exploring the Factors Associated with Web Site Success in the Context of Electronic Commerce. *Information & Management*, *38*(1), 23–33. doi:10.1016/S0378-7206(00)00049-5

Lynch, P. J., & Horton, S. (1997). *Web Style Guide Basic Design Principles for Creating Web sites*. Stanford, CT: Yale University Press. Online archive available at http://www.info.med.yale.edu/caim/manual

Maguire, M. C. (2000). Consumer Acceptance of Internet Services. In *Proceedings of Annual Conference of the Ergonomics Society*, (pp.207-211). New York: Taylor and Francis.

Mathieson, K. (1991). Predicting Use Intentions: Comparing the Technology Acceptance Model with the Theory of Planned Behaviour. *Information Systems Research*, *2*(3), 173–191. doi:10.1287/isre.2.3.173

Microsystems, S. U. N. (1996). *Guide to Web Style*. Online archive available at http://www.sun.com/styleguide/

Morganosky, M. A., & Cude, B. J. (2000). Consumer Response to Online Grocery Shopping. *International Journal of Retail & Distribution Management*, *28*(1), 17–26. doi:10.1108/09590550010306737

Morris, M. G., & Dillon, A. (1997). How User Perceptions Influence Software Use. *IEEE Software*, *14*(4), 58–65. doi:10.1109/52.595956

Nielsen, J. (1993). *Usability Engineering*. Boston: Academic Press.

Nielsen, J. (1999). Online archive available at http://www.useit.com/papers/heuristic/heuristic_list.html

Nielsen, J. (2000). *Designing Web Usability: The Practice of simplicity*. New York: New Riders Publishing.

Novak, T. P., Hoffman, D. L., & Yung, Y. F. (2000). Measuring the Customer Experience in Online Environments: A Structural Modeling Approach. *Marketing Science*, *19*(1), 22–42. doi:10.1287/mksc.19.1.22.15184

Preece, J., Rogers, Y., Sharp, H., Benyon, D., Holland, S., & Carey, T. (1994). *Human Computer Interaction*. Reading, MA: Addison Wesley.

Rajani, R., & Rosenberg, D. (1999). Usable Or Not? Factors Affecting the Usability of Web Sites. *CMC Magazine*. January 1999. Online archive available at http://www.december.com/cmc/mag/1999/jan/rakros.html

Ramsay, Barbesi, A., & Preece, J. (1998). A Psychological Investigation of Long Retrieval Times on the World Wide Web. *Interacting with Computers*, *10*(1), 77–86. doi:10.1016/S0953-5438(97)00019-2

Raskin, J. (1997). Looking for a Humane Interface: Will Computers Ever Become Easy to Use? *Communications of the ACM*, *40*(2), 98–101. doi:10.1145/253671.253737

Ravden, S., & Johnson, G. (1989). *Evaluating the Usability of Human-Computer Interfaces*. New York: John Wiley & Sons.

Rice, M. (1997). What makes users revisit a web site? *Marketing News*, *31*(6), 12.

Richtell, M., & Tedeschi, B. (2007, June 17). Online Sales Lose Steam. *New York Times*.

Rogers, E. M. (1995). *Diffusion of Innovations*, (4th Ed.). New York: The Free Press.

Schiffman, L. G., & Kanuk, L. L. (2000). *Consumer Behaviour*, (7th Ed.). Upper Saddle River, NJ: Prentice Hall.

Shackel, B. (1991). *Human Factors for Informatics Usability*. Cambrdige, UK: Cambridge University Press.

Shubin, H., & Meehan, M. M. (1997). Navigation in Web Applications. *Interaction*, *4*(6), 13–18. doi:10.1145/267505.267508

Sicilia, M., Ruiz, S., & Munuera, J. L. (2005). Effects of Interactivity in a Web Site: The Moderating Effect of Need for Cognition. *Journal of Advertising*, *34*(3), 31–44.

Smith, P. A., Newman, I. A., & Parks, L. M. (1997). Virtual Hierarchies and Virtual Networks: Some Lessons From Hypermedia Usability research Applied to the Web. *International Journal of Human-Computer Studies*, *47*(1), 67–95. doi:10.1006/ijhc.1997.0128

Spiller, P., & Lohse, G. L. (1998). A classification of Internet retail stores. *International Journal of Electronic Commerce*, *2*(2), 29–56.

Sullivan, T. (1998). *User Testing Techniques - A Reader-Friendliness Checklist*. Online archive available at http://www.pantos.org/atw/35317. html

Teo, T. S. H., Lim, V. K. G., & Lai, R. Y. C. (1999). Intrinsic and Extrinsic Motivation in Internet Usage. *Omega, 27*(1), 25–37. doi:10.1016/S0305-0483(98)00028-0

Thompson, R. L., Higgins, C. A., & Howell, J. M. (1991). Personal Computing: Toward a Conceptual Model of Utilisation. *MIS Quarterly, 15*(1), 125–143. doi:10.2307/249443

Tilson, R., Dong, J., Martin, S., & Kieke, E. (1998). A Comparison of Two Current E-commerce Sites. In *Proceedings of the 16th Annual Conference on Computer Documentation,* (pp.87-92). New York: ACM Press/Addison Wesley.

Venkatesh, V., & Davis, F. D. (2000). A Theoretical Extension of the Technology Acceptance Mode: Four Longitudinal Field Studies. *Management Science, 46*(2), 186–204. doi:10.1287/mnsc.46.2.186.11926

Ward, M. R., & Lee, M. J. (2000). Internet Shopping, Consumer Search and Product Branding. *Journal of Product and Brand Management, 9*(1), 6–18. doi:10.1108/10610420010316302

Wells, W. D., & Prensky, D. (1996). *Consumer Behaviour*. Chichester, UK: John Wiley.

Zviran, M., Glezer, C., & Anvi, I. (2006). User satisfaction from commercial web sites: The effect of design and use. *Information & Management, 43*(2), 157–178. doi:10.1016/j.im.2005.04.002

Chapter 14
The Influence of E-Commerce Website Colors on Usability

Jean-Eric Pelet
ISG Paris, IEMN Nantes, France

ABSTRACT

This chapter aims to study the effects of the colors of e-commerce websites on consumer behavior, in order to better understand website usability. Since color components (Hue, Brightness and Saturation) affect behavioral responses of the consumer (memorization and buying intention), this research reveals the importance of the interaction between hue and brightness, in enhancing the contrast necessary to ensure an easy navigation. By comparing graphic chart effects according to their level of saturation and brightness depending on the hue, it aims at focusing on particularly important consideration of webdesign, linked to choices of color. The obtained results were conveyed through the changes in internal states of the organism, which are emotions and mood. The interaction of hue and brightness, using chromatic colors (as opposed to Black & White) for the dominant (background) and dynamic (foreground) ones, supports memorization and the intent to purchase, reinforcing the importance to attach to usable websites. This is even more evident when contrast rests on a weak situation of brightness. The data collection was carried out during a laboratory experiment so as to ensure the accuracy of measurements regarding the color aspects of e-commerce websites.

INTRODUCTION

The impressive rise of e-commerce, while inspiring dismay in some and awe in others, merits closer examination. One of the factors which has contributed significantly to this success, is the enhanced "ease of movement" on the site, otherwise referred to as the "usability of the site". Moreover, the ease of recognizing functional zones such as the navigation bar, the search engine, the possibility to sort the information, constitutes a major aspect of this research. A significant part of this chapter is dedicated to the usability of websites, and to the quantity of information retained following a visit to an

DOI: 10.4018/978-1-60566-896-3.ch014

e-commerce website. By usability, we mean *"the extent to which a product can be used by specified users to achieve specified goals with effectiveness, efficiency and satisfaction in a specified context of use"* (ISO 9241-11). The possibility of identifying the links and the useful buttons to change pages constitute other key factors in the success of e-commerce. Characteristics such as hue, brightness and saturation, all of which are related to color are crucial in getting the consumers attention. Indeed, the design of e-commerce website interfaces is receiving increasing managerial and research attention in the online retail context.

People don't take the time to read the contents if they are not appealing enough: the consumer's decision is based on a first impression. This is especially true when people cannot read the text because of poor contrast, for example. Though the color variable is a widely researched topic (see the periodical published by Divard and Urien, 2001), to this day, very few studies focus on this phenomenon within the context of the Internet. Yet color is omnipresent on e-commerce websites. The lack of research on the effects of the colors used on e-commerce websites suggests that more study in this area is needed. In their effort to spur Internet users to buy, brands do not seem to focus systematically on color choice when conceiving or updating websites.

While several studies on the impact of colors on Internet site readability provide advice about how to choose the most harmonious colors (Hill and Scharff, 1997; Hall and Hanna, 2004), experts in research on usability such as Nielsen (2000) have made managerial recommendations. However studies have not addressed the variation of hue, brightness and saturation on e-commerce. In an attempt to address this gap, this paper aims to shed light on how customers perceive the usability of e-commerce website interfaces, and how colors can be helpful for them, in order to improve the usability of the website.

Definition of the Atmosphere Constructs

Atmosphere is a marketing tool which is used as the number of competitors on the market increases. More exactly, the action of the physical environment of the store can constitute a means of attracting new customers and of developing the loyalty of former customers. The same happens with e-commerce websites, where the interface is considered as the atmosphere of the store. From a cognitive point of view, the simple fact of getting lost on a webpage, for example, seems to be a consequence of a user's difficulty in simultaneously managing two cognitive activities, i.e. processing and locating (Tricot, 1995). A homepage simply indicates which actions are possible, which zones of the screen correspond to such and such an action (e.g. to visit the catalogue, look for the search engine, to recommend a page or a product to a contact); these actions constitute important control levers in the eyes of the consumer. He or she considers them attentively to feel comfortable and to be ready to return to the site as was revealed in the interviews conducted during the qualitative analysis.

Importance of the Visual Dimension on Internet

The fact that the state of a color changes when a user passes over a link counts among the standards recognized by consumers. It thus seems very important to change the color of this link when it is passed over because the users visiting a page, which does not respect this convention may:

- revisit the same pages unintentionally
- get lost more easily because his comprehension of the significance of each link is reduced
- badly interpret or be unaware of the difference between two similar links if he is not sure which ones he already visited

- give up the navigation more quickly because he or she has a diminished sense of control over the direction of the visual interface when the website does reflect his actions. The lack of "easy to find" links thus does not help him to continue using the interface (Nielsen, 2004)

By examining the customer's description of this type of electronic shopping environment, and the main constructs which are taken into account in the presented qualitative analysis, particularly those in the direction of color. This paper attempts to introduce some important recommendations to consider when conceiving an e-commerce website, especially when thinking about its usability. Results from recent work (Pelet, 2008) demonstrate the importance of considering chromatic colors vs. achromatic ones, taking into consideration the effects of the three color components: hue, brightness and saturation. These results will be presented below.

Among the many variables supporting a consumer's positive experience of an e-commerce website, color plays an important part. In an online environment, a vendor's competence will largely be assessed through the presentation of products and product information. Overall, most e-commerce websites present a product using images. These should be clear, of high quality and color precision (Papadopoulou, 2007).

The needs of disabled people don't seem to receive as much consideration with regard to website design and evaluation. Webdesigners are apparently not sufficiently aware of the community of people with disabilities (McMillan, 1992). Taking into account an increasingly older population, perhaps suffering from eye trouble, poor perception of color or, moreover, from cognition problems, online retailers will need to re-examine their e-commerce website's interface. Indeed it has been estimated that 95% of the commercial sites were inaccessible to the people with visual or auditive "handicaps" (Gignac, 2000). If they

want to avoid the cancellation of an order, due to an apparent lack of protection of the website or because it is impossible to carry out the transaction, online e-merchants have to consider the issue of accessibility of information in more depth. Inaccessibility should not slow down e-commerce websites, and the atmosphere of the website can help in this direction.

Research concerning the atmosphere of physical places of sale, postulates that it is essential to consider this in its entirety to obtain usable results related to the consumer's behavior (Filser, 2003b; Lemoine, 2003) since the five senses (sound, touch, sight, sense of smell, and taste sometimes) are stimulated. The situation is different when considering the atmosphere of e-commerce websites. Even if the Internet promises improvements, in this research dedicated to the field of e-commerce usability, consumer behavior depends mainly on the information retained and this thus characterizes his perception of the place of sale. Only two senses are stimulated on the Internet: sight and sound.

On the one hand, sight on an e-commerce website relates to colors, images and animations in the form of buttons, navigation bars, advertising and everything related to the iconicity of the website. Furthermore, hearing (the sound dimension) relates to the sounds of the site's interactivity; for example, the passage of the mouse over a link.

The visual dimension is particularly important for our subject as pertains to the impact of variables such as sight. In this case, color has evident importance. This study suggests that color serves largely to clarify and inform the consumer; therefore sound is not a focus of this research. Indeed, 80% of the information memorized by an individual comes from the visual sense, and other forms of perception of the environment are also heavily influenced by sight (Mattelart 1996). Consequently, we can show that on the Internet and in the context of e-commerce websites in particular, given the scarcity of the sites offering sound animation, sight is more frequently stimulated than hearing. It then makes sense that almost all information retained, determining the perception of the e-commerce website by the consumer, comes from sight.

We have chosen to measure the influence of e-commerce websites' colors on usability, with the help of system intended to measure retained information. Previous research on the effects of the colors of e-commerce websites on memorization and on the intent to purchase helps us to understand the utility of using a flexible measuring instrument for memorization and buying intention. The design of the experiment, carried out following a qualitative analysis based on 21 interviews, made it possible to develop constructs rarely encountered in the emerging literature, such as the "playability" of the interface. This refers to the pleasure of moving on the website as measured by the ease of use worked out by web designers. The conditions of the experiment, based on the use of exhaustive measurements of the perception of the website, have enabled us to deduce that the Internet consumer's environment also deserves to be taken into account when designing e-commerce websites.

Usability and E-Commerce

Since the birth of the Internet, e-commerce has experienced a constant expansion and its returns on investment speak for itself. All products and services together, e-commerce reached a global turnover of approximately 15 billion euros in 2008 (ACSEL, 2009) and has been able to preserve its image year after year. However, many consumers on the Internet give up the purchasing process prematurely (Cho, 2004). This is mainly due to access problems or to a complicated processes of payment (Ranganathan and Grandon, 2005). Navigation modes that make the understanding of the offer difficult, constitute a reason for giving up a purchase on an e-commerce website (Ladwein and Ben Mimoun, 2006). On the basis of the qualitative analysis we have undertaken, we

think that colors and the length of the text format, account, in part, for this weakness.

Color as a Main Variable of E-Commerce Website Interfaces

Color has always been used by human beings as an aid to distinguish important information from unimportant or irrelevant information. It is essential in strategies of camouflage, for example. It also aids an individual's memory in many uses such as presenting information, assisting in education or even with the intention to buy.

Color contains three principal components (Trouvé, 1999):

- Hue (or chromatic tonality), is the attribute of the visual sensation defined according to color denominations such as blue, green, red…;
- Saturation refers to the proportion of chromatically pure color contained in the total sensation;
- Brightness refers to the degree to which an illuminated surface seems to emit more or less light.

Unlike most empirical studies dealing with color which compare warm and cold colors, this study focuses on hue, brightness and saturation so as to demonstrate that the influence of color varies according to the intensity of each one of those components. These various levels occasion particular contrasts according to the chosen hue, which can then enhance or disturb the readability of the whole page. This can represent an obstacle for the website's usability.

Generally speaking, colors affect consumer behavior in compliance with Mehrabian and Russell's psycho environmental model, the SOR model (Stimulus Organism Response) (Mehrabian and Russell, 1974). Even within colors themselves, Bellizzi and Hite (1992), Dunn (1992), Drugeon-Lichtlé (1996), and Pantin-Sohier (2004) chose hue as the main variable. They also showed in their experiments that brightness and saturation should be taken into consideration when conducting experiments about color.

As Valdez (1993), Drugeon-Lichtlé (2002), Camgöz & alli. (2002) and Gorn & alli. (2004) demonstrated regarding the brightness component of color, it seems more pertinent to compare hue and brightness than to compare warm and cold colors when trying to ascertain what consumers recall and what spurs them to buy. Indeed, in everyday life, there is no trigger helping consumers to recall the content of an e-commerce website they visited or to compare it with another offer. The feeling of aggressiveness experienced by consumers when visiting an e-commerce website – partly due to the use of rather bright colors – does not result in a more effective retention of information, nor to a stronger buying intention.

When consulting a website, Internet users browse web pages designed to arouse their attention through the employment of various components such as color, sound, animation, texts, pictures, textures, graphic design and advertising. E-commerce website interfacing seeks to place consumers in a particular context by activating the sensory system (hearing or sight) so as to be able for web designers to perceive their emotional, cognitive, psychological, physiological and behavioral responses through their being altered.

Color Perception Within Interfaces

To this day the effects of the three color components on the Internet have been seldom documented. On a website, the interface represents the graphic chart, a set of rules composed of two colors: the foreground color, also called the "tonic" or "dynamic" color, and the background color, labeled the "dominant color" by webmasters. These colors reveal the contrast, which comes from a strong opposition between the foreground and the background colors, as the W3C defined it (Accessiweb, 2008). The main function of the

contrast serves to improve the readability of the displayed information, and, *a fortiori*, the memorization process. We contend that a better retention of information will enhance the perceived usability of the website.

Kiritani and Shirai (2003) show that the effects of background screen colors upon time perception vary according to the tasks performed by Internet users. When reading a text written on a white, blue or green background screen users have the feeling that time passes more slowly. When users are merely doing a simple search and only need to understand the meaning of the sentence, then the screen background color does not have any impact on how they perceive time duration. This temporal aspect figured significantly in the responses of interviewees to questions concerning usability.

Hill and Scharff (1997) have demonstrated the importance of contrast (dynamic color vs. dominant color) when searching for information within a page. They obtained better readability scores when resorting to chromatic colors (green dynamic color on yellow dominant color). This difference between colors (chromatic versus achromatic) merits some consideration since most current websites visited are black and white. Chromatic graphic charts and achromatic ones were differentiated during the experiment.

The results of the research undertaken by Corah and Gross (1967) suggest that recognition between the colors was achieved when the differences in contrast between the various forms and the standard forms were larger. The size and form of the displayed information contribute more than color to the perception of usability.

Camgöz & alli. (2002) observed that not only brightness and saturation but hue as well had a specific impact on each colored background screen they observed during an experiment where colored labels had been stuck on to background screens. Once again, a clear differentiation of the hue in association with particular brightness and saturation levels contributed to precise detailed recommendations with regard to the web designer's color choices while conceiving the website's interfaces.

Biers and Richards (2002) studied the impact of dominant color upon the perception of promoted items and found that backgrounds with cold hues such as blue display items to their advantage and reduced the risk of purchase postponement, especially as regards regular Internet users.

Hall and Hanna (2004) studied the readability of web pages according to their dominant and dynamic colors. According to them, sites promoting knowledge transfer must display black texts on white backgrounds and achromatic colors with maximum contrast. On the other hand, e-commerce websites should use chromatic colors due to the higher aesthetic appreciation score which is correlated to higher intents of purchase. These results underline the importance of taking into consideration the impact of the color's components (hue, brightness and saturation), as well as the contrasts occasioned by the foreground and background colors, to upgrade the usability of the e-commerce website interfaces. The consumer tends to remain longer on the e-commerce website according to certain criteria related to his or her perception of the interface. Pleasure, in particular, is thus increased by the deployment of colors whereas boredom can occur because of an inadequate deployment of them (Lemoine, 2008). The explanation of measures on the retention and buying intention variables reinforce the interest of these variables for this type of study.

From Ergonomics to Memorization

The concept of design on the Internet is often associated with ergonomics. The ergonomics of an e-commerce website refers to the readability of its pages, their composition, the whole structure of the website and its design. Its aim is to facilitate navigation inside the website. In the case of behavior directed towards a goal, ergonomics makes it possible to have easier access to the available,

relevant information (Helme-Guizon, 2001). Although the Internet frees the consumer from space and time constraints (Sheth and Sisodia, 1997), the products and services sought must be easily found thanks to the ease of navigation facilitated by the interface. The respondent of interview 1 underlines this: *"... yes I want to go quickly, because I look for pieces of music (profile of respondent: he is a musician) thus navigation must be fast"*.

The design and the readability of the Web pages influence the efficiency and the quality of the search for information. The consumer is able to act because of the interactivity of the computer which is, furthermore, under his control and so his fear of mishandling is overcome. *"Ensuring the readability of a web page, allows the visitor to obtain available information. Consequently, he has the optimal conditions under which to deliberate if purchasing on the commercial website is a possible goal. If the goal of the visit is to gather information with a view to purchasing later on the commercial website or at a sales outlet, then it is easier for him to memorize relevant information"* (Ladwein, 2001).

To measure the effects of color on interfaces, measures of the retained information allows us to identify which quality and which quantity of information an Internet user has memorized while visiting an e-commerce website. In agreement with the work of Hall and Hanna (2004), we suggest that retention varies according to the colors of the website, and especially according to the contrast arising from the dominant and dynamic colors. By taking the memorization variable into account, we wish to find a way of measuring how usable is an e-commerce website.

The Memorized Commercial Information

Memorization is a very important factor considering the large amount of information that exists on e-commerce websites. It is an important variable in this domain, since the users' tasks are often facilitated when they can retain information from one page to another. Thus, measures of high level processing, such as memorization, seem to be important in examining the impact of foreground and background color combinations on usability.

In general, information is stored according to an encoding process enabling one to sort out information thanks to criteria which will then allow one to retrieve this information. The role of these criteria is to connect one piece of information to other similar pieces of information already stored (Ladwein, 1999). In order to measure the information memorized by each participant, recognition and recall have been examined: two processes belonging to information retrieval based on overall stimulus in long-term memory. After visiting Musicashop.net – an e-commerce website selling music CD's especially designed for the experiment – participants were asked to answer questions related to the items they had just viewed. Users were instructed to look at, at least two items so as to make the survey accessible. Their memory had to be sufficiently complete in order to consider the questions related to memorization, that is why they had to consult two articles at least. Be it free or cued, recall enables individuals to mimic mentally a stimulus to which they are not exposed at the time of the evocation, for instance their past reaction to a promotional action (Filser, 1994).

Buying Intention

Intention is activated by a desire or a need (Darpy, 1997) and desire is viewed as an active process (O'Shaughnessy, 1992). Though buying intention is more than a mere desire, it is not a promise to buy (O'Shaughnessy, 1992), it is the outcome of a cognitively handled desire. Here is the definition given by Darpy (1997) echoing the studies of O'Shaughnessy (1992), Howard (1994) and Belk (1985): *"Intention results from a desire or*

a need handled on the cognitive level and leading the intention to purchase".

Among the environmental factors recognized to produce important emotional and behavioral reactions on the consumer, color seems to play a big role. It serves to retain consumers longer on the e-commerce website according to certain criteria related to their perception of the interface. This duration thanks to a proper use of colors can help maintain user interest in a site (Bucklin and Sismeiro, 2003, Hanson, 2000) and give users more time to consider and complete purchase transactions (Bucklin and Sismeiro, 2003).

Affect: A Mediating Variable

Another aspect we wish to bring to the fore concerns the effects of colors upon the affective response, which includes the emotions and moods experienced when visiting e-commerce websites. One can indeed think that the usability afforded can enhance the experienced affective response. Emotions are short-lived but extremely intense. Their cause is often apparent and their cognitive content is obvious (joy, sadness, anger, fear, disgust). Their most obvious features are brevity and intensity. While emotions imply some kind of awareness of the information about the background and consequences of actions, moods refer to affective states of mind less likely to reach our consciousness. Moreover, they last longer than emotions but are less intense (Forgeas, 1999).

Once we conducted our literature review and analyzed what the respondents said during the exploratory analysis, we were able to propose our research hypothesis described in the following section.

The Exploratory Qualitative Analysis

In order to adapt the conceptual model applied in our research to the literature, and in order to check and validate the nature of the constructs we wished to measure, we needed to conduct exploratory, qualitative analysis prior to the experiment. This was also a way to acquire primary data in order to explore and become familiar with the usability topic. Its form was based on a clinical approach in which semi-directing talks were conducted. It also incorporated a method of projection likely to bring the researcher(s) more details of what the respondents were really thinking about when describing a website. These interviews were appropriate since people felt freer to describe their experience than during focus groups or than if an open questionnaire had been solicited. The limits of our topic were then defined according to the exploration of the motivations, attitudes and values of our respondents. This analysis was a way to understand their behavior and decision-making processes, in order to prepare the confirmatory analysis. Both analyses (exploratory and confirmatory) are essential to this research project.

The interviews were carried out with consumers and webmasters. Our aim consisted of investigating whether changes on the Internet interface would lead to consumer satisfaction with respect to e-commerce websites.

The objectives of the qualitative study were pursued on the basis of the following questions:

- Is color one of the atmospheric elements which most influences the consumer's answers?
- Do consumers feel particular emotions while shopping on e-commerce websites? If yes, does color affect the emotions of the consumers?
- Does an e-commerce website's color make it possible to define the behavioral responses of the consumer?
- Which aspects of quality and quantity of information are retained following a period of shopping on an e-commerce website?

We thus used an interview guide to collect the needed information to accomplish our objectives. On the basis of semi-directing talks conducted with web designers and average consumers, topics referring to the emotional states experienced by the consumer were elicited while shopping on the Internet. These topics related to emotions and moods, demonstrate the importance attached to the ease of use of a website by the consumers. They also reinforce the effects of variables such as color as well as the quality of the images perceived by the consumers.

Participants

The consumers we questioned were chosen according to their expertise in the use of websites (webmaster/simple user), their age, their sex and their social background. The identification of experts as opposed to your average user was significant in meeting the qualitative criteria as regards the selection of people. The control question which we posed was: *"have you already conceived or built a website?"*

Method

For the criterion of saturation of the data being retained (Mucchielli, 1991, p. 114), we interviewed 21 people. The interviews were semi structured. This allowed us to obtain interviews based on subjects connected to the experience of consumption regarding the references on e-commerce websites. These interviews were often handled with a certain emotion. We adopted a neutral attitude with regard to the participants so as not to influence them in the way they answered. The participants had to respond to questions without being able to see a computer screen, so that they only answered by recalling the information gleaned during their navigation on the e-commerce website of their choice. Once every interview was transcribed, this amounted to one hundred pages. The interviews lasted from 13 to 47 minutes.

Results

The exploratory qualitative analysis enabled us to note that color was actually an integral part of the atmosphere on e-commerce websites. Color even seems to hold a more important role than we originally anticipated: it was referred to more than 79 times during the interviews. Some elements which appear essential to the interface are:

- elements related to usage and to the organization of the website, thanks to its clarity and the readability of its tree structure
- elements allowing a rapid navigation within the site, by the provision of search engines in particular

Color was actually mentioned by all the interviewees as a means of principal location within the interface of the site. It is perceived as an aid to move on the website and sometimes caused aggravation if it appeared too violent.

at times you feel aggravated, irritated, because it does not function well, because there are bugs or because it attacks you, yes it can attack you, when it is too "violent" at the level of the colors (respondent 14).

Not only is color part of the design of the website, but when soft, it also seems to comfort consumers thus filling them with enough self-confidence to buy an item in an environment to be "tamed":

What I like in the Boursorama website is that it is comfortable. Comfortable visually speaking I would say. (respondent 16)

Color serve the organization of the information by highlighting useful zones systematically sought by the surveyed Internet users:

it remains practical, therefore with really accessible doors, or in any case visible, where I am able to make my reference marks easily; by zones possibly defined by executives, and then zones of text in fact. A regrouping of texts on certain places. (respondent 5).

When used in compliance with the contrasts advocated by Itten (1970), color can prove very timesaving, a major asset in the relationship between consumers and websites.

I will spend more time on a site which has a large catalog, or products similar to what I seek, therefore always containing contents.

As we mentioned earlier, making the information search easier by implementing strategies specific to ergonomics and human computer interaction, the colors encountered when browsing an e-commerce website enable Internet users to appropriate it more easily, according to its layout.

Thus there is the speed already, it is important but it can be faster due to the material with ADSL or not, ... I do not know if one can control this, and if not, colors help to locate what one wants a little bit, how to explain that... if it is clear and neat if the screen were looked at by far, one knows what the various parts of the site contain more or less. But it is true that the most important things for me are the links.

The usability thus seems to play an important role in the consumer's perception of the e-commerce website's services and information provided. The content analysis allowed us to verify that the color played an important role in the emotional states experienced while of shopping on the Internet. This also allowed us to determine certain characteristics appropriate for the Internet purchase which differentiates this act from those used to traditional buying conditions. The respondent of interview 19 confirms this by saying that *"...the more readable the site, the more one wants to spend time on it"*. He further reinforces his assertion about the factors which discourage him from revisiting a particular website: *"... if the site is complicated to access, has a complicated address in the address bar which is completely unmemorizable in order to revisit the same page, difficult to read, too busy... "*. This testimony corresponds to that of the respondent of interview 3 who is more direct about the appearance of the e-commerce website: *"... its brightness encourages me to go and consult a commercial website, if it is clear and convivial. And what discourages me is if it is all the contrary"*.

Discussion

Links need to be easily located. Their recognition can be facilitated by color, which constitutes one of the characteristics of information systems: to make any zone of the page more easily interactive by the creation of an effect which changes the state of a textual link or a button when the mouse scans over it. Independently of the graphic style of the link, it is important that the visitor can discriminate very quickly what the important links are and understand where they lead (Spool & alii, 1999).

The non-recognition of these links can quickly become tiring and frustrating. Their recognition,

which corresponds to fast identification of the possible actions on the website, is crucial for the consumer to get the impression that he is in control of the website. The recourse to color is thus pivotal in making links easily recognizable.

A quantitative analysis follows, showing that the effects obtained by the colors of an e-commerce website on the Internet user, and in particular on his affective states, are not neutral.

RESEARCH MODEL AND HYPOTHESES

Our research is based on the "Stimulus-Organization-Answer" model of the atmosphere of an Internet website found in the Mehrabian and Russel (1974) model (Figure 1). The proposed hypotheses of these models are the following:

H1: The usability of the e-commerce website with regard to colors and text positively influences the memorizing of commercial information and the intention to purchase.

H2: The usability of the e-commerce website with regard to colors positively influences the affective response of the consumer.

Figure 1. Conceptual model of the research

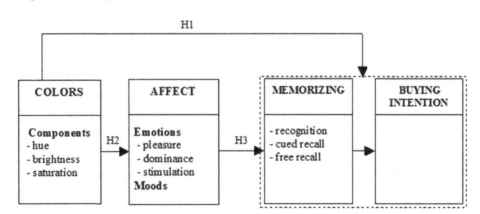

H3: A positive affective response felt by the consumer while shopping on an e-commerce website positively influences the memorizing of commercial information and the intention to purchase.

After this exploratory qualitative analysis, we conducted a quantitative analysis to confirm the results obtained so far. To do so, we carried out a lab experiment based on the conceptual model of the experiment. This is presented below, before describing the experimental design of the experiment conducted.

Research Model

The model explains how the atmosphere of an e-commerce website and particularly the color variable and its components (hue, brightness, saturation) can have an impact upon the buyer's emotional and cognitive state, upon his or her perception, which affects his or her buyer behavior on several levels as well as his memorization. Both can then lead to an appreciation of the perceived usability of the e-commerce website. This model draws inspiration from Mehrabian and Russell's SOR model (Stimuli Organism Response) used in environmental psychology (Mehrabian and Russell, 1974) (Figure 1).

Research Method

The essential purpose of the experiment is to measure the cause and effect relationship and thus to verify hypotheses of causality. This is accomplished by the comparison of various factorial plans, which were various graphic charts in our case.

Participants

Undergraduate students (440) from design school marketing classes participated in the experiment. After a few adjustments with the fictive e-com-

merce website and after deleting those participants who did not finish the questionnaire and those who were color bind, we finally obtained 296 useful responses. The sample of these final respondents is presented hereafter (Table 1).

Research Design

The experiment design included 8 treatments (4 x 2) related to the 8 graphic charts devised for the website dedicated to the experiment. We observed the results related to brightness and saturation, the variations of which depended on the hues carefully selected beforehand.

To devise our first experimental design we employed the graphic chart used by Hill et Scharff (1997) which registered the best readability rate

Table 1. Characteristics of the sample of respondents to the experiment

Characteristics		% of sample
Sex	Female Male	160 136
Age	Under 25 years old 25 to 34 years old 35 to 44 years old 45 to 54 years old 55 to 64 years old	242 29 13 11 1
Education	Certificate High school 2nd-year university diploma License / Master I /Master II Postgraduate / doctorate / post-graduate / Master degree no diploma	2 166 49 36 42 1
Job	Executives and academics Intermediate occupations Manual Workers Students Storekeepers and business managers Pensioners Other (to clarify)	32 3 2 244 4 1 10
Income per month	From 0 to 500 euros Under 1000 euros From 1000 to 1399 euros From 1400 to 1799 euros From 1800 to 2199 euros From 2200 to 2599 euros	247 15 11 5 9 9

in relation to contrast and we chose as chromatic colors a yellow dominant and a green dynamic. Starting from this chart, we inflected the brightness level of the two colors so as to obtain the second experimental design (Table 2). For experimental designs 3 and 4 we kept the same colors but switched dynamic and dominant colors. Experimental designs 5, 6, 7 and 8 are based on black and white (achromatic colors), the ones most frequently used on e-commerce websites with different brightness and saturation levels, such as the experimental designs we chose relying on green and yellow hues.

A lab experiment was conducted on 296 participants. Carrying out this experiment under laboratory conditions allowed us to draw valid conclusions about the groups surveyed (Jolibert and Jourdan, 2006). A study focusing on the color variable requires that at least three aspects of e-purchase be taken into consideration (Figure 3). (Read Appendices 1 for details)

Table 2. Effects of graphic chart colors upon cued and free recalls

Effects of graphic chart colors upon cued recall			
	DF	F	p-value
Hue	3	0.404	0.750
Brightness	1	0.771	0.381
Hue x Brightness	3	0.616	0.616
Effects of graphic chart colors upon free recall			
	DF	F	p-value
Hue	3	0.288	0.834
Brightness	1	0.049	0.835
Hue x Brightness	3	2.484	0.061*

Figure 2. Factorial design of the experiment

Graphic charts	Plan	Background				Foreground				*Plans explanations*
		Name	H	B	S	Name	H	B	S	
Chart 1 - chromatic colors- Green and Yellow	1	Magnolia yellow	60	100	20	Newsvine Green	120	40	100	(Hill and Scharff, 1997) showed that the sharp contrasts of his chart offered users the fastest reading speed possible.
	2	Magnolia yellow	60	100	20	Granny Apple Green	90	80	100	Same chart as in the **Plan 1** with increased dynamic color brightness (from 40 to 80).
	3	Newsvine Green	120	40	100	Magnolia yellow	60	100	20	Same colors as in **Plan 1.** Dynamic and dominant colors were switched.
	4	Newsvine Green	120	40	100	Sunflower yellow	60	100	60[1]	Same color chart as in **Plan 3** with a decrease in dynamic color brightness (from 80 to 40).
Chart 2 - Achromatic colors - Black et White	5	White	0	100	0	Black	0	0	0	This chart is the most widely used one on e-commerce websites.
	6	White	0	100	0	Grey	0	60	0	Same color chart as **Plan 5** with increased dynamic color brightness (from 0 to 60).
	7	Black	0	0	0	White	0	100	0	Same colors chart as in **Plan 5**. Dynamic and dominant colors have been switched.
	8	Black	0	0	0	Grey	0	60	0	Same color chart as in **Plan 7** with a decrease in dynamic color brightness (from 100 to 60).

1 The color which should have been used for the text of the experimental plan 4, in order to preserve rates of luminosity and saturation in relation to the background color, could not be preserved. Indeed, this chart could not be used given the lack of contrast between the two colors (foreground/background) which made the reading impossible on a more or less old or difficult screen, for an individual with difficulty distinguishing colors we refer to the directives of the w3c. We thus varied its degree of saturation.

Procedure

In order to measure the differences in color perception, we created 8 different graphic charts with varied hues, brightness and saturation levels. The color stimuli were modified in accordance with Munsell's system (Munsell, 1969), considered to be the most accurate system of this type (Aumont, 1994) which enabled us to precisely define several levels of brightness and saturation for each hue. Respondents were asked to enter a room where all conditions had been controlled before they started the procedure.

Measures

Memorization

Memorization was gauged by measuring recognition, cued recall and free recall. To measure recognition, we observed how participants recognized the CD cover when seeing it simultaneously with two other covers of different albums by the same artist. Recall scores varied from 0 to 2 at the minimum. It is worth noting that some participants had viewed more than two items.

Cued recall was measured by observing how users reacted to the seven commercial pieces of information appearing on each page of the catalogue, presented the same way for each item. Scores could thus be graded from 0 to 7 for each item visited. Since participants were required to

Figure 3. Conditions of the experiment

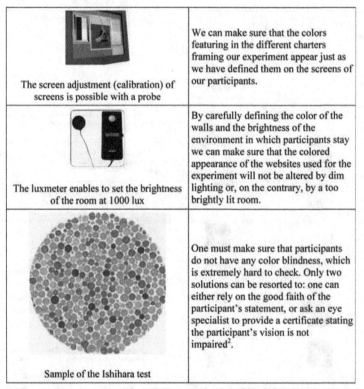

The screen adjustment (calibration) of screens is possible with a probe	We can make sure that the colors featuring in the different charters framing our experiment appear just as we have defined them on the screens of our participants.
The luxmeter enables to set the brightness of the room at 1000 lux	By carefully defining the color of the walls and the brightness of the environment in which participants stay we can make sure that the colored appearance of the websites used for the experiment will not be altered by dim lighting or, on the contrary, by a too brightly lit room.
Sample of the Ishihara test	One must make sure that participants do not have any color blindness, which is extremely hard to check. Only two solutions can be resorted to: one can either rely on the good faith of the participant's statement, or ask an eye specialist to provide a certificate stating the participant's vision is not impaired[2].

2 Asking a participant for such a certificate would assuredly have allowed him/her to guess that our experiment was focused on color, which would have biased the experiment. Following recommendations from eye specialist Professor Lanthony, we decided to have each participant take the Ishihara test in a room separate from the one where the experiment was conducted.

consult at least two items, scores for the cued recall could then range from 0 to 14 at the minimum. Participants had sometimes examined more than two items.

In order to measure free recall, participants typed their answer to an open-ended question related to the CD cover they had just examined. A certain number of items used in the product's description were expected to be identified. No matter what the item was, the description could not exceed 142 characters and there was an average number of 20 items per product. Since participants could visit more than two articles, the score to measure free recall could range from 0 to 40 at the minimum.

The score of commercial information memorization refers to the sum of the recognition score, cued recall score and free recall score.

Buying Intention

Considering that e-commerce's website's colors are likely to have an impact on the intent of purchase, we set out to measure these. We used a three item scale developed by Yoo and Donthu (2001) which had already been used in a similar context and in which its internal consistency proved reliable. The items were measured on a 5-point Likert scale ranging from strongly disagree (1) to strongly agree (5). Already used in a similar context, its internal consistency had proved to be reliable.

Emotions

In order to interpret colors one must go through a cognitive process which, in turn, arouses emotions in the Internet user. These emotions can fill users with a desire to buy, leading them to make a purchase or to leave the website. Perceived differently by each Internet user, depending on his or her own way of perceiving colors, emotions involve a shift in his or her behavior as a consumer.

Mehrabian and Russell (1974) point out two sets of methodological issues related to colors and emotions. The first one has to do with the lack of control or specification over the color stimulus; take, by way of illustration, the lack of control over saturation and brightness when focusing on hues. We endeavored to control this aspect by resorting to Munsell's system (Munsell, 1969) of defining the colors selected for our experiment's chart. The second methodological issue has to do with the question of reliability and validity of the tools used to measure emotional responses to color stimuli.

To measure the emotions of participants visiting an e-commerce website, we used Mehrabian and Russell's PAD scale (Pleasure Arousal Dominance) (Mehrabian and Russell, 1974).

- **Pleasure:** Pleasure / displeasure, assessing the well-being experienced by the individual;
- **Arousal (stimulation):** Arousal / nonarousal, assessing the consumer's level of awareness (to the item) and activation;
- **Dominance (domination):** Dominance / submission, assessing the feeling of freedom pervading the consumer when buying something on a website.

Since the reliability of the PAD scale remained continuously high and satisfactory throughout the experiments conducted by Valdez and Mehrabian (1994), this method was chosen. Originating in the studies of Osgood & alli. (1957) already centered on the "evaluation, activation and potency" triptych, this scale is still the most widely used to measure the consumer's affective state (Derbaix and Poncin, 2005).

Moods

An emotion related to a color is perceived either as positive or negative according to the individual's personal associations with this color (Boyatzis and Varghese, 1993). As a rule, different colors tend to call forth different moods (Odom and

Figure 4. Effects of brightness upon free recall

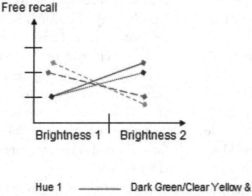

Sholtz, 2004). Therefore, we have chosen to measure the latter. To do so we utilized Mayer and Gaschke's BMIS 16-constructs scale (Mayer and Gaschke, 1988), the "Brief Mood Introspection Scale". We selected it because it provides a quite exhaustive range of moods and is easy to implement.

Results

We followed both the General Linear Model (GLM) to test the impact of the colors of the graphic chart and the analyses of variance (ANOVA) to analyze experimental data to define the meaning and accuracy of the variables. By incorporating interaction effects with a series of regressions for each of the dependant variables, we tested the interaction variables.

Direct Effects of the Colors of the Graphic Chart Upon Memorization

The colors did not show a significant impact upon cued recall, according to the GLM analysis. However, an interaction effect on free recall was noted ($F = 2.484$; $p \leq 0.061*$) (Table 2).

Participants managed to provide equivalent answers to closed questions about the content of the website, no matter which colors were featured in the graphic chart (cued recall). Those questions actually helped Internet users to retain information in that they accurately summarized the information that could be easily memorized by consumers. When no help was provided and visitors had to remember what they saw on the website (free recall), colors proved very helpful to them. This is significant in that it shows that color needs to be taken into consideration when conceiving usable graphic charts. Indeed, color helps to retain the information and memorization seems helpful to evaluate the e-commerce's website usability.

After studying the ANOVAs carried out, we noted that brightness affected free recall most significantly when hue 2 (green dominant color, yellow dynamic color) was implemented. Individuals exposed to a low level of brightness (brightness 1) remembered the content of the website better than individuals exposed to a high level of brightness (brightness 2) (Figure 4).

Through this result, we now understand that a lower contrast between dominant color and dynamic color enhances the retention of the commercial information provided on the website.

Direct Effects of the Colors of the Graphic Chart Upon Buying Intention

The results of the GLM analysis demonstrate that a graphic chart of an Internet website strongly influences buying intention. Brightness plays an important role in buying intention (F = 15.201, p ≤ 0.000***). Just as memorization does, we note that when the dominant and dynamic color brightness is not too strong, then buying intentions are the highest (Table 3).

The GLM analysis shows that hue and brightness have an effect upon buying intention (F = 3.732; p≤0.012*). The results of the ANOVA show that the effect of brightness on buying intention is only significant as regards hues 1 (yellow = dominant color, and green = dynamic color) and 2 (green = dominant color and yellow = dynamic color), with a chromatic color hue, but has no particular effect with a black and white hue chart. When contrast is higher and brightness increased, memorization decreases (Figure 4).

The Relationship Between Memorization and Buying Intention

A simple regression enables us to observe that free recall has a positive effect on buying intentions (F = 3.824; p ≤ 0.051*). The more information an individual memorizes about a product, the stronger his or her buying intention will be (Table 4).

Table 3. Effects of graphic chart colors upon buying intention

	DF	F	p-value
Hue	3	0.349	0.790
Brightness	1	**15.201**	**0.000***
Hue x Brightness	3	**3.732**	**0.012***

Table 4. Effects of graphic chart colors upon buying intention

	DF	F	p-value
Hue	3	0.349	0.790
Brightness	1	**15.201**	**0.000***
Hue x Brightness	3	**3.732**	**0.012***

Figure 5. Effects of brightness upon buying intention

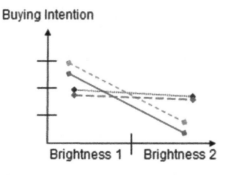

Hue 1	————	Dark Green/Clear Yellow & Clear Green/Clear Yellow
Hue 2	- - - - -	Clear Yellow/Dark Green & Dark Yellow/Dark Green
Hue 3	————	Black/White & Grey/Black
Hue 4	— — — —	White/Black & Grey/Black

Table 5. Effects of graphic chart colors upon emotions

Effects of graphic chart colors upon pleasure			
	DF	F	p-value
Hue	3	1.606	0.188
Brightness	1	0.330	0.566
Hue x Brightness	3	0.567	0.637

Effects of graphic chart colors upon stimulation			
Hue	3	1.243	0.294
Brightness	**1**	**3.167**	**0.076***
Hue x Brightness	3	0.154	0.927

Effects of graphic chart colors upon domination			
Hue	3	0.105	0.957
Brightness	1	0.705	0.402
Hue x Bightness	3	0.338	0.798

Observation of the Mediating Effect of Emotions

The GLM analysis demonstrates that the colors of the graphic chart affect emotions in a negative way because low brightness enhances stimulation (F = 3.167; p ≤ 0.076). However, the colors of the graphic chart do not affect pleasure nor domination in any way (Table 5).

Table 6. Effects of graphic chart colors upon mood

Effects of graphic chart colors on positive mood factor			
	DF	F	p-value
Hue	3	0.374	0.772
Brightness	1	0.041	0.840
Hue x Brightness	3	0.916	0.434

Effects of graphic chart colors on negative mood factor			
	DF	F	p-value
Hue	3	1.159	0.326
Brightness	1	0.334	0.564
Hue x Brightness	**3**	**3.042**	**0.029***

Stimulation does not affect memorization in a significant way (free recall) but does have a significant effect upon buying intention.

Observation of the Mediating Effect of Mood

GLM analyses show that hue and brightness have a significant interactive effect on negative mood (F = 3.042; p ≤ 0.029*) (Table 6).

ANOVAs show that a graphic chart based on hues 1 (dynamic = Newsvine Green / dominant = Magnolia Yellow and dynamic = Granny Apple Green / dominant = Magnolia Yellow) and 4 (dominant = black and dynamic = white) offers an interactive effect between hue and brightness. When resorting to hue 1 (Newsvine Green/Magnolia Yellow and Granny Apple Green/Magnolia Yellow), an increase in brightness entails a significant increase in negative mood, while with hue 4 (White/Black - Grey/Black), an increase in the brightness level contributes to toning down negative mood (F = 3.815; p ≤ 0.055*). Two simple regressions give evidence that negative mood has a significant and negative impact upon buying intention (t = -0.129; p ≤ 0.001*), but does not have any effect upon memorization (free recall) (Table 7).

DISCUSSION AND IMPLICATIONS

The results of the research suggest that the colors used on e-commerce websites have an effect on

Table 7. Regression between negative mood and buying intention

	Buying intention
Negative mood	**-0.129**
Constant	- 8.215E-17
F = 3.824 ; R² = 1.3%	

* p < 0.1 ** p < 0.01

consumer retention of information and buying intention. Two mediating variables – stimulation and negative mood – helped us to explain how colors reinforce these effects.

The possibility offered on certain e-commerce websites of seeing quality representations of the products contributes to the consumer experiencing a state of mind favorable to shopping. A representation of quality depends on the consumer being able to magnify the image so that the product appears larger. This is the case with the items on music websites or data processing websites, like the Apple website, for example. An image makes it possible for the consumer to see the product in another color, another pattern or another texture as with clothes and cars websites such as Smart, for example. This reinforces the feeling of well-being when shopping.

For the respondent of interview 17, *"… the fact that the images are clear is rather important, with products like music, books, photographs; there is need for at least a minimum of illustrations that hold my attention, especially if the image of the product is clear. I do not like to see a fuzzy image of a product, badly compressed"*. All the images that we see on the Internet are compressed so as to be exported in a readable format by the navigators such as Internet Explorer or Firefox.

The graphic composition of the website can affect the representation that the consumer retains when shopping. This composition thus should exploit the perception of the interface and the retention of the whole website and commercial information that is available on its pages.

Ergonomics and Design Rely on Color

Simplicity of movement on the website makes it possible to entertain consumers. This constitutes a new area of research which is starting to gain momentum. This does not seem surprising taking into account the usual population of Internet consumers and consumers in general, i.e. young people or those having a young "spirit". Ergonomics and a sought-after usability, thanks to a subtle use of colors, seem to encourage the likelihood of revisiting the website. The exploratory qualitative analysis conducted within the framework of this research has enabled us to emphasize topics such as "playability". At the same time, it has shown us to what extent the expertise of the consumer in the act of purchasing on the Internet was important. This could then facilitate the conceptual and practical grasp of the interface, making the act of buying simpler, and thus more pleasant.

Chromatic colors seem to be more likely to enhance the memorization of the displayed information than black and white (achromatic colors). These results are in keeping with the studies conducted by Silverstein (1987), who noticed that monochrome screens entailed more eye-strain and overall tiredness.

It appears indispensable to maintain the conditions under which we conducted our experiment – conditions complying with the criteria used to evaluate the color quality of digital interfaces – those which enable one to benefit from an accurate and easy to implement tool (Fernandez-Maloigne, 2004 ; Munsell, 1969). For future experiments related to the measurement of cybershopper perception, memorization or buying intention, one should undoubtedly take into consideration brightness and saturation rates. When focusing on textures, matte and glossy aspects, "an essential parameter of Japanese sensitivity that is all too often overlooked by Western standards" (Pastoureau, 1999), researchers can obtain more accurate outcomes in their studies dealing with screen colors in a business-driven context. Coupled with the use of auditory functions on e-commerce websites, these analyses would enable us to reach a better understanding of the effects of the atmosphere pervading such and such e-commerce websites upon consumers, especially according to a holistic rather than atomized approach to the phenomenon. The three-dimensional textures used on Flash billboards, videos or virtual worlds such as Second Life suggest greater complexity.

The psychobiological measurements based on the movement study of the muscles of the face and in particular on detection of electric activity in the muscles would surely also afford interesting results since the corrugator, the so called "muscle of the pathetic color", corresponds to the frown muscle, which is likely to function when the consumer is challenged by the difficulty of reading, including/understanding or retaining information posted on the screen.

The studies rising from electromyography (a technique of recording the electrical activity of the muscles and the nerves) from Haley, Staffaroni and Fox (1994), Crimmins (1997), as well as Hazlett and Hazlett (1999), relating to the treatment of advertisements, show that the zygomatics (put in action by negative emotional reactions) highlight a better recall of the televised advertisements by evoking more emotional reactions.

These requirements are now sufficiently known so that web designers take them into account before designing a website. Among these principles, let us not forget the regulations applying to public service sites of public service which force them to respect a minimum level of accessibility. Within a framework of sustainable development, the e-commerce websites sensitive to the problem of disabled people show a willingness to address their needs and as such serve as exemplars for other sites. To arrive at this level of accessibility by making it possible for the greatest number to discover the contents of a Web page, a certain number of principles of construction must be taken into account.

On the Internet, 80% of the information memorized by an individual comes from the visual sense and the other forms of perception of the environment are similarly influenced by the sight albeit to a lesser degree (Mattelart 1996). However, accessibility is not solely intended to help partially-sighted persons. Deaf people as well as physically handicapped persons must also be able to access the Internet. Among the various criteria of accessibility set up by consortium W3C and WAI (department of the W3C specializing in accessibility), worth mentioning are:

- a simple HTML code
- the use of cascade style sheets (CSS) functioning on HTML pages
- a separation between content and form
- the alternatives to purely graphic, audio, video elements

We see here that accessibility is not only related to ergonomics, but also to usability or "playability" and these do not prevent the creators from being creative. It is a question above all of indicating to the consumer the solutions which give access to information and services on the site. In addition to serving a greater number, accessibility, which is based on the use of a well structured HTML code separating the contents (commercial information) from the form (the style sheet), is easier to maintain and develop when the site loads more rapidly and is better referenced by search engines than a "normal" website. These characteristics related to the time of loading of the pages and the referencing of the Internet website constitute imperative reasons to take accessibility into account in a systematic manner in the design phase.

REFERENCES

Accessiweb. (2008). Publication du 9 juin 2008, *Version 1.1 du référentiel AccessiWeb créé par le consortium W3C*, Retrieved from http://www.accessiweb.org/

ACSEL. (2007). Association pour le Commerce et les Services en Ligne. Retrieved from http://www.acsel.asso.fr/barometres/barometres_e-commerce.asp

Aumont, J. (1994). *Introduction à la couleur: des discours aux images*. Paris: Armand Colin.

Baccino, T., & Colombi, T. (2001). L'analyse des mouvements des yeux sur le Web. In A. Vom Hofe (dir.). *Les interactions Homme-Système: perspectives et recherches psycho-ergonomiques* (127-148). Paris: Hermès.

Baker, J. (1986). The role of environment in marketing services: the consumer perspective. In Czpeil J.A., Congram C., Shanaham J., (Ed.), *The Services Marketing Challenge: Integrated for Competitive Advantage* (pp. 79–84). Chicago: American Marketing Association.

Belk, R. W. (1985). Issues in the Intention-Behavior Discrepancy. In Sheth Jagdish N., (eds.), *Research in Consumer Behavior*, (Vol. 1, pp. 1-34). Greenwich, CT: JAI Press.

Bellizzi, J. A., & Hite, R. E. (1992). Environmental Color, Consumer Feelings, and Purchase Likelihood. *Psychology and Marketing*, *9*(September-October), 347–364. doi:10.1002/mar.4220090502

Biers, K., & Richards, L. (2002). *Web Page Background Color Evaluative Effect On Selected Product Attributes*. Research paper, Utah State University.

Boyatzis, C. J., & Varghese, R. (1993). Children's emotional associations with colors. *The Journal of Genetic Psychology*, *155*, 77–85.

Bucklin, R. E., & Sismeiro, C. (2003). A model of web site browsing behavior estimated on clickstream data. *JMR, Journal of Marketing Research*, *40*, 249–267. doi:10.1509/jmkr.40.3.249.19241

Camgöz, N., Yener, N., & Güvenç, D. (2002). Effects of hue, saturation, and brightness on preference. *Color Research and Application*, *27*(3), 199–207. doi:10.1002/col.10051

Cho, J. (2004). Likelihood to abort an online transaction: influences from cognitive evaluations, attitudes, and behavioral variables. *Information & Management*, *41*, 827–838. doi:10.1016/j.im.2003.08.013

Churchill, G. A. Jr. (1979). A Paradigm for Developing Better Measures of Marketing Constructs. *JMR, Journal of Marketing Research*, *16*(1), 64–73. doi:10.2307/3150876

Corah, N. L., & Gross, J. B. (1967). Hue, Brightness, and Saturation Variables in Color Form Matching. *Child Development*, *38*(1), 137–142. doi:10.2307/1127135

Crimmins, J. C. (1997). *Inference and impact, Measuring advertising effectiveness*, (éd. W.D. Wells). Mahwah, NJ: Lawrence Erlbaum Associates.

Darpy, D. (1997). Une variable médiatrice du report d'achat: La procrastination. *Communication au 13ème Congrès International de l'AFM*, Toulouse, France.

Demers, E., & Lev, B. (2001). A rude awakening: internet shakeout in 2000. *Review of Accounting Studies*, *6*, 331–359. doi:10.1023/A:1011675227890

Derbaix, C. & Poncin, I. (2005). La mesure des réactions affectives en marketing: évaluation des principaux outils. *Recherche and Applications en Marketing, Numéro spécial sur La Mesure*, *20*(2), 55-76.

Divard, R. & Urien, B. (2001). The Consumer Lives in a Colored World. *Recherche et Applications en Marketing*, 3-24.

Donovan, R. J. & Rossiter, J. R. (1982). Store atmosphere: an environmental psychology approach. *J Retailing, Spring, 58*, 34-57.

Dreze, X., & Zufryden, F. (1997). Testing Web Site Design and Promotional Content. *Journal of AdGREENising Research*, *37*(2), 77–91.

Drugeon-Lichtlé M.-C. (1996). *Les effets des couleurs d'une annonce magazine sur les émotions du consumer: conceptualisation et résultats d'une étude exploratoire*. Actes de l'Association Française de Marketing, 12, Poitiers, 445-458.

Drugeon-Lichtlé, M.-C. (2002). *Couleur d'une annonce publicitaire, goûts des individus et perception des marque. Décisions Marketing, 26*(April/June), abi/inform global, 29.

Dunn, B. (1992, August 10). Choice of Color for Product Can Be Critical Factor. *Gazette*, 6.

Ekman, P., & Friesen, W. (1975). *Unmasking the face*. Upper Saddle River, NJ: Prentice Hall.

Fernandez-Maloigne, C. (2004). Quelle métrique pour l'évaluation de la qualité couleur d'une image numérique? *Application à la compression JPEG2000, CAM Conférence*, Paris, octobre.

Filser, M. (1994). *Le comportement du consommateur*. Paris: Précis Dalloz.

Filser, M. (2003a). Le marketing sensoriel: la quête de l'intégration théorique et managériale. *Revue Française du Marketing, 194*(4/5, Septembre), 5-11.

Filser, M. (2003b). Vingt ans de recherches en comportement du consumer. In Rémy, I. Garabuau-Moussaoui, D. Desjeux and M. Filser, (eds), *Sociétés, Consommation et Consommateurs* (pp. 15-20). L'Harmattan.

Fleury, P., & Imbert, C. (1996). Couleur. In *Encyclopeadia Universalis, 6*, 676-681.

Forgeas, J. P. (1999). *Network theories and beyond*. In T. Dalgleish & M. J. Power, (éds.), *Handbook of Cognition and Emotion*, (pp. 591-612). Chichester, UK: Wiley.

Gignac, T. (2000). Breaking the online barrier: an estimated 95 percent of Web sites are inaccessible to disabled users ± not a smart business move. *Calgary Herald* [Front.]. *Computers Section, 17*(August), V7.

Gorn, G., Chattopadhyay, A., Sengupta, J., & Tripathi, S. (2004). Waiting for the web: how screen color affects time perception. *JMR, Journal of Marketing Research, 41*(May), 215–225. doi:10.1509/jmkr.41.2.215.28668

Haley, R. I., Staffaroni, J., & Fox, A. (1994). The missing measures of copy testing. *Journal of Advertising Research, 34*(3), 46–61.

Hall, R. H., & Hanna, P. (2004). The Impact of Web Page Text-Background Color Combinations on Readability. *Retention, Aesthetics, and Behavioral Intention . Behaviour & Information Technology, 23*(3), 183–195. doi:10.1080/01449 290410001669932

Hanson, W. A. (2000). *Principles of Internet Marketing*. Cincinnati, OH: South-Western College Publishers.

Hazlett, R. L., & Hazlett, S. Y. (1999). Emotional response to television commercials: facial EMG vs. self-report. *Journal of Advertising Research, 39*(2), 7–23.

Helme-Guizon, A. (2001). Le comportement du consommateur sur un site web marchand est-il fondamentalement différent de son comportement en magasin? *Proposition d'un cadre d'appréhension de ses spécificités, Recherche et Applications en marketing*.

Hill, A., & Scharff, L. V. (1997). Readability of websites with various foreground/background color combinations, font types and word styles. In *Proceedings of 11th National Conference in Undergraduate Research, 2*, 742-746.

Howard, J. A. (1994). *Buyer Behavior in Marketing Strategy*. Englewood Cliffs, NJ: Prentice Hall.

Itten, J. (1970). *The elements of Color*. New York: Van Nostrand Reinhold Company.

Izard, C. E. (1971). *The face of emotion*. New York: Appleton-Century-Crofts.

Jacobs, L. W., & Suess, J. F. (1975). Effects of Four Psychological Primary Colors on Anxiety State. *Perceptual and Motor Skills, 41*(1), 207–210.

Jolibert, A., & Jourdan, P. (2006). Marketing Research. *Méthodes de recherche et d'études en marketing*. Paris: Dunod.

Kiritani, Y., & Shirai, S. (2003). Effects of background colors on user's experience in reading website. *Journal of the Asian Design International Conference, Academic Journal, 1*, 64.

Kotler, P. (1973). Atmosphere as a marketing tool. *Journal of Retailing, 49*(Winter), 48–64.

Kwallek, N., Lewis, C. M., & Robbin, A. S. (1998). Effects of Office Interior Color on Workers' Mood and Productivity. *Perceptual and Motor Skills, 66*(1), 123–128.

Ladwein, R. (1999). *Le comportement du consommateur et de l'acheteur*. Paris: Economica.

Ladwein, R. (2001). *L'impact de la conception des sites de e-commerce sur le confort d'utilisation: une proposition de modèle*. Actes du 17ème congrès international de l'AFM.

Ladwein, R. & Ben Mimoun, M.-S. (2006). *L'accès à l'offre sur un site web commercial: une approche expérimentale*. 5ème journée nantaise de recherche en e-marketing.

Lanthony, P. (2005). *La perception des couleurs sur écran*. Intervention dans le cadre d'un séminaire sur la couleur, 3C S.A., Abbaye de Royaumont - France, Juin 2005.

Lemoine, J.-F. (2003). Vers une approche globale de l'atmosphère du point de vente. *Revue Française du Marketing, 194*(Septembre), 83–101.

Lemoine, J.-F. (2008). *L'influence de l'atmosphère des sites web marchands sur les réponses des internautes*. 24ème congrès international de l'association française du marketing, Paris, 15 et 16 mai 2008, CDRom.

Lynch, J. G., & Ariely, D. (2000). Wine online: Search costs affect competition on price, quality and distribution. *Marketing Science, 19*(1), 83–103. doi:10.1287/mksc.19.1.83.15183

Mattelart, A. (1996). *The Invention of Communication*. Minneapolis: University Minnesota Press.

Mayer, J. D., & Gaschke, Y. N. (1988). The experience and meta-experience of mood. *Journal of Personality and Social Psychology, 55*, 102–111. doi:10.1037/0022-3514.55.1.102

Mehrabian, A., & Russell, J. A. (1974). *An Approach to Environmental Psychology*. Cambridge, MA: MIT Press.

Moe, W. W., & Fader, P. S. (2004b). Dynamic Conversion Behavior at E-Commerce Sites. *Management Science, 50*(3), 326–335. doi:10.1287/mnsc.1040.0153

Moss, G., Gunn, R., & Heller, J. (2006). Some men like it black, some women like it pink: consumer involvements of differences in male and female website design. *Journal of Consumer Behaviour, 5*(4), 328–342. doi:10.1002/cb.184

Mucchielli, A. (1991). *Les méthodes qualitatives, Que sais-je?* Paris: Presses Universitaires de France.

Munsell, A. (1969). *The Munsell Colour Atlas*. Munsell Color Corp.

Nakshian, J. S. (1964). The effects of red and green surroundings on behavior. *The Journal of General Psychology, 70*, 143–161.

Nielsen, J. (2000). *Designing Web Usability*. Indianapolis, IN: New Riders Publishers.

Nielsen, J. (2004). *Change the Color of Visited Links, useit.com*. Alertbox, May, Link colors.

O'Shaughnessy, J. (1992). *Explaining Buyer Behavior: Central concepts and Philosophy of Science issues*. New York: Oxford University Press.

Odom, A. S. & Sholtz, S. S. (2004). *The reds, whites, and blues of emotion: examinig color hue effects on mood tones.* Department of psychology Missouri Western State University.

Osgood, C. E., Suci, G. J., & Tannenbaum, P. H. (1957). *The measurement of meaning.* Chicago: University of Illinois Press.

Pantin-Sohier, G. (2004). *Le rôle de la couleur dans la perception des traits de personnalité de la marque: une étude comparative Etats-Unis/Suède.* 1ère journée de recherche AFM-AUDENCIA sur le Marketing et le Design - Janvier.

Papadopoulou, P. (2007). Applying virtual reality for trust-building e-commerce environments. *Virtual Reality, 11*(2-3), 107-127(21).

Pastoureau, M. (1999). *Dictionnaire des couleurs de notre temps, symbolique and société.* Paris: Bonneton.

Pelet, J.-É. (2008). *Effects of the color of e-commerce websites on the memorization and on the intention of purchase of the Net surfer.* Thesis in Management, Nantes University, France.

Plégat-Soutjis, F. (2004). *Sémantique graphique des interfaces. Représentations, valeurs, usages, communication et langages.* Dossier: le signe en scène, un enjeu politique, n°142, décembre 2004.

Pribadi, N. S., Wadlow, M. G., & Boyarski, D. (1990). *The use of color in computer interfaces: Preliminary Research.* Information technology Center, Carnegie Mellon University, Pittsburgh, PA.

Ranganathan & Grandon. (2005). *Converting browser to Buyers: key considerations in designing Business-to-Consumer Web sites.* In Y. Gao (ed.), *Web system design and online consumer Behavior,* (pp. 177-191). Hershey, PA: Idea Group Publishing.

Russel, J. A., & Fernandez-Dols, J. M. (1997). *The psychology of facial expressions.* Cambridge, UK: Cambridge University Press.

Sheth, J. N., & Sisodia, R. S. (1997). *Consumer Behavior in the Future.* In R. A. Peterson, (ed.), *Electronic Marketing and The Consumer,* (pp. 17-37). Thousand Oaks, CA: Sage Publications.

Silverstein, L. D. (1987). Human Factors for Color Display System: Concepts, Methods, and Research. In J. Durret (ed.), *Color and the Computer,* (pp. 27-61). San Diego, CA: Academic Press.

Spool, J. M., Scanlon, T., Schroeder, W., Snyder, C., & DeAngelo, T. (1999). *Web Site Usability, A Designer's Guide,* (pp. 17). San Francisco: Morgan Kaufmann Publishers.

Tricot, A. (1995). Un point sur l'ergonomie des interfaces hypermédia. *Le Travail Humain, 58*(1), 17–45.

Trouvé, A. (1999). *La mesure de la couleur.* Paris, CETIM, éd. Association française de normalisation (AFNOR).

Valdez, P. (1993). *Emotion responses to color.* Thèse de doctorat, University of California, Los Angeles.

Valdez, P., & Mehrabian, J. (1994). Effects of color on emotions. *Journal of Experimental Psychology. General, 123*(4), 394–409. doi:10.1037/0096-3445.123.4.394

Wilson, G. D. (1966). Arousal properties of red versus green. *Perceptual and Motor Skills, 23*(3), 947–949.

Wright, B., & Rainwater, L. (1962). The Meaning of color. *The Journal of General Psychology, 67*(1), 89–99.

Yoo, B., & Donthu, N. (2001). Developing and validating a multidimensional consumer-based brand equity scale. *Journal of Business Research, 52*(1), 1–14. doi:10.1016/S0148-2963(99)00098-3

APPENDIX 1

Devices and Installation Required to Conduct the Experiment Effectively

Experimental Room (Fernandez-Maloigne, 2004)

Measurements were taken at different intervals by a luxmeter:

- Keep a distance of about one meter between the back of the room and the screen
- A relationship between idle screen luminance and peak luminance (luminance is the Y coordinate of the XYZ model)
- Peak luminance of the screen
- Room lighting (ambient illumination)
- Background chromaticity related to the D65 illuminant
- Maximum observation angle (CRT screen) of 30°
- High-quality assessment monitor, size 50-60 cm (22" - 26")

Participants (Lanthony, 2005)

An Ishihara test for determining color blindness was conducted in another room than that of the experiment room so as to check that participants were not color-blind and were thus in a position to provide valid answers.

Screens

All the screens used during the experiment were calibrated:

- Ensure the screens warm up for an hour before calibration
- Ensure one can modulate Hue, Brightness, Saturation as well as the R, G, B channels for each screen used
- Use a CRT display rather than a plasma screen
- The target to be taken into account by the probe must be a 2.2 - 6500 Kelvin (Gamma, color temperature)
- Ambient light compensation must be disabled
- The BLACK point must have a light level of 0.8° while that of the WHITE must reach 90°. If the weakest screen is no higher than 80°, you must calibrate all the screens to this level°. This might very likely be the case with old screens
- The luminance of the WHITE for contrast must be set so that four more or less WHITE squares are visible to the naked eye
- The luminance of the BLACK, for brightness, must be set so that four more or less BLACK squares are visible to the naked eye
- Identification of color controls: press the radio button on "RGB slider"
- Place the probe which will then provide the test patterns on the screen using the suction pads enabling it to stay stuck
- The measurements mentioned above can be taken again two weeks afterwards, but they should not have been altered if no one has changed the screen settings
- The probe allows for the generation of the ICC profile: Save the ICC profile which will be set automatically afterwards

Section 4
Usability Methods and Techniques

Chapter 15
Whose Questionnaire
Is It, Anyway?

Andrew Saxon
Birmingham City University, UK

Shane Walker
Birmingham City University, UK

David Prytherch
Birmingham City University, UK

ABSTRACT

This chapter focuses on the adoption and adaptation of methodologies drawn from research in psychology for the evaluation of user response as a manifestation of the mental processes of perception, cognition and emotion. The authors present robust alternative conceptualizations of evaluative methodologies which allow the surfacing of views, feelings and opinions of individual users producing a richer, more informative texture for user centered evaluation of software. This differs from more usual user questionnaire systems such as the Questionnaire of User Interface Satisfaction (QUIS). (Norman et al, 1989) The authors present two different example methodologies so that the reader can firstly, review the methods as a theoretical exercise and secondly, applying similar adaptation principles, derive methods appropriate to their own research or practical context.

INTRODUCTION

Viewed from a design perspective, there appears to be a lack of empirical research investigating the determinants of important aspects of behavior such as emotion and motivation, and how an understanding of these may influence designers' decisions in the software evaluation process. The

DOI: 10.4018/978-1-60566-896-3.ch015

ubiquitous nature of information technology today means that the computer is no longer just a tool for those who are compelled to use it, or have to learn to use it, as was the case in the 1980s. Interfaces, in particular on the Internet, must appeal to a broad base of users with varying levels of skill and ability, and should work first time to ensure the user is not 'put off' the experience. Aesthetic considerations may also be considered significant in this context. (Hartmann, Sutcliffe & De Angeli, 2007) Modern psychological theories on motivation e.g. Ford, (1992) agree on a basic structure of component processes: goal directed activity, an individual's belief in their skills and the context within which they will work, and finally their emotions.

Motivation is a rather abstract term that historically has challenged psychologists to provide satisfactory definitions. Unified theories that attempt to satisfactorily explain human motivation have been developed only relatively recently and research on motivation within HCI such as the Technology Acceptance Model, (TAM) (Davis, 1989) supports the argument that visual communication and functionality (perceived ease of use) influence users' motivation, and change user behavior in a way that impacts on usability. Research has shown that highly motivated users experience less anxiety, have higher perceptions of self-efficacy and more positive attitudes towards the software. (Davis, *ibid.*)

In order to assess how far design techniques applied to the user interface can harmonize with psychological needs for optimal performance on specific tasks and attainment of goals, we must base questions on a fundamental understanding of key influencing variables of the interaction process, together with a clear knowledge of their relative importance to the individual user. In perceptual terms, interactive computer systems are not just representations of knowledge, but interactive *experiences* that should seek to fully exploit the user's senses and emotions, developing new ways to deliver effective communication.

Variables during interaction that can influence user motivation lie in the gulf between executing the task and its evaluation. The users evaluate their goals, their own ability to attain them and the potential of the context, (in this case the computer system) to support them in this activity. Evaluation is on-going as perception is regularly matched against expectations and is a good indicator of how successful the interface is. This gulf may be bridged by addressing issues from either direction, the computer or the user. The system designer can

bridge such issues by creating interaction mechanisms that better match the psychological needs of the user as evidenced by the task model.

We present two different examples, describing tested methodologies for addressing these needs, though many other comparable adaptations of different domain methodologies might be similarly useful.(e.g. Greenberg *et al*, 2000; Hollan, Hutchins & Kirshac, 2000; Duric, *et al*, 2002),

The first example is derived from Motivation Systems Theory (MST) (Ford, 1992) wherein components of human behavior are modeled as simple behavioral processes. MST integrates the conceptual frameworks of 32 motivational theories around its core concepts and was also found to compare well with models and theories already used to describe user interaction in HCI.

The second example is derived from Kelly's (1955) Repertory Grid Technique. This method uses a highly qualitative approach to the surfacing of a user's experience using his/her own frame of reference. The technique is highly amenable to customization by the experimenter, to suit the particular needs of his/her investigation, and details on customization carried out by the authors are described.

In order to prove these derived methodologies, they were used as part of a suite of usability tests that were run on *Webomatic*, a website design application aimed at UK Small and Medium sized Enterprises (SMEs) which itself was one of the outcomes of an earlier European Union Regional Development Fund (ERDF) part-funded project to investigate the implications of design for e-commerce.

TECHNIQUE 1: MOTIVATION SYSTEMS THEORY (MST)

MST is based on the Living Systems Framework (LSF) (Ford, 1987) which considers a person holistically on both a granular and global level, for example in considering goals, emotions, per-

Figure 1. Chapter structure

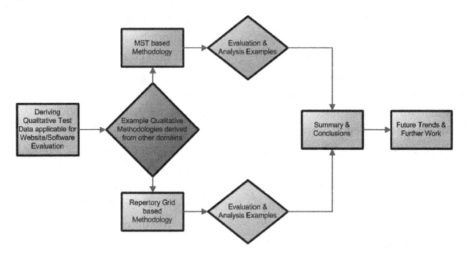

ceptions and actions. LSF also describes how the individual component processes work together to form organized patterns of behavior. The LSF breaks physical structure and organization of living systems into four sets of basic functions:

1. **Biological functions:** Life sustaining biological processes, the functioning of the body
2. **Transactional functions:** Exchange processes vital for life (sensory-perceptual actions, body movement etc)
3. **Cognitive functions:** Regulatory functions, evaluative thoughts
4. **Arousal functions:** Attention and consciousness arousal, emotional arousal

A person's behaviour can be represented as an organised flow of complex patterns. The LSF uses the concept of a behaviour episode, which is based on the premise that the individual will undertake goal directed activity until one of the following occurs:

*   The goal is accomplished
*   The person is distracted and another goal takes precedence
*   The goal is evaluated as unattainable

The behaviour episode is therefore organised by goals and context and the psychological constraints dictated by them.

The LSF integrates motivation with cognitive and arousal processes. MST emerged from an iterative process of integrating the basic framework provided by the LSF with concepts and data provided by existing work on motivation (both historical and contemporary). Motivation has often been considered a separate topic of research within the field of psychology leading to theories that cannot be compared. The theories and ideas have recently reached a level of maturity where referring to them to provide an extended view of the user can produce robust and enlightening findings. Unification and agreement of these processes has been found in psychology and HCI and this makes the study of users' motivation at the interface a more viable proposition. The importance of goals (intrinsic and extrinsic) and contexts for motivation highlighted by Ford (1992) suggests there may be value in attempting to apply the motivational theory to HCI. Most behaviour is goal directed, and goals can be considered as needs which when satisfied, generate positive emotions that energize motivation. An individual's personal goals illustrate the most distinctive characteristic of humans, the capability to use thought to construct models of action that can represent their past, present, and future activity and to then be able to utilise these to guide future decisions and behaviour. Designers may construct the conceptual design model for the interactive system through an understanding of the users' background experience, knowledge and expectations. Our expectations are initially fashioned by our prior experience however they are continually re-modelled during subsequent experiences.

MST attempts to represent three basic components of motivation. Firstly, the overall aim of the individual – what they are attempting to do. Secondly, what energises people and what does the opposite, and thirdly how people make decisions to continue or alternatively to give up. The theory describes the processes that guide these components: Goal setting activities will only be effective if (a) feedback is provided; the person/user must be able to evaluate any discrepancies between the current and desired consequences and (b) capability beliefs for realizing the desired consequences in the face of discouraging feedback. The person/user must have the skill (capability belief) and (c) a responsive and supporting environment (context belief) within which to attain their goals. Emotions play an evaluative and energizing role throughout these processes. The approach to the field of motivation taken by MST enables broader applications that are not possible with many other theories. Its unifying approach (32 other theories on motivation) and broad agreement with existing HCI models, e.g. TAM (Davis, 1989) makes it attractive for application to HCI, hence it was planned to adapt the model to analyse, measure and assess the role of motivation in the user experience at the software interface.

A novel qualitative user test based on MST was applied to twelve users whose roles had some involvement in web site design, content, construction and/or management. The descriptive terminology (for example, personal goals) used in MST required modification to improve semantic relevance to the HCI context. The application of the theory through the user tests provided a new 'lens' through which to view the users' experience and this proved to be an effective tool during the user tests to gauge motivational responses.

Data Analysis Methods

An assessment of the user's motivation prior to using the software will provide a point of reference so that assessments can be made whilst the software is being used, and post-use. This should provide a basis for determining the user's behavioural response and assist in the post-test interviews by suggesting lines for further investigation.

User's motivation assessment will require gathering information on the user's goals, emotions, and Personal Agency Beliefs (PABs) (Ford 1992). Personal Agency Beliefs consist of context and (the user's) capability beliefs. This will be achieved primarily by the use of a questionnaire that specifically links design attributes of the software with the components of motivation (identified by Ford 1992). Figure 2 provides an example of how context beliefs can be applied to HCI and how they relate to usability principles. The objective of this method is to obtain a user profile of behavioural response accumulated qualitatively through the user's experience of the software. Motivational theory can identify major influences on the user, but cannot necessarily provide answers with regard to the exact causes of motivational change. Through observation, video recording, asking the user to think aloud, and using keyword selection techniques it is possible to attribute motivational patterns to the user's experience of the software. The tests are designed to capture a broad range of impacts on the user that stem from user goals and needs. A specific focus is to elicit information about the user's response to the design of the software.

Figure 2. Example of how context beliefs can be applied to HCI and how they relate to usability principles

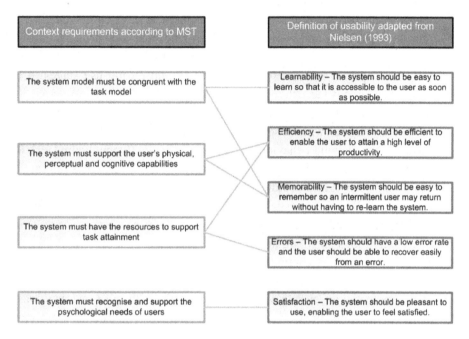

Pre-Test Stage

The pre-test questions provided a profile of the user, their background, previous experience, knowledge, psychological characteristics, attitudes and expectations before the test commenced. The task brief was set out as written text and was explained verbally to the user. After a demonstration of the software the user was asked to select from three keyword tables: emotions, aesthetics and usability. Following this a questionnaire was administered to assess the impact of the demonstration on the user.

During the Test

During the test, valuable data were obtained by combining traditional user observation techniques with MST. It was possible to elicit in-depth information on the user's behavioural response to the software during the test, indicating their progress towards conscious and unconscious goals, including an assessment of the user's own evaluative processes. To facilitate effective data gathering during the tests, lookup tables (See Figure 3) with representative keywords were used. This minimised cognitive load by reducing time off task. The purpose of the tables was to gauge emotional response and the users' view on the aesthetics and usability of the software. Emotions, although subjective, are good indicators of the user's experience, because of their evaluative role. The user was encouraged to think aloud describing their experience as they used the software. Recording this additional qualitative data during the test provided insight into the users' selection of keywords in the event of any notable conscious emotions experienced during use of the software (See Figure 4). Each conscious emotion event was recorded separately and a short one-page questionnaire was given at around the mid-point of task completion. These records could be reviewed together with video/audio recordings thus delivering a snapshot of the users' behavioural responses, underpinned by an assessment of their motivation over time.

The technique further enhances other information gathered during observation for example, by 'think aloud', as the user selects descriptions that they feel fit their current experience and view of the software.

On screen activity was captured and was synchronised with a camera that directly faced the user and recorded facial expression throughout the test. This video showing users' interaction with the software proved invaluable for explaining behaviour and mapping the user's response to the software over time. Most importantly the videos captured the strength of the user's feeling as an issue or event occurred at the interface, and provided the opportunity to make observations on strengthening or waning emotions as interaction continued. These recordings allowed the opportunity for further analysis of users' responses by linking closely with data collected through the questionnaires.

Post-Test

The post-test stage commenced with the completion of the three keyword selection tables that were identical to those completed at the post-demonstration and during-use stages. A questionnaire was completed and a reflective interview was conducted. The questionnaire was composed of closed questions using Likert and semantic differential scales (Oppenheim, 1992; Robson, 1993; Osgood *et al*, 1971). Questions at this stage were compared with questions at the pre-test stage so that it was possible to record and measure any shift in the user's responses as a result of using the software. A 'before and after' analysis was possible, including an explanation of the shift, if it occurred.

The aim of the post-test stage was to gather further qualitative data on the user's experience after

Figure 3. Example keyword selection table

Figure 4. Example emotion keyword sheet

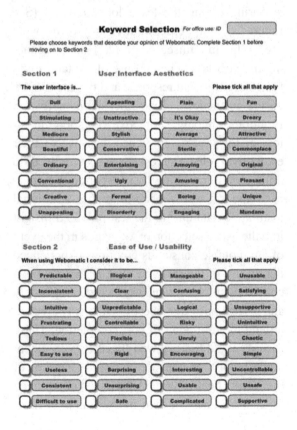

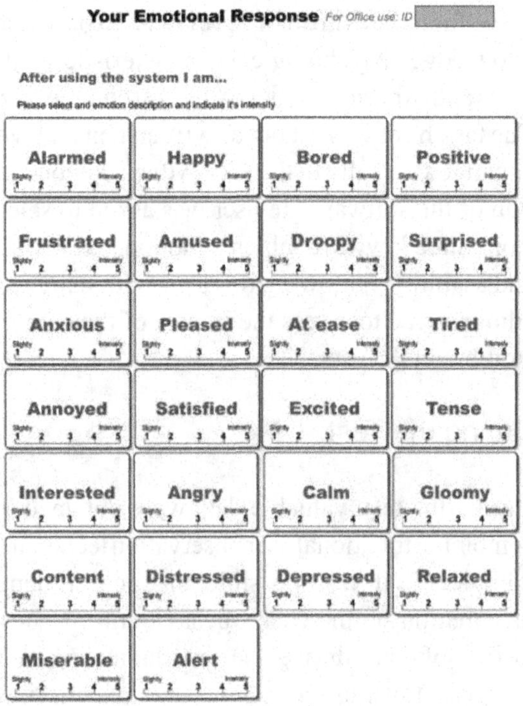

completion of the task. This was an opportunity to obtain insights into particular events to which the user had reacted strongly. User reflection and explanation were valuable aids to the subsequent assessment of their experience. The method used was an exploratory interview, semi-structured by the use of a questionnaire. This gathered data to support an assessment of user motivation after the experience and in anticipation of further use of the software. In depth interview techniques (Oppenheim, 1992) elicited information that indicated whether the user's goals had been accomplished and what types of goals they were, examples include task goals and personal goals. Additionally this included an assessment of the user's context and capability beliefs (Ford, 1992) to detect any shift during the experience.

Summary of MST Based Tests

The techniques described for pre-test and during test phases collect information on the user's motivation and emotions as it happens. The post-test phase seeks to identify the significance of earlier findings, reinforcing them with qualitative data collected from the in-depth interview. The post-test establishes the impact of the software users' experience on their motivation. It also assesses the users' motivation with regard to future use of the software.

A key requirement for the interview is to enhance the qualitative data gained from the questionnaires, confirm the user's responses and facilitate explorative open questioning on aspects of the experience that proved particularly interesting for different reasons. Another important role for the interview is to enable the user to reflect on their experience, to elicit their own opinions, which can then be compared with data collected during observation. This support for observational data will assist ranking of events that had a powerful motivational influence on the user, as conscious evaluations that can be recalled later to give an indication of the impact on the user's experience.

Throughout the development of the tests, comparisons and checks were made to establish comparability and validity with other models used to evaluate computer user's behaviour (Venkatesh, 2000; Norman *et al*, 2003). Reference to HCI user satisfaction questionnaires such as QUIS (Norman *et al*, *ibid*.) helped to define the scope of the questions and were extended by this research through reference to MST and other relevant theories and models in the field of psychology/HCI (Venkatesh, *ibid*.; Norman *et al*, *ibid*.) to deliver a predictive and explanatory framework. The understanding of the user derived from this approach can have a direct impact on the design of the interface with new requirements for design solutions.

The tests showed that it was possible to gain valuable information about the user with implications for designers, particularly when tracking the user over time, highlighting the significance of each user interaction. The strengthening and waning of emotions was particularly evident and the results indicated that the opportunity to manage and capitalize on the interaction process is under-recognized. *Satisfaction* is simply one of a number of goals the user is striving for. An optimal user experience may be partly dependent on recognising a broader range of goals and associated emotional response in the software design.

Using MST for understanding and measuring the strength of the users' response provided a robust framework that detected measurable shifts in the experience. These shifts indicated a link to the qualities of the software, highlighting virtues and shortfalls in the software design. The user tests established the importance of satisfying users' personal goals and additionally, this was recognized by the individuals as evidenced by user comments in interviews and questionnaires. This response depended to a large extent on successful use of the software, and also on qualities of the design and the users' experience.

Motivation embodies emotions and closer inspection of this readily observable aspect of the human response should inform an assessment of the software, providing valuable support to user surveys. Recognition of motivational aspects of the user response suggests the need to review information traditionally collected in user satisfaction surveys. It is possible that the user's psychological needs have been generally under-recognized by the HCI community. This view is supported by research on user emotion undertaken at MIT and IBM (Picard & Wexelblat, 2002, Norman *et al*, 2003, Bickmore and Picard, 2005).

TECHNIQUE 2: REPERTORY GRID TECHNIQUE

The Repertory Grid Technique was developed from Kelly's (1955) Personal Construct Theory. This theory had, at its starting point the belief that people are scientists. By this, it is meant that each of us has constructed our own point of view about the world (a theory), our own opinions on what will happen in a given situation (a hypothesis) and that in our day-to-day behavior, we continually test our views against our reality (we conduct experiments) and, based upon our day-to-day experiences (the experimental data,) we modify our world-view (our theory), forming new opinions on how the world works (a revised hypothesis).

According to Kelly (*ibid.*), as these constructs represent a set of individual qualitative judgments about the world, it is preferable to think of them as being scalar, having two contrasting poles. Kelly (*ibid.*) observed that our judgments are usually bipolar, rather than unipolar. The concept of *good* can only exist as the opposite of *bad;* the concept of *wet* can only exist as the opposite to *dry*. Therefore, when an individual offers a judgment, the question *'as opposed to what?'* needs always to be asked in order to further clarify the individual's meaning and the context. For example, the term *good* may mean *skilful* as opposed to *novice* when discussing sporting ability, or it may mean *virtuous* as opposed to *evil* when discussing the moral character of

another individual. The exact meaning of a word in a given context cannot therefore be assumed. Even where the opposite pole is thought obvious by the experimenter, it should still be sought in order to eliminate observer bias. Repertory Grid Technique sets out to measure subjective aspects of a participant's experience using a highly qualitative approach whose methods are amenable to customization by the experimenter.

Adherents of the quantitative approach, upon recognizing that a user's subjective response to the software under evaluation can be an important aspect of that evaluation, will often add a criterion that aims to deal with the subjective dimension of how much the user *liked* using the software. This is illustrated in Nielsen's (1993) model of the attributes of system acceptability, which explores and charts the notion of usability through consideration of such matters as: learnability, efficiency, memorability, user error-rate, and satisfaction. In so doing, they are acknowledging that no matter how well it performs in the other categories, if the software and its interface are not liked by the user, it may not actually be used much, and may even be discarded. On the World Wide Web, it is accepted that the competition is just one click away, so the importance of gaining a clear understanding of users' experience with web software cannot be overstated.

Data Analysis Methods

The application of Repertory Grid Technique requires the identification of a set of *elements*, or objects. These elements define the subject matter of the Repertory Grid interview. The interviewee is then asked to define some *constructs*, or attributes, to characterize the elements. These constructs are written down in a scalar, bipolar form, and each element is ranked along the bipolar scale. The *grid* or table is then created with the elements and constructs on its two axes, and the scores are entered at the element-construct intersections. The resulting grid is then available for analysis. This ability of Repertory Grid to help people articulate using their own range of convenience, *in their own terms,* that which they normally cannot coherently articulate, is of key importance as it is this facility that is used to help ascertain the particular quality of a specific user's experience.

Due to the widespread adoption of Repertory Grid outside of the particular domain for which it was originally devised it has been necessary to elaborate the technique for more applied uses. A selection of common elaborations, according to Fransella and Bannister (1977), would include: Grid (the original method); Rank Order Grid (which added rank ordering of elements to the Grid form); Ratings Grid (where each element is rated on a scale defined by the two construct poles) and the Implications Grid (which uses only one element, the self, concentrating on eliciting constructs relating to the self). This particular elaboration is designed to elicit tacit information from users. The addition of Rank Order Grid and Ratings Grid also make this a methodology which can very effectively combine qualitative with quantitative data providing an exceptionally rich information source.

There are obvious similarities between Repertory Grid and Osgood's Semantic Differential (Snider & Osgood, 1969), the latter being based to some extent upon the former. The major difference between the two is that Osgood's Semantic Differential supplies the bipolar constructs for the interviewee to use, thereby forcing them to use the construct system labels of the questionnaire designer, whereas the Repertory Grid elicits the bipolar constructs, actively engaging the construct system of the interviewee. This ensures that the constructs used in the interview lie within the range of convenience of the interviewee.

Choosing Elements and Eliciting Constructs

Repertory Grid elements can be identified by several means, but Stewart and Stewart (1981)

identify three main methods: the interviewer can provide them; or interviewees can be asked to think of a list of elements based upon a briefing which outlines what kinds of elements are sought; or the interviewer can supply a list of questions, the answers to which become the elements. Each of these methods has advantages and disadvantages.

Interviewer-provided elements can be closely targeted to the precise needs of the particular investigation by the interviewer, but can immediately introduce observer bias, in that the construct system of the interviewer (or questionnaire designer) is used as the basis for the interview, rather than the construct system of the interviewee.

Elements that are supplied free-form by the interviewee are, of course, making extensive use of the construct system of that interviewee, but the elements supplied may vary widely in relevance to the particular investigation at hand. The interviewee may supply elements that can seem irrelevant to the investigation. Stewart and Stewart (*ibid.*) point out that this technique will also introduce bias in the interviewee's choice of elements toward those with which he/she is familiar, and also toward those elements that are preferred by the interviewee.

Elements that are supplied by the interviewee in response to a pre-prepared list of questions appear to inhabit an optimal position. The pre-prepared list of questions will focus the interviewee's construing on the topic of the investigation, whilst the free-form nature of the interviewee's answers will extensively utilise the construct system of that interviewee. Observer bias is controlled due to the free-form nature of the resulting elements, and interviewee bias is controlled due to the strong focus provided by the need to work within the framework provided by the pre-prepared list of questions.

Eliciting Constructs

By far the most common method of construct elicitation is Kelly's (*op. cit.*) triadic method, where three elements are shown to the interviewee, who is then asked to specify some way in which two of these elements are alike and thereby different from the third. The reply, representing the *likeness* pole of the bipolar pair, is then recorded. Then, the interviewee is asked in what way the third element differs from the other two. This reply, representing the *contrast* pole in the bipolar pair is also recorded. The process is then repeated using as many triads of elements as the interviewer thinks appropriate.

Another less common, yet equally effective method according to Ryle and Lunghi (1970) is the dyadic method, where only two elements are shown to the interviewee, so that the two construct poles can be elicited more directly. The dyadic method is felt to be simpler in operation than the triadic method, without sacrificing either validity or reliability. Fransella and Bannister (*op. cit.*) note that the dyadic method is useful where constructs that are already present in the interviewee's mind are to be elicited, noting that in such cases there is no reason for using the triadic method.

Epting *et.al.* (1971) evaluated the two different formal methods proposed by Kelly (*op. cit.*) for identifying the contrast pole during the Repertory Grid interview. These are called the *opposite method* and the *difference method*, the latter, over time, becoming the more popular of the two. Using the *difference method*, after the likeness pole has been identified, as stated above, the interviewee is asked to specify some way in which two of the elements in the triad are alike and thereby *different* from the third.

Using the *opposite method*, after the likeness pole has been identified, as stated above, the interviewee is asked to specify what he/she considers to be the *opposite* of the characteristic given for the likeness pole. Epting *et.al.* (*op. cit.*) found that the *opposite method* produced a greater number of bipolar constructs than the *difference method* when using the Repertory Grid procedure.

Reliability and Validity

Fransella and Bannister (*op. cit.*) and Bannister and Fransella (1986) discuss the reliability and validity of Repertory Grid Technique, suggesting that the common experimental meaning attached to these terms needs a degree of contextualisation when applied to Repertory Grid.

Reliability

As Kelly (*op. cit.*) believed that living creatures were a form of motion, as opposed to being static objects, he envisaged that each of us is engaged in a constant and continuous re-evaluation and development of our personal construct systems. On this basis, it is highly likely that successive applications of Repertory Grid with the same interviewee over time would bring to light different results. This however, is not indicative of poor experimental reliability in the technique. Yin (1994, p. 37) notes that the objective of reliability is: "...to be sure that if a later investigator followed the same procedures as described by an earlier investigator and conducted the same case study all over again, the later investigator should arrive at the same findings and conclusions." If such a 'later investigator' were to find the interviewee 'frozen in time' and therefore completely unchanged, then this would be the case.

However, Bannister and Fransella (*op. cit.*) posit that: as people may maintain or alter how they construe their world over time, the reliability of Repertory Grid arises from its ability to permit effective investigation of this very issue,

Validity

Validity in an experimental sense is described by Yin (*op. cit.*, p. 37) as: "[dealing] with the problem of knowing whether a study's findings are generalizable beyond the immediate case..."

This widely used definition of validity causes immediate problems when considering Repertory Grid Technique. Our construct systems are different each to another, and furthermore, they are differently and personally expressed, often using private language (made-up words) to describe aspects of the world. At face value then, Repertory Grid Technique has low validity in the traditional experimental sense, as it is unwise to attempt generalisation from existing data to other as-yet-unknown situations.

In rebuttal of this view, Fransella and Bannister (*op. cit.*) argue that Repertory Grid is not actually a test, but rather a format into which information can be put in order to find out if relationships exist within the data.

Applications of the Repertory Grid Technique to Software Evaluation

When considering Repertory Grid Technique as the vehicle for gathering qualitative assessments of the user experience, as opposed to quantitative assessments of software usability, exemplars can be seen in the literature that demonstrate a precedent, and which may be shown to clarify the appropriateness of the theory for use in this context.

Baber (1996) provides an example of the use of Repertory Grid Theory in comparative product evaluation, suggesting that further use could be made of the technique in the early stages of product design, when compiling a list of desirable design characteristics. Baber (*ibid.*, p. 164) also envisages its use

...as a means of defining users' conceptions of usability, perhaps through a comparison of a range of products which users are encouraged to consider in terms of functionality, ease of use, etc.

Boy (1997) presents the Group Elicitation Method (GEM), which seeks to overcome the

problems experienced by different individuals when they are used as 'experts' on a product review panel. GEM has been used to facilitate the mutual understanding of terms and ideas among experts who have been gathered together in order to provide solutions to design or usability issues.

Much indebted to Personal Construct Theory, GEM acts as a decision support tool, producing clear and mutually understood outcomes. Boy (*ibid.*, p. 33) states: "Although we have used GEM to design new systems, we have observed that it would be useful for evaluating existing systems and suggesting alternatives."

Both Baber (*op.cit.*) and Boy (*op.cit.*) appear to have recognised a symmetry between initial product design and user testing that deploys an individual's personal construct system as a kind of yardstick against which to evaluate a product, either at the beginning or at the end of the design process.

Verlinden and Coenders (2000, p. 143) describing their approach to the use of Repertory Grid for the evaluation of a website state: "Most usability techniques are quantitative and measure the performance, retrieval times, success times/failure rates… Although [a quantitative method] might provide some information on experiences with respect to websites, it exposes a number of shortcomings."

Repertory Grid is offered as it "…facilitates an objective approach of capturing subjective aspects of web usability." (Verlinden & Coenders, ibid., p. 144)

The approach they use is comparative, but in this case the comparison is made between different pages of the website under evaluation, one against the other.

The experimental approach used by Verlinden and Coenders (*ibid.*) however can be criticised. One of the stated goals of the experimental approach was to exclude the observer's frame of reference and worldview from the evaluation.

In the interests of speeding up construct elicitation and of streamlining the analysis stages of the Repertory Grid process, interviewees were asked to select any two from a list of three pre-prepared elements, each with pre-prepared bipolar constructs attached. Whilst taking less time and producing more uniform data, this short cut may have compromised the main strength of the Repertory Grid technique by introducing observer bias at crucial early stages.

Hassenzahl and Trautmann (2001, p. 167) set out to evaluate the "holistic overall impression [or] 'character' of a web site." This approach was chosen (rather than merely evaluating isolated aspects of the site, such as usability) on the basis that the overall "character [of a site] will have an impact on interpretation, acceptance and further interaction..."

The method used was to employ Repertory Grid Technique to enable interviewees to compare a new website design, created for a German online bank, with the old design, along with the other six prominent online banking sites available in Germany. The experiment produced useful data, enabling a comparative evaluation of the eight websites to be conducted, facilitating a view on the success of the new site design in terms of its users' experience. (Hassenzahl & Trautmann, *ibid.*)

Hassenzahl et.al. (2001a) discuss the evolved needs of software product evaluation during the '00's, stating that the industry-wide focus on usability engineering over the last 30 years must now be extended to acknowledge contemporary users' needs. Citing 'joy of use' as an example, Hassenzahl et.al. (*ibid.*) argue that software possessing a high 'joy of use' factor tends to fare better with users on several levels, including: user acceptance and user satisfaction (Igbaria et.al., 1994); sustained quality of performance when using 'joy of use' enabled software at the customer interface (Millard et.al., 1999); enhanced ability to benefit from learning software (Draper, 1999);

and overall amount of system usage together with system enjoyment (Mundorf *et.al.,* 1993).

Hassenzahl et.al. (*op.cit.*), recognising that hedonic qualities in software can, in some cases reduce software usability and utility, perform a selective review of existing measurement methods and tools. Repertory Grid is cited as a valuable tool in this regard. The method used presents interviewees with a randomly drawn triad from the software product set occupying the design space of interest to the evaluators. The interviewee is then asked the classic question: *in what way are two of these three products similar to each other, but different from the third?* In this way, the personal construct systems of the interviewees are used as a means of communicating responses to the products under evaluation.

Hassenzahl et.al. (*ibid.*, p. 5) explain thus:

For example, if you perceive two software products as being different, you might come up with the personal construct 'too colourful—looks good' to name the opposed extremes. On the one hand, this personal construct tells something about you, namely that too many colours disturb your sense of aesthetics. On the other hand, it also reveals information about the product's attributes.

Hassenzahl *et al*, (2001b), seeking ways to better capture design requirements in the early stages of software design, introduce the Structured Hierarchical Interview for Requirement Analysis. (SHIRA).

A SHIRA interview aims to capture the interviewee's own point of view about desirable product qualities pertaining to a product under consideration *in his/her own terms* for later use in the design of the software. To this end, an open, non-directed approach is used in the interview. Data captured by a series of SHIRA interviews with different individuals can then be aggregated prior to use in the design stages of the product or system. To facilitate this use, the information gathering stage must also be highly structured.

As well as being useful in the early stages of designing, SHIRA has (as yet unexplored) potential for use as an evaluative tool. Hassenzahl *et al*, (*op. cit.*, p. 7) note that: "SHIRA is especially suited to gather information at early stages of the design process for interactive systems. However, it might also be possible to evaluate software at a later stage regarding how it fits the user's expectations."

Importantly, this technique avoids the need for the product or system under consideration to be viewed comparatively with other similar or competing systems. Instead, the experimenter takes a view of one product or system only at a time. Further, there appears to be a good 'fit' with the use of Personal Construct Theory in utilising an interviewee's own terms of reference in any evaluation.

The preceding exemplars from Baber (*op. cit.*), Boy (*op. cit.*), Verlinden and Coenders (*op. cit.*), Hassenzahl and Trautmann (*op. cit.*), Hassenzahl et.al. (*op. cit.*) and Hassenzahl et.al. (*op. cit.*) demonstrate that Repertory Grid Technique may be used successfully in the evaluation of designed artefacts in general, and websites and software products in particular.

Repertory Grid Technique has been successfully used in the synchronisation or co-ordination of the efforts of 'experts' so that they can better contribute to a review panel during the design of a new IT system, as seen in Boy (*op.cit.*), while Baber (*op.cit.*) has shown that the technique can be used for comparative product evaluation. Websites have been evaluated by taking a comparative view of the site under evaluation, either among its peers and competitors as seen in Hassenzahl and Trautmann (op.cit.) or by taking a comparative view within the different pages of the site itself as seen in Verlinden and Coenders (op.cit.). Also, Hassenzahl et.al. (*op. cit.*) have proposed that a software product's user experience, and hedonic quality could be comparatively evaluated by using Repertory Grid to expose the product under evaluation to the personal construct system of individual users, and in a controlled, structured manner to develop evaluative data.

Applying the Repertory Grid Technique

As has been shown above, Repertory Grid Technique has strong possibilities for application where a comparative view is needed of how one software product fares against its competitors in the eyes of its users. Where a software product must be evaluated in a stand-alone manner however, a novel approach is needed. Optimally, the required approach retains the many advantages offered by Repertory Grid Technique, whilst facilitating the stand-alone evaluation of the software user experience.

Our approach is described below: In brief, we use an initial card-sorting activity to identify precise themes for enquiry, after which an individualised questionnaire is created that can later be used to evaluate the test software. This questionnaire is made up of themes that were identified by the participant as important to him/her self. The specific questions used in the questionnaire were conceived and worded by the participant, thus ensuring that the terms of reference used fall within his/her range of convenience.

The specific method is explained below, step-by-step.

- Interviewees are sought from members of the target audience for the software under evaluation. The interviews are conducted singly. Interviewees are screened by questionnaire as to their IT skills.
- The interviewee is welcomed to the experimental venue. We use an office, provided with a round table, chairs, a desk and a computer connected to the Internet, running the software under evaluation. At the table, the interviewee is introduced to the aim and purpose of the experiment, and any initial questions are answered.

- A list of the software's design objectives is offered to the interviewee. These are written on index cards, one objective per card. The interviewee is asked to sort the cards, ranking them in order of importance according to his/her own opinion, by laying them out in a line on the table with 'most important' at one end and 'least important' at the other. Any questions asked by the interviewee are answered.
- The final card ranking arrived at by the interviewee is noted and recorded for future reference.
- The five cards ranked as most important are selected by the interviewer and the design objectives written on them are noted. These objectives correspond to the *elements* in a Repertory Grid interview.
- For each design objective (*element*), the interviewee is then asked to think of a characteristic that the software under evaluation would need, in order to fulfil that design objective in such a way that their experience of using the software would be positive. The resulting statement is written down on the Personal Statements Sheet form. Then the interviewee is asked to think of the opposite to the already stated characteristic, with the prompt "...as opposed to what?" This statement is also written down on the Personal Statements Sheet form. The two characteristics stated: one desirable, the other its opposite in the interviewee's own terms represent his/her personal construct relating to that design objective. The bipolar construct is written down as anchors, one at each end of a seven-point ratings scale.
- This step is repeated, to produce a total of three bipolar constructs for each of the five elements, making fifteen in total. The interviewer must take great care to avoid influencing the interviewee's choice of words at all times. Careful use of repetition and

reflecting during the interview will help the interviewee to state clearly what they mean, where difficulty is experienced.
- All fifteen constructs are written out to create a personal Ratings Form, in effect, creating a 'blank' user experience questionnaire that is completely personalised to the interviewee, being based on elements, that he/she has chosen from a large pool of design objectives, using dyadic personal constructs elicited by the *opposite method* (discussed earlier) from these elements.
- The interviewer and the interviewee then move to the desk with the computer, where the interviewer briefly introduces the software under evaluation. Any questions asked are answered.
- Each interviewee is invited to use the software under evaluation to achieve the same real-world task. During the process, any questions asked are answered.
- When the interviewee states that he/she had finished, he/she is invited to complete the personal Ratings Form, scoring the software under evaluation against their previously elicited constructs.
- The interviewee is asked to share any other comments or views that have not been captured by the personal Ratings Form, and these are noted.
- The interviewee is thanked, and the experiment is concluded.

The data gathered are then ready for analysis.

A Repertory Grid interview session as described above takes approximately two hours from beginning to end. We used 10 participants, each in a separate session. All interviews must be conducted in the same manner, preferably using the same venue.

Three methods are suggested for analysis of the data gathered, and these are described below:

Ranking of Design Objectives by Importance

As each participant had ranked all of the design objective cards in order of importance, the information may be tabulated in order to indicate an overall importance ranking as expressed by the whole group. This ranking may then be examined. On several occasions, this has produced surprising results where design objectives ranked 'most important' by the system designers were low-ranked by interviewees. The converse is also seen, where design objectives ranked 'least important' by the system designers were high-ranked by interviewees.

Tabulation of Each Participant's Personal Ratings with Mean of Overall Scores for Each Participant

This method tabulates scores taken from the Personal Ratings Sheets drawn up for each participant. The five design objectives selected by the participant as most important (the Repertory Grid elements) and the scores for each of the three sets of paired, bipolar statements associated with each design objective (the Repertory Grid constructs) are presented, summed and a mean score is calculated. The data are thus readily available for an 'eyeball' test. (Robson, 1993; Clegg, 1990), prior to further analysis.

Personal Ratings Sheet Discussion

Participants' Personal Ratings Sheets are reviewed and discussed. This discussion presents the individual subjective judgements made by each participant about their user experience of the software under review. Standard content analysis methods are useful here. Due to the Repertory Grid methodology used in the experiment, the judgements are stated using participants' own range of convenience and in their own terms of reference. These dimensions of judgement were hitherto hidden from view.

Summary of Repertory Grid Technique Applied to Software Evaluation

After all 15 personal constructs discussed above have been elicited, each participant is invited to use the software under review to perform the same real-world task. Once the participant has finished this task, he/she is invited to complete a Personal Ratings Sheet. This takes the form of a questionnaire, which uses the personal constructs elicited earlier in the session as questionnaire items. Each questionnaire item uses the personal construct 'likeness' and 'contrast' poles as anchors, separated by a seven-point ratings scale (1-7) with 7 representing greatest agreement with the 'likeness' pole and 1 representing greatest agreement with the 'contrast' pole.

The questionnaire items have therefore been elicited from the participant *before* using the software to perform any tasks. Participants must have no prior experience of using the software beforehand. Whilst participants are using the software, the experimenter transfers the personal constructs to the Personal Ratings Sheet, creating a questionnaire 'blank'. The questionnaire is administered *after* the user task is finished. Figures 5 and 6 show a blank Personal Statement Sheet (eliciting constructs) and a Personal Ratings sheet (post task questionnaire) used to elicit user data for analysis.

OVERALL SUMMARY AND CONCLUSION

Valuable data on the user experience is available if novel methods of investigation are applied. Many traditional HCI evaluation models have not been sufficiently sensitive to elicit data on user behavior, which has significant implications for software design. However, the need to understand more about the covert judgments made by users is now critical for the success of software applications.

Figure 5. Example blank personal statement sheet (eliciting constructs)

An important outcome has been the development of frameworks for surfacing these affective judgments in a structured manner. The two different techniques described here could be extended and applied to the design development of software capable of delivering a highly positive user experience.

The first technique showed that the design of the software does indeed influence the users' emotional response and motivation. An understanding of the relative importance of the differing and changing responses and how to address them in the design is derived from a theory of motivation that models this component of human behaviour as simple behavioural processes, (Ford, 1992) enabling the designer to attribute design features to components of motivated behaviour in the user. The MST – derived technique is compatible with current models and theories describing user interaction in HCI and this was an important reason for its selection.

The tests (pre, during and post test) revealed that tracking the user over time is valuable for gathering important information about the user's *changing* experience, which is not captured by previous methodologies. This extends beyond evaluation at specific stages, since the user records their emotional response as soon as they experience it. This technique reveals some variability in users' experience and the way that consecutive good or bad experiences appear to have a cumulative effect in terms of users' overall rating.

Video of facial expressions showing users' interaction with the software proves invaluable for explaining behaviour and mapping the user's response to the software over time. Most importantly the videos capture the strength of the user's feeling as an issue or event occurs at the interface, providing the opportunity to make observations on strengthening or waning emotions as interaction continues. Keyword selection successfully assists the tracking of specific emotional responses and their intensity over time. This information can then

Figure 6. Example personal ratings sheet (post task questionnaire)

Webomatic user experience survey
Personal Ratings Sheet

Now that you have finished making your website, please complete the evaluation form by circling the numbers which reflect your impressions about using Webomatic.

Form number ....

Attributes giving a **positive** experience...	...as opposed to...	...Attributes giving a **negative** experience
	7 6 5 4 3 2 1	
	7 6 5 4 3 2 1	
	7 6 5 4 3 2 1	
	7 6 5 4 3 2 1	
	7 6 5 4 3 2 1	
	7 6 5 4 3 2 1	
	7 6 5 4 3 2 1	
	7 6 5 4 3 2 1	

be analysed alongside the video/audio recordings of interaction events and the transcripts from interview and questionnaire analysis.

The second technique, derived from Repertory Grid Technique, begins with an initial card sorting activity which helps participants settle into the session. As questions arise, they are answered, helping to relax participants further. The card sorts are normally completed with no problems, and the five cards ranked as 'most important' are reserved. The Repertory Grid 'elements' are therefore elicited with great ease.

Completing the 'Personal Statements Sheet' form by taking each element and asking the question '…as opposed to what?' is very straightforward. In some cases long pauses occur while participants think through their answers. Timely follow up questions and focusing conversations may be needed in order to arrive at clear and unambiguous answers, taking great care at all times to avoid interviewer bias. Bipolar Repertory Grid construct elicitation requires deep thought on the part of the participant, but construction of the resulting Personal Ratings Form is very simple. This form constitutes the 'blank' user experience questionnaire for that individual, ready for use.

After using the software under evaluation, the Personal Ratings Forms are normally completed with no difficulty by participants. Some previous participants have commented on the ease and smoothness of the experiment, and seemed pleasantly surprised at this.

Data collected are well structured, and easily accessible to later content analysis. The initial 'eyeball test' of the data immediately highlights areas of interest. The data are, as can be expected, very rich and highly value laden, but the values seen are those of the respective interviewees whose covert judgments regarding the software under evaluation have been surfaced and recorded. In the interests of bias free construct elicitation, the interviewer must use good active listening skills (Richardson, 2002) and must deliberately and repeatedly reflect back the participant's utterances,

resisting the natural tendency to summarize them. This may need to be practiced beforehand in pilot sessions. Overall, the protocol is simple to deploy in the experimental setting.

FUTURE TRENDS

The philosophy underlying these two methodologies is fundamentally concerned with eliminating interviewer bias to the greatest extent possible whilst focusing on the user's own perceptions in his/her own terms. This is not done reductively by iterating draft questionnaire items, but constructively by simply asking users what is important to them. Qualitative methods as described, which produce "stackable" data for close analysis will change, due to the shift in emphasis, from merely measuring software usability to evaluating the quality and enjoyment of the software user's experience and will play an increasingly important role in software evaluation. (Blythe *et al*, 2004)

Further, whilst the prevailing view may be to discount less easily measurable aspects as not being worthwhile, these same less easily measured aspects will gradually take up centre stage in determining the value of software to its users.

The two approaches we have proposed, illuminating the general by close examination of the specific, (paraphrasing Denscombe, 2007) lend weight to theories of participatory design and amplify the user's voice in the software design cycle in ways that are authentic, genuine and transparent.

Work is now in progress on the development of a Qualitative User Experience Survey Tool (QUEST) which will be deeply rooted in our stated philosophy of "ask the user" and will incorporate key aspects of the two approaches described here.

REFERENCES

Baber, C. (1996). Repertory grid theory and its application to product evaluation. In Jordan, P., Thomas, B., Weerdmeester, B. & Mclelland, I. (Eds.), *Usability evaluation in industry*. London: Taylor and Francis.

Bannister, D., & Fransella, F. (1986). *Inquiring man: the psychology of personal constructs* (3rd ed.). London: Routledge.

Bickmore, T. W., & Picard, R. W. (2005). Establishing and maintaining long-term human-computer relationships. *ACM Transactions on Computer-Human Interaction, 12*(2), 293–327. doi:10.1145/1067860.1067867

Blythe, M., Overbeeke, K., Monk, A., & Wright, P. (Eds.). (2004). *Funology: From Usability to Enjoyment*. Berlin: Springer.

Boy, G. (1997). The group elicitation method for participatory design and usability testing. *Interactions of the ACM, 4*(2).

Clegg, F. (1990). *Simple Statistics*. Cambridge, UK: Cambridge University Press.

Davis, F. D. (1989). Perceived Usefulness, Perceived Ease of Use, and User Acceptance of Information Technology. *MIS Quart, 13*(3), 319–339. doi:10.2307/249008

Denscombe, M. (2007). *The Good Research Guide: For Small-scale Social Research Projects*. New York: McGraw-Hill International.

Draper, S. (1999). Analysing fun as a candidate software requirement. In *Personal technology*. Heidelberg, Germany: Springer Verlag.

Duric, Z., Gray, W. D., Heishman, R., Li, F., Rosenfeld, A., & Schoelles, M. (2002). 'Integrating perceptual and cognitive modeling for adaptive and intelligent human-computer interaction. *Proceedings of the IEEE, 90*(7), 1272–1289. doi:10.1109/JPROC.2002.801449

Epting, F., Suchman, D., & Nickeson, C. (1971). An evaluation of elicitation procedures for personal constructs. *The British Journal of Psychology, 62*(4), 513–517.

Ford, D. H. (1987). *Humans as Self-Constructing Living Systems: A Developmental Theory of Behaviour and Personality*. Hillsdale, NJ: Erlbaum.

Ford, M. E. (1992). *Motivating Humans, Goals, Emotions and Personal Agency Beliefs*. Thousand Oaks, CA: Sage.

Fransella, F., & Bannister, D. (1977). *A manual for repertory grid technique*. London: Academic Press.

Greenberg, S., Fitzpatrick, G., Gutwin, C., & Kaplan, S. (2000). Adapting the locales framework for heuristic evaluation of groupware. [AJIS]. *Australasian Journal of Information Systems, 7*(2), 102–108.

Hartmann, J., Sutcliffe, A., & De Angeli, A. (2007). 'Investigating attractiveness in web user interfaces. Paper presented at the SIGCHI Conference on Human Factors in Computing Systems, San Jose, CA.

Hassenzahl, M., Beu, A., & Burmester, M. (2001a). Engineering Joy. *IEEE Software, 18*(1). doi:10.1109/52.903170

Hassenzahl, M., & Trautmann, T. (2001). *Analysis of web sites with the repertory grid technique*. Paper presented at the CHI 2001: extended abstracts: interactive poster sessions, New York.

Hassenzahl, M., Wessler, R., & Hamborg, K. (2001b). *Exploring and understanding product qualities that users desire*. Paper presented at the Joint AFIHM-BCS conference on Human-Computer Interaction IHM-HCI'2001, Toulouse, France.

Hollan, J., Hutchins, E., & Kirshac, D. (2000). Distributed Cognition: Toward a New Foundation for Human-Computer Interaction Research. *ACM Transactions on Computer-Human Interaction*, *7*(2), 174–196. doi:10.1145/353485.353487

Igbaria, M., Schiffman, S., & Wieckowski, T. (1994). The respective roles of perceived usefulness and perceived fun in the acceptance of microcomputer technology. *Behaviour & Information Technology*, *13*(6). doi:10.1080/01449299408914616

Kelly, G. (1955). *The psychology of personal constructs,* (Vol. 1 & 2). New York: Norton.

Millard, N., Hole, L., & Crowle, S. (1999). Smiling through: motivation at the user interface. In Bullinger, H-J. & Ziegler, J. (Eds.), *Human-Computer Interaction Ergonomics and User Interfaces* (pp. 824-8). Mahwah, NJ: Lawrence Erlbaum.

Mundorf, N., Westin, S., & Dholakia, N. (1993). Effects of hedonic components and user's gender on the acceptance of screen-based information services. *Behaviour & Information Technology*, *12*(5), 293–303. doi:10.1080/01449299308924393

Nielsen, J. (1993). *Usability Engineering.* San Francisco: Morgan Kaufmann (Academic Press).

Norman, D. A., Ortony, A., & Russell, D. M. (2003). Affect and Machine Design: Lessons for the Development of Autonomous Machines. *IBM Systems Journal*, *42*(1), 38–44.

Norman, K. L., Shneiderman, B. A., Harper, B. D., & Slaughter, L. A. (1989). Questionnaire for User Interface Satisfaction. Maryland: University of Maryland.

Oppenheim, A. N. (1992). *Questionnaire design, interviewing and attitude measurement* (2nd Ed.). London: St Martins Press.

Osgood, C. E., Suci, G. J., & Tannenbaum, P. H. (1971). *The Measurement of Meaning*. London: University of Illinois Press.

Picard, R. W., & Wexelblat, A. (2002). *Future interfaces: social and emotional*. Paper presented at the CHI '02 Extended Abstracts on Human Factors in Computing Systems, Minneapolis, Minnesota, USA.

Richardson, J. T. E. (2002). *Handbook of Qualitative Research Methods for Psychology and the Social Sciences*. Oxford, UK: BPS Blackwell Publishing.

Robson, C. (1993). *Real World Research*. Oxford. UK: Blackwell.

Ryle, A., & Lunghi, M. (1970). The dyad grid: a modification of repertory grid technique. *The British Journal of Psychology*, 117.

Snider, J. G., & Osgood, C. E. (Eds.). (1969). *Semantic Differential Technique: A SourceBook*. Chicago: Aldine Transaction.

Stewart, V., & Stewart, A. (1981). *Business applications of the repertory grid*. Maidenhead, UK: McGraw-Hill.

Venkatesh, V. (2000). Determinants of Perceived Ease of Use: Integrating Control, Intrinsic Motivation, and Emotion into the Technology Acceptance Model. *Information Systems Research*, *11*(4), 342–365. doi:10.1287/isre.11.4.342.11872

Verlinden, J., & Coenders, M. (2000). *Qualitative usability measurement of websites by employing the repertory grid technique*. Paper presented at the CHI 2000: extended abstracts, The Hague, The Netherlands.

Yin, R. (1994). *Case study research: design and methods*. London: Sage.

Chapter 16
DEPTH:
A Method and a Web-Based Tool for Designing and Executing Scenario-Based Usability Inspections of E-Systems

Petros Georgiakakis
ITisART.Ltd, Greece

Symeon Retalis
University of Piraeus, Greece

ABSTRACT

Scenario based inspection methods are currently widely used for evaluating the usability of web-based information systems (e-systems). However, it is neither easy nor cheap to find usability experts who possess the competencies for performing a usability inspection while at the same time have deep knowledge of the context for which each e-system has been developed. Moreover, the effectiveness of these methods depends on the quality of the inspection scenarios. These issues can be tackled by finding potential users of the e-systems under inspection who have basic knowledge about human-computer interaction and adequately support them to execute the appropriate scenarios. Towards this goal, a new usability evaluation method called DEPTH along with a web based tool that supports its application, have been created. This chapter describes DEPTH's underlining philosophy which is the re-use of inspection scenarios per feature of genres of e-systems as well as the re-use design expertise which can be encoded in terms of design patterns.

POWERING NOVICE USABILITY EVALUATORS TO PERFORM INSPECTIONS

Nowadays most of the web based information systems (e-systems) are complex online systems with voluminous and complicated functionality. This complexity along with their high purchase and implementation cost, impose the necessity to determine whether an e-system meets users' expectations. Furthermore, since the number of available e-systems is enormous there is a great demand for finding trusted ways for e-system evaluation in order for a stakeholder to have the ability to choose the

DOI: 10.4018/978-1-60566-896-3.ch016

Table 1. Relative advantages and disadvantages of each category of usability evaluation methods

Usability method	Advantages	Disadvantages
User-based	Provides insights into user's options and understanding of the system. Can give clear record of important problems. Relatively inexpensive even for large sample of users. Intuitive; easy to motivate potential evaluators to use it. Rating scales can provide quantitative data.	Time consuming for preparation and analysis of data. Requires occurrence of prototype. Does not always suggest solutions for identified usability problems.
Expert-based	Fast. Can be used early in the development process. Advanced planning is not required. HCI experts can suggest appropriate and effective solutions.	Costly. Prone to reporting false alarms/problems that are not actual usability problems in application.

most reliable and usable one. On the other hand, usable systems facilitate user experiences which make the need of having those imperative.

Usability is the quality of a system that makes it easy to learn, easy to use, easy to remember, error tolerant, and subjectively pleasing (Nielsen, 2000). Usability is the extent to which a system can be used by specified users to achieve specified goals with effectiveness, efficiency and satisfaction in a specified context of use, according to ISO/DIS 9241-11. According to Bevan (1995) "usability must reflect the quality of a function of an e-system within a specific context of use." For this reason the usability evaluation of an e-system is two-fold: Being able to deal with technological aspects and the way the user interacts with the e-system, and being able to deal with the specific context of use which the e-system is connected to. Undoubtedly both usability aspects are closely affiliated and deeply associated.

Various usability evaluation methods and techniques for e-systems have been proposed (Frechtling & Sharp, 1997; Russell, 2001; Law, Hvannberg, and Cockton, 2007). They can be divided into two main categories: expert-based usability methods and user testing. The advantages and disadvantages of the two categories are summarized in Table 1. Although comparisons of evaluation methods have recently been reported by HCI researches (e.g. Andre et al., 1999), only very few, firm conclusions can yet be drawn.

The most well-adopted, in both academics and industry, are the expert-based – more specifically the heuristic evaluations (HE) – and the scenario-based inspections. HEs make the application of discount methods easier. HEs use and modulate the usability heuristics proposed by Nielsen (2000). It has been noted, however, that Nielsen's heuristics need to be configured to the specific context of use related to the genre of the e-system (Ling & Salvendy, 2005). For example for the genre of groupware systems, Baker at al. (2001) developed a set of specific heuristics on the basis of the Nielsen's heuristics. Furthermore, it is very difficult and expensive to find usability experts and especially "dual-usability experts" specializing in both HEs and context-of-use of the genre of the e-system under evaluation (Nielsen, 2000; Dix et al. 2003). A solution to that problem would be to replace usability experts (who are few and difficult to find) with potential end-users with some (but less) knowledge of HEs, who are more available, easier to find, and know very well the context of use of the e-system under evaluation.

Another shortcoming of HEs is that they do not provide a systematic way to generate fixes to usability problems identified, or a way to assess the probable quality of any proposal for redesign (Sears 1997). This is why Sears (1997) created a technique called "heuristic walkthrough" that combines benefits from the HE, cognitive walkthrough, and usability inspection. Evaluators are asked to identify usability problems while they examine in a systematic way the e-system against a heuristic set. With the use of inspection scenarios (i.e. a structured flow of activities) evaluators can concentrate on what needs to be evaluated and how this can be done. They do not neglect to check complex procedures, while at the same time they can identify context specific usability problems (Hertzum & Jacobsen, 2001) and suggest design solutions (Miller, 2006).

Nevertheless, the heuristic walkthroughs and scenario-based usability inspections demand a lot of resources for the preparation of the systematic usability inspection of the e-system. Analyzing the functionality of an e-system as well as creating good scenarios correlated to the e-system's functionality are not easy tasks. Scenarios need to be written in an accurate and comprehensive form so that evaluators can perform the tasks suggested (Cockton & Woolrych, 2001). Additionally, scenarios need to be easily reproduced, communicated, exploited and/or adapted to various usage contexts of e-systems (Garzotto & Matera, 1997).

Recently, in an attempt to overcome HE's shortcomings, various new usability methods were proposed (Ling & Salvendy, 2005). One such method is the DEPTH (usability evaluation based on DEsign PaTterns & Heuristics criteria) usability method. Usability studies using DEPTH can be performed by "novice evaluators". "Novice evaluators" refer to evaluators with no usability expertise, who are potential users of the e-system and have some knowledge of usability. DEPTH can be used for both formative and summative evaluations. When used as a formative method, novice evaluators, who will be future users, are connivers in the development of the e-system.

Within DEPTH, in order for novice evaluators to successfully perform usability inspections, guidance during the inspection is needed (what to check and how) as well as access to design best practices. Inspection scenarios provide a structured method for assessing an e-system in a stepwise fashion and reporting problems in a

way that encourages reflection on these assessments (Blandford & Buchanan, 2003; Cockton, Woolrych, Hall, & Hindmarch, 2003). With the design patterns novice evaluators can have access to best design practices, and compare the way an e-system is designed to these practices. Design patterns are more useful than usability guidelines since they embrace the expert knowledge (Graham 2003). Design patterns give a narrative solution to common design problems that appear frequently; the solution is accompanied by a rationale and well defined examples of its implementation (Goodyear et. al., 2004). Moreover, design patterns can be very valuable tools for novice evaluators in their attempt to propose design solutions for usability problems.

The DEPTH method is technologically supported by a web based tool, called DEPTH TOOL-KIT. It has been developed to ease necessary tasks performed during the preparatory phase as well as the execution phase of an e-system's usability inspection. DEPTH has already been successfully used in several case studies for evaluating the usability of e-sites such as e-travel sites, learning objects repositories, e-sites for pharmaceutical products, etc. In this chapter we analytically present the method and the tool. First we will give an overview of the design patterns and the benefits of their use in usability inspection. Then we will present the rationale behind the DEPTH method. The functionality of the DEPTH toolkit will be described through usage scenarios from a usability study in the domain of e-travel. Finally, comments about the open issues in the field of scenario based usability inspection methods will be made.

THE ADDED VALUE OF E-SYSTEMS DESIGN PATTERNS

Design practices can codify, make explicit and available to the community of designers, developers and end-users best design practices in a formal and practical manner. Designers of new or existing e-systems, especially inexperienced ones, can take advantage of design expertise, past experience, and save precious time and resources in their effort to build usable systems.

The history of design patterns and their proliferation is well known and broadly documented. It all began in the field of built architecture, when Christopher Alexander invented the idea of capturing design guidelines in the form of design patterns (Alexander, 1996; Alexander et. al., 1977). The 'Alexandrian' patterns found many followers in the computer science discipline, especially after the so-called 'GOF' book for object-oriented design (Gamma et al., 1994). Some of the fields that have adopted patterns are: hypermedia engineering (Garrido et al, 1997; Garzotto et al, 1999), pedagogy (Fincher, 1999; Lyardet et al., 1999; Carlson 1998), e-learning (Avgeriou et al., 2003) and, of course, human-computer interaction (HCI, 2005).

In the field of HCI, design patterns have many supporters who have created online interaction design pattern libraries. Some of them are the following:

- Yahoo! Design Pattern Library http://developer.yahoo.com/ypatterns/index.php
- Design patterns by Martijn van Welie http://www.welie.com/patterns/index.php
- Hypermedia Design Patterns Repository http://www.designpattern.lu.unisi.ch/PatternsRepository.htm
- The Interaction Design Patterns repository: http://www.visi.com/~snowfall/InteractionPatterns.html
- Interface Patterns and Widget Library http://groups.headshift.com/display/Lib/Home
- IAWiki Patterns: http://iawiki.net/WebsitePatterns#PatternRepositories
- Web Patterns Project: http://groups.ischool.berkeley.edu/ui_designpatterns/webpatterns2/webpatterns/home.php

- Patterns for Effective Interaction Design by Jenifer Tidwell http://designinginterfaces.com/

Interaction design patterns are tightly coupled to usability and quality in use. Alexander made reference to an inherent value of the design patterns called "quality without a name". He said that "Bad building creates stress. Good building nurtures." The same can be said for e-systems. Interaction design patterns can become a very productive way to collect, describe, and structure usability knowledge (Borchers, 2001). They describe well established solutions, together with preconditions and rationales, for usable design of user interfaces.

Basing a usability inspection method on patterns can be justified by the several advantages that patterns hold (Schmettow, 2005; Garzotto & Retalis, 2008), such as:

- Patterns state preconditions, forces, and a rationale for the proposed solution, which helps to identify an appropriate way of solving a design problem for a specific situation, while the decision of when to apply the specific solution is left to the evaluator.
- The descriptions of problems and solutions are far more vivid and problem-oriented than are heuristics/guidelines. This makes them easier for a (novice) evaluator to understand and apply correctly.
- By contrast to heuristics/guidelines, patterns describe usable solutions together with examples of their application; thus, they lend themselves naturally to design recommendations in an evaluation.

Furthermore, design patterns provide a unique means for sharing and re-using designers' knowledge among practitioners and between experts and novice designers. Designers can use patterns for sharing and transmitting to novices their instructional 'philosophy' and pragmatic approaches to their applications, how their experiences can be designed, built and associated with the specificities of the subject matter, the environmental context, the human actors, the different strategies, and the available resources and tools (Cagnin et. al., 2005). Thus, design patterns provide a 'reference model' that enables a novice evaluator to compare a proposed solution to already existing ones of acknowledged quality.

Moreover, design patterns are not ready-made pluggable solutions. The solution proposed by each design pattern can be applied with adaptation based on the particular e-system's user needs and context of use. Thus, design patterns can not only help novice evaluators compare an existing implementation with the solution of a design pattern, but they can also propose solutions to identified usability problems based on the ideas documented in the design patterns.

For all the reasons mentioned above, we make use of design patterns in the DEPTH method.

The DEPTH Usability Method

The DEPTH method has been proposed for two main reasons: i) to minimize the preparatory phase of a scenario based usability inspection process, and ii) to assist novice usability evaluators in identifying as many usability problems as experts would, by helping them systematically evaluate the functionality of an e-system, providing them with the experts' existing knowledge, and stimulating them to think about usability problems and possible solutions.

Like most scenario based usability inspection methods (e.g. MILE (Garzotto, et. al., 1998)), DEPTH requires two operational phases: a preparatory phase and an execution phase. The preparatory phase aims at defining the conceptual framework that allows the inspection to be carried out in a systematic and effective way. Although the preparatory phase can be time consuming and entirely dependent on the experience of the us-

ability expert/engineer (Paterno, 2000; Dix et al 2004), DEPTH tries to minimize the effort needed to complete this phase.

DEPTH's preparatory phase is being performed, by a domain-specialized, interaction-design expert, once for a specific genre of e-systems. The output of this phase is the creation and maintenance of a repository containing a set of features that an e-system of a specific genre should offer as well as scenarios for the inspection of these features which will be associated with design patterns for this specific genre. The term "genre" is used in a sense to refer to types of artifact, in our case the e-systems. Examples of genres are e-travel sites, e-shops, online newspapers, etc. The concept of genre has been suggested as a potential tool for structuring the design of e-systems (Brown & Duguid, 1996). For each e-system that needs to be evaluated, the preparatory process does not need to be performed from scratch since the list of features, the inspection scenarios, and the design patterns will be re-used (from the original application on the genre) and adapted to the specific case.

During the execution phase, novice evaluators will be guided while performing the inspections following the directives of the scenarios. The major objective of a scenario is to help the evaluator examine the e-system within its intended use by its envisaged type of user, performing standardized tasks in the specific context. The evaluator is called to answer questions related to the usability performance of the supported functionality according to the specific context of use in order to identify problems. The evaluator can access the design pattern to find best design practices for the features under inspection. Moreover, the novice evaluator is asked to report on the general usability performance according to context specific heuristic criteria.

The whole evaluation process provided by DEPTH is depicted in Figure 1. The left column presents the general steps/actions of the preparatory phase. The outcomes of these steps

Figure 1. The DEPTH evaluation process

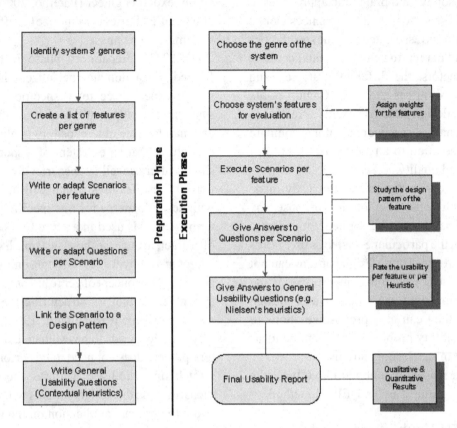

are reported into the "DEPTH-Repository". The right column shows the execution phase. Each evaluation study should start by first selecting the specific genre of the e-system under evaluation as well as the set of features of the e-system to be evaluated. Having as guide an analytical list of the features of the e-system under evaluation, the evaluator can easily perform the next step, which is an inspection walkthrough using the proposed scenarios. These scenarios act as an inspection wizard, guiding the evaluator. During the inspection, the evaluator can see the proposed design patterns. The evaluation report has two parts: a context-specific and a general part. The first reveals/measures the usability performance of the e-system under evaluation according to its specific context of use, while the second presents the general usability performance according to the expert/heuristic criteria. Thus, the comments that

a novice evaluator has made per scenario along with any proposed solutions to usability problems are collected and structured per feature of the e-system. Moreover, the evaluator is asked to give answers to questions about general aspects of the e-system's usability performance.

THE DEPTH TOOLKIT

The DEPTH TOOLKIT supports the tasks of the preparatory and execution phases. On the one hand, it facilitates the execution of the four main tasks of the preparatory phase for each genre of e-systems, namely:

i. Specifications of the features that could be offered by e-systems of a specific genre

ii. Editing and allocation of inspection scenarios and appropriate tasks to the features of genres

iii. Editing as well as linking of design patterns to features of a genre

From the novice usability evaluator perspective, the toolkit fully supports the execution phase. The initialization of an evaluation session occurs with the user (novice usability engineer) choosing the specific genre to which the e-system under inspection belongs. Then, as already said, the evaluator selects from a list the features of the genres the ones that will be evaluated. During the execution phase, the selected set of features is being inspected with the use of scenarios that are shown to the evaluator one after the other. Figure 2 shows a screenshot of the interface of the DEPTH_TOOLKIT. At the end of the evaluation process, a detailed report is automatically produced, containing the evaluator's notes about the usability performance of the examined e-system along with the evaluator's answers to general usability heuristic criteria (e.g. questions about the Nielsen's heuristics criteria (Nielsen, 1993).

APPLYING AND EVALUATING THE DEPTH METHOD

Scope of the Experimental Study

In order to evaluate our method we conducted an experiment with 18 novice usability evaluators (NUEs) who were postgraduate students of the Department of Educational Technology and Digital Systems at University of Piraeus. They had successfully completed an introductory course on Human - Computer Interaction. They were asked to evaluate two e-travel sites. E-travel sites allow users to search and book air tickets, hotels, renting a car, etc. The two e-systems had been carefully chosen since various usability problems had been identified within those by three usability experts.

The NUEs had average knowledge and experience with the specific genre, and none of them claimed to be an expert in using (nor designing) such e-systems. Actually only two (2) of them had used one of the e-sites under evaluation, and 14 of them had used less than 3 times some e-site for booking hotels, cars, or air tickets. Nevertheless, the students were quite accustomed to the concept of design patterns, through a 2-hour lecture they attended during the semester. They had also

Figure 2. A screen shot of the DEPTH TOOLKIT

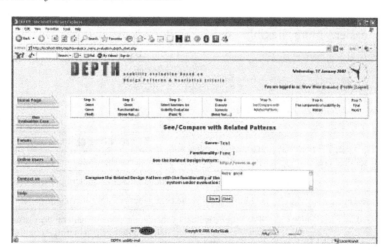

Figure 3. The functionality of e-travel sites

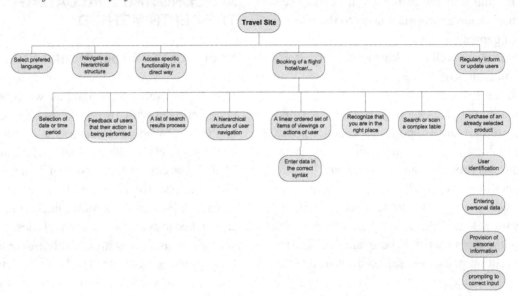

learned to apply design patterns when developing an e-system.

We used DEPTH only from the novice evaluator's point of view since we wanted to focus on this specific perspective. The main research questions of this evaluation study were:

- Can DEPTH help NUEs identify usability problems (especially complex ones)?
- Can DEPTH make NUEs improve their ability to propose solutions to the identified usability problems?
- Is DEPTH easy to apply?
- Does DEPTH make the NUEs' evaluation process easier, more flexible and enjoyable?

- Does DEPTH make NUEs feel confident that they performed a good evaluation study?
- Do the NUEs appreciate the added value of Design Patterns for usability evaluation?

EXPERIMENTAL PROCESS

According to the preparatory phase of the DEPTH method, several e-sites of the e-travel genre had been thoroughly examined with respect to the features they provide. Thus a superset of their features had been created, as shown in Figure 3.

In order to relate the features of the e-travel site to design patterns, we selected design patterns (DP) from Martijn van Welie's web design pat-

Table 2. Examples of relations between features and design patterns

FEATURES (F)	DESIGN PATTERNS (DP)
F1. Purchase of an already selected product	DP1.http://www.welie.com/patterns/showPattern.php?patternID=purchase-process
F2. User identification	DP2.http://www.welie.com/patterns/showPattern.php?patternID=login
F3. A list of search results process	DP3.http://www.welie.com/patterns/showPattern.php?patternID=search-results
F4. A hierarchical structure of user navigation	DP4a.http://developer.yahoo.com/ypatterns/pattern_breadcrumbs.php or DP4b.http://www.welie.com/patterns/showPattern.php?patternID=crumbs

terns repository (http://www.welie.com/) as well as from Yahoo's Design Pattern Library (http://developer.yahoo.com/ypatterns/). So, we created a table where each feature is related to one or more design patterns as shown in Table 2.

For each of these features we created a related usage scenario. For example to the functionality "F1: Booking of a flight/hotel/car/" we assigned the scenario "S1: Booking" as shown in Table3.

The NUEs had to conduct all the tasks of the proposed scenarios while having the ability to look at the related design patterns. After having fulfilled the inspection of the two e-travel sites, they had to express their overall opinion about each one of them according to Nielsen's heuristic criteria (Nielsen, 1993).

Not only did we analyze the reports written by the NUEs (and collected with the use of the DEPTH toolkit) but we also conducted focus-group interviews in teams of three students, in order to get a better insight of their opinion about DEPTH. The major advantage of conducting a focus group interview (Krueger, et. al., 2000) was the ability to obtain detailed information through group cooperation.

Evaluation Findings

After the experiment, we analyzed the performance of our NUEs by comparing their findings with the usability problems identified by the three (3) usability experts. The comparison was made based on three criteria:

- Validity or Accuracy (Sears, 1997; Hartson et al, 2003), i.e. the ratio of the number of real usability problems with respect to the total number of findings (whether problems or not) of each particular evaluation team.
- Thoroughness or Completeness (Sears, 1997; Hartson et al, 2003), i.e. the ratio of the number of real usability problems found by each evaluation team with respect to the total number of real usability problems that exist in the target system.
- Consistency (Hartson et al, 2003), i.e. the extent to which multiple applications of a particular usability inspection method produce similar results.

The results from this comparison are shown tin Tables 4, 5 and 6.

Table 3. Usage scenario and questions for the feature; booking a flight/hotel/car via an e-travel site

(S1)Description:	Booking
Task:	You are looking for the price of a ticket in association with date and time factors. Determine the item you wish to book or buy among (probably) some other options given. Select the town or airport you wish to leave from and go to. If you don't know the names or the abbreviations find out from information given within the site. Choose the departing date, time, booking class, and number of people travelling with you. Because you are looking for the best available price and you don't mind to be precise to the dates you've given, choose these dates to be flexible but close to those you initially chose. Submit your choices.
Questions:	Did you easily find the searching area where you can place your options? In the area where you can choose the departure and the arrival airport or town, did you have to type in the name or abbreviation of your location, or could you select from a list provided to you? If you had to type in the location was there any help provided for finding out the correct abbreviation or spelling? Were there any error messages in case something wrong was typed? In the departing and returning date forms was there a calendar available or did you have to type yourself the exact date? Could you select flexible dates (for example ±3 days from original choice)? When you selected other parties travelling with you, were you given the option of Adult or Senior, or Child? Could you search for a one way trip if you wished? When you submitted your choices for a query into their database, were you prompted that some action was taking place? Did you receive any results?

Table 4. Validity of usability findings

Evaluator	Total findings	Not a problem	%	Minor problems	%	Major Problems	%	Validity Real findings	%
1	35	2	5.71	20	57.14	13	37.14	33	94.29
2	36	4	11.11	18	50.00	14	38.89	32	88.89
3	32	3	9.38	17	53.13	12	37.50	29	90.63
4	35	1	2.86	20	57.14	14	40.00	34	97.14
5	32	0	0.00	20	62.50	12	37.50	32	100.00
6	34	3	8.82	19	55.88	12	35.29	31	91.18
7	30	1	3.33	17	56.67	12	40.00	29	96.67
8	33	1	3.03	20	60.61	12	36.36	32	96.97
9	34	3	8.82	17	50.00	14	41.18	31	91.18
10	35	5	14.29	18	51.43	12	34.29	30	85.71
11	32	1	3.13	19	59.38	12	37.50	31	96.88
12	36	2	5.56	20	55.56	14	38.89	34	94.44
13	34	2	5.88	18	52.94	14	41.18	32	94.12
14	36	5	13.89	18	50.00	13	36.11	31	86.11
15	37	6	16.22	19	51.35	12	32.43	31	83.78
16	34	4	11.76	18	52.94	12	35.29	30	88.24
17	32	1	3.13	17	53.13	14	43.75	31	96.88
18	34	3	8.82	17	50.00	14	41.18	31	91.18

Table 5. Thoroughness of DEPTH usability evaluation method

Evaluator	Real usability problems	Usability problems that exist in the system	Thoroughness (%)
1	33	36	91.67
2	32	36	88.89
3	29	36	80.56
4	34	36	94.44
5	32	36	88.89
6	31	36	86.11
7	29	36	80.56
8	32	36	88.89
9	31	36	86.11
10	30	36	83.33
11	31	36	86.11
12	34	36	94.44
13	32	36	88.89
14	31	36	86.11
15	31	36	86.11
16	30	36	83.33
17	31	36	86.11
18	31	36	86.11

Table 6. Consistency across the 18 novice usability evaluators

36 Evaluators	36 real problems	% of real usability problems found
found by 18 evaluators	28	77.78
found by 17 evaluators	29	80.56
found by 16 evaluators	29	80.56
found by 15 evaluators	29	80.56
found by 14 evaluators	30	83.33
found by 13 evaluators	30	83.33
found by 12 evaluators	30	83.33
found by 11 evaluators	30	83.33
found by 10 evaluators	30	83.33
found by 9 evaluators	31	86.11
found by 8 evaluators	31	86.11
found by 7 evaluators	31	86.11
found by 6 evaluators	31	86.11
found by 5 evaluators	32	88.89
found by 4 evaluators	32	88.89
found by 3 evaluators	32	88.89
found by 2 evaluators	33	91.67
found by 1 evaluator	34	94.44

The validity of usability evaluation results, as shown in Table 4, was considerably high. The validity percentage is oscillating from 83.78% to 100.00% which depicts that the large majority of the results were useful and valid. Also the percentage of false alarms within the reports was not high (13 out of 18 evaluators identified less than 10% problems that were not actual ones).

Concerning the criterion of thoroughness, the findings were very promising. As shown in Table 5, the percentage of the total number of real usability problems identified by each NUE divided by the total number of real problems that exist in the e-travel site was at least 80.56%.

In order to pinpoint the consistency of the evaluation results from the 18 different evaluators using DEPTH, we checked the extent to which the multiple usability evaluations produced similar results. As Table 6 shows, the results were also very satisfactory. All the evaluators found the same

28 (of 36) usability problems (77.78%). Only two (2) usability problems (out of 36) were not found by the NUEs and these were "banner blindness" which means that users never fixate their eyes on anything that looks like a banner ad due to shape or position on the page and "animation avoidance" which makes users ignore areas with blinking or flashing text or other aggressive animations Therefore, it is best to avoid any designs that look like advertisements since users almost never look at anything that looks like an advertisement, whether or not it's actually an ad.

This experiment helped us verify what we claimed to prove, i.e. the DEPTH method actually enables NUEs to perform reliable and high quality evaluations.

During the interviews, the NUEs clearly stated that the DEPTH method and the toolkit were user friendly and helped them in successfully executing the inspection of the e-travel sites. In many evaluation reports (10 out of 18) the NUEs were also suggesting solutions for each of the problems identified. Among other positive remarks, it was also mentioned that i) DEPTH can be used in evaluating isolated areas of interest by simply choosing only few features and ii) DEPTH helped NUEs acquire deeper knowledge about the use of patterns for interaction design.

However the method has some limitations. Design patterns are not that many. Therefore, it is difficult to find mature pattern languages to support the variety of e-system genres. That became obvious from the collection of design patterns we proposed as we deliberately chose some that are not completely mature yet. Even if we assume that the pattern language is there, pretty matured, will there always be a design pattern to validate all areas of interest in a digital genre? Luckily, there are some guidelines which are written in a form similar to design patterns (Shneiderman 2006).

CONCLUSION

Our main goal, in this chapter, was to provide an overview of DEPTH, which is an innovative method for performing scenario-based expert heuristic usability evaluation for e-systems.

A similar example of expert evaluation using design patterns has been performed by Van Welie et al. (2003) for evaluating the usability of web museums without user involvement. He analyzed the major sections of the museum websites in order to recognize patterns that had been applied. He commented that the evaluation is easier when the evaluator knows the pattern collection available (Van Welie et. al. 2003). The idea of re-usable scenarios in evaluation studies has also been proposed by the eLSE method (Lanzilotti, et al. 2006).

The DEPTH method is innovative since it uses the added value of design patterns in a very systematic way within the usability evaluation process. When DEPTH was applied by non us-

ability expert for the evaluation of e-travel sites, the results were satisfactory. The outcome of the presented case study shows that our method can be easily used by Novice Usability Evaluators. The expert knowledge, embedded in the form of design patterns and usage scenarios, was readily available to the novice evaluators, thus enhancing their inspection methods and improving their judgments about the usability of the functionality tested. As the field of design patterns grows and matures, this method seems very promising and highly applicable.

REFERENCES

Alexander, C. (1996). *The Origins of Pattern Theory: the Future of the Theory, And The Generation of a Living World*. Keynote speech at the 11th Annual ACM Conference on Object-Oriented Programs, Systems, Languages and Applications (OOPSLA), October 6-10, San Jose, CA. Retrieved from http://www.patternlanguage.com/archive/ieee/ieeetext.htm

Alexander, C., Ishikawa, S., Silverstein, M., Jacobson, M., Fiksdahl-King, I., & Angel, S. (1977). *A Pattern Language: Towns, buildings, constructions*. New York: Oxford University Press.

Andre, T., Williges, R., & Hartson, H. (1999). The effectiveness of usability evaluation methods: determining the appropriate criteria. In *Proceedings of the Human Factors and Ergonomics Society 43rd Annual Meeting*, Santa Monica CA, (pp. 1090-1094).

Avgeriou, P. Papasalouros A., Retalis S. & Skordalakis E. (2003). Towards a Pattern Language for Learning Management Systems. *Educational Technology & Society, 6*(2), 11-24. Retrieved from http://ifets.ieee.org/periodical/6-2/2.html

Baker, K., Greenberg, S., & Gutwin, C. (2001). Heuristic Evaluation of Groupware Based on the Mechanics of Collaboration. In *Proceedings of the 8th IFIP International Conference on Engineering for Human-Computer Interaction*, (pp.123-140).

Bevan, N. (1995). Measuring usability as quality of use. *Journal of Software Quality*, *4*, 115–130. doi:10.1007/BF00402715

Blandford, A. & Buchanan, G. (2003). Usability of digital libraries: a source of creative tensions with technical developments. *IEEE-CS Technical Committee on Digital Libraries' on-line newsletter.*

Borchers, J. (2001). *A Pattern Approach to Interaction Design.* Chichester, UK: John Wiley & Sons Ltd.

Branaghan, R. J. (2001). Design by People for People: Essays on Usability. *Cognetics.*

Brown, J. S., & Duguid, P. (1996). Keeping it simple. In Winograd, T. (ed), *Bringing Design to Software,* (pp. 129-145). New York: ACM Press.

Cagnin, M. I., Braga, R. T. V., Germano, F. S. R., Chan, A., & Maldonado, J. (2005). Extending Patterns with Testing Implementation. In *Fifth Latin American Conference on Pattern Languages of Programs, 2005, Campos do Jordão - SP. Proceedings do SugarLoafPLoP 2005, 2005. v. 1*

Carlson, P. (1998). Advanced Educational Technologies – Promise and Puzzlement. *Journal of Universal Computer Science*, *4*(3), 210–215.

Cockton, G., & Woolrych, A. (2001). Understanding inspection methods: lessons from an assessment of heuristic evaluation. In Blandford AJ, Vanderdonckt J (eds.) *People & Computers XV* (pp. 171–192). Berlin: Springer- Verlag.

Cockton, G., Woolrych, A., Hall, L., & Hindmarch, M. (2003). Changing analysts' tunes: The surprising impact of a new instrument for usability inspection method assessment. In P. Palanque, P. Johnson, & E. O'Neill (Eds.), People and computers XVII: Designing for society, Proceedings of HCI 2003, (pp. 145-162). Berlin: Springer-Verlag.

Dix, A., Finlay, J. E., Abowd, G. D., & Beale, R. (2003). *Human-Computer Interaction* (3rd Ed.). Upper Saddle River, NJ: Prentice Hall.

Dix, A. J., Finlay, J. E., Abowd, G. D., & Beale, R. (2004). *Human-Computer Interaction.* (3rd Ed.). Staffordshire Hemel Hempstead, UK: Prentice-Hall.

Fincher, S. (1999). Analysis of Design: an exploration of patterns and pattern languages for pedagogy. *Journal of Computers in Mathematics and Science Teaching. Special Issue CS-ED Research, 18*(3), 331–348.

Frechtling, J., & Sharp, L. (1997). *User-Friendly Handbook for Mixed Method Evaluations.* Washington, DC: National Science Foundation. Retrieved from http://www.nsf.gov/pubs/1997/nsf97153/start.htm

Gamma, E., Helm, R., Johnson, R., & Vlissides, J. (1994). *Design Patterns – Elements of reusable object oriented software.* Reading, MA: Addison Wesley.

Garrido, A., Rossi, G., & Schwabe, D. (1997). Patterns Systems for Hypermedia. In *Proceedings of PloP97 Pattern Language of Program.*

Garzotto, F., & Matera, M. (1997). A Systematic Method for Hypermedia Usability Inspection. *The New Review of Hypermedia and Multimedia, 3*, 39–65. doi:10.1080/13614569708914683

Garzotto, F., Matera, M., & Paolini, P. (1998). Model-based heuristic evaluation of hypermedia usability. In *Proceedings of the Working Conference on Advanced Visual Interfaces*, May 24–27, L'Aquila, Italy.

Garzotto, F., Paolini, P., Bolchini, D., & Valenti, S. (1999). "Modeling-by-patterns" of web applications. Chen P., Embley D., Kouloumdjian J. & Little S. (eds.), *Advances in Conceptual Modeling* (LNCS Vol. 1727, pp. 293-306). Berlin: Springer.

Garzotto, F., & Retalis, S. (2008). "Design-by-patterns" in e-learning: a critical perspective. In Lockyer, Bennett, Agostinho & Harper (eds.), *Handbook of Research on Learning Design and Learning Objects: Issues, Applications, and Technologies*. Hershey, PA: Idea Group Inc.

Goodyear, P., Avgeriou, P., Baggetun, R., Bartoluzzi, S., Retalis, S., Ronteltap, F., & Rusman, E. (2004). Towards a pattern language for networked learning. In *Proceedings of Networked Learning, 2004*, 449–455.

Graham, I. (2003). *A Pattern Language for Web Usability*. Reading, MA: Addison-Wesley.

Hartson, H. R., Andre, T. S., & Williges, R. C. (2003). Criteria for evaluating usability methods. *International Journal of Human-Computer Interaction, 13*, 373–410. doi:10.1207/S15327590IJHC1304_03

HCI design patterns. (2005). Retrieved from http://www.hcipatterns.org/

Hertzum, M., & Jacobsen, N. E. (2001). The evaluator effect: A chilling fact about usability evaluation methods. *International Journal of Human-Computer Interaction, 13*(4), 421–443. doi:10.1207/S15327590IJHC1304_05

Krueger, R. A., & Casey, M. A. (2000). *Focus Groups: A Practical Guide for Applied Research*, (3rd Ed.). Thousand Oaks, CA: Sage Publications.

Lanzilotti, R., Costabile, M., Ardito, C., & De Angeli, A. (2006). eLSE Methodology: a Systematic Approach to the e-Learning Systems Evaluation. *Educational Technology & Society, 9*(4), 42–53.

Law, E. L., Hvannberg, E., & Cockton, G. (2007). *Maturing Usability: Quality in Software, Interaction and Value* (Human-Computer Interaction Series). New York: Springer-Verlag.

Ling, C., & Salvendy, G. (2005). Extension of heuristic evaluation method: a review and reappraisal. *Ergonomia IJE&HF, 27*(3), 179–197.

Lyardet, F., Rossi, G., & Schwabe, D. (1999). Patterns for Adding Search Capabilities to Web Information Systems. In *Proc. of Europlop '99*, (pp. 134-147). Kloster Irsee, Germany: IEEE Press.

Miller, J. (2006). Usability Testing: A Journey, Not a Destination. *IEEE Internet Computing, 10*(6, Nov/Dec), 80-83.

Nielsen, J. (1993). *Usability Engineering*. Cambridge, MA: Academic Press.

Nielsen, J. (2000). *Designing Web Usability: The Practice of Simplicity*. Indianapolis: New Riders Publishing.

Paterno, F. (2000). Model-based design of interactive applications. *Intelligence, 11*(4), 26–38. doi:10.1145/355137.358311

Schmettow, M. (2005) Towards a Pattern Based Usability Inspection Method for Industrial Practitioners. In *Proceedings of the Workshop on Integrating Software Engineering and Usability Engineering* (held on Interact 2005). Retrieved from http://www.se-hci.org/bridging/interact2005/03_Schmettow_Towards_UPI.pdf

Sears, A. (1997). Heuristic walkthroughs: Finding the problems without the noise. *International Journal of Human-Computer Interaction, 9*(3), 213–234. doi:10.1207/s15327590ijhc0903_2

Sears, A. (1997). Heuristic walkthroughs: Finding the problems without the noise. *International Journal of Human-Computer Interaction, 9*(3), 213–234. doi:10.1207/s15327590ijhc0903_2

Shneiderman, B. (2006). Designing the User Interface. Reading, MA: Addison Wesley Longman.

Van Welie, M. & Van der Veer, G. C. (2003). *Pattern Languages in Interaction Design: Structure and Organization*. Interact 2003.

Chapter 17
Applying the WDP Technique to Usability Inspections in Web Development Organizations

Tayana Conte
Federal University of Amazonas, Brazil

Verônica T. Vaz
PESC – COPPE/UFRJ, Brazil

Jobson Massolar
PESC – COPPE/UFRJ, Brazil

Andrew Bott
Fundação COPPETEC, Brazil

Emilia Mendes
University of Auckland, New Zealand

Guilherme H. Travassos
PESC – COPPE/UFRJ, Brazil

ABSTRACT

This chapter presents the WDP (Web Design Perspectives-based Usability Evaluation), an inspection technique specifically designed to assess the usability of Web applications. This technique combines Web design perspectives and the heuristic evaluation method proposed by Nielsen (1994b). In addition to describing the components of the WDP technique this chapter also illustrates its use in practice by means of an industrial case study where the technique is applied to inspect a real Web application. In this case study, developers and requirement assessment staff applied the WDP technique to evaluate the usability of modules developed from scratch for a Web application. The results of this case study indicate the feasibility of performing usability inspections with the participation of a software project's stakeholders, even when stakeholders are not usability experts.

DOI: 10.4018/978-1-60566-896-3.ch017

INTRODUCTION

Due to the relevance of usability in Web applications the software development industry is investing in projects and evaluations that help improve this quality item in their Web applications (Matera *et al.* 2006). The most commonly adopted methods to evaluate usability are: (1) usability tests, in which real users take part; and (2) usability inspections, in which inspectors (usually specialists) examine aspects related to the usability of the application to detect violations of a set of usability principles.

Although usability testing is considered the most efficient way to test systems and prototypes from a user's standpoint, its costs are high as it involves user time and, many times, the use of specific usability labs. Apart from that, usability tests also have some inconveniences such as the difficulty in selecting a representative sample from a population and a possible difficulty in training the users in test execution that includes advanced application aspects (Matera *et al.* 2006). Usability inspection methods were proposed as an alternative with a good cost-benefit ratio in comparison to usability tests.

One of the methods for usability inspection is the Heuristics Evaluation (Nielsen 1994b) in which a small group of specialists study an application using a list of usability principles called heuristics. Studies have shown that this is a very efficient method, with a good cost-benefit ratio (Nielsen 1994a). However, a disadvantage to this method is the high dependency on the skills and experience of the evaluators (Matera *et al.* 2006).

Regarding the usability evaluation of Web applications, several techniques, methods and tools have been proposed. Insfran & Fernandez (2008) present a systematic review in which 51 articles were reviewed to investigate which methods for usability evaluation had been used by researchers to assess Web artefacts. Forty-five percent of the articles reviewed described the use of evaluation methods especially customized to evaluate Web applications, where usability testing is the most frequently used method.

However, despite the large number of techniques and tools proposed, many Web development organizations are not applying them (Insfran and Fernandez 2008). Possible causes to this are: lack of knowledge of these techniques and tools; or still budgetary limitations that prevent the hiring of usability specialists.

This chapter presents a usability inspection technique specific to Web applications named WDP (Web Design Perspectives-based Usability Evaluation), that can be used by the very stakeholders in software projects in the evaluation of their usability. WDP is based on the Heuristics Evaluation method with specific focus on Web applications, and was developed through an approach based on experimentation. Two feasibility studies have been carried out so far, one an observation study and two case studies where the WDP technique was evaluated (Conte *et al.* 2007a; Conte *et al.* 2007b; Conte *et al.* 2008; Vaz *et al.* 2008). This chapter clearly presents the application of the WDP technique in the Web development industry, along with an inspection process that is suggested to be used in usability evaluations. To this end, the chapter describes a case study in an industrial environment where a usability inspection was carried out where developers and requirement evaluators used this technique to assess recently-developed modules. An analysis is made of the efficiency indicators in the fault detection stage, effort in the detection stages and discrimination and learn ability degree as gathered throughout the case study. The purpose of this chapter is to provide information that may encourage other Web development organizations to carry out usability evaluations using techniques for the support of inspections.

The chapter is organized as follows: after the introduction on usability inspections for Web applications, the WDP technique is presented, describing the concept of perspectives, which form its basis, within the context of a Web project, and detailing the related Heuristics x Perspective pairs. Then the inspection process presented is suggested for use when inspecting the usability of Web applications with the WDP technique. After that, a case study executed at in an industrial setting is shown, where the usability inspection of three modules of a Web application and its results are discussed. Finally, conclusions and lessons learned are described as resulting from this practical experience.

The WDP Technique

According to Zhang *et al.* (1999), it is difficult for each inspector to detect all of the different usability issues at the same time. For that, Zhang *et al.* (1999) proposed a perspective-based usability inspection technique (UBR), in which each inspection session focuses on a sub-group of usability issues covered by a usability perspective. The assumption when using perspective-based inspections is that, thanks to the focus, each inspection session can detect a larger percentage of the issues related to the perspective used and that the combination of different perspectives can find more issues than the combination of the same number of inspection sessions that use a general inspection technique (Zhang *et al.* 1999).

Based on these facts, we prepared a new proposition in which we tested if the adoption of perspectives also renders a Heuristics Evaluation (Nielsen 1994b) more efficiently for the usability inspection of Web applications. For that, we propose the use of perspectives inherent to Web projects: Presentation, Conceptualization, and Navigation (Conte *et al.* 2007a). These perspectives were identified based on a study of eight development methods proposed specifically for Web applications:

- Object-Oriented Hypermedia Design Model (OHDM) (Schwabe *et al.* 1996)
- Web Modeling Language (WebML) (Ceri *et al.* 2000)

- W2000 (Baresi *et al.* 2000)
- Object-oriented Hypermedia method (OO-H) (Gómez *et al.* 2001)
- Web Application Extension (WAE) (Conallen 2002)
- UML-based Web Engineering (UWE) (Koch and Kraus 2002)
- Object Oriented Web Solution (OOWS) (Fons *et al.* 2003)
- Ariadne Development Method (ADM) (Díaz *et al.* 2005)

These development methods have tried to demonstrate the need to capture and represent design perspectives, which are particularly relevant for this class of applications, especially those related to domain concepts, navigation and presentation issues (Pastor, 2004). Although not all eight methods use the same names (Presentation, Conceptualization and Navigation), we could observe that they all consider these three perspectives. Some of the methods represent other perspectives (e.g. W2000 suggest the use of a service model, that comprises the definition of the business processes supplied by the application), but they are not a consensus.

We use these perspectives as a guide to interpret the Nielsen's heuristics with a specific focus on Web applications. This derived technique is called Web Design Perspectives-based Usability Evaluation (WDP). Table 1 shows the definitions for each Web project perspective and the related focus in the usability evaluations. Table 2 shows the heuristics as proposed by Nielsen (1994b). Finally, Table 3 shows the HxP pairs (Heuristics x Perspective) as obtained through the relating of the Web project perspectives with the Heuristics.

The next sub-section presents the full version of the WDP technique v4. For each perspective, we present the HxP pairs (Heuristics x Perspective) that show how a given heuristic is interpreted in the perspective at hand. It is important to note that not all the heuristics relate to all of the perspectives as shown in Table 3. For example, the Perspective Presentation is not related to Heuristic number 3,

Table 1. Web project perspectives employed in Usability evaluation

Web Design Perspectives		Usability Focus
Conceptual	Represents the **conceptual elements** that make up the application domain.	Relates to the clarity and the conciseness of the **domain elements** of the problem. Under this perspective, the usability is satisfactory if different users easily understand domain terms, such that it prevents mistakes caused by ambiguous, inconsistent, or unknown terms.
Presentation	Represents the characteristics related to the **application layout** and **interface element** arrangement.	Relates to how consistent **the information is as presented to the user**. Under this perspective, the usability is satisfactory if the arrangement of the interface's elements allow the user to accomplish one's tasks effectively, efficiently, and pleasantly.
Navigation	Represents the **navigational space**, defining the information access elements and their associations.	Relates to different **user accesses to system's functionalities**. According to this perspective, the usability is satisfactory if navigation options allow the user to accomplish one's tasks effectively, efficiently, and pleasantly.

and therefore there is no P.3 pair. For this reason, pair P.4 is presented after the P.2 pair.

HxP Pairs (Heuristics x Perspective) in WDP v4

Heuristics Related to the Perspective Presentation (Presentation)

The inspector should be concerned with what she/he is seeing and how it is being presented. The key question is: "Am I seeing?"

P.1. System status visibility

- Assess if system status is always visible to the user.
  - System status is the location of the application where the user is found or the status after a transaction.

P.2. Agreement between the system and the real world

- Assess if system information and options

Table 2. Nielsen's Heuristics Description (Dix et al. 2003)

1	Visibility of system status "Always keeps users informed of what is going on through appropriate feedback within reasonable time."
2	Matching between system and real world "The system should speak the user's language, with words, phrases and concepts that are familiar to the user, rather than system-oriented terms, pursuant to real-world conventions, making information appear in a natural and logical order."
3	User control and freedom "Users often choose system functions by mistake and need the clearly marked 'emergency exit' to leave the unwanted state without having to go through an extended dialog. Supports undo and redo."
4	Consistency and Standards "Users should not have to wonder whether words, situations or actions mean the same thing in different contexts. Follows platform conventions and accepted standards. "
5	Error prevention "Makes it difficult to make errors. Even better than good error messages is the careful design that prevents the problem from occurring in the first place."
6	Recognition rather than recall "Makes objects, actions and options visible. The user should not have to remember information from one part of the dialog to another. Instructions to use the system should be visible or easily retrievable whenever appropriate"
7	Flexibility and efficiency of use "Allows users to tailor frequent actions. Accelerators – unseen by the novice user – may often speed up the interaction for the expert user to such an extent that the system can cater to both inexperienced and experienced users."
8	Aesthetic and minimalist design "Dialogs should not contain information that is irrelevant or rarely needed. Every extra unit of information in the dialog competes with the relevant units of information and reduces their relative visibility."
9	Help users recognize, diagnose and recover from errors "Error messages should be conveyed in plain language (no codes), pinpoint the issue, and constructively suggest the solution."
10	Help and documentation "Few systems can be used with no instructions so it may be necessary to provide help and documentation. Any such information should be easily searchable, focused on the user's task, listing concrete steps to be carried out, and not be too large."

Table 3. Relationships between Heuristics and Design Perspectives in WDP v4

	Heuristics (Nielsen, 1994)	Web Design Perspective		
		Presentation	Conceptual	Navigation
1	Visibility of system status	P.1	C.1	
2	Matching between system and real world	P.2	C.2	
3	User control and freedom			N.3
4	Consistency and Standards	P.4	C.4	
5	Error prevention	P.5		N.5
6	Recognition rather than recall	P.6		
7	Flexibility and efficiency of use	P.7		N.7
8	Aesthetic and minimalist design	P.8		
9	Help users recognize, diagnose and recover from errors	P.9	C.9	N.9
10	Help and documenttion	P.10	C.10	N.10

are presented in a natural and logical order according to the concepts of the domain of the problem.

- Assess if the terms (words or symbols) used by the system comply with real-world conventions.
  - "Real-world conventions" cover both the conventions of the domain of the problem and the terminology conventions of similar applications.

P.4. Consistency and standards

- Discover if the terminology, graphs and symbols of the interface are consistent.
- Discover if there is compliance with the platform conventions and interface standards adopted in relation to the layout, formatting and controls.
- Verify if there is consistency in the interfaces for tasks that are equivalent.
- Verify if error messages are presented in a

Figure 1. Good example of the usage of the P.1 pair

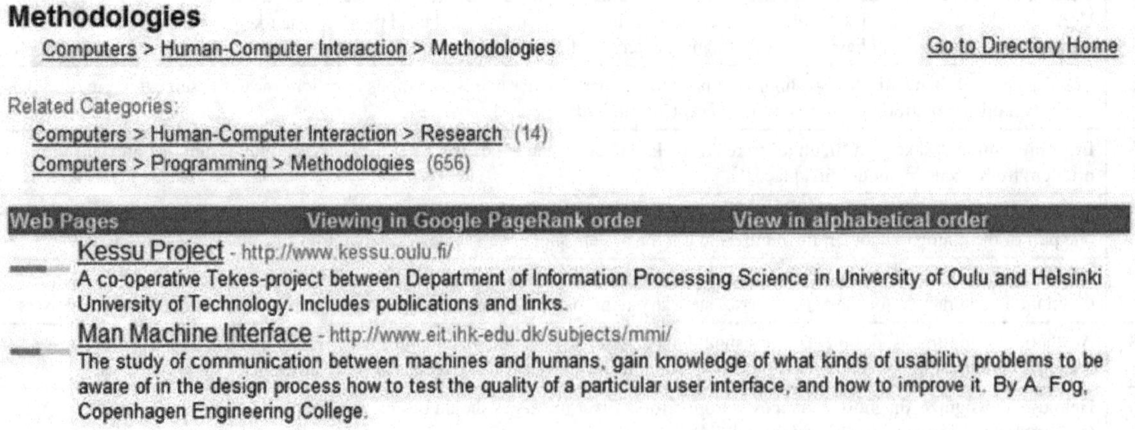

Methodologies

Computers > Human-Computer Interaction > Methodologies

Go to Directory Home

Related Categories:
Computers > Human-Computer Interaction > Research (14)
Computers > Programming > Methodologies (656)

Web Pages   Viewing in Google PageRank order   View in alphabetical order

Kessu Project - http://www.kessu.oulu.fi/
A co-operative Tekes-project between Department of Information Processing Science in University of Oulu and Helsinki University of Technology. Includes publications and links.

Man Machine Interface - http://www.eit.ihk-edu.dk/subjects/mmi/
The study of communication between machines and humans, gain knowledge of what kinds of usability problems to be aware of in the design process how to test the quality of a particular user interface, and how to improve it. By A. Fog, Copenhagen Engineering College.

way that is consistent with the presentation standards used.

P.5. Error Prevention

- Check if the mandatory data in data entry are clearly defined.
- Check if the interface indicates the correct format for a specific data entry.
- Check if the information is presented in a balanced way and in the natural order of the domain of the problem.
- Check if the interface facilitates the distinction between different tasks and data.

P.6. Recognizing instead of remembering

- Check if it is easy to recognize/visualize the option that is to be used to attain the intended goal.
- Check if system interface allows the user to visualize key data during the execution of a task.
- Check if it is easy to recognize/visualize already supplied data.

P.7. Flexibility and use efficiency

- Check if the arrangement of the elements in the system interface increased use efficiency, minimizing physical action efforts.
  - ○ N.B.: Disregard links and other access forms as 'interface elements'. These are considered as 'navigation elements' and will be dealt with in the navigation perspective.
- Check if the arrangement of the interface elements minimizes the effort in visual searches.
- Check if the interface supports specific and frequently repeated tasks.
- Check if the interface facilitates data entry, and if its elements are structurally simple or complex.
- Check if the interface allows the use of data search engines that aid the entering of mandatory data.

P.8. Minimalist or aesthetical design

- Check if the interface highlights the data that is relevant to the task under execution.
- Check if the interface DOES NOT highlight irrelevant information.
- Check if the interface presents error messages so that user attention is directed at them.
- Check if the interface is visually aggressive to the user (for example, through the use of colours that cause physical tiredness).
- Check if interface has illegible information or that which creates great difficulty in reading it (for example, due to the use of very small fonts, or due to low contrast).

P.9. Recognition, diagnosis and error recovery

Figure 2. Example of issue related to the P.5 pair

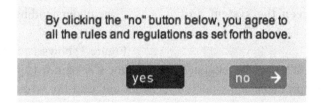

- Check if error messages are clearly visible to the user

P.10. Help and Documentation

- Check if the help information and options, as well as the documentation, are clearly visible to the user.
- Check if the help information and documentation are presented so that it helps task execution in an efficient manner as in a list of concrete steps.

Figure 1 shows a good example of the application of the P.1 pair, where it is possible to see that the user's location in the site is displayed as breadcrumbs, which tell the path taken by the user to reach the current page.

Figure 2 shows an example of problem related to the P.5 pair, which is using "No" as the button for the affirmative action (thus accepting the rules). Switching the meaning of Yes/No increases the chances of the user making a mistake instead of preventing it.

Heuristics Related to the Perspective Conceptualization

The inspector should be concerned if she/he understands what is being presented. The key question is: "Do I understand?"

C.1 System status visibility

- Check if system status is shown in a representation that is easily understood by the user – using symbols, words or sentences that are part of the domain of the problem.

C.2. Agreement between the system and the real world

- Check if system interface uses the language of the domain of the problem.

- Check if the definition of terms (words or symbols) specific to the domain of the problem is accessible to the users
  - ○ So that the definition can be consulted at the locations where these terms are used.

C.4. Consistency and standards

- Check if the terms of the domain of the problem are presented in a manner consistent to the user.
  - ○ Consistency of the terms refers to the use of a same term associated to a context.
  - ○ In the case of using synonyms, this equivalence should be clear to the user.

C.9. Recognition, diagnosis, and error recovery

- Check if error messages use simple language that is understood by the users, with concepts of the domain of the problem and according to the profile of the user.
- Check if error messages have an indication of recovery or procedure to be executed that can be understood by the user.
- Check if the alternative solutions presented in the error messages are clear to the user.

C.10. Help and Documentation

- Check if the user grasps the help provided by the system.
- Check if the system provides help or direction to the execution of complex tasks or the understanding of non-trivial concepts.

Figure 3 shows a good example of application for the C.9 pair. It is possible to see in Figure 3 that entering the wrong term in the search box

Figure 3. Good example related to the C.9 pair

causes the website to display the clear message indicating the possible typing mistake and the suggestion for the correct term.

Heuristics Related to the Navigation Perspective

The inspector should be concerned if she/he can access the different system options. The key question is: "Can I have access?"

N.3 Control and freedom to the user

- Check if the interface allows the user Undo and Redo functions or similar functions that allow the user to use "emergency exits" in the event of wrong choices or to exit an unexpected condition (or location).
- Check if the interface facilitates the return to the main stream of a task after the execution of a deviation or secondary task.

N.5. Error Prevention

- Check if the interface prevents the occurrence of navigation errors or, if the available navigation options clearly define what results or statuses will be attained.

N.7. Flexibility and use efficiency

- Check if the interface allows the user navigating with ease the different steps of a task.
  - Navigating with ease – refers to the clarity with which the system presents the navigation possibilities to the user in attaining a goal (executing a task)
- Check if the interface allows the user different access ways to the main tasks.
- Check if the interface allows the user the use of accelerators or shortcuts in the interaction with the main tasks.
- Check if the access forms offered by the system minimize the effort of physical actions.

N.9. Recognition, diagnosis and error recovery

- Check if the system shows how to access

Figure 4. Good example related to the N.9 pair

the alternative solutions presented in error messages.

N.10. Help and Documentation

• Check if the user can easily access the help information and documentation relevant to the desired task.

Figure 4 shows the same page as shown in Figure 3, now through the perspective of Navigation. Note the link highlighted in the figure - the website presents the link to the search page with the possible correct term.

INSPECTION PROCESS WITH THE USE OF THE WDP TECHNIQUE

To render the WDP technique adequate for the use in usability evaluations within an industrial context, the adoption of an inspection process was suggested, with resources and guidelines to support this process.

The inspection process suggested is divided into four activities, having the process suggested by Sauer et al. (2000) as a basis. The activities that form the process of usability inspection used are summarized in Table 4.

The Planning activity consists of the following sub-activities:

PLA.01 – Selection of the Modules/Applications to be evaluated and of the inspectors

PLA.02 – Preparation of the(s) script(s) for inspection

PLA.03 – Preparation of the environment for the Inspection

PLA.04 – Training in the WDP technique

The main product resulting from the Planning activity is the inspection plan, containing the selection of the modules and interactions of these modules that would be evaluated, the division of the groups of functionalities and the division of the inspectors by group. Apart from the inspection plan in itself, this activity also produces the environment prepared for the inspection, and the execution of the training on the WDP technique, when it is the first time the inspectors are using it.

Table 4. Inspection process activities

Planning	Activity where the scope of the inspection is defined (choice of the main interactions in the modules), preparation of the script with the interactions that have to be inspected, inspector selection, infrastructure preparation, inspector training in the WDP technique and assignment of tasks to each inspector
Detection	Each inspector individually executes this activity which consists of the search of usability issues in the chosen interactions
Collection	Elimination of recurring discrepancies (found by more than one inspector), generating a list of unique discrepancies (with no duplicates)
Discrimination and Prioritization	Classification of the discrepancies in real defects. Discrepancies not classified as defects are considered as false positives. After the classification, an analysis is made of the severity of the defects and the priorities for correction are defined.

Table 5. Detailing of the Planning activity

PLA.01 - Selection of the Modules/Applications to be evaluated and of the Inspectors	
Tasks:	Selecting the Application and the Inspectors
	Selecting the Modules that have to be inspected in each application
	Dividing the Modules into Interaction Scenarios: Grouping similar tasks in the same interaction scenario Listing the different players/roles in each scenario
	Dividing the inspectors in Groups of Inspection Grouping inspectors with supplementing views (based on the characterization form) Attributing the groups of inspectors to the inspection scenarios
Guidelines	Avoiding that an inspector inspects a module developed by him/her
PLA.02 – Preparation of the Inspection Script	
Tasks	Using client requirements and system specification as the basis for script preparation
Guidelines	In case system specification is described in the Utilization Cases: Remove system response from the use case flows. In case of complex Business Rules, prepare data according to the rules to be tested Describe the specific data to be used in the script
PLA.03 – Preparation of the Inspection Environment	
Tasks	Create an environment for the inspection with conditions similar to the production environment and with the system version that is to be inspected.
	Assess the data described in the inspection script
PLA.04 – Training on the WDP technique	
Tasks	The training on the technique should have the main usability concepts, usability evaluation and the WDP technique in a detailed manner, with examples of issues related to the HxP pairs
Guidelines	During the training, consideration should be given as to whether the inspectors have any prior knowledge on usability (and the level of such knowledge).

The Planning activity is the activity that undergoes most changes in its execution due to the direct dependence of the organizational context in which the usability inspection will be carried out. For this reason, the tasks and guidelines related to each sub-activity of the Planning activity were detailed. Table 5 describes each sub-activity.

The inspection team should consist of the following roles:

- Inspection Leader (or Moderator) – in charge of the execution of the inspection process as a whole, acts directly in the planning and collection activities.
- System Officer – role usually carried out by the technical manager for the project to develop the Web application under evaluation. This role does not take part in the detection of the discrepancies but acts

Figure 5. Excerpt from a Characterization Form

Kindly list the web applications/modules that you will be assessing during this usability evaluation. Please indicate if you had participated as developer in any of the related applications/modules.

Web Application/Module: _____

- Previous participation as developer of this application/module: (___) Yes   (___) No

- Current Application/Module Process Status:

(___) Initial Development   (___) Evolutive Maintenance   (___) in Use for ___ Months

decisively in the discrimination activity as his/her knowledge of system requirements supports the classification of the discrepancies found in defects or false positives.

- Inspectors – responsible for the detection of discrepancies, also take part in the discrimination activity. Should there be no professional evaluation from usability specialists, the inspectors of the developers themselves can be selected (from the project team or not) or requirement evaluators for the Web application under assessment.

In order to choose the inspectors, it is suggested that characterization forms are used to mark the roles played by each inspector in the development of the modules to be assessed. This data is important for the assembling of the groups of inspectors in sub-activity PLA.01 "Selection of the Modules/Applications to be evaluated and of the Inspectors", avoiding that an inspector who is a developer of the project team assess a module he/she may have developed him/herself. Figure 5 shows part of a characterization form used.

Apart from the guidelines for the inspection process, support material was also prepared for the inspections, containing two groups of materials with distinct objectives:

- Support materials for the use of the WDP technique – consists of the material for the training on the WDP technique and of the document containing the description of the technique and examples.

- Support materials for the usability inspection – consisting of a description of the process for the usability inspection and of a spreadsheet template to report the discrepancies found by each inspector.

These two groups of materials can be used in any usability inspections where one wishes to apply the WDP technique[1].

Industrial Case Study

The proposal of the WDP technique was strongly supported by the use of experimentation. A methodology was used that was based on experimentation (Shull *et al.* 2001; Mafra *et al.* 2006) throughout the development cycle of the WDP technique, starting with the support to the initial proposal and continuing through a series of experimental studies aimed at assessing and streamlining the technique until it would be ready for the use in the software industry.

The feasibility studies and the observation studies are described in (Conte *et al.* 2007a; Conte *et al.* 2007b; Conte *et al.* 2008), as carried out as part of the methodology based on experimentation through which the WDP technique has been evaluated and perfected. With the execution of these studies, we found signs of the effectiveness of the WDP technique. Following the experimental approach proposed in (Shull *et al.* 2001; Mafra *et al.* 2006), after the execution of the feasibility and observation studies, the next stage is the execution of case studies with the purpose of: (1)

characterizing the application of the technique in the context of a development life cycle and (2) checking if the application of the technology has any negative interaction with the industrial environment.

Case studies allow the analysis of a specific process within the context of a software lifecycle. At this point one can start to observe as the new process of usability inspection interacts with other aspects and processes of a real development cycle. This interaction can lead to issues that did not rise when evaluating the process in an isolated manner.

We present below one of the case studies carried out in an industrial environment. This study was executed in the context of an incremental development project of a Web system. The next sub-sections present the detailing of this case study, including the characterization of the object of the study, its planning, the execution of the activities of the inspection process, and the results and lessons learned.

Characterization of the Web Application

The object of this case study is a new Web application to manage the activities of Fundação COPPETEC[2], a foundation whose mission is to support the execution of technological development projects, as well as research, education and extension, for COPPE and other units within UFRJ – Federal University of Rio de Janeiro. This new application was named SiGIC – Integrated COPPETEC Management System, and its development was structured in an incremental lifecycle with the partial release of the functionalities so to gradually replace the previous application then in place at the Fundação COPPETEC. The application's specification is based on the description of use cases. At the time the case study was carried out, the modelling of the application consisted of 58 use cases, split into three modules: MGU – User Management Module (7 use cases), MSL – Request Module (27 use cases) and MPT – Protocol

Module (24 use cases). These three modules were the object of the usability inspection process.

Planning the Case Study

The purpose of this case study was to answer the following question: "Is the technique adequate in the context of a development lifecycle?" This study was executed from December 2007 to February 2008.

Objective (according to the GQM paradigm (Basili and Rombach, 1988)):

To analyze the WDP technique

With the purpose of understanding

In relation to the adequacy of the use of the WDP in a real lifecycle

From the standpoint of Stakeholders in Web applications

In the context of a usability evaluation of a Web organizational application by its developers and requirement evaluators.

To evaluate if the result of the application in a real lifecycle is satisfactory entailed measurement through the following indicators:

1. Efficiency in the Detection stage – according to Bolchini & Garzotto (2007), efficiency indicates the degree in which a method supports a 'rapid' detection of usability issues. It is calculated as the ratio between the number of defects by inspection time.

2. Effort in the Detection and Discrimination stages of the inspection – measured by each inspector – is the determining factor for the cost of execution of the inspection;

3. Learnability Degree – shows how easy it is to learn a method (Bolchini and Garzotto, 2007). In a similar manner by Bolchini & Garzotto (2007), this indicator was set in place through two factors:

    3.1. Effort with training on the technique – measured in man-hours, shows the time spent in training on the technique for the inspectors;

3.2. Perception of any difficulty in applying the technique – opinion of the inspectors on how difficult it was to apply the WDP technique during the usability inspection.

The indicators mentioned above were defined in accordance to the proposal of Bolchini & Garzotto (2007) regarding quality attributes to measure a Usability Evaluation Method. These indicators allow one to observe if it is possible have a good return on the inspection by using as usability inspectors the very developers and requirement evaluators of the project. It should be pointed that none of the inspectors in this case study is a specialist in usability, which allowed to see if the WDP technique guides non-specialist inspectors in the identification of usability issues.

As the number of existing usability issues was unknown, the Efficacy pointer was not calculated, measured through the ratio between the number of defects detected and the total number of defects.

Eight professionals (including two requirement evaluators) involved with the SiGIC project took part of the case study. Six of the eight professionals worked as inspectors. All of the inspectors signed a Consent form and filled out a characterization form with questions on the prior knowledge of the inspector on usability, experience with software inspections, and on the role played by the inspector in the development of the three modules of the SiGIC that were under assessment. The next sub-section of the agreement lists the different roles played in the inspection and describes the activities for each role.

Execution of the Usability Inspection

The inspection team consisted of the following roles:

- Inspection Leader (or Moderator) – this role was carried out by a developer from

the project team, with knowledge of usability evaluations and with experience with the use of the WDP technique.

- System Officer – role carried out by the project's technical manager.
- Inspectors –04 developers from the project team were selected as inspectors (with experience in development from 6 months and 7 years) and 02 requirement evaluators from the same team (both with over 20 years' experience in the organization). They also took part in the discrimination stage.

Table 6 shows the participation of each role from the inspection team in process activities.

In relation to the material used during the inspection process, the support materials for the use of the WDP technique and for the usability inspection were provided to the Inspection Leader by the researchers responsible for the technique. These researchers also discussed the main aspects of the process with the Inspection Leader. Apart from the above material, the Inspection Leader prepared the script for the detection activities containing the interactions that have to be inspected, using the description of the project's use cases as basis.

The conducting of the inspection, including inspector training on the WDP technique was done by

Table 6. Role participation in inspection activities

Role	Activities of the Inspection process			
	Planning	Detection	Collection	Discrimination and Prioritization
Inspection Leader	X		X	X
System Officer	X			X
Inspectos		X		X

a professional Inspection Leader without interference from the researchers abovementioned. This professional had knowledge on usability evaluations and experience with the WDP technique as he had already worked as an inspector in one of the previous studies. The responsible researchers only supported the leader in the planning activity for the inspection and did the analysis of the data after the end of the evaluation.

The execution of the activities is described below.

Planning - Firstly the application options that would be the object of the usability evaluation were selected. The selection of these options was based on the specification of the use cases of the system. The selection criteria were based on the kind of interaction of the use case and on who (which player) this was executed by. Apart from that, use cases with very similar interaction were eliminated. The three modules of the application were given a total 19 use cases (nearly 33% of the total) split into three groups according to the kind of functionality. Two inspectors were assigned to carry out the detection of discrepancies in each group of functionalities. The division of the inspectors by group was done so that the same use case would be inspected by supplementary perspectives in the identification of defects. Another criterion used was to avoid that one developer inspected an use case implemented by him/herself. After that, the leader prepared high level descriptions of the interactions for each critical path of the selected use cases, based on the specification document of the use cases that had already been evaluated from the presentation of interaction prototypes. Application responses to the flows of the use cases were removed from these descriptions. The reason for this change is that the descriptions should guide the inspector in the activities that are the focus of the inspection, however without previously telling how the application will behave after each action. The leader also prepared the inspection database with the data that would be needed for the interactions evaluated.

Finally, the qualification of the inspectors was made on the use of the WDP technique. Two training sessions were held on the technique with the same format and contents. Each inspector attended only one session, chosen according to one's agenda. Each training session lasted one hour. Training on the WDP technique was carried out by the very Inspection Leader professional after verification of the contents of the training session with the researchers responsible for the technique. This professional had knowledge on usability evaluations and experience with the WDP technique as he had already worked as an inspector in one of the previous studies and had, therefore, been trained on the technique.

Detection - In this activity, the inspectors executed the interactions described and reported the discrepancies found in a spreadsheet, filling in the following data: Activity (name of Interaction described), Step of the activity, Heuristics x Perspective Pair (HxP) as related to the problem, description of the problem and Degree of Severity (pursuant to the scale proposed by (NIELSEN 1994b)). One of the requirement evaluators did not do the inspection due to the need to execute other professional activities during the period of the detection. As a result only five inspectors did effectively work.

Collection - After receiving the spreadsheets with the discrepancies sent by each inspector, the Inspection Leader compared the spreadsheets from the inspectors in the same group, checking the existence of duplicates, that is, the same discrepancy being reported by more than one inspector. Similar discrepancies were reported many times but they referred to different use cases. These were not deemed as duplicates (29% of the defects reported were repetitions of similar defects reported during the execution of another activity). Only one duplicate defect (in the same use case) was assigned.

Discrimination and Prioritization of Defects – A discrimination meeting was held for each group, with the following attendants: inspection leader, System Officer, and the inspectors of the group at hand. In these meetings the interactions evaluated were re-executed thus allowing the in loco checking of each reported discrepancy. After the team discussion, the System Officer rated the discrepancies as defects or false-positives (non true defects). E.g., Table 7 shows part of a spreadsheet with two reported discrepancies and their classification according to the discrimination meeting. During these meetings, proposals were made for the solution of most of the defects found. After the execution of the three discrimination meetings the defects were analyzed and prioritized as follows: immediate solution, solution delayed (project decision) and non-defined solution (defects whose solution had not been proposed at the meeting). All of the defects were reported in a defect monitoring tool and those defects scheduled for immediate solution were prioritized for correction.

Results Obtained

One of the objectives to accomplish in this experience was to check whether it would be possible to have a good return on the inspection having the very developers and requirement evaluators of the project as usability inspectors, given that none of these inspectors is a specialist in usability. This type of team is common in the development of Web applications, so it was necessary to assess if the WDP technique met this kind of use where the inspection is made by the very stakeholders in the project.

Four of the five inspectors who carried out the detection already had previous experience in the execution of some kind of inspection. However, only two inspectors had previous experience in the execution of usability evaluations, with one of them having already used the WDP technique. The result in relation to this objective was positive as it can be seen in Tables 8 and 9. Table 8 shows, for each inspector, their previous experience in relation to the inspections, usability evaluations and use of the WDP technique, the number of

Table 7. Part of a Discrepancies Spreadsheet

HxP Pair	Discrepancy Description	Classification
P9	There is no error message if the provided agency code has alphabetical characters.	False positive (once agency codes can have alphabetical characters)
P10	The help text for bank and agency fields is not fully displayed, and it may omit important information.	Defect

Table 8. Characterization of the Inspectors and Inspection Results.

Inspector	Experience inspections	Experience with usability evaluations	Experience with the WDP technique	Number of Discrepancies	Number of False positives	Number of Defects
1	No	No	No	20	0	20
2	Yes	No	No	29	4	25
3	Yes	Yes	No	48	3	45
4	Yes	No	No	28	4	24
5	Yes	Yes	Yes	41	0	41

Table 9. General Results for the Usability Inspection

General Results	Total	Percentage
Number of Discrepancies	166	-
Number of False positives	11	6,63%
Number of Defects	155	93,37%

discrepancies reported and how many of these discrepancies were rated as defects or false positives. Table 9 shows the general results for the inspection.

When examining Tables 8 and 9 it is possible to see the low percentage of false positives (non true defects). This fact leads to a question that is to be observed in future studies: if the knowledge of the domain of the problem and of the system by the inspectors implies this low percentage of false positives. We believe that a positive reply to this question can point to an additional advantage in usability inspections with inspectors who are stakeholders of the project itself.

In terms of time and effort, the period given to the inspectors to detect discrepancies was of three working days. This timeframe considered that all of the inspectors were involved in other activities parallel to the inspection, and it was not possible to have all carry out the detection at a pre-set time. Average effort effectively spent by each inspector was of approximately 3 hours and 20 minutes. Thirty-one defects were found, on average by each inspector. With this data, the first indicator was calculated: *Efficiency in the Detection stage*. The Efficiency indicator was calculated as the ratio between the number of defects divided by inspection time. Efficiency in the Detection stage was of 9.3 defects/hour per inspector.

The second calculated indicator, Effort in the Detection and Discrimination stages, shows the largest cost part to execute the inspection as these are the activities that involve the largest number of professionals. To calculate this indica-

tor, it is necessary to consider the time spent in the discrimination activity, apart from the time spent in the detection. In relation to the effort in the discrimination activity, three meetings were held, one for each group. The first two meetings lasted two hours each with the participation of four people: the leader, the person responsible, and two inspectors. The third meeting lasted 1 hour and a half, with the participation of the leader, the responsible person and an inspector (as one of the inspectors did not execute the detection). In this case study, the total inspection effort was lower as the average effort of an inspector added by the effort in the detection (3 hours and 20 minutes) and discrimination (1 hour and 50 minutes) activities was of 5 hours and 10 minutes.

With regards to the third indicator, Learnability Degree, the effort needed with the training on the technique was of only 1 hour per inspector. To capture the perception of the difficulty in applying the technique, semi-structured interviews were made with the inspectors so that they could provide their impressions in relation to the usability inspection and the technique application. The five inspectors said they had found the technique easy to apply and adequate to the usability evaluation.

Although the results of one single case study cannot be generalized to other contexts the qualitative and quantitative result of this inspection is a pointer to the feasibility of its use by the members of the project team themselves as inspectors in a usability evaluation, with the use of the WDP technique. The training on an inspection technique that aids the inspectors in finding usability flaws reduces the dependence on the experience of the inspector, where such dependence can be one of the biggest problems when of the application of usability inspections (Garzotto *et al.* 1999; Matera *et al.* 2006). Apart from that, even though presentations of interaction prototypes occurred in previous stages of the project, the WDP technique guided the inspectors in the identification of usability issues that had not been captured before, thus highlighting the importance of its use.

With regards to the benefits to the development project itself, apart from the improvement in the usability of the modules inspected, the inspection provided an improvement of the adopted interaction standard which automatically produces benefits to the future modules to be developed usability. To illustrate this kind of problem, Figure 6 presents an example of this type of usability problem that spreads throughout the system as it is a problem of the adopted interaction standard. Figure 6 shows the Help link on the upper right hand corner of the page. This was a usability problem of the system as it led users to believe that, when clicking on it, they would have access to the generic Help contents of the system and not the contents of Help as related to the specific functionality (in Figure 6 the Help related to the Daily Allowances Request Help function. This problem was solved with the change of the interaction standard as shown in Figure 7, which shows a new Help link in the area

Figure 6. Example of Problem in Interaction standard

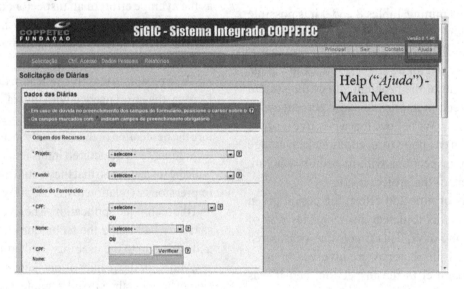

Figure 7. Example of Change in Interaction standard

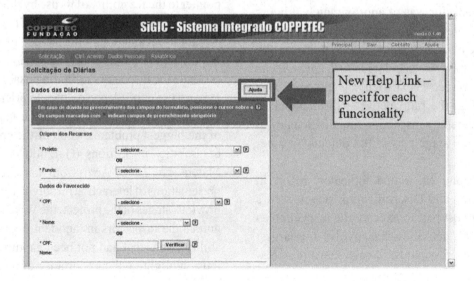

Figure 8. Defect Distribution after Solution Prioritization (Vaz et al. 2008)

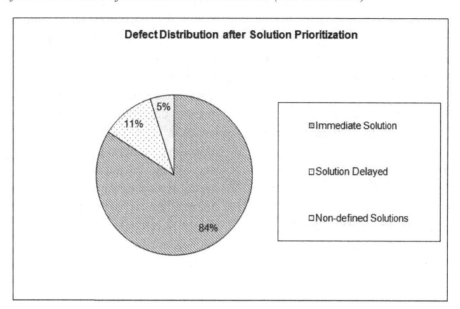

of the page related to the functionality itself. So, when solving this usability problem related to the help for the Daily Allowances Request functionality, this was solved for all of the other system functionalities as all of the pages started to adopt the new interaction standard.

Another important point found was the distribution of the defects after the discrimination and prioritization of the defects. As explained earlier, the defects rated with non-defined solution were rated as such, as no proposals were made for them during the discrimination meetings. Figure 8 shows the distribution of the defects after the Prioritization aiming at solution. We observe then that the defects with a non-defined solution represent only 5% of the total, that is, 95% of the defects received proposals for solution during the discrimination meeting itself.

CONCLUSION AND FUTURE TRENDS

This chapter presented a usability inspection technique for Web applications, the process to execute an inspection using this technique and the reporting of the execution of a usability inspection in a software development project. It is possible to see that it is feasible to carry out a usability inspection with the developers themselves and requirement evaluators of a software project. In this case study, three indicators were measured: (1) Efficiency in the Detection stage, (2) Effort in the Detection and Discrimination stages and (3) Learnability Degree. The Efficiency indicator was calculated as the ratio between the number of defects by inspection time, the result of its measurement being of 9.3 defects/hour, per inspector. The second indicator, Effort in the Detection and Discrimination stages, shows the largest part of the cost of execution of the inspection, as these are the activities that involve the largest number of professionals (inspectors). The average effort of an inspector was of 5 hours and 10 minutes, with 3 hours and 20 minutes spent on average in the detection activity and 1 hour and 50 minutes in the discrimination. In relation to the Learnability Degree, the effort needed with the training on the technique was of only 1 hour per inspector and the five inspectors stated they had found the technique easy to apply and adequate for the usability evaluation. They pointed that, even though presentations had been made of interaction prototypes in previous project stages the WDP technique supported the identification of usability issues that had not been previously detected, thus highlighting the importance of its use.

We consider the indicators assessed in this case study as important factors that define the method for usability evaluation quality. According to (Bolchini and Garzotto, 2007), the experimental evidence for the quality of the evaluation method is the key to promote it and make it accepted and adopted in the context of Web development organizations. We hope the results presented in this case study encourage more Web development organizations to adopt the use of methods for usability evaluation.

For the organization that carried out the inspection reported in this chapter, a relevant lesson learned was on the importance of undertaking usability evaluations from the first module that is completed or even from the first defined interaction prototype. The earliest the usability is evaluated, the greatest the gain; provided the system complies with an interaction standard. In the case of this experience, which involved the evaluation of three system modules, we can see that in many cases the same defect was found in different activities. This happened because the defect resided in the interaction standard adopted and not in a specific module interface. In total, 29% of the defects reported were repetitions of similar defects reported during another activity execution.

The running of this study led us to two questions that will be the focus of future work: the first one relates to the inspectors' ability to propose solutions for fixing the detected defects: "Does the use of the WDP technique facilitate the inspection team to prepare plans for fixing the detected defects?". This question had already been suggested by some participants when using the technique in previous inspection meetings. In this study, we observed that inspectors proposed solutions for 95% of the detected defects while the discrimination meeting

was taking place, which in turn contributed to reduce the application's development effort. This behaviour could have been facilitated by using the WDP technique; however, even if the WDP technique indeed facilitated the detection and correction plan of defects concomitantly, we still need to determine the extent of this facilitation, and whether a similar pattern would occur when developing other types of Web applications. The second research question relates to the learning of usability concepts by the developers throughout the reading activity: "Can the knowledge acquired by the developers while applying the WDP technique contribute to reduce the number of defects in future projects?". If so, the usability inspection technique would also present itself as an efficient guideline, as a contributor to reducing rework and improving the quality of the interface design.

ACKNOWLEDGMENT

The authors wish to thank all of the professionals who took part in the inspections and to research member Ulysses Vilela for his contributions to the WDP version used in this case study (WDP v4). We would also like to acknowledge the financial support received from Fundação COPPETEC, CNPq, FAPERJ, and FAPEAM.

REFERENCES

Baresi, L., Garzotto, F., & Paolini, P. (2000). From Web Sites to Web Applications: New Issues for Conceptual Modeling. In *Proceedings of the Workshops on Conceptual Modeling Approaches for E-Business and The World Wide Web and Conceptual Modeling,* (pp. 89 - 100), Salt Lake City, UT.

Basili, V., & Rombach, H. (1988). The tame project: towards improvement-oriented software environments. *IEEE Transactions on Software Engineering, 14*(6), 758–773. doi:10.1109/32.6156

Bolchini, D., & Garzotto, F. (2007). Quality of Web Usability Evaluation Methods: An Empirical Study on MiLE+. In *International Workshop on Web Usability and Accessibility (IWWUA) WISE 2007 Workshops*, (LNCS Vol. 4832, pp. 481-492), Nancy, France

Ceri, S., Fraternali, P., Bongio, A., (2000). Web Modeling Language (WebML): a modeling language for designing Web sites. *Computer Networks, 33*(1-6), 137-157.

Conallen, J. (2002). *Building Web Applications with Uml.* (2nd ed.). Reading, MA: Addison-Wesley Longman Publishing Co., Inc.

Conte, T., Massolar, J., Mendes, E., & Travassos, G. H. (2007a). Web Usability Inspection Technique Based on Design Perspectives. In *Proceedings of the 21th Brazilian Symposium on Software Engineering (SBES 2007)*, (Vol. 1, pp. 394-410), João Pessoa, Brazil.

Conte, T., Massollar, J., Mendes, E., & Travassos, G. H. (2007b, September). Usability Evaluation Based on Web Design Perspectives. In *Proceedings of the First International Symposium on Empirical Software Engineering and Measurement (ESEM 2007),* Madrid, Spain.

Conte, T., Vaz, V., Massolar, J., Mendes, E., & Travassos, G. H. (2008). Process Model Elicitation and a Reading Technique for Web Usability Inspections. In *International Workshop on Web Information Systems Engineering for Eletronic Businesses and Governments (E-BAG 2008)* (LNCS Vol. 5176 - Advances in Web Information Systems Engineering - WISE 2008 Workshops, pp. 36-47), Auckland, New Zealand

Díaz, P., Montero, S., & Aedo, I. (2005). Modelling hypermedia and web applications: the Ariadne development method. *Information Systems, 30*(8), 649–673. doi:10.1016/j.is.2004.09.001

Fons, J., Pelechano, V., Albert, M., & Pastor, O. (2003). Development of Web Applications from Web Enhanced Conceptual Schemas. In *Proceedings of the 22th Int. Conference on Conceptual Modeling (ER 2003),* (Vol. 2813/2003, pp. 232-245), Chicago.

Garzotto, F., Matera, M., & Paolini, P. (1999). Abstract tasks: a tool for the inspection of Web sites and off-line hypermedia. In *Proceedings of the tenth ACM Conference on Hypertext and hypermedia.* Darmstadt, Germany, ACM.

Gómez, J., Cachero, C., & Pastor, O. (2001). Conceptual Modeling of Device-Independent Web Applications. *IEEE MultiMedia, 8*(2), 26–39. doi:10.1109/93.917969

Insfran, E., & Fernandez, A. (2008). A Systematic Review of Usability Evaluation in Web Development. In *Proceedings of Second International Workshop on Web Usability and Accessibility (IWWUA 2008),* (LNCS Vol. 5176 - Advances in Web Information Systems Engineering - WISE 2008 Workshops, pp. 81-91), Auckland, New Zealand, September 1-4, 2008.

Koch, N., & Kraus, A. (2002). The expressive Power of UML-based Web Engineering. In *Proceedings of the Second International Workshop on Web-oriented Software Technology (IWWOST'02),* (pp. 105 – 119), Málaga, Spain.

Mafra, S., Barcelos, R., & Travassos, G. H. (2006). Aplicando uma Metodologia Baseada em Evidência na Definição de Novas Tecnologias de Software. In *Proceedings of the 20th Brazilian Symposium on Software Engineering (SBES 2006),* (vol. 1, pp. 239 – 254), Florianopolis. October.

Matera, M., Rizzo, F., & Carughi, G. T. (2006). Web Usability: Principles and Evaluation Methods. In Mendes, E., Mosley, N. (Eds.), *Web Engineering.* New York: Spinger Verlag.

Nielsen, J. (1994a). Guerrilla HCI: using discount usability engineering to penetrate the intimidation barrier. In *Cost-justifying usability*. Orlando: Academic Press, Inc.

Nielsen, J. (1994b). Heuristic evaluation. In Jakob Nielsen, Mack, R. L. (eds), *Usability inspection methods, Heurisitic Evaluation*. New York: John Wiley & Sons, Inc.

Pastor, O. (20040. Fitting the Pieces of the Web Engineering Puzzle. In *Proceedings of 18th Brazilian Symposium on Software Engineering (SBES2004)*, (Vol. 1, pp. 10 - 22).

Sauer, C., Jeffery, D. R., Land, L., & Yetton, P. (2000). The Effectiveness of Software Development Technical Reviews: A Behaviorally Motivated Program of Research. *IEEE Transactions on Software Engineering*, *26*(1), 1–14. doi:10.1109/32.825763

Schwabe, D., Rossi, G., & Barbosa, S. (1996). Systematic Hypermedia Design with OOHDM. In *Proceedings of the 7th ACM Conference on Hypertext,* (pp. 116 – 128), Washington, USA. March 1996.

Shull, F., Carver, J., & Travassos, G. H. (2001). An empirical methodology for introducing software processes. *ACM SIGSOFT Software Engineering Notes*, *26*(5), 288–296. doi:10.1145/503271.503248

Vaz, V., Conte, T., Bott, A., Mendes, E., & Travassos, G. H. (2008). Inspeção de Usabilidade em Organizações de Desenvolvimento de Software – Uma Experiência Prática. In *Proceedings of the 7th Brazilian Symposium on Software Engineering (SBQS 2008)*, (Vol. 1, pp. 369-378), Florianopolis - Brazil

Zhang, Z., Basili, V., & Shneiderman, B. (1999). Perspective-based Usability Inspection: An Empirical Validation of Efficacy. *Empirical Software Engineering*, *4*(1), 43–69. doi:10.1023/A:1009803214692

ENDNOTES

[1] Additional material on how to use the WDP technique can be requested to authors by email.

[2] Fundação Coordenação de Projetos, Pesquisas e Estudos Tecnológicos - www.coppetec. coppe.ufrj.br/

Chapter 18
Multiple–User Simultaneous Testing:
Experience with Two Methods

Borchuluun Yadamsuren
University of Missouri, USA

Anindita Paul
University of Missouri, USA

Sanda Erdelez
University of Missouri, USA

Joi L. Moore
University of Missouri, USA

ABSTRACT

Web developers and usability specialists face the challenge of dealing with the cost and quality of usability testing that must be implemented in a short period of time. Multiple-User Simultaneous Testing (MUST) can reduce usability testing time by allowing data collection from many users at the same time. This chapter reviews the literature on MUST and related methodologies for group users. It describes on a conceptual level two methods for setting up the MUST testing environment: self-paced and moderated. The authors do not aim to present which method is better from the empirical standpoint. Instead, the chapter describes the authors' comparative experiences with these methods, with a focus on the laboratory set up, data collection protocols, and data analysis issues. The chapter concludes with suggestions for future research and recommendations for usability specialists on how to conduct well designed MUST studies.

INTRODUCTION

Usability testing is one of many usability evaluation methods that help determine how easy or difficult it is to interact with websites and other computer applications or tools. Usability specialists observe how real users do what they do while interacting with the system to achieve their goals. Norman (1988) explains "to get something done, you have to start with some notion of what is wanted – the

DOI: 10.4018/978-1-60566-896-3.ch018

goal that is to be achieved" (p.56). He describes an action cycle of how users interact with systems to achieve their goals: forming the goal and intention, specifying an action, executing the action, perceiving the state of the world, and evaluating the outcome. While usability testing can also be a simple method to obtain information related to interface issues with a small number of subjects during the prototyping or development stage, Hackos & Reddish (1998) emphasize the importance of usability testing throughout the stages of interface design development.

Usability testing is usually conducted on an individual basis with different users. During usability testing, a study participant is asked to complete specific tasks on the website under evaluation. A facilitator observes the participant's behavior, takes notes, and assists if technical problems arise. Depending on the purpose and goals of the evaluation, the number and complexity of the tasks could require approximately 30 minutes to an hour to complete. According to Nielsen (1989) most usability issues can be found with a small sample size (i.e., 5 to 10 users). However, a small sample size is not sufficient when there is a need to correlate differences among participants' task performance and their personal characteristics. The process of testing one participant at a time can easily become time consuming for more than 10 participants. Hence, web developers and usability specialists face the challenge of balancing time, cost, and quality of usability tests that must be implemented in short time periods.

Usability research has focused on how users perform tasks in terms of the task completion rate and nodes they visit (Palmquist & Kim, 2000), task perception (Kim, 2005, 2006) and task type (Kim & Allen, 2002). Task performance is especially important during an iterative product development cycle that allows the usability testing outcomes to be included in the cyclical design decisions before dissemination to the public. However, data collected from a small number of users cannot be generalized with statistical significance to a broader population. For more comprehensive usability testing the number of study participants needs to be increased. When the needed sample of users is large, logistical issues arise related to the time and effort needed to collect data with one-user-at-a-time. Group testing (Allen, 2002; Downey, 2007) has emerged as a viable solution when there is a need to test a large number of users within a limited amount of time. Nielsen (2007) refers to this new breed of group testing as Multiple-User Simultaneous Testing (MUST). While some other researchers, such as Downey (2007) still continue to use the term "group usability testing," the authors of this chapter believe that MUST is a better term for representing this method.

Multiple-User Simultaneous Testing (MUST) can reduce usability testing time by allowing usability specialists to simultaneously collect data from multiple users. New usability evaluation tools, such as Morae (Techsmith) have emerged as viable solutions to facilitate MUST. Morae is an all-digital user-experience testing software that was designed to replace the complicated hardware setup of a traditional usability laboratory. With Morae, usability specialists can record several types of data streams from the user's interactions with a system, such as the user's voice, facial expressions, and detailed application and computer system data. Morae indexes the data recorded and makes them searchable so that the usability specialist can easily calculate various quantitative metrics, e.g., page changes, time on task, number of clicks, task completion rate, etc. In qualitative studies, one can quickly find a specific point in a session recording, a task that is typically very time-intensive when working with analog recordings. Furthermore, Morae can be used to conduct MUST in various settings -- in a laboratory, an office, conference room, or any other natural user setting.

One important decision when setting up a MUST session is whether to allow users to proceed through tasks on their own (self-paced MUST) or to have a moderator provide instructions and facilitate MUST (moderated MUST). Selection between these options has an impact on the data collection logistics and the process of data analysis. However, there is insufficient information in the literature about comparative benefits and drawbacks of these two approaches in terms of their impact on the quality of data collected in usability testing. This chapter will first introduce MUST as a method of usability testing and then describe the authors' experiences in using self-paced and moderated MUST. The objectives of this chapter are to present conceptual and pragmatic issues in conducting MUST and to discuss the effect of MUST on overall effectiveness of usability testing. Due to the nature of the pilot study presented in the chapter, the authors do not aim to compare the two methods empirically.

BACKGROUND

An implementation of group testing by Allen (2002) and Downey (2007) illustrates issues related to this testing methodology. The library staff at the University of South Florida evaluated their virtual library website (Allen, 2002). The staff needed a large group of subjects to test interface navigation, but they were concerned that it would require too much personnel time to have someone to observe and record user interactions for each participant. In order to select the best method for collecting data, the staff conducted an experimental comparison of unmediated and mediated test groups. The unmediated group in this study included 26 participants and the mediated group 4 participants. The evaluation tasks for both group consisted of 15 navigational exercises. For each exercise, the participants needed to find a specific resource by clicking on the links that were the most likely path to complete the task.

In the unmediated group the participants were asked to manually record their own navigational steps to the requested resources on a response sheet. In addition, the instructions directed participants to navigate through the website until they found the specific resource, but they could only go through 7 links/clicks. If the resource was not found within 7 clicks, then they were to stop the current task and proceed to the next one. Allen (2002) reported that the results showed several participants' errors as a result of the procedures. For example, the participants did not record all the links that were clicked on, leaving gaps in their notations on the response sheets. Because of this problem, it was difficult for the library staff to recreate the participants' task performance, which had a negative impact on the quality of data analysis. Also, some participants skipped an entire exercise or indicated that they could not find the resource even when there were clear hints about how to locate a specific resource. Another issue with the response sheets was the readability of some participants' handwriting.

During the mediated testing, evaluators assumed that they would obtain more precise results because a staff member sat beside the participant and recorded user interactions (Allen, 2002). The participants had the same instructions and exercises as the unmediated group, but the staff recorder stopped the participant when he or she reached 7 clicks during an exercises. The evaluators noticed that several participants were more nervous with this process because someone was watching their performance. At times, some participants sought approval from recorders for their actions by paying attention to what the recorders were writing and to their facial expressions. It was obvious that several participants seemed more self-conscious and less confident about their decisions while being observed. Another issue related to the mediated testing was the recorders' inability to capture all of the activities during the evaluation. The goal was to allow participants to freely work on the tasks without waiting for the recorder to document the interactions.

The unmediated group completed the exercises in 1.75 hours, compared to 45 minutes for the mediated group (Allen, 2002). Based on the issues revealed during the experimental test, there were many usability methodology errors that affected the results and analysis. Although the use of computerized applications to record user interactions with an interface had been implemented in previous studies (Nahl & Tenopir, 1996; Lazonder, Palmquist & Kim, 2000), the staff did not realize the importance of using these tools for data collection until the end of the study.

Taking the lessons learned from the experimental test, the evaluators implemented a second evaluation test that utilized an Apache web server to record all user activity within the library domain (Allen, 2002). Participants were divided into 2 groups of 16 participants, with one group completing the testing during the morning and the other during the afternoon of the same day. For both groups, the participants sat at different computer workstations. Each workstation was "locked" at the beginning of the test to prevent participants from exploring the website. Participants were instructed to complete a series of 15 questions and to document the start and end time of the entire testing session. An additional instruction requested that participants go to the virtual library homepage at the completion of each exercise. This step made it easier to detect the start and stop time of each exercise in the system logs. Each group completed all tasks in approximately 45 minutes.

Downey's (2007) usability evaluation of Kepler, a scientific workflow application, illustrates another example of group testing. During two identical training workshops for the application, a total of 33 scientists participated in this usability testing. Sets of 5 participants were seated in a circular shape, which decreased the ability to easily view another participant's computer screen. There were multiple observers (i.e., usability professional, trainer, and software developer), who walked among the participant workstations answering questions and trying to minimally probe the users during the testing. After each session, study participants discussed the usability

problems. The strength of this approach was the discovery of many usability issues in a short time span along with the design validations across multiple users. One drawback was the difficulty observers experienced in noting all issues in a group setting when individual tasks are performed simultaneously. This study did not record individual sessions. The study results were based on the observations during the group testing and final discussion after the testing.

Usability professionals and researchers in the previously mentioned studies faced numerous challenges in efficiently collecting, synchronizing, organizing, and analyzing rich data from the users' interactions with information systems. A better understanding of how to implement group testing is important for obtaining accurate data.

What is MUST?

Nielsen (2007) describes that MUST is useful when there is a need for quantitative data to measure statistical significance, for usability tests that include long duration tasks, to obtain more performance data than perception data from focus group discussions, and to improve game design. There is no upper limit to the number of users that can be tested in each session. The Microsoft Games Studios is an example of a high-end MUST lab that conducts approximately 8000 participants test games every year (Nielsen, 2007). Each user sits in a cubicle with headsets to minimize distractions. An additional strategy to alleviate distractions is to tell participants that they are working on different tasks. For the Halo 3 game, the company analyzed more than 3000 hours of 600 gamers interacting with the interface (Thompson, 2007). Multiple users are needed for game testing because it is more difficult to evaluate the user interface than a typical website (Nielsen, 2007).

The Microsoft Games Studio example illustrates the capacity of MUST methodology in facilitating collection of data from large groups of users. However, data collection is only one part of the usability testing process. Another important part is detailed data analysis, including logging beginning and ending of individual tasks for all participants, coding task completion, and marking any other issues that may be relevant for assessing usability. It is important to note that some MUST procedures can simplify not only data collection but also data analysis. For example, similar to the use of moderators in single participant studies, in moderated MUST moderators facilitate a MUST study. Their presence ensures that participants systematically move from one task to another. In contrast, in self-paced MUST moderators are not involved as facilitators and the participants complete the tasks independently at their own pace.

In moderated MUST, the participants should not begin a task until the facilitator provides a signal (e.g., a verbal or visual cue). In addition, participants have to signal the moderator when they have completed the task. When all participants have signaled task completion, the moderator announces the start of the next task. The participants who quickly complete their tasks receive instructions to close the browser and wait for the moderator to announce the beginning of the next task. The moderator's presence and instructions ensure consistency in the task initiation for all the participants and thus facilitate data coding and analysis. When implementing a self-paced MUST, the participants perform tasks individually without the guidance from a facilitator. They proceed from one task to another independent of others and can leave the testing facility after they complete all tasks. While self-paced MUST does not include a moderator, a study facilitator is available to answer logistical questions and resolve any technical problems that may emerge with the equipment.

A MUST session can be affected by protocol issues, such as the definition of a task, specific directions for the start and stop of a task, and talking during the testing. Defining how to start and stop each task is important, because it can affect time on task and the indicators for each in the recorded

data. For self-paced MUST, the protocol could ask users to open the browser at the beginning of a task, and close the browser at the end of the task. For moderated MUST, the same protocol can be used, but the moderator would still have each participant provide a physical signal of completion (e.g., raise hand, or sit back from computer) before everyone begins the next task.

Researchers and practitioners using MUST need more practical and empirical guidance about the effect of moderation in MUST on the processes and outcomes of usability evaluation. The authors of this chapter are members of a usability evaluation laboratory (Information Experience Laboratory at the University of Missouri – IE Lab) where MUST studies are in constant demand due to the efficiency they provide for data collection. But what is the price of the increased speed of data collection with MUST? Should one use moderated or self-paced MUST and what are the comparative implications of these two approaches on the quality of data collected? The next section of the chapter will attempt to address these questions by presenting highlights from a study conducted in the IE Lab.

IMPLEMENTATION OF SELF-PACED AND MODERATED MUST

The authors conducted a comparison of self-paced and moderated MUST within a larger website usability evaluation project for an academic unit at a university. The intended users of the website were students entering the program of study at the client's academic unit. The client requested usability testing of the current website in order to evaluate organization and presentation of information and to indentify changes that should be implemented in the redesign of the website. The timeline for this evaluation was very short given the firm deadline posed by the beginning of the new academic semester when the new website was expected to be launched. The nature of the evaluation tasks provided by the client and the need for a fast turnaround in usability evaluation suggested MUST as the most appropriate approach to usability testing.

With the client's help, 18 undergraduate students (6 male and 12 female) were recruited to participate in the study. All of them were attending the same course at the academic unit and were familiar with the client's existing website. The students were provided an incentive (extra credit) from the course instructors to participate in the study. The client also identified 10 typical tasks that the users should be able to complete on the website. These tasks were included in the usability evaluation protocol as mini-scenarios that provided instructions to the users to find specific information on the website. The scenarios included both factual questions ("Find out when the college was founded") and the open-ended questions ("Find information about scholarships that you may be interested in").

The usability evaluation team contemplated several options for MUST study set up. The literature review provided some information about generic characteristic of MUST protocols, but failed to elaborate about how different formats may impact the processes and outcomes of the data collection. To address this void the team decided to use the context of the client project as described above, to systematically collect comparative data on moderated and self-paced MUST. Conducting a study within a real-time client project created several problems. For example, there was a need for fast turnaround in data reporting and insufficient time for pre-testing and refinement of research protocols. Also, the client was responsible for recruiting the study participants, which resulted in a lack of predictability in how many participants are going to show up for the study and forced the research team to collect data in several separate data collection sessions, as described below.

The Study Set Up

The data collection was conducted in a usability laboratory with 6 data collection workstations, arranged along the wall in an "L" shape format. The participants were distributed over three moderated and two self-paced MUST data collection sessions. The moderated MUST sessions had a total of 11 participants (6, 3, and 2) while the self-paced sessions had a total of 7 participants (5 and 2). In the MUST sessions with a larger number of participants (i.e., 5 and 6) the participants were seated at computer workstations closer to each other. In the sessions with fewer participants (i.e., 2 and 3) there was more distance among the participants.

For each type of MUST data collection, the usability evaluation protocol consisted of 10 tasks. Each task was printed single-sided on a separate sheet of paper and all 10 sheets were collated on the top of left corner. All the tasks were provided in the same order for all the participants. In the moderated MUST sessions, the moderator facilitated the sessions by reading the tasks out loud to the participants. Special verbal and visual cues were implemented to facilitate the process of task coding during data analysis. The participants were instructed to follow the directions from the moderator about when to start new task. They were told that they should attempt to complete the tasks to the best of their abilities and that they should behave as they would normally do when looking for information on a website. The participants were also asked to raise their hand when they are done with the task. After all the participants have raised their hands, the moderator gave instructions for beginning of the next task. In the self-paced MUST sessions the participants read the instructions and performed the tasks on their own. The research team member was present in the laboratory and available to address only logistical problems that emerged, such as equipment malfunctioning, clarification of instructions, etc.

The participants' interaction with the website was recorded with Morae usability software. Morae Recorder 2.0 ran on each user's computer separately and recorded individual sessions separately. The data streams included interactive data (e.g., mouse movements and click) and a video recording of participants' behavior in front of the computer (e.g., body movements, and facial expressions). The think aloud data was not specifically collected due to the noise that it would generate in a MUST setting. However, the sound data recording was performed, which allowed collection of various incidental sounds that occurred around the participants' work stations (e.g., moderator's instructions in moderated MUST, chat among participants, etc.). All recorded MUST sessions were imported into Morae Manager 2.0 for analysis. During data analysis, the research team manually logged task performance details, such as task completion, beginning, and end. The researchers also recorded any additional observations about the participants' behavior, such as interruptions during task performance, communications with other participants, requests for assistance from the moderator, etc. The data from Morae Manager were exported into SPSS for simple descriptive statistical analysis. Due to the nature of this book chapter, in the following section only the highlights of the findings are presented.

Findings

The data averages revealed that participants in moderated MUST sessions completed the tasks faster than the participants in self-paced sessions. The participants in self-paced sessions completed the first few tasks more slowly than the participants in the moderated sessions. About halfway through the data collection, the participants across both types of MUST exhibited very similar performance in task completion. An interesting pattern was also observed in participants' comparative performance within each of the MUST types. In moderated

sessions, the participants' time on task seemed to be overall evenly distributed from slow to moderate and fast. However, in self-paced sessions, the participants' time on task was distributed mainly in the middle range and slower range.

The participants in moderated MUST sessions were on average more successful in completing assigned tasks than their counterparts in self-paced sessions. Their task completion rate (ratio of correctly completed and not completed tasks) was higher in 6 out of 10 tasks. Self-paced MUST participants had higher completion rate only in two tasks. In the remaining tasks, the completion rate for both MUST types was identical. The difference in average values and the patterns in time on task performance for two types of data collection may indicate that in moderated MUST there is increased awareness of how others are performing on their tasks. This awareness may create a competitive spirit among study participants and influence the faster pace of their task completion. However, as moderated MUST participants work faster to complete their tasks, they may pay less attention to the quality of their information search strategies. They may have given up sooner or stopped searching before the best answer was retrieved.

Challenges with MUST

Beyond the findings about the time on task and task completion the research team also made numerous observations about the characteristics of the testing environment and data collection protocol that may have influenced behavior of the study participants. These observations pertain to logistical issues such as the size of the room for data collection, the space between the data collection stations, mutual familiarity of the study participants, and the study instructions provided to them. Strengths and weaknesses of moderated and self-paced sessions are presented in *Table 1* and *Table 2*.

As mentioned above, the laboratory space where MUST sessions were conducted accom-

Table 1. Strengths and weaknesses of moderated MUST

Strengths	Weaknesses
• Well Structured • Moderator makes sure the participants stay on their tasks and do not become diverted by other activities • Moderator makes sure that participants follow the study protocol • Collects data from multiple participants in a short time • Fewer resources in terms of time and money required	• Too much control can make the testing environment unnatural • Presence of moderator in the room can affect participants' performance • The attempt to synchronize the beginning of each task for all participants can cause competition among them to rush through the process to finish tasks. This problem might affect overall performance of participants • Moderator-effect can increase social comparison among the participants of the session • Interaction between participants and moderator can affect performance of participants • Lab setting, including the distance between workstations and the position of the participants, might affect the study results

Table 2. Strengths and weaknesses of self-paced MUST

Strengths	Weaknesses
• More freedom and flexibility for participants to perform tasks on their own (more natural behavior compared to moderated session) • Fewer effects of social comparison and competition among participants compared to moderated session • Moderator is present to provide clarifications for participants • Collects data from multiple participants in a shorter time than the moderated session • As compared to single user studies, fewer resources in terms of time and money required	• Less control of participants' activities during the session. Some participants might divert to other sites or activities rather than focusing on the given task list. • Presence of multiple participants in the same room can affect their individual performance. Some participants can be distracted by others who leave the room before them • Presence of moderator can interfere in the participants' performance • Lab setting, including the distance between workstations and the position of the participants, might affect the study results.

modated 6 data collection workstations that were arranged along the side of the wall in an "L" shape format. The shape and the size of the room required close proximity of the workstations. In the groups that had 5 or 6 MUST participants it was easy for the participants to inadvertently notice the behavior of the people sitting next to them. The video recordings indicate that the participants in both types of MUST often looked away from their own computer screen. This behavior was more prominent in moderated MUST sessions where some participants appeared to be scanning the room for the signs of others raising their hands upon the task completion.

The closeness of the workstations and the fact that participants (who were recruited from the same class) knew each other, resulted in unexpected social interactions during data collection. Video recordings revealed that some participants became engaged in sporadic conversations. This behavior was especially noticeable in self-paced MUST sessions where the facilitator was not present to keep the pace of the study and deter social interactions among the participants. This social interaction was unrelated to the tasks at hand, but a lack of concentrated focus could have affected the outcomes of the study. Students who chatted with their colleagues were not completely focused on the assigned tasks, which may have influenced their time for completing the tasks. Also, the lack of concentration on their web search strategies may have impacted the quality of their searching and their ability to complete the tasks by finding the requested information.

Another observed characteristic of the self-paced MUST sessions was that many participants did not follow the pre-set order of the assigned tasks. Instead, the video recordings revealed that they moved back and forth among the tasks. For example, they would flip back through the pages of instructions and change the answers to the completed tasks. Also, they would flip forward through the instruction pages, skimming the tasks they still need to complete. Some self-paced MUST participants completely diverted from the assigned tasks and checked unrelated information on the web, such as local weather, news, and other websites of personal interest.

In the moderated MUST sessions, there was an indication that the participants' task performance was influenced not only by the presence of the fellow participants, but also by the presence of the moderator. In several instances when the moderator asked about the status of task completion and reminded participants to raise their hands when done, it was easy to detect that several participants began rushing to finish their current task. Furthermore, some participants asked the moderator to clarify various aspects of the task or to assist them with technical issues related to the performance of the lab computers. These interactions seem to distract some other participants in the room who would stop working on their own tasks while trying to hear the moderator's response.

Future Opportunities for MUST Usability Studies

Our implementation description illustrates that MUST in self-paced and moderated format can promote efficiency in data collection; however, researchers and usability specialists using these methods face many conceptual and practical challenges. These challenges also create opportunities for future research and practical refinement of MUST usability evaluation protocols.

On the conceptual level, the key question that requires additional research is how social comparison affects MUST usability evaluation. The preliminary findings of the study reported in this chapter indicate that participants in moderated MUST sessions performed better both in terms of

the time it took them to complete the tasks and in terms of the success in task completion. Because the study was conducted within the constraints of the time sensitive client project and with numerous logistical limitations, it is important to conduct additional comparative studies with different physical logistics for the testing environment. The researchers conducting these studies should pay specific attention to the impact of social comparison among the participants on the outcomes of the study.

Festinger's theory of social comparison (1954) could help understand the task performance under the two MUST conditions. The theory describes how individuals consider their external environment when evaluating their own opinions and abilities. A central proposition of this theory is the "similarity hypothesis," which identifies the common grounds between individuals for comparison (Wood, 1989). This hypothesis is based on the needs of three different interpersonal processes: the need for social comparison that leads to affiliation, the need for similar comparison that leads to pressure towards uniformity in groups, and the need for unidirectional drive upwards that leads to competition. Each of these processes could potentially affect the participants in MUST usability evaluation sessions. The results could be either slower performance on the tasks (e.g., participants' slowing down in self-paced MUST to conform to the slow pace of the group), or faster performance (e.g., slower participants catching up with the rest of the group in moderated MUST). Several researchers have proposed that social comparison is a common behavior, but some individuals are more inclined to engage in it than others (Gilbert, Giesler, & Morris, 1995; Hemphill & Lehman, 1991). Further research is needed to confirm these hypotheses and also to uncover any other possible influences of social comparison among study participants in MUST usability evaluation studies.

Practical Solutions and Recommendations

Although MUST helps collect more data in a shorter period of time than the typical one-user-at-a-time participant test, many challenges emerge in conducting MUST testing protocols. The presence of other users in the same room can impact users' behavior and performance outcomes during the testing period. Depending on the size and configuration of the testing facility, the physical problem of social comparison could be resolved with different solutions:

- increase distance between the participant workstations
- provide a physical divider among the workstations
- give each participant a headset for noise reduction
- provide additional activities at workstations for participants who finish early

Making adjustments in the data collection protocol can alleviate the psychological aspects of social comparison, for example:

- informing users that their tasks are different from other participants
- emphasizing that the objective of the test is not to evaluate participants, but to identify problems with the website
- determine the maximum length of the reasonable task completion and require participants to stop the task when they reach this point
- deter participants from communicating with each other during data collection and, if possible, do not recruit individuals who know each other

Many problems with the moderator's influence on participant behavior can be resolved by using sophisticated tools for data collection.

For example, Morae 3.0 provides a new feature called AutoPilot that allows automated delivery of instructions, tasks and satisfaction survey on the participants' computer screens. By presenting instructions and tasks on the computer rather than on the paper, this method improves the data collection process by eliminating the problem of participants going back to work on previous tasks in a self-paced MUST. An additional benefit of AutoPilot is that it automatically logs participants' time on task. This capability saves an enormous amount of time typically needed for data analysis and reporting. A drawback of collecting both interaction and survey data in Morae 3.0 is a danger of losing all participants' data in a case of technology malfunction. Also, ad hoc data collection is discouraged because testing configurations need to be carefully developed and pilot tested before conducting a MUST study. Nevertheless, AutoPilot and future advanced features of usability evaluation software, such as Morae, can open new creative possibilities for conducting MUST studies without moderation.

CONCLUSION

With the prevalence of web-based information services, the demand for usability testing of websites is expected to continue to grow. Usability evaluation specialists can meet the demands for timely and high quality usability evaluation by becoming more knowledgeable about options available for MUST studies. A key decision in implementing MUST studies is whether to conduct moderated MUST with a moderator who supervises participants' behavior during testing or to conduct self-paced MUST that allows participants to proceed through testing on their own. More research is still needed to identify in what way set up variations in MUST influence the usability evaluation outcomes. There is practical evidence that both moderated and self-paced MUST have strengths and weaknesses in terms of control imposed on the participants' behavior and ultimately the quality of data that are collected.

Usability specialists need to keep in mind the potential influence of social comparison among the study participants within a MUST environment. The layout of the testing facility and the characteristics of the recruited sample of participants may further increase the impact of social comparison on the quality of data. In such situations, various techniques are available to minimize the physical and psychological awareness of others' presence during usability testing. Finally, the usability specialists need to keep abreast of new technologies for usability testing. These technologies provide new solutions for automating data collection and should be evaluated in future MUST studies.

REFERENCES

Allen, M. (2002). A case study of the usability testing of the University of South Florida's virtual library interface design. *Online Information Review, 26*(1), 40–53. doi:10.1108/14684520210418374

Downey, L. (2007). Group Usability Testing: Evolution in Usability Techniques. *Journal of Usability Studies, 2*(3), 133–144.

Festinger, L. (1954). A theory of social comparison processes. *Human Relations, 7,* 117–140. doi:10.1177/001872675400700202

Gilbert, D. T., Giesler, R. B., & Morris, K. A. (1995). When comparisons arise. *Journal of Personality and Social Psychology, 69,* 227–236. doi:10.1037/0022-3514.69.2.227

Hackos, J., & Reddish, J. (1998). *User and Task Analysis for Interface Design.* New York: Wiley.

Hemphill, K. J., & Lehman, D. R. (1991). Social comparisons and their affective consequences: The importance of comparison dimensions and individual difference variables. *Journal of Social and Clinical Psychology, 10,* 372–394.

Kim, J. (2005). Task difficulty in information searching behavior: Expected difficulty and experienced difficulty. In *JCDL 2005: Proceedings of the 5th ACM/IEEE-CS joint conference on Digital libraries.*

Kim, J. (2006). Task difficulty as a predictor and indicator of a web searching interaction. In *CHI '06: CHI '06 extended abstracts on Human factors in computing systems.*

Kim, K. S., & Allen, B. (2002). Cognitive and task influences on web searching behavior. *Journal of the American Society for Information Science and Technology, 53*(2), 109–119. doi:10.1002/asi.10014

Lazonder, A. W., Biemens, H. J. A., & Wopereis, G. J. H. (2000). Differences between novice and experienced users in searching information on the World Wide Web. *Journal of American Society for Information Science, 51*(6), 576, 581.

Nahl, D., & Tenopir, C. (1996). Affective and cognitive searching behavior of novice end-users of a full-text database. *Journal of the American Society for Information Science and Technology, 47*(4), 276–286. doi:10.1002/(SICI)1097-4571(199604)47:4<276::AID-ASI3>3.0.CO;2-U

Nielsen, J. (1989). Usability engineering at a discount. In Salvendy, G., and Smith, M, J. (Eds.), *Designing and Using Human-Computer Interfaces and Knowledge Based Systems,* (pp. 394-401). Amsterdam: Elsevier Science Publishers.

Nielsen, J. (2007). Multiple Users Simultaneous Testing (MUST). *Jakob Nielsen's Alertbox.* Retrieved on December 3, 2008 at http://www.useit.com/alertbox/multiple-user-testing.html

Palmquist, R. A., & Kim, K. S. (2000). Cognitive style and on-line database search experience as predictors of web search performance. *Journal of the American Society for Information Science American Society for Information Science, 51*(6), 558–566. doi:10.1002/(SICI)1097-4571(2000)51:6<558::AID-ASI7>3.0.CO;2-9

Thompson, C. (2007). Halo 3: How Microsoft Labs Invented a New Science of Play. *Wired Magazine, 15*(09). Retrieved on December 1, 2008 at http://www.wired.com/gaming/virtualworls/magazine/15-09/ff-halo

Wood, J. V. (1989). Theory and research concerning social comparisons of personal attributes. *Psychological Bulletin, 106*(2), 231–248. doi:10.1037/0033-2909.106.2.231

Compilation of References

Abbott, K. R. (2001). *Voice Enabling Web Applications: VoiceXML and Beyond.* Berkeley, CA: Apress. Adobe Systems Incorporated. (n.d.). Retrieved from http://www.adobe.com/accessibility/products/flash/

Abels, E. G., White, M. D., & Hahn, K. (1998). A user-based design process for Web sites. *Internet Research: Electronic Networking Applications and Policy, 8*(1), 39–48. doi:10.1108/10662249810368879

Abels, E., Domas, M., & Hahn, K. (1997). Identifying user-based criteria for Web pages. *Internet Research: Electronic Networking Applications and Policy, 7*(4), 252–262. doi:10.1108/10662249710187141

AbilityNet. (2003a). *State of the e-nation report: UK on-line newspapers.* Retrieved June 1, 2009, from http://www.abilitynet.org.uk/content/oneoffs/Newspaper%20eNation%20report.pdf

AbilityNet. (2003b). *State of the e-nation report: UK airlines.* Retrieved June 1, 2009, from http://www.abilitynet.org.uk/content/oneoffs/Airlines%20eNation%20report.pdf

AbilityNet. (2004a). *State of the e-nation report: Premiership clubs.* Retrieved June 1, 2009, from http://www.abilitynet.org.uk/content/oneoffs/eNation%20report%20-%20Football%20Clubs.pdf

AbilityNet. (2004b). *State of the e-nation report: Online banks.* Retrieved June 1, 2009, from http://www.abilitynet.org.uk/content/oneoffs/eNation%20report%20-%20Online%20banks.pdf

AbilityNet. (2004c). *State of the e-nation report: Online supermarkets.* Retrieved June 1, 2009, from http://www.abilitynet.org.uk/content/oneoffs/eNation%20report%20-%20supermarkets.pdf

AbilityNet. (2004d). *State of the e-nation report: Retail websites.* Retrieved June 1, 2009, from http://www.abilitynet.org.uk/content/oneoffs/eNation%20report%20-%20Retail%20Sites.pdf

AbilityNet. (2007a). *State of the e-nation report: Online dating sites.* Retrieved June 1, 2009, from http://www.abilitynet.co.uk/docs/enation/2007datingSites.pdf

AbilityNet. (2007b). *State of the e-nation report: Utility and switching sites.* Retrieved June 1, 2009, from http://www.abilitynet.co.uk/docs/enation/2006utilitySites.pdf

AbilityNet. (2008a). *State of the e-nation report: Social networking sites.* Retrieved June 1, 2009, from http://www.abilitynet.co.uk/docs/enation/2008SocialNetworkingSites.pdf

AbilityNet. (2008b). *State of the e-nation report: The Beijing Olympics.* Retrieved June 1, 2009, from http://www.abilitynet.co.uk/docs/enation/2008BeijingSpecialReport.pdf

Abran, A., Khelifi, A., Suryn, W., & Seffah, A. (2003). Usability Meanings and Interpretations in ISO Standards. *Software Quality Journal, 11,* 325–338. doi:10.1023/A:1025869312943

Accessify. (2005). *Accessibility statement.* Retrieved May 10, 2009, from http://www.accessifyforum.com/viewtopic.php?t=2307

Accessiweb. (2008). Publication du 9 juin 2008, *Version 1.1 du référentiel AccessiWeb créé par le consortium W3C,* Retrieved from http://www.accessiweb.org/

ACSEL. (2007). Association pour le Commerce et les Services en Ligne. Retrieved from http://www.acsel.asso.fr/barometres/barometres_e-commerce.asp

Adamo-Villani, N., & Jones, D. (2007). A Study of Two Immotion Control Techniques. *Proc. of o Compuer Graphics and Visualization Conf, IADIS.*

Adams, D., Nelson, R., & Todd, P. (1992). Perceived Usefulness, Ease of Use, and Usage of Information Technology: a Replication. *MIS Quarterly, 16*(2), 227–247. doi:10.2307/249577

Adaptive Technology Resource Centre. (n.d). *Web accessibility verifier: Ensuring that your web pages are accessible to all people.* Retrieved November 21, 2008, from http://aprompt.snow.utoronto.ca/

Advertures. (2004). *Process Methodology.* Retrieved 16 Sept 2004, from http://www.advertures.cz/alt/index_en.php?cat=company&sub=methodology

Agarwal, R., & Prasad, J. (1997). The Role of Innovation Characteristics and Perceived Voluntariness in the Acceptance of Information Technologies. *Decision Sciences, 28*(3), 557–582. doi:10.1111/j.1540-5915.1997.tb01322.x

Agarwal, R., & Venkatesh, V. (2002). Assessing a Firm's Web Presence: A Heuristic Evaluation Procedure for the Measurement of Usability. *Information Systems Research, 13*(2), 168–186. doi:10.1287/isre.13.2.168.84

Ai, H., Raux, A., Bohus, D., Eskenazi, M., & Litman, D. (2007). Comparing spoken dialog corpora collected with recruited subjects versus real users. In *Proc. of the 8th SIGdial workshop on Discourse and Dialogue* (pp. 124–131).

Ajzen, I. (1991). The Theory of Planned Behaviour: Some Unresolved Issues. *Organizational Behavior and Human Decision Processes, 50,* 179–211. doi:10.1016/0749-5978(91)90020-T

Alexander, C. (1996). *The Origins of Pattern Theory: the Future of the Theory, And The Generation of a Living World.* Keynote speech at the 11th Annual ACM Conference on Object-Oriented Programs, Systems, Languages

and Applications (OOPSLA), October 6-10, San Jose, CA. Retrieved from http://www.patternlanguage.com/archive/ieee/ieeetext.htm

Alexander, C., Ishikawa, S., Silverstein, M., Jacobson, M., Fiksdahl-King, I., & Angel, S. (1977). *A Pattern Language: Towns, buildings, constructions.* New York: Oxford University Press.

Allen, M. (2002). A case study of the usability testing of the University of South Florida's virtual library interface design. *Online Information Review, 26*(1), 40–53. doi:10.1108/14684520210418374

Alter, S. L. (1980). *Decision Support Systems - Current Practice and Continuing Challenges.* London: Addison-Wesley.

Ambler, S. W. (2008). Tailoring Usability into Agile Software Development Projects. In *Maturing Usability* (pp. 75-95). Berlin: Springer.

Americans with Disabilities Act. (1990). Retrieved May 20, 2009, from http://www.ada.gov/pubs/adastatute08.htm

Anderson, J., Fleek, F., Garrity, K., & Drake, F. (2001). Integrating Usability Techniques into Software Development. *IEEE Software, 18*(1), 46–53. doi:10.1109/52.903166

Andre, T., Williges, R., & Hartson, H. (1999). The effectiveness of usability evaluation methods: determining the appropriate criteria. In *Proceedings of the Human Factors and Ergonomics Society 43rd Annual Meeting,* Santa Monica CA, (pp. 1090-1094).

Andreasen, M. S., Nielsen, H. V., Schrøder, S. O., & Stage, J. (2006). Usability in open source software development: Opinions and practice. *Information Technology and Control, 35A*(3), 303–312.

Andreasen, M. S., Nielsen, H. V., Schrøder, S. O., & Stage, J. (2007). What Happened to Remote Usability Testing? An Empirical Study of Three Methods. In *Proceedings of CHI 2007.* New York: ACM Press.

Andujar, C., Fairén, M., & Argelaguet, F. (2006). A Cost Effective Approach for Developing Application-Control GUIs for Virtual Environments. In *Proc. of the*

1st IEEE Symposium of 3D User Interfaces 3DUI'2006, Alexandria, March 25-26, pp. 45-52. Washington, DC: IEEE Comp. Society Press.

Aoyama, K., & Uno, Y. (2003). Modular design supporting system with a step-by-step design approach. In *Third International Symposium on Environmentally Conscious Design and Inverse Manufacturing, 2003 - EcoDesign '03.*

Apple Inc. (n.d.). Retrieved from http://www.apple.com

Arfé, B., & Boscolo, P. (2006). Causal Coherence in Deaf and Hearing Students' Written Narratives. *Discourse Processes, 42*(3), 271–300. doi:10.1207/s15326950dp4203_2

Arnold, S. J., Ma, S., & Tigert, D. J. (1978). A Comparative Analysis of Determinant Attributes in Retail Store Selection. *Advances in Consumer Research. Association for Consumer Research (U. S.), 5*(1), 663–667.

Asakawa, C., Takagi, H., Ino, S., & Ifukube, T. (2003). Maximum listening speeds for the blind. In Brazil, E. & Shinn-Cunningham, B. (Eds), *Proceedings of the 9th International Conference on Auditory Display 2003* (pp. 276-279). Boston: Boston University Publications Production Department.

Atterer, R., & Schmidt, A. (2005). *Adding Usability to Web Engineering Models and Tools.* Paper presented at the Fifth International Conference on Web Engineering (ICWE 2005), Sydney, Australia.

Aumont, J. (1994). *Introduction à la couleur: des discours aux images.* Paris: Armand Colin.

Avgeriou, P. Papasalouros A., Retalis S. & Skordalakis E. (2003). Towards a Pattern Language for Learning Management Systems. *Educational Technology & Society, 6*(2), 11-24. Retrieved from http://ifets.ieee.org/periodical/6-2/2.html

Avison, D. E., & Fitzgerald, G. (1993). *Information Systems Development: Methodologies, Techniques and Tools.* Oxfordshire, UK: Alfred Waller Ltd, Publishers.

Awad, E. M., & Gotterer, M. H. (1992). *Database management.* Danvers, MA: Boyd & Fraser.

Baber, C. (1996). Repertory grid theory and its application to product evaluation. In Jordan, P., Thomas, B., Weerdmeester, B. & Mclelland, I. (Eds.), *Usability evaluation in industry.* London: Taylor and Francis.

Baccino, T., & Colombi, T. (2001). L'analyse des mouvements des yeux sur le Web. In A. Vom Hofe (dir.). *Les interactions Homme-Système: perspectives et recherches psycho-ergonomiques* (127-148). Paris: Hermès.

Bach, C. (2004). *Elaboration et validation de Critères Ergonomiques pour les Interactions Homme-Environnements Virtuels.* Ph.D. Thesis, Metz University, France.

Baddeley, A. D. (1996). *Your Memory – A User's Guide.* London: Prion.

Badre, N. A. (2002). *Shaping Web Usability: Interaction Design in Context.* Boston: Addison-Wesley.

Baecker, M. R., & Buxton, A. S. W. (Eds.). (1987). *Readings in Human-Computer Interaction: A Multidisciplinary Approach.* Los Altos, CA: Morgan Kaufmann.

Bak, J. O., Nguyen, K., Risgaard, P., & Stage, J. (2008) Obstacles to Usability Evaluation in Practice: A Survey of Software Organizations. In *Proceedings of NordiCHI 2008.* New York: ACM Press.

Baker, D., Bridges, D., Hunter, R., Johnson, G., Krupa, J., Murphy, J., & Sorenson, K. (2002). *Guidebook to Decision-Making Methods.* USA, WSRC-IM-2002-00002, Department of Energy.

Baker, J. (1986). The role of environment in marketing services: the consumer perspective. In Czpeil J.A., Congram C., Shanaham J., (Ed.), *The Services Marketing Challenge: Integrated for Competitive Advantage* (pp. 79–84). Chicago: American Marketing Association.

Baker, K., Greenberg, S., & Gutwin, C. (2001). Heuristic Evaluation of Groupware Based on the Mechanics of Collaboration. In *Proceedings of the 8th IFIP International Conference on Engineering for Human-Computer Interaction,* (pp.123-140).

Bannister, D., & Fransella, F. (1986). *Inquiring man: the psychology of personal constructs* (3rd ed.). London: Routledge.

Baresi, L., Garzotto, F., & Paolini, P. (2000). From Web Sites to Web Applications: New Issues for Conceptual Modeling. In *Proceedings of the Workshops on Conceptual Modeling Approaches for E-Business and The World Wide Web and Conceptual Modeling,* (pp. 89 - 100), Salt Lake City, UT.

Baresi, L., Garzotto, F., & Paolini, P. (2001). Extending UML for modeling Web applications. In *Proceedings of the 34th Annual Hawaii International Conference on System Sciences* (pp. 1285-1294).

Bark, I., Folstad, A., & Gulliksen, J. (2005, 5-9 September). *Use and Usefulness of HCI Methods: Results from an Exploratory Study among Nordic HCI Practitioners.* Paper presented at the Human-Computer Interaction 2005: People and Computers XIX - The Bigger Picture, Edinburg.

Basili, V., & Rombach, H. (1988). The tame project: towards improvement-oriented software environments. *IEEE Transactions on Software Engineering, 14*(6), 758–773. doi:10.1109/32.6156

BBC. (2009). *My web, my way.* Retrieved June 26, 2009, from http://www.bbc.co.uk/accessibility/

Beck, K. (2000). *Extreme Programming Explained--Embrace Change.* Reading, MA: Addison-Wesley.

Beck, K., Beedle, M., van Bennekum, A., Cockburn, A., & Cunningham, W. (2001). *Manifesto for agile software development: Agile Manifesto Website.* Retrieved 01/2009 from http://agilemanifesto.org/

Becker, S. A. (2002). An Exploratory Study on Web Usability and the Internationalizational of US E-Businesses. *Journal of Electronic Commerce Research, 3*(4), 265–278.

Becker, S. A., & Mottay, F. E. (2001). A Global Perspective on Web Site Usability. *IEEE Software, 18*(1), 54–61. doi:10.1109/52.903167

Belk, R. W. (1985). Issues in the Intention-Behavior Discrepancy. In Sheth Jagdish N., (eds.), *Research in Consumer Behavior,* (Vol. 1, pp. 1-34). Greenwich, CT: JAI Press.

Bell, L., House, D., Gustafson, K., & Johansson, L. (1999). Child-directed speech synthesis: evaluation of prosodic variation for an educational computer program. In G. Olaszy, (Ed) *Proceedings / Eurospeech '99, 6th European Conference on Speech Communication and Technology* (pp. 1843-1846). Budapest: Dep. of Telecomm. and Telematics, Techn. Univ. of Budapest.

Bellizzi, J. A., & Hite, R. E. (1992). Environmental Color, Consumer Feelings, and Purchase Likelihood. *Psychology and Marketing, 9*(September-October), 347–364. doi:10.1002/mar.4220090502

Benavídez, C., Fuertes, J. L., Gutiérrez, E., & Martínez, L. (2006). Semi-Automatic Evaluation of Web Accessibility with HERA 2.0. In *Proceedings of the 10th International Conference on Computers Helping People with Special Needs (ICCHP 2006)* (pp. 199-106). Berlin: Springer.

Benson, C., Muller-Prove, M., & Mzourek, J. (2004). Professional usability in open source projects: Gnome, openoffice.org, netbeans. In *Proceedings of CHI 2004* (pp. 1083-1084). New York: ACM Press.

Benyon, D., Turner, P., & Turner, S. (2005). *Designing Interactive Systems, People, Activities, Context and Technology.* Edinburgh: Addison-Wesley.

Bernsen, N. O., & Dybkjær, L. (2000). A Methodology for Evaluating Spoken Language Dialogue Systems and Their Components. In *Proc. 2nd International Conference on Language Resources & Evaluation - LREC 2000* (pp.183-188).

Bernsen, N. O., & Dybkjær, L. (2004). Building Usable Spoken Dialogue Systems: Some Approaches. *Sprache und Datenverarbeitung, 28*(2), 111–131.

Bernsen, N. O., Dybkjaer, H., & Dybkjaer, L. (1998). *Designing Interactive Speech Systems: From First Ideas to User Testing.* New York: Springer-Verlag.

Berry, D. (2004). Requirements for Maintaining Web Access for Hearing-Impaired Individuals. *Software Quality Control, 12*(1), 9–28.

Bevan, N. (1995). Measuring usability as quality of use. *Journal of Software Quality, 4*, 115–130. doi:10.1007/BF00402715

Bevan, N. (1997). Usability Testing of World Wide Web Sites. *In Proceedings of Workshop at CHI'97: Usability Testing of World Wide Web Sites*, March 23-24, Atlanta, GA. Retrieved from http://www.acm.org/sigchi/webhci/chi97testing/bevan.htm

Bevan, N. (1998). Usability Issues in Web Site Design *In Proceedings of UPA'98: Usability Professional Association*. Online archive available at http://www.usability.serco.com

Bevan, N. (2005). Cost benefits framework and case studies. In R.G. Bias, & D.G. Mayhew (Eds.) *Cost-Justifying Usability: An update for the internet age*. San Francisco: Morgan Kaufmann.

Bevan, N. (2006). International Standards for HCI. In C. Ghaoui (Ed.), *Encyclopedia of Human-Computer Interaction*. Hershey, PA: Idea Group Reference.

Bevan, N. (2008). A framework for selecting the most appropriate usability measures. In *COST 294-MAUSE Workshop: Critiquing Automated Usability Evaluation Methods*. March.

Beyer, H., Holtzblatt, K., & Baker, L. (2004). An Agile Customer-Centered Method: Rapid Contextual Design. In *Extreme Programming and Agile Methods - XP/Agile Universe 2004. Proceedings,* (pp. 50-59). Berlin: Springer.

Bichler, M., Nusser, S., & Wien, W. (1996). *Modular Design of Complex Web-Applications with W3DT.* Paper presented at the 5th International Workshops on Enabling Technologies: Infrastructure for Collaborative Enterprises (WET ICE'96), Standord, CA.

Bickmore, T. W., & Picard, R. W. (2005). Establishing and maintaining long-term human-computer relationships. *ACM Transactions on Computer-Human Interaction, 12*(2), 293–327. doi:10.1145/1067860.1067867

Biers, K., & Richards, L. (2002). *Web Page Background Color Evaluative Effect On Selected Product Attributes*. Research paper, Utah State University.

Blandford, A. & Buchanan, G. (2003). Usability of digital libraries: a source of creative tensions with technical developments. *IEEE-CS Technical Committee on Digital Libraries' on-line newsletter.*

Bleser, T. W., & Sibert, J. (1990). Toto: a tool for selecting interaction techniques. *In Proc. of user interface software and technology,* Snowbird, Utah, Oct.3-5, pp. 135-142. New York: ACM.

Blythe, M., Overbeeke, K., Monk, A., & Wright, P. (Eds.). (2004). *Funology: From Usability to Enjoyment.* Berlin: Springer.

Bodart, F., & Vanderdonckt, J. (1994). On the Problem of Selecting Interaction Objects. In G. Cockton, S.W. Draper, G.R.S. Weir (eds.), *Proc. of BCS Conf. HCI'94 "People and Computers IX",* Glasgow, 23-26 August, (pp. 163-178). Cambridge, UK: Cambridge University Press.

Bohanec, M., & Rajkovič, V. (1990). DEX: an expert system shell for decision support. *Sistemica, 1*, 145–157.

Bohanec, M., & Rajkovič, V. (1995). Večparametrski odločitveni modeli. *Organizacija, 28*, 427–438.

Bohanec, M., & Rajkovič, V. (1999). Multi-Attribute Decision Modeling: Industrial Applications of DEX. *Informatica, 23*, 487–491.

Bolchini, D., & Garzotto, F. (2007). Quality of Web Usability Evaluation Methods: An Empirical Study on MiLE+. In *International Workshop on Web Usability and Accessibility (IWWUA) WISE 2007 Workshops,* (LNCS Vol. 4832, pp. 481 - 492), Nancy, France

Borchers, J. (2001). *A Pattern Approach to Interaction Design*. Chichester, UK: John Wiley & Sons Ltd.

Borg, A., Sandahl, K., & Patel, M. (2007). Extending the OpenUP/Basic Requirements Discipline to Specify Capacity Requirements. In *15th IEEE Internationalm, Requirements Engineering Conference, 2007 (RE '07), Proceedings*. Washington, DC: IEEE.

Borges, J. A., Morales, I., & Rodriguez, N. J. (1996). Guidelines for Designing Usabile World Wide Web Pages. In *Proceedings of CHI'96: Conference on Human Factors in Computing Systems,* Panel, (pp.277-278). New York: ACM Press/Addison Wesley.

Borges, J. A., Morales, I., & Rodriguez, N. J. (1998). Page Design Guidelines Developed Through Usability Testing. In E. G. J. R. Chris Forsythe (Ed.), *Human Factors and Web Development* (pp. 137-152). Mahwah, NJ: Lawrence Erlbaum Associates.

Borges, J. A., Morales, I., & Rodriguez, N. J. (2008). *Page Design Guidelines Developed through Usability Testing.* Retrieved 15 April, 2009, from http://ece.uprm.edu/hci/papers/Chapter.pdf

Bowman, D. A., Kruijff, E., & Laviola, J. J. (2004). *3D User Interfaces: Theory and Practice.* Reading, MA: Addison Wesley Publishing Company.

Bowman, D. Koller, D., & Hodges L. (1997). Travel in Immersive Virtual Environments: an Evaluation of Viewpoint Motion Control Techniques. In *Proceedings of Virtual Reality Annual International Symposium.*

Bowman, D., & Hodges, L. (1997). An evaluation of techniques for grabbing and manipulating remote objects in immersive virtual environments. In *Proceedings of Symposium on Interactive 3D Graphics,* (pp. 35-38).

Bowman, D., & Hodges, L. (1999). Formalizing the design, evaluation, and application of interaction techniques for immersive virtual environments. *Journal of Visual Languages and Computing, 10*(1), 37–53. doi:10.1006/jvlc.1998.0111

Bowman, D., Gabbard, J., & Hix, D. (2002). A Survey of Usability Evaluation in Virtual Environments: Classification and Comparison of Methods. *Presence (Cambridge, Mass.), 11*(4), 404–424. doi:10.1162/105474602760204309

Bowman, D., Wineman, J., Hodges, L., & Allison, D. (1998). Designing Animal Habitats Within an Immersive VE. *IEEE Computer Graphics and Applications, 18*(5), 9–13. doi:10.1109/38.708555

Boy, G. (1997). The group elicitation method for participatory design and usability testing. *Interactions of the ACM, 4*(2).

Boyatzis, C. J., & Varghese, R. (1993). Children's emotional associations with colors. *The Journal of Genetic Psychology, 155,* 77–85.

Boyer, M. A. (1999). Step 1: Satisfy the consumer. *Supermarket Business, 54*(4), 112.

Braiterman, J., Verhage, S., & Choo, R. (2000). Designing with Users in Internet Time. *Interactions, 7*(5, September–October), 23-27.

Brajnik, G. (2004). Comparing accessibility evaluation tools: a method for tool effectiveness. *Univers. Access Inf. Soc., 3*(3), 252–263. doi:10.1007/s10209-004-0105-y

Brajnik, G. (2006). Web Accessibility Testing: When the Method Is the Culprit. In *Proceedings of 10th International Conference on Computers Helping People with Special Needs* (pp. 156-163). Berlin: Springer.

Brajnik, G. (2008). A comparative test of web accessibility evaluation methods. In *Assets '08: Proceedings of the 10th international ACM SIGACCESS conference on Computers and accessibility* (pp. 113-120). Berlin: ACM.

Branaghan, R. J. (2001). Design by People for People: Essays on Usability. *Cognetics.*

Branson, J., & Miller, D. (1997). Research Methods for Studying the Language of the Signing Deaf. In N. Hornberger, & P. Corson (Eds), *Encyclopedia of Language and Education* (Vol. 8, pp. 175–184).

Bregman, A. S. (2002). *Auditory Scene Analysis: Perceptual Organization of Sound.* Cambridge, MA: MIT Press.

Brinck, T., Gergle, D., & Wood, S. D. (2002). *Usability for the Web: Designing Web Sites that Work.* San Francisco, CA: Morgan Kaufmann.

British Standards Institution. (2006). *PAS 78: 2006. Guide to good practice in commissioning accessible websites.* Retrieved June 1, 2009, from http://www.bsonline.bsi-global.com/server/PdfControlServlet/bsol?pdfId=GBM02%2F30129227&format=pdf

British Standards Institution. (2009). *BS 8788 Web accessibility: Building accessible experiences for disabled people* (in preparation). Retrieved June 26, 2009, from http://www.bsigroup.com/en/Standards-and-Publications/Industry-Sectors/ICT/ICT-standards/BS-8878/

Brown, J. S., & Duguid, P. (1996). Keeping it simple. In Winograd, T. (ed), *Bringing Design to Software,* (pp. 129-145). New York: ACM Press.

Brueggemann, B. J. (Ed.). (2004). *Literacy and Deaf People: Cultural and Contextual Perspectives.* Washington, DC: Gallaudet University Press.

Bruun, A., Gull, P., Hofmeister, L., & Stage, J. (2009). Let your users do the testing: a comparison of three remote asynchronous usability testing methods. *Proceedings of CHI 2009.* New York: ACM Press.

Bucklin, R. E., & Sismeiro, C. (2003). A model of web site browsing behavior estimated on clickstream data. *JMR, Journal of Marketing Research, 40,* 249 267. doi:10.1509/jmkr.40.3.249.19241

Bullet, D. (2002). *Introduction to Usability.* Retrieved 14 April 2004, from http://www.usabilityfirst.com/intro/index.txl

Burgoon, J. K., Bonito, J. A., Bengtsson, B., Cederberg, C., Lundeberg, M., & Allspach, L. (2000). Interactivity in Human-Computer Interaction: A Study Of Credibility, Understanding and Influence. *Computers in Human Behavior, 16*(6), 553–574. doi:10.1016/S0747-5632(00)00029-7

Burgstahler, S. (2006). Web accessibility: Guidelines for busy administrators. *Handbook of Business Strategy, 7*(1), 313-318. Retrieved June 1, 2009, from http://www.emeraldinsight.com/Insight/viewContentItem.do?contentType=Article&hdAction=lnkpdf&contentId=1523742

Bygstad, B., Ghinea, G., & Brevik, E. (2007). Systems Development Methods and Usability in Norway: An Industrial Perspective. In *Usability and Internationalization. HCI and Culture. Proceedings,* (pp. 258-266). Berlin: Springer.

Cagnin, M. I., Braga, R. T. V., Germano, F. S. R., Chan, A., & Maldonado, J. (2005). Extending Patterns with Testing Implementation. In *Fifth Latin American Conference on Pattern Languages of Programs, 2005, Campos do Jordão - SP. Proceedings do SugarLoafPLoP 2005, 2005. v. 1*

Caldwell, B., Cooper, M., Reid, L. G., & Vanderheiden, G. (2008). *Web content accessibility guidelines 2.0:* World Wide Web Consortium. Retrieved June, 2009 from http://www.w3.org/TR/WCAG20/

Calhoun, G. C., Arbak, C. L., & Boff, K. R. (1984). Eye-controlled switching for crew station design". In *Proceedings of the Human Factors Society 28th annual meeting,* (pp. 258-262). Santa Monica, CA: Human Factors Society.

Calvary, G., Coutaz, J., Thevenin, D., Limbourg, Q., Bouillon, L., & Vanderdonckt, J. (2003). A Unifying Reference Framework for Multi-Target User Interfaces. *Interacting with Computers, 15*(3), 289–308. doi:10.1016/S0953-5438(03)00010-9

Camgöz, N., Yener, N., & Güvenç, D. (2002). Effects of hue, saturation, and brightness on preference. *Color Research and Application, 27*(3), 199–207. doi:10.1002/col.10051

Card, S. K., Mackinlay, J. D., & Robertson, G. G. (1990). The design space of input devices. In *Proceedings of the SIGCHI conference on Human factors in computing systems: Empowering people,* (pp. 117-124). New York: ACM press.

Carey, K. (2005). Accessibility: The current situation and new directions. *Ariadne, 44.* Retrieved June 5, 2009, from http://www.ariadne.ac.uk/issue44/carey/

Carlson, P. (1998). Advanced Educational Technologies – Promise and Puzzlement. *Journal of Universal Computer Science, 4*(3), 210–215.

Carroll, J. M. (2002). *Human-Computer Interaction in the New Millennium.* New York: Addison-Wesley.

Carroll, J. M. (Ed.). (2003). *HCI Models, Theories, and Frameworks: Towards a Multidisciplinary Science.* Amsterdam: Morgan Kaufmann Publishers.

Carroll, M. (2004). *Usability testing leads to better ROI*. Retrieved 14 April 2004, from http://www.theus-abilitycompany.com/news/media_coverage/pdfs/2003/NewMediaAge_270303.pdf

Casaday, G. (2001). Whiteboard: online shopping: or, how I saved a trip to the store and receive my item in just 47 fun-filled days. *Interaction, 8*, 15–19.

Castillo, J. C., Hartson, H. R., & Hix, D. (1998). Remote usability evaluation: Can users report their own critical incidents? In *Proceedings of CHI 1998*, (pp. 253-254). New York: ACM Press.

Cato, J. (2001). *User-Centered Web Design*. Reading, MA: Addison Wesley.

CCIR-5. (1999). *User attitudes towards real and synthetic speech*. Edinburgh, UK: University of Edinburgh, Centre for Communication Interface Research.

Celentano, A., & Pittarello, F. (2001). A content cen-tred methodology for authoring 3d interactive worlds for cultural heritage. *International Cultural Heritage Informatics Meeting, 2*, 315-324.

Ceri, S., Fraternali, P., & Bongio, A. (2000). Web Modeling Language (WebML): a modeling language for designing Web sites. *Computer Networks, 33*(1-6), 137 - 157.

Chankong, V., & Haimes, Y. Y. (2008). *Multi-objective Decision Making: Theory and Methodology*. New York: Dover Publications.

Chavan, A., & Steins, C. (2003). Doing the right thing. *Planning, 69*(7), 10-13. Retrieved June 1, 2009, from http://proquest.umi.com/pqdweb?did=379258791&Fmt=3&clientId=5238&RQT=309&VName=PQD

Checkland, P., & Scholes, J. (2003). *Soft Systems Meth-odology in Action*. London: John Wiley & Sons, LTD.

Chen, H., Wigand, R. T., & Nilan, M. S. (1999). Op-timal Experience of Web Activities. *Computers in Human Behavior, 15*(5), 585–608. doi:10.1016/S0747-5632(99)00038-2

Chevalier, A., & Ivory, M. (2003). Web site design: In-fluences of designer's expertise and design constraints.

International Journal of Human-Computer Interaction Studies, 58, 57–87. doi:10.1016/S1071-5819(02)00126-X

Chikszentmihalyi, M. (1996). Go with the Flow. *Wired*. Online archive available at http://www.wired.com/wired/archive/4.09/czik_pr.html

Chisholm, W., & May, M. (2008). *Universal design for web applications*. Sebastopol, CA: O'Reilly.

Chisholm, W., Vanderheiden, G., & Jacobs, I. (1999). *Web content accessibility guidelines 1.0: World Wide Web Consortium*. Retrieved June, 2009 from http://www.w3.org/TR/WCAG10/

Cho, J. (2004). Likelihood to abort an online transaction: influences from cognitive evaluations, attitudes, and behavioral variables. *Information & Management, 41*, 827–838. doi:10.1016/j.im.2003.08.013

Choi, Y. S., Yi, J. S., Law, C. M., & Jacko, J. A. (2006). Are universal design resources designed for designers? In *Assets '06: Proceedings of the 8th international ACM SIGACCESS conference on Computers and accessibility* (pp. 87-94). New York: ACM.

Churchill, G. A. Jr. (1979). A Paradigm for Devel-oping Better Measures of Marketing Constructs. *JMR, Journal of Marketing Research, 16*(1), 64–73. doi:10.2307/3150876

Clare, S. (2002). Worldwide-friendly sites draw returns. *Marketing News, 36*(18), 24.

Clark, J. (2002). *Building accessible websites*. India-napolis: New Riders Publishing.

Clark, J. (2003). *How to save web accessibility from itself*. Retrieved June 10, 2009, from http://www.alistapart.com/articles/saveaccessibility/

Clegg, F. (1990). *Simple Statistics*. Cambridge, UK: Cambridge University Press.

Cluster, W. A. B. (2007). *Unified Web Evaluation Meth-odology (UWEM 1.2)*. Retrieved 01/2009 from www.w3c.org

Cockburn, A. & McKenzie (2001). 3D or not 3D? Evalu-ating the Effect of the Third Dimension in a Document

Management System. In *Proceedings of the SIGCHI conference on Human factors in computing systems,* Seattle, WA. (pp. 434 – 441). Retrieved from http://www.cosc.canterbury.ac.nz/andrew.cockburn/papers/chi01DM.pdf

Cockton, G. (2005). A development framework for value-centred design, Paper presented at the Conference on Human Factors in Computer Systems: CHI'05. Portland, USA.

Cockton, G., & Woolrych, A. (2001). Understanding inspection methods: lessons from an assessment of heuristic evaluation. In Blandford AJ, Vanderdonckt J (eds.) *People & Computers XV* (pp. 171–192). Berlin: Springer- Verlag.

Cockton, G., Woolrych, A., & Hindmarch, M. (2004) Reconditioned Merchandise: Extended Structured Report Formats in Usability Inspection. In *CHI 2004 Extended Abstracts,* (pp. 1433-36). New York: ACM Press.

Cockton, G., Woolrych, A., Hall, L., & Hindmarch, M. (2003). Changing analysts' tunes: The surprising impact of a new instrument for usability inspection method assessment. In P. Palanque, P. Johnson, & E. O'Neill (Eds.), People and computers XVII: Designing for society, Proceedings of HCI 2003, (pp. 145-162). Berlin: Springer-Verlag.

Cohen, M., Giancola, J. P., & Balogh, J. (2004*). Voice User Interface Design*. Boston: Addison-Wesley Professional.

Cole, R. (1999). New Tools for Interactive Speech and Language Training: Using Animated Conversational Agents in the Classrooms of Profoundly Deaf Children. In *Prof. of ESCA/SOCRA for Speech Science Education.*

Conallen, J. (2002). *Building Web Applications with Uml.* (2nd ed.). Reading, MA: Addison-Wesley Longman Publishing Co., Inc.

Conn, A. (1995). Time Affordances: The Time Factor in Diagnostic Usability Heuristics. *In Proceedings of CHI '95: Human Factors in Computing Systems,* (pp. 1836-913). New York: ACM Press/Addison Wesley.

Constantine, L. L. (2003). Canonical Abstract Prototypes for Abstract Visual and Interaction. In *Proceedings of the 10th International workshop on Design, Specification and Evaluation of Interactive Systems DSV-IS,* (LNCS Vol. 2844, pp. 1-15). Berlin: Springer Verlag.

Conte, T., Massolar, J., Mendes, E., & Travassos, G. H. (2007a). Web Usability Inspection Technique Based on Design Perspectives. In *Proceedings of the 21th Brazilian Symposium on Software Engineering (SBES 2007),* (Vol. 1, pp. 394-410), João Pessoa, Brazil.

Conte, T., Massollar, J., Mendes, E., & Travassos, G. H. (2007b, September). Usability Evaluation Based on Web Design Perspectives. In *Proceedings of the First International Symposium on Empirical Software Engineering and Measurement (ESEM 2007),* Madrid, Spain.

Conte, T., Vaz, V., Massolar, J., Mendes, E., & Travassos, G. H. (2008). Process Model Elicitation and a Reading Technique for Web Usability Inspections. In *International Workshop on Web Information Systems Engineering for Eletronic Businesses and Governments (E-BAG 2008)* (LNCS Vol. 5176 - Advances in Web Information Systems Engineering - WISE 2008 Workshops, pp. 36-47), Auckland, New Zealand

Corah, N. L., & Gross, J. B. (1967). Hue, Brightness, and Saturation Variables in Color Form Matching. *Child Development, 38*(1), 137–142. doi:10.2307/1127135

CornerStones. (1998). Retrieved 2008, from http://ncam.wgbh.org/cornerstones/cornerstones.html

Cox, K., & Walker, D. (1993). *User Interface Design* (2 ed.). New York: Prentice Hall.

Crasborn, O., et al. (2008). Construction and Exploration of Sign Language Corpora. *E-proc. of the 3rd Workshop on the Representation and Processing of Sign Languages, LREC 2008l.*

Crimmins, J. C. (1997). *Inference and impact, Measuring advertising effectiveness,* (éd. W.D. Wells). Mahwah, NJ: Lawrence Erlbaum Associates.

Culnan, M. (1984). The Dimensions of Accessibility to On-line Information: Implications for Implementing

Office Information Systems. *ACM Transactions on Information Systems*, *2*(2), 141–150. doi:10.1145/521.523

Cunliffe, D. (2000). Developing usable Web sites - a review and model. *Internet Research*, *10*(4), 295. doi:10.1108/10662240010342577

Dahlbäck, N., Wang, O., Nass, C. I., & Alwin, J. (2007). Similarity is More Important than Expertise: Accent Effects in Speech Interfaces. In *Proceedings of the SIGCHI conference on Human Factors in Computing Systems* (1553–1556). New York: ACM.

Darlington, K. (2005). *Effective Website Development*. Upper Saddle River, NJ: Pearson Education Limited.

Darpy, D. (1997). Une variable médiatrice du report d'achat: La procrastination. *Communication au 13ème Congrès International de l'AFM*, Toulouse, France.

Davidsson, O., et al. (2004). *Game Design Patterns for Mobile Game*. Project report to Nokia Research Center, Finland.

Davies, M. (2006). *Isolani, PAS 78 launch, 2006*. Retrieved June 10, 2009, from http://www.isolani.co.uk/blog/access/Pas78Launch

Davis, F. D. (1989). Perceived Usefulness, Perceived Ease of Use, and User Acceptance of Information Technology. *MIS Quarterly*, *13*(3), 319–340. doi:10.2307/249008

Day, P. N., Ferguson, R. K., & Holt, P. O'B., Hogg, S., & Gibson, D. (2005). Wearable Augmented VR for Enhancing Information Delivery in High Precision Defence Assembly: An Engineering Case Study. *Virtual Reality (Waltham Cross)*, *8*(3), 177–185. doi:10.1007/s10055-004-0147-8

De Boeck, J., González-Calleros, J. M., Coninx, K., & Vanderdonckt, J. (2006). Open Issues for the development of 3D Multimodal Applications from an MDE perspective. In A. Pleuss, J. Van den Bergh, H. Hussmann, S. Sauer, A. Boedcher, (ed.), *Proc. of 2nd Int. Workshop on Model Driven Development of Advanced User Interfaces MDDAUI'2006*, Geneva, October 2, (pp. 11-14).

December, J. (1996). An information development methodology for the World Wide Web. *Technical Communication in Cyberspace*, *43*(4), 369–374.

Demers, E., & Lev, B. (2001). A rude awakening: internet shakeout in 2000. *Review of Accounting Studies*, *6*, 331–359. doi:10.1023/A:1011675227890

Dempsey, B. J., Weiss, D., Jones, P., & Greenberg, J. (2002). Who is an open source software developer? *Communications of the ACM*, *45*(2), 67–72. doi:10.1145/503124.503125

Denscombe, M. (2007). *The Good Research Guide: For Small-scale Social Research Projects*. New York: McGraw-Hill International.

Denzin, N. K., & Lincoln, Y. S. (2005).The discipline and practice of qualitative research. In N.K. Denzin & Y. S. Lincoln, (Eds.) *The SAGE handbook of qualitative research*, (3rd Ed.). London: Sage.

Deque, (2008). *Deque RAMP™ product family*. Retrieved November 21, 2008, from http://deque.com/products/ramp/index.php

Derbaix, C. & Poncin, I. (2005). La mesure des réactions affectives en marketing: évaluation des principaux outils. *Recherche and Applications en Marketing, Numéro spécial sur La Mesure*, *20*(2), 55-76.

Deshpande, Y., Murugesan, S., Ginige, A., Hansen, S., Schwabe, D., & Gaedke, M. (2002). Web Engineering. *Journal of Web Engineering*, *1*(1), 3–17.

Dholakia, U. M., & Rego, L. L. (1998). What Makes Commercial Web Pages Popular? An empirical investigation of web page effectiveness. *European Journal of Marketing*, *32*(7/8), 724–736. doi:10.1108/03090569810224119

Di Mascio, T., & Gennari, R. (2008). An Intelligent Visual Dictionary for Italian Sign Language. *Journal of Web Engineering*, *7*(4), 318–338.

Diaper, D. (2006). Task Analysis is at the Heart of Human-Computer Interaction. In C. Ghaoui (Ed.), *Encyclopedia of Human-Computer Interaction* (pp. 579-587). Hershey, PA: Idea Group Reference.

Díaz, P., Montero, S., & Aedo, I. (2005). Modelling hypermedia and web applications: the Ariadne development method. *Information Systems*, *30*(8), 649–673. doi:10.1016/j.is.2004.09.001

Dillon, A. (1994). *Designing Usable Electronic Text: Ergonomic aspects of human information usage.* London: Taylor & Francis Ltd.

Disability Discrimination Act. (1995). (c.50) London: HMSO. Retrieved May 20, 2009, from http://www.opsi.gov.uk/acts/acts1995/ukpga_19950050_en_1

Disability Rights Commission. (2004). *The web, access and inclusion for disabled people: A formal investigation conducted by the Disability Rights Commission.* London: TSO. Retrieved May 25, 2009, from http://83.137.212.42/sitearchive/drc/PDF/2.pdf

Divard, R. & Urien, B. (2001). The Consumer Lives in a Colored World. *Recherche et Applications en Marketing*, 3-24.

Dix, A., Finlay, J. E., Abowd, G. D., & Beale, R. (2003). *Human-Computer Interaction* (3rd ed.). Upper Saddle River, NJ: Prentice Hall.

Doll, W. J., & Torkzadeh, G. (1989). A Discrepancy Model Of End-User Computing Involvement. *Management Science, 35*(10), 1151. doi:10.1287/mnsc.35.10.1151

Domingues, A. L. S., Bianchini, S. L., Re, R., & Ferrari, R. G. (2008). A Comparison Study of Web Development Methods. In *Proceedings of the 34th Latin-American Conference on Informatics* (pp. 10).

Donovan, R. J. & Rossiter, J. R. (1982). Store atmosphere: an environmental psychology approach. *J Retailing, Spring, 58*, 34-57.

Downey, L. (2007). Group Usability Testing: Evolution in Usability Techniques. *Journal of Usability Studies, 2*(3), 133–144.

Downton, A. (Ed.). (1993). *Engineering the Human-Computer Interface* (Student Ed.). London: McGraw-Hill.

Draper, S. (1999). Analysing fun as a candidate software requirement. In *Personal technology.* Heidelberg, Germany: Springer Verlag.

Dreze, X., & Zufryden, F. (1997). Testing Web Site Design and Promotional Content. *Journal of AdGREENising Research, 37*(2), 77–91.

Drugeon-Lichtlé M.-C. (1996). *Les effets des couleurs d'une annonce magazine sur les émotions du consumer: conceptualisation et résultats d'une étude exploratoire.* Actes de l'Association Française de Marketing, 12, Poitiers, 445-458.

Drugeon-Lichtlé, M.-C. (2002). *Couleur d'une annonce publicitaire, gôuts des individus et perception des marque. Décisions Marketing, 26*(April/June), abi/inform global, 29.

Duarte, C., & Carriço, L. (2008). Audio Interfaces for Improved Accessibility. In S.Pinder (Ed.), *Advances in Human Computer Interaction* (pp. 121-142). Vienna, Austria: I-Tech Education and Publishing.

Düchting, M., Zimmermann, D., & Nebe, K. (2007). Incorporating User Centered Requirement Engineering into Agile Software Development. In *Human-Computer Interaction. Interaction Design and Usability. Proceedings.* (pp. 58-67). Springer.

Dumas, J. S., & Redish, J. C. (1993). *A practical guide to usability testing.* Norwood, NJ: Ablex Publishing.

Dumas, J. S., & Redish, J. C. (1999). *A Practical Guide to Usability Testing.* Bristol, UK: Intellect Books.

Dunn, B. (1992, August 10). Choice of Color for Product Can Be Critical Factor. *Gazette*, 6.

Duric, Z., Gray, W. D., Heishman, R., Li, F., Rosenfeld, A., & Schoelles, M. (2002). 'Integrating perceptual and cognitive modeling for adaptive and intelligent human-computer interaction. *Proceedings of the IEEE, 90*(7), 1272–1289. doi:10.1109/JPROC.2002.801449

Dybkjær, L., & Bernsen, N. O. (2000). Usability Issues in Spoken Language Dialogue Systems. *Natural Language Engineering, 6*(3-4), 243–272. doi:10.1017/S1351324900002461

Dybkjær, L., & Bernsen, N. O. (2001). Usability Evaluation in Spoken Language Dialogue Systems. In. Proc. *ACL Workshop on Evaluation Methodologies for Language and Dialogue Systems*, (pp. 9-18).

Dybkjær, L., & Minker, W. (Eds.). (2008). *Recent Trends in Discourse and Dialogue.* Berlin: Springer-Verlag.

Dybkjær, L., Bernsen, N. O., & Minker, W. (2004). Evaluation and Usability of Multimodal Spoken Language Dialogue Systems. *Speech Communication, 43*(1-2), 33–54. doi:10.1016/j.specom.2004.02.001

Dybkjær, L., Hemsen, H., & Minker, W. (Eds.). (2007). *Evaluation of Text and Speech Systems.* Berlin: Springer-Verlag.

Eastgate, R. (2001). *The Structured Development of Virtual Environments: Enhancing Functionality and Interactivity.* Ph.D. Thesis, York University.

EduTools. (2008). *EduTools Course Management System Comparisons – Reborn.* Retrieved March 17, 2008, from http://www.edutools.info/course/index.jsp

Efstathiou, J., & Mamdani, E. H. (1986). *Expert Systems and How They are Applied to Industrial Decision Making.* North Holland: Computer Assisted Decision Making, Elsevier Science Publishers.

Eighmey, J., & McCord, L. (1998). Adding Value in the Information Age: Uses and Gratifications of Sites on the World Wide Web. *Journal of Business Research, 41*(3), 187–194. doi:10.1016/S0148-2963(97)00061-1

Ekman, P., & Friesen, W. (1975). *Unmasking the face.* Upper Saddle River, NJ: Prentice Hall.

e-LIS (2006). Retrieved 2008, from http://elis.eurac.edu/index_it

Elliot, S., & Fowell, S. (2000). Expectations versus Reality: A Snapshot of Consumer Experiences with Internet Retailing. *International Journal of Information Management, 20*(5), 323–336. doi:10.1016/S0268-4012(00)00026-8

Ellison, J. (2004). Assessing the accessibility of fifty United States government web pages. *First Monday, 9*(7). Retrieved April 23, 2009, from http://firstmonday.org/issues/issue9_7/ellison/index.html

Ellsworth, J. H., & Ellsworth, M. V. (1997). *Marketing on the Internet.* Mahwah, NJ: John Wiley & Sons, Inc.

EnSky. (1997). *EnSky's Unique Methodology.* Retrieved 16 Sept 2004, from http://www.ensky.com/company/process/methodology.php

Epting, F., Suchman, D., & Nickeson, C. (1971). An evaluation of elicitation procedures for personal constructs. *The British Journal of Psychology, 62*(4), 513–517.

Escalona, M. J., & Torres, J., Mejìas, M., GutìErrez, J. J., & Villadiego, D. (2007). The treatment of navigation in web engineering. *Advances in Engineering Software, 38*(4), 267–282. doi:10.1016/j.advengsoft.2006.07.006

Éthier, J., Hadaya, P., Talbot, J., & Cadieux, J. (2008). Interface design and emotions experienced on B2C Web Sites: empirical testing of a research model. *Computers in Human Behavior, 24*(6), 2771–2791. doi:10.1016/j.chb.2008.04.004

ETSI ETR-095. (1993). *Human Factors: Guide for Usability Evaluations of Telecommunications Systems and Services.* Sophia Antipolis, France: European Telecommunications Standards Institute.

European Commission. (2000). *Directive 2000/78/EC.* Retrieved May 20, 2009, from http://ec.europa.eu/employment_social/news/2001/jul/dir200078_en.html

European Commission. (2001). *Eurostat: Disability and social participation in Europe.* Retrieved June 11, 2009, from http://epp.eurostat.ec.europa.eu/cache/ITY_OFFPUB/KS-AW-01-001/EN/KS-AW-01-001-EN.PDF

European Commission. (2003). *Eurostat: One in six of the EU working-age population report disability.* Retrieved June 11, 2009, from http://epp.eurostat.ec.europa.eu/cache/ITY_PUBLIC/3-05122003-AP/EN/3-05122003-AP-EN.HTML

European Schoolnet. (2008). Virtual Learning Environments for European Schools. *A Survey and Commentary,* (pp. 1-36). Retrieved April 10, 2008, from http://www.eun.org/etb/vle/vle_eun_feb_2003.pdf

Fajardo, I. (2005). *Cognitive Accesibility to Hypertext Systems.* PhD thesis. U. of Granada, Spain.

Falk, L. K., & Sockel, H. (2005). Web Site Usability. In M. Pagani (Ed.), *Encyclopedia of Multimedia Technology and Networking* (Vol. 2, pp. 1078-1083). Hershey, PA: Idea Group reference.

Fath, J. L., Mann, T. L., & Holzman, T. G. (1994). A Practical Guide to Using Software Usability Labs: Lessons

Learned at IBM. *Behaviour & Information Technology, 13*(1-2), 25–35.

Fellbaum, K., & Kouroupetroglou, G. (2008). Principles of Electronic Speech Processing with Applications for People with Disabilities. *Technology and Disability, 20*(2), 55–85.

Fels, D. I., Richards, J., Hardman, J., Soudian, S., & Silverman, C. (2004). American sign language of the web. In *CHI '04 Extended Abstracts on Human Factors in Computing Systems* CHI '04 (pp. 1111-1114). New York: ACM.

Fernandez-Maloigne, C. (2004). Quelle métrique pour l'évaluation de la qualité couleur d'une image numérique? *Application à la compression JPEG2000, CAM Conférence*, Paris, octobre.

Ferreira, J., Noble, J., & Biddle, R. (2007). Agile Development Iterations and UI Design. In *Proceedings AGILE Conference*, (pp 50-58). Washington, DC: IEEE.

Ferrer, A., Romero, R., Martínez, M., Asensi, M., & Andreu, A. (2002). *Improving Reading Skills in Adult Deaf People: The Spanish MÀS Module*. Berlin.

Festinger, L. (1954). A theory of social comparison processes. *Human Relations, 7*, 117–140. doi:10.1177/001872675400700202

Fewster, R., & Mendes, E. (2001) Measurement, Prediction and Risk Analysis for Web Applications. In *Proceedings of IEEE Metrics'2001-7th International Software metrics Symposium*. Washington, DC: IEEE CS Press.

FFIEC IT Examination Handbook. (2005). *Systems Development Life Cycle*.

Filser, M. (1994). *Le comportement du consommateur*. Paris: Précis Dalloz.

Filser, M. (2003a). Le marketing sensoriel: la quête de l'intégration théorique et managériale. *Revue Française du Marketing, 194*(4/5, Septembre), 5-11.

Filser, M. (2003b). Vingt ans de recherches en comportement du consumer. In Rémy, I. Garabuau-Moussaoui, D.

Desjeux and M. Filser, (eds), *Sociétés, Consommation et Consommateurs* (pp. 15-20). L'Harmattan.

Fincher, S. (1999). Analysis of Design: an exploration of patterns and pattern languages for pedagogy. *Journal of Computers in Mathematics and Science Teaching: Special Issue CS-ED Research, 18*(3), 331–348.

Fishbein, M., & Ajzen, I. (1975). *Belief, Attitude, Intention and Behaviour: An Introduction to Theory and Research*. Reading, MA: Addison-Wesley.

Fleming, J. (1998). *Web Navigation: Designing the User Experience*. Sebastol, CA: O'Reilly & Associates.

Fleury, P., & Imbert, C. (1996). Couleur. In *Encyclopeadia Universalis, 6*, 676-681.

Fogg, B. J., Marshall, J., Laraki, O., Osipovich, A., Varma, C., Fang, N., et al. (2001). What Makes Web Sites Credible?: A Report on a Large Quantitative Study. In *Proceedings the SIG-CHI'01 Conference on Human Factors in Computing Systems*, (pp.61-680. Reading, MA: ACM Press/Addison Wesley.

Foley, V. W., & Chan, V. (1984). The human factors of computer graphics interaction techniques. *IEEE Computer Graphics and Applications*, (4): 13–48.

Fons, J., Pelechano, V., Albert, M., & Pastor, O. (2003). Development of Web Applications from Web Enhanced Conceptual Schemas. In *Proceedings of the 22th Int. Conference on Conceptual Modeling (ER 2003)*, (Vol. 2813/2003, pp. 232-245), Chicago.

Ford, D. H. (1987). *Humans as Self-Constructing Living Systems: A Developmental Theory of Behaviour and Personality*. Hillsdale, NJ: Erlbaum.

Ford, M. E. (1992). *Motivating Humans, Goals, Emotions and Personal Agency Beliefs*. Thousand Oaks, CA: Sage.

Forgeas, J. P. (1999). *Network theories and beyond*. In T. Dalgleish & M. J. Power, (éds.), *Handbook of Cognition and Emotion*, (pp. 591-612). Chichester, UK: Wiley.

Furnell, S. M., & Karweni, T. (1999). Security Implications of Electronic Commerce: A Survey of Consumers and Businesses. *Internet Research: Electronic Networking Applications and Policy, 9*(5), 372-382.

Frank, M., & Foley, J. (1993). Model-based user interface design by example and by answering questions. In *Proc. INTERCHI, ACM Conference on Human Factors in Computing Systems*, (pp. 161-162).

Fransella, F., & Bannister, D. (1977). *A manual for repertory grid technique*. London: Academic Press.

Frechtling, J., & Sharp, L. (1997). *User-Friendly Handbook for Mixed Method Evaluations*. Washington, DC: National Science Foundation. Retrieved from http://www.nsf.gov/pubs/1997/nsf97153/start.htm

Freire, A. P., Goularte, R., & de Mattos Fortes, R. P. (2007). Techniques for developing more accessible web applications: a survey towards a process classification. In *SIGDOC '07: Proceedings of the 25th annual ACM international conference on Design of communication* (pp. 162-169). New York: ACM.

Freire, A. P., Russo, C. M., & Fortes, R. P. M. (2008). A survey on the accessibility awareness of people involved in web development projects in Brazil. In *W4A '08: Proceedings of the 2008 international cross-disciplinary conference on Web accessibility (W4A)* (pp. 87-96). New York: ACM.

Freitas, D., & Kouroupetroglou, G. (2008). Speech Technologies for Blind and Low Vision Persons. *Technology and Disability, 20*(2), 135–156.

French, S. (1986). *Decision theory: An Introduction to the mathematics of rationality*. New York: Wiley.

Frishberg, N., Dirks, A. M., Benson, C., Nickell, S., & Smith, S. (2002). Getting to know you: Open source development meets usability. In *Proceedings of CHI 2002,* (pp. 932-933). New York: ACM Press.

Gabbard, J. L., Hix, D., & Swan, J. E. (1999). User-Centered Design and Evaluation of Virtual Environments. *IEEE Computer Graphics and Applications, 19*(6), 51–59. doi:10.1109/38.799740

Galitz, O. W. (1997). *The Essential Guide to User Interface Design: A Introduction to GUI Design Principles and Techniques*. New York: John Wiley & Sons.

Gamma, E., Helm, R., Johnson, R., & Vlissides, J. (1994). *Design Patterns – Elements of reusable object oriented software*. Reading, MA: Addison Wesley.

Gardner, D. (2003). Cool customer response? Hit their hot buttons! *Agri Marketing, 41*(4), 74.

Garrett, J. (2003). *The Elements of User Experience: User-Centered Design for the Web*. New York: New Riders.

Garrido, A., Rossi, G., & Schwabe, D. (1997). Patterns Systems for Hypermedia. In *Proceedings of PloP97 Pattern Language of Program*.

Garzotto, F., & Matera, M. (1997). A Systematic Method for Hypermedia Usability Inspection. *The New Review of Hypermedia and Multimedia, 3*, 39–65. doi:10.1080/13614569708914683

Garzotto, F., & Retalis, S. (2008). "Design-by-patterns" in e-learning: a critical perspective. In Lockyer, Bennett, Agostinho & Harper (eds.), *Handbook of Research on Learning Design and Learning Objects: Issues, Applications, and Technologies*. Hershey, PA: Idea Group Inc.

Garzotto, F., Matera, M., & Paolini, P. (1998). Model-based heuristic evaluation of hypermedia usability. In *Proceedings of the Working Conference on Advanced Visual Interfaces*, May 24–27, L'Aquila, Italy.

Garzotto, F., Matera, M., & Paolini, P. (1999). Abstract tasks: a tool for the inspection of Web sites and off-line hypermedia. In *Proceedings of the tenth ACM Conference on Hypertext and hypermedia*. Darmstadt, Germany, ACM.

Garzotto, F., Paolini, P., & Schwabe, D. (1993). HDM--a model-based approach to hypertext application design. *ACM Transactions on Information Systems, 11*(1), 1–26. doi:10.1145/151480.151483

Garzotto, F., Paolini, P., Bolchini, D., & Valenti, S. (1999). "Modeling-by-patterns" of web applications. Chen P., Embley D., Kouloumdjian J. & Little S. (eds.), *Advances in Conceptual Modeling* (LNCS Vol. 1727, pp. 293-306). Berlin: Springer.

Gehrke, D., & Turban, E. (1999). Determinants of successful web-site design: Relative importance and recommendations for effectiveness. In *HICSS '99: Proceedings of 32nd Hawaii International Conference on System Sciences.* Washington, DC: IEEE Computer Society.

Gennari, R., & Mich, O. (2008). Designing and Assessing an Intelligent E-Tool for Deaf Children. *Proc. of the IUI 2008 Conf.* ACM, pp. 325–328.

Gerber, A., Van Der Merwe, A., & Alberts, R. (2007). Practical implications of rapid development methodologies. In *Proceedings Computer Science and Information Technology Education Conference.*

Gibson, L. (2004). *Writing an accessibility statement.* Retrieved June 1, 2009, from http://www.dmag.org.uk/resources/design_articles/accessibilitystatement.asp

Gignac, T. (2000). Breaking the online barrier: an estimated 95 percent of Web sites are inaccessible to disabled users ± not a smart business move. *Calgary Herald* [Front.]. *Computers Section, 17*(August), V7.

Gilbert, D. T., Giesler, R. B., & Morris, K. A. (1995). When comparisons arise. *Journal of Personality and Social Psychology, 69,* 227–236. doi:10.1037/0022-3514.69.2.227

Ginige, A., & Murugesan, S. (2001). Guest Editors' Introduction: Web Engineering - An Introduction. *IEEE MultiMedia, 8*(1), 14–18. doi:10.1109/93.923949

Ginige, A., & Murugesan, S. (2001). Web engineering: an introduction. *Multimedia, IEEE, 8*(1), 14–18. doi:10.1109/93.923949

Gómez, J., Cachero, C., & Pastor, O. (2001). Conceptual Modeling of Device-Independent Web Applications. *IEEE MultiMedia, 8*(2), 26–39. doi:10.1109/93.917969

Gonzalez-Calleros, J. M. (2006, June). *A Method for Developing 3D User Interfaces for Information Systems.* DEA thesis, UCL, Louvain-la-Neuve.

González-Calleros, J. M., Vanderdonckt, J., & Arteaga, J. M. (2006). A Method for Developing 3D User Interfaces of Information Systems. In *Proc. of 6th Int. Conf. on Computer-Aided Design of User Interfaces CADUI'2006* (Bucharest, 6-8 June 2006), (pp. 85-100). Berlin: Springer-Verlag.

González-Calleros, J. M., Vanderdonckt, J., & Arteaga, J. M. (2009). Towards Canonical Task Types for User Interface Design. In *Proc. of 4th Int. Conf. on Latin-American Conference on Human-Computer Interaction CLIHC'2009,* Merida, November 9-11. Los Alamitos, CA: IEEE Computer Society Press.

Goodyear, P., Avgeriou, P., Baggetun, R., Bartoluzzi, S., Retalis, S., Ronteltap, F., & Rusman, E. (2004). Towards a pattern language for networked learning. In . *Proceedings of Networked Learning, 2004,* 449–455.

Google, (n.d.). Retrieved from https://www.google.com/accounts/DisplayUnlockCaptcha

Gorn, G., Chattopadhyay, A., Sengupta, J., & Tripathi, S. (2004). Waiting for the web: how screen color affects time perception. *JMR, Journal of Marketing Research, 41*(May), 215–225. doi:10.1509/jmkr.41.2.215.28668

Graham, I. (2003). *A Pattern Language for Web Usability.* Reading, MA: Addison-Wesley.

Grammenos, D., Mourouzis, A., & Stephanidis, C. (2006). Virtual prints: Augmenting virtual environments with interactive personal marks. *International Journal of Man-Machine Studies, 64*(3), 221–239.

Greenberg, S., Fitzpatrick, G., Gutwin, C., & Kaplan, S. (2000). Adapting the locales framework for heuristic evaluation of groupware. [AJIS]. *Australasian Journal of Information Systems, 7*(2), 102–108.

Greenstein, J. S., & Arnaut, L. Y. (1988). Input devices. In M. Helander, (Ed.), *Handbook of Human-Computer Interaction* (pp. 495-519). Amsterdam: North-Holland.

Guenther, K. (2006). Content Management Systems as "Silver Bullets". *Online, 30*(4), 54–55.

Hackett, S., Parmanto, B., & Zeng, X. (2004). *Accessibility of internet websites through time.* Paper presented at the 6th International ACM SIGACCESS Conference on Computers and Accessibility, 18-20 October 2004, Atlanta. Retrieved June 1, 2009, from http://delivery.acm.org/10.1145/1030000/1028638/p32-hackett.pdf?key1=1028638&key2=0515277511&coll=ACM&dl=ACM&CFID=486951&CFTOKEN=79021637

Hackos, T. J., & Redish, C. J. (1998). *User and Task Analysis for Interface Design*. New York: Wiley.

Haire, B., Henderson-Sellers, B., & D., a. L. (2001). Supporting web development in the OPEN process: additional tasks. In *Proceedings COMPSAC'2001: International Computer Software and Applications Conference*. New York: ACM.

Hajdinjak, M., & Mihelic, F. (2006). The PARADISE evaluation framework: Issues and findings. *Computational Linguistics, 32*(2), 263–272. doi:10.1162/coli.2006.32.2.263

Hales, B. M., & Provonost, P. J. (2006). The checklist. A tool for error management and performance improvement. *Journal of Critical Care, 21*, 231–235. doi:10.1016/j.jcrc.2006.06.002

Hales, B. M., Terblanche, M., Fowler, R., & Sibbald, W. (2008). Development of medical checklists for improved quality of patient care. *International Journal for Quality in Health Care, 20*(1), 22–30. doi:10.1093/intqhc/mzm062

Haley, R. I., Staffaroni, J., & Fox, A. (1994). The missing measures of copy testing. *Journal of Advertising Research, 34*(3), 46–61.

Hall, R. H., & Hanna, P. (2004). The Impact of Web Page Text-Background Color Combinations on Readability. *Retention, Aesthetics, and Behavioral Intention. Behaviour & Information Technology, 23*(3), 183–195. doi:10.1080/01449290410001669932

Hamilton, A. (1997). *Avoid The #1 Web Site Sin: Slow Loading Pages*. Online archive available at http://www4.zdnet.com/anchordesk/story/story/story_1244.html

Hanson, W. A. (2000). *Principles of Internet Marketing*. Cincinnati, OH: South-Western College Publishers.

Harper, S., Yesilada, Y., & Goble, C. (2004). Workshop report: W4A - International Cross Disciplinary Workshop on Web Accessibility 2004. *ACM SIGCAPH Computers and the Physically Handicapped, 76*, 2-3. Retrieved June 1, 2009, from http://portal.acm.org/ft_gateway.cfm?id=1037130&type=pdf&coll=ACM&dl=ACM&CFID=486951&CFTOKEN=79021637

Harris, R. A. (2005). *Voice Interaction Design: Crafting the New Conversational Speech Systems*. San Francisco: Morgan Kaufmann.

Harrison, C., & H., P. (2006). Impact of usability and accessibility problems in e-commerce and e-government websites. In *Proceedings HCI 2006*. (Vol. 1). London: British Computer Society.

Hartikainen, M., Salonen, E.-P., & Turunen, M. (2004). Subjective Evaluation of Spoken Dialogue Systems Using SERVQUAL Method. In *Proc. 8th International Conference on Spoken Language Processing - ICSLP*, (pp. 2273-2276).

Hartmann, J., Sutcliffe, A., & De Angeli, A. (2007). *'Investigating attractiveness in web user interfaces*. Paper presented at the SIGCHI Conference on Human Factors in Computing Systems, San Jose, CA.

Hartson, H. R. (1998). Human-Computer Interaction: Interdisciplinary Roots and Trends. *Journal of Systems and Software, 43*, 103–118. doi:10.1016/S0164-1212(98)10026-2

Hartson, H. R., & Castillo, J. C. (1998). Remote evaluation for post-deployment usability improvement. In *Proceedings of AVI 1998*, (pp. 22-29). New York: ACM Press.

Hartson, H. R., & Hix, D. (1989). Human-Computer Interface Development: Concepts and Systems for Its Management. *ACM Computing Surveys, 21*(1), 5–92. doi:10.1145/62029.62031

Hartson, H. R., Castillo, J. C., Kelso, J., & Neale, W. C. (1996). Remote evaluation: The network as an extension of the usability laboratory. In *Proceedings of CHI 1996*, (pp. 228-235). ACM Press

Hartson, H., Andre, T., & Williges, R. (2001). Criteria for Evaluating Usability Evaluation Methods. *International Journal of Human-Computer Interaction, 13*(4), 373–410. doi:10.1207/S15327590IJHC1304_03

Hartson, R. H. (1998). Human-Computer Interaction: Interdisciplinary Roots and Trends. *Journal of Systems and Software, 43*(2), 103–118. doi:10.1016/S0164-1212(98)10026-2

Hartwick, J., & Barki, H. (1994). Explaining the role of user participation in information Systems. *Management Science, 40*(4), 440. doi:10.1287/mnsc.40.4.440

Hartwick, J., & Barki, H. (2001). Communications as a Dimension of User Participation. *IEEE Transactions on Professional Communication, 44*(1), 21–36. doi:10.1109/47.911130

Hassanein, K., & Head, M. (2006). The Impact of Infusing Social Presence in the Web Interface: An Investigation Across Product Types. *International Journal of Electronic Commerce, 10*(2), 31–55. doi:10.2753/JEC1086-4415100202

Hassenzahl, M., & Trautmann, T. (2001). *Analysis of web sites with the repertory grid technique.* Paper presented at the CHI 2001: extended abstracts: interactive poster sessions, New York.

Hassenzahl, M., Beu, A., & Burmester, M. (2001a). Engineering Ioy. *IEEE Software, 18*(1). doi:10.1109/52.903170

Hassenzahl, M., Wessler, R., & Hamborg, K. (2001b). *Exploring and understanding product qualities that users desire.* Paper presented at the Joint AFIHM-BCS conference on Human-Computer Interaction IHM-HCI'2001, Toulouse, France.

Hatch, M. J., & Cunliffe, A. L. (2006). *Organization Theory. Modern, Symbolic, and Postmodern Perspectives (2ⁿᵈ ed.).* Oxford, UK: Oxford University Press.

Hatch, M. J., & Yanow, D. (2008). Methodology by Metaphor: Ways of Seeing in Painting and Research. *Organization Science, 29*(1), 23–44. doi:10.1177/0170840607086635

Hayes, P. H., & Rosson, M. B. Schneider, M. L., & Whiteside, J. A. (1986). Classifying Users: A Hard Look at some Controversial Issues. In *Panel Proceedings of CHI'86: Conference on Human Factors in Computing Systems,* (pp.84-88). Reading, MA: ACM Press/Addison Wesley.

Hazlett, R. L., & Hazlett, S. Y. (1999). Emotional response to television commercials: facial EMG vs. self-report. *Journal of Advertising Research, 39*(2), 7–23.

HCI design patterns. (2005). Retrieved from http://www.hcipatterns.org/

Head, A. J. (1999). *Design Wise.* Medford, NJ: Thomas H Hogan Sr.

HearSay Browser, (n.d.). Stony Brook University, NY, NSF Award-IIS-0534419. Retrieved from http://www.cs.sunysb.edu/~hearsay/.

Helander, M. (2006). *A Guide to Human Factors and Ergonomics,* (2nd ed.). Boca Raton, FL: CRC Press.

Helander, M. G., & Khalid, H. M. (2000). Modeling the Customer in Electronic Commerce. *Applied Ergonomics, 31*(6), 609–619. doi:10.1016/S0003-6870(00)00035-1

Helme-Guizon, A. (2001). Le comportement du consommateur sur un site web marchand est-il fondamentalement différent de son comportement en magasin? *Proposition d'un cadre d'appréhension de ses spécificités, Recherche et Applications en marketing.*

Hémard, D. (2003). Language Learning Online: Designing Towards User Acceptability, In Felix, U. (Ed.) *Language Learning Online: Towards Best Practice* (pp. 21–42). Hawaii, USA: University of Hawaii, National Foreign Language Resource Center.

Hemphill, K. J., & Lehman, D. R. (1991). Social comparisons and their affective consequences: The importance of comparison dimensions and individual difference variables. *Journal of Social and Clinical Psychology, 10,* 372–394.

Henderson, R., Rickwood, D., & Roberts, P. (1998). The Beta Test of An Electronic Supermarket. *Interacting with Computers, 10,* 385–399. doi:10.1016/S0953-5438(98)00037-X

Hertzum, M., & Jacobsen, N. E. (2001). The evaluator effect: A chilling fact about usability evaluation methods. *International Journal of Human-Computer Interaction, 13*(4), 421–443. doi:10.1207/S15327590IJHC1304_05

Hesse, W. (2003). Dinosaur meets Archaeopteryx? or: Is there an alternative for Rational's Unified Process? *Software and Systems Modeling, Springer, 2*(4), 240–247. doi:10.1007/s10270-003-0033-y

Highsmith, J. (2004). *Agile Project Management: Creating Innovative Products*. New York: Addison Wesley.

Hill, A., & Scharff, L. V. (1997). Readability of websites with various foreground/background color combinations, font types and word styles. In *Proceedings of 11th National Conference in Undergraduate Research, 2*, 742-746.

Hix, D., & Hartson, H. R. (1993). *Developing user interfaces: Ensuring usability through product and process*. New York: John Wiley & Sons.

Ho, C. F., & Wu, W. H. (1999) Antecedents of customer satisfaction on the Internet: An empirical study of online shopping. In HICSS '99 - *Proceedings of 32ⁿᵈ Hawaii International Conference on System Sciences*. Washington, DC: IEEE Computer Society.

Hochheiser, H., & Shneiderman, B. (2001). Universal usability statements: marking the trail for all users. *Interactions, 8*(2), 16-18. Retrieved June 1, 2009, from http://portal.acm.org/citation.cfm?id=361897.361913

Hoekstra, G. (2000). *History of Web Design*. Retrieved 27 May 2003, from http://www.weballey.net/webdesign/history.html

Hollan, J., Hutchins, E., & Kirshac, D. (2000). Distributed Cognition: Toward a New Foundation for Human-Computer Interaction Research. *ACM Transactions on Computer-Human Interaction, 7*(2), 174–196. doi:10.1145/353485.353487

Holleran, P. A. (1991). A methodological note on pitfalls in usability testing. *Behaviour & Information Technology, 10*, 345–357. doi:10.1080/01449299108924295

Holmes, J. N., & Holmes, W. (2002). *Speech Synthesis and Recognition*. New York: Taylor and Francis.

Holmes, M. (2002). *Web Usability & Navigation: A Beginner's Guide*. New York: McGraw-Hill.

Holzinger, A. (2005). Usability Engineering Methods for Software Developers. *Communications of the ACM, 48*, 71–74. doi:10.1145/1039539.1039541

Hornbæk, K., & Frøkjær, E. (2004). Usability Inspection by Metaphors of Human Thinking Compared to

Heuristic Evaluation. *International Journal of Human-Computer Interaction, 17*(3), 357–374. doi:10.1207/s15327590ijhc1703_4

Howard, J. A. (1994). *Buyer Behavior in Marketing Strategy*. Englewood Cliffs, NJ: Prentice Hall.

Huang, H. A. (2002). *A Research Taxonomy for e-Commerce System Usability*. Paper presented at the Eight Americans Conference on Information Systems.

Huang, X., Acero, A., & Hon, H.-W. (2001). *Spoken Language Processing: A Guide to Theory, Algorithm and System Development*. Upper Saddle River, NJ: Prentice Hall PTR.

Huizingh, E. K. R. E. (2000). The Content and Design of Web Sites: An Empirical Study. *Information & Management, 37*(3), 123–134. doi:10.1016/S0378-7206(99)00044-0

Humphreys, C. P., & Wisudha, D. A. (1987). *Methods and Tools for Structuring and Analysing Decision Problems, Decision Analysis Unit* (Tech. Rep. No. 87-1). London: The London School of Economics and Political Sciences.

Hutchinson, T. E., White, K. P. Jr, Martin, W. N., Reichert, K. N., & Frey, L. A. (1989). Human-Computer Interaction Using Eye-Gaze Input. *IEEE Transactions on Systems, Man, and Cybernetics, 19*(6), 1527–1533. doi:10.1109/21.44068

IBM. (1998). *Ease of Use Web Design Guidelines*. Online archive available at http://www-3.ibm.com/ibm/easy/eou_ext.nsf/Publish/572

ICICLE. (2008). Retrieved 2008, from http://www.eecis.udel.edu/research/icicle/.

IEEE. Computer Society. (2002). *Learning Technology Standards Committee LTSC, IEEE, Draft Standard for Learning Objects Metadata (LOM)* (Tech. Rep. 1484.12/D4.0). Washington, DC: IEEE Computer Society.

Igbaria, M., Schiffman, S., & Wieckowski, T. (1994). The respective roles of perceived usefulness and perceived fun in the acceptance of microcomputer technology. *Behaviour & Information Technology, 13*(6). doi:10.1080/01449299408914616

IGDA. (2004). *Accessibility in games: motivations and approaches.* Retrieved May 29, 2009, from http://www.igda.org/accessibility/IGDA_Accessibility_WhitePaper.pdf

Insfran, E., & Fernandez, A. (2008). A Systematic Review of Usability Evaluation in Web Development. In *Proceedings of Second International Workshop on Web Usability and Accessibility (IWWUA 2008),* (LNCS Vol. 5176 - Advances in Web Information Systems Engineering - WISE 2008 Workshops, pp. 81-91), Auckland, New Zealand, September 1-4, 2008.

Insight, S. (Producer), & Tibbetts, J. (Director). (2007). *A world denied* [DVD]. Extract retrieved June 26, 2009, from http://www.socitm.gov.uk/NR/rdonlyres/8B648F2B-B602-4224-8DA9-FD70BD822CAE/0/Aworlddenied-video.wmv

International Community for Auditory Display. (n.d.). Retrieved from http://www.icad.org

International Standards Organization. (1992 - 2000). *Standard 9241: Ergonomic requirements for office work with visual display terminals.* Retrieved November 21, 2008, from http://www.iso.org

Inversini, A., Botturi, L., & Triacca, L. (2006). Evaluating LMS Usability for Enhanced eLearning Experience. In *the proceedings of EDMEDIA 2006,* (pp. 595-601), Orlando, GA.

Isakowitz, T. a., Stohr, E. A., & Balasubramanian, P. (1995). RMM: a methodology for structured hypermedia design. *Communications of the ACM, 38*(8), 34–44. doi:10.1145/208344.208346

ISO (1998). *Guidance on Usability,* (Vol. ISO 9141-11).

ISO (1999). *Human Centred Design Processes for Interactive Systems* (Vol. ISO 13407).

ISO 9241-11 (1998). *Ergonomic requirements for office work with visual display terminals* (VDTs), (Part 11: Guidance on usability). New York: ISO.

ISO. (1995). ISO/DIS 9241-11 *Draft International Standard, Ergonomic Requirements for Office Work with Visual Display Terminals (VDTs). Part 10: Dialogue*

Principles. Genève, Switzerland: International Organisation for Standardisation.

Issa, T. (2008). *Development and Evaluation of a Methodology for Developing Websites - PhD Thesis, Curtin University, Western Australia.* Retrieved from http://espace.library.curtin.edu.au:1802/view/action/nmets.do?DOCCHOICE=17908.xml&dvs=1235702350272~864&locale=en_US&search_terms=17908&usePid1=true&usePid2=true

Itten, J. (1970). *The elements of Color.* New York: Van Nostrand Reinhold Company.

Ivory, M. Y. (2003). *Automated Web Site Evaluation: Researchers and Practitioners Perspectives.* Amsterdam: Kluwer Academic Publishers.

Ivory, M. Y., & Hearst, M. A. (2001). The state of the art in automating usability evaluation of user interfaces. *ACM Computing Surveys, 33*(4), 470–516. doi:10.1145/503112.503114

Iwarsson, S., & Stahl, A. (2003). Accessibility, usability and universal design: Positioning and definition of concepts describing person-environment relationships. *Disability and Rehabilitation, 25*(2), 57–66.

Izard, C. E. (1971). *The face of emotion.* New York: Appleton-Century-Crofts.

Jacko, J. A., Sears, A., & Borella, M. (2000). The Effect of Network Delay and Media on User Perceptions of Web Resources. *Behaviour & Information Technology, 19*(6), 427–439. doi:10.1080/014492900750052688

Jacobs, L. W., & Suess, J. F. (1975). Effects of Four Psychological Primary Colors on Anxiety State. *Perceptual and Motor Skills, 41*(1), 207–210.

Jacobsen, N. E., Hertzum, M., & John, B. E. (1998) The Evaluator Effect in Usability Tests. In *Proc. CHI'98.* New York: ACM Press

Jahng, J., Jain, H. K., & Ramamurthy, K. (2006). An Empirical Study of the Impact of Product Characteristics and Electronic Commerce Interface Richness on Consumer Attitude and Purchase Intentions. *Systems, Man and Cybernetics, Part A: Systems and Humans . IEEE Transactions, 36*(6), 1185–1201.

Jansen, B. J. (2006). Using Temporal Patterns of Interaction to Design Effective Automated Searching engines. *Communications of the ACM, 49*(4), 72–74. doi:10.1145/1121949.1121986

Jarvenpaa, S. L., & Todd, P. A. (1997). Consumer reactions to electronic shopping on the World Wide Web. *International Journal of Electronic Commerce, 1*(2), 59–88.

Jaspers, M. W. M. (2006). The Think Aloud Method and User Interface Design. In C. Ghaoui (Ed.), *Encyclopedia of Human-Computer Interaction* (pp. 597-602). Hershey, PA: Idea Group Reference.

JAWS Screen Reader. (n.d.). Retrieved from http://www.freedomscientific.com

Jayaratna, N. (1994). *Understanding and Evaluating Methodologies -NIMSAD- A Systemic Framework.* London: McGraw-Hill International.

Jeffries, R., Miller, J. R., Wharton, C., & Uyeda, K. M. (1991) User Interface Evaluation in the Real World: A Comparison of Four Techniques. In *Proceedings of CHI '91*, (pp. 119-124). New York: ACM Press.

Jerman Blažič, B., & Klobučar, T. (2005). Privacy provision in e-learning standardized systems: status and improvements. *Computer Standards & Interfaces, 27*, 561–578. doi:10.1016/j.csi.2004.09.006

JISC. (2008). *JISC Technology Applications Programme.* Retrieved February 8, 2008, from http://www.leeds.ac.uk/educol/documents/00001237.htm

John, E. B. (2003). Information Processing and Skilled Behavior. In J. M. Carroll (Ed.), *HCI Models, Theories and Frameworks: Towards a Multidisciplinary Science* (pp. 55-101). Amsterdam: Morgan Kaufmann.

Johnsgard, T. J., & Page, S. R., Wilson, R.D. & Zeno, R., J. (1995). A Comparison of Graphical User Interface Widgets for Various Tasks. In *Proceedings of the Human Factors & Ergonomics Society - 39th Annual Meeting, Human Factors and Ergonomics Society*, (pp. 287-291).

Johnson, R., & Hegarty, J. R. (2003). Websites as Educational Motivators for Adults with Learning Disabil-

ity. *British Journal of Educational Technology, 34*(4), 479–486. doi:10.1111/1467-8535.00344

Jokela, T. (2008). Characterizations, Requirements, and Activities of User-Centered Design—the KESSU 2.2Model. In E. L-C. Law, E.T. Hvannberg & G. Cockton, (Eds.), *Maturing Usability. Quality in interaction, software and value.* London: Springer-Verlag Limited.

Jolibert, A., & Jourdan, P. (2006). Marketing Research. *Méthodes de recherche et d'études en marketing.* Paris: Dunod.

Jones, D. M., & Macken, W. J. (1993). Irrelevant Tones Produce an Irrelevant Speech Effect: Implications for Phonological Coding in Working Memory. *Journal of Experimental Psychology. Learning, Memory, and Cognition, 19*(2), 369–381. doi:10.1037/0278-7393.19.2.369

Jones, D. M., Madden, C., & Miles, C. (1992). Privileged access by irrelevant speech to short-term memory: The role of changing state. *Quarterly Journal of Experimental Psychology, 44*(4), 645–669.

Jordan, P. W. (2002). *An Introduction To Usability.* London: Taylor and Francis.

Jurafsky, D., & Martin, J. H. (2008). *Speech and Language Processing. An Introduction to Natrural Language Processing, Computational Linguistics, and Speech Recognition.* Upper Saddle River, NJ: Prentice-Hall.

Kaklanis, N., González Calleros, J. M., Vanderdonckt, J., & Tzovaras, D. (2008). Hapgets, Towards Haptically-enhanced widgets Based on a User Interface Description Language. In *Proc. of Workshop on Multimodal Interaction Through Haptic Feedback MITH'2008* Naples, May 31. New York: ACM Press.

Kambil, A., & Eselius, E. (2000). Where the interaction is. *Across the Board, 37*(10), 36.

Kamm, C. A., & Walker, M. A. (1997). Design and Evaluation of Spoken Dialogue Systems. In Proc. *IEEE Workshop on Automatic Speech Recognition and Understanding*, (pp. 14–17).

Kamm, C. A., Litman, D. J., & Walker, M. A. (1998). From novice to expert: The effect of tutorials on user expertise with spoken dialogue systems. In *Proc. 5ᵗʰ International Conference on Spoken Language Processing - ICSLP.*

Kamm, C. A., Walker, M. A., & Litman, D. J. (1999). Evaluating spoken language systems. In *Proc. Applied Voice Input/Output Society Conference - AVIOS*, (pp. 187–197).

Kaplan, B., & Duchon, D. (1988). Combining Qualitative and Quantitative Methods in Information Systems Research: A Case Study. *MIS Quarterly/December 1988*, 571 - 586.

Karat, C.-M., Campbell, R., & Fiegel, T. (1992) Comparison of Empirical Testing and Walk-through Methods in User Interface Evaluation. In *Proceedings of CHI '92*, (pp. 397-404). New York; ACM Press

Kaur, K. (1997). Designing Virtual Environments for Usability. *INTERACT, 1997*, 636–639.

Kaur, K. (1998). *Designing virtual environments for usability.* Ph. D. Thesis, City University, London.

Kaur, K., Maiden, N. A. M., & Sutcliffe, A. G. (1999). Interacting with virtual environments: an evaluation of a model of interaction. *Interacting with Computers, 11*(4), 403–426. doi:10.1016/S0953-5438(98)00059-9

Keeker, K. (1997) *Improving Web site Usability and Appeal.* Online archive available at http://msdn.microsoft.com/workshop/management/planning/improvingsiteusa.asp

Keeling, K. A. (1999). *Customer Acceptance of Electronic Service Delivery: Extending the Technology Acceptance Model.* Unpublished PhD Thesis, School of Management, University of Manchester Institute of Science and Technology, Manchester, UK.

Keen, P. G. W., & Scott Morton, M. S. (1978). *Decision Support Systems – An Organizational Perspective.* Reading, MA: Addison-Wesley.

Keeney, R. L. (1999). The Value of Internet Commerce to the Customer. *Management Science, 45*(4), 533–542. doi:10.1287/mnsc.45.4.533

Keeney, R. L., & Raiffa, H. (1976). *Decisions with Multiple Objectives.* New York: John Wiley & Sons.

Kelly, B., Sloan, D., Phipps, L., Petrie, H., & Hamilton, F. (2005). *Forcing standardization or accommodating diversity? A framework for applying the WCAG in the real world.* Paper presented at the International Cross-Disciplinary Workshop on Web Accessibility (W4A), 10-14 May 2005, Chiba, Japan. Retrieved June 1, 2009, from http://portal.acm.org/citation.cfm?id=1061811.1061820

Kelly, G. (1955). *The psychology of personal constructs,* (Vol. 1 & 2). New York: Norton.

Kennaugh, P., & Petrie, H. (2006). *Enhanced Access to Television (EAT): humanITy.*

Kennedy, R. S., Lane, N. E., Berbaum, K. S., & Lilienthal, M. G. (1993). Simulator sickness questionnaire (SSQ): A new method for quantifying simulator sickness. *The International Journal of Aviation Psychology, 3*, 203–220. doi:10.1207/s15327108ijap0303_3

Kim, J. (2005). Task difficulty in information searching behavior. Expected difficulty and experienced difficulty. In *JCDL 2005: Proceedings of the 5th ACM/IEEE-CS joint conference on Digital libraries.*

Kim, J. (2006). Task difficulty as a predictor and indicator of a web searching interaction. In *CHI '06: CHI '06 extended abstracts on Human factors in computing systems.*

Kim, K. S., & Allen, B. (2002). Cognitive and task influences on web searching behavior. *Journal of the American Society for Information Science and Technology, 53*(2), 109–119. doi:10.1002/asi.10014

King, N. (2004). Using interviews in Qualitative Research. In C. Cassell, & G. Symon, (Ed.), *Essential Guide to Qualitative Methods in Organizational Research.* Thousand Oaks, CA: Sage Publications.

Kirakowski, J., Claridge, N., & Whitehand, R. (1998) Human Centred Measures of Success in Web site Design, In *Proceedings 4th Conference on Human Factors and the Web.* Online archive available at http://www.research.att.com/conf/hfweb/proceedings/kirakowski/index.html

Kirakowski, J., Gould, J., Dillon, A., & Sweeny, M. (1987). *Parameters of Change in User Development. HUFIT Document Code:HUFIT/HFRG-2-2.*

Kiritani, Y., & Shirai, S. (2003). Effects of background colors on user's experience in reading website. *Journal of the Asian Design International Conference, Academic Journal, 1*, 64.

Kirkpatrick, D. (1994). *Evaluating Training Programs.* San Francisco, CA: Berrett Koehler Publishers Inc.

Kirwan, B., & Ainsworth, L. K. (Eds.). (1992). *A Guide to Task Analysis.* London: Taylor and Francis.

Knight, J., Heaven, C., & Christie, I. (2002). *Inclusive citizenship.* London: Leonard Cheshire.

Koch, N. (2001). *Software engineering for adaptive hypermedia applications.* Munich, Germany: Uni-Druck Publishing Company.

Koch, N., & Kraus, A. (2002). The expressive Power of UML-based Web Engineering. In *Proceedings of the Second International Workshop on Web-oriented Software Technology (IWWOST'02)*, (pp. 105 – 119), Málaga, Spain.

Koch, N., & Kraus, A. (2003). Towards a Common Metamodel for the Development of Web Applications. In *Web Engineering* (pp. 419-422). Berlin: Springer.

Kotelly, B. (2003). *The Art and Business of Speech Recognition: Creating the Noble Voice.* Reading, MA: Addison-Wesley Professional.

Kotler, P. (1973). Atmosphere as a marketing tool. *Journal of Retailing, 49*(Winter), 48–64.

Kotze, P., & Johnson, C. W. (2001). *Human-Computer Interaction 1.* Study Guide for INF120-8, INF120-8/502/2001, University of South Africa.

Kouroupetroglou, G. (2009). Universal Access in Public Terminals: Information Kiosks and Automated Teller Machines (ATMs). In C. Stephanidis (Ed.), *The Universal Access Handbook*, (pp. 761-780). Boca Raton, FL: CRC Press.

Kroll, P., & Kruchten, P. (2003). *The Rational Unified Process Made Easy: A Practitioner's Guide to the RUP.* Reading, MA: Addison-Wesley.

Kruchten, P. (2003). *The Rational Unified Process: An Introduction.* Reading, MA: Addison-Wesley.

Krueger, R. A., & Casey, M. A. (2000). *Focus Groups: A Practical Guide for Applied Research*, (3rd Ed.). Thousand Oaks, CA: Sage Publications.

Krug, S. (2000) *Don't Make Me Think – A Common Sense Approach to Web Usability.* Circle.com Library, USA

Kuan, H. H., Vathanophas, V., & Bock, G. (2003). *The Impact of Usability on the Intention of Planned Purchases in e-Commerce Service Websites.* Paper presented at the 7th Pacific Asia Conferece on Information Systems, Adelaide, South Australia.

Kubilus, N. J. (2000). Designing an e-commerce site for users. *Crossroads, 7*, 23–26. doi:10.1145/351092.351099

Kumar, N. and Benbasat, I. (2002). Para-Social Presence and Communication Capabilities of a Web Site: A Theoretical Perspective. *e-Service Journal, 1*(3), 5-24

Kumar, R. L., Smith, M. A., & Bannerjee, S. (2004). User interface features influencing overall ease of use and personalization. *Information & Management, 41*(3), 157–178. doi:10.1016/S0378-7206(03)00075-2

Kuniavsky, M. (2003). *Observing the user experience. A practitioner's guide to user research.* San Francisco: Elsevier.

Kurniawan, S. H. (2003). Aging. In *Web Accessibility: A foundation for research* (pp.47-58). Berlin: Springer

Kwallek, N., Lewis, C. M., & Robbin, A. S. (1998). Effects of Office Interior Color on Workers' Mood and Productivity. *Perceptual and Motor Skills, 66*(1), 123–128.

Labuschagne, L., & Eloff, J. H. P. (2000). Electronic Commerce: The Information-Security Challenge. *Information Management & Computer Security, 8*(3), 154–157. doi:10.1108/09685220010372582

Ladwein, R. & Ben Mimoun, M.-S. (2006). *L'accès à l'offre sur un site web commercial: une approche expérimentale.* 5ème journée nantaise de recherche en e-marketing.

Ladwein, R. (1999). *Le comportement du consommateur et de l'acheteur*. Paris: Economica.

Ladwein, R. (2001). *L'impact de la conception des sites de e-commerce sur le confort d'utilisation: une proposition de modèle*. Actes du 17ème congrès international de l'AFM.

Lai-Chong Law, E., & Pipan, M. (2003). *International Usability Tests on the Multilingual EducaNext Portal - Universal Exchange for Pan-European Higher Education* (Usability Tech. Rep. v.2.0). Zurich, Switzerland: Swiss Federal Institute of Technology Zurich.

Lai-Chong Law, E., Jerman Blažič, B., & Pipan, M. (2007). Analysis of user rationality and system learnability: Performing task variants in user tests. *Behavior & Information Technology, 7, 26*(5), 421-436.

Lanthony, P. (2005). *La perception des couleurs sur écran*. Intervention dans le cadre d'un séminaire sur la couleur, 3C S.A., Abbaye de Royaumont - France, Juin 2005.

Lanzilotti, R., Costabile, M., Ardito, C., & De Angeli, A. (2006). eLSE Methodology: a Systematic Approach to the e-Learning Systems Evaluation. *Educational Technology & Society, 9*(4), 42–53.

Larsen, L. B. (2003). Issues in the Evaluation of Spoken Dialogue Systems using Objective and Subjective Measures. In *Proc. 8th IEEE Workshop on Automatic Speech Recognition and Understanding -ASRU*, (pp. 209-214).

Larson, J. A. (2000). *Introduction and Overview of W3C Speech Interface Framework*. Retrieved August 2, 2009, from http://www.w3.org/TR/voice-intro/

Larson, J. A. (2002). *Voicexml: Introduction to Developing Speech Applications*. Upper Saddle River, NJ: Prentice Hall.

Larson, J. A., Raman, T. V., & Raggett, D. (2003). *W3C Multimodal Interaction Framework*. Retrieved August 2, 2009, from http://www.w3.org/TR/mmi-framework/

Laurel, B. (1990). *The Art of Human-Computer Interface Design*. Mountford S. Joy.

Lavery, D., Cockton, G., & Atkinson, M. P. (1997). Comparison of Evaluation Methods Using Structured Usability Problem Reports. *Behaviour & Information Technology, 16*(4), 246–266. doi:10.1080/014492997119824

Lavie, T., & Tactinsky, N. (2004). Assessing dimensions of perceived visual aesthetics of web sites. *International Journal of Human-Computer Studies, 60*(3), 269–298. doi:10.1016/j.ijhcs.2003.09.002

Law, E. L., Hvannberg, E., & Cockton, G. (2007). *Maturing Usability: Quality in Software, Interaction and Value* (Human-Computer Interaction Series). New York: Springer-Verlag.

Law, E. L.-C., Hvannberg, E. T., & Cockton, G. (2008). A Green Paper on Usability Maturation. In Law, E. L-C., Hvannberg, E.T., & Cockton, G. (Eds). *Maturing Usability. Quality in interaction, software and value*. London: Springer-Verlag Limited.

Law, E., Hvannberg, E., & Cockton, G. (Eds.). (2008). *Maturing Usability: Quality in Software, Interaction and Value*, (Human Computer Interaction Series). Berlin: Springer Verlag.

Lazar, J. (2006). *Web Usability*. Upper Saddle River, NJ: Pearson Education, Inc.

Lazar, J., Dudley-Sponaugle, A., & Greenidge, K. (2004). Improving Web Accessibility: A Study of Webmaster Perceptions. *Computers in Human Behavior, 20*(2), 269–288. doi:10.1016/j.chb.2003.10.018

Lazonder, A.W., Biemens, H. J. A., & Wopereis, G. J. H. (2000). Differences between novice and experienced users in searching information on the World Wide Web. *Journal of American Society for Information Science, 51*(6), 576, 581.

Lederer, A. L., Maupin, D. J., Sena, M. P., & Zhuang, Y. (2000). The Technology Acceptance Model and the World Wide Web. *Decision Support Systems, 29*(3), 269–282. doi:10.1016/S0167-9236(00)00076-2

Lee, J. C., & McCrickard, D. S. (2007). Towards Extreme(ly) Usable Software: Exploring Tensions Between Usability and Agile Software Development. In *Proceedings AGILE Conference*, (pp. 59-71). Berlin: IEEE.

Lee, J., Kim, J., & Moon, J. Y. (2000). What Makes Users Visit Cyber Stores Again? Key Design Factors for Customer Loyalty. In *Proceedings of CHI'2000: Computers and Human Interface*, (pp. 305-312). New York: ACM Press/Addison Wesley.

Lemeni, G., & Miclea, M. (2004). *Consiliere şi orientare. Ghid de educaţie pentru carieră*. Editura ASCR, Cluj-Napoca.

Lemoine, J.-F. (2003). Vers une approche globale de l'atmosphère du point de vente. *Revue Française du Marketing, 194*(Septembre), 83–101.

Lemoine, J.-F. (2008). *L'influence de l'atmosphère des sites web marchands sur les réponses des internautes*. 24ème congrès international de l'association française du marketing, Paris, 15 et 16 mai 2008, CDRom.

Lemon, G. (2005). *Writing a good accessibility statement*. Retrieved June 1, 2009, from http://juicystudio.com/article/writing-a-good-accessibility-statement.php

Lenhart, A., Horrigan, J., Rainie, L., Allen, K., Boyce, A., & Madden, M. (2003). *The ever shifting internet population: A new look at internet access and the digital divide*. Retrieved May 28, 2009, from http://www.pewinternet.org/~/media//Files/Reports/2003/PIP_Shifting_Net_Pop_Report.pdf.pdf

Lenorovitz, D. R., Phillips, M. D., Ardrey, R. S., & Kloster, G. V. (1984). A taxonomic approach to characterizing human-computer interaction. In G. Salvendy (Ed.), *Human-Computer Interaction*, (pp. 111-116). Amsterdam: Elsevier Science Publishers.

Levi, M. D., & Conrad, F. G. (1996). A Heuristic Evaluation of a World Wide Web Prototype . *Interaction, 3*(4), 50–61. doi:10.1145/234813.234819

Lewis, C., & Rieman, J. (2007). *Task-Centered User Interface Design: A Practical Introduction*. Retrieved May 17, 2007, from http://hcibib.org/tcuid/tcuid.pdf

Lewis, J. R. (1991). Psychometric evaluation of an after-scenario questionnaire for computer usability studies: the ASQ. *SIGCHI Bulletin, 23*(1), 78–81. doi:10.1145/122672.122692

Lewis, J. R. (1996). IBM Computer Usability Satisfaction Questionnaires: Psychometric evaluation and instructions for use. *International Journal of Human-Computer Interaction, 7*(1), 57–78. doi:10.1080/10447319509526110

Liang, T. P., & Huang, J. S. (1998). An Empirical Study on Consumer Acceptance of Products in Electronic Markets: A transaction cost model. *Decision Support Systems, 24*(1), 29–43. doi:10.1016/S0167-9236(98)00061-X

Liang, T. P., & Lai, H. (2000). Electronic Store Design and Consumer Choice: An Empirical Study. In *Proceedings of HICSS'00: 33rd Hawaii International Conference on System Sciences*. Washington, DC: IEEE Computer Society.

Lif, M., & Goransson, B. (2007). Usability Design: A New Rational Unified Process Discipline. In *Proceedings Human-Computer Interaction; INTERACT 2007*, (pp. 714-715). New York: ACM.

Lightner, N. J., Bose, I., & Salvendy, G. (1996). What is Wrong with the World-Wide Web? A Diagnosis of Some Problems and Prescription of Some Remedies. *Ergonomics, 39*(8), 995–1004. doi:10.1080/00140139608964523

Limayem, M., Khalifa, M., & Frini, A. (2000). What makes Consumers Buy from Internet? A longitudinal Study of Online Shopping. *IEEE Transactions on Systems, Man, and Cybernetics. Part A, Systems and Humans, 30*(4), 421–432. doi:10.1109/3468.852436

Limbourg, Q. (2004). *Multi-path Development of User Interfaces*. Ph.D. thesis, Université catholique de Louvain Press, France.

Limbourg, Q., Vanderdonckt, J., Michotte, B., Bouillon, L., & Lopez, V. (2004): UsiXML: a Language Supporting Multi-Path Development of User Interfaces. In R. Bastide, P. Palanque, & J. Roth (Eds.), *Engineering Human Computer Interaction and Interactive Systems*. (LNCS Vol. 3425, pp. 200–220).

Lin, H. X., Choong, Y., & Salvendy, G. (1997). A Proposed Index of Usability: A Method for Comparing the Relative Usability of Different Software Systems. *Behaviour & Information Technology, 16*(4/5), 267–278.

Lin, J. C., & Lu, H. (2000). Towards an Understanding of the Behavioural Intention to Use a Web Site. *International Journal of Information Management, 20*(3), 197–208. doi:10.1016/S0268-4012(00)00005-0

Lindquist, J. D. (1974). Meaning of image: a survey of empirical and hypothetical evidence . *Journal of Retailing, 50*(4), 29–38.

Ling, C., & Salvendy, G. (2005). Extension of heuristic evaluation method: a review and reappraisal. *Ergonomia IJE&HF, 27*(3), 179–197.

Litman, D. J., & Pan, S. (2002). Designing and evaluating an adaptive spoken dialogue system. *User Modeling and User-Adapted Interaction, 12*(2-3), 111–137. doi:10.1023/A:1015036910358

Litman, D. J., Pan, S., & Walker, M. A. (1998). Evaluating Response Strategies in a Web-Based Spoken Dialogue Agent. In *Proc. 36th Annual Meeting of the Association for Computational Linguistics and 17th International Conf. on Computational Linguistics (ACL/COLING)*, (pp. 780–786).

Liu, C., & Arnett, K. P. (2000). Exploring the Factors Associated with Web Site Success in the Context of Electronic Commerce. *Information & Management, 38*(1), 23–33. doi:10.1016/S0378-7206(00)00049-5

LMS Evaluation Committee. (2009). LMS Evaluation Committee Report. *University of North Carolina at Charlotte*. Retrieved January 15, 2009, from http://www.lmseval.uncc.edu

LODE. (2008). Retrieved 2008, from http://www.inf.unibz.it/lode

Loeterman, M., Paul, P., & Donahue, S. (2002). Reading and Deaf Children. *Reading Online, 6*(5). Retrieved 2008, from http://www.readingonline.org/articles/art_index.asp?HREF=loeterman/index.html.

Loiacono, E., & McCoy, S. (2004). Web site accessibility: An online sector analysis. *Information Technology & People, 17*(1), 87-101. Retrieved June 1, 2009, from http://www.emeraldinsight.com/Insight/ViewContentServlet?Filename=/published/emeraldfulltextarticle/pdf/1610170105.pdf

Luce, P. A., Feustel, T. C., & Pisoni, D. B. (1983). Capacity demands in short-term memory for synthetic and natural word lists. *Human Factors, 25*, 17–32.

Lyardet, F., Rossi, G., & Schwabe, D. (1999). Patterns for Adding Search Capabilities to Web Information Systems. In *Proc. of Europlop'99*, (pp. 134-147). Kloster Irsee, Germany: IEEE Press.

Lynch, J. G., & Ariely, D. (2000). Wine online: Search costs affect competition on price, quality and distribution. *Marketing Science, 19*(1), 83–103. doi:10.1287/mksc.19.1.83.15183

Lynch, P. J., & Horton, S. (1997). *Web Style Guide Basic Design Principles for Creating Web sites*. Stanford, CT: Yale University Press. Online archive available at http://www.info.med.yale.edu/caim/manual

MacKenzie, D. (2000). *A View from the Sonnenbichl: On the Historical Sociology of Software and System Dependability*. Paper presented at the International Conference on the History of Computing: Software Issues, Paderborn, Germany.

MacLean, A., Young, R. M., Bellotti, V., & Moran, T. P. (1991). Questions, Options, and Criteria: Elements of Design Space Analysis. *Human-Computer Interaction, 6*(3-4), 201–250. doi:10.1207/s15327051hci0603&4_2

Mafra, S., Barcelos, R., & Travassos, G. H. (2006). Aplicando uma Metodologia Baseada em Evidência na Definição de Novas Tecnologias de Software. In *Proceedings of the 20th Brazilian Symposium on Software Engineering (SBES 2006)*, (vol. 1, pp. 239 – 254), Florianopolis. October.

Maguire, M. (1997). *RESPECT User Requirements Framework Handbook*. Leicester, UK: HUSAT Research Institute.

Maguire, M. C. (2000). Consumer Acceptance of Internet Services. In *Proceedings of Annual Conference of the Ergonomics Society*, (pp.207-211). New York: Taylor and Francis.

Mahemoff, M. J., & Johnston, L. J. (2001).Usability Pattern Languages: the "Language" Aspect. In Hirose M.

(ed.), *Human-Computer? Interaction: Interact '01, Tokyo, Japan,* (pp. 350-358). Amsterdam: IOS Press.

Mandel, T. (1997). *The Elements of User Interface Design.* New York: John Wiley & Sons.

Mandić, J. N., & Mamdani, H. E. (1984). A multi-attribute decision-making model with fuzzy rule-based modification of priorities. In Zimmerman, Zadeh, & Gaines (Ed.), *Fuzzy Sets and Decision Analysis* (pp. 285-306). North-Holland: Elsevier Publishers.

Mankelow, T. (2006). Optimal Usability. *NZ Business, 20*(1), 53.

Mapes, D., & Moshell, J. (1995). A Two-Handed Interface for Object Manipulation in virtual Environments. *Presence (Cambridge, Mass.), 4*(4), 403–426.

Maria, E., Alva, O., Ana, B., Martínez, P., Juan, M., Cueva, L., et al. (2003). Comparison of Methods and Existing Tools for the Measurement of Usability in the Web. In J. M. Cueva Lovelle (Ed.), *Lecture Notes in Computer Science* (Vol. 2722/2003, pp. 386–389). Berlin: Springer-Verlag.

Mariage, C., & Vanderdonckt, J. (2005). Creating Contextualised Usability Guides for Web Sites Design and Evaluation. *Computer-Aided Design of User Interfaces, IV,* 147–158. doi:10.1007/1-4020-3304-4_12

Market-Vantage. (2003). *Internet Marketing Methodology.* Retrieved 16 Sept 2004, from http://www.market-vantage.com/about/methodology.htm

Marschark, M., & Spencer, P. (Eds.). (2003). *Oxford Handbook of Deaf Studies, Language and Education.* New York: Oxford University Press.

Marschrak, M., & Wauters, L. (2008). *Language Comprehension and Learning by Deaf Students.* In M. Marschark & P.C. Hauser (Eds) *Deaf Cognition* (pp. 309–350). Oxford, UK: Oxford University Press.

Marshall, C., & Rossman, G. B. (2006). *Designing Qualitative Research,* 93rd Ed.). London: Sage

Martens, A. (2003). Usability of Web Services. *International Conference on Web Information Systems Engineering Workshops,* (pp. 182-190). Washington, DC: IEEE.

Massie, B. (2005). *Bert Massie BSI Conference, London July 2005.* Retrieved August 30, 2006, from http://www.drc-gb.org/library/drc_speeches/bert_massie_-_bsi_conference_.aspx

Matera, M., Rizzo, F., & Carughi, G. T. (2006). Web Usability: Principles and Evaluation Methods. In Mendes, E., Mosley, N. (Eds.), *Web Engineering.* New York: Spinger Verlag.

Mathieson, K. (1991). Predicting Use Intentions: Comparing the Technology Acceptance Model with the Theory of Planned Behaviour. *Information Systems Research, 2*(3), 173–191. doi:10.1287/isre.2.3.173

Mattelart, A. (1996). *The Invention of Communication.* Minneapolis: University Minnesota Press.

Mayer, J. D., & Gaschke, Y. N. (1988). The experience and meta-experience of mood. *Journal of Personality and Social Psychology, 55,* 102–111. doi:10.1037/0022-3514.55.1.102

Mayhew, D. J. (1999). *The Usability Engineering Lifecycle: a practitioner's handbook for user interface design.* San Francisco: Morgan Kaufmann.

McCracken, D. D., & Wolfe, R. J. (2004). *User-Centered Website Development A Human-Computer Interaction Approach.* Upper Saddle River, NJ: Pearson Education, Inc.

McDonald, A., & Welland, R. (2004). Evaluation of Commercial Web Engineering Processes. In *Web Engineering* (pp. 166-170). Berlin: Springer.

McGovern, G. (2003). *Usability is good management.* Retrieved 14 April 2004, from http://www.gerrymcgovern.com/nt/2003/nt_2003_04_07_usability.htm

McTear, M. F. (2004). *Spoken Dialogue Technology: Towards the Conversational User Interface.* London: Springer-Verlag.

Mehrabian, A., & Russell, J. A. (1974). *An Approach to Environmental Psychology.* Cambridge, MA: MIT Press.

Memmel, T., Reiterer, H., & Holzinger, A. (2007). Agile Methods and Visual Specification in Software Development: A Chance to Ensure Universal Access. In *Proceedings of Universal Access in Human Computer Interaction Coping with Diversity.* (pp. 453-462). Berlin: Springer.

Meszaros, G., & Aston, J. (2006). Adding usability testing to an agile project. In *Proceedings of Agile Conference, 2006.* Washington, DC: IEEE.

Meyer, B. (1985). On Formalism in Specification. *IEEE Software,* 6–25. doi:10.1109/MS.1985.229776

Michaud, L., & McCoy, K. (2006). Capturing the Evolution of Grammatical Knowledge in a CALL System for Deaf Learners of English. [IJAIED]. *International Journal of Artificial Intelligence in Education, 16*(1), 65–97.

Microsoft Corporation. (n.d.). Retrieved from http://msdn.microsoft.com/en-us/library/bb980024(VS.95).eapx

Microsystems, S. U. N. (1996). *Guide to Web Style.* Online archive available at http://www.sun.com/styleguide/

Miles, R. (1992). Combining 'Hard' and 'Soft' systems practice: Grafting and Embedding Revisited. *Systemist, 14*(2), 62–66.

Millard, N., Hole, L., & Crowle, S. (1999). Smiling through: motivation at the user interface. In Bullinger, H-J. & Ziegler, J. (Eds.), *Human-Computer Interaction Ergonomics and User Interfaces* (pp. 824-8). Mahwah, NJ: Lawrence Erlbaum.

Miller, J. (2006). Usability Testing: A Journey, Not a Destination. *IEEE Internet Computing, 10*(6, Nov/Dec), 80-83.

Mine, M. (1995). *Virtual environment interaction techniques.* UNC Chapel Hill CS Dept., Technical Report TR95-018, Chapel Hill, NC.

Moe, W. W., & Fader, P. S. (2004b). Dynamic Conversion Behavior at E-Commerce Sites . *Management Science, 50*(3), 326–335. doi:10.1287/mnsc.1040.0153

Moggridge, B. (1999). Design, expressing experience in design. *Interaction, 6*(July), 17–25. doi:10.1145/306412.306430

Mohamad, Y., Stegemann, D., Koch, J., & Velasco, C. A. (2004). imergo: Supporting Accessibility and Web Standards to Meet the Needs of the Industry via Process-Oriented Software Tools. In *Proceedings of the 9th International Conference on Computers Helping People With Special Needs (ICCHP 2004),* (pp. 310-316). Berlin: Springer.

Molich, R. (2000). *User-Friendly Web Design* (in Danish). Copenhagen: Ingeniøren Books.

Molich, R., & Nielsen, J. (1990). Improving a human-computer dialogue. *Communications of the ACM, 33*(3), 338–348. doi:10.1145/77481.77486

Molina Massó, J. P. (2008). *A Structured Approach to the Development of 3D User Interfaces.* Ph.D. thesis, University of Castilla-La Mancha, Albacete, Spain, February 29.

Moller, S., Engelbrecht, K., & Schleicher, R. (2008). Predicting the quality and usability of spoken dialogue services. *Speech Communication, 50*(8-9), 730–744. doi:10.1016/j.specom.2008.03.001

Moller, S., Englert, R., Engelbrecht, K., Hafner, V., Jameson, A., Oulasvirta, A., et al. (2006). MeMo: Towards Automatic Usability Evaluation of Spoken Dialogue Services by User Error Simulations. In *Proc. 9th International Conference on Spoken Language Processing - ICSLP,* (pp. 1786-1789).

Monk, A., Wright, P., Haber, J., & Davenport, L. (1993). *Improving your human-computer interface: a practical technique.* Bath, UK: Redwood Books.

Montero, F., & Vanderdonckt, J. (2008). *Generative Pattern-Based Design of User Interfaces.* Working paper 08/13, Louvain School of Management, Université catholique de Louvain, Louvain-la-Neuve, April 2008. Accessible at http://www.uclouvain.be/cps/ucl/doc/iag/documents/WP_08-13.pdf

Moreno, N. Romero, J. R. & Vallecillo (2007), A. An overview Model Driven Web Engineering and the MDA. In L. Olsina, O. Pastor, & G. D. Schwabe, (Eds.), *Web Engineering and Web Applications Design Methods*, (vol. 12 of Human-Computer Interaction Series). Berlin: Springer.

Morgan, D. L., Krueger, R. A., & King, J. A. (1998). *Focus Group Kit*. London: SAGE.

Morganosky, M. A., & Cude, B. J. (2000). Consumer Response to Online Grocery Shopping. *International Journal of Retail & Distribution Management, 28*(1), 17–26. doi:10.1108/09590550010306737

Morris, M. G., & Dillon, A. (1997). How User Perceptions Influence Software Use. *IEEE Software, 14*(4), 58–65. doi:10.1109/52.595956

Morrissey, W., & Zajicek, M. (2001). Remembering how to use the Internet: An investigation into the effectiveness of VoiceHelp for older adults, In Stephanidis, C (Ed.) *Proceedings of the 9th International Conference on Human-Computer Interaction, New Orleans* (pp. 700-704). Mahwah, NJ: Lawrence Erlbaum

Moss, G., Gunn, R., & Heller, J. (2006). Some men like it black, some women like it pink: consumer involvements of differences in male and female website design. *Journal of Consumer Behaviour, 5*(4), 328–342. doi:10.1002/cb.184

Motschnig-Pitrik, R. (2002). Employing the Unified Process for Developing a Web-Based Application - A Case-Study. In *Practical Aspects of Knowledge Management: 4th International Conference, PAKM 2002 Vienna, Austria, December 2-3, 2002, Proceedings,* (pp. 97-113). Berlin: Springer.

Mucchielli, A. (1991). *Les méthodes qualitatives, Que sais-je?* Paris: Presses Universitaires de France.

Mumford, E. (1995). *Effective Systems Design and Requirements Analysis*. London: Macmillan Press Ltd.

Mundorf, N., Westin, S., & Dholakia, N. (1993). Effects of hedonic components and user's gender on the acceptance of screen-based information services.

Behaviour & Information Technology, 12(5), 293–303. doi:10.1080/01449299308924393

Munsell, A. (1969). *The Munsell Colour Atlas*. Munsell Color Corp.

Murphy, J., Howard, S., Kjeldskov, K., & Goschnick, S. (2004). Location, location, location: Challenges of outsourced usability evaluation. In *Proceedings of the Workshop on Improving the Interplay between Usability Evaluation and User Interface Design, NordiCHI 2004,* Aalborg University, Department of Computer Science, HCI-Lab Report no. 2004/2, (pp. 12-15).

Myers, M. D., & Avison, D. (2002). *Qualitative Research in Information Systems* (1st, Ed.). London: SAGE Publications Ltd.

Nagel, S. (1993). *Computer-Aided Decision Analysis: Theory and Application*. Westport, CT: Quorum Books.

Nahl, D., & Tenopir, C. (1996). Affective and cognitive searching behavior of novice end-users of a full-text database. *Journal of the American Society for Information Science and Technology, 47*(4), 276–286. doi:10.1002/(SICI)1097-4571(199604)47:4<276::AID-ASI3>3.0.CO;2-U

Nakshian, J. S. (1964). The effects of red and green surroundings on behavior. *The Journal of General Psychology, 70,* 143–161.

Nass, C., & Brave, S. (2005). *Wired for Speech: How Voice Activates and Advances the Human-Computer Relationship*. Cambridge, MA: MIT Press.

National Cancer Institute. (2002, 5 August 2002). *Is Usability Testing Always Conducted the Same Way?* Retrieved 12 August, 2003, from http://usability.gov/methods/same_way.html

NCAM. (n.d.). *Accessible Digital Media: Design Guidelines for Electronic Publications, Multimedia and the Web*. Retrieved 2008, from http://ncam.wgbh.org/publications/adm/

Ncube, C., Lockerbie, J., & Maiden, N. A. M. (2007). Automatically Generating Requirements from \it * Models:

Experiences with a Complex Airport Operations System. In *Proceedings REFSQ,* (pp. 33-47).

Neale, H., & Nichols, S. (2001). *Designing and Developing Virtual Environments: Methods and Applications.* Visualization and Virtual Environments Community Club (VVECC) Workshop: Design of Virtual Environments, Oxfordshire, England.

Nedel, L. P., & Freitas, C. M. D. S. (2006). 3D User Interfaces: from Pragmatics to Formal Description. *Research in Interactive Design, 1,* 1–13.

Newell, A. F., & Gregor, P. (2000). Designing for extraordinary people and situations. *CSERIAC Gateway, 11*(1), 12–13.

Newman, W. M., & Lamming, M. G. (1995). *Interactive System Design.* Wokingham: Addison Wesley.

News, B. B. C. (2002a). *Europe's ageing workforce.* Retrieved November 21, 2008, from http://news.bbc.co.uk/1/hi/world/europe/2053581.stm

News, B. B. C. (2002b). *Asia strained by ageing population.* Retrieved November 21, 2009, from http://news.bbc.co.uk/1/hi/world/south_asia/3025289.stm

NIAR - National Institute for Aviation Research. (2007). *Think-Aloud Protocol.* Retrieved July 6, 2007, from http://www.niar.wichita.edu/humanfactors/toolbox/T_A%20Protocol.htm

Nielsen, J. (1989). Usability engineering at a discount. In Salvendy, G., and Smith, M, J. (Eds.), *Designing and Using Human-Computer Interfaces and Knowledge Based Systems,* (pp. 394-401). Amsterdam: Elsevier Science Publishers.

Nielsen, J. (1992). Finding Usability Problems Through Heuristic Evaluation. In *Proceedings of CHI '92,* (pp. 373-380). New York: ACM Press.

Nielsen, J. (1993). *Usability Engineering.* Boston: Academic Press.

Nielsen, J. (1994). *Enhancing the explanatory power of usability heuristics.* Paper presented at the SIGCHI conference on Human factors in computing systems, Boston, MA.

Nielsen, J. (1994a). Guerrilla HCI: using discount usability engineering to penetrate the intimidation barrier. In *Cost-justifying usability.* Orlando: Academic Press, Inc.

Nielsen, J. (1994b). Heuristic evaluation. In Jakob Nielsen, Mack, R. L. (eds), *Usability inspection methods, Heurisitic Evaluation.* New York: John Wiley & Sons, Inc.

Nielsen, J. (1996). *Top Ten Mistakes in Web design.* Retrieved 25 June, 1999, from http://www.useit.com/alerbox/9605.html

Nielsen, J. (1999). Online archive available at http://www.useit.com/papers/heuristic/heuristic_list.html

Nielsen, J. (2000). *Designing Web Usability: The Practice of simplicity.* New York: New Riders Publishing.

Nielsen, J. (2001). *Beyond Accessibility: Treating Users with Disabilities as People.* Retrieved 2008, from Alertbox: Current Issues in Web Usability http://www.useit.com/alertbox/20011111.html

Nielsen, J. (2001). *Did Poor Usability Kill e-Commerce.* Retrieved 3 June, 2003, from http://www.useit.com/alertbox/200110819.html

Nielsen, J. (2003). *Usability 101.* Retrieved 14 April 2004, from http://www.useit.com/alertbox/20030825.html

Nielsen, J. (2004). *Change the Color of Visited Links, useit.com.* Alertbox, May, Link colors.

Nielsen, J. (2007). Multiple Users Simultaneous Testing (MUST). *Jakob Nielsen's Alertbox.* Retrieved on December 3, 2008 at http://www.useit.com/alertbox/multiple-user-testing.html

Nielsen, J. (2009). *useit.com: Jakob Nielsen's website.* Retrieved June 11, 2009, from http://www.useit.com/

Nielsen, J., & Mack, R. (1994). *Usability Inspection Methods.* New York: John Wiley & Sons.

Nielsen, J., & Molich, R. (1990). Heuristic Evaluation of User Interfaces. In *Proc. of ACM CHI'90 Conf.*

Nielsen, J., & Molich, R. (1990, 1-5 April). *Heuristic evaluation of user interfaces.* Paper presented at the ACM CHI'90 Conf, Seattle, WA.

Nielsen, J., & Tahir, M. (2002). Homepage Usability – 50 Websites Deconstructed. New York: New Riders Publishing.

Nielsen, J., Bush, R. M., Dayton, T., Mond, N. E., Muller, M. J., & Root, R. W. (1992). Teaching experienced developers to design graphical user interfaces. In *Proceedings of CHI 1992*, (pp. 557-564). New York: ACM Press.

Norman, D. (1998). *The Design of Everyday Things.* Cambridge, MA: MIT.

Norman, D. A., Ortony, A., & Russell, D. M. (2003). Affect and Machine Design: Lessons for the Development of Autonomous Machines. *IBM Systems Journal, 42*(1), 38–44.

Norman, K. L., Shneiderman, B. A., Harper, B. D., & Slaughter, L. A. (1989). Questionnaire for User Interface Satisfaction. Maryland: University of Maryland.

Novak, T. P., Hoffman, D. L., & Yung, Y. F. (2000). Measuring the Customer Experience in Online Environments: A Structural Modeling Approach. *Marketing Science, 19*(1), 22–42. doi:10.1287/mksc.19.1.22.15184

O'Shaughnessy, J. (1992). *Explaining Buyer Behavior: Central concepts and Philosophy of Science issues.* New York: Oxford University Press.

Obendorf, H., & Finck, M. (2008). Scenario-based usability engineering techniques in agile development processes. In *CHI '08: CHI '08 extended abstracts on Human factors in computing systems* (pp. 2159-2166). New York: ACM.

Odom, A. S. & Sholtz, S. S. (2004). *The reds, whites, and blues of emotion: examinig color hue effects on mood tones.* Department of psychology Missouri Western State University.

Olle, T. W., Hagelstein, J., Macdonald, I. G., Rolland, C., Sol, H. G., Assche, F. J. M. V., et al. (1988). *Information Systems Methodologies "A framework for understanding."*: Reading, MA: Addison-Wesley Publishing Company.

Olson, M. H., & Ives, B. (1981). User Involvement in System Design: An Empirical Test of Alternative Approaches. *Information & Management, 4*(4), 183. doi:10.1016/0378-7206(81)90059-8

Onacă (Andrei), D.M., Tarţa, A.M., & Pitariu, H.D. (2006). The development of a theatre/opera website pattern based on a user need assessment approach. *Psihologia Resurselor Umane, 4*(1).

Onaca (Andrei). D.M., & Guran, A.M. (2008). A User-centred approach in developing an intelligent web assistant for supporting career related decision making. In *Proceedings of the Romanian Computer Human Interaction Conference,* Matrix Rom.

Oppenheim, A. N. (1992). *Questionnaire design, interviewing and attitude measurement* (2nd Ed.). London: St Martins Press.

Oravec, J. A. (2002). Virtually accessible: Empowering students to advocate for accessibility and support universal design. *Library Hi Tech, 20*(4), 452-461. Retrieved June 1, 2009, from http://www.emeraldinsight.com/Insight/ViewContentServlet?Filename=/published/emeraldfulltextarticle/pdf/2380200407.pdf

Osgood, C. E., Suci, G. J., & Tannenbaum, P. H. (1957). *The measurement of meaning.* Chicago: University of Illinois Press.

Paciello, M. G. (2000). *Web accessibility for people with disabilities.* Lawrence, KS: CMP Books.

Paddison, C., & Englefield, P. (2004). Applying heuristics to accessibility inspections. *Interacting with Computers, 16*(3), 507–521. doi:10.1016/j.intcom.2004.04.007

Palmer, J. W. (2002). Web site usability, design, and performance metrics. *Information Systems Research, 13*(2), 151–167. doi:10.1287/isre.13.2.151.88

Palmer, S. R., & Felsing, J. M. (2002). *A Practical Guide to Feature-Driven Development.* Upper Saddle River, NJ: Prentice Hall PTR.

Palmquist, R. A., & Kim, K. S. (2000). Cognitive style and on-line database search experience as predictors of web search performance. *Journal of the American Society for Information Science American Society for Information Science, 51*(6), 558–566. doi:10.1002/(SICI)1097-4571(2000)51:6<558::AID-ASI7>3.0.CO;2-9

Pantin-Sohier, G. (2004). *Le rôle de la couleur dans la perception des traits de personnalité de la marque: une étude comparative Etats-Unis/Suède.* 1ère journée de recherche AFM-AUDENCIA sur le Marketing et le Design - Janvier.

Papadopoulou, P. (2007). Applying virtual reality for trust-building e-commerce environments. *Virtual Reality, 11*(2-3), 107-127(21).

Park, J. Y. (2008). A model of experience test for web designers: Design Principles and Practices. *International Journal (Toronto, Ont.), 2*(1), 175–182.

Parkinson, C. M. (2007). Website accessibility statements: a comparative investigation of local government and high street sectors. *Library and Information Research, 31*(98), 29-44. Retrieved November 19, 2008, from http://www.lirg.org.uk/lir/ojs/index.php/lir/article/viewFile/40/50

Pastor, O. (20040. Fitting the Pieces of the Web Engineering Puzzle. In *Proceedings of 18th Brazilian Symposium on Software Engineering (SBES2004),* (Vol. 1, pp. 10 - 22).

Pastoureau, M. (1999). *Dictionnaire des couleurs de notre temps, symbolique et société.* Paris: Bonneton.

Paternò, F. (1999). Model-based design and evaluation of interactive applications. *Applied Computing.* Berlin: Springer.

Paterno, F. (2000). Model-based design of interactive applications. *Intelligence, 11*(4), 26–38. doi:10.1145/355137.358311

Pausch, R., Burnette, T., Brockway, D., & Weiblen, M. E. (1995). Navigation and locomotion in virtual worlds via flight into hand-held miniatures. In *Proceedings of ACM SIGGRAPH 95,* (pp. 399-400).

Pederick, C. (2009). *The web developer toolbar.* Retrieved June 26, 2009, from http://chrispederick.com/work/web-developer/

Pelet, J.-É. (2008). *Effects of the color of e-commerce websites on the memorization and on the intention of purchase of the Net surfer.* Thesis in Management, Nantes University, France.

Perry, T. J., & Schneider, P. G. (2001). *New Perspectives on E-Commerce.* Australia: Thomson Learning.

Persons with Disabilities (Equal Opportunities, Protection of Rights and Full Participation) Act. (1995). Retrieved May 28, 2009, from http://www.disabilityindia.org/pwdacts.cfm

Petrie, H., & Kheir, O. (2007). The relationship between accessibility and usability of websites. In *CHI '07: Proceedings of the SIGCHI conference on Human factors in computing systems* (pp. 397-406). New York: ACM.

Petrie, H., Hamilton, F., & King, N. (2003). *Tension? What tension?: Website accessibility and visual design.* Paper presented at the 2004 International Cross-Disciplinary Workshop on Web Accessibility (W4A) 17-22 May, 2004, New York. Retrieved June 1, 2009, from http://portal.acm.org/citation.cfm?id=990660&coll=ACM&dl=ACM&CFID=486951&CFTOKEN=79021637&ret=1#Fulltext

Petric, H., Hamilton, F., King, N., & Pavan, P. (2006). Remote usability evaluations with disabled people. In *CHI '06: Proceedings of the SIGCHI conference on Human Factors in computing systems* (pp. 1133-1141). New York: ACM.

Petrie, H., King, N., & Hamilton, F. (2005). *Accessibility of museum, library and archive websites: the MLA audit.* Retrieved 01/2009 from http://www.mla.gov.uk/webdav/harmonise?Page/@id=73&Document/@id=23090&Section%5B@stateId_eq_left_hand_root%5D/@id=4302

Petrie, H., Weber, G., & Fisher, W. (2005). Personalization, interaction and navigation in rich multimedia documents for print disabled users. In *IBM Systems Journal.* Armonk NY: IBM.

Philips, B., & Dumas, J. (1990). Usability testing Functional requirements for data logging software. In Human Factors Society (Ed.), *Proceedings of the Human Factors Society 34th Annual Meeting: Countdown to the 21st Century,* (pp. 295–299). Santa Monica, CA: Human Factors & Ergonomics Society.

Phillips, L. D. (1986). Decision Analysis and its Applications in Industry. In G. Mitra (Ed.), *Computer*

Assisted Decision Making. North-Holland: Elsevier Science Publishers.

Phipps, L., Harrison, S., Sloan, D., & Willder, B. (2004). Developing and publicising a workable accessibility strategy. *Ariadne, 38*. Retrieved June 1, 2009, from http://www.ariadne.ac.uk/issue38/phipps/intro.html

Phipps, L., Witt, N., & McDermott, A. (n.d.). *To logo or not to logo?* Retrieved June 1, 2009, from http://www.techdis.ac.uk/index.php?p=3_8_8

Picard, R. W., & Wexelblat, A. (2002). *Future interfaces: social and emotional*. Paper presented at the CHI '02 Extended Abstracts on Human Factors in Computing Systems, Minneapolis, Minnesota, USA.

Pierce, J. S., Forsberg, A. S., & Conway, M. J. (1997), Image Plane Interaction Techniques in 3D Immersive Environments. In *Proceedings symposium on Interactive 3D graphics*, 39-ff.

Pilgrim, M. (2002). *Dive into accessibility: 30 days to a more accessible website. Day 30: creating an accessibility statement*. Retrieved June 1, 2009, from http://diveintoaccessibility.org/day_30_creating_an_accessibility_statement.html

Pipan, M. (2007). *Methods and techniques for usability evaluation of software solutions*. Unpublished dissertation, University of Ljubljana, Ljubljana, Slovenia.

Pipan, M., Arh, T., & Jerman Blažič, B. (2006). Development of the model for a usability and applicability assessment of learning management systems. In Lillemaa, T (Ed.), *Is information technology shaping the future of higher education?: Proceedings of the 12th International Conference of European University Information Systems EUNIS 2006* (pp. 325-332). Tartu, Estonia: University of Tartu press.

Pitariu, H.D. (2003). The influence of personality traits upon human computer interaction. *Cognition, Brain, Behavior, 8*(3).

Plégat-Soutjis, F. (2004). *Sémantique graphique des interfaces. Représentations, valeurs, usages, communication et langages*. Dossier: le signe en scène, un enjeu politique, n°142, décembre 2004.

Poupyrev, I. Weghorst, S., Billinghurst, M., & Ichikawa, T. (1997). A framework and testbed for studying manipulation techniques for immersive VR. In *Proceedings of the ACM symposium on Virtual reality software and technology*, (pp. 21-28).

Poupyrev, I., Billinghurst, M., Weghorst, S., & Ichikawa, T. (1996), The Go-Go Interaction Technique: Nonlinear Mapping for Direct Manipulation in VR. In *Proc. UIST'96*, (pp. 79-80).

Preece, J., Rogers, Y., & Sharp, H. (2002). *Interaction Design: Beyond human-computer interaction*. New York: John Wiley & Sons.

Preece, J., Rogers, Y., & Sharp, H. (2002). *Interaction design: beyond human-computer interaction*. New York: John Wiley & Sons.

Preece, J., Rogers, Y., Keller, L., Davies, G., & Benyon, D. (1993). A Guide to Usability. In J. Preece (Ed.), *Human Factors in Computing*. London: Addison Wesley.

Preece, J., Rogers, Y., Sharp, H., Benyon, D., Holland, S., & Carey, T. (1994). *Human Computer Interaction*. Reading, MA: Addison Wesley.

Presser, S. (2004). *Methods for Testing and Evaluating Survey Questionnaires*. New York: Wiley-IEEE.

Pressman, R. (2006). *Software Engineering: A Practitioner's Approach* (6th ed.). New York: McGraw-Hill.

Pressman, R. S. (2000). What a Tangled Web We Weave. *IEEE Software, 17*(1), 18–21. doi:10.1109/52.819962

Pribadi, N. S., Wadlow, M. G., & Boyarski, D. (1990). *The use of color in computer interfaces: Preliminary Research*. Information technology Center, Carnegie Mellon University, Pittsburgh, PA.

Pribeanu, C., & Vanderdonckt, J. M. (2003). A Pattern-based Approach to User Interface Development. In *Proceedings of the Tenth International Conference on Human-Computer Interaction 2003*, (pp. 1524-1528).

Providenti, M. (2005). The art of the accessibility statement. *Internet Reference Services Quarterly, 10*(1), 47–62. doi:10.1300/J136v10n01_04

Puerta, A. R. (1997). A Model-Based Interface Development Environment. *IEEE Software, 14*(4), 41–47. doi:10.1109/52.595902

Pulichino, J. (2004). *Usability and e-learning.* The E-learning Guide Survey series: Vol. January 2004.

RACE. 1065-ISSUE. (1992). *ISSUE Usability Evaluation Guidelines.* Brussels: Commission of the European Communities.

Rajani, R., & Rosenberg, D. (1999). Usable Or Not? Factors Affecting the Usability of Web Sites. *CMC Magazine.* January 1999. Online archive available at http://www.december.com/ cmc/mag/1999/jan/rakros.html

Rajkovič, V., Bohanec, M., & Batagelj, V. (1988). Knowledge Engineering Techniques for Utility Identification. *Acta Psychologica, 68,* 37–46. doi:10.1016/0001-6918(88)90060-1

Ramey, J. (2000). Guidelines for Web Data Collection: Understanding and Interacting with Your Users. *Technical Communication, 47*(3), 397–410.

Ramsay, Barbesi, A., & Preece, J. (1998). A Psychological Investigation of Long Retrieval Times on the World Wide Web. *Interacting with Computers, 10*(1), 77–86. doi:10.1016/S0953-5438(97)00019-2

Ranganathan & Grandon. (2005). *Converting browser to Buyers: key considerations in designing Business-to-Consumer Web sites.* In Y. Gao (ed.), *Web system design and online consumer Behavior,* (pp. 177-191). Hershey, PA: Idea Group Publishing.

Raskin, J. (1997). Looking for a Humane Interface: Will Computers Ever Become Easy to Use? *Communications of the ACM, 40*(2), 98–101. doi:10.1145/253671.253737

Ravden, S., & Johnson, G. (1989). *Evaluating the Usability of Human-Computer Interfaces.* New York: John Wiley & Sons.

Redmond-Pyle, D., & Moore, A. (1995). *Graphical User Interface Design and Evaluation: A Practical Process.* London: Prentice Hall.

Reusch, P. J. A., Stoll, B., & Studnik, D. (2005). VoiceX-ML-Applications for E-Commerce and E-Learning. *Intelligent Data Acquisition and Advanced Computing Systems: Technology and Applications, 2005. IDAACS 2005,* (pp. 709-712). Washington, DC: IEEE.

Reynolds, C., & Fletcher-Janzen, E. (2001). Concise Encyclopedia of Special Education: A Reference for the Education of the Handicapped and Other Exceptional Children and Adults. Hoboken, NJ: Wiley.

Rhodes, J. S. (2000). *Usability can save your company.* Retrieved 5 Dec 2003, from http://webword.com/moving/savecompany.html

Rice, M. (1997). What makes users revisit a web site? *Marketing News, 31*(6), 12.

Richardson, J. T. E. (2002). *Handbook of Qualitative Research Methods for Psychology and the Social Sciences.* Oxford, UK: BPS Blackwell Publishing.

Richtell, M., & Tedeschi, B. (2007, June 17). Online Sales Lose Steam. *New York Times.*

RIT. (2008). *Hearing Loss.* Retrieved 2008, from RIT, Hearing Loss, http://www.ntid.rit.edu/media/hearing_loss.php

Robb, D. (2005). One site fits all: Companies find web sites that comply with accessibility guidelines mean more customers. *Computerworld, 39*(13), 29-30. Retrieved June 1, 2009, from http://www.computerworld.com/action/article.do?command=viewArticleBasic&articleId=100607

Robson, C. (1993). *Real World Research.* Oxford. UK: Blackwell.

Rogers, E. M. (1995). *Diffusion of Innovations,* (4th Ed.). New York: The Free Press.

Rohn, J. A. (1994). The Usability Engineering Laboratories at Sun Microsystems. *Behaviour & Information Technology, 13*(1-2), 25–35. doi:10.1080/01449299408914581

Rohn, J. A. (1998, September). Creating Usable e-Commerce Sites. *StandardView, 6,* 110–115. doi:10.1145/324042.324046

Rosenbaum, S. (2008). The Future of Usability Evaluation: Increasing Impact on Value. In Law, E. L-C., Hvannberg, E.T., & Cockton, G. (Eds). *Maturing Usability. Quality in interaction, software and value.* London: Springer-Verlag Limited.

Rosmaita, B. (2006). *Accessibility first! A new approach to web design.* Paper presented at the 37th SIGCSE Technical Symposium on Computer Science Education, 1-5 March 2006, Houston, Texas. Retrieved June 1, 2009, from http://portal.acm.org/citation.cfm?id=1124706.1121426

Rosson, M. B., & Carroll, J. M. (2002). *Usability Engineering: Scenario-Based Development of Human-Computer Interaction.* San Francisco: Morgan Kaufmann.

Rubin, J. (1994). *Handbook of Usability Testing: How to plan, design and conduct effective tests.* New York: John Wiley & Sons, Inc.

Rubin, J., & Chisnell, D. (2008). *Handbook of Usability Testing: How to Plan, Design, and Conduct Effective Tests.* Indianapolis, IN: Wiley Publishing, Inc.

Ruse, K. (2005). *Web standards design guide.* Boston: Charles River Media.

Russel, J. A., & Fernandez-Dols, J. M. (1997). *The psychology of facial expressions.* Cambridge, UK: Cambridge University Press.

Ryle, A., & Lunghi, M. (1970). The dyad grid: a modification of repertory grid technique. *The British Journal of Psychology*, 117.

Sampson, J. P., Carr, D. L., Panke, J., Arkin, S., Minvielle, M., & Vernick, S. H. (2001). *An Implementation Model for Web Site Design and Use in Counseling and Career Services.* Retrieved 14 June 2004, from http://www.career.fsu.edu/documents/implementation/Implementing%20Web%20Sites.ppt.

San Murugesan, Y. D., Hansen, S., & Ginige, A. (2001). Web Engineering: A New Discipline for Development of Web-Based Systems. In *Web Engineering Managing Diversity and Complexity of Web Application Development*, (LNCS Vol. 2016, pp. 3-13). Berlin: Springer.

Sauer, C., Jeffery, D. R., Land, L., & Yetton, P. (2000). The Effectiveness of Software Development Technical Reviews: A Behaviorally Motivated Program of Research.

IEEE Transactions on Software Engineering, 26(1), 1–14. doi:10.1109/32.825763

Schaffer, E., & Sorflaten, J. (1999). Web Usability Illustrated: Breathing Easier with Your Usable E-Commerce Site. *Journal of Economic Commerce, 11*(4), 1–10.

Schamel, J. (2008). *How the pilot's checklist came about.* Retrieved from http://www.atchistory.org/History/checklst.htm

Schiffman, L. G., & Kanuk, L. L. (2000). *Consumer Behaviour,* (7th Ed.). Upper Saddle River, NJ: Prentice Hall.

Schirmer, B. R., & Williams, C. (2003). Approaches to Teaching Reading. In M. Marschark, & P. Spencer (Eds), *Handbook of Deaf Studies, Language and Education* (pp. 110–122). Oxford, UK: Oxford University Press.

Schmettow, M. (2005) Towards a Pattern Based Usability Inspection Method for Industrial Practitioners. In *Proceedings of the Workshop on Integrating Software Engineering and Usability Engineering* (held on Interact 2005). Retrieved from http://www.se-hci.org/bridging/interact2005/03_Schmettow_Towards_UPI.pdf

Scholtz, J. (1995). Usability: What's it all about? *Software Quality Journal, 4*(2), 95–100. doi:10.1007/BF00402713

Scholtz, J., Laskowski, S., & Downey, L. (1998). Developing Usability Tools and Techniques for Designing and Testing Web Sites. In *Proceedings of the 4th Conference on Human Factors & the Web.* AT&T.

Schwabe, D., & Rossi, G. (1995). The Object-Oriented Hypermedia Design Model. *Communications of the ACM, 38*(8), 45–46. doi:10.1145/208344.208354

Schwabe, D., & Rossi, G. (1998). An object oriented approach to web-based applications design. *Theory and Practice of Object Systems, 4*(4), 207–225. doi:10.1002/(SICI)1096-9942(1998)4:4<207::AID-TAPO2>3.0.CO;2-2

Schwabe, D., Rossi, G., & Barbosa, S. (1996). Systematic Hypermedia Design with OOHDM. In *Proceedings of the 7th ACM Conference on Hypertext,* (pp. 116 – 128), Washington, USA. March 1996.

Sears, A. (1997). Heuristic walkthroughs: Finding the problems without the noise. *International Journal of Human-Computer Interaction, 9*(3), 213–234. doi:10.1207/s15327590ijhc0903_2

Seilheimer, S. (2004). Productive development of World Wide Web sites intended for international use. *International Journal of Information Management, 24*(5), 363. doi:10.1016/j.ijinfomgt.2004.06.001

Sekaran, U. (2003). *Research Methods for Business "A Skill Building Approach"* (4th ed.). Mahwah, NJ: John Wiley & Sons.

Shackel, B., & Richardson, D. (1991). *Human Factors for Informatics Usability.* Cambridge, UK: Cambridge University Press.

Sharp, H., Rogers, Y., & Preece, J. (2007). *Interaction Design: Beyond Human-Computer Interaction.* West Sussex, UK: John Wiley & Sons, Inc.

Shepherd, A. (1989). Analysis and Training in Information Technology Tasks. In D. Diaper (Ed.), *Task Analysis for Human-Computer Interaction* (pp. 15-55). Chichester, UK: Ellis Horwood Limited.

Sheridan, W. (1999). *Web Design is Changing.* Retrieved 27 May 2003, from http://www3.sympatico.ca/cypher/web-design.htm

Sherry, R. (2006). *Showing web accessibility statements the door.* Retrieved October 19, 2008, from http://www.usabilitynews.com/news/article3516.asp

Sheth, J. N., & Sisodia, R. S. (1997). *Consumer Behavior in the Future.* In R. A. Peterson, (ed.), *Electronic Marketing and The Consumer,* (pp. 17-37). Thousand Oaks, CA: Sage Publications.

Shneiderman B. (2003). Why Not Make Interfaces Better than 3D Reality. *Virtualization Viewpoints,* (November-December).

Shneiderman, B. (1998). *Design the User Interface: Strategies for effective Human-Computer Interaction* (3 ed.). Reading, MA: Addison-Wesley.

Shneiderman, B. (2000). Universal usability. *Communications of the ACM, 43*(5), 85–91. doi:10.1145/332833.332843

Shneiderman, B. (2002). 3D or Not 3D: When and Why Does it Work? Human-Computer Interaction Laboratory & Department of Computer Science University of Maryland. *Talk in Web3D.* Phoenix, AZ, February 26, 2002.

Shneiderman, B. (2003). Promoting universal usability with multi-layer interface design. In *Proceedings of the 2003 Conference on Universal Usability (CUU 2003).* New York: ACM.

Shneiderman, B. (2006). Designing the User Interface. Reading, MA: Addison Wesley Longman.

Shneiderman, B., Byrd, D. & Croft, W.B. (1997). Clarifying Search: A User-Interface Framework for Text Searches. *D-Lib Magazine, January.*

Shubin, H., & Meehan, M. M. (1997), Navigation in Web Applications. *Interaction, 4*(6), 13–18. doi:10.1145/267505.267508

Shull, F., Carver, J., & Travassos, G. H. (2001). An empirical methodology for introducing software processes. *ACM SIGSOFT Software Engineering Notes, 26*(5), 288–296. doi:10.1145/503271.503248

Sicilia, M., Ruiz, S., & Munuera, J. L. (2005). Effects of Interactivity in a Web Site: The Moderating Effect of Need for Cognition. *Journal of Advertising, 34*(3), 31–44.

Silverstein, L. D. (1987). Human Factors for Color Display System: Concepts, Methods, and Research. In J. Durret (ed.), *Color and the Computer,* (pp. 27-61). San Diego, CA: Academic Press.

SIMICODE. (2002). Retrieved 2008, from http://acceso.uv.es/preacceso/typo/index.php/simicole.html

Simon, A. H. (1977). *The New Science of Management Decision.* New York: Prentice-Hall.

Sims, R. (1997). *Interactivity: A Forgotten Art?* Retrieved 4 Dec 2003, from http://www.gsu.edu/~wwwitr/docs/interact/

Singh, S., & Erwin, J. G. (2002, 4-5 April). *Electronic Business Accepted Practices (e-BAP): Standardized HCI for E-Commerce.* Paper presented at the ISOneWorld, Las Vegas, NV.

Skov, M. B., & Stage, J. (2001). A Simple Approach to Web-Site Usability Testing. In *Proceedings of 1st International Conference on Universal Access in Human-Computer Interaction*, (pp. 737-741). Mahwah, NJ: Lawrence-Erlbaum.

Skov, M. B., & Stage, J. (2004) Integrating Usability Design and Evaluation: Training Novice Evaluators in Usability Testing. In K. Hornbæk & J. Stage (Eds.), *Proceedings of the Workshop on Improving the Interplay between Usability Evaluation and User Interface Design, NordiCHI 2004*, (pp. 31-35), Aalborg University, Department of Computer Science, HCI-Lab Report no. 2004/2.

Skov, M. B., & Stage, J. (2005) Supporting Problem Identification in Usability Evaluations. In *Proceedings of the Australian Computer-Human Interaction Conference 2005 (OzCHI'05)*. New York: ACM Press.

Slatin, J. (2002). The imagination gap: Making web-based instructional resources accessible to students and colleagues with disabilities. *Currents in Electronic Literacy, 6*. Retrieved June 26, 2009, from http://www.cwrl.utexas.edu/currents/spring02/slatin.html

Slavkovic, A., & Cross, K. (1999). Novice heuristic evaluations of a complex interface. In *Proceedings of CHI 1999*, (pp. 304-305). New York: ACM Press.

Sloan, D., Dickinson, A., McIlroy, N., & Gibson, L. (2006). *Evaluating the usability of online accessibility information.* Retrieved June 1, 2009, from http://www.techdis.ac.uk/index.php?p=3_10_10_1

Sloan, D., Heath, A., & Hamilton, F. (2006). *Contextual web accessibility: maximizing the benefit of accessibility guidelines.* Paper presented at the International Cross-Disciplinary Workshop on Web Accessibility (W4A), 10-14 May 2005, Chiba, Japan. Retrieved June 1, 2009, from http://portal.acm.org/citation.cfm?id=1133242&coll=ACM&dl=ACM&CFID=553412&CFTOKEN=75424160&ret=1#Fulltext

Sloan, M. (2001). *Institutional websites and legislation.* Retrieved June 1, 2009, from http://www.techdis.ac.uk/index.php?p=3_8_14

SMILE. (2006). Retrieved 2008, from http://www2.tech.purdue.edu/cg/i3/SMILE/

Smith, P. A., Newman, I. A., & Parks, L. M. (1997). Virtual Hierarchies and Virtual Networks: Some Lessons From Hypermedia Usability research Applied to the Web. *International Journal of Human-Computer Studies, 47*(1), 67–95. doi:10.1006/ijhc.1997.0128

Smith, S. P., & Marsh, T. (2004). Evaluating design guidelines for reducing user disorientation in a desktop virtual environment. *Virtual Reality (Waltham Cross), 8*(1), 55–62. doi:10.1007/s10055-004-0137-x

Snider, J. G., & Osgood, C. E. (Eds.). (1969). *Semantic Differential Technique: A SourceBook.* Chicago: Aldin-eTransaction.

Soares, K., & Furtado, E. (2003). RUPi - A Unified Process that Integrates Human-Computer Interaction and Software Engineering. In *Workshop Bridging the Gap Between Software-Engineering and Human-Computer Interaction at ICSE 2003, Proceedings,* (pp. 41-48).

Sousa, K., & Furtado, E. (2005). A Unified Process Supported by a Framework for the Semi-Automatic Generation of Multi-Context UIs. In *12th International Workshop on Design, Proceedings.*

Sousa, K., Mendonça, H., & Vanderdonckt, J. (2007). Towards Method Engineering of Model-Driven User Interface Development. In *Task Models and Diagrams for User Interface Design* (pp. 112-125). Berlin: Springer.

Spiller, P., & Lohse, G. L. (1998). A classification of Internet retail stores. *International Journal of Electronic Commerce, 2*(2), 29–56.

Spool, J. M., Scanlon, T., Schroeder, W., Snyder, C., & DeAngelo, T. (1999). *Web Site Usability – A Designer's Guide.* San Francisco: Morgan Kaufmann Publishers, Inc.

Spyridakis, J. H. (2000). Guidelines for authoring comprehensible Web pages and evaluating their success. *Technical Communication, 47*(3), 359.

SSB BART Group. (2006). *InFocus suite overview.* Retrieved November 21, 2008, from http://ssbtechnologies.com

Stanton, N. A., Salmon, P. M., Walker, G. H., Baber, C., & Jenkins, D. P. (2005). *Human Factors Methods: A Practical Guide for Engineering and Design.* London: Ashgate.

Stapleton, J. (2003). *DSDM: Business Focused Development* (2nd ed.). Harlow, UK.: Addison-Wesley.

Steed, A., & Tromp, J. (1998), Experiences with the evaluation of CVE applications. In *Proc. of the conf. Collaborative Virtual Environments* (CVE'98), Manchester, UK, June 17-19th.

Stephanidis, C. (Ed.). (2001). *User Interfaces for All: Concepts, Methods and Tools.* Mahwah, NJ: Lawrence Erlbaum Associates.

Stephanidis, C. (Ed.). (2009). *The Universal Access Handbook.* Boca Raton, FL: CRC Press.

Stephens, R. (1996). *Principles for design of auditory interfaces to present complex information to blind people.* Unpublished doctorial dissertation, University of York, UK.

Stewart, V., & Stewart, A. (1981). *Business applications of the repertory grid.* Maidenhead, UK: McGraw-Hill.

Stoakley, R., Conway, M. J., & Pausch, R. (1995), Virtual Reality on a WIM: Interactive Worlds in Miniature. In *Proceedings of ACM CHI 95,* (pp. 265-272).

Strauss, J., El-Ansary, A., & Frost, R. (2006). *E-Marketing* (4th ed.). Upper Saddle River, NJ: Pearson Prentice Hall.

Sullivan, T. (1998). *User Testing Techniques - A Reader-Friendliness Checklist.* Online archive available at http://www.pantos.org/atw/35317.html

Sullivan, T., & Matson, R. (2000). Barriers to Use: Usability and Content Accessibility on the Web's Most Popular Sites. In *Proceedings of Conference on Universal Usability,* November 16-17, Washington, (pp. 139-144). New York: ACM.

Sutcliffe, A. (1988). *Human-Computer Interface Design.* London: Macmillan Education LTD.

Sutcliffe, A. (2001). Heuristic Evaluation of Website Attractiveness and Usability. *Interactive Systems: Design, Specification, and Verification,* (. *LNCS, 2220,* 183–198.

Szalvay, V. (2004). *An Introduction to Agile Software Development.* Bellevue, WA: Danube Technologies, Inc.

Tatham, M., & Morton, K. (2005). *Developments in Speech Synthesis.* West Sussex, UK: John Wiley & Sons, Inc.

Taylor, H. (2000). *How the internet is improving the lives of Americans with disabilities.* Retrieved June 1, 2009, from http://www.harrisinteractive.com/harris_poll/index.asp?PID=93

Teo, T. S. H., Lim, V. K. G., & Lai, R. Y. C. (1999). Intrinsic and Extrinsic Motivation in Internet Usage. *Omega, 27*(1), 25–37. doi:10.1016/S0305-0483(98)00028-0

Thatcher, J., Waddell, C. D., Henry, S. L., Swierenga, S., Urban, M. D., Burks, M., et al. (2003). *Constructing accessible web sites.* San Francisco: glasshaus.

Thatcher, J., Waddell, C., Henry, S., Swierenga, S., Urban, M., Burks, M., et al. (2002). *Constructing accessible websites.* Birmingham: Glasshaus.

The Learning Technologies Resource Centre. (2008). *LMS Evaluation Information.* Retrieved March 30, 2008, from http://www.ltrc.mcmaster.ca/lmseval/index.html

The World Bank. (2009). *Disability and development.* Retrieved May 29, 2009, from http://go.worldbank.org/19SCI890L0

Thimbley, H. (1990). *User Interface Design.* Wokingham, UK: Addison-Wesley.

Thompson, C. (2007). Halo 3: How Microsoft Labs Invented a New Science of Play. *Wired Magazine, 15*(09). Retrieved on December 1, 2008 at http://www.wired.com/gaming/virtualworls/magazine/15-09/ff-halo

Thompson, R. L., Higgins, C. A., & Howell, J. M. (1991). Personal Computing: Toward a Conceptual

Model of Utilisation. *MIS Quarterly, 15*(1), 125–143. doi:10.2307/249443

Tilson, R., Dong, J., Martin, S., & Kieke, E. (1998). A Comparison of Two Current E-commerce Sites. In *Proceedings of the 16th Annual Conference on Computer Documentation,* (pp.87-92). New York: ACM Press/ Addison Wesley.

Tingling, P., & Saeed, A. (2007). Extreme Programming in Action: A Longitudinal Case Study. In *Human-Computer Interaction. Interaction Design and Usability, Proceedings,* (pp. 242-251).

Travis, D. (2003). *Bluffers' Guide to ISO 9241.* Retrieved 19 August, 2003, from www.userfocus.co.uk

Travis, D. (2003). *e-Commerce Usability: Tools and Techniques to Perfect the On-line Experience.* London: Taylor & Francis.

Tricot, A. (1995). Un point sur l'ergonomie des interfaces hypermédia. *Le Travail Humain, 58*(1), 17–45.

Trouvé, A. (1999). *La mesure de la couleur.* Paris, CETIM, éd. Association française de normalisation (AFNOR).

Troyer, O. D. (1998). *Designing Well-Structured Websites: Lessons to Be Learned from Database Schema Methodology.* Paper presented at the Conceptual Modeling – ER '98: 17th International Conference on Conceptual Modeling, Singapore.

Troyer, O. M. F. D., & Leune, C. J. (1998). *WSDM: a user centered design method for Web sites.* Paper presented at the Computer Networks and ISDN systems, Proceedings of the 7th International World Wide Web Conference, Elsevier, Vrijdag.

Troyer, O. M. F. D., & Leune, C. J. (1998). WSDM: a user centered design method for Web sites. *Computer Networks and ISDN Systems, 30*(1-7), 85 - 94.

Turban, E. (1988). *Decision Support and Expert Systems.* New York: Macmillian.

Turban, E., & Aronson, J. E. (1998). *Decision Support Systems and Intelligent Systems.* Englewood Cliffs, NJ: Prentice Hall.

Turk, A. (2001). *Towards Contingent Usability Evaluation of WWW Sites.* Paper presented at the Proceedings of OZCHI, Perth, Australia.

Turunen, M., Hakulinen, J., & Kainulainen, A. (2006). Evaluation of a Spoken Dialogue System with Usability Tests and Long-term Pilot Studies: Similarities and Differences. In *Proc. 9th International Conference on Spoken Language Processing - INTERSPEECH* (pp. 1057—1060).

Tzanidou, E., Minocha, S., Petre, M., & Grayson, A. (2005, 5-9 September). *Revisiting Web Design Guidelines by Exploring Users' Expectations, Preferences and Visual Search Behaviour.* Paper presented at the The 19th British HCI Group Annual Conference: the Bigger Picture, Edinburgh.

United Nations General Assembly. (1948). *Universal declaration of human rights.* Retrieved November 21, 2008, from http://www.un.org/Overview/rights.html

Valdez, P. (1993). *Emotion responses to color.* Thèse de doctorat, University of California, Los Angeles.

Valdez, P., & Mehrabian, J. (1994). Effects of color on emotions. *Journal of Experimental Psychology. General, 123*(4), 394–409. doi:10.1037/0096-3445.123.4.394

Van Dyk, T. (1999). *Usability and Internet-Based Banking.* Unpublished Masters, University of South Africa, Pretoria.

van Kuppevelt, J., Dybkjær, L., & Bernsen, N. O. (Eds.). (2005). *Advances in natural multimodal dialogue.* Dordrecht, The Netherlands: Springer.

Van Maanen, J. (1998). *Qualitative studies of organizations.* The Administrative Science Quarterly, Series in Organization Theory and Behaviour. London: Sage Publications.

Van Welie, M. & Van der Veer, G. C. (2003). *Pattern Languages in Interaction Design: Structure and Organization.* Interact 2003.

Van Welie, M. (2001). *Task-Based user interface design.* Amsterdam: SIKS.

van Welie, M., & Traetteberg, H. (2000). Interaction Patterns in User Interfaces. In *7th. Pattern Languages of Programs Conference*, 13-16 August, Allerton Park Monticello, Illinois. Retrieved June 20, 2005, from http://www.welie.com/about.html

van Welie, M., van der Veer, G. C., & Eliëns, A. (2000). Patterns as Tools for User Interface Design. In *International Workshop on Tools for Working with Guidelines*, (pp. 313-324), October 7-8, Biarritz, France. Retrieved June 17, 2005, from http://www.welie.com/about.html

Vanden Bossche, P. (2006). Développement d'un outil de critique d'interface intelligent: UsabilityAdviser. M.Sc. thesis, *Université catholique de Louvain*, Louvain-la-Neuve, Septembre 1, 2006.

Vanderdonckt, J. (1999). Development Milestones towards a Tool for Working with Guidelines. *Interacting with Computers*, *12*(2), 81–118. doi:10.1016/S0953-5438(99)00019-3

Vanderdonckt, J. (2005), A MDA-Compliant Environment for Developing User Interfaces of Information Systems. In *Proc. of 17th Conf. on Advanced Information Systems Engineering CAiSE'05,* Porto, June 13-17, 2005, (LNCS Vol. 3520, pp.16-31). Berlin: Springer-Verlag.

Vanderdonckt, J., & Beirekdar, A. (2005). Automated Web Evaluation by Guideline Review. *Journal of Web Engineering*, *4*(2), 102–117.

Vanderdonckt, J., & Bodart, F. (1993), Encapsulating Knowledge for Intelligent Automatic Interaction Objects Selection. In: *Proc. of the ACM Conf. on Human Factors in Computing Systems INTERCHI'93,* Amsterdam, 24-29 April 1993, (pp. 424–429). New York: ACM Press.

Vanderdonckt, J., Bouillon, L., Chieu, K. C., & Trevisan, D. (2004): Model-based Design, Generation, and Evaluation of Virtual User Interfaces. In *Proc. of 9th ACM Int. Conf. on 3D Web Tech. Web3D'2004,* Monterey, April 5-8, 2004. New York: ACM Press.

Vanderheiden, G., Reid, L. G., Caldwell, B., & Henry, S. L. (Eds.). (2008), *The Web Content Accessibility Guidelines*, W3C. Retrieved from http://www.w3.org/WAI/

Van-Duyne, D. K., Landay, J. A., & Hong, J. I. (2003). *The Design of Sites: Patterns, Principles and processes for Crafting a Costumer-Centered Web Experience.* Boston: Addison-Wesley.

Vaz, V., Conte, T., Bott, A., Mendes, E., & Travassos, G. H. (2008). Inspeção de Usabilidade em Organizações de Desenvolvimento de Software – Uma Experiência Prática. In *Proceedings of the 7th Brazilian Symposium on Software Engineering (SBQS 2008)*, (Vol. 1, pp. 369-378), Florianopolis - Brazil

Venkatesh, V. (2000). Determinants of Perceived Ease of Use: Integrating Control, Intrinsic Motivation, and Emotion into the Technology Acceptance Model. *Information Systems Research*, *11*(4), 342–365. doi:10.1287/isre.11.4.342.11872

Venkatesh, V., & Davis, F. D. (2000). A Theoretical Extension of the Technology Acceptance Mode: Four Longitudinal Field Studies. *Management Science*, *46*(2), 186–204. doi:10.1287/mnsc.46.2.186.11926

Verdaasdonk, E. G. G., Stassen, L. P. S., Widhiasmara, P. P., & Dankelman, J. (2008) Requirements for the design and implementation of checklists for surgical processes. *Surgical Endoscopy.*

Verlinden, J., & Coenders, M. (2000). *Qualitative usability measurement of websites by employing the repertory grid technique.* Paper presented at the CHI 2000: extended abstracts, The Hague, The Netherlands.

Vora, P. (1998). Human Factors Methodology for Designing Web Sites. In E. G. J. R. Chris Forsythe (Ed.), *Human Factors and Web Development* (pp. 153 - 172). Mahwah, NJ: Lawrence Erlbaum Associates.

W1. (2009). The South African Revenue Services. Retrieved 10 June, 2009, from http://www.sars.gov.za/

W2. (2004). *e-Commerce Usability Guide.* Retrieved 7 October, 2005, from http://www.bonasource.com/print/page/e-commerce-usability-guide.htm

Wahlster, W. (Ed.). (2006). *SmartKom: Foundations of Multimodal Dialogue Systems.* Berlin: Springer-Verlag.

WAI Working Group (2008). Retrieved from http://www.w3.org/WAI/GL/WCAG20/implementation-report/Silverlight_accessibility_support_statement

Walker, M. A., Borland, J., & Kamm, C. A. (1999). The utility of elapsed time as a usability metric for spoken dialogue systems. In *Proc. IEEE Automatic Speech Recognition and Understanding Workshop - ASRU*, (pp. 317–320).

Walker, M. A., Kamm, C. A., & Litman, D. J. (2000). Towards developing general models of usability with PARADISE. *Natural Language Engineering, 6*(3-4), 363–377. doi:10.1017/S1351324900002503

Walker, M. A., Litman, D. J., Kamm, C. A., & Abella, A. (1998). Evaluating spoken dialogue agents with PARADISE: Two case studies. *Computer Speech & Language, 12*(3), 317–347. doi:10.1006/csla.1998.0110

Wallis, J. (2005). The web, accessibility and inclusion: Networked democracy in the United Kingdom. *Library Review, 54*(8), 479-85. Retrieved June 6, 2009, from http://www.emeraldinsight.com/Insight/viewPDF.jsp?Filename=html/Output/Published/EmeraldFullTextArticle/Pdf/0350540806.pdf

Ward, M. R., & Lee, M. J. (2000). Internet Shopping, Consumer Search and Product Branding. *Journal of Product and Brand Management, 9*(1), 6–18. doi:10.1108/10610420010316302

Ward, N., & Tsukahara, W. (2003). A Study in Responsiveness in Spoken Dialog. *International Journal of Human-Computer Studies, 59*, 603–630. doi:10.1016/S1071-5819(03)00085-5

Watanabe, T. (2007). Experimental evaluation of usability and accessibility of heading elements. In *Proceedings of International Cross-Disciplinary Conference on Web Accessibility (W4A)* (pp. 157-164). New York: ACM Press.

Web Accessibility Initiative. (2005). *Involving users in web accessibility evaluation.* Retrieved June 11, 2009, from http://www.w3.org/WAI/eval/users.html

Web Accessibility Initiative. (2006a). *Improving the accessibility of your web site.* Retrieved June 11, 2009, from http://www.w3.org/WAI/impl/improving.html

Web Accessibility Initiative. (2008a). *Web content accessibility guidelines (WCAG) 2.0.* Retrieved June 10, 2009, from http://www.w3.org/TR/WCAG20/

Web Accessibility Initiative. (2008b). *Evaluating web sites for accessibility: Overview.* Retrieved June 10, 2009, from http://www.w3.org/WAI/eval/Overview.html

Web Accessibility Initiative. (2008c). *Understanding conformance.* Retrieved June 24, 2009, from http://www.w3.org/TR/UNDERSTANDING-WCAG20/conformance.html#uc-conformance-claims-head

Web Accessibility Tools Consortium. (2005). *Colour contrast analyser.* Retrieved June 26, 2009, from http://www.wat-c.org/tools/CCA/1.1/

WebAIM. (2005). *Check of an accessibility statement.* Retrieved May 10, 2009, from http://www.webaim.org/discussion/mail_thread.php?thread=2341&id=6773

WebAIM. (2009a). *The web content accessibility guidelines.* Retrieved June 11, 2009, from http://www.webaim.org/standards/wcag/

WebAIM. (2009b). *The WAVE web accessibility evaluation tool.* Retrieved June 26, 2009, from http://wave.webaim.org/

Weinschenk, S., & Barker, D. T. (2000). *Designing effective speech interfaces.* New York: John Wiley & Sons, Inc.

Welie, M., & Trétteberg, H. (2000). Interaction Patterns in User Interfaces. In *Proc. Seventh Pattern Languages of Programs Conference: PLoP 2000*, Allerton Park Monticello, IL.

Wells, W. D., & Prensky, D. (1996). *Consumer Behaviour.* Chichester, UK: John Wiley.

Wesson, J., & Cowley, N. L. O. (2003). Designing with patterns: Possibilities and pitfalls. In *2nd Workshop on Software and Usability Cross-Pollination: The Role of Usability Patterns 2003.*

Wharton, C., Rieman, J., Lewis, C., & Polson, P. (1994). The Cognitive Walkthrough Method: a Practitioner's Guide. In J. Nielsen, & R. Mack (Eds), *Usability Inspection Methods* (pp. 105–140). Hoboken, NJ: John Wiley and Sons, Inc.

Wickens, C., & Hollands, J. (2000). *Engineering Psychology and Human Performance.* Upper Saddle River, NJ: Prentice-Hall.

Wilcox, S. (2003). The Multimedia Dictionary of American Sign Language: Learning Lessons about Language, Technology, and Business. *Sign Language Studies, 3*(4), 379–392. doi:10.1353/sls.2003.0019

Wilson, G. D. (1966). Arousal properties of red versus green. *Perceptual and Motor Skills, 23*(3), 947–949.

Wilson, J. R., Eastgate, R., & D'Cruz, M. (2002). Structured Development of Virtual Environments. In J. Jacko (ed.), *Handbook of Virtual Environments: Design, Implementation, and Applications.* Mahwah, NJ: Lawrence Erlbaum Associates.

Witmer, B. G., & Singer, M. J. (1998). Measuring Presence in Virtual Environments: A Presence Questionnaire. *Presence (Cambridge, Mass.), 7*(3), 225–240. doi:10.1162/105474698565686

Witt, N., & McDermott, A. (2004). Web site accessibility: what logo will we use today? *British Journal of Educational Technology, 35*(1), 45-56. Retrieved June 1, 2009, from http://www.blackwell-synergy.com/doi/pdf/10.1111/j.1467-8535.2004.00367.x

Wolkerstorfer, P., Tscheligi, M., Sefelin, R., Milchrahm, H., Hussain, Z., Lechner, M., et al. (2008). Probing an agile usability process. In *CHI '08. Extended abstracts on Human factors in computing systems Proceedings,* (pp. 2151-2158). New York: ACM.

Wood, J. V. (1989). Theory and research concerning social comparisons of personal attributes. *Psychological Bulletin, 106*(2), 231–248. doi:10.1037/0033-2909.106.2.231

Woodson, W. (1981). *Human Factors Design Handbook.* New York: McGraw-Hill Education.

Woordenboek (2004). Retrieved 2008, from http://gebaren.ugent.be/information.php

World Health Organisation. (2009). *International classification of functioning, disability and health (ICF).* Retrieved May 22, 2009, from http://www.who.int/classifications/icf/en/

Wright, B., & Rainwater, L. (1962). The Meaning of color. *The Journal of General Psychology, 67*(1), 89–99.

Wrigley, S. N., & Brown, G. J. (2000). *A model of auditory attention.* Technical Report CS-00-07, Speech and Hearing Research Group, University of Sheffield, UK.

Yagita, Y., Aikawa, Y., & Inaba, A. (2001). *A Proposal of the Quantitative Evaluation Method for Social Acceptability of Products and Services.* Tokyo: Ochanomizu University.

Yesilada, Y., Stevens, R., Goble, C. A., & Hussein, S. (2004). Rendering tables in audio: the interaction of structure and reading styles. In *Proceedings of the ACM SIGACCESS Conference on Computers and Accessibility (ASSETS),* (pp. 16-23). Berlin: Springer.

Yin, R. (1994). *Case study research: design and methods.* London: Sage.

Yoo, B., & Donthu, N. (2001). Developing and validating a multidimensional consumer-based brand equity scale. *Journal of Business Research, 52*(1), 1–14. doi:10.1016/S0148-2963(99)00098-3

Younossi, O., Arena, M. V., Leonard, R. S., Roll, C. R., Jain, A., & Sollinger, J. M. (2007). Is Weapon System Cost Growth Increasing? *(A Quantitative Assessment of Completed and Ongoing Programs), (Monograph MG-588-AF).* Santa Monica, CA: RAND Corporation.

Yu, H. (2002). Web accessibility and the law: recommendations for implementation. [from http://www.emeraldinsight.com/Insight/viewPDF.jsp?Filename=html/Output/Published/EmeraldFullTextArticle/Pdf/2380200403.pdf]. *Library Hi Tech, 20*(4), 406–419. Retrieved May 10, 2009. doi:10.1108/07378830210452613

Zhang, Z., Basili, V., & Shneiderman, B. (1999). Perspective-based Usability Inspection: An Empirical Validation of Efficacy. *Empirical Software Engineering, 4*(1), 43–69. doi:10.1023/A:1009803214692

Zviran, M., Glezer, C., & Anvi, I. (2006). User satisfaction from commercial web sites: The effect of design and use. *Information & Management, 43*(2), 157–178. doi:10.1016/j.im.2005.04.002

About the Contributors

Tasos Spiliotopoulos is a researcher at the Department of Informatics and Telecommunications, National and Kapodistrian University of Athens, Greece. As a member of the Information Systems Laboratory Research Group since 2000 he has participated in numerous EU and national research projects. His current research focuses on human-computer interaction, computer systems usability, the social web and online security and privacy.

Panagiota Papadopoulou is currently a research associate at the Department of Informatics, University of Athens. She holds a B.Sc (Hons) from the Department of Informatics, University of Athens, an MSc with distinction in Distributed and Multimedia Information Systems from Heriot-Watt University, U.K. and a PhD from the Department of Informatics, University of Athens. She has worked as a visiting professor at the University of Athens, University of Pireaus and the University of Peloponnese. Dr. Papadopoulou has also actively participated in a number of European Community and National research projects. Her current research interests focus on web-based information systems, interface design and online trust.

Drakoulis Martakos is an associate professor and head of the Sector of Computer Systems and Applications at the Department of Informatics and Telecommunications of the National and Kapodistrian University of Athens, Greece. He is also director of the Information Systems Laboratory (ISLab) Research Group within the department. Professor Martakos is a consultant to public and private organizations, a project leader in numerous national and international projects and the author or co-author of more than 70 scientific publications and a number of technical reports and studies.

Georgios Kouroupetroglou holds a B.Sc. in physics and a Ph.D. in Communications and Signal Processing. He is the Director of the Speech Laboratory, Department of Informatics and Telecommunications, University of Athens and Head of the e-Accessibility Unit for Students with Disabilities. His current research interests focuses on the area of Speech Communication and Accessibility, as parts of the major domain of Multimedia and Human-Computer Interaction. Dr. Kouroupetroglou has actively participated in a number of European Union funded and National research projects. He has been reviewer/evaluator and member of working groups/technical panels of various European Union's projects/programs.

* * *

Jim Aitchison currently works as an international trade and compliance manager at Selex Galileo, UK, which is part of the Finmeccanica group. Jim has worked in the Aerospace Industry for over 25 years working on import and export control and international licensing. For the past five years Jim has been focusing on the introduction of new export controls within the UK and also in design and implementation of compliance systems for international trade. Jim is currently involved in numerous projects to ensure compliance with international legislation covering the import and export of commercial and military goods and the wide ranging controls required by Customs. He has also been involved in a number of prizes for innovation within his field of expertise and remains committed to improving business processes at all levels within a fast moving and complex environment.

Daniela Andrei is an assistant professor and PhD student at the Faculty of Psychology and Education Sciences, Babes-Bolyai University, Cluj-Napoca, Romania. She is a licensed psychologist and holds a Master degree in Human Resources Management and Marketing. She has participated in several international training programs in the field of human-computer interaction and interaction design and recently became involved in COST Action IC0904 on the Integration of Transectorial IT Design and Evaluation. Her current research focuses on integrating the use social sciences methods in interactive systems design, implementation of interactive systems in organizations, compatibility between interactive systems' design and organizational culture.

Tanja Arh, M.Sc. graduated of Computer Science at the Faculty of Organizational Sciences, University of Maribor. She obtained her Master's degree at the Faculty of Organizational Sciences, University of Maribor. She is a PhD candidate at Faculty of Economics, University of Ljubljana. She works in Laboratory for Open Systems and Networks at Jožef Stefan Institute as a researcher in the field of e-learning and organizational learning. Her current research is performed mostly for European-wide research programmes (e4VET, MeRLab, iCooper, etc.) with focus on e-learning, applications of ICT in education, education and transfer of knowledge, human resource development and organizational learning. Tanja Arh is member of Executive Board of Slovenian Project Management Association. She is Technical editor of Slovenian scientific journal Project Management Review.

Andrew H. Bott, Metallurgical Engineer from Sheffield, UK, worked in industrial research and development at the British Steel Corporation in England, before becoming a visiting lecturer at Sheffield City Polytechnic (SCP). As a UKAEA CASE Award Associate and EURATOM Research Fellow at SCP he worked on alloy design for fast breeder fission and tokomak fusion reactors. From 1986 to 1998 he continued in metallurgical and electron microscopy research at the Federal University of Rio de Janeiro (UFRJ) in Brazil. In 1998 Andrew accepted an administrative post as Coordinator at the COPPETEC Foundation, a non-profit institution which administers the R&D projects of UFRJ's post-graduate and engineering research school, COPPE. His work at COPPETEC has involved strategic planning and organizational reengineering, including integrated management software development. He is a Director of the Brazilian National Council for Higher Education Scientific and Technological Research Support Foundations (CONFIES).

Tayana Conte is an Assistant Professor of Computer Science Department at UFAM - Federal University of Amazonas – Brazil. She received her doctorate degree from COPPE/UFRJ (Federal University of Rio de Janeiro) in 2009. Her current research interests include Usability Evaluation for Web, Web Engineering, Experimental Software Engineering and VV&T. Tayana Conte is member of the Brazilian Computer Society (SBC).

Tania Di Mascio obtained a Ph.D. degree in Electric and Information Engineering at the DIEI of L'Aquila University, working on HCI, more precisely, on UCDM, usability and information visualisation. Since 2006, Di Mascio is employed at the University of L'Aquila. Since 2008, Di Mascio is also a researcher at IASI LEKS of CNR, in Rome. Her research works are mainly in HCI design, information visualisation and usability.

Sanda Erdelez is an Associate Professor at the University of Missouri, U.S.A., School of Information Science and Learning Technologies and the founder of the Information Experience Laboratory (http://ielab.missouri.edu). She obtained bachelors and masters degrees from the University of Osijek, Croatia; and a Ph.D. from Syracuse University, where she studied as a Fulbright Scholar. Dr Erdelez conducts research, teaching, and consulting in human information behavior, Internet search behavior, and usability evaluation. Her research in accidental aspects of information behavior (information encountering) has been funded by SBC Communication and Dell Inc and she also served as a research team member and a co-PI on research projects funded by the U.S. Department of Education and the National Science Foundation. Dr. Erdelez co-edited (with K. Fisher and L. McKechnie) the Theories of Information Behavior (Information Today, 2005) and authored more than 80 research papers and presentation.

André P. Freire is a researcher at the University of York. His research interests are related to techniques and methods to help in the inclusive design and evaluation of web systems. In his previous research projects at the University of São Paulo, he conducted research on the awareness of web developers in Brazil regarding web accessibility. He has also conducted wide studies on the accessibility of governmental web sites at Brazil over time. His current work is focused on the investigation of issues regarding the impact of the involvement of users with disabilities on quantitative metrics in the accessibility evaluation of web sites.

Rosella Gennari obtained a Ph.D. degree in Computer Science at the ILLC institute of the University of Amsterdam, working on constraint programming and automated reasoning for modal logic. Since 2005, Gennari is employed as assistant professor at the Department of Computer Science of the Free University of Bozen-Bolzano. Previously, she was post-doc ERCIM fellow at CWI, Amsterdam, The Netherlands, and then post-doc fellow at the Automated Reasoning Systems division of ITC-irst (now FBK-irst), Trento, Italy. Her research work is in constraint programming, modal automated reasoning and, more recently, AI educational tools. Lately, she has worked on e-LIS and LODE, two projects and intelligent educational web tools for deaf people.

Petros P. Georgiakakis holds a PhD from Department of Technology Education and Digital Systems, University of Piraeus. His research interests include Usability Evaluation of Network Supported Collaborative Learning systems, based in advanced educational technologies with the use of Design Patterns. He has participated in a great number of European R & D projects. He is member of the CoSy LLab (Computer Supported Learning Engineering Laboratory) [http://cosy.ted.unipi.gr]. He has written more than 20 papers which have been presented in international workshops and conferences. He is the CEO of ITisART.Ltd [http://www.itisart.com.gr], which is a company specialising in creating integrated innovative interactive technological solutions mainly in the sectors of e-commerce, e-learning and digital art. He is also one of the founders of VideoAnnotator.Ltd [http://www.vannotator.com]. He is a member of many International Forums such as the Educational Technology & Society and the International Forum Community "Quality Assurance in VET".

Juan Manuel González Calleros is a Researcher assistant of the University catholic of Louvain (UCL). He is member of the Belgian Lab of Human Computer Interaction and of the UsiXML consortium. Having received a scholarship award, he came to Belgium and completed his DEA in computer Science at UCL. He received a master degree in Computer Sciences at National Institute of Astrophysics, Optics and Electronic (Mexico). Juan Manuel Gonzalez Calleros is pursuing a PhD in Computer Sciences with the thesis model Driven engineering of 3D User Interfaces at UCL, Louvain School of Management (IAG-LSM). He is responsible of HCI activities of the Human project (The European project to develop a methodology with techniques and prototypical tools based on a cognitive model of the crew behaviour, to support the prediction of human errors in ways that are usable and practical for human centred design of systems operating in complex cockpit environments).

Adriana-Mihaela Guran is lecturer at the Department of Computer Science of the Faculty of Mathematics and Computer Science, Babeş-Bolyai University of Cluj-Napoca (Romania). She holds a bachelor's degree in computer science and a master's degree in computer science (both from the University of Cluj-Napoca). She has a PhD focusing on ergonomic modeling of user interfaces obtained from the same university. Her current research focuses on integrating social sciences methods in interactive systems design, automatic usability evaluation methods, and intelligent interfaces.

Steven Hogg is currently working as an IT Business Analyst at Selex Galileo, UK, which is part of the Finmeccanica group. He studied Computer Science at Heriot-Watt University (Edinburgh) and was awarded an MPhil by research. Steven has been in the Aerospace Industry for over 30 years working mostly in Manufacturing and Operations. For the past seven years Steven has been focusing on the design of web systems to support manufacture. Through the years Steven has been involved in numerous high technology projects to improve manufacture and these e.g. include the design and development of wearable computers with augmented virtual reality displays. He has been awarded a number of prizes for innovation. Steven's current work is focused on the design of a new web portal system to enhance ITAR compliance within the USA.

Tomayess Issa is a Lecturer at school of Information Systems – Curtin University of Technology, Western Australia. She is holding a Doctor of Philosophy degree from Curtin University – Western Australia, Master of Science (Telecommunication Management) and Bachelor of Science (Information Systems) from Murdoch University – Western Australia. From 2001, she worked at Curtin University, as Unit Leader for Undergraduate and Postgraduate units, which are focusing on Business Technology, Networking Telecommunication Management, Web Design and Usability. In addition, she is supervising postgraduate students. Her research interest included Web Design, Usability, Websites Methodologies, Human Computer Interaction, and Social Networking. She is also interested in establishing teaching methods and styles to define the positive aspects of learning experiences and problems, which are facing students during the semester in order to enhance the positives and address concerns.

Borka Jerman Blažič is working as a head of the Department for Open Systems and Networks at Jožef Stefan Institute and in the Department of Economics, University of Ljubljana as Full Professor teaching Telecommunication Services and Technologies (post-graduate) and Legal aspects and standards in ICT. The main field of applications and research are computer communications, internet technologies, security in networking, privacy and internationalisation of Internet services, etc. Borka Jerman-Blažič is a member of many professional associations and is appointed expert to UNECE UN (Economic Commission for Europe), appointed member of UNECE/CEFAT Team of specialist on Internet enterprise development, appointed member of eTEN management committee of EU, member of FP7 PC on security, chair of the Execom of the Internet Society of Europe (www.isoc-ecc.org), member of New York Academy of science 1999, IEEE, ACM, distinguished member of Slovene Society for Informatics, member of IEEE on Computers, ACM. She is also chair of Slovenian Standardisation Committee on ICT as well as chair of the Slovenian chapter of Internet Society and a member of the European ICT Standardisation Board. She is holding Plaque of appreciation of Thai branch of IFIP and ACM for her services in Internet development. She has published more than 80 papers in refereed journals, 154 communications scientific meetings, 15 chapters in scientific books, 6 books and other 142 non-classified contributions.

Kathy Keeling is a Senior Lecturer in Marketing Research at Manchester Business School. She has worked closely and gained research support from many organisations, the larger including Boots, British Airways, the Co-operative Bank (now Co-operative Financial Services), CWS, Manchester Evening News and Microsoft; cross-disciplinary interests are reflected in the research funding obtained from both the ESRC and EPSRC. Her most recent project under the Realising Our Potential Award (ROPA) scheme is entitled Human Computer Relationships And Persuasiveness In E-Retailing. She has published a number of papers across retailing, marketing, e-commerce and human-computer interaction and universal access to IT fields.

Aidan Kehoe has worked in industry for more than 20 years in a variety of software development roles, including at Logitech USA as Director of Software Engineering. He has worked on product and middleware development for peripherals on a variety of gaming platforms including PC, Sony and Nintendo. He recently completed his PhD studies at the Department of Computer Science at University College Cork, Ireland where he is also a researcher for the IDEAS Research Group. His area of research is multimodal user assistance and he currently works for Logitech, Ireland in product development for the Gaming Business Unit.

Georgios Kouroupetroglou holds a B.Sc. in Physics and a Ph.D. in Communications and Signal Processing. He is the Director of the Speech Laboratory, Department of Informatics and Telecommunications, University of Athens and Head of the e-Accessibility Unit for Students with Disabilities. His current research interests focuses on the area of Speech Communication and Accessibility, as parts of the major domain of Multimedia and Human-Computer Interaction. Dr. Kouroupetroglou has actively participated in a number of European Union funded and National research projects. He has been reviewer/evaluator and member of working groups/technical panels of various European Union's projects/programs.

Linda Macaulay (B.Sc, M.Sc, PhD, CEng, Cert. Ed., FBCS) Professor of System Design at Manchester Business School (MBS) is twice holder of the prestigious IBM Faculty Award 2004 and 2006 for work on e-business patterns. She is Director of the MBS Centre for Service Research and Principal

Investigator on the EPSRC funded SSME UK network project. She has led over 25 externally funded projects won through competitive bids and her work is widely published in over one hundred journal papers and articles.

Jobson Massolar has B.Sc. in Computer Science from Universidade Federal Fluminense (1990) and M.Sc. in Systems and Computer Engineering from COPPE / UFRJ (1993). Currently he is a doctoral student in Systems and Computer Engineering at COPPE / UFRJ, with emphasis on Software Engineering. He have taught disciplines regarding Project Management, Software Project Planning and Estimation, ER and OO modeling, Modeling with UML and Programming for Web in several post-graduate courses. In the area of Software Engineering, he has worked in the following subjects: Web Engineering, Experimental Software Engineering, Usability Evaluation for Web and VV&T. He has extensive experience in software systems development, participating for more than fifteen years in various projects in the areas of sales, marketing, logistics, HR and finance.

Emilia Mendes is Associate Professor in Computer Science at the University of Auckland (New Zealand). She has active research interests in the areas of Empirical Web & Software Engineering, Evidence-based research, Hypermedia, Computer Science & Software Engineering education, in which areas she has published widely and over 120 refereed publications, which include two books (one edited (2005) and one authored (2007)). A/Prof. Mendes is on the editorial board of the International Journal of Web Engineering and Technology, the Journal of Web Engineering, the Journal of Software Measurement, the International Journal of Software Engineering and Its Applications, the Empirical Software Engineering Journal, the Advances in Software Engineering Journal, and the Software Quality Journal. She worked in the software industry for ten years before obtaining in 1999 her PhD in Computer Science from the University of Southampton (UK), and moving to Auckland (NZ).

Joi L. Moore is an Associate Professor in the School of Information Science & Learning Technologies at the University of Missouri where she manages and teaches courses in the Digital Media Curriculum. Dr Moore's current research interests include: constructing knowledge in online learning environments; analyzing information architecture in Electronic Performance Support Systems and Interactive Learning Environments; and designing user-centered web applications (Human Computer Interaction and Human Information Behavior).

Jaime Muñoz Arteaga is Professor in Computer Science at Universidad Autónoma de Aguascalientes in Mexico. He is a researcher in Human-Computer Interaction, and web technologies. He holds a Ph.D. in Computer Science, Human-Computer Interaction (University Toulouse 1 (UT1), Toulouse, France, 2000). He has reported his work in journals, book chapters, conference papers, and technical reports, and so far has supervised several students at the graduate and undergraduate level. He is coordinator of Instructional Technology for Multicultural Learning Objects project .His current research interests include topics on: Human-Computer Interaction, Software Engineering and E-learning.

Flaithrí Neff is a researcher for the IDEAS Research Group at the Department of Computer Science, University College Cork, Ireland where he has recently completed his PhD studies. He is also an assistant lecturer at the Limerick Institute of Technology, Ireland since September 2009. His research interests are in virtual sonic interface design and intelligent hearing systems. He is particularly focused on applying his research to accessibility issues pertaining to visually disabled users of technology. In 2002 he attained a first class honours MSc degree at the University of Limerick, Ireland specializing in Audio Technology.

Patrik O'Brian Holt is Research Professor of Computing (Human Factors Engineering) at the School of Computing, the Robert Gordon University, Aberdeen. He is also Director of the Computational Systems Joint Research Institute, which is part of the Northern Research Partnership in Engineering, a joint venture by the Universities of Dundee, Aberdeen and Robert Gordon. Professor Holt has been a Computer Scientist for over 20 years but has a background in Experimental Cognitive Psychology, Statistical Modelling and Cognitive Science. He has published widely and has received research funding from diverse sources, including EPSRC, BBSRC, Scottish Executive, New Opportunities Fund (UK National Lottery) and various industrial organisations such as BAE SYSTEMS (Edinburgh) and Lockheed-Martin (Atlanta, USA). Professor Holt's current research interests are focused on modelling human errors in telehealth and advanced visualisation in tele-operation.

Wendy Olphert is a Senior Research Fellow in the Department of Information Science at Loughborough University. Wendy's broad research area is the human, social and organisational aspects of information and communication technologies, and in particular the way in which such technologies can be designed and shaped to meet human, organisational and social requirements. ICTs. She has led numerous research and consultancy projects around these themes. Her current research focus is the use of ICTs by older people and in the voluntary sector. Wendy has previously published in journals including the Journal of the Association for Information Systems, the Journal of the Operational Research Society, Behaviour and Information Technology, and the European Journal of Work and Organizational Psychology. She is co-author (with Leela Damodaran) of a book entitled "Informing Digital Futures: Strategies for Citizen Engagement" (Springer, 2006).

Catherine Parkinson is a freelance researcher and information scientist, with a background in information provision for disabled people. She trained in information science at Loughborough University and was the winner of the Dunn and Wilson Ltd. Prize for best performance on the MA/MSc Information and Library Management Programme. She was also awarded the Library and Information Research Group (LIRG) postgraduate prize in 2007 for her dissertation 'Website accessibility statements: A comparative investigation of local government and high street sectors.' The dissertation was supervised by Wendy Olphert.

Anindita Paul is a Doctoral Candidate at the School of Information Science and Learning Technologies at the University of Missouri. She is also a senior usability researcher at the Information Experience Lab where she is actively involved in planning, conducting, managing, and reporting usability related issues of the different projects. She is also actively involved in training in the usability area and has done cross-cultural training for the labs many international collaborators and visitors. Her dissertation research is in web analytics and its use for understanding the users' online behavior. Her research interests include online users' information behavior, usability techniques, and cultural aspects of information behavior. Anindita did her Masters in Business Administration, and then gained industry experience before joining the school.

Jean-Eric Pelet has a phd in marketing with distinction from Nantes University (France) and a MBA in information systems with distinction from Laval University (Québec, Québec, Canada). He works as a research associate at ISG Paris on issues dedicated to the interface and to the consumer behaviour facing a website or any information system (e-learning, CRM, ERP, KM, BI, SCM platforms). His main interest lies on the variables that enhance navigation in order to help people to be more efficient. He works as a visiting professor in several places in France in Design School (Nantes), Business Schools (Paris, Reims), and Universities (Paris Dauphine – Nantes), on lectures focused on e-marketing, ergonomics, usability, and consumer behaviour. Dr. Pelet has also actively participated in a number of research projects around e-commerce.

Helen Petrie is Head of the HCI Group as a Professor of Human-Computer Interaction in the Department of Computer Science. She has been involved in many research projects on the design and evaluation of technology for disabled and elderly people, including 12 EU-funded projects; for the EU-funded MultiReader Project she was Project Leader. She led the team that conducted the largest and most comprehensive study of web site accessibility for the Disability Rights Commission of Great Britain and the same team conducted a similar study of web accessibility for the UK Council of Museums, Libraries and Archives (MLA). She also led the academic work on the UK funded VISTA Project on the accessibility of digital television which won the Royal Television Society Award for Technical Innovation in 2003. She is on the board of a number of academic journals, is a Lay Advisor to the Royal College of Ophthalmologists and is a trustee of the Foundation for Assistive Technology (FAST).

Matija Pipan, M.Sc. obtained his Master's degree at Faculty of Economics, University of Ljubljana. His master thesis was Methods and Techniques for Usability Evaluation of Software Solutions. He works in Laboratory for Open Systems and Networks at Jožef Stefan Institute as a researcher. His key qualifications are focused on usability evaluation of information communication technologies (ICTs) and on development of technology enhanced learning systems and technologies. Currently he is involved in several EU research projects from the field of usability evaluation and e-learning. Matija Pipan is representative of Slovenia in EU COST project MAUSE - Towards the MAturation of Information Technology USability Evaluation.

Horia D. Pitariu is a professor of work and personnel psychology at the Faculty of Psychology and Education Sciences, Babes-Bolyai University, Cluj-Napoca, Romania. His expertise is in personnel selection, professional performance assessment, stress and emotions in organizations and human-computer interaction. He was involved in several projects and actions in the field of human computer interaction at the European level (program of the Institut fur Arbeitsphysiologie Universität Dortmund - Germany: Psycho physiological correlates in learning a novel VDU task, COST Action 294 (MAUSE) on usability evaluation, COST Action IC0904 on the Integration of Transectorial IT Design and Evaluation). He introduced courses of cognitive ergonomics and human computer interaction at undergraduate and postgraduate levels at the Faculty of Psychology and Education Sciences. His current research interests in this field are represented by the role of emotions and personality variables in interactive systems usability and acceptance.

Ian Pitt is a lecturer in Usability Engineering and Multimedia at University College Cork, Ireland. He attained his PhD at the University of York, UK, then spent a year as a post-doctoral research fellow at Otto-von-Guericke University, Magdeburg, Germany, before moving to Cork in 1997. His research interests include the use of speech and non-speech sound in human-machine interfaces and he leads the IDEAS Research Group at the Department of Computer Science, UCC.

Christopher Power is a Research Fellow in the University of York HCI Group. Coming from a software engineering background, he has participated in multiple research projects relating to web accessibility, specifically working on the development of test methodologies for web accessibility. Further, he has worked in the management of requirements for people with disabilities in the creation of websites and in the establishing the accessibility of web authoring tools.

David Prytherch is Senior Research Fellow in Haptics and Computer Interface Design working in User-lab, a dedicated research and development lab in User Centred Design, Human Computer Interaction and Haptics. Prior to this, he had 30 years professional experience as a freelance glass engraver/sculptor and is a Fellow of the Guild of Glass Engravers. Research interests include Haptic (tacit) learning and teaching, the role of haptics in skill development, particularly in the arts, haptic implications in activity satisfaction and motivation, and issues surrounding tool use and material embodiment, particularly with regard to computer interface systems. A particular interest lies in the development of inclusive interface systems that facilitate transparent access to creative processes for people with disabilities.

Symeon Retalis is associate professor at the Department of Digital Systems, University of Piraeus, Greece. He has performed research in the field of elearning engineering since many years. He is coordinating the activities of the research group called CoSy Learning Lab. He has participated in and coordinated various EU funded projects in the area of technology enhanced learning. His publications concern the creation of elearning design patterns, design of learning tools for children and lifelong e-learning and human computer interaction.

Andy Saxon is Director of e-Learning at Birmingham City University's Institute of Art and Design, and a University Senior Learning and Teaching Fellow. His research interests lie in the application of arts-based models of designing to software user interface development, the evaluation of the software user interface and user experience design for software. The main focus of this work has been toward web and multimedia software. He is also involved in the development of e-learning initiatives within the Institute's Learning and Teaching Centre, which he leads. These include the design and evaluation of reusable learning objects, and research into e-pedagogies for art and design. He supervises Doctoral and Masters' students in the School of Visual Communication, where he is also Head of Research.

Shawren Singh is a PhD candidate at the University of South Africa and a faculty member. His research interest include: Problem-Based Research in Information Systems, Human Computer Interaction (HCI), Web-based Courseware Tools, Internet Applications, Blended Education, E-commerce and Accounting Information Systems.

Mikael B. Skov is an associate professor at the HCI Lab, Department of Computer Science, Aalborg University, Denmark. Mikael completed his PhD in 2002 at Aalborg University on design of interactive narratives. He teaches general human-computer interaction to undergraduate computer science and informatics students as well as advanced human-computer interaction to graduate students. Mikael has supervised more than 25 Masters students on various topics within interaction design or human-computer interaction. His research interests are human-computer interaction and interaction design especially within mobile, pervasive, and ubiquitous computing. Mikael is currently involved in a major research project on improving web portal usability in close collaboration with several industry partners.

Dimitris Spiliotopoulos holds a BSc in Computation, an MA in Linguistics, an MPhil in Computation and studying towards a PhD in Language Technology. He is a researcher of the Speech Laboratory, Department of Informatics and Telecommunications, University of Athens. His research focuses on speech processing, human-computer interaction, universal accessibility and natural language dialogue systems. He has participated in several EU and National projects.

Jan Stage is full professor at the HCI Lab, Department of Computer Science, Aalborg University, Denmark. Jan holds a PhD in computer science from University of Oslo. His current research interests are in usability evaluation and user interaction design, with emphasis on reduction on the effort needed to conduct usability evaluations. He has published several journal and conference articles in these topics as well as in information system development and methods for software development. Jan teaches human-computer interaction and usability engineering to undergraduate, graduate and PhD students in computer science, informatics and information technology. He is also conduction training and consulting in software companies. Jan is currently involved in a major research project on improving web portal usability in close collaboration with several industry partners.

Guilherme H. Travassos is an Associate Professor of Software Engineering in the Systems Engineering and Computer Science Program at COPPE – Federal University of Rio de Janeiro – Brazil CNPq – Brazilian Research Council researcher and FAPERJ State Scientist. He received his doctorate degree from COPPE/UFRJ in 1994. He has been with the Experimental Software Engineering Group at the University of Maryland – College Park for a post-doctoral position (1998/2000). He leads the Experimental Software Engineering Group at COPPE/UFRJ. His current research interests include experimental software engineering, e-science, software quality, software engineering environments and verification, validation and testing concerned with object-oriented software. He is member of the ISERN, ACM and SBC – Brazilian Computer Society. Director of Planning and Administration of COPPE/UFRJ. Most of the information regarding his research projects and working activities can be found at http://www.cos.ufrj.br/~ght

Andrew Turk has degrees in Surveying, Applied Science (Cartography) and Arts (Psychology Honours and Philosophy) and a PhD. From 1993 he worked at Murdoch University, Western Australia, teaching undergraduate students, supervising postgraduate students and carrying out research and consultancy projects specializing in: design and usability evaluation of user interfaces and websites; ethnographic and socio-technical methodologies for developing information systems; Geographic Information Systems; human factors aspects of interactive television; and cultural and ethical aspects of Information and Communications Technology. He has worked on projects with Indigenous communities in the Pilbara and the Ngaanyatjarra Lands areas of WA. Currently his main research concentrates on Ethnophysiography (cultural / linguistic aspects of conceptions of landscape). In July 2007 he retired but continues as an Adjunct Associate Professor at Murdoch University.

Jean Vanderdonckt is Full Professor in Computer Science at Université catholique de Louvain (Belgium), Louvain School of Management (IAG-LSM) where he leads the Belgian Laboratory of Computer-Human Interaction (BCHI). This laboratory is conducting research, development, and consulting services in the domain of user interface engineering, a domain that is located midway between software engineering, human-computer interaction, and usability engineering. Jean Vanderdonckt is the founder and the coordinator of the UsiXML Consortium that structures activities towards the definition and the usage of UsiXML (User Interface eXtensible Markup Language) as a common User Interface Description Language. He is the scientific coordinator of the ITEA2 Call 3 project on UsiXML. He is the coordinator of HCI activities within the Similar network of excellence (The European research taskforce creating human-machine interfaces SIMILAR to human-human communication). He is also a member of the European COST n°294 Action MAUSE on usability engineering and of the SESAMI Working Group. He is a Senior member of IEEE, ACM, and SIGCHI. He is also co-editor in chief of Springer HCI Series of books.

Konstantina Vassilopoulou (B.Sc, M.B.A., M.Sc, PhD) is a Lecturer in Usability and Electronic Commerce at Harokopio University in Athens Greece. She has worked in numerous EU funded and National research projects, both in UK and Greece. Her main research interests are directed towards the role of usability and social attitude theories in designing e-commerce sites (i.e. retail, e-government and e-learning sites). She has published a number of papers across human computer interaction and social attitude theories and the usability of retail sites and e-learning.

Verônica Taquette Vaz is an undergraduate student in Computer Engineering of the Federal University of Rio de Janeiro. Her current research interests are: Requirements Engineering, Software Quality e Experimental Software Engineering.

Shane Walker is Director of Knowledge Transfer Partnerships at Birmingham City University's Institute of Art and Design. This role determines current opportunities to develop capability and identify barriers to growth faced by creative industries in the West Midlands region and beyond. As a member of the University's Human Computer Interaction Design Research Group his research centres on the role of the users' motivation and emotion in software user interface evaluation and user experience design for software.

Martin West is Associate Professor in the School of Information Systems at Curtin University of Technology, in Perth Australia. His current research interests information systems strategy, supply chain management and logistics information systems.

Borchuluun Yadamsuren is a doctoral candidate at the School of Information Science and Learning Technologies of the University of Missouri. She has worked as a senior researcher at the Information Experience Laboratory since 2005. She has been involved in managing various usability studies of websites in the laboratory and remote setting applying various usability techniques. She was involved in the planning and management of more than 20 client and research projects on usability of different websites and information systems. She has an extensive experience in conducting training sessions on usability testing with the usage of Morae both in house and internationally (Croatia, and Taiwan). Her research interests are in user behavior studies, user-centered design and usability. Borchuluun Yadam-suren received her Master's degree in Journalism from the University of Missouri, master's degree in computer science from the Mongolian Technical University and bachelor's degree in computer science from the Novosibirsk State Technology University in Russia.

Index